CRIMINAL LAW

The One-State Solution

ASPEN SELECT SERIES

CRIMINAL LAW

The One-State Solution

Second Edition

Thaddeus Hoffmeister
Professor of Law
University of Dayton

Published by Wolters Kluwer in New York.

Wolters Kluwer Legal & Regulatory U.S. serves customers worldwide with CCH, Aspen Publishers, and Kluwer Law International products. (www.WKLegaledu.com)

To contact Customer Service, e-mail customer.service@wolterskluwer.com, call 1-800-234-1660, fax 1-800-901-9075, or mail correspondence to:

> Wolters Kluwer
> Attn: Order Department
> PO Box 990
> Frederick, MD 21705

Printed in the United States of America.

2 3 4 5 6 7 8 9 0

ISBN 978-1-4548-9813-9

About Wolters Kluwer Legal & Regulatory U.S.

Wolters Kluwer Legal & Regulatory U.S. delivers expert content and solutions in the areas of law, corporate compliance, health compliance, reimbursement, and legal education. Its practical solutions help customers successfully navigate the demands of a changing environment to drive their daily activities, enhance decision quality and inspire confident outcomes.

Serving customers worldwide, its legal and regulatory portfolio includes products under the Aspen Publishers, CCH Incorporated, Kluwer Law International, ftwilliam.com and MediRegs names. They are regarded as exceptional and trusted resources for general legal and practice-specific knowledge, compliance and risk management, dynamic workflow solutions, and expert commentary.

About Wolters Kluwer Legal & Regulatory U.S.

This book is dedicated to A and Z.

--TH

"If I were giving a young man advice as to how he might succeed in life, I would say to him, pick out a good father and mother, and begin life in Ohio"

--Wilbur Wright (1910)

Summary of Contents

Part VI: Defenses

Contents

Acknowledgments

The author would like to thank Mary Boston, who had the arduous task of transcribing 18th Century English criminal law cases. This book also benefitted from the efforts of my Research Assistants, Marty Gehres, Elizabeth Watson, Stephen Slawinski and Ann Charles Watts. These hard working third-year law students were instrumental in getting this book project completed on time. I would also like to thank the individuals and entities who granted me permission to republish the following works:

American Law Institute, Model Penal Code copyright 1962, 1985, and 2007 by the American Law Institute

Frank R. Baumgartner, *The Impact of Race, Gender, and Geography on Ohio Executions,* January 28, 2016

Guyora Binder, *Making the Best of Felony Murder*, 91 B.U.L. Rev. 403 (2011)

Dana Cole, *Expanding Felony-Murder in Ohio: Felony-Murder or Murder Felony?* 63 Ohio St. L.J. 15 (2002)

John F. Decker, *The Mental State Requirement for Accomplice Liability in American Criminal Law,* 60 S.C. L. Rev. 237 (2008)

Patricia J. Falk, *Husbands Who Drug Their Wives: The Injustice of the Marital Exception in Ohio's Sexual Offenses,* 36 Women's Rts. L. Rep. 265 (2015)

Chad Flanders, *The One State-Solution to Teaching Criminal Law, or, Leaving the Common Law and the MPC Behind*, 8 Ohio St. J. Crim. L. 167 (2010).

Jessica Foxx, *Dementia Sex Culture: Out with the Old, in with the New,* 91 J. Am. Acad. Matrim. Law. 187 (2016)

Robert Higgs, *Lawmaker Proposes Death Penalty for Murder of First Responders, Military Personnel,* Columbus Dispatch (Feb. 10, 2017)

Thaddeus Hoffmeister, *Social Media in the Courtroom, A New Era for Criminal Justice*, Praeger Publishing (2014)

Thea Johnson and Andrew Gilden, *Common Sense and the Cannibal Cop* , 11 Stan. J. Civ. Rits. & Civ. Liberties 313 (2015)

Eric Johnson, *Rethinking the Presumption of Mens Rea* , 47 WFLR (2012)

S. Adele Shank, *The Death Penalty in Ohio: Fairness, Reliability, and Justice at Risk--A Report on Reforms in Ohio's Use of the Death Penalty Since the 1997 Ohio State Bar Association Recommendations Were Made,* 63 Ohio St. L. J. 371 (2002)

James J. Tomkovicz, *The Endurance of the Felony Murder Rule: A Study of the Forces that Shape Our Criminal Law,* 51 Wash & Lee L. Rev. 1429 (1994)

Ian Urbina, *New Murder Charge in '66 Shooting* , NY Times (Sept. 19, 2007)

James Q. Whitman, *The Origins of Reasonable Doubt: Theological Roots of the Criminal Trial,* Yale University Press (2008)

Jonathan Witmer-Rich, *Unpacking Affirmative Consent: Not as Great as You Hope, Not as Bad as You Fear,* 49 Tex. Tech. L. Rev. 57 (2016)

PART I
Background and Punishment

Chapter 1
Background

A. The Book

This criminal law book consists of six parts. Part I serves as an introduction to criminal law. Here, the book provides background information on criminal law and an overview of punishment. Part II examines the general components of a crime to include (1) actus reus; (2) mens rea; (3) causation; and (4) concurrence of elements. In Part III, the book examines specific crimes. This part discusses crimes against the person which include murder, manslaughter, assault, kidnapping, and robbery. In Part IV, the book looks at property crimes such as larceny, false pretenses, embezzlement, receipt of stolen property, and burglary. Part V concludes the discussion on specific crimes by examining inchoate crimes and accomplice liability. The last section of the book, Part VI, discusses defenses to crimes such as self-defense, insanity, infancy, intoxication, entrapment, necessity, and duress.

Unlike most criminal law texts that examine cases and statutes from across the country, this book concentrates on one particular jurisdiction, Ohio. While there are a few non-Ohio cases and laws sprinkled throughout, the focus is on Ohio case law and statutes. Ohio was selected as the jurisdiction of choice because it is one of the few states of size that has both significant urban and rural populations. Furthermore, Ohio, as most presidential candidates are aware, has historically reflected the overall view and mood of the country. This is because the population tends to split fairly evenly to both the right and the left. Thus, Ohio case law, especially opinions from the Ohio Supreme Court, doesn't tend to skew too far in any one direction.

A criminal law course focused on one particular jurisdiction offers numerous benefits to students. Professor Chad Flanders discusses some of those advantages in his article, *The One State-Solution to Teaching Criminal Law, or, Leaving the Common Law and the MPC Behind,* 8 Ohio St. J. Crim. L. 167 (2010):

A. One Set of Laws

The first, and I think nearly overwhelming, advantage of the state-centered approach is that it gives students experience digging into the statutes of one state. In the introduction to the class, I am able to say that we will be looking at the "real law on the books in Missouri" and that, to a large extent, the book of statutes will be their "answer key" for the class (although it is certainly not a self-interpreting answer key, and sometimes the answers it gives will be puzzling—students have to learn how to "crack the code"). Students are expected to know, even to master, the statutes assigned to them for each class and to bring their copy of the criminal code to class every day (when they forget, they can easily look up the statutes online). Moreover, students are able to gain familiarity with the laws of one state rather than just jumping around and learning bits and pieces of the laws of several states. Proceeding in this way has a number of subsidiary benefits.

First, it hammers home the point that criminal law in the modern state today is, to a great extent, statutory law and the cases interpreting those statutes.***

A second and related advantage of focusing on one code is that it teaches students to look at the entire architecture of a statute. For example, my students had the entire first-degree murder statute in front of them on the page of the criminal code, including the punishment for the crime and various cross-references to other statutes. Students also had in front of them, on the same page or the next, the statutes for second-degree murder and voluntary manslaughter and, on the page before, the definitions of various terms in the criminal statutes. With the relevant materials right there, students learn to see both how various parts of a statute interact and also how statutes interact with one another. In the lesson on kidnapping, for instance, students were able to look across the page at false imprisonment and analyze how the two crimes are both similar and different. Students further see patterns in how statutes are constructed and can refer back to statutes which use the same language that they are currently studying (does "unlawful remaining" have the same meaning in the self-defense statute as it does in the statute defining burglary?). This is something a casebook cannot do for the laws of a particular state, which again will usually, at best, be excerpted at the bottom of the page a perfect place for students to skip over them. There is no reason why students should be introduced to "intratextualism" only when it comes to interpreting constitutions.

Third, by reading the Missouri criminal code along with Missouri case law, students are more fully exposed to the history of the changes in the code and how case law and the code interact. In teaching felony-murder, I assigned *Bouser*, a case which looks at the fascinating evolution of Missouri's felony-murder statute, including the shift from making only so-called inherently dangerous felonies, such as arson and burglary, predicate felonies, to making any felony sufficient for felony murder. (This led to a discussion of whether this was the right move and also to a somewhat convoluted discussion of the "merger" doctrine.) In addition, when I taught particular crimes near the end of the course, I handed out the legislative comments that Missouri appended to many of its criminal statutes when it undertook a comprehensive statutory reform in 1973. Such comments are helpful in showing why Missouri went in one direction rather than another and why it differs or agrees with the Model Penal Code. The comments also give students an insight into the use of legislative history in interpreting statutes. Finally, in my unit on rape, I had the class read several nineteenth century Missouri opinions to show how the presumption used to be very strongly against the veracity of victim testimony to see both how far we have come from the common law to our modern day statutes and how far we have left to go in changing our attitudes and our laws regarding rape.

There is also a deeper, historical point to be made about reading the statutes of one state and then reading how state courts have interpreted those statutes. The history of the case law on these statutes makes up what Walker has recently called the "new common law." After the Model Penal Code was promulgated, states—to a greater or lesser extent adopted it for their own, and indeed "[t]he fact that there is a significant degree of agreement in the definition of crimes in state codes is due to a large extent to the Model Penal Code." But it was still left to courts to puzzle out how to interpret various ambiguities in the MPC as adopted in their state. This is what state courts have been doing for a while now and will continue to do.***

B. The Local Connection

Despite the "One-State Solution" title, Ohio cases in this book are substantially supplemented by both foreign and federal cases. These non-Ohio cases serve several purposes. First, they fill in gaps in Ohio law. For example, Ohio does not have a generic solicitation statute; therefore, it is necessary to rely on federal cases to thoroughly explore the elements of the crime and potential defenses.

Another purpose of the non-Ohio cases is to help explain the common law and Model Penal Code (MPC). While the focus of this book is Ohio law, it is not done at the expense of learning either the MPC or the common law. Quite the opposite, the reader is exposed to both the common law and MPC through federal and foreign cases and at times even Ohio case law. In fact, the reader is regularly asked throughout the text to compare and contrast the MPC and common law with the laws of Ohio.

1. Common Law

The common law serves as the foundation upon which the criminal law is built. In the early common law, judges did not have statutes by which to guide them on the cases currently before them. Instead, they relied on precedent or past case decisions. While many associate the common law with pre-nineteenth century jurisprudence, it is not necessarily static. Like the norms and customs of society, the common law can evolve in certain situations. This fact will be illustrated later in *Montana v. Egelhoff*, which examines the history of involuntary intoxication.

This case-by-case approach to determining what conduct is illegal has been abandoned by approximately half of the jurisdictions in the United States—e.g., neither the federal government nor Ohio rely on common law crimes. This movement away from the common law occurred as more and more states codified their criminal laws. This is not to say, however, that the common law is no longer relevant to attorneys or law students. Learning the common law adds value to a law student's education in a variety of ways.

Arguably, the biggest benefit of the common law today is that it helps clarify ambiguous criminal statutes. No matter how well legislatures draft a criminal statute, it cannot cover every conceivable real-life situation. Thus, judges are forced to look to the common law for help. This point is illustrated in *State v. Boggs*.

State v. Boggs, 2003 WL 22994531 (Ohio Ct. App. 2003)

WILLIAM M. O'NEILL, J.

***Appellant was married to Angela Boggs ("Angela"), the victim in this case. During the relevant times of this matter, the couple lived in a trailer in Portage County with their two-year-old daughter.

Angela testified that on February 21, 2001, appellant arrived home early from work because he had been laid off. Angela and appellant went to a grocery store and purchased items for dinner and rented a movie. They returned home, where they cooked dinner and drank strawberry daiquiris. After dinner, they watched the movie.

During the movie, one of Angela's male friends, Mr. Foster, called her. Mr. Foster was a kidney dialysis patient at a medical center where Angela worked. Shortly after the call, appellant asked Angela who had called, and she told him it was Mr. Foster. Appellant decided to go to Mr. Foster's residence to tell him to stop calling Angela. He told Angela not to warn Mr. Foster he was coming, or it "would be bad for [her.]"

Angela did page Mr. Foster to warn him appellant was on his way. Mr. Foster was not home when appellant arrived. Appellant returned home and violently confronted Angela about warning Mr. Foster. During this confrontation, their daughter was sleeping in her room.

Appellant struck Angela in the head a few times. She dropped to the floor with her hands over her head to protect herself. Appellant left the trailer and picked up a five-gallon container of kerosene, which was full. The couple used kerosene in heaters to heat their home. As appellant returned with the kerosene, he commented that it would be funny if the place burned down and he and their daughter were the only ones to escape. Appellant doused Angela with about half of the kerosene in the container. Her hair, shirt, and pants were soaked. Angela was near a heater when this occurred, and appellant remarked that she would catch on fire if the heater sparked.

Appellant briefly stopped the assault, and Angela went to the bathroom to rinse the kerosene off her face. Appellant followed her into the bathroom and smacked her. Thereafter, appellant pulled out a cigarette lighter, lit it, and proceeded to waive it in front of Angela. He also poked her with it. As appellant was waiving the lighter, he stated that he would bring their daughter to see Angela's grave.

While still in the bathroom, appellant told Angela her pants were on fire, although, actually, they were not. As a result, Angela removed her pants in a panic and fell backwards into the bathtub. Appellant struck her a few more times when she was in the bathtub. Appellant then left the bathroom and retrieved the container of kerosene. When he returned, Angela was standing in the bathtub. Appellant struck her again, and she fell down. Appellant dumped the remainder of the kerosene on Angela in the bathtub. After dousing Angela a second time, appellant resumed waiving his lit lighter near her. According to Angela's testimony, appellant dropped the lighter, or it fell, into the bathtub. The lighter went out prior to landing in the bathtub.

The events in the bathroom were interrupted by the telephone ringing. Mr. Foster called the trailer, and engaged in an argument with appellant. Angela stated that the remainder of the evening was uneventful.

Two days later, appellant arrived home intoxicated. He began yelling at Angela and accusing her of having an affair with Mr. Foster. Angela testified he hit her in the face twice. Angela then called her mother and informed her of these events. Her mother called the sheriff's office, and two deputies responded to the trailer. Angela testified that appellant was heavily intoxicated when the officers arrived and "couldn't even stand up." Appellant was arrested.

As a result of these events, appellant was indicted on one count of aggravated arson, one count of arson, one count of felonious assault, one count of endangering children, and two counts of domestic violence. Appellant pled not guilty to these charges, and a jury trial was held. Following the state's case-in-chief, the defense moved for a judgment of acquittal pursuant to Crim. R. 29. The trial court granted appellant's motion regarding the endangering children charge. The trial court denied the motion with respect to the remaining charges. The jury found appellant guilty of these remaining charges.

The trial court sentenced appellant to a five-year term on the aggravated arson conviction, a five-year term on the felonious assault conviction, a one-year term on the arson conviction, and a nine-month term for each of the domestic violence convictions. These sentences were ordered to be served consecutively.

Appellant raises the following assignment of error on appeal:

> "The conviction of the appellant was against the manifest weight of the evidence and based on evidence that was insufficient as a matter of law."***

In his brief, appellant only challenges his convictions for arson and aggravated arson. Therefore, we will not engage in a detailed analysis of the other convictions. A review of the record, including Angela's testimony, reveals the state presented sufficient evidence to sustain appellant's convictions for domestic violence and felonious assault.

Aggravated arson is codified in R.C. 2909.02, which states, in pertinent part:

> "(A) No person, by means of fire or explosion, shall knowingly do any of the following:
> "(1) Create a substantial risk of serious physical harm to any person other than the offender[.]"

Arson is codified in R.C. 2909.03, which states, in part:

> "(A) No person, by means of fire or explosion, shall knowingly do any of the following:
> "(1) Cause, or create a substantial risk of, physical harm to any property of another without the other person's consent."
> "A person acts knowingly, regardless of his purpose, when he is aware that his conduct will probably cause a certain result or will probably be of a certain nature. A person has knowledge of circumstances when he is aware that such circumstances probably exist.

At specific issue in this case is whether there was sufficient evidence presented that there was a "fire" and that a substantial risk of harm was created.

There was evidence presented that appellant lit his cigarette lighter on two separate occasions. "Fire" is not defined in the Revised Code Section relating to arson offenses. Therefore, it will be given the meaning generally understood in common usage. The ordinary definition of fire is "[a] rapid, persistent chemical reaction that releases heat and light, esp. the exothermic combination of a combustible substance with oxygen." The flame of the cigarette lighter was a rapid, persistent chemical reaction that produced both heat and light. In addition, the flame was an exothermic combination of the cigarette lighter's fluid (a combustible substance) and oxygen. Accordingly, the flame from appellant's cigarette lighter was a "fire."

The characterization of a flame from a lighter as fire is not unprecedented. In *State v. Herring,* the Second Appellate District held that there was sufficient evidence presented to sustain an aggravated arson conviction where the victim was burned on her unclothed vagina and buttock with a lighter. We agree with the Second District's holding that a flame from a lighter can be a fire for the purposes of R.C. 2909.02 and 2909.03.

Detective Scott Witkosky testified that kerosene is flammable. He also testified that if one to two gallons of kerosene were ignited inside the trailer, the entire trailer would be engulfed. This evidence, combined with the fact that the victim was in the bathtub covered in gallons of kerosene while appellant was waving his lit cigarette lighter, is sufficient to show that a substantial risk of harm was created.

Historically, arson required a malicious burning of the dwelling house of another. However, as noted above, the current statutes only require that a substantial risk of harm is created by fire. A review of the committee comment to R.C. 2909.02 is helpful in recognizing this distinction. The comment states, in part:

"This section substantially broadens former law by defining the offense not only in terms of burning an occupied structure, but also in terms of endangering any person or damaging any occupied structure by means of fire or explosion. In addition, the section represents a significant shift in emphasis from the way in which the relative severity of arson offenses was formerly determined, by using the degree of danger to persons as the key factor and placing only secondary reliance on the kind of property involved in the offense."

This comment is extremely helpful in the analysis of this case. Not only was there a risk to property as a result of appellant's conduct, there was a grave degree of danger to Angela and the couple's two-year-old daughter.

After soaking Angela in kerosene, appellant waived the flame from a lit cigarette lighter in front of her kerosene soaked body. At the end of this rampage, the victim ended up in the bathtub, where another two-and-a-half gallons of kerosene was poured upon her. Finally, in the words of the terrified victim, "he lit [his lighter] and waving it a little and then it, I don't know if he dropped it or if fell but [it] went out before it landed in the tub." As a matter of law, deliberately waving a flame in the presence of a person soaked in kerosene is aggravated arson.

Appellant asserts that there was insufficient evidence that he placed the property of another at risk. He claims the trailer was in his name and none of Angela's personal belongings were in danger. An individual may be prosecuted for arson relating to a spouse's property when they are living together. Angela testified that several of her belongings were inside the trailer when appellant doused her with kerosene. Detective Witkosky testified that the entire trailer would have been engulfed had the kerosene ignited. Taken together, this is sufficient evidence to show that appellant created a substantial risk of harm to Angela's property.

Finally, Appellant claims that he could not have acted knowingly, due to his impairment from alcohol. R.C. 2901.21 has been amended, effective October 27, 2000, and now provides, in pertinent part, "[v]oluntary intoxication may not be taken into consideration in determining the existence of a mental state that is an element of a criminal offense." Thus, appellant was not entitled to use the defense of voluntary intoxication.

There was sufficient evidence presented to sustain the appellant's convictions for aggravated arson and arson.

In addition to his sufficiency argument, Boggs claims the convictions were against the manifest weight of the evidence.***

Boggs did not testify on his own behalf, and the defense did not call any witnesses. Therefore, the version of events as presented by the state's witnesses was the only evidence before the jury. There were not conflicting versions of these events. Thus, it was the jury's decision whether to believe the state's witnesses, including the victim, as to what happened. We cannot say the jury lost its way or created a manifest miscarriage of justice by believing the state's witnesses.***

DONALD R. FORD, P.J., dissenting.

I respectfully dissent. R.C. 2909.02(A)(1) states in part that "[n]o person, by means of fire or explosion, shall knowingly *** [c]reate a substantial risk of serious physical harm to any person other than the offender ***." Criminal offenses in Ohio were codified by the General Assembly in the early nineteenth century with the effect that common law crimes were abrogated in Ohio. R.C. 2901.03; see, also, Committee Comment to H 511. Any act, to be criminal, must be declared so by some statute or ordinance. *In re The Grand Jury* (1907), 5 Ohio N.P. (N.S.) 33. Nevertheless, the common law has been referenced since then for pertinent interpretive purposes. At common law, arson primarily focused on the burning of property and did not include a substantial risk of physical harm to any person. Today, the crime of arson has been considerably broadened by modern legislation. As such, R.C. 2909.02 takes the common law definition of arson a step further to include a substantial risk of serious physical harm to any person.

At common law, arson is the malicious burning of the dwelling house of another. Consequently, an accidental or negligent burning is not sufficient. *Morris v. State* (1900), 124 Ala. 44. Arson is not committed unless some part of the structure of the dwelling house is actually damaged by fire. Blackening or discoloration is insufficient; the fiber of some part of the structural material of the building must be at least slightly damaged. *People v. Oliff* (1935), 361 Ill. 237. The word "burn" means to consume by fire; charring is sufficient. *People v. Haggerty* (1873), 46 Cal. 354.

Thus, both common law arson and the Revised Code require a "fire" in order for something to be consumed, at least in part, by flames. It is this writer's position that the word "fire" as used in this statutory section is not intended to be interpreted in derogation of the common law. Certainly no legislative intent is expressed in the statute which would support that position. "Fire" is not defined by R.C. 2909.01, the section relating to arson offenses. The majority contends that the flame from the lighter is sufficient to constitute a "fire" for purposes of R.C. 2909.02 and 2909.03, with which I disagree wholeheartedly. I feel it is the legislature's role to address whether it wishes to depart from the common law meaning of "fire," to an expanded version of what the majority advances.

The majority relies on the Second District in *State v. Herring* (Jan. 31, 1993), 2d Dist. No. 13128, 1993 Ohio App. LEXIS 179, which determined that a flame from a lighter can be a "fire" for purposes of R.C. 2909.02 and 2909.03. However, the facts in that case are quite distinct from those in the case sub judice. As such, the majority's emphasis on *Herring* is misplaced. In *Herring,* the court held that there was sufficient evidence presented to sustain an aggravated arson conviction where the victim was burned on her unclothed vagina and buttock with a lighter. *Id.* at 13. Thus, in *Herring,* the victim was actually burned by the flame produced from the lighter.

In the case at bar, on the other hand, although appellant ignited and dropped his lighter, it was out by the time that it hit the bathtub. There was no evidence which indicated that the victim's clothing caught on fire. Also, there was no evidence that the victim was physically burned or singed in any way. Thus, the flame from the lighter never produced a "fire" that physically damaged the victim's person. Therefore, while appellant's behavior was heinous and reprehensible, he never set a "fire" within the meaning of the statute. Based on the facts in this case, the desire to prosecute this matter under the arson penumbra rather than a lesser offense is understandable. Again, it remains a legislative prerogative to broaden the statutory scope to make a charge of arson applicable to the facts predicated here. Although the majority argues that appellant created a substantial risk of serious physical harm to the victim by pouring kerosene over her body and waving a lighter about, no "fire" or "explosion" was created pursuant to R.C. 2909.02(A)(1).

I would reverse the judgment of the trial court.

2. Model Penal Code (MPC)

The MPC was created by the American Law Institute in 1962 and last updated in 1985. The MPC was initially drafted in order to help guide states as they modernized their criminal statutes. Another purpose or goal of the MPC was to harmonize the criminal laws in the various jurisdictions around the country. While the MPC itself is not binding law, numerous jurisdictions around the country have borrowed from the MPC and codified its provisions.

Arguably, the most lasting contribution of the MPC on criminal law was its standardization of mens rea terms. Before the MPC, jurisdictions around the country relied on various terms and phrases to describe the mental state required for specific crimes. The MPC brought not only uniformity to the topic of mens rea but also clarity by relying on only four terms (knowingly, purposely, negligently, and recklessly). Furthermore, the MPC offered concrete definitions of those terms.

When initially drafted, the MPC was thought to be very cutting-edge and many states quickly adopted portions of it. However, because the MPC has not been regularly updated, many view it today as antiquated. Nonetheless, some judges when interpreting statutes will look to the MPC for guidance. However, this practice is much more likely to occur with the common law. The following case, *State v. Woods,* illustrates how judges rely on the MPC to interpret Ohio's attempt statute.

State v. Woods, 48 Ohio St. 2d 127 (1976)

Syllabus by the Court

***Shortly after midnight on July 17, 1974, the Cincinnati police received a telephone call from a woman who said that she had seen a man on the roof of the United Dairy Farmers store at 2373 Florence Avenue in Cincinnati. That information was broadcast to patrol cars in the area and several officers responded. One of the officers, Patrolman Terry Kramer, observed two men looking over their shoulders while walking on Florence Avenue in the vicinity of the store, and he reported that information over the police radio. Another officer, Patrolman David Cole, also responded to the broadcast and was approaching the scene along Florence Avenue.

Just after he made his broadcast, Patrolman Kramer heard a series of gunshots. Other officers also heard the shots and came to the scene. Patrolman Cole was lying in the street at the rear of his cruiser, dying from multiple gunshot wounds. Cole was pronounced dead on arrival at the hospital, and the subsequent autopsy and ballistics examination disclosed that he had been shot by both a .22 and a .38 caliber weapon.

Roland Reaves, the defendant in case No. 76-155, was arrested on July 18, 1974, in Cincinnati and subsequently made statements to investigating officers which implicated Ricardo Woods, the defendant in case No. 76-137. Woods was arrested on July 19, 1974, in West Virginia at the home of his mother. After the arrival of Cincinnati police, Woods made a complete statement as to his part in the events leading up to and following the homicide.

Both defendants were charged with multiple counts of aggravated murder with specifications. Reaves was tried before a jury, and Woods before a three-judge panel. The evidence presented at the two trials was virtually identical. It established that Woods had been living with Reaves' sister for some time and had recently been laid off from his construction job. Woods and Reaves met for the first time, about two weeks before the killing, when Reaves came to Cincinnati from Chicago. Woods stated that on July 16, he and Reaves agreed that they needed money, and, using Woods' unemployment check as funds, Reaves negotiated the purchase of a .38 caliber revolver, which Reaves told the seller he planned to use to rob a loan company. Later, around midnight, Reaves, accompanied by Woods, parked his car close to the United Dairy Farmers store, and both men began to "case" the store. According to Woods' statement, they could see the store manager inside. The plan was to wait until the manager came out and to "hold him up and take the money." Reaves had the .38 caliber revolver and Woods had a .22 caliber pistol which Reaves had brought from Chicago. Reaves then left Woods as a lookout across the street, and climbed onto the roof of the store.

Reaves descended from the roof and joined Woods who said that "things looked funny." Apparently, they had heard the sirens of a fire department unit making a run nearby. Woods and Reaves were walking away from the store and down Florence Avenue when Patrolman Cole skidded to a stop near the curb. Woods stated that he leaned in the front passenger window of the police cruiser to talk to Cole just as the officer was getting out on the opposite side of the car, and that when Cole got to the rear of the cruiser, Reaves began to fire at him, the first bullet striking Cole in the chest. Reaves fired three or four times, and Woods also shot at Cole, who at that time was lying on the street, as he and Reaves fled the scene. Cole fired four shots without hitting the fleeing men.

The pair ran to the house of a friend nearby, changed clothes, and drove away in the friend's car. Woods left the next morning for his mother's home in West Virginia.

At their separate trials, Reaves and Woods were each found guilty of aggravated murder, under a count in the indictment charging that they had purposely caused the death of Patrolman Cole while fleeing immediately after attempting to commit aggravated robbery, and guilty of the second specification, that at the time of the offense the victim was a law-enforcement officer whom they knew to be such, and who at the time was engaged in his duties. Following mitigation hearings, both defendants were sentenced to death. The Court of Appeals affirmed both judgments in separate opinions, and the causes are now before this court as a matter of right.***

STERN, Justice.

II

In case No. 76-137, appellant Woods raises similar claims relating to the constitutionality of Ohio's death penalty statutes, and also contends that the evidence was insufficient to prove an attempted robbery, or, in the alternative, that the defense had proved an abandonment of the offense, and that the charge of aggravated murder against Woods should accordingly have been reduced to murder.

There is no serious dispute concerning the facts of this case. Defendants Reaves and Woods decided to rob the manager of the United Dairy Farmers store by accosting him as he came out with the day's receipts; they "cased" the premises; Reaves climbed onto the roof, while Woods stayed behind as a lookout; Reaves then climbed back down, apparently having heard the nearby fire engine siren; and Reaves and Woods then walked away, leaving Reaves' car behind.

R.C. 2923.02(A) provides that: "No person, purposely or knowingly, and when purpose or knowledge is sufficient culpability for the commission of an offense, shall engage in conduct which, if successful, would constitute or result in the offense."

The committee comment for this section states, in part, that: "In order to prove an attempt to commit an offense, it must be shown that particular conduct directed toward commission of the offense took place and that such conduct, if successful, would constitute or result in the offense. ***" This language establishes that the essential elements of a criminal attempt are the mems rea of purpose or knowledge, and conduct directed toward the commission of an offense. The statute does not, however, indicate how far this conduct must proceed toward the actual consummation of the crime in order to be considered an attempt to commit that crime. There is also little case law in Ohio on this question, although this court has held that the conduct necessary for a criminal attempt "need not be the last proximate act prior to the consummation of the felony." State v. Farmer (1951), 156 Ohio St. 214. In Farmer, an assault with intent to rob was held, 156 Ohio St. at page 217, "sufficient to justify the triers of the facts in determining beyond a reasonable doubt that the action of the defendant at the time for *** (an) altercation was action taken to carry out that intent and therefore amounted to an attempt to perpetrate robbery." In this case, Reaves committed no assault, and the question arises as to whether his acts nevertheless amounted to an attempt to rob.

American courts have generally agreed that intent to commit a crime does not of itself constitute an attempt, nor does mere preparation. The difficulty is to formulate a standard that excludes preparations prior to an actual attempt to commit a crime, while including, as punishable, those acts which are so dangerously close to resulting in a crime that intervention and arrest by the police are justified, even before the "last proximate act." Various tests have been suggested and followed in other jurisdictions. There is a good discussion of this problem and the various approaches in Wechsler, Jones and Korn, The Treatment of Inchoate Crimes in the Model Penal Code of the American Law Institute: Attempt, Solicitation, and Conspiracy. 61 Columbia L. Rev. 571, 573-621. It is not necessary to consider each of the alternative approaches here. Ohio's statutory definitions of criminal offenses in the Revised Code are based largely upon the American Law Institute's Model Penal Code, and the standard adopted in the latter Code appears to us workable, reasonable, and consistent with the language of R.C. 2923.02(A). Under Section 5.01 of the Model Penal Code, an attempt is when one "purposely does or omits to do anything which is *** an act or omission constituting a substantial step in a course of conduct planned to culminate in his commission of the crime." To constitute a "substantial step," the conduct must be "strongly corroborative of the actor's criminal purpose." The application of this standard will of course depend upon both the nature of the intended crime and the facts of the particular case. A substantial step in the commission of a robbery may be quite different from that in arson, rape, or some other crime. But this standard does properly direct attention to overt acts of the defendant which convincingly demonstrate a firm purpose to commit a crime, while allowing police intervention, based upon observation of such incriminating con...[d]uct, in order to prevent the crime when the criminal intent becomes apparent.

Reaves' act of climbing onto the store roof with a gun, apparently to lie in wait for the store manager, was plainly a substantial step in the planned robbery, and certainly was strongly corroborative of the criminal purpose. We find no error in the trial court's holding that this conduct could constitute attempted robbery, or in the verdict of the three-judge panel that the defendant Woods was guilty beyond a reasonable doubt.

There was also sufficient evidence from which to conclude that the defendants had not "completely and voluntarily" renounced their criminal purpose. Abandoning an attempt out of fear that the police might be coming cannot reasonably be considered voluntary. Nor is it clear in this case that the attempt was completely abandoned, for the defendants left the car parked near the store and walked away, behavior from which a jury might properly infer that they intended only to wait at a distance and observe whether the robbery might still be possible despite the siren they had heard.[1] We find no error in the guilty verdict rendered by the three-judge panel.

---

[1] Cf., Model Penal Code, Section 501(4):

> *** Within the meaning of this Article, renunciation of criminal purpose is not voluntary if it is motivated, in whole or in part, by circumstances, not present or apparent at the inception of the actor's course of conduct, which increase the probability of detection or apprehension or which make more difficult the accomplishment of the criminal purpose. Renunciation is not complete if it is motivated by a decision to postpone the criminal conduct until a more advantageous time or to transfer the criminal effort to another but similar objective or victim.

3. Criminal Procedure

Criminal law focuses on the elements of crimes and how they should be defined and punished. In contrast, criminal procedure examines the constitutional issues that arise in the investigation and prosecution of crimes. While it is possible to teach both topics together, most law schools have separate courses for criminal law and criminal procedure. Some law schools further divide criminal procedure into adjudication and investigation or Criminal Procedure I and II. As one might imagine, criminal law and criminal procedure on occasion bleed over into each other. In addition, certain criminal procedure topics give students the necessary foundation to understand why particular conduct cannot be criminalized or why statutes have to be drafted in a specific manner. The following case, which examines the constitutionality of a federal criminal statute, illustrates these last two points.

United States v. Drew, 259 F.R.D. 449 (C.D. Cal. 2009)

I. INTRODUCTION

This case raises the issue of whether (and/or when will) violations of an Internet website's terms of service constitute a crime under the Computer Fraud and Abuse Act ("CFAA"), 18 U.S.C. § 1030.... [T]he question arose in the present motion...is whether an intentional breach of an Internet website's terms of service, without more, is sufficient to constitute a misdemeanor violation of the CFAA; and, if so, would the statute, as so interpreted, survive constitutional challenges on the grounds of vagueness and related doctrines.

II. BACKGROUND

A. Indictment

In the Indictment, Drew was charged with one count of conspiracy in violation of 18 U.S.C. § 371 and three counts of violating a felony portion of the CFAA, i.e., 18 U.S.C. §§ 1030(a)(2)(C) and 1030(c)(2)(B)(ii), which prohibit accessing a computer without authorization or in excess of authorization and obtaining information from a protected computer where the conduct involves an interstate or foreign communication and the offense is committed in furtherance of a crime or tortious act.

The Indictment included, inter alia, the following allegations (not all of which were established by the evidence at trial). Drew, a resident of O'Fallon, Missouri, entered into a conspiracy in which its members agreed to intentionally access a computer used in interstate commerce without (and/or in excess of) authorization in order to obtain information for the purpose of committing the tortious act of intentional infliction of emotional distress upon "M.T.M.," subsequently identified as Megan Meier ("Megan"). Megan was a 13 year old girl living in O'Fallon who had been a classmate of Drew's daughter Sarah. Pursuant to the conspiracy, on or about September 20, 2006, the conspirators registered and set up a profile for a fictitious 16 year old male juvenile named "Josh Evans" on the www.MySpace.com website ("MySpace"), and posted a photograph of a boy without that boy's knowledge or consent. Such conduct violated MySpace's terms of service. The conspirators contacted Megan through the MySpace network (on which she had her own profile) using the Josh Evans pseudonym and began to flirt with her over a number of days. Id. On or about October 7, 2006, the conspirators had "Josh" inform Megan that he was moving away. On or about October 16, 2006, the conspirators had "Josh" tell Megan that he no longer liked her and that "the world would be a better place without her in it." Later on that same day, after learning that Megan had killed herself, Drew caused the Josh Evans MySpace account to be deleted.

B. Verdict

The jury did find Defendant "guilty" "of [on the dates specified in the Indictment] accessing a computer involved in interstate or foreign communication without authorization or in excess of authorization to obtain information in violation of Title 18, United States Code, Section 1030(a)(2)(C) and (c)(2)(A), a misdemeanor."

IV. DISCUSSION

A. The Misdemeanor 18 U.S.C. § 1030(a)(2)(C) Crime Based on Violation of a Website's Terms of Service***

In this particular case, as conceded by the Government, the only basis for finding that Drew intentionally accessed MySpace's computer/servers without authorization and/or in excess of authorization was her and/or her co-conspirator's violations of the MSTOS by deliberately creating the false Josh Evans profile, posting a photograph of a juvenile without his permission and pretending to be a sixteen year old O'Fallon resident for the purpose of communicating with Megan. Therefore, if conscious violations of the MySpace terms of service were not sufficient to satisfy the first element of the CFAA misdemeanor violation as per 18 U.S.C. §§ 1030(a)(2)(C) and 1030(b)(2)(A), Drew's Rule 29(c) motion would have to be granted on that basis alone. However, this Court concludes that an intentional breach of the MSTOS can potentially constitute accessing the MySpace computer/server without authorization and/or in excess of authorization under the statute.***

B. Contravention of the Void-for-Vagueness Doctrine
1. Applicable Law

Justice Holmes observed that, as to criminal statutes, there is a "fair warning" requirement. As he stated in *McBoyle v. United States*:

> Although it is not likely that a criminal will carefully consider the text of the law before he murders or steals, it is reasonable that a fair warning should be given to the world in language that the common world will understand, of what the law intends to do if a certain line is passed. To make the warning fair, so far as possible the line should be clear.

As further elaborated by the Supreme Court in *United States v. Lanier*:

> There are three related manifestations of the fair warning requirement. First, the vagueness doctrine bars enforcement of "a statute which either forbids or requires the doing of an act in terms so vague that men of common intelligence must necessarily guess at its meaning and differ as to its application." *Connally v. General Constr. Co.*, 269 U.S. 385, 391 (1926) . . . . Second, as a sort of "junior version of the vagueness doctrine," H. Packer, The Limits of the Criminal Sanction 95 (1968), the canon of strict construction of criminal statutes, or rule of lenity, ensures fair warning by so resolving ambiguity in a criminal statute as to apply it only to conduct clearly covered . . . . Third, although clarity at the requisite level may be supplied by judicial gloss on an otherwise uncertain statute, . . . due process bars courts from applying a novel construction of a criminal statute to conduct that neither the statute nor any prior judicial decision has fairly disclosed to be within its scope. . . . In each of these guises, the touchstone is whether the statute, either standing alone or as construed, made it reasonably clear at the relevant time that the defendant's conduct was criminal.

The void-for-vagueness doctrine has two prongs: 1) a definitional/notice sufficiency requirement and, more importantly, 2) a guideline setting element to govern law enforcement. In *Kolender v. Lawson*, the Court explained that:

> As generally stated, the void-for-vagueness doctrine requires that a penal statute define the criminal offense with sufficient definiteness that ordinary people can understand what conduct is prohibited and in a manner that does not encourage

arbitrary and discriminatory enforcement . . . . Although the doctrine focuses both on actual notice to citizens and arbitrary enforcement, we have recognized recently that the more important aspect of the vagueness doctrine "is not actual notice, but the other principal element of the doctrine – the requirement that a legislature establish minimal guidelines to govern law enforcement." *Smith* [*v. Goguen*], 415 U.S. [566,] 574 [1974]. Where the legislature fails to provide such minimal guidelines, a criminal statute may permit "a standardless sweep [that] allows policemen, prosecutors, and juries to pursue their personal predilections."

To avoid contraving the void-for-vagueness doctrine, the criminal statute must contain "relatively clear guidelines as to prohibited conduct" and provide "objective criteria" to evaluate whether a crime has been committed. *Gonzalez v. Carhart*.***

2. Definitional/Actual Notice Deficiencies

The pivotal issue herein is whether basing a CFAA misdemeanor violation as per 18 U.S.C. §§ 1030(a)(2)(C) and 1030(c)(2)(A) upon the conscious violation of a website's terms of service runs afoul of the void-for-vagueness doctrine. This Court concludes that it does primarily because of the absence of minimal guidelines to govern law enforcement, but also because of actual notice deficiencies.

As discussed in Section IV(A) above, terms of service which are incorporated into a browsewrap or clickwrap agreement can, like any other type of contract, define the limits of authorized access as to a website and its concomitant computer/server(s). However, the question is whether individuals of "common intelligence" are on notice that a breach of a terms of service contract can become a crime under the CFAA. Arguably, they are not.

First, an initial inquiry is whether the statute, as it is written, provides sufficient notice. Here, the language of section 1030(a)(2)(C) does not explicitly state (nor does it implicitly suggest) that the CFAA has "criminalized breaches of contract" in the context of website terms of service. Normally, breaches of contract are not the subject of criminal prosecution. Thus, while "ordinary people" might expect to be exposed to civil liabilities for violating a contractual provision, they would not expect criminal penalties. This would especially be the case where the services provided by MySpace are in essence offered at no cost to the users and, hence, there is no specter of the users "defrauding" MySpace in any monetary sense.

Second, if a website's terms of service controls what is "authorized" and what is "exceeding authorization"—which in turn governs whether an individual's accessing information or services on the website is criminal or not, section 1030(a)(2)(C) would be unacceptably vague because it is unclear whether any or all violations of terms of service will render the access unauthorized, or whether only certain ones will. For example, in the present case, MySpace's terms of service prohibits a member from engaging in a multitude of activities on the website, including such conduct as "criminal or tortious activity," "gambling," "advertising to . . . any Member to buy or sell any products," "transmit[ting] any chain letters," "covering or obscuring the banner advertisements on your personal profile page," "disclosing your password to any third party," etc. The MSTOS does not specify which precise terms of service, when breached, will result in a termination of MySpace's authorization for the visitor/member to access the website. If any violation of any term of service is held to make the access unauthorized, that strategy would probably resolve this particular vagueness issue; but it would, in turn, render the statute incredibly overbroad and contravene the second prong of the void-for-vagueness doctrine as to setting guidelines to govern law enforcement.

Third, by utilizing violations of the terms of service as the basis for the section 1030(a)(2)(C) crime, that approach makes the website owner—in essence—the party who ultimately defines the criminal conduct. This will lead to further vagueness problems. The owner's description of a term of service might itself be so vague as to make the visitor or member reasonably unsure of what the term of service covers. For example, the MSTOS prohibits members from posting in "band and filmmaker profiles . . . sexually suggestive imagery or any other unfair . . . [c]ontent intended to draw traffic to the profile." It is unclear what "sexually suggestive imagery" and "unfair content" mean. Moreover, website owners can establish terms where either the scope or the application of the provision are to be decided by them ad hoc and/or pursuant to undelineated standards. For example, the MSTOS provides that what constitutes "prohibited content" on the website is determined "in the sole discretion of MySpace.com . . . ." Additionally, terms of service may allow the website owner to unilaterally amend and/or add to the terms with minimal notice to users.

Fourth, because terms of service are essentially a contractual means for setting the scope of authorized access, a level of indefiniteness arises from the necessary application of contract law in general and/or other contractual requirements within the applicable terms of service to any criminal prosecution. For example, the MSTOS has a provision wherein "any dispute" between MySpace and a visitor/member/user arising out of the terms of service is subject to arbitration upon the demand of either party. Before a breach of a term of service can be found and/or the effect of that breach upon MySpace's ability to terminate the visitor/member/user's access to the site can be determined, the issue would be subject to arbitration. Thus, a question arises as to whether a finding of unauthorized access or in excess of authorized access can be made without arbitration.

Furthermore, under California law, a material breach of the MSTOS by a user/member does not automatically discharge the contract, but merely "excuses the injured party's performance, and gives him or her the election of certain remedies." 1 Witkin, Summary of California Law (Tenth Ed.). Those remedies include rescission and restitution, damages, specific performance, injunction, declaratory relief, etc. The contract can also specify particular remedies and consequences in the event of a breach which are in addition to or a substitution for those otherwise afforded by law. The MSTOS does provide that: "MySpace.com reserves the right, in its sole discretion . . . to restrict, suspend, or terminate your access to all or part of the services at any time, for any or no reason, with or without prior notice, and without liability." However, there is no provision which expressly states that a breach of the MSTOS automatically results in the termination of authorization to access the website. Indeed, the MSTOS cryptically states: "you are only authorized to use the Services . . . if you agree to abide by all applicable laws and to this Agreement."

3. The Absence of Minimal Guidelines to Govern Law Enforcement

Treating a violation of a website's terms of service, without more, to be sufficient to constitute "intentionally access[ing] a computer without authorization or exceed[ing] authorized access" would result in transforming section 1030(a)(2)(C) into an overwhelmingly overbroad enactment that would convert a multitude of otherwise innocent Internet users into misdemeanant criminals. As noted in Section IV(A) above, utilizing a computer to contact an Internet website by itself will automatically satisfy all remaining elements of the misdemeanor crime in 18 U.S.C. §§ 1030(a)(2)(C) and 1030(c)(2)(A). Where the website's terms of use only authorizes utilization of its services/applications upon agreement to abide by those terms (as, for example, the MSTOS does herein), any violation of any such provision can serve as a basis for finding access unauthorized and/or in excess of authorization.

One need only look to the MSTOS terms of service to see the expansive and elaborate scope of such provisions whose breach engenders the potential for criminal prosecution. Obvious examples of such breadth would include: 1) the lonely-heart who submits intentionally inaccurate data about his or her age, height and/or physical appearance, which contravenes the MSTOS prohibition against providing "information that you know is false or misleading"; 2) the student who posts candid photographs of classmates without their permission, which breaches the MSTOS provision covering "a photograph of another person that you have posted without that person's consent"; and/or 3) the exasperated parent who sends out a group message to neighborhood friends entreating them to purchase his or her daughter's girl scout cookies, which transgresses the

MSTOS rule against "advertising to, or solicitation of, any Member to buy or sell any products or services through the Services." However, one need not consider hypotheticals to demonstrate the problem. In this case, Megan (who was then 13 years old) had her own profile on MySpace, which was in clear violation of the MSTOS which requires that users be "14 years of age or older." No one would seriously suggest that Megan's conduct was criminal or should be subject to criminal prosecution.

Given the incredibly broad sweep of 18 U.S.C. §§ 1030(a)(2)(C) and 1030(c)(2)(A), should conscious violations of a website's terms of service be deemed sufficient by themselves to constitute accessing without authorization or exceeding authorized access, the question arises as to whether Congress has "establish[ed] minimal guidelines to govern law enforcement." *Kolender*, 461 U.S. at 358; see also *City of Chicago v. Morales*, 527 U.S. 41, 60 (1999). Section 1030(a)(2)(C) does not set forth "clear guidelines" or "objective criteria" as to the prohibited conduct in the Internet/website or similar contexts. See generally *Posters 'N' Things, Ltd.*, 511 U.S. at 525-26. For instance, section 1030(a)(2)(C) is not limited to instances where the website owner contacts law enforcement to complain about an individual's unauthorized access or exceeding permitted access on the site. Nor is there any requirement that there be any actual loss or damage suffered by the website or that there be a violation of privacy interests.

The Government argues that section 1030(a)(2)(C) has a scienter requirement which dispels any definitional vagueness and/or dearth of guidelines***

Here, the Government's position is that the "intentional" requirement is met simply by a conscious violation of a website's terms of service. The problem with that view is that it basically eliminates any limiting and/or guiding effect of the scienter element. It is unclear that every intentional breach of a website's terms of service would be or should be held to be equivalent to an intent to access the site without authorization or in excess of authorization. This is especially the case with MySpace and similar Internet venues which are publically available for access and use. However, if every such breach does qualify, then there is absolutely no limitation or criteria as to which of the breaches should merit criminal prosecution. All manner of situations will be covered from the more serious (e.g. posting child pornography) to the more trivial (e.g. posting a picture of friends without their permission). All can be prosecuted. Given the "standardless sweep" that results, federal law enforcement entities would be improperly free "to pursue their personal predilections." 31 *Kolender*, 461 U.S. at 358.

In sum, if any conscious breach of a website's terms of service is held to be sufficient by itself to constitute intentionally accessing a computer without authorization or in excess of authorization, the result will be that section 1030(a)(2)(C) becomes a law "that affords too much discretion to the police and too little notice to citizens who wish to use the [Internet]." *City of Chicago*, 527 U.S. at 64.

V. CONCLUSION

For the reasons stated above, the Defendant's motion under F.R. Crim. P. 29(c) is GRANTED.

Notes and Questions

1. What are the potential disadvantages of focusing on one particular jurisdiction in a criminal law course? Do you think those disadvantages outweigh the advantages?

2. Who had the stronger argument in *State v. Boggs*, the majority or the dissent? Which side stayed true to the common law? Does Ohio's current statute on arson stay true to the common law? Why was it even necessary for the judges to consult the common law?

3. In what way did the court in *State v. Woods* rely on the MPC?

4. *United States v. Drew* raises a number of interesting criminal procedure points that are relevant to students studying criminal law. The holding of the case centers on whether or not the CFAA is vague and thus unconstitutional as applied to the defendant. Ultimately, the court found the statute to be vague and struck it down as applied. This book will re-examine the Void-for-Vagueness Doctrine in the section on statutory rape.

Other criminal procedure topics related to *Drew* include the enactment of ex post facto laws. One of the reasons that the federal government prosecuted Mrs. Drew instead of the state of Missouri is that Missouri's harassment statute at the time did not cover online activities. Missouri subsequently modified its harassment statute to cover the online conduct of people like Mrs. Drew. This change, however, will not allow the state of Missouri to prosecute Mrs. Drew for any past conduct. Making new criminal laws retroactive violates the ex post facto clause of the United States constitution. Can you think of why the constitution would prohibit the government from prosecuting individuals for committing acts that were not criminal when first performed?

B. Criminal Law

Criminal law, generally studied in the first year of law school, is different from all other first-year courses. First, criminal law does not involve a dispute between two private parties. Rather, it concerns the state and an individual defendant. Also, the outcomes in criminal matters are far different than in civil matters where most disputes are resolved through the award of monetary damages or compensation. A defendant found guilty of violating a criminal law may be incarcerated and, in extreme cases, sentenced to death.

Another major difference involves the collateral consequences of a criminal conviction. Since one of the parties in criminal law is the state, a guilty verdict in a criminal trial carries with it the moral authority of society. Thus, a criminal conviction leads not only to the possibility of incarceration but also the attachment of a moral stigma for violating the rules of society. This stigma, among other things, greatly reduces an individual's opportunities in life.

Due to the differences between civil and criminal law, each has developed its own set of rules and procedures. The next case, *In re Winship*, examines the applicable legal standard to be applied when determining whether the defendant is guilty or innocent. While reading *In re Winship*, think about whether legal standards for civil and criminal cases should be the same or different. What justifications, if any, support a higher legal standard in criminal law?

In re Winship, 397 U.S. 358 (1970)

Mr. Justice BRENNAN delivered the opinion of the Court.

***This case presents the single, narrow question whether proof beyond a reasonable doubt is among the "essentials of due process and fair treatment" required during the adjudicatory stage when a juvenile is charged with an act which would constitute a crime if committed by an adult.

Section 712 of the New York Family Court Act defines a juvenile delinquent as "a person over seven and less than sixteen years of age who does any act which, if done by an adult, would constitute a crime." During a 1967 adjudicatory hearing, conducted pursuant to § 742 of the Act, a judge in New York Family Court found that appellant, then a 12-year-old boy, had entered a locker and stolen $112 from a woman's pocketbook. The petition which charged appellant with delinquency alleged that his act, "if done by an adult, would constitute the crime or crimes of Larceny." The judge acknowledged that the proof might not establish guilt beyond a reasonable doubt, but rejected appellant's contention that such proof was required by the Fourteenth Amendment. The judge relied instead on § 744(b) of the New York Family Court Act, which provides that [a]ny determination at the conclusion of [an adjudicatory] hearing that a [juvenile] did an act or acts must be based on a preponderance of the evidence.***

The requirement that guilt of a criminal charge be established by proof beyond a reasonable doubt dates at least from our early years as a Nation. The demand for a higher degree of persuasion in criminal cases was recurrently expressed from ancient times, [though] its crystallization into the formula "beyond a reasonable doubt" seems to have occurred as late as 1798. It is now accepted in common law jurisdictions as the measure of persuasion by which the prosecution must convince the trier of all the essential elements of guilt.

Although virtually unanimous adherence to the reasonable doubt standard in common law jurisdictions may not conclusively establish it as a requirement of due process, such adherence does "reflect a profound judgment about the way in which law should be enforced and justice administered."

Expressions in many opinions of this Court indicate that it has long been assumed that proof of a criminal charge beyond a reasonable doubt is constitutionally required. Justice Frankfurter stated that:

> [i]t is the duty of the Government to establish . . . guilt beyond a reasonable doubt. This notion—basic in our law and rightly one of the boasts of a free society—is a requirement and a safeguard of due process of law in the historic, procedural content of "due process."

In a similar vein, the Court said in *Brinegar v. United States*, supra, at 174, that:

> [g]uilt in a criminal case must be proved beyond a reasonable doubt and by evidence confined to that which long experience in the common law tradition, to some extent embodied in the Constitution, has crystalized into rules of evidence consistent with that standard. These rules are historically grounded rights of our system, developed to safeguard men from dubious and unjust convictions, with resulting forfeitures of life, liberty and property.

Davis v. United States stated that the requirement is implicit in "constitutions . . . [which] recognize the fundamental principles that are deemed essential for the protection of life and liberty." In *Davis*, a murder conviction was reversed because the trial judge instructed the jury that it was their duty to convict when the evidence was equally balanced regarding the sanity of the accused. This Court said:

> On the contrary, he is entitled to an acquittal of the specific crime charged if, upon all the evidence, there is reasonable doubt whether he was capable in law of committing crime. . . . No man should be deprived of his life under the forms of law unless the jurors who try him are able, upon their consciences, to say that the evidence before them . . . is sufficient to show beyond a

reasonable doubt the existence of every fact necessary to constitute the crime charged.

The reasonable doubt standard plays a vital role in the American scheme of criminal procedure. It is a prime instrument for reducing the risk of convictions resting on factual error. The standard provides concrete substance for the presumption of innocence—that bedrock "axiomatic and elementary" principle whose "enforcement lies at the foundation of the administration of our criminal law." As the dissenters in the New York Court of Appeals observed, and we agree,

> a person accused of a crime . . . would be at a severe disadvantage, a disadvantage amounting to a lack of fundamental fairness, if he could be adjudged guilty and imprisoned for years on the strength of the same evidence as would suffice in a civil case.

The requirement of proof beyond a reasonable doubt has this vital role in our criminal procedure for cogent reasons. The accused, during a criminal prosecution, has at stake interests of immense importance, both because of the possibility that he may lose his liberty upon conviction and because of the certainty that he would be stigmatized by the conviction. Accordingly, a society that values the good name and freedom of every individual should not condemn a man for commission of a crime when there is reasonable doubt about his guilt. As we said in *Speiser v. Randall*:

> There is always, in litigation, a margin of error, representing error in factfinding, which both parties must take into account. Where one party has at stake an interest of transcending value— as a criminal defendant his liberty—this margin of error is reduced as to him by the process of placing on the other party the burden of . . . persuading the factfinder at the conclusion of the trial of his guilt beyond a reasonable doubt. Due process commands that no man shall lose his liberty unless the Government has borne the burden of . . . convincing the factfinder of his guilt.

To this end, the reasonable doubt standard is indispensable, for it "impresses on the trier of fact the necessity of reaching a subjective state of certitude of the facts in issue."

Moreover, use of the reasonable doubt standard is indispensable to command the respect and confidence of the community in applications of the criminal law. It is critical that the moral force of the criminal law not be diluted by a standard of proof that leaves people in doubt whether innocent men are being condemned. It is also important in our free society that every individual going about his ordinary affairs have confidence that his government cannot adjudge him guilty of a criminal offense without convincing a proper factfinder of his guilt with utmost certainty.

Lest there remain any doubt about the constitutional stature of the reasonable doubt standard, we explicitly hold that the Due Process Clause protects the accused against conviction except upon proof beyond a reasonable doubt of every fact necessary to constitute the crime with which he is charged.***

Mr. Justice HARLAN, concurring

***[W]e have before us a case where the choice of the standard of proof has made a difference: the juvenile court judge below forthrightly acknowledged that he believed by a preponderance of the evidence, but was not convinced beyond a reasonable doubt, that appellant stole $112 from the complainant's pocketbook. Moreover, even though the labels used for alternative standards of proof are vague, and not a very sure guide to decisionmaking, the choice of the standard for a particular variety of adjudication does, I think, reflect a very fundamental assessment of the comparative social costs of erroneous factual determinations.

To explain why I think this so, I begin by stating two propositions, neither of which I believe can be fairly disputed. First, in a judicial proceeding in which there is a dispute about the facts of some earlier event, the factfinder cannot acquire unassailably accurate knowledge of what happened. Instead, all the factfinder can acquire is a belief of what *probably* happened. The intensity of this belief— the degree to which a factfinder is convinced that a given act actually occurred— can, of course, vary. In this regard, a standard of proof represents an attempt to instruct the factfinder concerning the degree of confidence our society thinks he should have in the correctness of factual conclusions for a particular type of adjudication. Although the phrases "preponderance of the evidence" and "proof beyond a reasonable doubt" are quantitatively imprecise, they do communicate to the finder of fact different notions concerning the degree of confidence he is expected to have in the correctness of his factual conclusions.

A second proposition, which is really nothing more than a corollary of the first, is that the trier of fact will sometimes, despite his best efforts, be wrong in his factual conclusions. In a lawsuit between two parties, a factual error can make a difference in one of two ways. First, it can result in a judgment in favor of the plaintiff when the true facts warrant a judgment for the defendant. The analogue in a criminal case would be the conviction of an innocent man. On the other hand, an erroneous factual determination can result in a judgment for the defendant when the true facts justify a judgment in plaintiff's favor. The criminal analogue would be the acquittal of a guilty man.

The standard of proof influences the relative frequency of these two types of erroneous outcomes. If, for example, the standard of proof for a criminal trial were a preponderance of the evidence, rather than proof beyond a reasonable doubt, there would be a smaller risk of factual errors that result in freeing guilty persons, but a far greater risk of factual errors that result in convicting the innocent. Because the standard of proof affects the comparative frequency of these two types of erroneous outcomes, the choice of the standard to be applied in a particular kind of litigation should, in a rational world, reflect an assessment of the comparative social disutility of each.

When one makes such an assessment, the reason for different standards of proof in civil, as opposed to criminal, litigation becomes apparent. In a civil suit between two private parties for money damages, for example, we view it as no more serious in general for there to be an erroneous verdict in the defendant's favor than for there to be an erroneous verdict in the plaintiff's favor. A preponderance of the evidence standard therefore seems peculiarly appropriate, for, as explained most sensibly, it simply requires the trier of fact to believe that the existence of a fact is more probable than its nonexistence before [he] may find in favor of the party who has the burden to persuade the [judge] of the fact's existence.

In a criminal case, on the other hand, we do not view the social disutility of convicting an innocent man as equivalent to the disutility of acquitting someone who is guilty. As Mr. Justice Brennan wrote for the Court in *Speiser v. Randall*:

> There is always in litigation a margin of error, representing error in factfinding, which both parties must take into account. Where one party has at stake an interest of transcending value— as a criminal defendant his liberty—this margin of error is reduced as to him by the process of placing on the other party the burden . . . of persuading the factfinder at the conclusion of the trial of his guilt beyond a reasonable doubt.

In this context, I view the requirement of proof beyond a reasonable doubt in a criminal case as bottomed on a fundamental value determination of our society that it is far worse to convict an innocent man than to let a guilty man go free. It is only because of the nearly complete and longstanding acceptance of the reasonable doubt standard by the States in criminal trials that the Court has not, before today, had to hold explicitly that due process, as an expression of fundamental procedural fairness, requires a more stringent standard for criminal trials than for ordinary civil litigation.

II

When one assesses the consequences of an erroneous factual determination in a juvenile delinquency proceeding in which a youth is accused of a crime, I think it must be concluded that, while the consequences are not identical to those in a criminal case, the differences will not support a distinction in the standard of proof. First, and of paramount importance, a factual error here, as in a criminal case, exposes the accused to a complete loss of his personal liberty through a state-imposed confinement away from his home, family, and friends. And second, a delinquency determination, to some extent at least, stigmatizes a youth in that it is, by definition, bottomed on a finding that the accused committed a crime. Although there are no doubt costs to society (and possibly even to the youth himself) in letting a guilty youth go free, I think here, as in a criminal case, it is far worse to declare an innocent youth a delinquent. I therefore agree that a juvenile court judge should be no less convinced of the factual conclusion that the accused committed the criminal act with which he is charged than would be required in a criminal trial.

Notes and Questions

1. Most law schools make criminal law a required first-year course. If you were designing a law school curriculum, would you place criminal law in the first-year? What rationale would support placing criminal law in the first, second, or third year?

2. *In re Winship* holds that the beyond a reasonable doubt standard is applied because the consequences of a criminal trial are more severe than in a civil trial. Is this assertion always true? Under what circumstances might someone be more concerned with a civil matter than a criminal matter?

3. Do you agree with Justice Harlan's concurring opinion in which he writes, "it is far worse to convict an innocent man than to let a guilty man go free"? What if the guilty man goes on to commit additional crimes, some of which are quite heinous?

4. After reading *In re Winship,* do you think it is permissible for a judge to give the following instructions? Why or why not?

> The law presumes that a person intends the ordinary consequences of his voluntary acts.

In *Sandstrom v. Montana*, 442 U.S. 510 (1979), these same instructions were given in a case where the defendant was charged with "deliberate homicide."

Defense argued that the defendant did not kill the victim "purposely or knowingly." Thus, the defendant was not guilty of deliberate homicide but of a lesser crime. Defense counsel then objected to the proposed instructions ("The law presumes that a person intends the ordinary consequences of his voluntary acts") arguing that they had "the effect of shifting the burden of proof on the issue of" purpose and knowledge to the defense.

In siding with the defense, the Supreme Court found that a reasonable juror could have interpreted the instructions in one of two ways; (1) the juror could have interpreted the presumption as "conclusive," that is, not a presumption at all, but as an irrebutable direction by the court to find intent once convinced of the facts triggering the presumption; or (2) the juror could have interpreted the instruction as a direction to find intent upon proof of the defendant's voluntary actions, unless the defendant proved the contrary by some quantum of proof. Since a reasonable juror could have given the presumption conclusive or persuasion-shifting effect, the court found the instructions unconstitutional.

5. If you were before a jury and had to explain the difference between proof beyond a reasonable doubt and preponderance of evidence, how would you do it? Quantify those terms mathematically.

6. How does one define "reasonable doubt"? Here is the definition of reasonable doubt taken from the Ohio Jury Instructions:

> "Reasonable doubt" is a doubt based on reason and common sense. Reasonable doubt is not mere possible doubt, because everything relating to human affairs is open to some possible or imaginary doubt. "Reasonable doubt" exists when an ordinary person would hesitate to act on the evidence in the most important of his or her own affairs. Proof beyond a reasonable doubt is the highest standard of proof in our legal system.

Is this definition helpful? Why or why not?

7. Historical Note: According to Professor James Q. Whitman who wrote *The Origins of Reasonable Doubt: Theological Roots of Criminal Trial*, Yale University Press (2008),

> The reasonable doubt formula seems mystifying today because we have lost sight of its original purpose. At its origins the rule was not intended to perform the function we ask it to perform today: It was not primarily intended to protect the accused. Instead, strange as it may sound, the reasonable doubt

formula was originally concerned with protecting the souls against damnation.

. . . Convicting an innocent defendant was regarded, in the older Christian tradition as a potential mortal sin. The reasonable doubt rule developed in response to this disquieting possibility. It was originally a theological doctrine, intended to reassure jurors that they could convict the defendant without risking their own salvation.

8. Why do we have criminal laws? What is the purpose behind criminal law? According to Professor Paul Robinson, criminal law serves three functions. First, criminal law announces to society what conduct is prohibited. Second, criminal law determines whether a violation of a societal rule warrants condemnation. Third, criminal law serves a grading function to assess the seriousness of the offense.

Chapter 2
Punishment

A. Theories of Punishment: Retributivism and Utilitarianism

After every criminal conviction, the court must determine the defendant's punishment. At present, there are two underlying theories of punishment, retributivism and utilitarianism. Retributivists believe that punishment is justified because people deserve it. Retributivism tends to be backward looking and seeks to justify punishment on the basis of the defendant's behavior in the past. Utilitarians believe that justification for punishment lies in the useful purpose that punishment seeks. Utilitarianism tends to be forward looking and seeks to justify punishment on the basis of the good consequences it is expected to produce in the future.

B. Principles of Punishment

In addition to the two theories of punishment, there are several principles of punishment. The following explains each principle of punishment.

<u>Incapacitation or Restraint</u>: Removing the criminal from society reduces the opportunity to commit future harm. The criminal defendant cannot commit crime if he is isolated from society.

<u>Rehabilitation</u>: Punishment allows for reform of the criminal who will hopefully conform to the rules of society. Some question whether it is appropriate to classify rehabilitation as punishment.

<u>Specific and General Deterrence</u>: Specific deterrence punishment is used to deter the criminal defendant from committing future criminal acts. General deterrence punishment of the criminal defendant hopes to deter the public at large. The

challenge here is measuring the effect of general deterrence on society as a whole.

Education: The trial phase, conviction, and punishment of the criminal defendant serve to show the public the repercussions of running afoul of the law. Education is especially important for malum prohibitum crimes.

Retribution: Punishment is imposed to satisfy the need for revenge by some in society. Retribution, the oldest form of punishment, is viewed disfavorably by some who see it as retaliation. Others argue that retribution is necessary to prevent private vengeance.

United States v. Blarek, 7 F. Supp. 2d 192 (E.D.N.Y. 1998)

I. Introduction

This sentencing presents the unusual case of two talented decorators whose desires to rise in the ranks of their profession while having access to unlimited funding for their creative endeavors induced them to become the facilitators, through money washing, of a ruthless and notorious Colombian drug cartel's operations.

A long term of incarceration and severe monetary penalties that will strip defendants of all their assets is required. The sentences are designed to penalize the defendants for their criminal behavior and to deter other business and professional people from assisting drug traffickers.

II. Facts

A. Charges

Defendants Blarek and Pellecchia were arrested in March 1996. They were charged with Racketeering, 18 U.S.C. § 1962(c), Racketeering Conspiracy, 18 U.S.C. § 1962(d), and Conspiring to Launder Monetary Instruments, 18 U.S.C. §§ 371 and 1956(h), for their alleged involvement in the activities of the Santacruz faction of the Cali Colombia drug mob. Blarek was additionally charged with one count of Interstate Travel in Aid of Racketeering. 18 U.S.C. § 1952(a)(1). By way of indictment, the government sought the forfeiture of defendants' property traceable to their alleged criminality. Both defendants pleaded not guilty.

B. Evidence

Blarek, while operating his own interior design firm in Coconut Grove, Florida, met Pellecchia in 1980. They worked together, and became intimate, cohabitating as homosexual partners.

Quickly they established a new decorating company. Blarek was President and Pellecchia Vice-President. The venture was successful. Defendants designed, remodeled, and renovated homes and offices for a broad range of private persons and businesses.

Beginning in the early 1980's, the nature of defendants' operation changed. From that time forward they worked almost exclusively for a single, ill-famed and powerful criminal client—Jose Santacruz Londono.

Blarek met Santacruz by chance in 1979 during a visit to friends in Colombia. He agreed to work for Santacruz, designing the interior of the drug lord's new ostentatious home. Blarek was paid a handsome sum for this work. So extraordinary was the dwelling, its furnishings, and its equipment that its photograph appeared on the cover of a major American interior design magazine.

Other dealings with Santacruz followed. Over a twelve year period, the defendants designed and decorated a number of offices and living spaces for Santacruz, his wife, his mistresses, and his children. Defendants provided everything from blueprints and construction designs to lighting, appliances for huge kitchens, carpeting, draperies, furniture, artwork, and even specially produced crockery and flatware.

The projects presented no simple decorating task. Some homes contain their own beauty salons, others have ornate marble and granite work with stone that was selected by the defendants in Italy. Defendants were responsible for obtaining unblemished cattle for leather, as well as the very best equipment and electrical materials from the United States and abroad for Santacruz and the various apartments of his wife and mistresses. Some residences were refurbished with elaborate secret compartments. Expense was of almost no significance as an inhibitor to artistic imagination.

Defendants were extraordinarily proud of their designs. At the trial every facet of their work was described by them in great detail with the aid of video cassettes, photographs, and samples.

It was clear that designing was more than a livelihood for these defendants. It was their passion. Yet, they were apparently unaware of the irony of their trial situation. While listening to a defendant's descriptions of the embellished bedrooms and recreation areas created for the children of Jose Santacruz, and how much fun they would provide for these young people, the jury could not help but reflect on the thousands of teens whose lives had been ruined by Cali cartel drugs sold for the cash used to pay for Santacruz's extravagant lifestyle.

There is little doubt that defendants delivered exceptional design services to Santacruz. They also knowingly provided something even more valuable to him— method for laundering his drug cash in the United States and converting it to assets movable to Colombia. Defendants laundered, spent, and were compensated with millions of dollars, the proceeds of the cartel's profitable drug trade in the United States.

Defendants knowingly laundered tainted cash for Santacruz in the United States in order to continue exercising their own craft and to enhance their own lives. They could not help but be aware of the illegal drug-related activities of their client. Both Blarek and Pellecchia knew who Jose Santacruz was, what he did, and from where his money was derived. Yet, each voluntarily agreed to, and in fact did, "wash" his drug proceeds. They converted huge amounts of currency that was delivered to them secretly in boxes, paper sacks, duffel bags, and an expensive designer sachel into assets the drug cartel could remove from this country.

Elaborate and elusive bookkeeping methods were developed in order to keep track of the funds received from Santacruz, while at the same time protecting his identity. Defendants' secretary, a key government witness at the trial, was told not to record Santacruz's name on any company documents or bookkeeping ledgers, and not disclose when the defendants traveled to meet with him or his agents in Colombia.

Feigned trips to countries like Spain hid the fact that defendants were in Colombia meeting with a drug lord. Defendants lied about the identity of their client to others, informing a number of suppliers that they worked for Spanish royalty or prominent individuals in other countries. Defendant Blarek even bleached out entries in his passport to hide the extent of his travel to Colombia.

Nearly all transactions between Santacruz and defendants were in cash. Defendants traveled to Miami, New York City, and other pre-determined locations to receive large sums of money from Santacruz's couriers. Payments as high as one million dollars at a time were hand-delivered to defendants in piles of fifty and one-hundred dollar bills. Defendants moved the cash between cities, traveling by car or train to avoid airport searches.

Portions of the funds were deposited in defendants' safe deposit boxes, or in bank accounts in amounts of less than $10,000 at a time to avoid federal bank transaction reporting requirements. *See* 31 C.F.R. § 103.22; *see also* 31 U.S.C. § 5324. In addition, defendants' own accountant, who pleaded guilty to money laundering and testified as a government witness, converted some one million dollars of the drug cash into checks for the defendants, thus "cleaning" the money for routine use in defendants' business operations.

Over the years, defendants were visited on a number of occasions by members of the United States Drug Enforcement Agency. They informed defendants that Santacruz was a drug trafficker and inquired if the defendants knew where he could be found. On at least one occasion, in 1987, Blarek lied to the agents, telling them that he had not seen Santacruz since 1980 even though he and his co-defendant in fact had, and continued to have, extensive contact with Santacruz until his death in March, 1996.

Taped telephone conversations between defendant Blarek and a government witness unequivocally proved that both defendants were aware of the nature of Santacruz's business, and that, if caught, they would attempt to conceal the fact that they were engaged in illegal activity for the drug trafficking organization.

Despite their covert actions and plans, defendants flaunted their own illegal income. On Santacruz's drug money, defendants lived lavish lives. Their home, "Villa Vecchia," in an exclusive area in San Francisco, California, reflects an affluent lifestyle. Their vehicles included a Mercedes-Benz automobile and Harley Davidson motorcycles. Their clothing was impeccable and of the highest quality. For their fine work, they were well paid by their drug lord client, and they did not stint in enjoying their profits.

C. Verdict

After a two week trial, in February, 1997, defendants were each found guilty of the Racketeering Conspiracy and Money Laundering Conspiracy counts. The jury also returned a verdict of Blarek's guilt of Interstate Travel in Aid of Racketeering.***

E. Presentence Report Computations

According to the Presentence Reports prepared by the United States Probation Office, defendants' offense conduct after 1986 involved at least $5.5 million dollars. In the process of "grouping" the counts, Guideline level 20 was used as an appropriate base offense level reflecting a determination that violation of section 1956(a)(1)(b)(i) of Title 18 of the United States Code was one of the underlying objectives of the conspiracies. See U.S.S.C. § 2S1.1(a)(2). Additionally, enhancements were made to the initial offense levels based upon defendants' knowledge that the monies received were drug proceeds and for their supervisory role in the crimes. Further upward adjustment to Blarek's offense level was predicated upon obstruction of justice for his alleged false testimony at the trial.

Taking these factors into account, the Presentence Report indicates Blarek has a combined adjusted offense level of 33 based upon the three counts for which he was convicted. His criminal history category is I, since he has no prior record. His Guidelines imprisonment range would then be 135 to 168 months. A fine range for Blarek's crimes of $20,000 to $14,473,063, as well as a required period of supervised release of at least two but not more than three years is also indicated.

Pellecchia's combined adjusted offense level, according to the Presentence Report, is 33. He, too, was assigned a criminal history category of I by the Probation Office since he has no prior convictions. This assessment results in an imprisonment range of 135 to 168 months. The Presentence Report also indicates a fine range of $17,500 to $14,473,063 and a required period of supervised release of at least two but not more than three years.***

III. Law

A. Sentencing Statute: 18 U.S.C. § 3553

1. Sufficient But Not Greater Than Necessary

Congress restructured the federal sentencing law in the 1980's to create the current Guidelines-based system. See Sentencing Reform Act of 1984, Pub.L. No. 98-473, § 211, 98 Stat.1987, 1989-90 (1984). It expressly stated that courts "shall impose a sentence sufficient, but not greater than necessary," to comply with the purposes of criminal sanctions. 18 U.S.C. § 3553(a). Harshness greater than that required is statutorily prohibited by this portion of the Sentencing Reform Act. Excessive leniency is also forbidden.

2. Seriousness of the Offense, Adequate Deterrence, Protection of the Public, and Correctional Treatment

The Sentencing Reform Act went on to explicitly delineate the purposes of criminal sanctions. Section 3551(a) provides that every defendant "shall be sentenced . . . so as to achieve the purposes set forth in subparagraphs (A) through (D) of section 3553(a)(2) to the extent that they are applicable in light of all the circumstances of the case."

Subparagraphs (A) through (D) of section 3553(a)(2) instruct courts to consider the necessity of the sentence imposed:

> (A) to reflect the seriousness of the offense, to promote respect for the law, and to provide just punishment for the offense;
> (B) to afford adequate deterrence to criminal conduct;
> (C) to protect the public from further crimes of the defendant; and
> (D) to provide the defendant with needed educational or vocational training, medical care, or other, correctional treatment in the most effective manner.***

(A) above largely constitutes a summary of the just deserts theory and (B), (C), and (D) encompass utilitarian concerns. In creating the sentencing statutes, Congress spelled out the four traditional justifications of the criminal sentence—deterrence, incapacitation, retribution and rehabilitation—and expressly instructed the sentencing court to keep these purposes in mind . . . .***

Sentencing is a critical stage of a criminal prosecution. It represents an important moment in the law, a fundamental judgment determining how, where, and why the offender should be dealt with for what may be much or all of his remaining life. It is significant not only for the individual before the court, but for his family and friends, the victims of his crime, potential future victims, and society as a whole. Four core considerations, in varying degrees and permutations, have traditionally shaped American sentencing determinations:

incapacitation of the criminal, rehabilitation of the offender, deterrence of the defendant and of others, and just deserts for the crime committed.***

Ascertaining priorities among these potentially conflicting notions has long been a point of contention amongst legislators, scholars, jurists, and practitioners. Somewhat oversimplifying, there are two basic camps. Retributivists contend that just deserts are to be imposed for a crime committed. Utilitarians, in their various manifestations, suggest that penalties need to be viewed more globally by measuring their benefits against their costs. The debate between the desert justification and the various utilitarian justifications such as deterrence, incapacitation, and rehabilitation has continued to divide criminal law thinkers. . . .***

Implied in this debate are questions about our basic values and beliefs: Why do we impose punishment? Or is it properly to be named punishment? Is our purpose retributive? Is it to deter the defendant himself or others in the community from committing crimes? Is it for reform? Rehabilitation? Incapacitation of dangerous people? Questions like these have engaged philosophers and students of the criminal law for centuries.

In the nineteenth and most of the twentieth century American prison and punishment system reforms were designed primarily to rehabilitate the prisoner as a protection against further crime. In more recent years there has been a perception by many that attempts at rehabilitation have failed; a movement towards theoretically-based, more severe, fixed punishments, based upon the nature of the crime gained momentum. Two eighteenth and nineteenth century philosophers set the terms of the current late twentieth century debate.

[B. Traditional Sentencing Rationales]
1. Kant's Retributive Just Deserts Theory

Immanuel Kant, born in East Prussia in 1724, is regarded by some as one of the most important philosophers in Western culture. On the ascendency of law, he wrote:

> Duty is the necessity to act out of reverence for the law. . . .
> Thus, the moral worth of an action does not depend on the result expected from it, and so too does not depend on any principle of action that needs to borrow its motive from this expected result . . . nothing but the idea of law in itself . . . can constitute that preeminent good which we call moral, a good which is already present in the person acting on this idea. . . .

It is said that Kant accepted as fundamental the principle . . . that the only absolutely good thing in the universe is the human will governed by respect for the moral law or the consciousness of duty. Kant's anti-utilitarian thesis on criminal penalties is reflected in an oft-cited passage from his work, The Metaphysical Elements of Justice: Juridical punishment can never be used merely as a means to promote some other good for the criminal himself or for civil society, but instead it must in all cases be imposed on him only on the ground that he has committed a crime; for a human being can never be manipulated merely as a means to the purposes of someone else and can never be confused with the objects of the Law of things. . . . It follows from this position that the sole justification for criminal punishment is retribution or jus talionis.

The average man or woman on the streets of New York, struggling to exist with some dignity, would hardly recognize as words to live by Kant's merciless doctrine: The law concerning punishment is a categorical imperative, and woe to him who rummages around in the winding paths of a theory of happiness looking for some advantage to be gained by releasing the criminal from punishment or by reducing the amount of it—in keeping with the Pharisaic motto: It is better that one man should die than the whole people should perish. If legal justice perishes, then it is no longer worthwhile for men to remain alive on this earth.

For Kant and his adherents, [p]unishment that gives an offender what he or she deserves for a past crime is a valuable end in itself and needs no further justification. It is not inflicted because it will give an opportunity for reform, but because it is merited. Kantian just deserts theory, therefore, focuses almost exclusively on the past to determine the level of punishment that should be meted out to right the wrong that has already occurred as a result of the defendant's delict. Some softening of this cold and relentless rigidity by simultaneously integrating the Benthamite utilitarian approach is possible.

2. Bentham's Utilitarian Theory

Jeremy Bentham, an English philosopher born in 1748, advocated a far different, more prospective approach through his Principle of Utility. Fifty Major Philosophers. For him, law in general, and criminal jurisprudence in particular, was intended to produce the greatest happiness for the greatest number, a concept sometimes referred to as the felicity calculus. This is not to say that Bentham did not believe in sanctions. It was his view that punishment was sometimes essential to ensure compliance with public laws.***

Unlike his contemporary, Kant, Bentham was not interested in criminal punishment as a way of avenging or canceling the theoretical wrong suffered by society through a deviation from its norms. Rather, a criminal sanction was to be utilized only when it could help ensure the greater good of society and provide a benefit to the community.***

Under the Benthamite approach, deterring crime, as well as correction and reformation of the criminal, are primary aspirations of criminal law. While the theory of retribution would impose punishment for its own sake, the utilitarian theories of deterrence and reformation would use punishment as a means to [a practical] end—the end being community protection by the prevention of crime.

3. Sanctions in Strict Retributive and Utilitarian Models

Given the divergence in underlying assumptions and theory, the competing retributivist and utilitarian theories suggest opposing methods for ascertaining proper penalties. Under a Kantian model, the extent of punishment is required to neatly fit the crime. Whoever commits a crime must be punished in accordance with his desert. In the case of murder, some believe that just desert is clear. A taker of life must have his own life taken. Even in the case of killings, however, there are degrees of mens rea, and over large portions of the world capital punishment is outlawed on a variety of just deserts and utilitarian grounds. For lesser offenses, reaching a consensus on the proper price for the criminal act under the Kantian approach is even more difficult.

As one scholar has written:

> The retributivist can perhaps avoid the question of how we decide that one crime is morally more heinous than another by hewing to his position that no such decision is necessary so long as we make the punishment equal to the crime. To accomplish this, he might argue, it is not necessary to argue to the relative wickedness of crimes. But at best this leaves us with the problem of how we do make punishments equal to crimes, a problem which will not stop plaguing retributivists.

Two main theoretical problems are presented by this just deserts approach. The degree of the earned desert—that is to say the extent or length of the appropriate punishment—is subjective. The upper and lower limits of the punishment can be very high or very low, justified on personal views and taste. The earned punishment may be quite cruel and do more harm to society, the criminal, and his family, than can be justified on utilitarian grounds.

Determining the appropriateness of sanction differs under Bentham's utilitarian approach, although it too poses challenging theoretical and practical tasks for the sentencer. Under this model, among: the factors . . . [to be considered] are the need to set penalties in such a way that where a person is tempted to commit one of two crimes he will commit the lesser, that the evil consequences . . . of the crime will be minimized even if the crime is committed, that the least amount possible of punishment be used for the prevention of a given crime. Obviously, one problem with utilizing a system based only upon this approach is that [i]t is difficult . . . to determine when more good than harm has been achieved. . . . As in the case of Kantian just deserts, the felicity calculation is subject to considerable difficulty and dispute. Another major problem with the utilitarian approach is that the individual criminal can be treated very cruelly, to gain some societal advantage even through the crime is minor—or very leniently, despite the shocking nature of the crime—if that will on balance benefit society. Given these problems, it may make sense to continue to equivocate, oscillating between these poles, tempering justice with mercy, just deserts with utility calculations, in varying pragmatic ways.

C. Utility and Retribution Under Sentencing Guidelines

The Sentencing Guidelines, written by the United States Sentencing Commission pursuant to the Sentencing Reform Act purport to comport with the competing theoretical ways of thinking about punishment. The Guidelines state that they provided for the development of guidelines that will further the basic purposes of criminal punishment: deterrence, incapacitation, just punishment, and rehabilitation. A systematic, theoretical approach to these four purposes was not, however, employed by the Commission:

> A philosophical problem arose when the Commission attempted to reconcile the differing perceptions of the purposes of criminal punishment. Most observers of the criminal law agree that the ultimate aim of the law itself, and of punishment in particular, is the control of crime. Beyond this point, however, the consensus seems to break down. Some argue that appropriate punishment should be defined primarily on the basis of the principle of just deserts. Under this principle, punishment should be scaled to the offender's culpability and the resulting harms. Others argue that punishment should be imposed primarily on the basis of practical crime control considerations. This theory calls for sentences that most effectively lessen the likelihood of future crime, either by deterring others or incapacitating the defendant.

The Commission decided not to create a solely retributivist or utilitarian paradigm, or accord one primacy over the other.***

Blarek faces a period of imprisonment of 121 to 151 months. Pellecchia faces 97 to 121 months' incarceration.***

[IV. Law Applied to Facts]

B. Traditional and Statutory Sentencing Rationales
1. Incapacitation

Incapacitation seeks to ensure that offenders . . . are rendered physically incapable of committing crime. In colonial America, incapacitation was sometimes imposed in a literal sense (loss of organs). With the development of the penitentiary system, incarceration was seen as a more reliable means of incapacitation. In the instant case, incapacitation is not an important factor. First, these defendants have no prior criminal record indicating any propensity towards crime. Second, their connection to the criminal world, Santacruz, is now deceased. Third, it does not appear that long term restriction is necessary to ensure that defendants do not reenter a life of crime. Consistent with utilitarian-driven analysis, little would be gained if the sentences emphasized incapacitation.

2. Rehabilitation

Rehabilitation is designed to instill in the offender proper values and attitudes, by bolstering his respect for self and institutions, and by providing him with the means of leading a productive life. . . . Neither of these men is wayward or in need of special instruction on the mores of civilized society. They have in place strong community support systems, as evidenced by the many letters submitted to the court by family and friends. They know how to live a law abiding life. It is not required that a penalty be fashioned that teaches them how to be moral in the future. This criterion, rehabilitation, therefore, is not one that is useful in assessing a penalty.

3. Deterrence

Of the two forms of deterrence that motivate criminal penalties—general and specific—only one is of substantial concern here. Specific deterrence is meant to disincline individual offenders from repeating the same or other criminal acts. Such dissuasion has likely already occurred. Defendants regret their actions. The ordeal of being criminally prosecuted and publically shamed by being denominated felons and the imposition of other penalties has taught them a sobering lesson.

General deterrence attempts to discourage the public at large from engaging in similar conduct. It is of primary concern in this case. Defendants' activities have gained a great deal of attention. Notorious cases are ideal vehicles for capturing the attention of, and conveying a message to, the public at large. While it is not appropriate under just deserts views for defendants in famous cases to be treated more harshly than defendants in less significant ones simply for the sake of making an example of them, under a utilitarian view the notoriety of particular a defendant may be taken into account by sentencing courts provided the punishment is not disproportionate to the crime.

4. Retribution

Retribution is considered by some to be a barbaric concept, appealing to a primal sense of vengeance. It cannot, however, be overlooked as an appropriate consideration. When there is a perception on the part of the community that the courts have failed to sensibly sanction wrongdoers, respect for the law may be reduced. This is a notion applicable under both just deserts and utilitarian balancing concepts that has had some resurgence with the current growth of the rights of victims to be heard at sentencing.

Should punishment fail to fit the crime, the citizenry might be tempted to vigilantism. This may be why, according to one group of scholars, a criminal law based on the community's perceptions of just deserts, from a utilitarian perspective, the more effective strategy for reducing crime. White collar victimless offenses, such as the ones committed by these defendants, are harmful to all society, particularly since drugs are involved. It is important, therefore, that the imposition of a penalty in this case capture, to some rational degree, the worth of defendants' volitional criminal acts.

5. Sufficient But Not Greater Than Necessary

Mercy is seldom included on the list of traditional rationales for sentencing. It is, however, evinced by the federal sentencing statute, 18 U.S.C. § 3553(a), which provides, as noted above, that the lowest possible penalty consistent with the goals of sentencing be imposed. The notion that undue harshness should be avoided by those sitting in judgment has long been a part of the human fabric and spirit. Lenity is often the desirable route.***

For reasons already indicated, the sentence imposed should reflect a downward departure of six levels to offense level 26. Blarek is sentenced towards the lower end of the Guidelines' range for level 26 to a concurrent term of 68 months' incarceration for his conviction on the three counts.***Pellecchia's total offense level is computed at 30. The sentence should reflect a downward departure of seven levels to offense level 23. This represents the same six level departure granted for defendant Blarek with an addition level of downward departure based upon defendant's health as well as his lesser culpability. A concurrent term of incarceration of 48 months.***

Notes and Questions

1. Under the utilitarian approach, should an innocent person ever be convicted? If yes, under what circumstances would this occur?

2. How does the judge in *United States v. Blarek* know that the defendants have been specifically deterred? Was Blarek's sentence of 68 months imposed for deterrence or more for retribution purposes?

3. Do you agree with the downward departure taken by the judge? According to the judge, "[d]efendants regret their actions. The ordeal of being criminally

prosecuted and publically shamed by being denominated felons and the imposition of other penalties has taught them a sobering lesson." Is this an accurate statement? Would you feel differently if the defendants had pled guilty at the outset and avoided a two-week trial that required witnesses and jurors? What if the defendants had cooperated with the government?

4. Historical Note: The first part of this chapter introduced the term malum prohibitum. This phrase refers to crimes that are not inherently wrong but made criminal by statute (e.g., driving under the influence). In contrast, malum in se crimes are inherently wrong (e.g., rape).

Regina v. Dudley and Stephens, 14 Q.B.D. 273
(Queen's Bench Division 1884)

INDICTMENT for the murder of Richard Parker on the high seas within the jurisdiction of the Admiralty:

[T]hat on July 5, 1884, the prisoners, Thomas Dudley and Edward Stephens, with one Brooks, all able-bodied English seamen, and the deceased also an English boy, between seventeen and eighteen years of age, the crew of an English yacht, a registered English vessel, were cast away in a storm on the high seas 1600 miles from the Cape of Good Hope, and were compelled to put into an open boat belonging to the said yacht. That in this boat they had no supply of water and no supply of food, except two 1 lb. tins of turnips, and for three days they had nothing else to subsist upon. That on the fourth day they caught a small turtle, upon which they subsisted for a few days, and this was the only food they had up to the twentieth day when the act now in question was committed. That on the twelfth day the turtle were entirely consumed, and for the next eight days they had nothing to eat. That they had no fresh water, except such rain as they from time to time caught in their oilskin capes. That the boat was drifting on the ocean, and was probably more than 1000 miles away from land. That on the eighteenth day, when they had been seven days without food and five without water, the prisoners spoke to Brooks as to what should be done if no succour came, and suggested that someone should be sacrificed to save the rest, but Brooks dissented, and the boy, to whom they were understood to refer, was not consulted. That on the 24th of July, the day before the act now in question, the prisoner Dudley proposed to Stephens and Brooks that lots should be cast who should be put to death to save the rest, but Brooks refused consent, and it was not put to the boy, and in point of fact there was no drawing of lots. That on that day the prisoners spoke of their having families, and suggested it would be better to kill the boy that their lives should be saved, and Dudley proposed that if there was no vessel in sight by the morrow morning the boy should be killed. That next day, the 25th of July, no vessel appearing, Dudley told Brooks that he had better go and have a sleep, and made signs to Stephens and Brooks that the boy had better be killed. The prisoner Stephens agreed to the act, but Brooks dissented from it. That the boy was then lying at the bottom of the boat quite helpless, and extremely weakened by famine and by drinking sea water, and unable to make any resistance, nor did he ever assent to his being killed. The prisoner Dudley offered a prayer asking forgiveness for them all if either of them should be tempted to commit a rash act, and that their souls might be saved. That Dudley, with the assent of Stephens, went to the boy, and telling him that his time was come, put a knife into his throat and killed him then and there; that the three men fed upon the body and blood of the boy for four days; that on the fourth day after the act had been committed the boat was picked up by a passing vessel, and the prisoners were rescued, still alive, but in the lowest state of prostration. That they were carried to the port of Falmouth, and committed for trial at Exeter. That if the men had not fed upon the body of the boy they would probably not have survived to be so picked up and rescued, but would within the four days have died of famine. That the boy, being in a much weaker condition, was likely to have died before them. That at the time of the act in question there was no sail in sight, nor any reasonable prospect of relief. That under these circumstances there appeared to the prisoners every probability that unless they then fed or very soon fed upon the boy or one of themselves they would die of starvation. That there was no appreciable chance of saving life except by killing someone for the others to eat. That assuming any necessity to kill anybody, there was no greater necessity for killing the boy than any of the other three men. But whether upon the whole matter by the jurors found the killing of Richard Parker by Dudley and Stephens be felony and murder the jurors are ignorant, and pray the advice of the Court thereupon, and if upon the whole matter the Court shall be of opinion that the killing of Richard Parker be felony and murder, then the jurors say that Dudley and Stephens were each guilty of felony and murder as alleged in the indictment.

Notes and Questions

1. Under what theory or theories of punishment were Dudley and Stephens prosecuted?

2. The defendants ultimately had their sentences of death commuted to six months confinement. Under what theory of punishment did the Crown reduce the sentences of the defendants?

3. Historical Note: The term "Rex" or "Regina" used in the title of a case refers to the king or queen of England respectively.

C. Defining Punishment

Merriam-Webster's dictionary defines "punishment" as "suffering, pain, or loss that serves as retribution" or "a penalty inflicted on an offender through judicial procedure." While this definition may seem fairly straightforward, the Supreme Court has taken a rather nuanced view of punishment. The following case illustrates the challenges the court faces when it attempts to determine whether or not certain actions taken by the state are indeed punishments.

Kansas v. Hendricks, 521 U.S. 346 (1997)

Justice THOMAS delivered the opinion of the Court.

In 1994, Kansas enacted the Sexually Violent Predator Act, which establishes procedures for the civil commitment of persons who, due to a "mental abnormality" or a "personality disorder," are likely to engage in "predatory acts of sexual violence." Kan. Stat. Ann. §59-29a01 *et seq.* (1994). The State invoked the Act for the first time to commit Leroy Hendricks, an inmate who had a long history of sexually molesting children, and who was scheduled for release from prison shortly after the Act became law. Hendricks challenged his commitment on, *inter alia,* "substantive" due process, double jeopardy, and *ex post-facto* grounds. The Kansas Supreme Court invalidated the Act, holding that its pre-commitment condition of a "mental abnormality" did not satisfy what the court perceived to be the "substantive" due process requirement that involuntary civil commitment must be predicated on a finding of "mental illness." The State of Kansas petitioned for certiorari. Hendricks subsequently filed a cross petition in which he reasserted his federal double jeopardy and *ex post-facto* claims. We granted certiorari on both the petition and the cross petition, and now reverse the judgment below.

The Kansas Legislature enacted the Sexually Violent Predator Act (Act) in 1994 to grapple with the problem of managing repeat sexual offenders. Although Kansas already had a statute addressing the involuntary commitment of those defined as "mentally ill," the legislature determined that existing civil commitment procedures were inadequate to confront the risks presented by "sexually violent predators."***

The initial version of the Act, as applied to a currently confined person such as Hendricks, was designed to initiate a specific series of procedures. The custodial agency was required to notify the local prosecutor 60 days before the anticipated release of a person who might have met the Act's criteria. §59-29a03. The prosecutor was then obligated, within 45 days, to decide whether to file a petition in state court seeking the person's involuntary commitment. §59-29a04. If such a petition were filed, the court was to determine whether "probable cause" existed to support a finding that the person was a "sexually violent predator" and thus eligible for civil commitment. Upon such a determination, transfer of the individual to a secure facility for professional evaluation would occur. §59-29a05. After that evaluation, a trial would be held to determine beyond a reasonable doubt whether the individual was a sexually violent predator. If that determination were made, the person would then be transferred to the custody of the Secretary of Social and Rehabilitation Services (Secretary) for "control, care and treatment until such time as the person's mental abnormality or personality disorder has so changed that the person is safe to be at large." §59-29a07(a).

In addition to placing the burden of proof upon the State, the Act afforded the individual a number of other procedural safeguards. In the case of an indigent person, the State was required to provide, at public expense, the assistance of counsel and an examination by mental health care professionals. §59-29a06. The individual also received the right to present and cross examine witnesses, and the opportunity to review documentary evidence presented by the State. §59-29a07.

Once an individual was confined, the Act required that "[t]he involuntary detention or commitment . . . shall conform to constitutional requirements for care and treatment." §59-29a09. Confined persons were afforded three different avenues of review: First, the committing court was obligated to conduct an annual review to determine whether continued detention was warranted. §59-29a08. Second, the Secretary was permitted, at any time, to decide that the confined individual's condition had so changed that release was appropriate, and could then authorize the person to petition for release. §59-29a10. Finally, even without the Secretary's permission, the confined person could at any time file a release petition. §59-29a11. If the court found that the State could no longer satisfy its burden under the initial commitment standard, the individual would be freed from confinement.

We granted Hendricks' cross petition to determine whether the Act violates the Constitution's double jeopardy prohibition or its ban on *ex post-facto* lawmaking. The thrust of Hendricks' argument is that the Act establishes criminal proceedings; hence confinement under it necessarily constitutes punishment. He contends that where, as here, newly enacted "punishment" is predicated upon past conduct for which he has already been convicted and forced to serve a prison sentence, the Constitution's Double Jeopardy and *Ex Post-Facto* Clauses are violated. We are unpersuaded by Hendricks' argument that Kansas has established criminal proceedings.

The categorization of a particular proceeding as civil or criminal "is first of all a question of statutory construction." We must initially ascertain whether the legislature meant the statute to establish "civil" proceedings. If so, we ordinarily defer to the legislature's stated intent. Here, Kansas' objective to create a civil proceeding is evidenced by its placement of the Sexually Violent Predator Act within the Kansas probate code, instead of the criminal code, as well as its description of the Act as creating a *"civil commitment procedure."* Kan. Stat. Ann.,

Article 29 (1994) ("Care and Treatment for Mentally Ill Persons"), §59-29a01 (emphasis added). Nothing on the face of the statute suggests that the legislature sought to create anything other than a civil commitment scheme designed to protect the public from harm.

Although we recognize that a "civil label is not always dispositive," we will reject the legislature's manifest intent only where a party challenging the statute provides "the clearest proof" that "the statutory scheme [is] so punitive either in purpose or effect as to negate [the State's] intention" to deem it "civil." In those limited circumstances, we will consider the statute to have established criminal proceedings for constitutional purposes. Hendricks, however, has failed to satisfy this heavy burden.***

As a threshold matter, commitment under the Act does not implicate either of the two primary objectives of criminal punishment: retribution or deterrence. The Act's purpose is not retributive because it does not affix culpability for prior criminal conduct. Instead, such conduct is used solely for evidentiary purposes, either to demonstrate that a "mental abnormality" exists or to support a finding of future dangerousness. We have previously concluded that an Illinois statute was nonpunitive even though it was triggered by the commission of a sexual assault, explaining that evidence of the prior criminal conduct was "received not to punish past misdeeds, but primarily to show the accused's mental condition and to predict future behavior." In addition, the Kansas Act does not make a criminal conviction a prerequisite for commitment—persons absolved of criminal responsibility may nonetheless be subject to confinement under the Act. See Kan. Stat. Ann. §59-29a03(a) (1994). An absence of the necessary criminal responsibility suggests that the State is not seeking retribution for a past misdeed. Thus, the fact that the Act may be "tied to criminal activity" is "insufficient to render the statut[e] punitive."

Moreover, unlike a criminal statute, no finding of scienter is required to commit an individual who is found to be a sexually violent predator; instead, the commitment determination is made based on a "mental abnormality" or "personality disorder" rather than on one's criminal intent. The existence of a scienter requirement is customarily an important element in distinguishing criminal from civil statutes. The absence of such a requirement here is evidence that confinement under the statute is not intended to be retributive.

Nor can it be said that the legislature intended the Act to function as a deterrent. Those persons committed under the Act are, by definition, suffering from a "mental abnormality" or a "personality disorder" that prevents them from exercising adequate control over their behavior. Such persons are therefore unlikely to be deterred by the threat of confinement. And the conditions surrounding that confinement do not suggest a punitive purpose on the State's part. The State has represented that an individual confined under the Act is not subject to the more restrictive conditions placed on state prisoners, but instead experiences essentially the same conditions as any involuntarily committed patient in the state mental institution. Because none of the parties argues that people institutionalized under the Kansas general civil commitment statute are subject to punitive conditions, even though they may be involuntarily confined, it is difficult to conclude that persons confined under this Act are being "punished."

Although the civil commitment scheme at issue here does involve an affirmative restraint, "the mere fact that a person is detained does not inexorably lead to the conclusion that the government has imposed punishment." The State may take measures to restrict the freedom of the dangerously mentally ill. This is a legitimate nonpunitive governmental objective and has been historically so regarded. The Court has, in fact, cited the confinement of "mentally unstable individuals who present a danger to the public" as one classic example of nonpunitive detention. If detention for the purpose of protecting the community from harm *necessarily* constituted punishment, then all involuntary civil commitments would have to be considered punishment. But we have never so held.***

Hendricks next contends that the State's use of procedural safeguards traditionally found in criminal trials makes the proceedings here criminal rather than civil. In *Allen*, we confronted a similar argument. There, the petitioner "place[d] great reliance on the fact that proceedings under the Act are accompanied by procedural safeguards usually found in criminal trials" to argue that the proceedings were civil in name only. We rejected that argument, however, explaining that the State's decision "to provide some of the safeguards applicable in criminal trials cannot itself turn these proceedings into criminal prosecutions." The numerous procedural and evidentiary protections afforded here demonstrate that the Kansas Legislature has taken great care to confine only a narrow class of particularly dangerous individuals, and then only after meeting the strictest procedural standards. That Kansas chose to afford such procedural protections does not transform a civil commitment proceeding into a criminal prosecution.

Finally, Hendricks argues that the Act is necessarily punitive because it fails to offer any legitimate "treatment." Without such treatment, Hendricks asserts, confinement under the Act amounts to little more than disguised punishment. Hendricks' argument assumes that treatment for his condition is available, but that the State has failed (or refused) to provide it. The Kansas Supreme Court, however, apparently rejected this assumption, explaining:

"It is clear that the overriding concern of the legislature is to continue the segregation of sexually violent offenders from the public. Treatment with the goal of reintegrating them into society is incidental, at best. The record reflects that treatment for sexually violent predators is all but nonexistent. The legislature concedes that sexually violent predators are not amenable to treatment under [the existing Kansas involuntary commitment statute]. If there is nothing to treat under [that statute], then there is no mental illness. In that light, the provisions of the Act for treatment appear somewhat disingenuous."

It is possible to read this passage as a determination that Hendricks' condition was *untreatable* under the existing Kansas civil commitment statute, and thus the Act's sole purpose was incapacitation. Absent a treatable mental illness, the Kansas court concluded, Hendricks could not be detained against his will.***

Where the State has "disavowed any punitive intent"; limited confinement to a small segment of particularly dangerous individuals; provided strict procedural safeguards; directed that confined persons be segregated from the general prison population and afforded the same status as others who have been civilly committed; recommended treatment if such is possible; and permitted immediate release upon a showing that the individual is no longer dangerous or mentally impaired, we cannot say that it acted with punitive intent. We therefore hold that the Act does not establish criminal proceedings and that involuntary confinement pursuant to the Act is not punitive.***

Justice BREYER, with whom Justices STEVENS and SOUTER join, and with whom Justice GINSBURG joins as to Parts II and III, dissenting.

***Certain resemblances between the Act's "civil commitment" and traditional criminal punishments are obvious. Like criminal imprisonment, the Act's civil commitment amounts to "secure" confinement, Kan. Stat. Ann. §59-29a07(a) (1994), and "incarceration against one's will." *In re Gault*. See Testimony of Terry Davis, SRS Director of Quality Assurance (App. 52-54, 78-81) (confinement takes place in the psychiatric wing of a prison hospital where those whom the Act confines and ordinary prisoners are treated alike). Cf. *Browning Ferris Industries of Vt., Inc. v. Kelco Disposal, Inc.* (O'Connor, J., concurring in part and dissenting in part). In addition, a basic objective of the Act is incapacitation, which, as Blackstone said in describing an objective of criminal law, is to "depriv[e] the party injuring of the power to do future mischief." 4 W. Blackstone (incapacitation is one important purpose of criminal punishment); see also *Foucha* ("Incapacitation for the protection of society is not an unusual ground for incarceration"); *United States v. Brown* (punishment's "purposes: retributive, rehabilitative, deterrent and preventative. One of the reasons society imprisons those convicted of crimes is to keep them from inflicting future harm, but that does not make imprisonment any the less punishment").

Moreover, the Act, like criminal punishment, imposes its confinement (or sanction) only upon an individual who has previously committed a criminal offense. Kan. Stat. Ann. §§59-29a02(a), 59-29a03(a) (1994). Cf. *Department of Revenue of Mont. v. Kurth Ranch* (fact that a tax on marijuana was "conditioned on the commission of a crime" is "significant of [its] penal and prohibitory intent"). And the Act imposes that confinement through the use of persons (county prosecutors), procedural guarantees (trial by jury, assistance of counsel, psychiatric evaluations), and standards ("beyond a reasonable doubt") traditionally associated with the criminal law. Kan. Stat. Ann. §§59-29a06, 59-29a07 (1994).

These obvious resemblances by themselves, however, are not legally sufficient to transform what the Act calls "civil commitment" into a criminal punishment. Civil commitment of dangerous, mentally ill individuals by its very nature involves confinement and incapacitation. Yet "civil commitment," from a constitutional perspective, nonetheless remains civil. Nor does the fact that criminal behavior triggers the Act make the critical difference. The Act's insistence upon a prior crime, by screening out those whose past behavior does not concretely demonstrate the existence of a mental problem or potential future danger, may serve an important noncriminal evidentiary purpose. Neither is the presence of criminal law type procedures determinative. Those procedures can serve an important purpose that in this context one might consider noncriminal, namely helping to prevent judgmental mistakes that would wrongly deprive a person of important liberty.

If these obvious similarities cannot by themselves prove that Kansas' "civil commitment" statute is criminal, neither can the word "civil" written into the statute, §59-29a01, by itself prove the contrary. This Court has said that only the "clearest proof" could establish that a law the legislature called "civil," was, in reality a "punitive" measure. But the Court has also reiterated that a "civil label is not always dispositive," *Allen v. Illinois*; it has said that in close cases the label is "not of paramount importance," and it has looked behind a "civil" label fairly often.

In this circumstance, with important features of the Act pointing in opposite directions, I would place particular importance upon those features that would likely distinguish between a basically punitive and a basically nonpunitive purpose. *United States v. Ursery* (asking whether a statutory scheme was so punitive "either in purpose or effect" to negate the legislature's "intention to establish a civil remedial mechanism") (citations omitted). And I note that the Court, in an earlier civil commitment case, *Allen v. Illinois,* looked primarily to the law's concern for treatment as an important distinguishing feature. I do not believe that *Allen* means that a particular law's lack of concern for treatment, by itself, is enough to make an incapacitative law punitive. But, for reasons I will point out, when a State believes that treatment does exist, and then couples that admission with a legislatively required delay of such treatment until a person is at the end of his jail term (so that further incapacitation is therefore necessary), such a legislative scheme begins to look punitive.

In *Allen*, the Court considered whether, for Fifth Amendment purposes, proceedings under an Illinois statute were civil or "criminal." The Illinois statute, rather like the Kansas statute here, authorized the confinement of persons who were sexually dangerous, who had committed at least one prior sexual assault, and who suffered from a "mental disorder." The *Allen* Court, looking behind the statute's "civil commitment" label, found the statute civil—in important part because the State had "provided for the treatment of those it commits" (also referring to facts that the State had "disavowed any interest in punishment" and that it had "established a system under which committed persons may be released after the briefest time in confinement").

In reaching this conclusion, the Court noted that the State Supreme Court had found the proceedings "essentially civil" because the statute's aim was to provide "treatment, not punishment." It observed that the State had "a statutory obligation to provide 'care and treatment . . . designed to effect recovery'" in a "facility set aside to provide psychiatric care." And it referred to the State's purpose as one of "*treating* rather than punishing sexually dangerous persons." ("Had petitioner shown, for example, that the confinement . . . imposes . . . a regimen which is essentially identical to that imposed upon felons with no need for psychiatric care, this might well be a different case").

The *Allen* Court's focus upon treatment, as a kind of touchstone helping to distinguish civil from punitive purposes, is not surprising, for one would expect a nonpunitive statutory scheme to confine, not simply in order to protect, but also in order to cure. That is to say, one would expect a nonpunitively motivated legislature that confines *because of* a dangerous mental abnormality to seek to help the individual himself overcome that abnormality (at least insofar as professional treatment for the abnormality exists and is potentially helpful, as Kansas, supported by some groups of mental health professionals, argues is the case here). Conversely, a statutory scheme that provides confinement that does not reasonably fit a practically available, medically oriented treatment objective, more likely reflects a primarily punitive legislative purpose.***

Notes and Questions

1. Do you agree with Justice Thomas's statement in *Kansas v. Hendricks* that the "the Act does not implicate either of the two primary objectives of criminal punishment: retribution or deterrence"? Are incapacitation and rehabilitation also important objectives of punishment? If so, has the Supreme Court argued that these are absent here? What factors did the Court look at to ultimately determine that the Act in question was not punishment?

2. If pedophiles like Hendricks are unable to control their actions, are they worthy of punishment? Should it be a crime at all if you cannot conform your conduct to the rules of society?

3. If the state of Kansas failed to provide treatment to Hendricks, would that constitute punishment? Why or why not?

4. Would you expect the Supreme Court to rule differently if a state enacted a statute that employed the same post-sentence hearing and confinement used in *Hendricks* for all sex-related crimes or crimes involving children?

PART II
General Principles

Chapter 3
Actus Reus

A. Background

Generally speaking, most crimes require (1) actus reus, (2) mens rea, (3) causation, and (4) concurrence. Thus, the prosecution must prove these four parts of a crime in order to successfully convict the defendant. Actus reus will be the first of the four to be discussed in this book.

Actus reus loosely translates to "guilty act." The defendant cannot be found guilty for merely having criminal thoughts or even criminal fantasies see e.g., *United States v. Valle*, 301 F.R.D. 53 (S.D.N.Y. 2014). The defendant must commit some wrongful act or omission which is deemed the "actus reus."

B. Voluntary Act

The first two cases to be examined in this chapter look at the voluntariness of the defendant's wrongful act. The third case in this chapter, *Jones v. United States*, explores actus reus as an omission by the defendant.

State v. Cargile, 2008 WL 2350644

CHRISTINE T. McMONAGLE, P.J.

Defendant-appellant, Cleveland L. Cargile, appeals from his conviction for illegally conveying drugs onto the grounds of a detention facility in violation of R.C. 2921.36(A)(2). We vacate his conviction, because the State's evidence was insufficient to render Cargile criminally liable for a violation of R.C. 2921.36(A)(2).

The evidence presented by the State at trial revealed the following. On March 10, 2007, an individual waiting at a bus stop near Tower City in Cleveland was assaulted twice by a group of young men. After the assaults, his cell phone was missing from his pocket. When the police responded to the scene, the individual and his friend identified Cargile, as he was walking out of Tower City, as one of the assailants. The police arrested Cargile, handcuffed him, and patted him down. The pat-down failed to reveal any weapons or contraband.

The police then transported Cargile to jail for booking and detention. Prior to entering the jail, one of the police officers admonished Cargile that conveying drugs into the jail would be a crime and advised him that he should tell the officer if he had any contraband. Cargile denied that he had any contraband on his person.

An officer then escorted Cargile into the jail and began the booking process. Another officer searched Cargile. The officers saw Cargile move his right leg during the pat-down, allegedly so the officer would avoid making contact with that part of his leg. The officers then found three bags of marijuana concealed in the cuff of Cargile's right pant leg.

Cargile was charged with two counts of robbery, in violation of R.C. 2911.02, and one count of illegal conveyance of a controlled substance into a detention facility, in violation of R.C. 2921.36(A)(2). The jury found him not guilty of both robbery counts, but guilty with regard to the prohibited conveyance count, and the trial court sentenced him to two years in prison.

In his third assignment of error, which we find dispositive, Cargile contends that the trial court erred in denying his Crim. R. 29 motion for acquittal regarding the illegal conveyance count, because the evidence was insufficient to support his conviction. We agree.

Crim. R. 29(A) governs motions for acquittal and provides for a judgment of acquittal "if the evidence is insufficient to sustain a conviction." An appellate court's function in reviewing the sufficiency of the evidence to support a criminal conviction is to examine the evidence admitted at trial to determine whether such evidence, if believed, would convince the average mind of the defendant's guilt beyond a reasonable doubt. The relevant inquiry is whether, after viewing the evidence in a light most favorable to the prosecution, any rational trier of fact could have found the essential elements of the crime proven beyond a reasonable doubt. *State v. Jenks* (1991), 61 Ohio St. 3d 259, paragraph two of the syllabus.

Under R.C. 2921.36(A)(2), no one shall "knowingly convey, or attempt to convey, onto the grounds of a detention facility *** any drug of abuse, as defined in section 3719.011 of the Revised Code."

It is undisputed that the marijuana found in the cuff of Cargile's pant leg when he was brought to jail is a drug of abuse as defined by R.C. 3719.011. It is also undisputed that the county jail is a detention facility for purposes of R.C. 2921.36(A)(2).

Under R.C. 2901.21(A), a person is not guilty of a criminal offense unless 1) the person's liability is based on either a voluntary act or an omission to perform an act or duty; and 2) the person has the requisite degree of culpability for each element as to which a culpable mental state is specified in the statute defining the offense.

Cargile argues that, on these facts, he cannot be convicted of illegally conveying drugs into the jail, because his act was not voluntary, as required by R.C. 2901.21(A). We agree.

In *State v. Sowry,* 155 Ohio App. 3d 742, 2004-Ohio-399, the Second District Court of Appeals considered a similar situation. The defendant in that case was arrested for disorderly conduct and resisting arrest and a pat-down failed to reveal any weapons or contraband. At the jail, the defendant was asked whether he had any drugs on his person, and he responded negatively. A more thorough search at booking revealed a baggie of marijuana in his right front pants pocket.

The Second District found that "any act that is not the product of the actor's conscious determination is not a voluntary act." *Sowry* at ¶ 17, citing Katz/Gianelli, Criminal Law, Baldwin's Ohio Practice, Vol. 2, Section 85:3, at p. 871. Therefore, it concluded, because the officers controlled the defendant's person by arresting him and conveying him to jail, the fact "that [the defendant's] 'person' and the possessions on his person were in the jail was *** not a product of a voluntary act on [the defendant's] part. Rather, those events were, as to him, wholly involuntary." *Id.* at ¶ 19.

The Second District held that "at most, [the defendant] might be charged with knowing that drugs were on his person when officers conveyed him to jail. However, *** the law will not punish for a guilty mind alone. Because [the defendant's] conduct with respect to the R.C. 2921.36(A)(2) violation with which he was charged cannot satisfy the requirement for criminal liability that R.C. 2901.22(A)(1) imposes, the trial court erred when it denied defendant-appellant Sowry's Crim. R. 29 motion for acquittal." *Sowry* at ¶ 22.

This court adopted the reasoning of *Sowry* in *State v. Lee,* Cuyahoga App. No. 89087, 2007-Ohio-5952, reversed on other grounds, *State v. Lee,* Cuyahoga App. No. 89087, 2008-Ohio-143.

Despite the State's argument that this case in different than *Sowry,* we find no distinction between the two cases. Accordingly, the trial court erred in denying Cargile's Crim. R. 29 motion for acquittal on the offense of illegally conveying a prohibited substance onto the grounds of a detention facility.

Appellant's third assignment of error is sustained. Our resolution of the third assignment of error renders the other assignments of error moot. See App. R. 12(A)(1)(c).

Having sustained the third assignment of error, we reverse and vacate Cargile's conviction for violation of R.C. 2921.36(A)(2), enter a judgment of acquittal on that charge, and order him discharged from any penalty imposed upon his conviction for that offense.

State v. Cargile, 123 Ohio St. 3d 343 (2009)

CUPP, J.

III

A

The court of appeals held that entering the detention facility with drugs in his pants cuff was not a voluntary act by Cargile, because at the time of his entry, he was under arrest. Because his arrest and transport to the detention facility deprived him of the fundamental right to freedom, the court of appeals held, his presence in the facility was a wholly involuntary act on his part.

We disagree with the court's analysis and conclude that Cargile's conduct constituted a voluntary act. Although Cargile did not have any choice whether to go to jail following his arrest, the fact that his entry into the jail was not of his volition does not make his conveyance of drugs into the detention facility an involuntary act. He was made to go into the detention facility, but he did not have to take the drugs with him.

Conscious and aware of the physical presence of the drugs hidden in his pants cuff, Cargile did not reveal his possession of the drugs during any of the searches. Moreover, Cargile affirmatively concealed the drugs by stating to the arresting officer that he did not possess anything the officer needed to be concerned about, despite the warning Cargile received that if he brought drugs into the detention facility he would be committing a felony. Cargile declined opportunities to end his possession of the drugs before entering the facility. Accordingly, Cargile's possession of the drugs when he entered the detention facility was a voluntary act, and thus he was criminally liable under R.C. 2921.36(A)(2).

B

Cargile argues that once he was arrested, he had a constitutional right to remain silent, and if he had admitted to possessing drugs, he would have incriminated himself. However, there is no indication that Cargile invoked his constitutional privilege to remain silent and avoid self-incrimination at the time of the arrest or that he argued a violation of this right before the trial court. Cargile failed to raise this claim and has thereby waived it. *State v. Awan* (1986), 22 Ohio St. 3d 120, 22 OBR 199, 489 N.E.2d 277, syllabus.

Moreover, this challenge lacks merit. Cargile's argument is based on a faulty premise: that the right to remain silent and avoid self-incrimination also includes the privilege of lying or providing false responses to direct questions. Despite the several warnings the officer gave Cargile about bringing drugs into a detention facility, Cargile actively denied possessing any drugs. The constitutional right to remain silent does not confer upon a defendant the privilege to lie, *Brogan v.* **778 *United States* (1998), 522 U.S. 398, or the right to be protected from having to make difficult choices regarding whether to invoke the right to remain silent, *State v. Canas* (Iowa 1999), 597 N.W.2d 488, 496, overruled on other grounds by *State v. Turner* (Iowa 2001), 630 N.W.2d 601; *State v. Carr* (Sept. 26, 2008), Tenn. Crim. App. No. M2007-01759-CCA-R3-CD, 2008 WL 4368240. Thus, this constitutional protection does not apply to Cargile's conduct.

Cargile additionally asserts that R.C. 2921.36 is not aimed at prisoners. He claims that the intent of R.C. 2921.36 is to prevent visitors, employees, or other nonprisoners from bringing drugs or other contraband into a detention facility, and because he was not a visitor, employee, or other nonprisoner, R.C. 2921.36 does not apply to him.

In reviewing statutory provisions, courts are constrained to look to the statutory language and the "purpose to be accomplished." *State ex rel. Richard v. Bd. of Trustees of the Police & Firemen's Disability & Pension Fund* (1994), 69 Ohio St. 3d 409, quoting *State v. S.R.* (1992), 63 Ohio St. 3d 590. "Words used in a statute must be taken in their usual, normal or customary meaning *** [and it] is the duty of the court to give effect to the words used and not to insert words not used." Id. at 412.

We find no language within the statute to support Cargile's interpretation. R.C. 2921.36 applies uniformly to all persons and provides a blanket prohibition: "*No person* shall knowingly convey" weapons or drugs onto the grounds of a detention facility. (Emphasis added.) This statute is broadly written. We reject Cargile's interpretation, which would not only change the language of the statute but would also limit the purposes to be accomplished by its proscriptions.

IV

For the foregoing reasons, we hold that a person who is taken to a detention facility after his arrest and who possesses a drug of abuse at the time he enters the facility meets the actus reus requirement for a violation of R.C. 2921.36(A)(2). The judgment of the court of appeals is reversed, and the cause is remanded to the appellate court to consider the assignments of error that it held were moot.

Notes and Questions

1. Should there be an actus reus requirement? What is wrong with punishing people for criminal thoughts or criminal fantasies? Does it matter whether you view the world as a retributivist or utilitarian? Before answering the aforementioned questions, consider the case of the so-called "Cannibal Cop."

Thea Johnson and Andrew Gilden, *Common Sense and the Cannibal Cop*
11 Stan. J. Civ. Rts. & Civ. Liberties 313 (2015)

The trial of New York City's so-called "Cannibal Cop" seemed ripped from an episode of *Law & Order: Special Victims Unit*. New York City Police Officer Gilberto Valle was caught chatting online with men from New Jersey to Pakistan about kidnapping, killing, and eating women he knew -- including his wife, college friends, and a local teenager. For almost a year, he took actions like exchanging photos with his cohorts, discussing various methods of torture, and googling the uses of chloroform. He adopted the pseudonym "girlmeathunter."

This all sounds heinous. However, by the time of his arrest in 2013, he had made no effort to kidnap, kill, or eat anyone, and there was no evidence that his online discussions went beyond graphic exchanges of dark sexual fantasies. Indeed, in these discussions, Valle repeatedly gave false identifying information about the alleged victims, concocted false stories about his own "kidnapper-for-hire" past, lied about his location, and omitted any mention of the various weapons he had access to as a police officer. Nonetheless, Valle was charged with and tried for conspiracy to kidnap and conducting an unauthorized computer search of a federal database. At trial, the government repeatedly pressed the jury to use its "common sense" and find that it was not "okay" for an NYPD officer to have these types of conversations. On March 12, 2013, the jury convicted Valle on both counts. But on June 30, 2014, Judge Gardephe issued a 118-page opinion vacating the decision of the jury as to the conspiracy to kidnap charge and overturned Valle's conviction on that count.

Although it provoked outrage in some circles, Judge Gardephe's decision is a useful starting point for thinking about the knotty ethical boundaries of applying criminal laws to the precarious realm of Internet-mediated sexuality.***

The prosecutor in the "Cannibal Cop" case called on jurors to rely on their "common sense" about Valle's fantasy life. It is unlikely, however, that the jury had much or any "common sense" about the issues that arose in the "Cannibal Cop" case. And missing from the trial was any expert testimony to educate jurors about the paraphilia, fantasy, and role-play at the center of the case. Moreover, there is no evidence that the FBI or the U.S. Attorney's Office made any effort to better understand the context or meaning of the conversations they sought to criminalize.***

While the "Cannibal Cop" case may seem like an outlier, the punch line to a joke even, it sheds light on a troubling dynamic within the contemporary criminal justice system. How does the system handle the reality of the Internet's endless ability to give people an easy outlet for sexual desires that may make others deeply uncomfortable? How do we decide what is "fantasy" and what is "reality?" And who should be making those decisions? In order to begin to tackle these difficult questions, all actors within the criminal justice system -- law enforcement, prosecutors, judges, and juries—need a better understanding about the contexts in which individuals explore their desires online. The prosecution, conviction, and ultimate acquittal of Gilberto Valle demonstrate the need for education, expertise, and social science data both in and outside the courtroom.

2. After reading the two *Cargile* cases, are you clear on what consitutes a "voluntary act"? What conduct of the defendant in *Cargile* was truly voluntary? Do you think the court would have reached a different outcome had the defendant remained silent during his arrest and subsequent transportation to the jail? Jurisdictions around the country take contrasting views on whether a defendant upon arrest "voluntarily" brings in contraband to the jail. See, e.g., Wayne R. LaFave, Criminal Law 5th Edition, Sec. 6.1(c).

In determining what constitutes a voluntary act, most states follow the guidelines set out by the MPC.

Model Penal Code
Section 2.01. Requirements of Voluntary Act: Omission as Basis of Liability; Possession as an Act

(2) The following are not voluntary acts within the meaning of this Section:

(a) a reflex or convulsion;

(b) a bodily movement during unconsciousness or sleep;

(c) conduct during hypnosis or resulting from hypnotic suggestion;

(d) a bodily movement that otherwise is not a product of the effort or determination of the actor, either conscious or habitual.

C. Omission

Jones v. United States, 308 F.2d 307 (D.C. Cir. 1962)

Appellant, together with one Shirley Green, was tried on a three-count indictment charging them jointly with (1) abusing and maltreating Robert Lee Green, (2) abusing and maltreating Anthony Lee Green, and (3) involuntary manslaughter through failure to perform their legal duty of care for Anthony Lee Green, which failure resulted in his death. At the close of evidence, after trial to a jury, the first two counts were dismissed as to both defendants. On the third count, appellant was convicted of involuntary manslaughter. Shirley Green was found not guilty.

Appellant urges several grounds for reversal. We need consider but two. First, appellant argues that there was insufficient evidence as a matter of law to warrant a jury finding of breach of duty in the care she rendered Anthony Lee. Alternatively, appellant argues that the trial court committed plain error in failing to instruct the jury that it must first find that appellant was under a legal obligation to provide food and necessities to Anthony Lee before finding her guilty of manslaughter in failing to provide them. The first argument is without merit. Upon the latter we reverse.

A summary of the evidence, which is in conflict upon almost every significant issue, is necessary for the disposition of both arguments. In late 1957, Shirley Green became pregnant, out of wedlock, with a child, Robert Lee, subsequently born August 17, 1958. Apparently to avoid the embarrassment of the presence of the child in the Green home, it was arranged that appellant, a family friend, would take the child to her home after birth. Appellant did so, and the child remained there continuously until removed by the police on August 5, 1960. Initially appellant made some motions toward the adoption of Robert Lee, but these came to nought, and shortly thereafter it was agreed that Shirley Green was to pay appellant $72 a month for his care. According to appellant, these payments were made for only five months. According to Shirley Green, they were made up to July, 1960.

Early in 1959 Shirley Green again became pregnant, this time with the child Anthony Lee, whose death is the basis of appellant's conviction. This child was born October 21, 1959. Soon after birth, Anthony Lee developed a mild jaundice condition, attributed to a blood incompatability with his mother. The jaundice resulted in his retention in the hospital for three days beyond the usual time, or until October 26, 1959, when, on authorization signed by Shirley Green, Anthony Lee was released by the hospital to appellant's custody. Shirley Green, after a two or three day stay in the hospital, also lived with appellant for three weeks, after which she returned to her parents' home, leaving the children with appellant. She testified she did not see them again, except for one visit in March, until August 5, 1960. Consequently, though there does not seem to have been any specific monetary agreement with Shirley Green covering Anthony Lee's support, appellant had complete custody of both children until they were rescued by the police.

With regard to medical care, the evidence is undisputed. In March, 1960, appellant called a Dr. Turner to her home to treat Anthony Lee for a bronchial condition. Appellant also telephoned the doctor at various times to consult with him concerning Anthony Lee's diet and health. In early July, 1960, appellant took Anthony Lee to Dr. Turner's office where he was treated for "simple diarrhea." At this time the doctor noted the "wizened" appearance of the child and told appellant to tell the mother of the child that he should be taken to a hospital. This was not done.

On August 2, 1960, two collectors for the local gas company had occasion to go to the basement of appellant's home, and there saw the two children. Robert Lee and Anthony Lee at this time were age two years and ten months respectively. Robert Lee was in a "crib" consisting of a framework of wood, covered with a fine wire screening, including the top which was hinged. The "crib" was lined with newspaper, which was stained, apparently with feces, and crawling with roaches. Anthony Lee was lying in a bassinet and was described as having the appearance of a "small baby monkey." One collector testified to seeing roaches on Anthony Lee.

On August 5, 1960, the collectors returned to appellant's home in the company of several police officers and personnel of the Women's Bureau. At this time, Anthony Lee was upstairs in the dining room in the bassinet, but Robert Lee was still downstairs in his "crib." The officers removed the children to the D. C. General Hospital where Anthony Lee was diagnosed as suffering from severe malnutrition and lesions over large portions of his body, apparently caused by severe diaper rash. Following admission, he was fed repeatedly, apparently with no difficulty, and was described as being very hungry. His death, 34 hours after admission, was attributed without dispute to malnutrition. At birth, Anthony Lee weighed six pounds, fifteen ounces—at death at age ten months, he weighed seven pounds, thirteen ounces. Normal weight at this age would have been approximately 14 pounds.

Appellant argues that nothing in the evidence establishes that she failed to provide food to Anthony Lee. She cites her own testimony and the testimony of a lodger, Mr. Wills, that she did in fact feed the baby regularly. At trial, the defense made repeated attempts to extract from the medical witnesses opinions that the jaundice, or the condition which caused it, might have prevented the baby from assimilating food. The doctors conceded this was possible but not probable since the autopsy revealed no condition which would support the defense theory. It was also shown by the disinterested medical witnesses that the child had no difficulty in ingesting food immediately after birth, and that Anthony Lee, in the last hours before his death, was able to take several bottles, apparently without difficulty, and seemed very hungry. This evidence, combined with the absence of any physical cause for nonassimilation, taken in the context of the condition in which these children were kept, presents a jury question on the feeding issue.

Moreover, there is substantial evidence from which the jury could have found that appellant failed to obtain proper medical care for the child. Appellant relies upon the evidence showing that on one occasion she summoned a doctor for the child, on another took the child to the doctor's office, and that she telephoned the doctor on several occasions about the baby's formula. However, the last time a doctor saw the child was a month before his death, and appellant admitted that on that occasion the doctor recommended hospitalization. Appellant did not hospitalize the child, nor did she take any other steps to obtain medical care in the last crucial month. Thus there was sufficient evidence to go to the jury on the issue of medical care, as well as failure to feed.

Appellant also takes exception to the failure of the trial court to charge that the jury must find beyond a reasonable doubt, as an element of the crime, that appellant was under a legal duty to supply food and necessities to Anthony Lee. Appellant's attorney did not object to the failure to give this instruction, but urges here the application of Rule 52(b).

The problem of establishing the duty to take action which would preserve the life of another has not often arisen in the case law of this country. The most commonly cited statement of the rule is found in *People v. Beardsley*, 150 Mich. 206:

> The law recognizes that under some circumstances the omission of a duty owed by one individual to another, where such omission results in the death of the one to whom the duty is owing, will make the other chargeable with manslaughter.
>
> *** This rule of law is always based upon the proposition that the duty neglected must be a legal duty, and not a mere moral obligation. It must be a duty imposed by law or by contract, and the omission to perform the duty must be the immediate and direct cause of death. ***

There are at least four situations in which the failure to act may constitute breach of a legal duty. One can be held criminally liable: first, where a statute imposes a duty to care for another; second, where one stands in a certain status relationship to another; third, where one has assumed a contractual duty to care for another; and fourth, where one has voluntarily assumed the care of another and so secluded the helpless person as to prevent others from rendering aid.

It is the contention of the Government that either the third or the fourth ground is applicable here. However, it is obvious that in any of the four situations, there are critical issues of fact which must be passed on by the jury—specifically in this case, whether appellant had entered into a contract with the mother for the care of Anthony Lee or, alternatively, whether she assumed the care of the child and secluded him from the care of his mother, his natural protector. On both of these issues, the evidence is in direct conflict, appellant insisting that the mother was actually living with appellant and Anthony Lee, and hence should have been taking care of the child herself, while Shirley Green testified she was living with her parents and was paying appellant to care for both children.

In spite of this conflict, the instructions given in the case failed even to suggest the necessity for finding a legal duty of care. The only reference to duty in the instructions was the reading of the indictment which charged, inter alia, that the defendants "failed to perform their legal duty." A finding of legal duty is the critical element of the crime charged and failure to instruct the jury concerning it was plain error.

Notes and Questions

1. Generally speaking, one does not expose himself or herself to criminal liability for failing to warn or aid another. While it might be morally objectionable to ignore the plight of another human being, it is neither criminal nor illegal. The exception to this rule arises when one has a duty to act. In *Jones v. United States*, the court listed four instances in which a person has a duty to act. Can you think of any other instances where an individual might have a duty to act?

2. In *Jones*, appellant and the mother of the children, Shirley Green, were tried together. In finding the mother not guilty and the appellant guilty, did the jury essentially determine that the appellant, not the mother, had a duty of care for Anthony? Could the jury find that neither appellant nor Shirley Green had an obligation to provide for the children?

3. Many states now impose affirmative reporting requirements for certain occupations (e.g., teachers, health care workers, social workers, etc.) whenever they come across potential instances of child abuse. Other states, like Ohio, have gone even further and impose a general reporting duty. Consider R.C. 2921.22 which reads as follows:

> Failure to report a crime or knowledge of a death or burn injury.
> (A)
> (1) Except as provided in division (A)(2) of this section, no person, knowing that a felony has been or is being committed, shall knowingly fail to report such information to law enforcement authorities.***

Do you think this law is necessary? What concerns, if any, do you have with this statute? Before answering these questions, read about notorious sex assault case that involved members of the Steubenville High School football team.

Thaddeus Hoffmeister, *Social Media in the Courtroom, A New Era for Criminal Justice*, Praeger Publishing (2014)

Ohio's failure to report statute was recently put to the test in the 2012 Steubenville football rape case in which two juvenile defendants were found delinquent (the juvenile equivalent of a guilty finding) of digitally penetrating an intoxicated 16-year-old girl at a high-school party. The case came to the attention of investigators and the public at large after evidence of the assault including a video and photos appeared on social media. In fact, the social media evidence was critical to the actual conviction of the two juveniles because the victim remembered very little from the night in question.

One unique and unfortunate aspect of the case involved the role of bystanders who actually saw the girl firsthand or viewed videos and photos of her in a semiconscious state. One of the bystanders was a young college freshman who shortly after viewing the photos and videos of the young girl made his own video in which he said:

"She is so raped right now."

This young man's video was posted on YouTube on the same night of the assault.

Not surprisingly, this comment drew outrage from across the country. Groups and Organizations like the National Organization of Women (NOW) have called upon the Ohio Attorney General to investigate and prosecute this individual as well as others who viewed the video and photos of the young girl and then failed to alert authorities or report that a crime had occurred. Despite the push by groups like NOW to have this young man prosecuted under Ohio's failure to report statute, it has not happened to date. The state of Ohio is probably hesitant to charge him because of the precedent it might set.

D. Vicarious Liability

While vicarious liability is more common in the civil arena, it occasionally arises in criminal law, e.g., where the employer or owner of a business is made criminally liable for the bad conduct of an employee. In contrast to strict liability that dispenses with mens rea, vicarious liability removes the actus reus requirement for the defendant, which runs contrary to the common law notion that guilt be personal and individual.

Those who support criminal vicarious liability argue that the law is necessary because of the nature and inherent danger of certain business activities and the challenges of establishing wrongdoing in the way those businesses function. Since vicarious liability imposes criminal liability for faultless conduct by the defendant, courts have been hesitant to apply it in certain situations. The second case in this section, *State v. Tomaino*, illustrates this view.

United States v. Park, 421 U.S. 658 (1975)

MR. CHIEF JUSTICE BURGER delivered the opinion of the Court.

We granted certiorari to consider whether the jury instructions in the prosecution of a corporate officer under § 301(k) of the Federal Food, Drug, and Cosmetic Act, 52 Stat. 1042, as amended, 21 U.S.C. § 331(k), were appropriate under _United States v. Dotterweich,_ 320 U.S. 277 (1943).

Acme Markets, Inc., is a national retail food chain with approximately 36,000 employees, 874 retail outlets, 12 general warehouses, and four special warehouses. Its headquarters, including the office of the president, respondent Park, who is chief executive officer of the corporation, are located in Philadelphia, Pa. In a five-count information filed in the United States District Court for the District of Maryland, the Government charged Acme and respondent with violations of the Federal Food, Drug, and Cosmetic Act. Each count of the information alleged that the defendants had received food that had been shipped in interstate commerce and that, while the food was being held for sale in Acme's Baltimore warehouse following shipment in interstate commerce, they caused it to be held in a building accessible to rodents and to be exposed to contamination by rodents. These acts were alleged to have resulted in the food's being adulterated within the meaning of 21 U.S.C. §§ 342(a)(3) and (4),[2] in violation of 21 U.S.C. § 331(k).[3]

Acme pleaded guilty to each count of the information. Respondent pleaded not guilty. The evidence at trial demonstrated that, in April, 1970, the Food and Drug Administration (FDA) advised respondent by letter of insanitary conditions in Acme's Philadelphia warehouse. In 1971, the FDA found that similar conditions existed in the firm's Baltimore warehouse. An FDA consumer safety officer

---

[2] Section 402 of the Act, 21 U.S.C. § 342, provides in pertinent part:

A food shall be deemed to be adulterated—

"a) . . . (3) if it consists in whole or in part of any filthy, putrid, or decomposed substance, or if it is otherwise unfit for food; or (4) if it has been prepared, packed, or held under insanitary conditions whereby it may have become contaminated with filth, or whereby it may have been rendered injurious to health. . . .

[3] Section 301 of the Act, 21 U.S.C. § 331, provides in pertinent part:

The following acts and the causing thereof are prohibited:

(k) The alteration, mutilation, destruction, obliteration, or removal of the whole or any part of the labeling of, or the doing of any other act with respect to, a food, drug, device, or cosmetic, if such act is done while such article is held for sale (whether or not the first sale) after shipment in interstate commerce and results in such article being adulterated or misbranded.

testified concerning evidence of rodent infestation and other insanitary conditions discovered during a 12-day inspection of the Baltimore warehouse in November and December, 1971.[4] He also related that a second inspection of the warehouse had been conducted in March, 1972.[5] On that occasion, the inspectors found that there had been improvement in the sanitary conditions, but that "there was still evidence of rodent activity in the building and in the warehouses and we found some rodent-contaminated lots of food items."

The Government also presented testimony by the Chief of Compliance of the FDA's Baltimore office, who informed respondent by letter of the conditions at the Baltimore warehouse after the first inspection. There was testimony by Acme's Baltimore division vice-president, who had responded to the letter on behalf of Acme and respondent and who described the steps taken to remedy the insanitary conditions discovered by both inspections. The Government's final witness, Acme's vice-president for legal affairs and assistant secretary, identified respondent as the president and chief executive officer of the company and read a bylaw prescribing the duties of the chief executive officer. He testified that

---

[4] The witness testified with respect to the inspection of the basement of the "old building" in the warehouse complex:

> We found extensive evidence of rodent infestation in the form of rat and mouse pellets throughout the entire perimeter area and along the wall.

> We also found that the doors leading to the basement area from the rail siding had openings at the bottom or openings beneath part of the door that came down at the bottom large enough to admit rodent entry. There were also roden[t] pellets found on a number of different packages of boxes of various items stored in the basement, and looking at this document, I see there were also broken windows along the rail siding.

> App. 221. On the first floor of the "old building," the inspectors found: Thirty mouse pellets on the floor along walls and on the ledge in the hanging meat room. There were at least twenty mouse pellets beside bales of lime Jello and one of the bales had a chewed rodent hole in the product. . . .

[5] The letter, dated January 27, 1972, included the following:

> We note with much concern that the old and new warehouse areas used for food storage were actively and extensively inhabited by live rodents. Of even more concern was the observation that such reprehensible conditions obviously existed for a prolonged period of time without any detection, or were completely ignored. . . .

> We trust this letter will serve to direct your attention to the seriousness of the problem and formally advise you of the urgent need to initiate whatever measures are necessary to prevent recurrence and ensure compliance with the law.

respondent functioned by delegating "normal operating duties," including sanitation, but that he retained "certain things, which are the big, broad, principles of the operation of the company," and had "the responsibility of seeing that they all work together." *Id.* at 41.

At the close of the Government's case in chief, respondent moved for a judgment of acquittal on the ground that "the evidence in chief has shown that Mr. Park is not personally concerned in this Food and Drug violation." The trial judge denied the motion, stating that *United States v. Dotterweich,* 320 U.S. 277 (1943), was controlling.

Respondent was the only defense witness. He testified that, although all of Acme's employees were, in a sense, under his general direction, the company had an "organizational structure for responsibilities for certain functions" according to which different phases of its operation were "assigned to individuals who, in turn, have staff and departments under them." He identified those individuals responsible for sanitation, and related that, upon receipt of the January, 1972, FDA letter, he had conferred with the vice-president for legal affairs, who informed him that the Baltimore division vice president "was investigating the situation immediately and would be taking corrective action and would be preparing a summary of the corrective action to reply to the letter." Respondent stated that he did not "believe there was anything [he] could have done more constructively than what [he] found was being done."

On cross-examination, respondent conceded that providing sanitary conditions for food offered for sale to the public was something that he was "responsible for in the entire operation of the company," and he stated that it was one of many phases of the company that he assigned to "dependable subordinates." Respondent was asked about and, over the objections of his counsel, admitted receiving, the April, 1970, letter addressed to him from the FDA regarding insanitary conditions at Acme's Philadelphia warehouse. [6] He

---

[6] The April, 1970, letter informed respondent of the following "objectionable conditions" in Acme's Philadelphia warehouse:

> 1. Potential rodent entryways were noted via ill-fitting doors and door in irrepair at Southwest corner of warehouse; at dock at old salvage room, and at receiving and shipping doors which were observed to be open most of the time.
>
> 2. Rodent nesting, rodent excreta pellets, rodent-stained bale bagging and rodent-gnawed holes were noted among bales of flour stored in warehouse.
>
> 3. Potential rodent harborage was noted in discarded paper, rope, sawdust and other debris piled in corner of shipping and receiving dock near bakery and warehouse doors. Rodent excreta pellets were observed among bags of sawdust (or wood shavings).

acknowledged that, with the exception of the division vice-president, the same individuals had responsibility for sanitation in both Baltimore and Philadelphia. Finally, in response to questions concerning the Philadelphia and Baltimore incidents, respondent admitted that the Baltimore problem indicated the system for handling sanitation "wasn't working perfectly," and that, as Acme's chief executive officer, he was responsible for "any result which occurs in our company." *Id.* at 48-55.

At the close of the evidence, respondent's renewed motion for a judgment of acquittal was denied. The relevant portion of the trial judge's instructions to the jury challenged by respondent is set out in the margin.[7] Respondent's counsel objected to the instructions on the ground that they failed fairly to reflect our decision in *United States v. Dotterweich, supra,* and to define *"responsible relationship.'"*

The trial judge overruled the objection. The jury found respondent guilty on all counts of the information, and he was subsequently sentenced to pay a fine of $50 on each count. The Court of Appeals reversed the conviction and remanded for a new trial. That court viewed the Government as arguing "that the conviction may be predicated solely upon a showing that . . . [respondent] was the President of the offending corporation," and it stated that as "a general proposition, some act of commission or omission is an essential element of every crime." 499 F.2d 839, 841 (CA4 1974). It reasoned that, although our decision in United States v. Dotterweich, supra, at 320 U.S. 281, had construed the statutory provisions under which respondent was tried to dispense with the traditional element of

---

[7] "In order to find the Defendant guilty on any count of the Information, you must find beyond a reasonable doubt on each count . . . "
"*** *"

"Thirdly, that John R. Park held a position of authority in the operation of the business of Acme Markets, Incorporated."

"However, you need not concern yourselves with the first two elements of the case. The main issue for your determination is only with the third element, whether the Defendant held a position of authority and responsibility in the business of Acme Markets"

"The statute makes individuals, as well as corporations, liable for violations. An individual is liable if it is clear, beyond a reasonable doubt, that the elements of the adulteration of the food as to travel in interstate commerce are present. As I have instructed you in this case, they are, and that the individual had a responsible relation to the situation, even though he may not have participated personally."

"The individual is or could be liable under the statute even if he did not consciously do wrong. However, the fact that the Defendant is pres[id]ent and is a chief executive officer of the Acme Markets does not require a finding of guilt. Though he need not have personally participated in the situation, he must have had a responsible relationship to the issue. The issue is, in this case, whether the Defendant, John R. Park, by virtue of his position in the company, had a position of authority and responsibility in the situation out of which these charges arose."

"'awareness of some wrongdoing,'" the Court had not construed them as dispensing with the element of "wrongful action." The Court of Appeals concluded that the trial judge's instructions "might well have left the jury with the erroneous impression that Park could be found guilty in the absence of 'wrongful action' on his part," 499 F.2d at 841-842, and that proof of this element was required by due process. It held, with one dissent, that the instructions did not "correctly state the law of the case," id. at 840, and directed that, on retrial the jury be instructed as to "wrongful action," which might be "gross negligence and inattention in discharging . . . corporate duties and obligations or any of a host of other acts of commission or omission which would 'cause' the contamination of food." *Id.* at 842. (Footnotes omitted.)***

We granted certiorari because of an apparent conflict among the Courts of Appeals with respect to the standard of liability of corporate officers under the Federal Food, Drug, and Cosmetic Act as construed in *United States v. Dotterweich, supra,* and because of the importance of the question to the Government's enforcement program. We reverse.***

II

The rule that corporate employees who have "a responsible share in the furtherance of the transaction which the statute outlaws" are subject to the criminal provisions of the Act was not formulated in a vacuum. *Cf. Morissette v. United States,* 342 U.S. 246 (1952). Cases under the Federal Food and Drugs Act of 1906 reflected the view both that knowledge or intent were not required to be proved in prosecutions under its criminal provisions and that responsible corporate agents could be subjected to the liability thereby imposed. *See, e.g., United States v. Mayfield,* 177 F. 765 (ND Ala. 1910). Moreover, the principle had been recognized that a corporate agent, through whose act, default, or omission the corporation committed a crime was himself guilty individually of that crime. The principle had been applied whether or not the crime required "consciousness of wrongdoing," and it had been applied not only to those corporate agents who themselves committed the criminal act, but also to those who by virtue of their managerial positions or other similar relation to the actor could be deemed responsible for its commission.

In the latter class of cases, the liability of managerial officers did not depend on their knowledge of, or personal participation in, the act made criminal by the statute. Rather, where the statute under which they were prosecuted dispensed with "consciousness of wrongdoing," an omission or failure to act was deemed a sufficient basis for a responsible corporate agent's liability. It was enough in such cases that, by virtue of the relationship he bore to the corporation, the agent had the power to prevent the act complained of. *See, e.g., State v. Burnam,* 71 Wash. 199 (1912).

The rationale of the interpretation given the Act in *Dotterweich,* as holding criminally accountable the persons whose failure to exercise the authority and supervisory responsibility reposed in them by the business organization resulted in the violation complained of, has been confirmed in our subsequent cases. Thus, the Court has reaffirmed the proposition that "the public interest in the purity of its food is so great as to warrant the imposition of the highest standard of care on distributors." *Smith v. California,* 361 U.S. 147 (1959). In order to make "distributors of food the strictest censors of their merchandise," *ibid.,* the Act punishes "neglect where the law requires care, or inaction where it imposes a duty." *Morissette v. United States, supra* at 342 U.S. 255.

"The accused, if he does not will the violation, usually is in a position to prevent it with no more care than society might reasonably expect and no more exertion than it might reasonably exact from one who assumed his responsibilities." *Id.* at 342 U.S. 256. *Cf.* Hughes, Criminal Omissions, 67 Yale L.J. 590 (1958). Similarly, in cases decided after *Dotterweich,* the Courts of Appeals have recognized that those corporate agents vested with the responsibility, and power commensurate with that responsibility, to devise whatever measures are necessary to ensure compliance with the Act bear a "responsible relationship" to, or have a "responsible share" in, violations.

Thus, *Dotterweich* and the cases which have followed reveal that, in providing sanctions which reach and touch the individuals who execute the corporate mission—and this is by no means necessarily confined to a single corporate agent or employee—the Act imposes not only a positive duty to seek out and remedy violations when they occur, but also, and primarily, a duty to implement measures that will insure that violations will not occur. The requirements of foresight and vigilance imposed on responsible corporate agents are beyond question demanding, and perhaps onerous, but they are no more stringent than the public has a right to expect of those who voluntarily assume positions of authority in business enterprises whose services and products affect the health and wellbeing of the public that supports them. *Cf.* Wasserstrom, Strict Liability in the Criminal Law, 12 Stan. L. Rev. 731, 741-745 (1960).

The Act does not, as we observed in *Dotterweich,* make criminal liability turn on "awareness of some wrongdoing" or "conscious fraud." The duty imposed by Congress on responsible corporate agents is, we emphasize, one that requires the highest standard of foresight and vigilance, but the Act, in its criminal aspect, does not require that which is objectively impossible. The theory upon which responsible corporate agents are held criminally accountable for "causing" violations of the Act permits a claim that a defendant was "powerless" to prevent or correct the violation to "be raised defensively at a trial on the merits." *United States v. Wiesenfeld Warehouse Co.,* 376 U.S. 86 (1964). If such a claim is made, the defendant has the burden of coming forward with evidence, but this does not alter the Government's ultimate burden of proving beyond a reasonable doubt the defendant's guilt, including his power, in light of the duty imposed by the Act, to prevent or correct the prohibited condition. Congress has seen fit to enforce the accountability of responsible corporate agents dealing with products which may affect the health of consumers by penal sanctions cast in rigorous terms, and the obligation of the courts is to give them effect so long as they do not violate the Constitution.

III

We cannot agree with the Court of Appeals that it was incumbent upon the District Court to instruct the jury that the Government had the burden of establishing "wrongful action" in the sense in which the Court of Appeals used that phrase. The concept of a "responsible relationship" to, or a "responsible share" in, a violation of the Act indeed imports some measure of blameworthiness; but it is equally clear that the Government establishes a *prima facie* case when it introduces evidence sufficient to warrant a finding by the trier of the facts that the defendant had, by reason of his position in the corporation, responsibility and authority either to prevent in the first instance, or promptly to correct, the violation complained of, and that he failed to do so. The failure thus to fulfill the duty imposed by the interaction of the corporate agent's authority and the statute furnishes a sufficient causal link. The considerations which prompted the imposition of this duty, and the scope of the duty, provide the measure of culpability.

Turning to the jury charge in this case, it is of course arguable that isolated parts can be read as intimating that a finding of guilt could be predicated solely on respondent's corporate position. But this is not the way we review jury instructions, because "a single instruction to a jury may not be judged in artificial isolation, but must be viewed in the context of the overall charge." *Cupp v. Naughten,* 414 U.S. 141 (1973).

Reading the entire charge satisfies us that the jury's attention was adequately focused on the issue of respondent's authority with respect to the conditions that formed the basis of the alleged violations. Viewed as a whole, the charge did not permit the jury to find guilt solely on the basis of respondent's position in the corporation; rather, it fairly advised the jury that to find guilt it must find respondent "had a responsible relation to the situation," and "by virtue of his position . . . had . . . authority and responsibility" to deal with the situation. The situation referred to could only be

> "food . . . held in unsanitary conditions in a warehouse with the result that it consisted, in part, of filth or . . . may have been contaminated with filth."

Moreover, in reviewing jury instructions, our task is also to view the charge itself as part of the whole trial.

"Often isolated statements taken from the charge, seemingly prejudicial on their face, are not so when considered in the context of the entire record of the trial." *United States v. Birnbaum,* 373 F.2d 250, 257 (CA2) (1967). (Emphasis added.)

The record in his case reveals that the jury could not have failed to be aware that the main issue for determination was not respondent's position in the corporate hierarchy, but rather his accountability, because of the responsibility and authority of his position, for the conditions which gave rise to the charges against him.

We conclude that, viewed as a whole and in the context of the trial, the charge was not misleading, and contained an adequate statement of the law to guide the jury's determination. Although it would have been better to give an instruction more precisely relating the legal issue to the facts of the case, we cannot say that the failure to provide the amplification requested by respondent was an abuse of discretion. *See United States v. Bayer,* 331 U.S. 532 (1947). Finally, we note that there was no request for an instruction that the Government was required to prove beyond a reasonable doubt that respondent was not without the power or capacity to affect the conditions which founded the charges in the information. In light of the evidence adduced at trial, we find no basis to conclude that the failure of the trial court to give such an instruction *sua sponte* was plain error or a defect affecting substantial rights. Fed. Rule Crim. Proc. 52(b).

IV

Our conclusion that the Court of Appeals erred in its reading of the jury charge suggests as well our disagreement with that court concerning the admissibility of evidence demonstrating that respondent was advised by the FDA in 1970 of insanitary conditions in Acme's Philadelphia warehouse. We are satisfied that the Act imposes the highest standard of care and permits conviction of responsible corporate officials who, in light of this standard of care, have the power to prevent or correct violations of its provisions. Implicit in the Court's admonition that "the ultimate judgment of juries must be trusted," *United States v. Dotterweich,* 320 U.S. at 320 U.S. 285, however, is the realization that they may demand more than corporate bylaws to find culpability.

Respondent testified in his defense that he had employed a system in which he relied upon his subordinates, and that he was ultimately responsible for this system. He testified further that he had found these subordinates to be "dependable" and had "great confidence" in them. By this and other testimony, respondent evidently sought to persuade the jury that, as the president of a large corporation, he had no choice but to delegate duties to those in whom he reposed confidence, that he had no reason to suspect his subordinates were failing to insure compliance with the Act, and that, once violations were unearthed, acting through those subordinates he did everything possible to correct them.

Although we need not decide whether this testimony would have entitled respondent to an instruction as to his lack of power, *see supra* at 421 U.S. 676, had he requested it, the testimony clearly created the "need" for rebuttal evidence. That evidence was not offered to show that respondent had a propensity to commit criminal acts, *cf. Michelson v. United States,* 335 U.S. 469, 335 U.S. 475-476 (1948), or, as in *United States v. Woods,* 484 F.2d 127, that the crime charged had been committed; its purpose was to demonstrate that respondent was on notice that he could not rely on his system of delegation to subordinates to prevent or correct insanitary conditions at Acme's warehouses, and that he must have been aware of the deficiencies of this system before the Baltimore violations were discovered. The evidence was therefore relevant, since it served to rebut respondent's defense that he had justifiably relied upon subordinates to handle sanitation matters. And, particularly in light of the difficult task of juries in prosecutions under the Act, we conclude that its relevance and persuasiveness outweighed any prejudicial effect.

Mr. Justice STEWART, with whom Mr. Justice MARSHALL and Mr. Justice POWELL join, dissenting.

Although agreeing with much of what is said in the Court's opinion, I dissent from the opinion and judgment, because the jury instructions in this case were not consistent with the law as the Court today expounds it.

As I understand the Court's opinion, it holds that, in order to sustain a conviction under § 301(k) of the Federal Food, Drug, and Cosmetic Act, the prosecution must at least show that, by reason of an individual's corporate position and responsibilities, he had a duty to use care to maintain the physical integrity of the corporation's food products. A jury may then draw the inference that, when the food is found to be in such condition as to violate the statute's prohibitions, that condition was "caused" by a breach of the standard of care imposed upon the responsible official. This is the language of negligence, and I agree with it.

To affirm this conviction, however, the Court must approve the instructions given to the members of the jury who were entrusted with determining whether the respondent was innocent or guilty. Those instructions did not conform to the standards that the Court itself sets out today.

The trial judge instructed the jury to find Park guilty if it found beyond a reasonable doubt that Park "had a responsible relation to the situation. . . . The issue is, in this case, whether the Defendant, John R. Park, by virtue of his position in the company, had a position of authority and responsibility in the situation out of which these charges arose." Requiring, as it did, a verdict of guilty upon a finding of "responsibility," this instruction, standing alone, could have been construed as a direction to convict if the jury found Park "responsible" for the condition in the sense that his position as chief executive officer gave him formal responsibility within the structure of the corporation. But the trial judge went on specifically to caution the jury not to attach such a meaning to his instruction, saying that "the fact that the Defendant is pres[id]ent and is a chief executive officer of the Acme Markets does not require a finding of guilt." "Responsibility" as used by the trial judge therefore had whatever meaning the jury in its unguided discretion chose to give it.

The instructions, therefore, expressed nothing more than a tautology. They told the jury: "You must find the defendant guilty if you find that he is to be held accountable for this adulterated food." In other words: "You must find the defendant guilty if you conclude that he is guilty." The trial judge recognized the infirmities in these instructions, but he reluctantly concluded that he was required to give such a charge under *United States v. Dotterweich,* 320 U.S. 277, which, he thought, in declining to define "responsible relation" had declined to specify the minimum standard of liability for criminal guilt.

As the Court today recognizes, the *Dotterweich* case did not deal with what kind of conduct must be proved to support a finding of criminal guilt under the Act. *Dotterweich* was concerned, rather, with the statutory definition of "person"—with what kind of corporate employees were even "subject to the criminal provisions of the Act." *Ante* at 421 U.S. 670. The Court held that those employees with "a responsible relation" to the violative transaction or condition were subject to the Act's criminal provisions, but all that the Court had to say with respect to the kind of conduct that can constitute criminal guilt was that the Act "dispenses with the conventional requirement for criminal conduct—awareness of some wrongdoing." 320 U.S. at 320 U.S. 281.

In approving the instructions to the jury in this case—instructions based upon what the Court concedes was a misunderstanding of *Dotterweich*—the Court approves a conspicuous departure from the long and firmly established division of functions between judge and jury in the administration of criminal justice. As the Court put the matter more than 80 years ago:

> "We must hold firmly to the doctrine that, in the courts of the United States it is the duty of juries in criminal cases to take the law from the court and apply that law to the facts as they find them to be from the evidence. Upon the court rests the responsibility of declaring the law; upon the jury, the responsibility of applying the law so declared to the facts as they, upon their conscience, believe them to be. Under any other system, the courts, although established in order to declare the law, would for every practical purpose be eliminated from our

system of government as instrumentalities devised for the protection equally of society and of individuals in their essential rights. When that occurs our government will cease to be a government of laws, and become a government of men. Liberty regulated by law is the underlying principle of our institutions." *Sparf v. United States,* 156 U.S. 51, 156 U.S. 102-103.

More recently, the Court declared unconstitutional a procedure whereby a jury, having acquitted a defendant of a misdemeanor, was instructed to impose upon him such costs of the prosecution as it deemed appropriate to his degree of "responsibility." *Giaccio v. Pennsylvania,* 382 U.S. 399. The state statute under which the procedure was authorized was invalidated because it left "to the jury such broad and unlimited power in imposing costs on acquitted defendants that the jurors must make determinations of the crucial issue upon their own notions of what the law should be instead of what it is." *Id.* at 382 U.S. 403. And in *Jackson v. Denno,* 378 U.S. 368, the Court found unconstitutional a procedure whereby a jury was permitted to decide the question of the voluntariness of a confession along with the question of guilt, in part because that procedure permitted the submergence of a question of law, as to which appellate review was constitutionally required, in the general deliberations of a jury.

These cases no more than embody a principle fundamental to our jurisprudence: that a jury is to decide the facts and apply to them the law as explained by the trial judge. Were it otherwise, trial by jury would be no more rational and no more responsive to the accumulated wisdom of the law than trial by ordeal. It is the function of jury instructions, in short, to establish in any trial the objective standards that a jury is to apply as it performs its own function of finding the facts.

To be sure, "the day [is] long past when [courts] . . . parsed instructions and engaged in nice semantic distinctions," *Cool v. United States,* 409 U.S. 100, 409 U.S. 107 (Rehnquist, J., dissenting). But this Court has never before abandoned the view that jury instructions must contain a statement of the applicable law sufficiently precise to enable the jury to be guided by something other than its rough notions of social justice. And while it might be argued that the issue before the jury in this case was a "mixed" question of both law and fact, this has never meant that a jury is to be left wholly at sea, without any guidance as to the standard of conduct the law requires. The instructions given by the trial court in this case, it must be emphasized, were a virtual nullity, a mere authorization to convict if the jury thought it appropriate. Such instructions—regardless of the blameworthiness of the defendant's conduct, regardless of the social value of the Food, Drug, and Cosmetic Act, and regardless of the importance of convicting those who violate it—have no place in our jurisprudence.

We deal here with a criminal conviction, not a civil forfeiture. It is true that the crime was but a misdemeanor and the penalty in this case light. But under the statute even a first conviction can result in imprisonment for a year, and a subsequent offense is a felony carrying a punishment of up to three years in prison. So the standardless conviction approved today can serve in another case tomorrow to support a felony conviction and a substantial prison sentence. However highly the Court may regard the social objectives of the Food, Drug, and Cosmetic Act, that regard cannot serve to justify a criminal conviction so wholly alien to fundamental principles of our law.

The *Dotterweich* case stands for two propositions, and I accept them both. First, "any person" within the meaning of 21 U.S.C. § 333 may include any corporate officer or employee "standing in responsible relation" to a condition or transaction forbidden by the Act. 320 U.S. at 320 U.S. 281. Second, a person may be convicted of a criminal offense under the Act even in the absence of "the conventional requirement for criminal conduct—awareness of some wrongdoing." *Ibid.*

But before a person can be convicted of a criminal violation of this Act, a jury must find—and must be clearly instructed that it must find—evidence beyond a reasonable doubt that he engaged in wrongful conduct amounting at least to common law negligence. There were no such instructions, and clearly, therefore, no such finding in this case.

For these reasons, I cannot join the Court in affirming Park's criminal conviction.

Notes and Questions

1. After reading *United States v. Park*, who do you think had the better argument the majority or the dissent? What exactly is the dissent concerned with? The dissent appears to agree with the rule of law but is troubled with the jury instructions. Specifically, the dissent is bothered by the word "responsibility."

2. What more should the defendant have done in *Park*? It appears as though he was attempting to take corrective action. If you were the general counsel to Acme Markets, what advice would you have given Park?

State v. Tomaino, 135 Ohio App. 3d 309 (1999)

Appellant owns VIP Video, a video sales and rental store in Millville, Ohio. VIP Video's inventory includes only sexually-oriented videotapes and materials. On October 13, 1997, Carl Frybarger, age thirty-seven, and his son Mark, age seventeen, decided that Mark should attempt to rent a video from VIP. Mark entered the store, selected a video, and presented it to the clerk along with his father's driver's license and credit card. The purchase was completed and the Frybargers contacted the Butler County Sheriff's Department. After interviewing Mark and his father, Sergeant Greg Blankenship, supervisor of the Drug and Vice Unit, determined that Mark should again attempt to purchase videos at VIP Video with marked money while wearing a radio transmitter wire. On October 14, 1997, Mark again entered the store. A different clerk was on duty. Following Blankenship's instructions, Mark selected four videos and approached the clerk. He told her that he had been in the store the previous day and that he was thirty-seven. Mark told the clerk that he had used a credit card on that occasion and that he was using cash this time and thus did not have his identification with him. The clerk accepted the cash ($100) and did not require any identification or proof of Mark's age. It is this video transaction that constitutes the basis of the indictment.

The clerk, Billie Doan, was then informed by Blankenship that she had sold the videos to a juvenile and that she would be arrested. Doan said that she needed to call appellant and made several unsuccessful attempts to contact appellant at different locations.

The grand jury indicted appellant, Doan, and VIP Video on two counts. Count One charged the defendants with recklessly disseminating obscene material to juveniles and Count Two charged the defendants with disseminating matter that was harmful to juveniles.

Doan was tried separately from appellant. Appellant moved to dismiss the indictment against him. During pretrial proceedings, appellant argued that criminal liability could not be imputed to him based on the actions of the clerk. The state moved to amend the bill of particulars to provide that appellant "recklessly failed to supervise his employees and agents." The trial court denied appellant's motion to dismiss and the case against appellant proceeded to a jury trial on August 25, 1998.***

The state argued that appellant was reckless by not having a sign saying "no sales to juveniles." Appellant argued in part that he was not liable for the clerk's actions. The jury was instructed that in order to convict they must find beyond a reasonable doubt that appellant, recklessly and with knowledge of its character or content, sold to a juvenile any material that was obscene (Count One) and harmful to a juvenile (Count Two). The jury was also instructed on the definitions of knowingly and recklessly and on the definitions of obscene material and of material harmful to juveniles. The jury found appellant not guilty on Count One (disseminating obscene material) and guilty on Count Two (disseminating matter harmful to juveniles).

***The court stated that the jury could find that appellant was the owner of the store and thus had knowledge of the character or content of the material being sold in his store. The court also stated that appellant "did not implement any policies, plans or procedures to prohibit entrance of juveniles into his store or the sale of material to juveniles."

Appellant has raised one assignment of error:

> The trial court erred as a matter of law when it denied Mr. Tomaino's Rule 29(C) motion for judgment of acquittal and, in the alternative, motion for a new trial.

Appellant raises five different issues under this assignment of error; we find that appellant's first issue is dispositive. Appellant argues that his Crim. R. 29 motion should have been granted because no statute imposed criminal liability for his actions or inactions. Having carefully reviewed the state's arguments, we must agree, although we hold that the court erred in its instructions to the jury rather than in denying the motion for acquittal.

Appellant was convicted of disseminating matter harmful to juveniles. R.C. 2907.31 provides in relevant part:

> (A) No person, with knowledge of its character or content, shall recklessly do any of the following:
> (1) Sell, deliver, furnish, disseminate, provide, exhibit, rent, present to a juvenile any material or performance that is obscene or harmful to juveniles.

We begin with a proposition that the state does not and cannot dispute: Ohio has no common law offenses. R.C. 2901.03 provides:

> (A) No conduct constitutes a criminal offense against the state unless it is defined as an offense in the Revised Code.
> (B) An offense is defined when one or more sections of the Revised Code state a positive prohibition or enjoin a specific duty and provide a penalty for violation of such prohibition or failure to meet such duty."

In interpreting this language, the Ohio Supreme Court has noted that criminal liability is "rigidly and precisely limited to those situations that the General Assembly has specifically delineated by statute." *State v. CECOS Intern., Inc.* (1988), 38 Ohio St. 3d 120. In R.C. 2901.21, the legislature has further provided that a person is not guilty of an offense unless both of the following apply:

(1) His liability is based on conduct which includes either a voluntary act, or an omission to perform an act or duty which he is capable of performing;

(2) He has the requisite degree of culpability for each element as to which a culpable mental state is specified by the section defining the offense.

The state argues that because appellant was "capable of performing" actions to prevent juveniles from entering his store he can be held criminally liable for the clerk's actions. However, the state's theory would create a common law crime based on appellant's failure to act. The legislature, under R.C. 2907.31, the offense charged in this case, has not specifically provided a penalty for the failure to meet the duty the state has posited, i.e. the duty to keep juveniles out of such stores. As the legislative comments indicate, R.C. 2901.21 codified the "fundamental distinction between criminal conduct on the one hand and innocent conduct or accident on the other: that, generally, an offense is not committed unless a person not only does a forbidden act or fails to meet a prescribed duty, but also has a guilty state of mind at the time of his act or failure."

Vicarious liability for another's criminal conduct or failure to prevent another's criminal conduct can be delineated by statute; it cannot be created by the courts. Statutes defining offenses are to be strictly construed against the state and liberally construed in favor of the accused. R.C. 2901.04. The elements of a crime must be gathered wholly from the statute. *State v. Warner* (1990), 55 Ohio St. 3d 31. Where a duty of supervision is specifically enjoined by a statute, a failure to meet such a duty can be the basis for criminal liability. For instance, criminal liability for endangering children can be based on the combination of one's status as a parent, guardian, or person having custody and control of a child with either positive acts such as abuse or allowing the child to act in nudity oriented matter, or by "violating a duty of care, protection, or support." (Emphasis added.) R.C. 2919.22.

Liability based on ownership or operation of a business may also be specifically imposed by statute. For instance, the owner of premises used for gambling—even if he is not present while gambling occurs—can be criminally liable under the statute prohibiting operating a gambling house. Such premises oriented liability is specifically imposed by the statute, which provides in part that "no person being the owner * * * of premises, shall * * * [r]ecklessly permit such premises to be used or occupied for gambling." R.C. 2915.03.

Significantly, the legislature has also made it an offense for one who "has custody, control, or supervision of a commercial establishment * * * [to] display at the establishment any material that is harmful to juveniles and that is open to view by juveniles as part of the invited general public." R.C. 2907.311.

However, appellant was not prosecuted under this statute or under any statute that purports to impose criminal liability for allowing one's premises to be used for the offense of selling proscribed material. Inexplicably, the jury was not instructed on the issue of whether appellant aided and abetted the clerk in the commission of the crime that was charged, i.e., R.C. 2907.31. The jury was instructed that appellant was charged as a principal offender in recklessly disseminating material harmful to juveniles. While an aider and abettor may be charged as a principal, appellant's absence from direct participation required the jury to decide the issue of aiding and abetting before rendering a guilty finding.

As noted above, the state posited, and the trial court apparently accepted, that appellant could be criminally liable because he failed to supervise his employees and take affirmative steps to keep juveniles from entering his store and purchasing videos. However, as we have determined, no statute specifically criminalizes this failure. Although such failure may provide circumstantial evidence of appellant's complicity in the clerk's criminal actions, appellant was not indicted or prosecuted and the jury was not instructed under a complicity theory. It is undisputed that the clerk furnished the video to the minor and that appellant was not present. Because we find that a plain reading of the disseminating matter harmful to juveniles statute requires personal action by a defendant unless the issue of aiding and abetting is submitted, and does not by its terms impose vicarious or premises oriented liability, the jury was not correctly instructed in this case.

Reduced to its essence, the trial court was presented with a question of statutory interpretation, i.e., whether personal criminal liability for recklessly disseminating matter could be imposed based on evidence that appellant recklessly supervised the clerk and the premises where the offense occurred. Because the legislature has not criminalized such conduct or more particularly such inaction, the trial court erred by submitting the case to the jury without any instructions on aiding and abetting as it is only under a complicity theory that the appellant could be lawfully adjudged guilty of the charged offense.

After arguments are completed, a trial court must fully and completely give the jury all instructions that are relevant and necessary for the jury to weigh the evidence and discharge its duty as the fact finder. *State v. Comen* (1990), 50 Ohio St. 3d 206. In light of this analysis, we have concluded that the trial court committed plain error in its instructions to the jury by failing to instruct on aiding and abetting. As given, the court's instructions implied that appellant could be found guilty based on the sale alone regardless of his lack of direct participation in that sale.

We emphasize that our reversal is predicated upon the error of law committed by the trial court. It is not based upon insufficient evidence. Thus, on remand, the state is not precluded by the Double Jeopardy Clause from retrying appellant as a complicitor with the clerk in the commission of the offense. See

State v. Thompkins (1997), 78 Ohio St. 3d 380, (explaining that retrial is barred if a reversal is based upon a finding that the evidence was legally insufficient to support the conviction).

Appellant's remaining arguments for acquittal or a new trial are rendered moot by our decision to reverse on the ground that the trial court's jury instructions constituted plain error. Accordingly, the judgment of the trial court is reversed, and the case is hereby remanded for further proceedings consistent with this opinion.

Judgment reversed and cause remanded.

Notes and Questions

1. What did the court in *State v. Tomaino* mean when it said the state was attempting to "create a common law crime based on appellant's failure to act"? What was the prosecution's theory in this case?

2. The court held that "[l]iability based on ownership or operation of a business may also be specifically imposed by statute." If this statement is accurate, why was the court unwilling to impose liability on Tomaino? Would it have made a difference if Tomaino was present in the store when the clerk sold the video to the juvenile? What additional conduct by Tomaino was necessary for prosecutors to have succeeded in this case?

3. In your opinion, did the clerk violate the statute in question? Why or why not? Is it reckless behavior to mistake a 17-year-old for a 37-year-old? To answer this question, you first may want to read the definition of "recklessness" provided in the chapter on Mens Rea.

4. After reading *United States v. Park*, why do you think the government shifted its argument in *Tomaino*?

5. What would happen if the 17-year old son in *Tomaino* had actually gone in the video store on his own and purchased or rented an adult video? Could the father have been held criminally liable for the actions of his son? Based on *City of Maple Heights v. Ephraim*, 178 Ohio. App. 3d 439 (2008) it is highly unlikely. In *City of Maple Heights*, the appellate court struck down a local ordinance that held "the parent or legal guardian of child under the age of 18 criminally liable, in the absence of intent or action, if that child commits a delinquent act that would be considered a felony or misdemeanor if committed by an adult."

E. Corporate Liability

United States v. Hilton, 467 F. 2d 1000 (9th Cir. 1972)

BROWNING, Circuit Judge:

This is an appeal from a conviction under an indictment charging a violation of section 1 of the Sherman Act, 15 U.S.C. § 1.

Operators of hotels, restaurants, hotel and restaurant supply companies, and other businesses in Portland, Oregon, organized an association to attract conventions to their city. To finance the association, members were asked to make contributions in predetermined amounts. Companies selling supplies to hotels were asked to contribute an amount equal to one per cent of their sales to hotel members. To aid collections, hotel members, including appellant, agreed to give preferential treatment to suppliers who paid their assessments, and to curtail purchases from those who did not.

I

The jury was instructed that such an agreement by the hotel members, if proven, would be a per se violation of the Sherman Act. Appellant argues that this was error.

We need not explore the outer limits of the doctrine that joint refusals to deal constitute per se violations of the Act, for the conduct involved here was of the kind long held to be forbidden without more. "Throughout the history of the Sherman Act, the courts have had little difficulty in finding unreasonable restraints of trade in agreements among competitors, at any level of distribution, designed to coerce those subject to a boycott to accede to the action or inaction desired by the group or to exclude them from competition." Barber, Refusals to Deal under the Federal Anti-trust Laws, 103 U. Pa. L. Rev. 847, 872-873 (1955).***

II

Appellant's president testified that it would be contrary to the policy of the corporation for the manager of one of its hotels to condition purchases upon payment of a contribution to a local association by the supplier. The manager of appellant's Portland hotel and his assistant testified that it was the hotel's policy to purchase supplies solely on the basis of price, quality, and service. They also testified that on two occasions they told the hotel's purchasing agent that he was to take no part in the boycott. The purchasing agent confirmed the receipt of these instructions, but admitted that, despite them, he had threatened a supplier with loss of the hotel's business unless the supplier paid the association assessment. He testified that he violated his instructions because of anger and personal pique toward the individual representing the supplier.

Based upon this testimony, appellant requested certain instructions bearing upon the criminal liability of a corporation for the unauthorized acts of its agents. These requests were rejected by the trial court. The court instructed the jury that a corporation is liable for the acts and statements of its agents "within the scope of their employment," defined to mean "in the corporation's behalf in performance of the agent's general line of work," including "not only that which has been authorized by the corporation, but also that which outsiders could reasonably assume the agent would have authority to do." The court added:

> "A corporation is responsible for acts and statements of its agents, done or made within the scope of their employment, even though their conduct may be contrary to their actual instructions or contrary to the corporation's stated policies."

Appellant objects only to the court's concluding statement.

Congress may constitutionally impose criminal liability upon a business entity for acts or omissions of its agents within the scope of their employment. United States v. A & P Trucking Co., 358 U.S. 121, (1958); New York Central & Hudson R. R. Co. v. United States, 212 U.S. 481, (1909); *cf.* United States v. Illinois Central R. R. Co., 303 U.S. 239, (1938). Such liability may attach without proof that the conduct was within the agent's actual authority, and even though it may have been contrary to express instructions. United States v. American Radiator & Standard Sanitary Corp., 433 F.2d 174, 204-205 (3d Cir. 1970).

The intention to impose such liability is sometimes express, New York Central & Hudson R. R. Co. v. United States, *supra*, 212 U.S. 481, but it may also be implied. The text of the Sherman Act does not expressly resolve the issue. For the reasons that follow, however, we think the construction of the Act that best achieves its purpose is that a corporation is liable for acts of its agents within the scope of their authority even when done against company orders.

It is obvious from the Sherman Act's language and subject matter that the Act is primarily concerned with the activities of business entities. The statute is directed against "restraint upon commercial competition in the marketing of *1005 goods or services." Apex Hosiery Co. v. Leader, 310 U.S. 469, 495, (1940). In 1890, as now, the most significant commercial activity was conducted by corporate enterprises. *See* New York Central & Hudson R. R. Co. v. United States.

Despite the fact that "the doctrine of corporate criminal responsibility for the acts of the officers was not well established in 1890", United States v. Wise, 370 U.S. 405, (1962), the Act expressly applies to corporate entities. 15 U.S.C. § 7. The preoccupation of Congress with corporate liability was only emphasized by the adoption in 1914 of section 14 of the Clayton Act to reaffirm and emphasize that such liability was not exclusive, and that corporate agents also were subject to punishment if they authorized, ordered, or participated in the acts constituting the violation. United States v. Wise, *supra*, 3704.

Criminal liability for the acts of agents is more readily imposed under a statute directed at the prohibited act itself, one that does not make specific intent an element of the offense. *See* Standard Oil Co. v. United States, *supra*, 307 F.2d at 125; *cf.* Empire Printing Co. v. Roden, 247 F.2d 8, 17 (9th Cir. 1957); Note, Corporate Criminal Liability for Acts in Violation of Company Policy, 50 Geo. L.J. 547, 562 (1962); Perkins on Criminal Law 638, 640 (2d ed. 1969). The Sherman Act is aimed at consequences. Specific intent is not an element of any offense under the Act except attempt to monopolize under section 2, and conscious wrongdoing is not an element of that offense. The Sherman Act is violated if "a restraint of trade or monopoly results as the consequence of a defendant's conduct or business arrangements." United States v. Griffith, *supra*, 334 U.S. 100, (1948).

The breadth and critical character of the public interests protected by the Sherman Act, and the gravity of the threat to those interests that led to the enactment of the statute, support a construction holding business organizations accountable, as a general rule, for violations of the Act by their employees in the course of their businesses. In enacting the Sherman Act, "Congress was passing drastic legislation to remedy a threatening danger to the public welfare. . . ." United Mine Workers v. Coronado Coal Co., 259 U.S. 344, (1922). The statute "was designed to be a comprehensive charter of economic liberty aimed at preserving free and unfettered competition as the rule of trade. It rests on the premise that the unrestrained interaction of competitive forces will yield the best allocation of our economic resources, the lowest prices, the highest quality and the greatest material progress, while at the same time providing an environment conducive to the preservation of our democratic political and social institutions." Northern Pacific Ry. v. United States, *supra*, 356 U.S. at 4.

With such important public interests at stake, it is reasonable to assume that Congress intended to impose liability upon business entities for the acts of those to whom they choose to delegate the conduct of their affairs, thus stimulating a maximum effort by owners and managers to assure adherence by such agents to the requirements of the Act. *See* Note, *supra*, 50 Geo. L.J. 547, 558; Note, 60 Harv. L. Rev. 283, 285-286, 289 (1946).

Legal commentators have argued forcefully that it is inappropriate and ineffective to impose criminal liability upon a corporation, as distinguished from the human agents who actually perform the unlawful acts (*see* Francis, Criminal Responsibility of the Corporation, 18 Ill. L. Rev. 305 (1924); Canfield, Corporate Responsibility for Crime, 14 Colum. L. Rev. 469 (1914)), particularly if the acts of the agents are unauthorized. *See* Mueller, Mens Rea and the Corporation, 19 U. Pitt. L. Rev. 21, 45 (1957). But it is the legislative judgment that controls, and "the great mass of legislation calling for corporate criminal liability suggests a widespread belief on the part of legislators that such liability is necessary to effectuate regulatory policy." ALI Model Penal Code, Comment on § 2.07, Tentative Draft No. 4, p. 149 (1956). Moreover, the strenuous efforts of corporate defendants to avoid conviction, particularly under the Sherman Act, strongly suggests that Congress is justified in its judgment that exposure of the corporate entity to potential conviction may provide a substantial spur to corporate action to prevent violations by employees. Note, *supra*, 60 Harv. L. Rev. 283, 286.

Because of the nature of Sherman Act offenses and the context in which they normally occur, the factors that militate against allowing a corporation to disown the criminal acts of its agents apply with special force to Sherman Act violations.

Sherman Act violations are commercial offenses. They are usually motivated by a desire to enhance profits. They commonly involve large, complex, and highly decentralized corporate business enterprises, and intricate business processes, practices, and arrangements. More often than not they also involve basic policy decisions, and must be implemented over an extended period of time.

Complex business structures, characterized by decentralization and delegation of authority, commonly adopted by corporations for business purposes, make it difficult to identify the particular corporate agents responsible for Sherman Act violations. At the same time, it is generally true that high management officials, for whose conduct the corporate directors and stockholders are the most clearly responsible, are likely to have participated in the policy decisions underlying Sherman Act violations, or at least to have become aware of them.

Violations of the Sherman Act are a likely consequence of the pressure to maximize profits that is commonly imposed by corporate owners upon managing agents and, in turn, upon lesser employees. In the face of that pressure, generalized directions to obey the Sherman Act, with the probable effect of foregoing profits, are the least likely to be taken seriously. And if a violation of the Sherman Act occurs, the corporation, and not the individual agents, will have realized the profits from the illegal activity.

In sum, identification of the particular agents responsible for a Sherman Act violation is especially difficult, and their conviction and punishment is peculiarly ineffective as a deterrent. At the same time, conviction and punishment of the business entity itself is likely to be both appropriate and effective.

For these reasons we conclude that as a general rule a corporation is liable under the Sherman Act for the acts of its agents in the scope of their employment, even though contrary to general corporate policy and express instructions to the agent.

Thus the general policy statements of appellant's president were no defense. Nor was it enough that appellant's manager told the purchasing agent that he was not to participate in the boycott. The purchasing agent was authorized to buy all of appellant's supplies. Purchases were made on the basis of specifications, but the purchasing agent exercised complete authority as to source. He was in a unique position to add the corporation's buying power to the force of the boycott. Appellant could not gain exculpation by issuing general instructions without undertaking to enforce those instructions by means commensurate with the obvious risks.

Appellant asserts that the evidence connecting appellant with the conspiracy was not sufficient.

The argument rests largely upon three erroneous premises of law.

The first is that because of the acquittal of appellant's manager, evidence connecting him with the conspiracy cannot be considered against appellant. Acts and statements of appellant's employees within the scope of their employment bind appellant. *See* Part II. It makes no difference whether such acts and statements are sufficient to convict the employee of participation in the conspiracy. A fortiori, it is irrelevant that the employee was charged with the offense and acquitted. United States v. American Stevedore, Inc., 310 F.2d 47, 48-49 (2d Cir. 1962). Secondly, appellant erroneously asserts that the acts and statements of appellant's purchasing agent did not bind appellant because they were contrary to express instructions. *See* Part II.

Finally, appellant asks us to test the sufficiency of the evidence by inquiring whether "reasonable minds could find that the evidence excludes every reasonable hypothesis but that of guilt." Remmer v. United States, 205 F.2d 277, 288 (9th Cir. 1953). We specifically rejected this standard in United States v. Nelson, 419 F.2d 1237, 1243-1245 (9th Cir. 1969). The question is whether the fact-finder could reasonably conclude that defendant's guilt was free of the kind of doubt that would make a person hesitate to act in the more serious and important affairs of his life.

We have examined the government's evidence in light of this standard and conclude that it is sufficient.

Affirmed.

State v. CECOS International, 38 Ohio St. 3d. 120 (1988)

WRIGHT, Justice.

The modern corporation is nearly omnipresent in American society. Yet, legal sanctions on corporate criminal activity are difficult to enforce because a corporation is but an intangible, ethereal being created by the state. Its actions affect employees, assets, the economy, and finally, society; yet, it remains, in Lord Thurlow's words, a being that "has no soul to be damned, and no body to be kicked."[1] Deterring and punishing corporate criminal conduct thus has become a difficult and sometimes elusive quest.

One of the most controversial aspects of enterprise criminal liability concerns the problem of identifying who represents the corporation for purposes of indictment and prosecution. We address this question today in the setting of a discovery dispute between the state and the criminal defendant, CECOS International, Inc.

We begin by noting that the trial court's decision to disclose grand jury testimony may not be disturbed unless we find an abuse of discretion. *State v. Greer* (1981), 66 Ohio St. 2d 139, paragraph one of the syllabus. With this in mind, we now analyze the arguments posed by the state and defendant, as well as the applicable statutes and case precedent.

I

Crim. R. 16(B)(1)(a) permits disclosure of statements made by a "defendant" during grand jury proceedings. A corporation operates through its employees, officers, and directors. Logic dictates that the employees whose criminal conduct may be imputed to the corporation constitute the corporate defendant. The gravamen of this appeal, therefore, rests in the question of whose criminal conduct may be imputed to the corporation.

The criminal liability of an enterprise has evolved through three phases. The early common-law view was that a corporate body could not be criminally liable because it was incapable of forming the requisite criminal intent to commit a crime and could not be imprisoned. Under the revised common-law view, criminal conduct of any employee acting on behalf of the corporation and within the scope of employment was generally imputed to the business entity upon the theory of vicarious liability. The modern trend limits the revised common law by imputing criminal liability to high managerial personnel only.

CECOS suggests Ohio follows the revised common-law view while the prosecution suggests Ohio subscribes to the modern trend. This issue is addressed, in part, by the Revised Code. R.C. 2901.03(A) states, in pertinent part, that "[n]o conduct constitutes a criminal offense against the state unless it is defined as an offense in the Revised Code." Thus, in Ohio, criminal liability is rigidly and precisely limited to those situations that the General Assembly has specifically delineated by statute.

In R.C. 2901.23, the General Assembly carefully identified which employees may create criminal liability for a business entity. R.C. 2901.23 provides in pertinent part:

> "(A) An organization may be convicted of an offense under any of the following circumstances:
> " ***
> "(4) If, acting with the kind of culpability otherwise required for the commission of the offense, its commission was authorized, requested, commanded, tolerated, or performed by the board of directors, trustees, partners, or by a high managerial

officer, agent, or employee acting on behalf of the organization
and within the scope of his office or employment. *** "

Appellee suggests *any* employee's criminal conduct may be imputed to the
corporation. CECOS correctly notes there is no Ohio case law on point that
construes the statute. In support of its position, appellee cites cases from several
federal courts that have determined a "corporation may be criminally bound by
the acts of subordinate, even menial, employees." *Standard Oil Co. of Texas v.
United States* (C.A.5, 1962), 307 F.2d 120. *United States v. Illinois Central Railroad*
(1938), 303 U.S. 239 (corporation subject to penalty liable for acts of manual
laborers); *United States v. George F. Fish, Inc.* (C.A.2, 1946), 154 F.2d 798
(corporation may be criminally liable for acts of salesman); *Riss & Co. v. United
States* (C.A.8, 1958), 262 F.2d 245 (criminal conduct of clerical workers imputed
to corporation).

Appellee relies primarily on *United States v. Hughes* (C.A.5, 1969), 413 F.2d
1244. *Hughes* applies the reasoning of *Standard Oil* to a dispute under former
Fed. R. Crim. P. 16(a)(3). The court observed at 1252:

"The significance of a witness' testimony to the inquiry into potential
corporate criminal liability, and to the defense in preparing its case, does not
depend upon organizational charts. *** If the door to Rule 16(a)(3) is to be open
to corporations at all-and we are of the opinion that it must-its availability should
not be based upon corporate titles."

Hughes dealt with Fed. R. Crim. P. 16(a)(3) prior to its amendment. The
amended rule, Fed. R. Crim. P. 16(a)(1)(A), effectively overruled *Hughes* by
requiring that the employee have authority to "legally *** bind the defendant."
Nevertheless, the assertion that organizational charts and titles should not
determine potential criminal liability remains viable in many jurisdictions. It is not
the only viable argument on this subject, however.

The state submits the corporate defendant, for purposes of criminal liability,
is composed of those employees with the assigned authority and function to act
on behalf of the corporation with regard to the matter that gave rise to the
criminal offense. In support of its argument, the state relies on a strict
construction of R.C. 2901.23.

Inherent in the state's argument is that R.C. 2901.23(A)(4) requires
authorization by "a *high managerial* officer, agent, or employee ***," while
subsection (A)(1), which refers to misdemeanors, permits authorization by "*an*
officer, agent, or employee." (Emphasis added.) Conspicuously absent in the
description of the (A)(1) class are the adjectives "high managerial."

The state submits the language in subsection (A)(4), therefore, should be
construed to mean "high managerial officers, high managerial agents, or high
managerial employees." Although the state concedes there is no Ohio precedent

to support such a view, it suggests that any other construction would read the phrase "high managerial" out of the statute.

Accordingly, the state contends the high managerial personnel directly responsible for the proper disposal of waste at the site are the only employees whose criminal conduct may be imputed to the corporation. Those individuals constitute the "corporate defendant," and, consequently, only their grand jury testimony may be discovered and inspected by CECOS, pursuant to Crim. R. 16.

Both arguments may be maintained from a public policy standpoint. Nevertheless, a reasonable and appropriate construction of R.C. 2901.23 indicates a business entity may be found guilty of a criminal offense only if the criminal act or omission was approved, recommended, or implemented by high managerial personnel with actual or implied authority to approve, recommend or implement same. High managerial personnel are those who make basic corporate policies.

Consequently, we hold a corporate employee's grand jury testimony is discoverable under Crim. R. 16(B)(1)(a) when the statement concerns an alleged criminal act or omission performed on behalf of the corporation and within the scope of employment. The declarant must hold sufficient authority to impute criminal culpability to the corporation.

As noted above, we cannot disturb the trial court's ruling releasing the grand jury testimony unless we find an abuse of discretion. In *Warner v. Waste Management, Inc.* (1988), 36 Ohio St. 3d 91, we noted a mere analytical error does not constitute an abuse of discretion, but "where the trial court completely misconstrues the letter and spirit of the law, it is clear that the court has been unreasonable and has abused its discretion." *Id.* at 99, 521 N.E.2d at 1099, fn. 10. In the case before us, the trial court's analysis went beyond mere analytical error. Indeed, we believe the court misconstrued the letter and spirit of the law. Hence, we reverse the trial court's ruling on this issue.***

Accordingly, the judgment of the court of appeals is reversed and the cause is remanded to the trial court for further proceedings consistent with this opinion.

Judgment reversed and cause remanded.

MOYER, C.J., and SWEENEY, LOCHER, HOLMES, DOUGLAS and HERBERT R. BROWN, JJ., concur.

Notes and Questions

(1) Why did the 9th Circuit uphold the conviction of Hilton Hotels? It appears that the court wanted to hold someone or something liable and that it is often difficult in large organizations to determine who is responsible for the wrongful conduct. Plus, the court noted that it is the company that ultimately benefits from the wrongful conduct of its employees. Do you agree with the court's rationale?

F. Status Crimes

Robinson v. California, 370 U.S. 660 (1962)

Mr. Justice STEWART delivered the opinion of the Court.

A California statute makes it a criminal offense for a person to "be addicted to the use of narcotics." This appeal draws into question the constitutionality of that provision of the state law, as construed by the California courts in the present case.

The appellant was convicted after a jury trial in the Municipal Court of Los Angeles. The evidence against him was given by two Los Angeles police officers. Officer Brown testified that he had had occasion to examine the appellant's arms one evening on a street in Los Angeles some four months before the trial. The officer testified that at that time he had observed "scar tissue and discoloration on the inside" of the appellant's right arm, and "what appeared to be numerous needle marks and a scab which was approximately three inches below the crook of the elbow" on the appellant's left arm. The officer also testified that the appellant under questioning had admitted to the occasional use of narcotics.

Officer Lindquist testified that he had examined the appellant the follow morning in the Central Jail in Los Angeles. The officer stated that at that time he had observed discolorations and scabs on the appellant's arms, and he identified photographs which had been taken of the appellant's arms shortly after his arrest the night before. Based upon more than ten years of experience as a member of the Narcotic Division of the Los Angeles Police Department, the witness gave his opinion that "these marks and the discoloration were the result of the injection of hypodermic needles into the tissue into the vein that was not sterile." He stated that the scabs were several days old at the time of his examination, and that the appellant was neither under the influence of narcotics nor suffering withdrawal symptoms at the time he saw him. This witness also testified that the appellant had admitted using narcotics in the past.

The appellant testified in his own behalf, denying the alleged conversations with the police officers and denying that he had ever used narcotics or been addicted to their use. He explained the marks on his arms as resulting from an allergic condition contracted during his military service. His testimony was corroborated by two witnesses.

The trial judge instructed the jury that the statute made it a misdemeanor for a person "either to use narcotics, or to be addicted to the use of narcotics *** That portion of the statute referring to the 'use' of narcotics is based upon the 'act' of using. That portion of the statute referring to 'addicted to the use' of narcotics is based upon a condition or status. They are not identical. *** To be addicted to the use of narcotics is said to be a status or condition and not an act.

It is a continuing offense and differs from most other offenses in the fact that (it) is chronic rather than acute; that it continues after it is complete and subjects the offender to arrest at any time before he reforms. The existence of such a chronic condition may be ascertained from a single examination, if the characteristic reactions of that condition be found present."

The judge further instructed the jury that the appellant could be convicted under a general verdict if the jury agreed either that he was of the "status" or had committed the "act" denounced by the statute. "All that the People must show is either that the defendant did use a narcotic in Los Angeles County, or that while in the City of Los Angeles he was addicted to the use of narcotics ***."

Under these instructions the jury returned a verdict finding the appellant "guilty of the offense charged."***

It would be possible to construe the statute under which the appellant was convicted as one which is operative only upon proof of the actual use of narcotics within the State's jurisdiction. But the California courts have not so construed this law. Although there was evidence in the present case that the appellant had used narcotics in Los Angeles, the jury were instructed that they could convict him even if they disbelieved that evidence. The appellant could be convicted, they were told, if they found simply that the appellant's "status" or "chronic condition" was that of being "addicted to the use of narcotics." And it is impossible to know from the jury's verdict that the defendant was not convicted upon precisely such a finding. ***

Indeed, in their brief in this Court counsel for the State have emphasized that it is "the proof of addiction by circumstantial evidence *** by the tell-tale track of needle marks and scabs over the veins of his arms, that remains the gist of the section."

This statute, therefore, is not one which punishes a person for the use of narcotics, for their purchase, sale or possession, or for antisocial or disorderly behavior resulting from their administration. It is not a law which even purports to provide or require medical treatment. Rather, we deal with a statute which makes the "status" of narcotic addiction a criminal offense, for which the offender may be prosecuted "at any time before he reforms." California has said that a person can be continuously guilty of this offense, whether or not he has ever used or possessed any narcotics within the State, and whether or not he has been guilty of any antisocial behavior there.

It is unlikely that any State at this moment in history would attempt to make it a criminal offense for a person to be mentally ill, or a leper, or to be afflicted with a venereal disease. A State might determine that the general health and welfare require that the victims of these and other human afflictions be dealt with by compulsory treatment, involving quarantine, confinement, or sequestration. But, in the light of contemporary human knowledge, a law which made a criminal offense of such a disease would doubtless be universally thought to be an infliction of cruel and unusual punishment in violation of the Eighth and Fourteenth Amendments. See State of Louisiana ex rel. Francis v. Resweber, 329 U.S. 459.

We cannot but consider the statute before us as of the same category. In this Court counsel for the State recognized that narcotic addiction is an illness. Indeed, it is apparently an illness which may be contracted innocently or involuntarily. We hold that a state law which imprisons a person thus afflicted as a criminal, even though he has never touched any narcotic drug within the State or been guilty of any irregular behavior there, inflicts a cruel and unusual punishment in violation of the Fourteenth Amendment. To be sure, imprisonment for ninety days is not, in the abstract, a punishment which is either cruel or unusual. But the question cannot be considered in the abstract. Even one day in prison would be a cruel and unusual punishment for the "crime" of having a common cold.

We are not unmindful that the vicious evils of the narcotics traffic have occasioned the grave concern of government. There are, as we have said, countless fronts on *668 which those evils may be legitimately attacked. We deal in this case only with an individual provision of a particularized local law as it has so far been interpreted by the California courts.

Reversed.

Mr. Justice FRANKFURTER took no part in the consideration or decision of this case.

Mr. Justice DOUGLAS, concurring.

While I join the Court's opinion, I wish to make more explicit the reasons why I think it is "cruel and unusual" punishment in the sense of the Eighth Amendment to treat as a criminal a person who is a drug addict.

Sixteenth Century England one prescription for insanity was to beat the subject "until he had regained his reason." Deutsch, The Mentally Ill in America (1937), p. 13. In America "the violently insane went to the whipping post and into prison dungeons or, as sometimes happened, were burned at the stake or hanged"; and "the pauper insane often roamed the countryside as wild men and from time to time were pilloried, whipped, and jailed." Action for Mental Health (1961), p. 26.

As stated by Dr. Isaac Ray many years ago:

> "Nothing can more strongly illustrate the popular ignorance respecting insanity than the proposition, equally objectionable in its humanity and its logic, that the insane should be punished for criminal acts, in order to deter other insane persons from doing

the same thing." Treatise on the Medical Jurisprudence of Insanity (5th ed. 1871), p. 56.

Today we have our differences over the legal definition of insanity. But however insanity is defined, it is in end effect treated as a disease. While afflicted people may be confined either for treatment or for the protection of society, they are not branded as criminals.

Yet terror and punishment linger on as means of dealing with some diseases. As recently stated:

> "*** the idea of basing treatment for disease on purgatorial acts and ordeals is an ancient one in medicine. It may trace back to the Old Testament belief that disease of any kind, whether mental or physical, represented punishment for sin; and thus relief could take the form of a final heroic act of atonement. This superstition appears to have given support to fallacious medical rationales for such procedures as purging, bleeding, induced vomiting, and blistering, as well as an entire chamber of horrors constituting the early treatment of mental illness. The latter included a wide assortment of shock techniques, such as the 'water cures' (dousing, ducking, and near-drowning), spinning in a chair, centrifugal swinging, and an early form of electric shock. All, it would appear, were planned as means of driving from the body some evil spirit or toxic vapor." Action for Mental Health (1961), pp. 27-28.

That approach continues as respects drug addicts. Drug addiction is more prevalent in this country than in any other nation of the western world. S. Rep. No. 1440, 84th Cong., 2d Sess., p. 2. It is sometimes referred to as "a contagious disease." Id., at p. 3. But those living in a world of black and white put the addict in the category of those who could, if they would, forsake their evil ways.

The first step toward addiction may be as innocent as a boy's puff on a cigarette in an alleyway. It may come from medical prescriptions. Addiction may even be present at birth. Earl Ubell recently wrote:

> "In Bellevue Hospital's nurseries, Dr. Saul Krugman, head of pediatrics, has been discovering babies minutes old who are heroin addicts.
>
> "More than 100 such infants have turned up in the last two years, and they show all the signs of drug withdrawal: irritability, jitters, loss of appetite, vomiting, diarrhea, sometimes convulsions and death.

" 'Of course, they get the drug while in the womb from their mothers who are addicts,' Dr. Krugman said yesterday when the situation came to light. 'We control the symptoms with Thorazine, a tranquilizing drug.

" 'You should see some of these children. They have a high-pitched cry. They appear hungry but they won't eat when offered food. They move around so much in the crib that their noses and toes become red and excoriated.'

"Dr. Lewis Thomas, professor of medicine at New York University-Bellevue, brought up the problem of the babies Monday night at a symposium on narcotics addiction sponsored by the New York County Medical Society. He saw in the way the babies respond to treatment a clue to the low rate of cure of addiction.

" 'Unlike the adult addict who gets over his symptoms of withdrawal in a matter of days, in most cases,' Dr. Thomas explained later, 'the infant has to be treated for weeks and months. The baby continues to show physical signs of the action of the drugs.

" 'Perhaps in adults the drugs continue to have physical effects for a much longer time after withdrawal than we have been accustomed to recognize. That would mean that these people have a physical need for the drug for a long period, and this may be the clue to recidivism much more than the social or psychological pressures we've been talking about.' " N.Y. Herald Tribune, Apr. 25, 1962, p. 25, cols. 3-4.

The addict is under compulsions not capable of management without outside help. As stated by the Council on Mental Health:

"Physical dependence is defined as the development of an altered physiological state which is brought about by the repeated administration of the drug and which necessitates continued administration of the drug to prevent the appearance of the characteristic illness which is termed an abstinence syndrome. When an addict says that he has a habit, he means that he is physically dependent on a drug. When he says that one drug is habit-forming and another is not, he means that the first drug is one on which physical dependence can be developed and that the second is a drug on which physical dependence cannot be developed. Physical dependence is a real physiological disturbance. It is associated with the development of hyperexcitability in reflexes mediated through multineurone arcs. It can be induced in animals, it has been shown to occur in the paralyzed hind limbs of addicted chronic spinal dogs, and also has been produced in dogs whose cerebral cortex has been removed." ***

The extreme symptoms of addiction have been described as follows:

"To be a confirmed drug addict is to be one of the walking dead. *** The teeth have rotted out; the appetite is lost and the stomach and intestines don't function properly. The gall bladder becomes inflamed; eyes and skin turn a billious yellow. In some cases membranes of the nose turn a flaming red; the partition separating the nostrils is eaten away—breathing is difficult. Oxygen in the blood decreases; bronchitis and tuberculosis develop. Good traits of character disappear and bad ones emerge. Sex organs become affected. Veins collapse and livid purplish scars remain. Boils and abscesses plague the skin; gnawing pain racks the body. Nerves snap; vicious twitching develops. Imaginary and fantastic fears blight the mind and sometimes complete insanity results. Often times, too, death comes—much too early in life. *** Such is the torment of being a drug addict; such is the plague of being one of the walking dead." N.Y. L.J., June 8, 1960, p. 4, col. 2.

Some States punish addiction, though most do not. See S.Doc. No. 120, 84th Cong., 2d Sess., pp. 41, 42. Nor does the Uniform Narcotic Drug Act, first approved in 1932 and now in effect in most of the States. Great Britain, beginning in 1920 placed "addiction and the treatment of addicts squarely and exclusively into the hands of the medical profession." Lindesmith, The British System of Narcotics Control, 22 Law & Contemp. Prob. 138 (1957). In England the doctor "has almost complete professional autonomy in reaching decisions about the treatment of addicts." Schur, British Narcotics Policies, 51 J. Crim. L. & Criminology 619, 621 (1961). Under British law "addicts are patients, not criminals." Ibid. Addicts have not disappeared in England but they have decreased in number (id., at 622) and there is now little "addict-crime" there. Id., at 623.

The fact that England treats the addict as a sick person, while a few of our States, including California, treat him as a criminal, does not, of course, establish the unconstitutionality of California's penal law. But we do know that there is "a hard core" of "chronic and incurable drug addicts who, in reality, have lost their power of self-control." S. Rep. No. 2033, 84th Cong., 2d Sess., p. 8. There has been a controversy over the type of treatment—whether enforced hospitalization or ambulatory care is better. H.R. Rep. No. 2388, 84th Cong., 2d Sess., pp. 66-68. But there is little disagreement with the statement of Charles Winick: "The hold of drugs on persons addicted to them is so great that it would be almost appropriate to reverse the old adage and say that opium derivatives represent the religion of the people who use them." Narcotics Addiction and its Treatment, 22 Law & Contemp. Prob. 9 (1957). The abstinence symptoms and their treatment are well known. Id., at 10-11. Cure is difficult because of the complex of forces that make for addiction. Id., at 18—23. "After the withdrawal period, vocational activities, recreation, and some kind of psycho-therapy have a major role in the treatment program, which ideally lasts from four to six months." Id., at 23-24. Dr. Marie Nyswander tells us that normally a drug addict must be hospitalized in order to be cured. The Drug Addict as a Patient (1956), p. 138.

The impact that an addict has on a community causes alarm and often leads to punitive measures. Those measures are justified when they relate to acts of transgression. But I do not see how under our system being an addict can be punished as a crime. If addicts can be punished for their addiction, then the insane can also be punished for their insanity. Each has a disease and each must be treated as a sick person. As Charles Winick has said:

> "There can be no single program for the elimination of an illness as complex as drug addiction, which carries so much emotional freight in the community. Cooperative interdisciplinary research and action, more local community participation, training the various healing professions in the techniques of dealing with addicts, regional treatment facilities, demonstration centers, and a thorough and vigorous post-treatment rehabilitation program would certainly appear to be among the minimum requirements for any attempt to come to terms with this problem. The addict should be viewed as a sick person, with a chronic disease which requires almost emergency action." 22 Law & Contemp. Prob. 9, 33 (1957).

The Council on Mental Health reports that criminal sentences for addicts interferes "with the possible treatment and rehabilitation of addicts and therefore should be abolished." 165 A.M.A.J. 1968, 1972.

The command of the Eighth Amendment, banning "cruel and unusual punishments," stems from the Bill of Rights of 1688. See State of Louisiana ex rel. Francis v. Resweber, 329 U.S. 459. And it is applicable to the States by reason of the Due Process Clause of the Fourteenth Amendment. Ibid.

The historic punishments that were cruel and unusual included "burning at the stake, crucifixion, breaking on the wheel" (In re Kemmler, 136 U.S. 436), quartering, the rack and thumbscrew (see Chambers v. Florida, 309 U.S. 227), and in some circumstances even solitary confinement (see In re Medley, 134 U.S. 160).

The question presented in the earlier cases concerned the degree of severity with which a particular offense was punished or the element of cruelty present. A punishment out of all proportion to the offense may bring it within the ban against "cruel and unusual punishment." See O'Neil v. Vermont, 144 U.S. 323. So may the cruelty of the method of punishment, as, for example, disemboweling a person alive. See Wilkerson v. Utah, 99 U.S. 130. But the principle that would deny power to exact capital punishment for a petty crime would also deny power to punish a person by fine or imprisonment for being sick.

The Eighth Amendment expresses the revulsion of civilized man against barbarous acts—the "cry of horror" against man's inhumanity to his fellow man.

By the time of Coke, enlightenment was coming as respects the insane. Coke said that the execution of a madman "should be a miserable spectacle, both against law, and of extreame inhumanity and cruelty, and can be no example to others." 6 Coke's Third Inst. (4th ed. 1797), p. 6. Blackstone endorsed this view of Coke. 4 Commentaries (Lewis ed. 1897), p. 25.

We should show the same discernment respecting drug addiction. The addict is a sick person. He may, of course, be confined for treatment or for the protection of society. Cruel and unusual punishment results not from confinement, but from convicting the addict of a crime. The purpose of s 11721 is not to cure, but to penalize. Were the purpose to cure, there would be no need for a mandatory jail term of not less than 90 days. Contrary to my Brother CLARK, I think the means must stand constitutional scrutiny, as well as the end to be achieved. A prosecution for addiction, with its resulting stigma and irreparable damage to the good name of the accused, cannot be justified as a means of protecting society, where a civil commitment would do as well. Indeed, in s 5350 of the Welfare and Institutions Code, California has expressly provided for civil proceedings for the commitment of habitual addicts. Section 11721 is, in reality, a direct attempt to punish those the State cannot commit civilly. This prosecution has no relationship to the curing *678 of an illness. Indeed, it cannot, for the prosecution is aimed at penalizing an illness, rather than at providing medical care for it.

We would forget the teachings of the Eighth Amendment if we allowed sickness to be made a crime and permitted sick people to be punished for being sick. This age of enlightenment cannot tolerate such barbarous action.

Mr. Justice HARLAN, concurring.

I am not prepared to hold that on the present state of medical knowledge it is completely irrational and hence unconstitutional for a State to conclude that narcotics addiction is something other than an illness nor that it amounts to cruel and unusual punishment for the State to subject narcotics addicts to its criminal law. Insofar as addiction may be identified with the use or possession of narcotics within the State (or, I would suppose, without the State), in violation of local statutes prohibiting such acts, it may surely be reached by the State's criminal law. But in this case the trial court's instructions permitted the jury to find the appellant guilty on no more proof than that he was present in California while he was addicted to narcotics.[*] Since addiction alone cannot reasonably be thought to amount to more than a compelling propensity to use narcotics, the effect of this instruction was to authorize criminal punishment for a bare desire to commit a criminal act.

If the California statute reaches this type of conduct, and for present purposes we must accept the trial court's construction as binding, Terminiello v. Chicago, 337 U.S. 1, it is an arbitrary imposition which exceeds the power that a State may exercise in enacting its criminal law. Accordingly, I agree that the application of the California statute was unconstitutional in this case and join the judgment of reversal.

Mr. Justice CLARK, dissenting.

The Court finds s 11721 of California's Health and Safety Code, making it an offense to "be addicted to the use of narcotics," violative of due process as "a cruel and unusual punishment." I cannot agree.

The statute must first be placed in perspective. California has a comprehensive and enlightened program for the control of narcotism based on the overriding policy of prevention and cure. It is the product of an extensive investigation made in the mid-Fifties by a committee of distinguished scientists, doctors, law enforcement officers and laymen appointed by the then Attorney General, now Governor, of California. The committee filed a detailed study entitled "Report on Narcotic Addiction" which was given considerable attention. No recommendation was made therein for the repeal of s 11721, and the State Legislature in its discretion continued the policy of that section.

Apart from prohibiting specific acts such as the purchase, possession and sale of narcotics, California has taken certain legislative steps in regard to the status of being a narcotic addict—a condition commonly recognized as a threat to the State and to the individual. The Code deals with this problem in realistic stages. At its incipiency narcotic addiction is handled under s 11721 of the Health and Safety Code which is at issue here. It provides that a person found to be addicted to the use of narcotics shall serve a term in the county jail of not less than 90 days nor more than one year, with the minimum 90-day confinement applying in all cases without exception. Provision is made for parole with periodic tests to detect readdiction.

The trial court defined "addicted to narcotics" as used in s 11721 in the following charge to the jury:

> "The word 'addicted' means, strongly disposed to some taste or practice or habituated, especially to drugs. In order to inquire as to whether a person is addicted to the use of narcotics is in effect an inquiry as to his habit in that regard. Does he use them habitually. To use them often or daily is, according to the ordinary acceptance of those words, to use them habitually."

There was no suggestion that the term "narcotic addict" as here used included a person who acted without volition or who had lost the power of self-control. Although the section is penal in appearance—perhaps a carry-over from a less sophisticated approach—its present provisions are quite similar to those for civil commitment and treatment of addicts who have lost the power of self-control, and its present purpose is reflected in a statement which closely follows s 11721: "The rehabilitation of narcotic addicts and the prevention of continued addiction to narcotics is a matter of statewide concern." California Health and Safety Code, s 11728.

Where narcotic addiction has progressed beyond the incipient, volitional stage, California provides for commitment of three months to two years in a state hospital. California Welfare and Institutions Code, s 5355. For the purposes of this provision, a narcotic addict is defined as "any person who habitually takes or otherwise uses to the extent of having lost the power of self-control any opium, morphine, cocaine, or other narcotic drug as defined in Article 1 of Chapter 1 of Division 10 of the Health and Safety Code." California Welfare and Institutions Code, s 5350. (Emphasis supplied.)

This proceeding is clearly civil in nature with a purpose of rehabilitation and cure. Significantly, if it is found that a person committed under s 5355 will not receive substantial benefit from further hospital treatment and is not dangerous to society, he may be discharged—but only after a minimum confinement of three months. s 5355.1.

Thus, the "criminal" provision applies to the incipient narcotic addict who retains self-control, requiring confinement of three months to one year and parole with frequent tests to detect renewed use of drugs. Its overriding purpose is to cure the less seriously addicted person by preventing further use. On the other hand, the "civil" commitment provision deals with addicts who have lost the power of self-control, requiring hospitalization up to two years. Each deals with a different type of addict but with a common purpose. This is most apparent when the sections overlap: if after civil commitment of an addict it is found that hospital treatment will not be helpful, the addict is confined for a minimum period of three months in the same manner as is the volitional addict under the "criminal" provision.

In the instant case the proceedings against the petitioner were brought under the volitional-addict section. There was testimony that he had been using drugs only four months with three to four relatively mild doses a week. At arrest and trial he appeared normal. His testimony was clear and concise, being simply that he had never used drugs. The scabs and pocks on his arms and body were caused, he said, by "overseas shots" administered during army service preparatory to foreign assignment. He was very articulate in his testimony but the jury did not believe him, apparently because he had told the clinical expert while being examined after arrest that he had been using drugs, as I have stated above. The officer who arrested him also testified to like statements and to scabs—some 10 or 15 days old—showing narcotic injections. There was no evidence in the record of withdrawal symptoms. Obviously he could not have been committed under s 5355 as one who had completely "lost the power of self-control." The jury was instructed that narcotic "addiction" as used in s 11721 meant strongly disposed to a taste or practice or habit of its use, indicated by the use of narcotics often or daily. A general verdict was returned against petitioner, and he was ordered confined for 90 days to be followed by a two-year parole during which he was required to take periodic Nalline tests.

The majority strikes down the conviction primarily on the grounds that petitioner was denied due process by the imposition of criminal penalties for nothing more than being in a status. This view point is premised upon the theme that s 11721 is a "criminal" provision authorizing a punishment, for the majority admits that "a State might establish a program of compulsory treatment for those addicted to narcotics" which "might require periods of involuntary confinement." I submit that California has done exactly that. The majority's error is in instructing the California Legislature that hospitalization is the only treatment for narcotics addiction—that anything less is a punishment denying due process. California has found otherwise after a study which I suggest was more extensive than that conducted by the Court. Even in California's program for hospital commitment of nonvolitional narcotic addicts—which the majority approves—it is recognized that some addicts will not respond to or do not need hospital treatment. As to these persons its provisions are identical to those of s 11721—confinement for a period of not less than 90 days. Section 11721 provides this confinement as treatment for the volitional addicts to whom its provisions apply, in addition to parole with frequent tests to detect and prevent further use of drugs. The fact that s 11721 might be labeled "criminal" seems irrelevant, not only to the majority's own "treatment" test but to the "concept of ordered liberty" to which the States must attain under the Fourteenth Amendment. The test is the overall purpose and effect of a State's act, and I submit that California's program relative to narcotic addicts—including both the "criminal" and "civil" provisions—is inherently one of treatment and lies well within the power of a State.

However, the case in support of the judgment below need not rest solely on this reading of California law. For even if the overall statutory scheme is ignored and a purpose and effect of punishment is attached to s 11721, that provision still does not violate the Fourteenth Amendment. The majority acknowledges, as it must, that a State can punish persons who purchase, possess or use narcotics. Although none of these acts are harmful to society in themselves, the State constitutionally may attempt to deter and prevent them through punishment because of the grave threat of future harmful conduct which they pose. Narcotics addiction—including the incipient, volitional addiction to which this provision speaks—is no different. California courts have taken judicial notice that "the inordinate use of a narcotic drug tends to create an irresistible craving and forms a habit for its continued use until one becomes an addict, and he respects no convention or obligation and will lie, steal, or use any other base means to gratify his passion for the drug, being lost to all considerations of duty or social position." People v. Jaurequi, 142 Cal. App. 2d 555, (1956). Can this Court deny the legislative and judicial judgment of California that incipient, volitional narcotic addiction poses a threat of serious crime similar to the threat inherent in the purchase or possession of narcotics? And if such a threat is inherent in addiction, can this Court say that California is powerless to deter it by punishment?

It is no answer to suggest that we are dealing with an involuntary status and thus penal sanctions will be ineffective and unfair. The section at issue applies only to persons who use narcotics often or even daily but not to the point of losing self-control. When dealing with involuntary addicts California moves only through s 5355 of its Welfare Institutions Code which clearly is not penal. Even if it could be argued that s 11721 may not be limited to volitional addicts, the petitioner in the instant case undeniably retained the power of self-control and thus to him the statute would be constitutional. Moreover, "status" offenses have long been known and recognized in the criminal law. 4 Blackstone, Commentaries (Jones ed. 1916), 170. A ready example is drunkenness, which plainly is as involuntary after addiction to alcohol as is the taking of drugs.

Nor is the conjecture relevant that petitioner may have acquired his habit under lawful circumstances. There was no suggestion by him to this effect at trial, and surely the State need not rebut all possible lawful sources of addiction as part of its prima facie case.

The argument that the statute constitutes a cruel and unusual punishment is governed by the discussion above. Properly construed, the statute provides a treatment rather than a punishment. But even if interpreted as penal, the sanction of incarceration for 3 to 12 months is not unreasonable when applied to a person who has voluntarily placed himself in a condition posing a serious threat to the State. Under either theory, its provisions for 3 to 12 months' confinement can hardly be deemed unreasonable when compared to the provisions for 3 to 24 months' confinement under s 5355 which the majority approves.

I would affirm the judgment.

Powell v. Texas, 392 U.S. 514 (1968)

THE CHIEF JUSTICE, Mr. Justice BLACK, and Mr. Justice HARLAN join.

In late December, 1966, appellant was arrested and charged with being found in a state of intoxication in a public place, in violation of Texas Penal Code, Art. 477 (1952), which reads as follows:

> Whoever shall get drunk or be found in a state of intoxication in any public place, or at any private house except his own, shall be fined not exceeding one hundred dollars.

Appellant was tried in the Corporation Court of Austin, Texas, found guilty, and fined $20. He appealed to the County Court at Law No. 1 of Travis County, Texas, where a trial *de novo* was held. His counsel urged that appellant was "afflicted with the disease of chronic alcoholism," that "his appearance in public [while drunk was] . . . not of his own volition," and, therefore, that to punish him criminally for that conduct would be cruel and unusual, in violation of the Eighth and Fourteenth Amendments to the United States Constitution.

I

The principal testimony was that of Dr. David Wade, a Fellow of the American Medical Association, duly certificated in psychiatry.***

Dr. Wade sketched the outlines of the "disease" concept of alcoholism; noted that there is no generally accepted definition of "alcoholism;" alluded to the ongoing debate within the medical profession over whether alcohol is actually physically "addicting" or merely psychologically "habituating," and concluded that, in either case a "chronic alcoholic" is an "involuntary drinker," who is "powerless not to drink," and who "loses his self control over his drinking." He testified that he had examined appellant, and that appellant is a "chronic alcoholic," who "by the time he has reached [the state of intoxication] . . . , is not able to control his behavior, and [who] . . . has reached this point because he has an uncontrollable compulsion to drink."

Dr. Wade also responded in the negative to the question whether appellant has "the willpower to resist the constant excessive consumption of alcohol." He added that, in his opinion, jailing appellant without medical attention would operate neither to rehabilitate him nor to lessen his desire for alcohol.

On cross-examination, Dr. Wade admitted that, when appellant was sober, he knew the difference between right and wrong, and he responded affirmatively to the question whether appellant's act of taking the first drink in any given instance when he was sober was a "voluntary exercise of his will." Qualifying his answer, Dr. Wade stated that "these individuals have a compulsion, and this compulsion, while not completely overpowering, is a very strong influence, an exceedingly strong influence, and this compulsion, coupled with the firm belief in their mind that they are going to be able to handle it from now on, causes their judgment to be somewhat clouded."

Appellant testified concerning the history of his drinking problem. He reviewed his many arrests for drunkenness; testified that he was unable to stop drinking; stated that, when he was intoxicated, he had no control over his actions and could not remember them later, but that he did not become violent, and admitted that he did not remember his arrest on the occasion for which he was being tried.***

Following this abbreviated exposition of the problem before it, the trial court indicated its intention to disallow appellant's claimed defense of "chronic alcoholism." Thereupon, defense counsel submitted, and the trial court entered, the following "findings of fact":

> (1) That chronic alcoholism is a disease which destroys the afflicted person's willpower to resist the constant, excessive consumption of alcohol.
> (2) That a chronic alcoholic does not appear in public by his own volition, but under a compulsion symptomatic of the disease of chronic alcoholism.
> (3) That Leroy Powell, defendant herein, is a chronic alcoholic who is afflicted with the disease of chronic alcoholism.

Whatever else may be said of them, those are not "findings of fact" in any recognizable, traditional sense in which that term has been used in a court of law; they are the premises of a syllogism transparently designed to bring this case within the scope of this Court's opinion in *Robinson v. California*. Nonetheless, the dissent would have us adopt these "findings" without critical examination; it would use them as the basis for a constitutional holding that

> a person may not be punished if the condition essential to constitute the defined crime is part of the pattern of his disease and is occasioned by a compulsion symptomatic of the disease.

The difficulty with that position, as we shall show, is that it goes much too far on the basis of too little knowledge. In the first place, the record in this case is utterly inadequate to permit the sort of informed and responsible adjudication which alone can support the announcement of an important and wide-ranging new constitutional principle. We know very little about the circumstances surrounding the drinking about which resulted in this conviction, or about Leroy Powell's drinking problem, or indeed about alcoholism itself. The trial hardly reflects the sharp legal and evidentiary clash between fully prepared adversary litigants which is traditionally expected in major constitutional cases. The State put on only one witness, the arresting officer. The defense put on three—a policeman who testified to appellant's long history of arrests for public drunkenness, the psychiatrist, and appellant himself.

Furthermore, the inescapable fact is that there is no agreement among members of the medical profession about what it means to say that "alcoholism" is a "disease." One of the principal works in this field states that the major difficulty in articulating a "disease concept of alcoholism" is that "alcoholism has too many definitions, and disease has practically none." This same author concludes that *"a disease is what the medical profession recognizes as such."* In other words, there is widespread agreement today that "alcoholism" is a "disease," for the simple reason that the medical profession has concluded that it should attempt to treat those who have drinking problems. There, the agreement stops. Debate rages within the medical profession as to whether "alcoholism" is a separate "disease" in any meaningful biochemical, physiological or psychological sense, or whether it represents one peculiar manifestation in some individuals of underlying psychiatric disorders.

Nor is there any substantial consensus as to the "manifestations of alcoholism." E. M. Jellinek, one of the outstanding authorities on the subject, identifies five different types of alcoholics which predominate in the United States, and these types display a broad range of different and occasionally inconsistent symptoms. Moreover, wholly distinct types, relatively rare in this country, predominate in nations with different cultural attitudes regarding the consumption of alcohol. Even if we limit our consideration to the range of alcoholic symptoms more typically found in this country, there is substantial disagreement as to the manifestations of the "disease" called "alcoholism."***

The trial court's "finding" that Powell "is afflicted with the disease of chronic alcoholism," which "destroys the afflicted person's willpower to resist the constant, excessive consumption of alcohol" covers a multitude of sins. Dr. Wade's testimony that appellant suffered from a compulsion which was an "exceedingly strong influence," but which was "not completely overpowering," is at least more carefully stated, if no less mystifying. Jellinek insists that conceptual clarity can only be achieved by distinguishing carefully between "loss of control" once an individual has commenced to drink and "inability to abstain" from drinking in the first place. Presumably, a person would have to display both characteristics in order to make out a constitutional defense, should one be recognized. Yet the "findings" of the trial court utterly fail to make this crucial distinction, and there is serious question whether the record can be read to support a finding of either loss of control or inability to abstain.

Dr. Wade did testify that, once appellant began drinking, he appeared to have no control over the amount of alcohol he finally ingested. Appellant's own testimony concerning his drinking on the day of the trial would certainly appear, however, to cast doubt upon the conclusion that he was without control over his consumption of alcohol when he had sufficiently important reasons to exercise such control. However that may be, there are more serious factual and conceptual difficulties with reading this record to show that appellant was unable to abstain from drinking. Dr. Wade testified that, when appellant was sober, the act of taking the first drink was a "voluntary exercise of his will," but that this exercise of will was undertaken under the "exceedingly strong influence" of a "compulsion" which was "not completely overpowering." Such concepts, when juxtaposed in this fashion, have little meaning.

Moreover, Jellinek asserts that it cannot accurately be said that a person is truly unable to abstain from drinking unless he is suffering the physical symptoms of withdrawal. There is no testimony in this record that Leroy Powell underwent withdrawal symptoms, either before he began the drinking spree which resulted in the conviction under review here or at any other time. In attempting to deal with the alcoholic's desire for drink in the absence of withdrawal symptoms, Jellinek is reduced to unintelligible distinctions between a "compulsion" (a "psychopathological phenomenon" which can apparently serve in some instances as the functional equivalent of a "craving" or symptom of withdrawal) and an "impulse" (something which differs from a loss of control, a craving or a compulsion, and to which Jellinek attributes the start of a new drinking bout for a "gamma" alcoholic). Other scholars are equally unhelpful in articulating the nature of a "compulsion." It is one thing to say that, if a man is deprived of alcohol, his hands will begin to shake, he will suffer agonizing pains, and ultimately he will have hallucinations; it is quite another to say that a man has a "compulsion" to take a drink, but that he also retains a certain amount of "free will" with which to resist. It is simply impossible, in the present state of our knowledge, to ascribe a useful meaning to the latter statement. This definitional confusion reflects, of course, not merely the undeveloped state of the psychiatric art, but also the conceptual difficulties inevitably attendant upon the importation of scientific and medical models into a legal system generally predicated upon a different set of assumptions.

II

Despite the comparatively primitive state of our knowledge on the subject, it cannot be denied that the destructive use of alcoholic beverages is one of our principal social and public health problems. The lowest current informed estimate places the number of "alcoholics" in America (definitional problems aside) at 4,000,000, and most authorities are inclined to put the figure considerably higher. The problem is compounded by the fact that a very large percentage of the alcoholics in this country are "invisible"—they possess the means to keep their drinking problems secret, and the traditionally uncharitable attitude of our society toward alcoholics causes many of them to refrain from seeking treatment from any source. Nor can it be said that the legislative response to this enormous problem has in general been inadequate.

There is as yet no known generally effective method for treating the vast number of alcoholics in our society. Some individual alcoholics have responded to particular forms of therapy with remissions of their symptomatic dependence upon the drug. But just as there is no agreement among doctors and social workers with respect to the causes of alcoholism, there is no consensus as to why particular treatments have been effective in particular cases, and there is no generally agreed-upon approach to the problem of treatment on a large scale. Most psychiatrists are apparently of the opinion that alcoholism is far more difficult to treat than other forms of behavioral disorders, and some believe it is impossible to cure by means of psychotherapy; indeed, the medical profession as a whole, and psychiatrists in particular, have been severely criticised for the prevailing reluctance to undertake the treatment of drinking problems. Thus, it is entirely possible that, even were the manpower and facilities available for a full-scale attack upon chronic alcoholism, we would find ourselves unable to help the vast bulk of our "visible"—let alone our "invisible"—alcoholic population.

However, facilities for the attempted treatment of indigent alcoholics are woefully lacking throughout the country. It would be tragic to return large numbers of helpless, sometimes dangerous and frequently unsanitary inebriates to the streets of our cities without even the opportunity to sober up adequately which a brief jail term provides. Presumably no State or city will tolerate such a state of affairs. Yet the medical profession cannot, and does not, tell us with any assurance that, even if the buildings, equipment and trained personnel were made available, it could provide anything more than slightly higher-class jails for our indigent habitual inebriates. Thus, we run the grave risk that nothing will be accomplished beyond the hanging of a new sign—reading "hospital"—over one wing of the jailhouse.

One virtue of the criminal process is, at least, that the duration of penal incarceration typically has some outside statutory limit; this is universally true in the case of petty offenses, such as public drunkenness, where jail terms are quite short on the whole. "Therapeutic civil commitment" lacks this feature; one is typically committed until one is "cured." Thus, to do otherwise than affirm might subject indigent alcoholics to the risk that they may be locked up for an indefinite period of time under the same conditions as before, with no more hope than before of receiving effective treatment and no prospect of periodic "freedom."

Faced with this unpleasant reality, we are unable to assert that the use of the criminal process as a means of dealing with the public aspects of problem drinking can never be defended as rational. The picture of the penniless drunk propelled aimlessly and endlessly through the law's "revolving door" of arrest, incarceration, release and re-arrest is not a pretty one. But before we condemn the present practice across the board, perhaps we ought to be able to point to some clear promise of a better world for these unfortunate people. Unfortunately, no such promise has yet been forthcoming. If, in addition to the absence of a coherent approach to the problem of treatment, we consider the almost complete absence of facilities and manpower for the implementation of a rehabilitation program, it is difficult to say in the present context that the criminal process is utterly lacking in social value. This Court has never held that anything in the Constitution requires that penal sanctions be designed solely to achieve therapeutic or rehabilitative effects, and it can hardly be said with assurance that incarceration serves such purposes any better for the general run of criminals than it does for public drunks.***

III

Appellant, however, seeks to come within the application of the Cruel and Unusual Punishment Clause announced in *Robinson v. California,* which involved a state statute making it a crime to "be addicted to the use of narcotics." This Court held there that

> a state law which imprisons a person thus afflicted [with narcotic addiction] as a criminal, even though he has never touched any narcotic drug within the State or been guilty of any irregular behavior there, inflicts a cruel and unusual punishment.
>
> . . .

On its face, the present case does not fall within that holding, since appellant was convicted not for being a chronic alcoholic, but for being in public while drunk on a particular occasion. The State of Texas thus has not sought to punish a mere status, as California did in *Robinson;* nor has it attempted to regulate appellant's behavior in the privacy of his own home. Rather, it has imposed upon appellant a criminal sanction for public behavior which may create substantial health and safety hazards both for appellant and for members of the general public, and which offends the moral and esthetic sensibilities of a large segment of the community. This seems a far cry from convicting one for being an addict, being a chronic alcoholic, being "mentally ill, or a leper. . . ."

Robinson, so viewed, brings this Court but a very small way into the substantive criminal law. And unless *Robinson* is so viewed, it is difficult to see any limiting principle that would serve to prevent this Court from becoming, under the aegis of the Cruel and Unusual Punishment Clause, the ultimate arbiter of the standards of criminal responsibility in diverse areas of the criminal law throughout the country.

It is suggested in dissent that *Robinson* stands for the "simple" but "subtle" principle that "[c]riminal penalties may not be inflicted upon a person for being in a condition he is powerless to change." In that view, appellant's "condition" of public intoxication was "occasioned by a compulsion symptomatic of the disease" of chronic alcoholism, and thus, apparently, his behavior lacked the critical element of *mens rea*. Whatever may be the merits of such a doctrine of criminal responsibility, it surely cannot be said to follow from *Robinson*. The entire thrust of *Robinson's* interpretation of the Cruel and Unusual Punishment Clause is that criminal penalties may be inflicted only if the accused has committed some act, has engaged in some behavior, which society has an interest in preventing, or perhaps, in historical common law terms, has committed some *actus reus*. It thus does not deal with the question of whether certain conduct cannot constitutionally be punished because it is, in some sense, "involuntary" or "occasioned by a compulsion."

Likewise, as the dissent acknowledges, there is a substantial definitional distinction between a "status," as in *Robinson,* and a "condition," which is said to be involved in this case. Whatever may be the merits of an attempt to distinguish between behavior and a condition, it is perfectly clear that the crucial element in this case, so far as the dissent is concerned, is whether or not appellant can legally be held responsible for his appearance in public in a state of intoxication. The only relevance of *Robinson* to this issue is that, because the Court interpreted the statute there involved as making a "status" criminal, it was able to suggest that the statute would cover even a situation in which addiction had been acquired involuntarily. That this factor was not determinative in the case is shown by the fact that there was no indication of how *Robinson* himself had become an addict.

Ultimately, then, the most troubling aspects of this case, were *Robinson* to be extended to meet it, would be the scope and content of what could only be a constitutional doctrine of criminal responsibility. In dissent, it is urged that the decision could be limited to conduct which is "a characteristic and involuntary part of the pattern of the disease as it afflicts" the particular individual, and that "[i]t is not foreseeable" that it would be applied "in the case of offenses such as driving a car while intoxicated, assault, theft, or robbery." That is limitation by fiat. In the first place, nothing in the logic of the dissent would limit its application to chronic alcoholics. If Leroy Powell cannot be convicted of public intoxication, it is difficult to see how a State can convict an individual for murder if that individual, while exhibiting normal behavior in all other respects, suffers from a "compulsion" to kill which is an "exceedingly strong influence," but "not completely overpowering." Even if we limit our consideration to chronic alcoholics, it would seem impossible to confine the principle within the arbitrary bounds which the dissent seems to envision.

It is not difficult to imagine a case involving psychiatric testimony to the effect that an individual suffers from some aggressive neurosis which he is able to control when sober; that very little alcohol suffices to remove the inhibitions which normally contain these aggressions, with the result that the individual engages in assaultive behavior without becoming actually intoxicated, and that the individual suffers from a very strong desire to drink, which is an "exceedingly strong influence," but "not completely overpowering." Without being untrue to the rationale of this case, should the principles advanced in dissent be accepted here, the Court could not avoid holding such an individual constitutionally unaccountable for his assaultive behavior.

Traditional common law concepts of personal accountability and essential considerations of federalism lead us to disagree with appellant. We are unable to conclude, on the state of this record or on the current state of medical knowledge, that chronic alcoholics in general, and Leroy Powell in particular, suffer from such an irresistible compulsion to drink and to get drunk in public that they are utterly unable to control their performance of either or both of these acts, and thus cannot be deterred at all from public intoxication. And, in any event, this Court has never articulated a general constitutional doctrine of *mens rea*.

We cannot cast aside the centuries-long evolution of the collection of interlocking and overlapping concepts which the common law has utilized to assess the moral accountability of an individual for his antisocial deeds. The doctrines of *actus reus, mens rea,* insanity, mistake, justification, and duress have historically provided the tools for a constantly shifting adjustment of the tension between the evolving aims of the criminal law and changing religious, moral, philosophical, and medical views of the nature of man. This process of adjustment has always been thought to be the province of the States.

Nothing could be less fruitful than for this Court to be impelled into defining some sort of insanity test in constitutional terms. Yet that task would seem to follow inexorably from an extension of *Robinson* to this case. If a person in the "condition" of being a chronic alcoholic cannot be criminally punished as a constitutional matter for being drunk in public, it would seem to follow that a person who contends that, in terms of one test, "his unlawful act was the product of mental disease or mental defect," would state an issue of constitutional dimension with regard to his criminal responsibility had he been tried under some different, and perhaps lesser, standard, *e.g.,* the right-wrong test of *M'Naghten's Case* experimentation, and freeze the developing productive dialogue between law and psychiatry into a rigid constitutional mold. It is simply not yet the time to write into the Constitution formulas cast in terms whose meaning, let alone relevance, is not yet clear either to doctors or to lawyers.
Affirmed.

Mr. Justice FORTAS, with whom Mr. Justice DOUGLAS, Mr. Justice BRENNAN, and Mr. Justice STEWART join, dissenting.***

I

The issue posed in this case is a narrow one. There is no challenge here to the validity of public intoxication statutes in general or to the Texas public intoxication statute in particular. This case does not concern the infliction of punishment upon the "social" drinker—or upon anyone other than a "chronic alcoholic" who, as the trier of fact here found, cannot "resist the constant, excessive consumption of alcohol." Nor does it relate to any offense other than the crime of public intoxication.

The sole question presented is whether a criminal penalty may be imposed upon a person suffering the disease of "chronic alcoholism" for a condition—being "in a state of intoxication" in public—which is a characteristic part of the pattern of his disease and which, the trial court found, was not the consequence of appellant's volition but of "a compulsion symptomatic of the disease of chronic alcoholism." ***

II

As I shall discuss, consideration of the Eighth Amendment issue in this case requires an understanding of "the disease of chronic alcoholism" with which, as the trial court found, appellant is afflicted, which has destroyed his "will power to resist the constant, excessive consumption of alcohol," and which leads him to "appear in public [not] by his own volition but under a compulsion symptomatic of the disease of chronic alcoholism."

III

*** It is settled that the Federal Constitution places some substantive limitation upon the power of state legislatures to define crimes for which the imposition of punishment is ordered. In *Robinson v. California,* 370 U.S. 660 (1962), the Court considered a conviction under a California statute making it a criminal offense for a person to "be addicted to the use of narcotics." At Robinson's trial, it was developed that the defendant had been a user of narcotics. The trial court instructed the jury that "[t]o be addicted to the use of narcotics is said to be a status or condition and not an act. It is a continuing offense and differs from most other offenses in the fact that [it] is chronic rather than acute; that it continues after it is complete and subjects the offender to arrest at any time before he reforms." *Id.,* at 662-663.

This Court reversed Robinson's conviction on the ground that punishment under the law in question was cruel and unusual, in violation of the Eighth Amendment of the Constitution as applied to the States through the Fourteenth Amendment. The Court noted that narcotic addiction is considered to be an illness and that California had recognized it as such. It held that the State could not make it a crime for a person to be ill. Although Robinson had been sentenced to only 90 days in prison for his offense, it was beyond the power of the State to prescribe such punishment. As Mr. Justice Stewart, speaking for the Court, said: "[e]ven one day in prison would be a cruel and unusual punishment for the 'crime' of having a common cold." 370 U.S. at 667.

Robinson stands upon a principle which, despite its subtlety, must be simply stated and respectfully applied because it is the foundation of individual liberty and the cornerstone of the relations between a civilized state and its citizens: Criminal penalties may not be inflicted upon a person for being in a condition he is powerless to change. In all probability, Robinson at some time before his conviction elected to take narcotics. But the crime as defined did not punish this conduct. The statute imposed a penalty for the offense of "addiction"—a condition which Robinson could not control. Once Robinson had become an addict, he was utterly powerless to avoid criminal guilt. He was powerless to choose not to violate the law.

In the present case, appellant is charged with a crime composed of two elements—being intoxicated and being found in a public place while in that condition. The crime, so defined, differs from that in *Robinson.* The statute covers more than a mere status. But the essential constitutional defect here is the same as in *Robinson,* for in both cases the particular defendant was accused of being in a condition which he had no capacity to change or avoid. The trial judge sitting as trier of fact found, upon the medical and other relevant testimony, that Powell is a "chronic alcoholic." He defined appellant's "chronic alcoholism" as "a disease which destroys the afflicted person's will power to resist the constant, excessive consumption of alcohol." He also found that "a chronic alcoholic does not appear in public by his own volition but under a compulsion symptomatic of the disease of chronic alcoholism." I read these findings to mean that appellant was powerless to avoid drinking; that having taken his first drink, he had "an uncontrollable compulsion to drink" to the point of intoxication; and that, once intoxicated, he could not prevent himself from appearing in public places.

Article 477 of the Texas Penal Code is specifically directed to the accused's presence while in a state of intoxication, "in any public place, or at any private house except his own." This is the essence of the crime. Ordinarily when the State proves such presence in a state of intoxication, this will be sufficient for conviction, and the punishment prescribed by the State may, of course, be validly imposed. But here the findings of the trial judge call into play the principle that a person may not be punished if the condition essential to constitute the defined crime is part of the pattern of his disease and is occasioned by a compulsion symptomatic of the disease. This principle, narrow in scope and applicability, is implemented by the Eighth Amendment's prohibition of "cruel and unusual punishment," as we construed that command in *Robinson.* It is true that the command of the Eighth Amendment and its antecedent provision in the Bill of Rights of 1689 were initially directed to the type and degree of punishment inflicted. But in *Robinson* we recognized that "the principle that would deny power to exact capital punishment for a petty crime would also deny power to punish a person by fine or imprisonment for being sick." 370 U.S. at 676 (Mr. Justice Douglas, concurring).

The findings in this case, read against the background of the medical and sociological data to which I have referred, compel the conclusion that the infliction upon appellant of a criminal penalty for being intoxicated in a public place would be "cruel and inhuman punishment" within the prohibition of the Eighth Amendment. This conclusion follows because appellant is a "chronic alcoholic" who, according to the trier of fact, cannot resist the "constant excessive consumption of alcohol" and does not appear in public by his own volition but under a "compulsion" which is part of his condition.

I would reverse the judgment below.

Notes and Questions

1. Who has the better argument in *Powell v. Texas,* the majority or the dissent? What limitations can be placed on the dissent's argument? According to the dissent, would alcoholics be excused for crimes they committed in order to obtain alcohol?

2. Is *Powell* consistent with *Robinson v. California*, why or why not? What portion of *Robinson* do you think concerned the majority in *Powell*?

3. Do you agree with the language from *Robinson* cited by the dissent in *Powell*, "to be addicted to the use of narcotics is said to be a status and not an act." If you do agree, did the Court in *Powell* reach the right conclusion?

4. Historical Note: The defendant in *Robinson* never received the news about his Supreme Court victory. This is because Lawrence Robinson died of an overdose ten months prior to the court's ruling. Does this fact make you reassess Justice Clark's dissenting opinion in *Robinson,* which included the following language?

> The majority strikes down the conviction primarily on the grounds that petitioner was denied due process by the imposition of criminal penalties for nothing more than being in a status. This view point is premised upon the theme that s 11721 is a "criminal" provision authorizing a punishment, for the majority admits that "a State might establish a program of compulsory treatment for those addicted to narcotics" which

"might require periods of involuntary confinement." I submit that California has done exactly that. The majority's error is in instructing the California Legislature that hospitalization is the only treatment for narcotics addiction—that anything less is a punishment denying due process. California has found otherwise after a study which I suggest was more extensive than that conducted by the Court. Even in California's program for hospital commitment of nonvolitional narcotic addicts—which the majority approves—it is recognized that some addicts will not respond to or do not need hospital treatment.

Chapter 4
Mens Rea

A. Background

In addition to the defendant committing a wrongful act or omission (actus reus), he or she must have a specific mental state or mens rea to meet the elements of a crime. Like actus reus, mens rea has numerous definitions. Many equate mens rea with the defendant having a "guilty mind" or "a culpable state of mind." It should be clear, however, that mens rea does not mean motive. A motive, which hardly ever has to be proven by the prosecution in order to convict the defendant, is the reason or explanation for why the defendant committed the crime.

Most but not all crimes require a mens rea. Those crimes that don't require a mens rea are classified as strict liability offenses. Section D of this chapter examines strict liability crimes in greater detail.

Common law judges used a number of different adverbs to describe the mens rea required for a person to be found guilty of committing a crime, e.g., maliciously, wantonly, designedly, willfully, corruptly, etc. In addition, common law judges classified offenses as either specific or general intent crimes. The challenge here was the inconsistency in how these terms were used. Oftentimes, the definitions of these terms would vary by statute and courthouse. Thus, few, to include practitioners, were entirely clear on what constituted "maliciously" and what offenses were deemed specific intent crimes as opposed to general intent crimes.

This ultimately led most jurisdictions, including Ohio, to abandon the language used by the common law to describe a defendant's mental state in favor of the terms used by the MPC: purposely, knowingly, recklessly, and negligently.

B. Purposely, Knowingly, Recklessly, and Negligently

O.R.C. 2901.22 Degrees of Mental States

(A) A person acts **purposely** when it is the person's specific intention to cause a certain result, or, when the gist of the offense is a prohibition against conduct of a certain nature, regardless of what the offender intends to accomplish thereby, it is the offender's specific intention to engage in conduct of that nature.

(B) A person acts **knowingly**, regardless of purpose, when the person is aware that the person's conduct will probably cause a certain result or will probably be of a certain nature. A person has knowledge of circumstances when the person is aware that such circumstances probably exist. When knowledge of the existence of a particular fact is an element of an offense, such knowledge is established if a person subjectively believes that there is a high probability of its existence and fails to make inquiry or acts with a conscious purpose to avoid learning the fact.

(C) A person acts **recklessly** when, with heedless indifference to the consequences, the person disregards a substantial and unjustifiable risk that the person's conduct is likely to cause a certain result or is likely to be of a certain nature. A person is reckless with respect to circumstances when, with heedless indifference to the consequences, the person disregards a substantial and unjustifiable risk that such circumstances are likely to exist.

(D) A person acts **negligently** when, because of a substantial lapse from due care, the person fails to perceive or avoid a risk that the person's conduct may cause a certain result or may be of a certain nature. A person is negligent with respect to circumstances when, because of a substantial lapse from due care, the person fails to perceive or avoid a risk that such circumstances may exist.

(E) When the section defining an offense provides that negligence suffices to establish an element thereof, then recklessness, knowledge, or purpose is also sufficient culpability for such element. When recklessness suffices to establish an element of an offense, then knowledge or purpose is also sufficient culpability for such element. When knowledge suffices to establish an element of an offense, then purpose is also sufficient culpability for such element.

1. Purposely vs. Knowingly

State v. Collier, 1979 WL 209245

McCORMAC, J.

Timothy Collier was convicted of two counts of rape and one count of kidnapping after trial before a jury, following which the trial court sentenced him concurrently to four to twenty-five years imprisonment on the rape convictions, and two to fifteen years on the kidnapping conviction.

Collier has appealed, setting forth the following assignments of error:

> 1. "The court committed error prejudicial to the defendant in failing to instruct the jury on the lesser included offense of rape, sexual battery. R.C. 2907.03(A)(1)."
> 2. "The trial court committed reversible error in permitting the jury to convict on both the offense of rape as defined by R.C. 2907.02(A) (1), and kidnapping, as defined by R.C. 2905.01 (A)(4), since kidnapping is an 'offense of similar import' to rape. R.C. 2941.25(A)."

There is no dispute but that defendant, age 19, and his alleged victim, age 15, engaged in sexual conduct on several occasions after having met at a roller skating rink and having departed therefrom in defendant's automobile. As to whether the sexual conduct was consensual or involuntary is hotly disputed. The only two witnesses to what actually happened were the defendant and the alleged victim. The victim testified that the defendant induced her to accompany him in his car by falsely promising to take her to a nearby restaurant and that she engaged in sexual conduct because defendant held a knife on her and told her that she would "get it if she did not." The defendant testified that the alleged victim actually propositioned him and that what happened thereafter was with her complete consent. The victim's version was corroborated in part by a special duty police officer at the roller skating rink who testified that the prosecuting witness was confused, crying, and in a nervous state when she returned to the roller rink and her clothes were mussed, her hair disarrayed, and one of her pants legs was twisted around her leg. The defendant testified that her clothing was not mussed and she was not crying when he dropped her off at the skating rink.

Appellant does not contest, nor can he, that there was sufficient evidence to convict him of two counts of rape and one count of kidnapping if the state's testimony is believed. However, appellant contends that the trial court erred in denying his request to charge the jury on the lesser offense of sexual battery. The trial court denied the request, stating that there was no reasonable basis for a jury to find sexual battery as defendant either used force or a threat of force, clearly amounting to rape, or defendant was not guilty if the prosecuting witness consented, there being no basis for an in between verdict.

R.C. 2907.02, defining rape, provides as pertinent as follows:

"(A) No person shall engage in sexual conduct with another, not the spouse of the offender, when any of the following apply:
"(1) The offender purposely compels the other person to submit by force or threat of force."

R.C. 2907.03 defines sexual battery as pertinent as follows:

"(A) No person shall engage in sexual conduct with another, not the spouse of the offender, when any of the following apply:
"(1) The offender knowingly coerces the other person to submit by any means that would prevent resistance by a person of ordinary resolution."

Appellant argues that even if it is believed that defendant threatened the prosecuting witness with a knife to induce her to enter into sex with him that the jury should be given the option of considering whether this action constituted purposely compelling her to submit by force or threat of force to constitute rape, or whether it constituted knowingly coercing her to submit by any means that would prevent resistance by a person of ordinary resolution.

Appellant's argument is not valid. If defendant used a knife to threaten or coerce his victim into complying with his sexual wishes, rape by purposely compelling the other to submit by force or threat of force was clearly proved even though that conduct may also have met the lesser test of knowingly coercing her to submit by any means that would prevent resistance by a person of ordinary resolution. The argument made by appellant is comparable to arguing in a murder case that the jury should also be charged as to aggravated assault because there was also serious physical harm caused to another, even though it is undisputed that death was caused, or arguing in a case where, if a theft occurred, the value stolen was undisputably $1,000 that petty larceny should be charged as $100 had been stolen. There is no basis for the jury to find guilt of an offense less than rape. Defendant either used force or threat of force or there was consent.

Appellant cites *State v. Tolliver* (1976). 49 Ohio App. 2d 258, as authority for his argument. In *Tolliver*, the First District Court of Appeals affirmed a conviction of sexual battery on the basis that rape requires the culpable mental state of purposely and sexual battery requires the culpable mental state of knowingly, which in that case permitted a jury determination of whether the threat of force was done knowingly or purposely.

R.C. 2901.22 defines purposely and knowingly as follows:

"(A) A person acts purposely when it is his specific intention to cause a certain result, or, when the gist of the offense is a prohibition against conduct of a certain nature, regardless of what the offender intends to accomplish thereby, it is his specific intention to engage in conduct of that nature.

"(B) A person acts knowingly, regardless of his purpose, when he is aware that his conduct will probably cause a certain result or will probably be of a certain nature. A person has knowledge of circumstances when he is aware that such circumstances probably exist."

If defendant threatened the prosecuting witness with a knife, there is no doubt that it was his specific intention to coerce her to engage in sexual conduct with him against her will. Thus, if the state's version of the testimony is believed, it is clear that defendant acted purposely. The difference between purposely and knowingly is that one may act knowingly irrespective of a specific intention to cause a certain result, whereas a specific intention is required for purposely. Knowingly is a culpable mental state requiring less proof than purposely. However, if defendant acted as claimed by the state, he acted purposely. It could not be reasonably found that he acted knowingly, but not purposely.

We do not disagree with the basic principal of *Tolliver* that in an appropriate case a jury may be permitted to consider that the defendant acted knowingly rather than purposely when a threat of force ultimately culminated in sexual conduct. However, in line with the well-established principle that a charge on a lesser included offense should be given only if the trier of the fact could reasonably find against the state and for the accused upon one or more of the elements of the crime charged and for the accused on the remaining elements we affirm the trial court's overruling of defendant's request for a charge on sexual battery. See *State v. Nolton* (1969), 19 Ohio St. 2d 133.

Appellant's first assignment of error is overruled.

Appellant next contends that the trial court erred in permitting the jury to convict him of the offense of kidnapping in addition to the rape offense, contending that kidnapping is an offense of similar import to rape.

R.C. 2941.25 provides as follows:

"(A) Where the same conduct by defendant can be construed to constitute two or more allied offenses of similar import, the indictment or information may contain counts for all such offenses, but the defendant may be convicted of only one.

"(B) Where the defendant's conduct constitutes two or more offenses of dissimilar import, or where his conduct results in two or more offenses of the same or similar kind committed separately or with a separate animus as to each, the indictment or information may contain counts for all such offenses, and the defendant may be convicted of all of them."

Appellant contends that even if he is guilty of both rape and kidnapping, the offenses are of similar import and committed with a single animus as the kidnapping of the victim was done solely for the purpose of taking her to a place where he could engage in sexual conduct with her.

Appellant primarily relies upon *State v. Donald* (1979), 57 Ohio St. 2d 73. In *Donald*, the defendant raped a hospital employee after forcing her to accompany him from one room to another in the hospital. The Supreme Court held that kidnapping was an offense of similar import to rape for the purpose of applying R.C. 2941.25(A), where the victim was removed or restrained solely for the purpose of engaging in sexual activity where the same force or threat was used for both the kidnapping and rape. As the court pointed out necessarily in the crime of rape, the victim must be restrained of her liberty which can constitute an element of kidnapping.

However, the court pointed out that no issue had been raised or determined as to whether the kidnapping and rape offenses were "committed separately or with a separate animus as to each," which would permit conviction of two or more similar offenses pursuant to R.C. 2941.25(B).

The state argues that there is a separate animus as to each pointing out that the victim was removed and restrained of liberty by conduct preceding the first rape and in between the first and second rape. Defendant argues that any kidnapping was for the sole purpose to engage in sexual activity, thus requiring a finding of offenses of similar import.

This case differs from *Donald* in that the initial removal or restraint of liberty was by deception in leading the victim to believe that she was being taken to a restaurant and that additional threats of force were used to coerce her to comply with defendant's sexual desires. Also, the time and distance factors were different as the kidnapping force was not part and parcel of the succeeding rapes. In *Donald*, the victim was removed only to an adjacent room and the restraint was only for the period of time necessary to conduct the sexual activity. Moreover, in *Donald*, the Supreme Court did not decide whether there was a separate animus.

The Supreme Court later decided *State v. Frazier* (1979), 58 Ohio St. 2d 253. In *Frazier*, the defendant forced his way into the victim's house knocking her to the floor and beating her and her husband, after which items from the house were stolen. The Supreme Court pointed out that, although the offenses may be allied offenses of similar import within the contemplation of R.C. 2941.25(A), there could be a conviction for both as there was a separate animus as to each. The court pointed out that, when the defendant forced the victim's door open with intent to assault her and take her property, a burglary was completed and there was a separate animus when the victim and her husband were beaten and their property taken.

In this case, the kidnapping was not solely part and parcel of the rapes but had been completed before the sexual conduct took place. The crime of kidnapping was complete when the victim was removed by deception and restrained of liberty for the purpose of engaging in sexual activity against the victim's will. There was one animus in deceptively removing and restraining the victim and another animus when the sexual acts were actually committed upon the victim. In addition, the force used to accomplish the kidnapping was deception, a different act than the later threats with the knife used to coerce the victim into submitting. Thus, there was different conduct under R.C. 2941.25(A) and more than one animus under R.C. 2941.25(B).

Appellant's second assignment of error is overruled.

Appellant's assignments of error are overruled and the judgment of the trial court is affirmed.

Judgment affirmed.

2. Knowingly vs. Recklessly

State v. Robinson, 2013-Ohio-4375 (Ohio Ct. App. 2013)

*** Robinson and codefendant Jeremy Logan were charged in a ten-count indictment: aggravated murder and two counts of murder involving one victim (Counts 1-3), six counts of felonious assault involving six different named victims (Counts 4-9), and discharging a firearm on or near prohibited premises (Count 10). All counts included one-, three-, and five-year firearm specifications.

Robinson pleaded not guilty to the charges, and the state voluntarily dismissed the aggravated murder charge prior to trial. The matter proceeded to a jury trial. The charges arose out of the fatal shooting of Dena'Jua Delaney ("Bubbles") on February 22, 2012, around 3:15 in the afternoon. The incident took place on Garfield Road (a.k.a. "The One Way"), a one-way residential street in East Cleveland, stemming from two competing groups of people squaring off to fight.

At trial, the state presented 25 witnesses, including 17 eyewitnesses, each who offered slightly varied accounts of the events in question. We summarize the following pertinent facts from the evidence presented at trial.

The night before the fatal shooting, on February 21, 2012, Russell Stokes and Latima Brown got into a heated altercation after a night of hanging out and drinking at Latima and Bubbles's East Cleveland apartment. Russell ultimately left the apartment after threatening Latima. At the time, Russell was "staying" nearby at his aunt's house on The One Way.

The next day, Russell called his best friend, S.P., who was Robinson's girlfriend at the time, and told her to "beat up" Latima. Consequently, S.P., along with her sister and two friends, D.B. and B.D., went over to The One Way to fight Latima.

According to Latima, she received a call the next day from Russell, telling her to go outside, where she encountered three females coming down The One Way to meet her. Although witnesses offered various accounts of the fight that ensued, Latima returned to her apartment after the fight with apparent injuries, including a "bloody face," and was upset. This prompted Bubbles to call many of her family and friends, asking them to meet on The One Way "to fight."

According to Latima, approximately 15 people—nine females and six males—congregated outside of her and Bubbles's apartment building in response to Bubbles's calls. Other witnesses estimated approximately 20 to 30 people gathered. The group ranged in ages from late teens to early 20s.

Amongst the calls Bubbles made, Russell received one. He testified that Bubbles stated "you all jump my best friend" and now "you just signed your death certificate."

Russell, in turn, called S.P. According to S.P., she got a call, "saying that they was trying to jump Russell, they outside trying to jump Russell and stuff. And then I called—my boyfriend"—Robinson. S.P. told Robinson, "come get me, they're about to jump my best friend Russell." Robinson, who drove a two-door gold Saturn, picked up codefendant, Jeremy Logan, S.P., and her two friends, D.B. and B.D., and drove to The One Way. According to Logan, Robinson called and asked him to accompany him to The One Way "because he didn't want to be up there by himself in a fight."

When Robinson arrived on The One Way, a mob quickly convened near Robinson's car, which had stopped near Russell's aunt's house. According to Russell, he ran back inside his aunt's house once he realized that they were "outnumbered." According to S.P., she jumped out of the car, and a heated altercation ensued. D.B. and B.D. never left the car. Ultimately, when all five occupants were seated in the car, Devere Ealom, a friend of Bubbles, ran up to the front seat passenger side of the vehicle and punched Logan in the face. The eyewitnesses' accounts of what happened next, including the fatal shooting of Bubbles, conflict.

According to the majority of the eyewitnesses present, after Logan was punched, the car moved slightly forward, allowing Logan to position himself on the door jamb and hang his upper body outside the car while he fired several shots above the car toward the crowd of people behind the car on Garfield Road. The witnesses characterized this as the first round of shots. Following Logan's firing of his gun, Robinson fired his gun out his window and toward "the back of the car." This was characterized as the second round of shots. Several witnesses testified that Bubbles was standing after the first round of shooting but not after the driver (Robinson) shot his gun. After Bubbles fell to the ground, Robinson drove off.

According to Bubbles's friends and family, no one from the crowd ever fired any shots at the car until after Bubbles had already fallen down. Instead, these witnesses testified that someone from the crowd fired what sounded like a shotgun following the screaming that Bubbles was down. Even Russell Stokes—Robinson's girlfriend's best friend—testified that first there were shots fired from the car, a couple of people hit the ground, the car took off, and then someone from the crowd "got to busting [shooting]" toward the car while the car was moving away. The same shooter then apparently spotted Russell in the window, "[h]e shoot toward the house, shot in the corner of the window, the room that we was in."

Conversely, Robinson (through his statement to the police) and Logan (through his testimony at trial) stated that someone from the crowd was shooting at their car. According to B.D. and D.B., also passengers in Robinson's car, there were gunshots at the car. D.B. testified, however, that the first shots came from the "boys in the front seat"—Robinson and Logan. S.P. never mentioned any shooting directed at the car.

According to her, Logan fired at least four or five shots toward the crowd of people. She further testified that after they pulled away from The One Way, Logan said, "Ah, I shot someone. I'm going to break my phone. What am I going to do?"

East Cleveland police responded to the call of gunshots and victim down. East Cleveland police detective Reginald Holcomb testified that, through initial interviews at the scene, the police quickly learned that Jeremy Logan was a passenger in the car and had fired his gun into the crowd. They further recovered Logan's gun, a Rossie .38 Special revolver, based on an anonymous tip called into the station, which Logan acknowledged as being his gun after being called in by the police. Robinson, likewise, turned himself into the police and ultimately admitted to firing a single shot "out the window towards the back of [his] car." According to Robinson's statement, someone from the crowd fired a single round first, then Logan fired his gun, and then someone from the crowd fired another one or two shots. At that point, Logan told Robinson that "his gun was messing up" so Robinson fired a single shot and then they drove away. Based on Robinson's admission, the police also recovered Robinson's gun, a .38 caliber Smith & Wesson revolver.***

Under R.C. 2903.11(A)(2), felonious assault, "[n]o person shall knowingly *** [c]ause or attempt to cause physical harm to another *** by means of a deadly weapon or dangerous ordnance.***

The jury ultimately acquitted Robinson of the murder count contained in Count 3, a violation of R.C. 2903.02(A), but found him guilty of felony murder, a violation of R.C. 2903.02(B), as contained in Count 2. The jury further found Robinson guilty of five counts of felonious assault, violations of R.C. 2903.11(A)(2) (Counts 4-8), and one count of discharging a firearm on or near prohibited premises, a violation of R.C. 2923.162(A)(3) (Count 10).***

Next, Robinson argues that the state failed to prove that he acted "knowingly." He contends that the evidence only established that he acted "recklessly." We disagree.

> A person acts knowingly, regardless of his purpose, when he is aware that his conduct will probably cause a certain result or will probably be of a certain nature. A person has knowledge of circumstances when he is aware that such circumstances probably exist.

R.C. 2901.22(B).

It is common knowledge that a firearm is an inherently dangerous instrumentality, use of which is reasonably likely to produce serious injury or death. *State v. Widner*, 69 Ohio St. 2d 257. This court has consistently held that "shooting a gun in a place where there is risk of injury to one or more persons supports the inference that the offender acted knowingly." *State v. Hunt*, 8th Dist. Cuyahoga No. 93080, 2010-Ohio-1419, Notably, "[e]ven firing a weapon randomly at victims arguably within range of the shooter is sufficient to demonstrate actual intent to cause physical harm." *State v. Phillips*, 75 Ohio App.3d 785.

Here, Robinson admitted to shooting his gun into the crowd of people. Further, the majority of the eyewitnesses who testified indicated that Robinson fired his gun several times into the crowd and that Bubbles "went down" after Robinson fired. The state presented, through both direct and circumstantial evidence, that Robinson fired his gun out of his car toward Bubbles.

As for Robinson's claim that his conduct was merely "reckless" because the crowd had already dispersed, we find his claim unsupported by the record. Based on the collective testimony of the eyewitnesses, a crowd of at least 15 to 20 people was congregated behind Robinson's car when he fired his gun into the crowd. While the scene was definitely chaotic, we cannot say that the evidence established that the crowd had dispersed. To the contrary, one witness testified that she was standing behind the car "in shock" when Robinson started firing toward the crowd. Accordingly, we find that there was sufficient evidence that Robinson acted "knowingly" rather than "recklessly" in firing his gun.

Having found that the state presented sufficient evidence to support the single count of felony murder, we overrule Robinson's first assignment of error.

Notes and Questions

1. If you were a juror in *State v. Robinson,* would you have found the defendant's conduct reckless even if you believed his story that he fired his gun after the crowd had dispersed? What facts would turn the defendant's mens rea from knowingly to recklessly?

2. Could the prosecution have proven that Robinson acted purposely? What facts would support a finding that Robinson purposely caused the death of Bubbles?

State v. Chambers, 2011-Ohio-4352

ABELE, J.

This is an appeal from an Adams County Common Pleas Court judgment of conviction and sentence. David Chambers, defendant below and appellee herein, was convicted of two counts of felony murder in violation of R.C. 2903.02(B), with the predicate offenses being felonious assault and child endangering, respectively. The trial court merged the two counts for sentencing purposes and sentenced appellant to serve fifteen years to life in prison.

During the early morning hours of September 15, 2009, appellant was home with his eighteen-month old daughter. Around 7:30 a.m., appellant went to the nearby apartment of Marla Striblen to summon help for the child. He told Striblen, who had training as a medical emergency technician, that he believed the child was having a seizure and asked if she would check on the child. Striblen obliged and when she entered the apartment, she observed appellant's sister holding the child. Striblen noticed that the child was unresponsive, with shallow breathing. Striblen asked what happened, and appellant stated that the child had fallen down steps. Striblen directed appellant to phone 9-1-1 and performed mouth-to-mouth resuscitation until medical responders arrived.

The child eventually was life-flighted to Cincinnati Children's Hospital. Sadly, the child did not survive her injuries. An autopsy reported that the child died from blunt force trauma to the head and the cause of death homicide.

The Adams County Grand Jury returned an indictment that charged appellant with: (1) felony murder in violation of R.C. 2903.02(B), as a result of committing or attempting to commit felonious assault; and (2) felony murder in violation of R.C. 2903.02(B), as a result of committing or attempting to commit endangering children. Appellant entered not guilty pleas.

At trial, Vickie Barr, the child's great-aunt, happened to be one of the first medical responders. Like Striblen, she explained that upon her arrival at the apartment, the child was unresponsive and had shallow breathing. Barr observed facial bruising and swelling. Barr stated that appellant told her that the child had fallen down the steps. Barr additionally stated that when she was at the hospital with appellant, appellant told her that "he was the one that killed his daughter." She also indicated that appellant felt that he may not have sought medical assistance in a timely manner.

Village of Manchester Police Chief Randy Walters testified that he interviewed appellant shortly after the child was transported to the hospital. Appellant informed Chief Walters that when he awoke that morning, between 5 and 6 a.m., he changed the child's diaper and the two went downstairs, where appellant played video games while the child had milk and fell asleep. At some point, appellant had to use the bathroom, which was located upstairs. He stated that while in the bathroom, he heard the child walking on the stairs and he then heard her falling down the stairs. Appellant left the bathroom and found the child at the bottom of the stairs. When he examined her, she cried for a second and then stiffened. Appellant then put her on the living room couch and went to Striblen's apartment for help.

Kenneth Dick, an investigator for the Adams County prosecutor's office, testified that he interviewed appellant the day after the child's alleged fall. Dick advised appellant that the doctors determined that appellant's story about the fall down the stairs did not explain the child's injuries. Appellant explained that when he observed the child at the bottom of the steps, he thought she was "faking," which made him mad, so he yelled at her to get up. He then stated that he moved her to the living room rug to attempt to wake her up, then ran her head under water, but his efforts didn't succeed. He stated that he then shook the child in an attempt to revive her and that while doing so, her head struck the carpeted floor. Appellant stated that approximately twenty minutes after the child fell, he summoned his sister for help.

Investigator Dick interviewed appellant again on September 17, 2009. At that time appellant stated that after he observed the child at the bottom of the stairs, he yelled "get the fuck up" and that he was upset because she did not respond. He stated that he shook her in an attempt to make her respond. Appellant explained that he was not certain whether the child's head struck the tile floor at the bottom of the steps. Later in the interview, he stated that her head hit the tile floor three times and that he could hear it hitting the floor. He then stated that he moved her to the living room rug and shook her stomach and chest, then grabbed her by the head and shook it. He stated that he "shook it up and down." Appellant explained that the child then started to stiffen, at which point he sought his sister's help. Appellant continually stated that he was only trying to wake up the child and that although he knew he was "too rough," he had not meant to hurt her.

Doctor Kathy Makaroff, a child abuse pediatric physician at Cincinnati Children's Hospital, testified that she examined the child on September 15, 2009 and reviewed the CAT scans. She stated that the first CAT scan showed brain swelling and bleeding on the top of the child's brain and on one side that extended into the middle of her brain. Doctor Makaroff stated that bleeding on top of the brain is most commonly caused by a "pretty significant injury." She further testified that the child had retinal hemorrhages—"some of the worst bleeding in the back of her eyes that [Makaroff] had ever seen." Makaroff explained that the child had puddles of blood in each eye that extended into the vitreous or the jelly of her eye. The doctor stated that a "very significant amount of trauma," caused both the bleeding in the brain and the retinal hemorrhages. She emphasized that not just any trauma would cause the injuries but, rather, "a very significant, and I'm going to stress that, very significant amount of trauma to cause both the bleeding in her brain and the retinal hemorrhages." Makaroff stated that the child's injuries were not consistent with a fall down the stairs but, instead, were consistent with "a very violent hitting" onto a tile or carpeted floor.

Karen Looman conducted the autopsy and found hemorrhaging surrounding the atlanto-occipital joint (the area between the base of the skull and the top of the spine), which would be caused by a whiplash-type injury or movement of the head back and forth. She also observed hemorrhaging and bleeding in the child's eyes. Looman stated that the injuries indicated "significant trauma to the head" resulting from a whipping or extreme shaking action. Looman testified that the child's injuries were not consistent with a fall, but, rather, an extreme trauma caused her injuries. Looman identified the cause of death as "traumatic brain injury due to blunt trauma to the head." Looman stated that the child's injuries were "extreme" and "lethal," and further explained that even if the injuries had occurred in the emergency room of a hospital, the child still would not have survived. She concluded that the child's manner of death resulted from homicide.

After the prosecution rested, appellant presented the testimony of an expert witness who opined that the child's injuries could have resulted from a fall down the stairs. Appellant also testified and denied that he possessed any intent to hurt or kill the child. He stated that he was "bothered" that the child would not respond to him and that he "panicked" when he saw her at the bottom of the steps. Appellant testified that his "first instinct" was to shake her to see if she would wake up. He stated that he was not certain whether the child's head hit the tile floor and that if it did, "it was just a stupid mistake." On cross-examination, appellant stated that the child's injury resulted from an accident.

After the court submitted the case to the jury, the jury posed several questions. The jury first requested a "copy of the elements from the prosecution." The court referred the jury to its instructions. The jury next asked whether it could "have a definition of violence as stated on verdict form two." The court responded, "child endangering *** is statutorily defined as an offense of violence." The jury then advised the court that it was "blocked by a question regarding the actual definition of the term violence, rather than child endangerment." The jury explained that it was debating the term violence, "in regards to its inclusion of intent within its definition." The court requested the jury to clarify its question and the jury responded: "*** we are requesting a definition of the term 'violence.' *** Further, we need to know if the term 'violence,' includes intent in any way." The court responded: "*** the term violence is not statutorily defined in Ohio Revised Code. In the absence of a statutory definition, you should employ the common ordinary meaning of words appearing in a statute. Webster's dictionary defines violence as, 'an exertion of physical force so as to injure or abuse.' " The court further instructed the jury that the term violence does not include intent.

The jury next requested to review the transcripts of the three doctors' testimony. The court advised the jury that it must rely upon its collective memory.

The jury then posed a multi-part question that requested: (1) the definition of felonious assault; (2) whether "attempting" includes intent; (3) whether the term "knowingly" includes intent; and (4) whether "aware" as used in knowingly includes intent. As to first three questions, the court referred the jury to the court's instructions. As to the last question, the court answered "no."

The jury subsequently sent another note to the court that stated: "We feel we have reached a standstill, in that the determination remains divided. Regarding verdict one, the voting remains at ten to two. Regarding verdict two, the voting remains at eleven to one. The obstacle *** seems to be based on wording of the verdict forms, that is, the concern of which forms designate intent. Please advise us regarding direction or further instruction."

The court brought the jury into the courtroom and asked: "[I]s the question or issue whether purposeful intent is an essential element that must be proven beyond a reasonable doubt in either or both counts of the indictment." The foreperson responded that she believed that to be the issue. The court then instructed: "Felony murder does not require purposeful intent pursuant to Revised Code Section 2903.02(B)." The foreperson then asked, "Intent is not an issue?" The court responded: "Felony murder does not require purposeful intent ***."

The jury then continued deliberating and subsequently posed the following question: "We question if the term knowingly or aware implies that the defendant was in control of his thoughts and actions, or if they mean that, prior to the incident he understood that the actions or conduct (in this case shaking) could produce, in this case, severe injury." The court directed the jury to the jury instructions' definition of knowingly.

The jury additionally asked if "finding [appellant] guilty/not guilty of verdict form 1 and 1A designate that we believe the action committed was an accident; that is—will we claim by signing that he did this on purpose." The court responded: "[D]epending on your verdict or verdicts, on verdict forms 1 and 1 A, you are only determining whether the State of Ohio did or did not prove beyond a reasonable doubt each and every essential element of the offense designated on verdict forms 1 and 1A. No more, no less."

On May 20, 2010, the jury found appellant guilty of both counts. The court merged the two counts for sentencing purposes and sentenced appellant to serve fifteen years to life in prison. This appeal followed.

I

In his first assignment of error, appellant asserts that his conviction is against the manifest weight of the evidence. He contends that the evidence shows that he attempted to "revive and resuscitate" the child and that his "lack of training and failure to maintain his composure" led to the child's death. He argues that the jury lost its way when it found that he acted either knowingly (to support the felony murder felonious assault count) or recklessly (to support the felony murder chid endangering count). Appellant contends that he did not knowingly cause serious physical harm to the child: "When he picked up his unconscious daughter, he was not aware that shaking her would cause the injuries described by the medical witnesses. He was attempting to revive or resuscitate his injured daughter." Appellant further argues that he did not act recklessly, but, instead, "acted deliberately in an effort to aid his daughter following her injury." In support of his argument, appellant points to the jury's questions to the court, which he asserts demonstrate that the jury "was struggling with the question of why [appellant] shook his daughter after she had fallen down the steps and appeared to be unconscious."***

In the case at bar, the predicate offenses are felonious assault and child endangering. R.C. 2903.11(A)(1) sets forth the offense of felonious assault and states: "No person shall knowingly do either of the following: (1) Cause serious physical harm to another or to another's unborn[.]" R.C. 2919.22(B) defines the offense of child endangering and states:

> (B) No person shall do any of the following to a child under
> eighteen years of age or a mentally or physically handicapped
> child under twenty-one years of age:
> (1) Abuse the child;
> (2) Torture or cruelly abuse the child;

In the case sub judice, appellant disputes whether the jury lost its way in finding that he acted "knowingly" or "recklessly."[8] He argues that he did not

---

[8] Although a mental state is not specified in the child endangering statute, the Ohio Supreme Court has stated that the appropriate mental state under R.C. 2919.22(B) is recklessness.

knowingly or recklessly cause serious physical harm to the child, but rather, simply attempted to revive the child.

R.C. 2901.22(B) defines "knowingly" as follows:

> (B) A person acts knowingly, regardless of his purpose, when he is aware that his conduct will probably cause a certain result or will probably be of a certain nature. A person has knowledge of circumstances when he is aware that such circumstances probably exist.

Recklessness is defined as follows:

> "A person acts recklessly when, with heedless indifference to the consequences, he perversely disregards a known risk that his conduct is likely to cause a certain result or is likely to be of a certain nature. A person is reckless with respect to circumstances when, with heedless indifference to the consequences, he perversely disregards a known risk that such circumstances are likely to exist."

R.C. 2901.22(C).

We further observe that proof of knowledge is also proof of recklessness. See *State v. Journey*, Scioto App. No. 09CA3270, 2010-Ohio-2555, ¶ 25. Thus, in the case at bar, if substantial competent and credible evidence shows that appellant acted knowingly, then such evidence also suffices to show that appellant acted recklessly. We therefore begin by analyzing whether the evidence shows that appellant acted knowingly.

To act "knowingly" is not to act "purposely," or with a specific intent to do the prohibited act.[9] See *State v. Huff* (2001), 145 Ohio App. 3d 555, 563 (stating

---

[9] In Katz & Gianelli, Ohio Criminal Law (2010 Ed.), Section 85.7, the authors further define the distinction between "knowingly" and "purposely" as follows:

> "An offender acts purposely when he or she intends the proscribed result. An offender acts knowingly when, although he or she may be indifferent to the result, the actor was nevertheless conscious that the unlawful result would occur. For example, one 'purposely' kills another when he discharges a firearm in the direction of the intended victim seeking to bring about his death. However, one would 'knowingly' kill another if she simply discharged the same firearm in the direction of the victim, not seeking to effect death (she may well have committed the act for the purpose of testing the weapon) but knowing full well that death would result. In other words, 'purpose' depends on an intended result, while 'knowledge' is consciousness that the proscribed result will occur."

that "'[k]nowingly' does not require the offender to have the specific intent to cause a certain result. That is the definition of 'purposely'"); see, also, *State v. Dixon*, Cuyahoga App. No. 82951, at ¶ 16, 2004-Ohio-2406. "Motive, purpose or mistake of fact is no significance" when determining whether a defendant acted knowingly. *State v. Wenger* (1979), 58 Ohio St. 2d 336, 339, fn. 3.

Because knowing precisely what existed in a defendant's mind at the time of the wrongful act may be impossible, the trier of fact may consider circumstantial evidence, i.e., the facts and circumstances surrounding the defendant's wrongful act, when determining if the defendant was subjectively "aware that his conduct will probably cause a certain result or will probably be of a certain nature." See *Huff,* 145 Ohio App. 3d 563, ("Whether a person acts knowingly can only be determined, absent a defendant's admission, from all the surrounding facts and circumstances, including the doing of the act itself."). Even when a defendant testifies as to his lack of knowledge, a trier of fact may disbelieve his testimony and examine the surrounding facts and circumstances to determine whether the defendant possessed "knowledge." Cf. *State v. Browning,* Highland App. No. 09CA36, 2010-Ohio-5417, ¶ 41 (stating that trier of fact may believe "all, some, or none" of a witness's testimony). Thus, a defendant's testimony regarding his lack of knowledge is not determinative.

In the case sub judice, we believe that the record contains substantial competent and credible evidence that appellant knowingly caused serious physical harm to the child. Appellant admitted to shaking the child and hitting her head at least three times on a tile floor. He admitted that he heard the child's head hitting the tile floor. The prosecution's expert medical witness stated that the child's injuries resulted from a "very significant trauma." The coroner stated that the child's injuries resulted from an extreme shaking motion. It is inconceivable that any person would not have realized that hitting a child's head on a tile floor would lead to serious physical harm. Even if appellant argues that he did not possess the specific intent to cause serious physical harm and intended only to "revive" the child, the facts nonetheless show, by any reasonable interpretation, that even the densest of individuals would be aware that slamming a child's head into a tile floor at least three times, continuing to shake the child's head, and then hitting the child's head on carpeted floor would probably result in serious physical harm. See *State v. Freeman,* Stark App. No.2010CA19, 2010-Ohio-5818, ¶ 16 (concluding that a defendant who violently strikes another individual already knocked to the ground "must be held to know that this action will probably cause serious physical harm to such person"). It simply defies belief to suggest that an individual would not be aware that hitting an eighteen-month old child's head into a tile floor at least three times, and yet again on a carpeted floor, and then shaking the child in an extreme manner, according to the state's witnesses, would cause the child serious physical harm. We recognize that appellant's remorse may indeed be genuine, but his actions nonetheless caused serious physical harm. His claims that he did not know that slamming the child's head into the floor and shaking the child "too rough" would probably result in serious physical harm are not worthy of belief.

We also recognize that the jury appeared to be concerned with appellant's intent. As we previously stated, however, a defendant need not possess a specific or purposeful intent to cause serious physical harm to a person in order to support a felony murder felonious assault conviction. Rather, the appropriate mental state is "knowingly," which does not require a specific intent to cause serious physical harm. Thus, although appellant attempts to demonstrate that the jury's questions regarding intent shows that it lost its way, the jury's questions actually demonstrate an initial misunderstanding of the elements. The jury apparently initially believed that appellant must possess the intent to harm or kill the child. Once the court corrected this misunderstanding, the jury returned guilty verdicts. Appellant may well have lacked an intent to kill his child, but the prosecution is not required to prove that he possessed the intent to kill. Rather, the prosecution is required to prove that appellant knowingly caused the child serious physical harm that proximately resulted in the child's death. Here, the prosecution presented substantial competent and credible evidence to demonstrate that appellant knowingly caused the child serious physical harm that proximately resulted in the child's death. Thus, appellant's conviction for felony murder as a result of committing felonious assault is not against the manifest weight of the evidence.

Moreover, because substantial competent and credible evidence establishes that appellant acted "knowingly," that same evidence also establishes that he acted "recklessly." Thus, appellant's conviction for felony murder as a result of committing child endangering is not against the manifest weight of the evidence.

Accordingly, based upon the foregoing reasons, we hereby overrule appellant's first assignment of error.

II

In his second assignment of error, appellant asserts that the trial court committed plain error by failing to give the jury an accident instruction. ***

When a defendant raises an accident defense, " 'the defendant denies any intent ***. He denies that he committed an unlawful act and says that the result is accidental.' " *State v. Poole* (1973), 33 Ohio St. 2d 18, 20, quoting 4 Ohio Jury Instructions (1970) 177, Section 411.01. The defense of accident is "tantamount to a denial that an unlawful act was committed; it is not a justification for the defendant's admitted conduct. *** Accident is an argument that supports a conclusion that the state has failed to prove the intent element of the crime beyond a reasonable doubt." *State v. Atterberry* (1997), 119 Ohio App. 3d 443, 447.

An accident is defined as an unfortunate event occurring casually or by chance. *State v. Brady* (1988), 48 Ohio App. 3d 41. Accident is defined as a "mere physical happening or event, out of the usual order of things and not reasonably (anticipated) (foreseen) as a natural or probable result of a lawful act." 4 Ohio Jury Instructions 75, Section 411.01(2). Moreover, "[a]n accidental result is one that occurs unintentionally and without any design or purpose to bring it about." *Id.*

In general, a trial court errs by failing to provide a jury instruction on the accident defense when the facts of a case warrant such an instruction. See *State v. Smiley,* Cuyahoga App. No. 03853, 2010-Ohio-4349, ¶ 16. "[I]f [, however,] the trial court's general charge was otherwise correct, it is doubtful that this error of omission would ever satisfy the tests for plain error or ineffective assistance of counsel." *Id.,* quoting *State v. Stubblefield* (Feb. 13, 1991), Hamilton App. No. C-890597, citing *State v. Sims* (1982), 3 Ohio App. 3d 331, 335. "This is so '[b]ecause the accident defense is not an excuse or justification for the admitted act,' and the effect of such an instruction 'would simply *** remind the jury that the defendant presented evidence to negate the requisite mental element,' such as purpose. In this regard, '[i]f the jury had credited [the defendant's] argument, it would have been required to find [the defendant] not guilty *** pursuant to the court's general instructions.'" *Id.,* quoting *State v. Johnson,* Franklin App. No. 06AP-878, 2007-Ohio-2792, ¶ 63 (internal citations omitted).

In *Smiley,* for example, the court held that in a prosecution for felonious assault, trial counsel's failure to request an accident instruction did not prejudice the defendant when the trial court properly instructed the jury regarding the requisite mental state of knowingly. The court reasoned that the court's knowingly instruction clearly informed the jurors that "knowing conduct *** goes beyond that considered to be an accident" and that "an accident instruction would not have added anything to the general instructions." *Id.* at ¶ 19. The court stated that if the jury had believed the defendant's accident claim, then it would have returned a not guilty verdict in accordance with the general instructions that the trial court did provide. *Id.*

In the case sub judice, the trial court properly instructed the jury regarding the applicable mental state, knowingly. By definition, the term "knowingly" means that the defendant's conduct was not an accident. By finding that appellant acted knowingly, the jury necessarily concluded that he was aware of his conduct and thus, that his conduct could not have simply been accidental. Thus, the court's knowingly instruction adequately conveyed to the jury the requisite mental state, and had the jury believed appellant's claimed accident theory at trial, it could not have found that he acted knowingly. We therefore see no danger that the jury wrongly convicted appellant due to the absence of an accident instruction.

Moreover, we do not believe that the facts adduced at trial support an accident instruction. Appellant admits that he shook the child and hit her head into the tile floor and the carpet. Thus, his admission reveals that his conduct was not simply an unfortunate event, but rather that he made a conscious decision to shake the child. Additionally, the child's resulting serious physical harm was not an unforeseen consequence of appellant's shaking and smacking of the child's head. Although the child's death may have arguably occurred unintentionally, the serious physical harm and her death was not an unforeseeable consequence of appellant's actions. In appellant's mind, the child's death may have been an accident because he did not intend to kill her. According to law, however, appellant's conduct was not an accident. The evidence shows that he was aware that his conduct would probably result in serious physical harm to the child, which negates any claim of accident.

Accordingly, based upon the foregoing reasons, we hereby overrule appellant's second assignment of error.***

JUDGMENT AFFIRMED.

3. Recklessly vs. Negligently

State v. Beasley, 1995 WL 453082

SUNDERMANN, J.

Defendant-appellant Rodney Beasley has taken this appeal from his conviction for aggravated vehicular homicide in the Hamilton County Court of Common Pleas.

On June 23, 1994, Mack Germany, along with his son and grandson, was proceeding west on I-275 with a U-Haul trailer. Germany noticed the load had come loose and pulled off into the emergency lane. His vehicle was entirely within the emergency lane. Germany left the truck to effect repairs.

Germany's son observed a truck, operated by appellant, approaching them partially in the emergency lane. Before he could shout a warning, appellant's truck struck and killed Germany.

On June 30, 1994, the grand jury of Hamilton County returned an indictment, with specifications, charging appellant with aggravated vehicular homicide for recklessly causing the death of Mack Germany while operating a motor vehicle, in violation of R.C. 2309.06(A). Following a trial to a jury, appellant was convicted of aggravated vehicular homicide. On appeal, appellant advances two assignments of error.

Appellant first claims the trial court erred in refusing to instruct the jury on the lesser-included offense of vehicular homicide. For the reasons that follow, we agree.

In *State v. Campbell* (1991), 74 Ohio App. 3d 352, we held that a criminal defendant is entitled to an instruction on a lesser-included offense if: (1) the offense on which the instruction is requested is lesser than and included within the charged offense under the analysis set forth in *State v. Deem* (1988), 40 Ohio St. 3d 205; and (2) the jury could reasonably conclude that the evidence supports a finding of guilt on the lesser offense and not the greater offense. R.C. 2945.74; *State v. Thomas* (1988), 40 Ohio St. 3d 213.

R.C. 2903.06, which defines aggravated vehicular homicide, reads in part:

> (A) No person, while operating or participating in the operation of a motor vehicle, motorcycle, snowmobile, locomotive, watercraft, or aircraft, shall recklessly cause the death of another.

R.C. 2903.07, which defines vehicular homicide, reads in part:

> (A) No person, while operating or participating in the operation of a motor vehicle, motorcycle, snowmobile, locomotive, watercraft, or aircraft: shall negligently cause the death of another.

These statutes proscribe identical conduct, except for the required culpable mental state: "recklessly" for aggravated vehicular homicide, "negligently" for vehicular homicide. These mental states are defined in R.C 2901.22 as follows:

> (C) A person acts recklessly when, with heedless indifference to the consequences, he perversely disregards a known risk that his conduct is likely to cause a certain result or is likely to be of a certain nature. A person is reckless with respect to circumstances when, with heedless indifference to the consequences, he perversely disregards a known risk that such circumstances are likely to exist.
> (D) A person acts negligently when, because of a substantial lapse from due care, he fails to perceive or avoid a risk that his conduct may cause a certain result or may be of a certain nature. A person is negligent with respect to circumstances when, because of a substantial lapse from due care, he fails to perceive or avoid a risk that such circumstances may exist.

It is beyond cavil that, under the test enunciated in *State v. Deem,* upon these facts, vehicular homicide is a lesser included offense of aggravated vehicular homicide. See *State v. Chippendale* (1990), 52 Ohio St. 3d 118.

The next step of our analysis requires us to review the evidence adduced at trial to determine if the jury could reasonably conclude that the evidence supports a finding of guilt on the lesser offense and not the greater offense. There was no evidence presented that appellant was either speeding or under the influence of alcohol or drugs. Other drivers testified that appellant was weaving from side to side before the accident and was driving in the emergency lane before striking Germany. Appellant claimed to have been checking his load constantly to see if it had shifted. He applied his brakes before striking Germany. He stopped his vehicle and returned to the scene of the accident.

We conclude that the jury reasonably could have determined from the circumstances of the accident that appellant acted not with a heedless indifference to the consequences and a perverse disregard for a known risk, but rather with a substantial lapse from due care, and failed to perceive or avoid the risk of striking a motorist stopped in the emergency lane; that is, the jury could reasonably have concluded that appellant acted negligently and not recklessly in causing the death of Germany. Thus, we hold that appellant was entitled to a jury instruction on the lesser-included offense of vehicular homicide. The first assignment of error is sustained.

Appellant's second assignment of error, in which he challenges the manifest weight of the evidence adduced to support his conviction for aggravated vehicular homicide, is rendered moot by our disposition of this case in the first assignment of error. App. R. 12(A)(1)(c).

Therefore, the judgment of the trial court, finding the appellant guilty of aggravated vehicular homicide, in violation of R.C. 2903.06, is reversed and this cause is remanded for a new trial.

PAINTER, J., concurring separately.

Many cases present difficult or at least arguable issues of law; this case is not one of those. It is so manifestly clear that the proper instruction was required to be given to the jury that I am baffled, to say the least, by the refusal of the trial judge to follow the law. Now, because of this refusal, this case must be reversed, perhaps putting the victim's survivors, the prosecution, the defense and the court through a retrial of this case----at a cost in human, as well as financial terms. This unfortunate result could have been avoided by the simple expedient of following the law in the first place.

C. Transferred Intent

State v. Mullins, 76 Ohio App. 3d 633 (1996)

TYACK, Judge.

Ten-year-old Jasper Moffitt was with his parents near the family's store on the east side of Columbus when shots rang out. A bullet struck Jasper in the head and he died from the wound.

The ensuing police investigation indicated that Allen Brian Mullins had fired the fatal shot while shooting at third parties in a white Cadillac over a city block away.

Mullins was indicted on a charge of aggravated murder with a gun specification. Ultimately, a jury trial was conducted and Mullins was convicted of murder with a gun specification. Accordingly, he was sentenced to a term of imprisonment of fifteen years to life for the murder conviction. He received an additional sentence of three years' actual incarceration to be served prior to the indefinite term because he was found to have used a firearm in committing the murder.

Mullins ("appellant") has timely appealed, assigning a single error for our consideration:

"The evidence does not support appellant's conviction for murder. Viewed in the manner most favorable to the prosecution, the evidence at best supports conviction of the lesser-included offense of involuntary manslaughter and leaves in doubt identification of the defendant as the perpetrator."

Addressing the latter part of the assignment of error first, the testimony as to identity presented to the trial court clearly met the standard for sufficiency of evidence set forth in *State v. Jenks* (1991), 61 Ohio St. 3d 259. In *Jenks,* the Supreme Court of Ohio held at paragraph two of the syllabus:

"*** The relevant inquiry is whether, after viewing the evidence in a light most favorable to the prosecution, any rational trier of fact could have found the essential elements of the crime proven beyond a reasonable doubt. ***" (Citation omitted.)

Testimony at trial indicated that appellant was seen in possession of a silver nine millimeter pistol on the day Jasper died. Appellant was alleged to have said that he was going to kill "the Detroit dudes." Appellant supposedly saw a white Cadillac in the neighborhood, indicated that it contained the men from Detroit, and began firing at the white Cadillac. After the shooting, a woman was heard crying out down the street that her baby had been shot. Appellant then fled and later concealed himself from the police, even to the point of attempting to hide his identity when arrested.

To the extent that the assignment of error alleges insufficient proof of identification as the perpetrator, the assignment of error is overruled.

The first portion of the assignment of error alleges that the evidence was insufficient to establish a conviction for murder, as opposed to involuntary manslaughter.

"Murder" is defined in R.C. 2903.02(A) as follows:

> "No person shall purposely cause the death of another."

"Involuntary manslaughter" is defined in R.C. 2903.04(A) thus:

> "No person shall cause the death of another as a proximate result of the offender's committing or attempting to commit a felony."

The least crime appellant could be found guilty of committing is involuntary manslaughter. He apparently at least was knowingly attempting to do physical harm with a deadly weapon to the persons in the white Cadillac. Thus, he was guilty of felonious assault, which is defined in R.C. 2903.11(A) as follows:

> "No person shall knowingly:
> " ***
> "(2) Cause or attempt to cause physical harm to another by means of a deadly weapon or dangerous ordnance, as defined in section 2923.11 of the Revised Code."

As a direct and proximate result of the felonious assault, Jasper Moffitt was struck and killed by a stray bullet-hence, the observation above that appellant was at least guilty of involuntary manslaughter, an aggravated felony of the first degree.

The more difficult question is whether appellant is guilty of purposely causing the death of Jasper Moffitt, thereby making him guilty of the greater offense of murder. No reason exists to believe that appellant wanted to kill a ten-year-old child, as opposed to the "Detroit dudes" in the white Cadillac who he apparently believed were gunning for him. However, appellant may still be guilty of murder if the doctrine of transferred intent is applicable.

The doctrine of transferred intent indicates that where an individual is attempting to harm one person and as a result accidentally harms another, the intent to harm the first person is transferred to the second person and the individual attempting harm is held criminally liable as if he both intended to harm and did harm the same person.

The doctrine has been applied for many years in Ohio but has apparently been removed by the legislature from application in aggravated murder cases. In revising R.C. 2903.01(D), the legislature mandated:

"No person shall be convicted of aggravated murder unless he is specifically found to have intended to cause the death of another. *** [T]he jury *** is to consider all evidence introduced by the prosecution to indicate the person's intent and by the person to indicate his lack of intent in determining whether the person specifically intended to cause the death of the person killed ***."

The legislature did *not* remove the doctrine of transferred intent from application in determining the absence or presence of purpose to kill in murder, as opposed to aggravated murder, convictions. The limitation of the legislative reference to aggravated murder implies to a point that the legislature intended for the doctrine of transferred intent to have applicability in situations involving lesser crimes such as murder.

The applicable case law does not indicate that transferred intent applies only **772 to victims whose presence is known to the perpetrator. In fact, the case law implies that the proximity of the victim and the knowledge of the perpetrator about the ultimate victim are immaterial. Thus, in *Wareham v. State* (1874), 25 Ohio St. 601, 607, the Supreme Court of Ohio stated:

"*** The intent to kill and the malice followed the blow, and if another was killed the crime is complete ***. The purpose and malice with which the blow was struck is not changed in any degree by the circumstance that it did not take effect upon the person at whom it was aimed. The purpose and malice remain, and if the person struck is killed, the crime is as complete as though the person against whom the blow was directed had been killed, the lives of all persons being equally sacred in the eye of the law, and equally protected by its provisions. A blow given with deliberate and premeditated malice and with the intent and purpose to kill another, if it accomplish its purpose, can not be said to have been given without malice and unintentionally, although it did not take effect upon the person against whom it was directed ***."

Recent case law has even allowed transferred intent to be the basis for transferring prior calculation and design from one victim or intended victim to the victim who actually dies, even though the latter victim's death was not originally contemplated. See *State v. Solomon* (1981), 66 Ohio St. 2d 214, and *State v. Sowell* (1988), 39 Ohio St. 3d 322.

Given the action of the legislature and the existing case law regarding transferred intent, we are bound to hold that transferred intent is the appropriate legal theory to apply in assessing the sufficiency of the evidence. Appellant's apparent intention to kill one or more of the occupants of the white Cadillac, combined with the actual death of Jasper Moffitt resulting from the gunshots fired in an attempt to kill the occupants of the car, presents sufficient proof of the elements of a charge of murder.

The first part of the assignment of error is also overruled.

The assignment of error having been overruled *in toto,* the judgment and sentence of the Franklin County Court of Common Pleas is affirmed.

Judgment affirmed.

D. Strict Liability

Strict liability crimes have no mens rea requirement for some, if not all, elements of the crime. Strict liability crimes are generally reserved for low-level offenses that involve public health, safety, or welfare. See, e.g., *United States v. Park.* However, this is not always the case. For example, the chapter on sexual assault discusses statutory rape, which many jurisdictions treat as a strict liability crime at least with respect to the defendant's knowledge of the victim's age.

By removing the mens rea requirement and punishing solely for fulfilling the actus reus, it is hoped that criminal defendants will take extra precautions when engaging in activity that implicates strict liability. This removal of mens rea, however, leads to the major criticism of strict liability crimes—defendants are convicted without moral blameworthiness.

One of the major questions with strict liability crimes is whether the lack of mens rea was an intentional or unintentional act by the legislature. *State v. Collins* illustrates the difficulties courts have in deciding whether to read in a mens rea requirement for an offense when the statutory language of the crime and the intent of the legislators are less than clear.

State v. Collins, 89 Ohio St. 3d 524 (2000)

The parties have argued this case as presenting the legal issue whether the crime set forth in R.C. 2919.21(B), *i.e.,* failure to pay in accordance with a court order of child support, requires the state to prove a specific *mens rea.* The state asserts, as its sole proposition of law, that "R.C. 2919.21(B) is a strict-liability offense," thereby challenging the conclusion of the court of appeals that the state was required to prove recklessness on the part of Collins as an element of the crime charged of him in the second count of the indictment.

The second count filed against appellee by the grand jury charged him with a violation of the current version of R.C. 2919.21(B), which reads:

> No person shall abandon, or fail to provide support as established by a court order to, another person whom, by court order or decree, the person is legally obligated to support.

The court of appeals found that this statute does not specify the degree of culpability the state must prove beyond a reasonable doubt, and therefore applied R.C. 2901.21(B), which provides:

> When the section defining an offense does not specify any degree of culpability, and plainly indicates a purpose to impose strict criminal liability for the conduct described in such section, then culpability is not required for a person to be guilty of the offense. When the section neither specifies culpability nor plainly indicates a purpose to impose strict liability, recklessness is sufficient culpability to commit the offense.

The court of appeals determined that the legislature did not specify a mental element for culpability in R.C. 2919.21, or plainly indicate a purpose to impose strict liability. It concluded that the state therefore had the burden to prove that appellee recklessly failed to provide adequate support to his minor children as mandated by a court order, in order to demonstrate a violation of R.C. 2919.21(B). The court of appeals held contrary to the trial court on this issue, as the trial court expressly struck the word "reckless" from the second count of the indictment, and declined to instruct the jury that recklessness was an element of R.C. 2919.21(B).

However, the focus of the parties in the court of appeals was on Collins's assertion of prosecutorial misconduct. His argument focused solely on the ground that the prosecutor's statements included what he asserted to be unfair comments implying that the burden of proving a criminal violation had shifted from the state to the defendant. As discussed earlier, the trial court appropriately overruled those objections. The state did not argue that the prosecutor's statements were legitimate because R.C. 2919.21(B) was a strict-liability offense.

We acknowledge the convincing public policy arguments presented by the state and *amicus* Ohio Prosecuting Attorneys' Association in support of the proposition that failure to follow a court-ordered child support order should be a strict liability offense. However, the General Assembly itself has established the test for determining strict criminal liability in R.C. 2901.21(B). That statute provides that where a statute defining a criminal offense fails to expressly specify a mental culpability element, *e.g.*, negligence, recklessness, or intentional conduct, proof of a violation of the criminal provision requires a showing of recklessness, absent a plain indication in the statute of a legislative purpose to impose strict criminal liability. R.C. 2901.21(B). It is not enough that the General

Assembly in fact intended imposition of liability without proof of mental culpability. Rather the General Assembly must plainly indicate that intention in the language of the statute. There are no words in R.C. 2919.21(B) that do so.

Were we to accept the state's argument that public policy considerations weigh in favor of strict liability, thereby justifying us in construing R.C. 2919.21(B) as imposing criminal liability without a demonstration of any *mens rea,* we would be writing language into the provision which simply is not there—language which the General Assembly could easily have included, but did not. Cf. *State v. Young* (1988), 37 Ohio St. 3d 249, providing that "[n]o person shall," *e.g.*, possess or view, any material or performance involving a minor who is in a state of nudity, requires showing of recklessness); *State v. McGee* (1997), 79 Ohio St. 3d 193, which provides that "no person, who is the parent *** of a child under eighteen years of age ***, shall" endanger that child, requires showing of recklessness). Clearly, society has just as compelling a need to protect children from sexual exploitation and child endangerment as it does to ensure payment of court-ordered child support obligations.

Moreover, we find more than sufficient evidence in the record in the case at bar to support a jury finding of recklessness. The state most commonly proves criminal intent through circumstantial evidence. Where, after notice and opportunity to be heard, a court order is issued mandating a person to submit child support payments to a specific agency of government, and that agency shows no record of any payments having been received from that person over a period of many years, a circumstantial inference arises that the person was aware of the obligation to pay and yet did not do so. Payment in accordance with such an obligation is an either-or proposition—the obligor either takes intentional actions to pay, or does not. Where no payments reach the agency over a period of many years, it may be inferred that the obligor took no action to ensure payment, and, in fact, intended not to pay. Accordingly, where no evidence is presented to counter that inference, such as evidence of mistake or misdirected payments, a jury has evidence before it sufficient to establish a culpable mental state of at least recklessness, beyond a reasonable doubt. The fact that a defendant may then realistically find himself with a burden of producing evidence to counter that inference does not mean that the ultimate burden of proof has shifted to the defendant.

Such an inference of recklessness is reinforced in the case at bar by the fact that, subsequent to the 1990 wage assignment executed by Collins, a second lump-sum judgment was entered against Collins in 1994 totaling nearly $137,000 in child support and spousal support arrearages. Clearly at that time Collins was on notice that the child support agency was not receiving child support payments from his employer pursuant to his signing a wage assignment authorization form in 1990. Yet the agency received no payments whatsoever from 1991 through the 1997 date specified in the indictment. The evidence presented by the state is more than sufficient to support a finding of at least a reckless failure to comply with the 1990 and 1994 court orders.

The trial was free of reversible error. The judgment of the court of appeals is reversed, and the cause is remanded for reinstatement of Collins's conviction on the second count of the indictment.

Judgment reversed, and cause remanded.

LUNDBERG STRATTON, J., concurring in part and dissenting in part.

I concur with the majority as to the lack of prosecutorial misconduct and that the evidence was more than sufficient to prove recklessness. However, I respectfully dissent with its conclusion that recklessness is the necessary *mens rea* to establish a violation of R.C. 2919.21(B).

The majority declines to impose strict liability in R.C. 2919.21(B) on the basis that "[t]here are no words in R.C. 2919.21(B) that do so." The majority relies upon R.C. 2901.21(B), which provides that where a statute does not specify the degree of culpability but "plainly indicates a purpose to impose strict criminal liability," then culpability is not required to find a person guilty of the offense. I believe the majority's analysis should also have considered the legislative intent and public policy behind the statute to determine whether strict liability for the conduct described in R.C. 2919.21(B) was intended. See *State v. Schlosser* (1997), 79 Ohio St. 3d 329.

On numerous occasions, this court has determined that strict liability applies in a statute that defines a criminal offense despite the statute's silence on the applicable mental state. See *Schlosser* (strict liability imposed under the RICO statute, R.C. 2923.32[A][1], despite the lack of specific *mens rea* language); *Greeley v. Miami Valley Maintenance Contractors, Inc.* (1990), 49 Ohio St. 3d 228 (strict liability imposed for discharging an employee on the basis of an order to withhold child support from employee's paycheck in violation of R.C. 3113.213[D]); and *State v. Wac* (1981), 68 Ohio St. 2d 84 (strict liability imposed for gambling under R.C. 2915.03[A][1] but not R.C. 2915.03[A][2] because of language differentiation).

Likewise, appellate courts have imposed strict liability, despite the absence of a specific statement of *mens rea*. See *State v. Larbi (June 21, 1999), Stark App. No. 1998CA00192, unreported, 1999 WL 437007* (strict liability standard imposed for violation of R.C. 4301.69, selling alcohol to a minor); *State v. Hull* (1999), 133 Ohio App. 3d 401 (strict liability standard imposed for violation of R.C. 3599.12, illegally voting in Ohio elections); *State v. Donnelly (Feb. 2, 1999), Ashland App. No. 98COA01272, unreported, 1999 WL 172772* (strict liability standard imposed for violation of R.C. 959.13[A][1], which states that "no person shall" cruelly treat an animal); *Cleveland v. Criss (Dec. 10, 1998), Cuyahoga App. No. 72862, unreported, 1998 WL 855630* (strict liability standard imposed for violation of city ordinance, which states that no person with a temporary driving permit shall drive without a licensed driver); *State v. Workman* (1998), 126 Ohio App. 3d 422 (strict liability standard imposed for violation of R.C. 3599.12, which states that "no person shall" impersonate another in order to vote); *State v. Shaffer* (1996), 114 Ohio App. 3d 97 (strict liability standard imposed for violation of R.C. 1721.21[B], which states that "no person shall" operate or continue to operate a cemetery without establishing or maintaining an endowment care fund); *State v. Harr* (1992), 81 Ohio App. 3d 244 (strict liability standard imposed for violation of R.C. 4507.02[B][1], which states that "no person shall" drive with a suspended license); *State v. Cheraso* (1988), 43 Ohio App. 3d 221 (strict liability standard imposed for violation of R.C. 4301.69, which states that "no person shall" sell beer to a minor); *State v. Grimsley* (1982), 3 Ohio App. 3d 265 (strict liability for violation of R.C. 4511.19, driving under the influence).

The majority cites *State v. Young (1988)*, 37 Ohio St. 3d 249, and *State v. McGee (1997)*, 79 Ohio St. 3d 193, in support of its conclusion. However, the statutes at issue in those cases do not evidence an intent to impose strict liability. Violation of those statutes could arise in a perfectly innocent situation, *i.e.*, viewing a photograph of a child in a bathtub, or failing to prevent a child from running into the street. Where an innocent or negligent act *could* subject a parent to criminal liability, recklessness should be required in order to establish a violation of the statute. This case, however, involves a much different scenario, the violation of a *court order.*

In *Schlosser,* this court looked to the statutory language, the legislative intent, and public policy to determine whether the statute was intended to impose strict liability for the conduct described. *Schlosser*, 79 Ohio St. 3d at 331-332. I believe that the General Assembly clearly intended there to be strict liability for a violation of the conduct proscribed in R.C. 2919.21(B). R.C. 2919.21(A), in existence for decades, imposes criminal liability for failing to provide "adequate" support to one's obligees. In July 1996, the General Assembly passed a law that added a new section to address the failure to provide support as already established by court order. 146 Ohio Laws, Part VI, 10862. R.C. 2919.21(B) states: "*No person shall* abandon, or *fail to provide support as established* by a court order to, another person whom, *by court order or decree,* the person is legally obligated to support." (Emphasis added.)

In addition, newly enacted R.C. 2919.21(D) creates an affirmative defense when the failure to provide support established by court order under section (B) is due to lack of ability or means. These statutory changes remove the state's burden to prove the inadequacy of the support when a court order has already established the legal obligation to pay. The state need only establish the violation of a court order. It is apparent that R.C. 2919.21(B) expands the scope of criminal liability beyond what is "adequate" support, and that the new affirmative defense recognizes situations where the obligor lacks that means or ability to pay. These changes plainly indicate a purpose to impose strict liability as the culpable mental state for a violation of R.C. 2919.21(B).

In this case, the divorce resolved issues of responsibility, income, and needs of the child, and the final decree established the amount of the father's child support obligation. When he failed to follow that court order and arrearages had grown within four years to more than $136,000, the state was called upon to obtain yet another court order to resolve support issues and arrearages. At that time, the father was both negligent *and* reckless in his failure to pay support, necessitating the state to take additional action based on the existing court order that already placed upon the father an *affirmative duty* to pay support.

The General Assembly intentionally differentiated between the liability imposed under R.C. 2919.21(A) and that for *disobeying a court order* under R.C. 2919.21(B). The state had already obtained a court order against the father for arrearages and proven that he was negligent and reckless and perhaps willful in failing to pay child support. The state should not have to prove its case again.

The plain language of the statute also implies the application of strict liability. The use of the operative words "no person shall" clearly indicates the General Assembly's intent to impose strict liability. *Schlosser.* There is no doubt that the defendant understood his duties and obligations under the court order. The court order, part of the foundation of any orderly society, demands compliance.

An offense designed to protect the public health, safety, or welfare need not contain intent as a necessary element. *Morissette v. United States (1952), 342 U.S. 246.* "While such offenses do not threaten the security of the state in the manner of treason, they may be regarded as offenses against its authority, for their occurrence impairs the efficiency of controls deemed essential to the social order as presently constituted. In this respect, whatever the intent of the violator, the injury is the same, and the consequences are injurious or not according to fortuity.

Hence, legislation applicable to such offenses, as a matter of policy, does not specify intent as a necessary element. The accused, if he does not will the violation, usually is in a position to prevent it with no more care than society might reasonably expect and no more exertion than it might reasonably exact from one who assumed his responsibilities." *Id.,* 342 U.S. at 256.

Clearly, this statute was designed to protect our most vulnerable population, our children, and we can reasonably expect a parent to assume his or her responsibility to support that child.

Finally, public policy supports such an interpretation. Strict enforcement of child support obligations "clearly serves the public purpose of advancing the welfare of children by enforcing a child's right to be supported by his parents, fostering parental responsibility and parental involvement with the child, and preventing the child and custodial parent from having to turn to welfare." *In re Lappe* (1997), 176 Ill.2d 414.

A failure to support one's child is also morally wrong and ultimately imposes the burden of support upon the public. The custodial parent carries the entire financial responsibility of support and the state is faced with prosecuting the failure to adhere to a court order *already* in place. The state need not have to prove one's state of mind for failing to obey a court order. As the Illinois Supreme Court explained:

> The focus of this legislation is on *effective* enforcement. The provisions simply create a mechanism whereby custodial parents of dependent children can, *with minimal time and expense,* obtain assistance with the paperwork involved in child support enforcement, with locating the person obligated to pay support and with taking the necessary steps, including judicial action, to ensure that the proper amount of money is collected. (Emphasis added in part.)

In re Lappe, 176 Ill.2d at 432.

The state proved this defendant's recklessness. However, the state prosecutes hundreds of persons under this section. The next case may not be so easy. Recklessness is a more difficult standard to prove. In the event of nonpayment of child support, must a parent gather evidence of "recklessness" before the state will assist in enforcement? If a defendant is negligent in failing to abide by the order, but not reckless, is there criminal liability? Or do we merely warn the defendant to try harder and to pay attention to court orders?

The answer is simple. If a court order requires a parent to pay child support, that parent must obey it unless the parent proves that he or she is financially *unable* to do so. If the parent does not pay the court-ordered child support, the parent is guilty of violating R.C. 2919.21(B). The mere fact of nonpayment should be sufficient to establish culpability. Therefore, I respectfully dissent from the majority's conclusion on *mens rea*.

Notes and Questions

1. Why do you think the state legislature would "require a showing of recklessness, absent a plain indication in the statute of legislative purpose to impose strict criminal liability"?

2. In *State v. Collins*, the court writes, "proof of a violation of the criminal provision requires a showing of recklessness, absent a plain indication in the statute of a legislative purpose to impose strict criminal liability." What type of

language is required to provide the average person "plain indication" that the crime is one of strict liability? According to the dissent, "appellate courts have imposed strict liability, despite the absence of a specific statement of mens rea."

3. After reading *Collins*, are you confident that you can read a statute and determine whether it imposes strict liability? How might you re-write the statute in *Collins* to make it clear that strict liability is to be imposed?

4. Why do you think the majority in *Collins* was hesitant to apply strict liability?

5. Although the court ultimately disagreed with the prosecutor's argument, it still reinstated the defendant's conviction. What reasoning did the court rely on to reinstate the defendant's conviction?

E. Specific and General Intent

As stated previously, in addition to relying on a number of different adverbs to describe a defendant's mens rea, common law judges categorized criminal offenses as either specific or general intent crimes. There have been a variety of definitions applied to both "specific intent" and "general intent." This is because these definitions are not codified, and courts vary in their interpretation of the terms. The most common definition of specific intent is as follows: a crime that requires a mental state above and beyond what is necessary to commit the actus reus.

Specific intent is probably best understood by looking at particular crimes. For example, burglary, at common law, was the breaking and entering of the dwelling house of another at night with the intent to commit a felony therein. Burglary is a specific intent crime because the defendant must go beyond the initial conduct of trespass and breaking and entering. The defendant must intend to commit a felony therein. The next category of specific intent crimes involves the defendant intending for his conduct to have some future impact. An example here would be the crime of hindering prosecution. This crime involves the defendant giving the police misinformation with the intention that the misinformation hinder or prevent the police from apprehending or investigating another person. The third category of specific intent crimes is defendant's knowledge of a specific element of the crime. The example here is receiving stolen property. To be convicted of this crime, the defendant must know that the property in question is stolen.

In contrast, general intent crimes only require that the defendant have knowledge of the actus reus and does not require that the criminal defendant intended any specific result. Another difference arises with what the prosecution has to prove. With specific intent crimes, the prosecution must introduce independent evidence of what the defendant intended, while with general intent crimes, the defendant's intent can be inferred from his conduct. Some view general intent crimes as the residual category where all crimes go that do not fit any other category. The distinctions between specific and general intent crimes, while not always clear, are important because certain defenses available to specific intent crimes like intoxication may be unavailable for general intent crimes. Some believe that the real reason for creating the labels of specific and general intent and making a distinction between them was to limit the availability of certain defenses.

Eric Johnson, *Rethinking the Presumption of Mens Rea* 47 WFLR 769 (2012)

To explain, the terms "general intent" and "specific intent" do not describe mental states, or at least they do not describe mental states in the way that terms like intentionally, purposely, knowingly, recklessly, negligently, willfully, and maliciously do. When a legislature defines the mental state for an element, it uses terms like purposely, knowingly, recklessly, and so on. It never uses the terms general intent and specific intent. Nor, in most places, do judges use the terms general intent and specific intent in instructing juries. Rather, they use terms like purposely, knowingly, recklessly, and so on.

If general and specific intent are not the names of mental states, though, what are they? The answer is that whether a particular mental state counts as a general intent or a specific intent will depend not just on the nature of the mental state itself but also on the kind of objective element to which it is attached. The mental state of "intentionally," for example, sometimes will count as a general intent and sometimes will count as a specific intent, depending on what objective element the mental state attaches to. When the mental state of intentionally attaches to an element that is designed to measure the harm from the offense — say, the element of serious bodily injury in the crime of aggravated assault — the mental state of intentionally will usually be classified as a specific intent. When the mental state of intentionally attaches instead to an element that is designed to measure the risk posed by an offense — say, the element of discharge of a firearm — it will be classified as a general intent.

Granted, this isn't what the courts actually say when they articulate the distinction between general and specific intent. What the courts typically say is that a crime is a general-intent offense if it requires the government to prove only that "the defendant intended to do the proscribed act," and that, by contrast, a crime is a specific-intent offense if it requires the government to prove that the defendant also intended to "achieve some additional consequence." But the only way to make sense of this distinction between an "additional consequence" and "the proscribed conduct" is to differentiate the (1) the social harm that is the statute's ultimate target from (2) earlier events in the causal sequence leading up to the social harm, whose significance lies in their contribution to the risk.

To illustrate, imagine a case where the defendant uses a firearm to kill another person. The event can be broken down into several steps: first, the shooter squeezes the trigger of the firearm; second, the firearm goes off, sending a bullet in the direction of the victim; third, the bullet strikes the victim's body; and fourth, the damage inflicted by the bullet causes the victim's death. The act of squeezing the trigger clearly seems to be part of the "act," rather than an "additional consequence." And the last event in the causal sequence--the death of the victim--is clearly an "additional consequence." (Courts uniformly classify intent-to-kill homicide as a specific intent crime.) But what of the two events that mediate the causal connection between the squeezing of the trigger and the death of the victim? Are they "additional consequences" or just part of "the proscribed act"?

At first glance, the discharge of the firearm might appear to be an "additional consequence." In causal terms, the discharge of the firearm is a consequence of squeezing the trigger. What is more, it appears to be a truly separate or "additional" event. After all, sometimes pulling the trigger of a gun causes a gun to discharge, and sometimes it does not.

But courts have said that the discharge of a firearm does not qualify as an "additional consequence." Consider, for example, California decisions interpreting a state statute that prohibits "discharg[ing] a firearm in a grossly negligent manner." The California courts have held that this statute requires proof that the defendant actually intended that the firearm go off; it is not enough that he intended to squeeze the trigger. Nevertheless, the courts have said that this statute defines a "general intent crime, because . . . its mental state consists of an intent to do the act that causes the harm." Thus, the discharge of the firearm cannot be an "additional consequence" for purposes of the definition of specific intent.

Nor, in our original illustration, is the bullet's initial contact with the victim's body "an additional consequence." Granted, in purely causal terms, the bullet's contact with the victim's body plainly is a consequence both of the squeezing of the trigger and the firearm's discharge. What is more, this initial contact appears to be a truly separate event; the discharge of a firearm sometimes causes a bullet to strike another person's body, and it sometimes does not. Nevertheless, courts uniformly have held--in interpreting statutes that define the crime of battery--that an intent to bring about physical contact with another person's body is a form of general intent, not specific intent. This means that the bullet's initial contact with the other person's body cannot be considered an "additional consequence" for purposes of our definition of specific intent.

So what's going on here? All three of the events that followed the squeezing of the trigger--the discharge of the firearm, the bullet's initial contact with the victim's body, and the death of the victim—appear to be consequences of the conduct. Why is only one of these events—the death of the victim--treated as an "additional consequence" for purposes of the definition of specific intent? The answer, as I have said, lies in the distinction between (1) the ultimate harm at which the statute is targeted and (2) the intermediate events that contribute to the risk of that harm occurring. In our hypothetical shooting, only the death of the victim is the kind of harm at which criminal statutes are targeted. Statutes that proscribe, say, the intentional discharge of a firearm are not ultimately targeted at the discharge of firearms. These statutes proscribe the discharge of firearms not because the discharge of a firearm is harmful in itself but because the discharge of a firearm creates or enhances a risk of death or physical injury.

There are other facets to the complex distinction between general and specific intent. But this facet defines the real content of the distinction. When courts say that an offense will qualify as a specific-intent offense if it requires proof that the defendant intended to "achieve some additional consequence" beyond "the proscribed act," what they really mean (usually) is that an offense will qualify as a specific-intent offense if it requires proof that the defendant intended to bring about the social harm at which the statute is targeted. And when the courts say that an offense will qualify as general-intent offense if it requires only proof that the defendant intended to do "the prohibited act," what they really mean is that an offense will qualify as a general-intent offense if it requires only proof that the defendant intended to do something, or to cause something to exist or occur, that creates a risk or increases the magnitude of the risk.

F. Mistake of Fact and Mistake of Law

1. Mistake of Fact

United States v. Oney Langley, 33 M.J. 278 (1991)

EVERETT, Senior Judge:

Contrary to his pleas, a general court-martial with officer and enlisted members convicted appellant of assault with intent to commit rape, as charged, in violation of Article 134, Uniform Code of Military Justice, 10 USC § 934. The court-martial sentenced appellant to a bad-conduct discharge, confinement for 5 years, total forfeitures, and reduction to the lowest enlisted grade. The convening authority approved these results. In turn, the Court of Military Review reduced the confinement to 3 years but in all other respects affirmed. 29 MJ 1015, 1017 (1990).

We granted appellant's petition for review to consider whether, in this prosecution for assault with intent to commit rape, the military judge erred by instructing the members that appellant's claimed mistake of fact as to the victim's consent must be both honest and reasonable rather than merely honest. We conclude that he did.

I

Essentially, Langley defended against the charge on the basis of voluntary intoxication and mistake of fact as to the victim's lack of consent. Near the end of the contest on guilt, counsel and the military judge discussed proposed findings at a session pursuant to Article 39(a), UCMJ, 10 USC § 839(a).

At the outset, the judge indicated that he intended to instruct on attempted rape, indecent assault, indecent acts with another, and assault consummated by a battery as lesser-included offenses of the one charged. Defense counsel objected that attempted rape did not appear in the Manual as a lesser-included offense. *See* para. 64d(3), Part IV, Manual for Courts–Martial, United States, 1984. Moreover, the defense complained that attempted rape was only "a general-intent crime,"[10] while the charged assault with intent to commit rape was "a specific-intent crime" and that the trial defenses of mistake-of-fact and voluntary intoxication were aimed at specific intent.[11] When trial counsel disagreed and urged an instruction on attempted rape, the military judge ruled:

> I'll give the instruction. I'll give the instruction on circumstantial evidence, both generally and on the issue of

---

[10] We are unsure how defense counsel reached this view—and why no one else at trial disagreed with it—in light of the clear language of Article 80, Uniform Code of Military Justice, 10 USC § 880, as follows:

> An act, *done with specific intent to commit an offense* under this chapter, amounting to more than mere preparation and tending, even though failing, to effect its commission, is an attempt to commit that offense.

(Emphasis added.) Moreover, while there may be some difference under certain fact patterns between attempted rape and assault with intent to commit rape, typically where an assault is the predicate act, as here, the offenses are the same. *See United States v. Gibson,* 11 MJ 435 (CMA 1981); and n. 4 of this opinion, *infra.* Accordingly, the requisite intent involved, whether general or specific, would be the same. It would seem that counsel's more legitimate objection to including attempted rape as a lesser-included offense here is that it is multiplicious with the charged offense. *See United States v. Gibson, supra.*

[11] Even if defense counsel had been correct in his view concerning the nature of the intent involved in attempted rape, his objection is curious in light of the fact that all the other lesser-included offenses cited by the military judge are only general-intent crimes.

> intent; mistake of fact, I'll give both facets as to specific intent
> crimes and as to general intent crimes.

(Emphasis added.)

At this point, in reference to the last-emphasized language above, trial counsel interceded. He made reference to a written brief in which he argued that no instruction at all should be given concerning mistake of fact and that, if one was given, the instruction should require that the mistake be both honest and reasonable, not just honest. Defense counsel, of course, argued that an instruction on mistake was appropriate and that, since the charged offense was a specific-intent crime, a mistake need only be honest.

A short while later, after the remainder of the evidence had been heard and he had taken a brief recess to consider his instructions, the judge ruled as follows:

Okay, I'm going to give the instruction on mistake of fact; however, I will instruct that there must have been an honest and reasonable mistake of fact. I will give that on all of the offenses, with the exception of indecent acts with another.

In due course, the military judge instructed as he had said he would:

> Apply this next instruction to the offense[s] of assault with
> intent to commit rape, attempted rape, indecent assault and
> assault consummated by a battery. This instruction does not
> apply to indecent acts with another. This instruction pertains to
> ignorance or mistake of fact.

The evidence in this trial has raised the issue of mistake of fact on the part of the accused concerning the existence of consent on the part of Kim Myra Herresthal. If the accused mistakenly believed that Miss Herresthal was consenting to his attempt to have intercourse, then he is not guilty of the offenses I enumerated, if his mistake or belief was reasonable. To be reasonable the belief must have been based on information or lack of it which would indicate to a reasonable person that Miss Herresthal was consenting to intercourse.

***

Now, the burden is on the prosecution to establish the accused's guilt. If you are convinced beyond a reasonable doubt that at the time of the charged offense and lesser offenses that the accused was not under the mistaken belief that she was consenting to his actions, then the asserted ignorance or mistake does not exist. Even if you conclude that the accused was under the mistaken belief that she was going to consent, if you are convinced beyond a reasonable doubt that at the time of the charged offense the accused's ignorance or mistake was unreasonable, then the defense of ignorance or mistake does not exist.

II

The issue before us first was addressed by this Court nearly 4 decades ago in *United States v. Short,* 4 USCMA 437, 16 CMR 11 (1954). On that occasion, however, no majority was able to agree on the answer.

There, as here, the accused was charged with assault with intent to rape under circumstances where the assault stopped before actual penetration. He did not deny the incident at his trial, but he explained that he had "thought she was a prostitute" and that they had negotiated agreement on a business arrangement. *Id.* at 440, 16 CMR at 14. At the conclusion of the evidence, defense counsel requested but was denied the following instruction:

> In order to constitute an offense, the accused must think victim is not consenting because he must intend not only to have carnal knowledge of the woman but to do so by force. *Id.* at 441, 16 CMR at 15.

In the lead opinion, Chief Judge Quinn observed that "[t]he assault and the intent may unite to complete the offense before any attempt to effect penetration." Accordingly, a conviction for assault with intent to commit rape is proper, even though the woman actually consents to the final act. The offense is complete if there is an assault and "at any moment during the assault" the accused intends to have carnal knowledge of the victim against her will, and to use, for that purpose, whatever force may be required. *Id.* at 443-44, 16 CMR at 17-18. In an apparent non sequitur, however, the Chief Judge later analogized assault with intent to rape with rape and, on this basis, concluded that any mistake as to the victim's consent must be both honest and reasonable. He explained:

> When consent is in issue, whether or not it was given is a question of fact for the court. It, not the accused, must determine whether the woman's conduct was such as to lead the accused to believe she had consented to his acts. The accused's personal evaluation of the circumstances is but one factor to be considered by the court; it is not conclusive. *Id.* at 445, 16 CMR at 19.

Judge Latimer concurred in the result with Chief Judge Quinn, but he did not reach the issue addressed in the lead opinion and involved in this case. Instead, he viewed the evidence as presenting a simple question of fact: Was the woman a prostitute who "agreed to the act for a consideration of 500 yen." He did not view the evidence as presenting a possibility that the accused was mistaken in that regard. *Id.*

Judge Brosman dissented from that portion of the lead opinion which concerns us here. He wrote:

Rape—like unpremeditated murder—has ordinarily been treated as requiring only a general criminal intent. Thus, drunkenness, even in excessive degree, would probably not constitute a defense to this crime—that is, as serving to belie the accused's necessary intent. However, assault with intent to commit rape would seem to occupy a quite different position—since the very designation of the offense indicates the requirement of specific intent. Clearly, then, drunkenness could operate to negate the intent required for conviction of such an assault.

An *unreasonable* mistake of fact could perhaps not serve to deny criminal liability for a consummated rape. But could it negative the prerequisites for a finding of guilt of assault with intent to commit rape—just as an unreasonable mistake of fact is said to destroy liability for larceny by false pretenses? *See United States v. Rowan*, 4 USCMA 430, 16 CMR 4.

***

It may be regarded as anomalous to conclude that an accused may be exonerated from guilt of assault with intent to commit rape because of an unreasonable mistake, whereas he could have been convicted lawfully of rape had penetration been effected under the same misapprehension. It is to be observed, however, that the anomaly is no greater than that involved in holding that an assault with intent to murder requires a specific intent to kill, whereas the crime of murder may be made out with a lesser intent. *See United States v. Woodson,* 3 USCMA 372, 12 CMR 128. The fact of the matter is that a specific intent is, by definition, required for the present finding. The evidence, in my view, raised the possibility that a mistake of fact on the accused's part precluded that intent. *Id.* at 446-47, 16 CMR 20-21.

III

We revisit *Short* in detail here because the views expressed on each side of the present issue by Chief Judge Quinn and Judge Brosman represent, as well, the different views argued on that issue today. We believe that the matter may be resolved by a sensitive examination of precisely what intent is involved in the crime of assault with intent to commit rape, as distinguished from rape.

Rape is defined in Article 120, UCMJ, 10 USC § 920, as "an act of sexual intercourse with a female not his wife, by force and without her consent." No specific intent is mentioned in the statute—only general criminal *mens rea* is involved. Accordingly, if an accused mistakenly believed that his victim consented to intercourse, that is not enough. Instead, because the "mistake goes to . . . [an] element requiring only general intent or knowledge, the ignorance or mistake must have existed in the mind of the accused and must have been reasonable under all the circumstances." RCM 916(j), Manual, *supra*.

By contrast, assault with intent to commit rape—charged under Article 134 and defined in paragraph 64, Part IV, Manual, *supra*—contains as an expressed element "[t]hat, at the time of the assault, the accused . . . intended to commit rape. . . ." Para. 64b(2). "In assault with intent to commit rape, the accused must have intended to overcome any resistance by force, and to complete the offense. Any lesser intent will not suffice." Para. 64c(4). More than a general criminal *mens rea* is involved; instead, the prosecution must affirmatively prove that, at the time of the assault, the accused specifically intended to forcibly accomplish sexual intercourse. As Judge Brosman put it in his separate opinion in *Short,* "[T]he very designation of the offense indicates the requirement of a specific intent." 4 USCMA at 446, 16 CMR at 20.

The Court of Military Review in this case relied almost exclusively on that court's earlier opinion in *United States v. McFarlin,* 19 MJ 790, *pet. denied,* 20 MJ 314 (1985). There, the accused had been charged with indecent assault and had claimed mistake of fact as to the victim's consent in his defense. In challenging the military judge's instructions that such a mistake must have been both honest and reasonable, McFarlin urged that it need only have been honest because indecent assault was a specific-intent crime.

The *McFarlin* court correctly noted, however, that the specific intent involved in indecent assault goes only to "the intent to gratify the lust or sexual desires of the accused," not to the offense as a whole. *See* para. 63b(2), Part IV, Manual, *supra.* Thus, any purported mistake as to the victim's consent is not a claim of mistake as to anything about which the accused must have had any specific intent. Instead, such a claim of mistake would tend to negate only his general criminal *mens rea*—his general willingness to do a criminal act.

As we just noted, however, that is not the case in the circumstance of assault with intent to commit rape. This crime involves essentially two components: An *actus reus*—an assault—and a specific *mens rea*—a coexisting specific intent to accomplish "sexual intercourse with a female not his wife, by force and without her consent." Art. 120. The Court of Military Review here, in superimposing its sound reasoning in *McFarlin* as to indecent assault, erred by not recognizing the fundamental difference in the objects of the specific intent: In indecent assault, the intent goes only to the element of gratifying his lust; in assault with intent to commit rape, the specific intent goes to the element that itself includes the entire crime of rape—including taking his victim without her consent.

Chief Judge Quinn took this same misstep in *Short.* As pointed out earlier, he correctly recognized that assault with intent to commit rape "is complete [only] if there is an assault and, [at some point] 'during the assault', the accused intends to have carnal knowledge of the victim against her will, and to use, for that purpose, whatever force may be required." 4 USCMA at 444, 16 CMR at 18. That is, it is complete only if there is an assault and, at some point during the assault, the accused intends to commit rape. Later in the opinion, however, he lost track of the full scope of the required intent. But for that slip of the pen, he might well have reached the correct result along with Judge Brosman.

Accordingly, we hold that, in a prosecution for assault with intent to commit rape, at some point during the assault, the accused must have had the specific intent to commit each element of rape. Accordingly, the Court of Military Review erred in affirming the military judge's ruling that appellant's claimed mistake of fact as to his victim's consent must have been both honest and reasonable, instead of just honest.***

State v. Rawson, 2006 WL 279003 (Ohio Ct. App. 2006)

DEGENARO, J.

This timely appeal comes for consideration upon the record in the trial court and the parties' briefs. Defendant-Appellant, Douglas Rawson, appeals the decision of the Jefferson County Court of Common Pleas that found him guilty of felonious assault and sentenced him to two years imprisonment. On appeal, Rawson argues the trial court erred by refusing to specifically instruct the jury on the defense of mistake of fact.

Ignorance or mistake of fact is a defense if it negates a mental state required to establish an element of a crime. In this case, the trial court instructed the jury on what "knowingly" means and the mistake of fact defense is implicit in this instruction. Furthermore, the only fact which Rawson was mistaken about, according to his own testimony, is the identity of his victim. This mistake does not negate any element of the offense. Accordingly, the trial court did not err when it refused to give that instruction.

The trial court's decision is affirmed.

Facts

On August 7, 2004, Greg Metcalf was celebrating at the Mingo Community Days in Mingo Junction, Ohio, with his wife and some friends. The street fair ended at about 11:00 p.m. that night and the group went to the Town House, a restaurant and bar in Mingo Junction, to listen to a band. Sometime after midnight, Metcalf had to go to the restroom, but when he arrived at the men's room, he noticed a man was using the facilities. So he waited in the hall and spoke with a woman he knew, Virginia Ruckman, who was waiting to enter the ladies' restroom with a friend of hers. After the man left the restroom, Metcalf entered it.

Rawson was also at the Town House that evening with his wife and some friends, Virginia Ruckman among them. At some point Ruckman accompanied Rawson's wife, Kelly Quinn, to the restroom. While they were standing outside, they spoke with Metcalf. According to Rawson, he saw this from across the bar and mistook Metcalf for one of his stepdaughter's friends. Those friends would commonly pretend to flirt with Quinn and Rawson would good-naturedly pretend to be angry with them for doing so. According to Rawson, since he believed that Metcalf was one of those friends, he thought he would good-naturedly tease him about flirting with Rawson's wife and headed to the restroom.

Metcalf testified that as he was getting ready to use the facilities a man walked in and struck him in the face. Metcalf's memory was hazy after the initial blow, but other witnesses testified that they saw Metcalf crawling out of the restroom while Rawson was standing over him kicking him.

Rawson testified that he went into the restroom, slammed his hand against the wall, and said something along the lines of, "Stop hitting on my old lady." He then said that he saw Metcalf's face and discovered his mistake. According to Rawson, he turned to leave the restroom when Metcalf started punching him. Rawson said he never struck Metcalf. He further testified that they each fell out the restroom door and that Metcalf fell onto Rawson's feet. He denied kicking Metcalf.

After the incident, Rawson had superficial injuries, a cut lip and bruises. He did not require medical attention before leaving the Town House. Metcalf was covered in blood and required immediate medical attention. Metcalf's nose and teeth were broken and displaced and he was suffering from numerous scrapes and bruises. A doctor subsequently performed surgery on Metcalf to fix his broken nose and a dentist had to repair his teeth.

The Jefferson County Grand Jury indicted Rawson for one count of felonious assault in violation of R.C. 2903.11(A)(1), a second degree felony, on October 6, 2004. The matter proceeded to a jury trial. Before the trial court gave the jury its instructions, Rawson requested that the trial court instruct the jury on the defense of mistake of fact, among other things. The trial court denied this request. The jury found Rawson guilty and the trial court sentenced him to the minimum prison sentence for a second degree felony.

Mistake of Fact
Rawson's sole assignment of error on appeal argues:

> The trial court abused its discretion by failing to instruct the jury on the defense of mistake of fact.***

Rawson's argument that the trial court erred by not including a jury instruction on the defense of "mistake of fact" fails for the following two reasons: 1) the trial court's jury instructions accurately described the mental state required to commit a felonious assault, and 2) the facts in the case do not demonstrate that Rawson was mistaken about any fact which would show that he did not have the requisite mental state.

"Ignorance or mistake of fact is a defense if it negates a mental state required to establish an element of a crime." *State v. Pecora (1993)*, 87 Ohio App. 3d 687. It can only be used as a defense "to specific intent crimes such as theft since, when the defendant has an honest purpose, such a purpose provides an excuse for an act that would otherwise be deemed criminal." *State v. Snowden*, 7 Ohio App. 3d 358, citing *Farrell v. State (1877)*, 32 Ohio St. 456. In other words, mistakes of fact can, in an appropriate circumstance, negate either the "knowingly" or "purposely" elements of a criminal offense. Id.; see also *State v. Pinkney (1988)*, 36 Ohio St. 3d 190.

Rawson was convicted of violating R.C. 2903.11(A)(1), which provides that "[n]o person shall knowingly *** [c]ause serious physical harm to another ***." Thus, the defense of mistake of fact could negate an element of this offense. He requested that the trial court give the following instruction:

> Unless the defendant had the required knowledge he is not guilty of the crime of felonious assault.
>
> In determining whether the defendant had the required knowledge you will consider whether he acted under a mistake of fact regarding his conduct in relation to Gregory R. Metcalf.
>
> If the defendant had an honest belief arrived at in good faith in the existence of such facts and acted in accordance with the facts as he believed them to be, he is not guilty of felonious assault as knowledge of the result or nature of his conduct is an essential element of that offense.

The trial court refused to give that instruction. Instead, it instructed the jury on how to assess Rawson's state of mind.

Knowingly: A person acts knowingly regardless of his purpose when he is aware that his conduct will probably cause a certain result or he is aware that his conduct will probably be of a certain nature. A person has knowledge of circumstances when he is aware that such circumstances probably exist.

Since you can not look into the mind of another, knowledge is determined from all the facts and circumstances in evidence. You will determine from these facts and circumstances whether there existed at the time in the mind of the Defendant an awareness of the probability that his conduct would probably cause serious physical harm to Mr. Metcalf.

Although the trial court did not give the instruction Rawson requested, the instruction it gave incorporates the defense of "mistake of fact" into the definition of knowingly. It tells the jury to consider the facts and circumstances in the case to determine whether Rawson knew at the time that his conduct would seriously harm Metcalf. Under the terms of this instruction, if Rawson was mistaken about a fact which would nullify the "knowingly" element of the offense, then the jury should acquit him. Thus, although the trial court did not highlight that particular defense or use the proposed instruction verbatim, the instruction given is substantively the same as the requested instruction.

Importantly, a mistake of fact defense clearly cannot apply to the facts in this case, even if we only considered the facts in the light most favorable to Rawson. Rawson testified that he saw Metcalf talking to his wife and her friend and mistook him for a friend of Rawson's stepdaughter. A common joke between Rawson and his stepdaughter's male friends was that he would angrily tell them, "Hey, you better not be hitting on my wife."

He decided to play this same joke now. Rawson "slammed open the door to the bathroom" and hit the partition separating the urinal from the toilet while saying, "Hey, what are you doin' hitting on my old lady." Rawson testified that he then pushed Metcalf, discovered that he had mistaken Metcalf for one of his stepdaughter's friends, and turned to leave the bathroom. He said that Metcalf then turned around and hit him in the jaw. Rawson said he put his arm up to protect himself and Metcalf hit his arm. Rawson then pushed Metcalf into the wall and turned to leave the bathroom again. Metcalf grabbed his shoulder from behind, the two wrestled and fell in different directions, and Rawson's arm struck something, but he did not know what it struck. He and Metcalf then tried getting out the door. On the way out of the bathroom door, Metcalf fell down in front of Rawson's feet. Rawson denied kicking Metcalf while he was on the ground. He also denied having ever punched Metcalf with his fists.

This version of events is completely inconsistent with a mistake of fact defense. The crime for which he was convicted required him to knowingly cause serious physical harm to another. The only fact which Rawson was mistaken about was the identity of the man he spoke with in the bathroom, but this fact is unrelated to any of the elements of the crime he committed. Thus, a mistake of fact defense is simply inapplicable in this situation.

The jury instruction given by the trial court implicitly incorporated the mistake of fact defense. Moreover, that defense is inapplicable to the facts of this case. Accordingly, Rawson's sole assignment of error is meritless and the judgment of the trial court is affirmed.

Notes and Questions

1. Can a defendant raise a mistake of fact defense for a general intent crime? According to *State v. Rawson,* the answer to that question is in the negative. At common law, a defendant could raise a mistake of fact defense for both general and specific intent crimes. However, if the defendant was accused

of committing a general intent crime, the mistake had to be reasonable. Why do you think they made that exception for general intent crimes?

2. Given that assault is "to knowingly cause physical harm to another," can you imagine a scenario where mistake of fact would ever be a viable defense?

2. Mistake of Law

Lambert v. California, 355 U.S. 225 (1957)

Mr. Justice DOUGLAS delivered the opinion of the Court.

Section 52.38(a) of the Los Angeles Municipal Code defines "convicted person" as follows:

> Any person who, subsequent to January 1, 1921, has been or hereafter is convicted of an offense punishable as a felony in the State of California, or who has been or who is hereafter convicted of any offense in any place other than the State of California, which offense, if committed in the State of California, would have been punishable as a felony.

Section 52.39 provides that it shall be unlawful for "any convicted person" to be or remain in Los Angeles for a period of more than five days without registering; it requires any person having a place of abode outside the city to register if he comes into the city on five occasions or more during a 30-day period; and it prescribes the information to be furnished to the Chief of Police on registering.

Section 52.43(b) makes the failure to register a continuing offense, each day's failure constituting a separate offense.

Appellant, arrested on suspicion of another offense, was charged with a violation of this registration law. The evidence showed that she had been, at the time of her arrest, a resident of Los Angeles for over seven years. Within that period, she had been convicted in Los Angeles of the crime of forgery, an offense which California punishes as a felony. Though convicted of a crime punishable as a felony, she had not, at the time of her arrest, registered under the Municipal Code. The case having been argued and reargued, we now hold that the registration provisions of the Code as sought to be applied here violate the Due Process requirement of the Fourteenth Amendment.

The registration provision, carrying criminal penalties, applies if a person has been convicted "of an offense punishable as a felony in the State of California" or, in case he has been convicted in another State, if the offense "would have been punishable as a felony" had it been committed in California. No element of willfulness is, by terms, included in the ordinance, nor read into it by the California court as a condition necessary for a conviction.

We must assume that appellant had no actual knowledge of the requirement that she register under this ordinance, as she offered proof of this defense, which was refused. The question is whether a registration act of this character violates due process where it is applied to a person who has no actual knowledge of his duty to register, and where no showing is made of the probability of such knowledge.

We do not go with Blackstone in saying that "a vicious will" is necessary to constitute a crime, for conduct alone, without regard to the intent of the doer, is often sufficient. There is wide latitude in the lawmakers to declare an offense and to exclude elements of knowledge and diligence from its definition. But we deal here with conduct that is wholly passive—mere failure to register. It is unlike the commission of acts, or the failure to act under circumstances that should alert the doer to the consequences of his deed. The rule that "ignorance of the law will not excuse" (*Shevlin-Carpenter Co. v. Minnesota*) is deep in our law, as is the principle that, of all the powers of local government, the police power is "one of the least limitable." On the other hand, due process places some limits on its exercise. Engrained in our concept of due process is the requirement of notice. Notice is sometimes essential so that the citizen has the chance to defend charges. Notice is required before property interests are disturbed, before assessments are made, before penalties are assessed. Notice is required in a myriad of situations where a penalty or forfeiture might be suffered for mere failure to act.***

Registration laws are common, and their range is wide. Many such laws are akin to licensing statutes in that they pertain to the regulation of business activities. But the present ordinance is entirely different. Violation of its provisions is unaccompanied by any activity whatever, mere presence in the city being the test. Moreover, circumstances which might move one to inquire as to the necessity of registration are completely lacking. At most, the ordinance is but a law enforcement technique designed for the convenience of law enforcement agencies through which a list of the names and addresses of felons then residing in a given community is compiled. The disclosure is merely a compilation of former convictions already publicly recorded in the jurisdiction where obtained. Nevertheless, this appellant, on first becoming aware of her duty to register, was given no opportunity to comply with the law and avoid its penalty, even though her default was entirely innocent. She could but suffer the consequences of the ordinance, namely, conviction with the imposition of heavy criminal penalties thereunder. We believe that actual knowledge of the duty to register or proof of the probability of such knowledge and subsequent failure to comply are necessary before a conviction under the ordinance can stand. As Holmes wrote in The Common Law,

> A law which punished conduct which would not be blameworthy in the average member of the community would be too severe for that community to bear.

Its severity lies in the absence of an opportunity either to avoid the consequences of the law or to defend any prosecution brought under it. Where a person did not know of the duty to register, and where there was no proof of the probability of such knowledge, he may not be convicted consistently with due process. Were it otherwise, the evil would be as great as it is when the law is written in print too fine to read or in a language foreign to the community.

Reversed.

Mr. Justice FRANKFURTER, whom Mr. Justice HARLAN and Mr. Justice WHITTAKER join, dissenting.

The present laws of the United States and of the forty-eight States are thick with provisions that command that some things not be done and others be done, although persons convicted under such provisions may have had no awareness of what the law required or that what they did was wrongdoing. The body of decisions sustaining such legislation, including innumerable registration laws, is almost as voluminous as the legislation itself. The matter is summarized in *United States v. Balint*:

> Many instances of this are to be found in regulatory measures in the exercise of what is called the police power, where the emphasis of the statute is evidently upon achievement of some social betterment rather than the punishment of the crimes as in cases of mala in se.

Surely there can hardly be a difference as a matter of fairness, of hardship, or of justice, if one may invoke it, between the case of a person wholly innocent of wrongdoing, in the sense that he was not remotely conscious of violating any law, who is imprisoned for five years for conduct relating to narcotics, and the case of another person who is placed on probation for three years on condition that she pay $250, for failure, as a local resident, convicted under local law of a felony, to register under a law passed as an exercise of the State's "police power." Considerations of hardship often lead courts, naturally enough, to attribute to a statute the requirement of a certain mental element—some consciousness of wrongdoing and knowledge of the law's command—as a matter of statutory construction. Then too, a cruelly disproportionate relation between what the law requires and the sanction for its disobedience may constitute a violation of the

Eighth Amendment as a cruel and unusual punishment, and, in respect to the States, even offend the Due Process Clause of the Fourteenth Amendment.

But what the Court here does is to draw a constitutional line between a State's requirement of doing and not doing. What is this but a return to Year Book distinctions between feasance and nonfeasance—a distinction that may have significance in the evolution of common law notions of liability, but is inadmissible as a line between constitutionality and unconstitutionality. One can be confident that Mr. Justice Holmes would have been the last to draw such a line. What he wrote about "blameworthiness" is worth quoting in its context:

> It is not intended to deny that criminal liability, as well as civil, is founded on blameworthiness. Such a denial would shock the moral sense of any civilized community; or, to put it another way, a law which punished conduct which would not be blameworthy in the average member of the community would be too severe for that community to bear.

(This passage must be read in the setting of the broader discussion of which it is an essential part. Holmes, The Common Law at 49-50.)

If the generalization that underlies, and alone can justify, this decision were to be given its relevant scope, a whole volume of the United States Reports would be required to document in detail the legislation in this country that would fall or be impaired. I abstain from entering upon a consideration of such legislation, and adjudications upon it, because I feel confident that the present decision will turn out to be an isolated deviation from the strong current of precedents—a derelict on the waters of the law. Accordingly, I content myself with dissenting.

This case does not involve a person who, convicted of a crime in another jurisdiction, must decide whether he has been convicted of a crime that "would have been punishable as a felony" had it been committed in California. Appellant committed forgery in California, and was convicted under California law. Furthermore, she was convicted in Los Angeles itself, and there she resided for over seven years before the arrest leading to the present proceedings.

Notes and Questions

1. Historically, mistake of law or ignorance of the law was not a defense. There are very strong policy arguments supporting why citizens should be encouraged to know the law. In *Lambert v. California*, the Supreme Court carved out an exception to the long-standing rule that ignorance of the law is not a defense. Do you think the majority in this closely decided case (5-4) was influenced by the fact that the appellant had to take an affirmative step (i.e., she had to register with

law enforcement)? Were other factors at play to support ruling in favor of the appellant?

2. Could the majority have reached the same result by finding that this was not a strict liability offense, but rather a crime that imposes a mens rea of recklessness? What would the outcome be with a recklessness standard?

3. In 1988, the Ohio Supreme Court in *State v. Pickney* stated "that it is well-settled that the mistake-of-law defense is not recognized in Ohio." 36 Ohio St. 3d 190 (1988). Other states have recognized the mistake of law in limited circumstances, including when:

(1) The mistake negates a mental state.
(2) The statute in question has not been published or made available.
(3) The defendant reasonably relied upon a prior judicial decision or statute.
(4) The defendant reasonably relied upon an official interpretation of the law which he is accused of violating.

Chapter 5
Causation and Concurrence of Elements

A. Actual and Proximate Cause

Causation consists of both actual cause and proximate cause. If both actual and proximate cause are satisfied, the defendant is said to have caused the prohibited result.

The defendant's conduct is the cause in fact or actual cause of the prohibited result if the prohibited result (1) would not have occurred "but for" the defendant's conduct, or (2) the defendant's act was a substantial factor of the prohibited result.

The defendant's conduct is the proximate or legal cause of the prohibited result if the prohibited result is a natural and probable consequence of the conduct, even if the defendant did not anticipate the precise manner in which the prohibited result occurred.

State v. Beaver, 119 Ohio App. 3d 385 (1997)

NADER, Judge.

On May 12, 1995, the state filed an indictment charging appellant, Richard Darnell Beaver, with one count of murder. R.C. 2903.02. A second indictment, which was filed on June 6, 1995, contained a firearm specification pursuant to R.C. 2941.141.

The first trial was commenced on June 27, 1995. At the close of the state's case, appellant moved for a judgment of acquittal pursuant to Crim. R. 29(A), arguing that the state failed to produce enough evidence to prove that appellant caused the death of the victim, Fred Butler. The court denied the motion, after which appellant called his sister, Latanya Beaver, as a witness in order to assert a self-defense claim. Defense counsel then requested an instruction on a lesser-included offense, felonious assault. R.C. 2903.11. The trial court granted the request and instructed the jury on murder, felonious assault, the firearm specification, and self-defense. The jury returned a verdict of not guilty to the murder charge but was unable to reach a unanimous verdict on the felonious assault charge. The court later ordered appellant to be retried for felonious assault.***

The second trial began on October 11, 1995. On October 16, 1995, the second jury found appellant guilty of felonious assault with a firearm. The trial judge sentenced appellant to the maximum term of imprisonment allowed by law for the assault, eight to fifteen years, to be served consecutively to a three-year term of actual incarceration on the firearm specification. From his conviction, appellant appeals.***

In the section of his July 22, 1996 brief prepared by the attorney, appellant asserts the following as error:

> "1. The trial court erred, to the detriment of appellant, by not discharging the first case at the close of the state's evidence.
>
> "2. The trial court erred, to the detriment of appellant, by issuing the first improper jury instructions.
>
> "3. The trial court erred, to the detriment of appellant, by ordering a second trial, since appellant had been placed once in jeopardy.
>
> "4. The trial court erred, to the detriment of appellant, by issuing the second improper jury instructions.
>
> "5. The second trial verdict was against the manifest weight of the evidence."

In his first assignment of error, appellant challenges the trial court's decision, in the first trial, to deny his motion for judgment of acquittal, pursuant to Crim. R. 29(A), at the close of the state's case. Appellant repeats the argument initially made to the trial court that the state failed to produce sufficient evidence to prove that the three bullets he admitted to firing into Butler's chest, stomach, and left knee proximately caused his death.

A motion for a judgment of acquittal is properly denied when the evidence is such that reasonable minds can reach different conclusions as to whether each material element of a crime had been proved beyond a reasonable doubt. *State v. Robinson* (Apr. 26, 1996), Ashtabula App. No. 95-A-0034, unreported, at 7, 1996 WL 297036, citing *State v. Bridgeman* (1978), 55 Ohio St. 2d 261, syllabus. The evidence is to be viewed in the light most favorable to the prosecution. *State v. Jenks* (1991), 61 Ohio St. 3d 259.

During the first trial, the state called several witnesses who claimed that, on the night of April 7, 1995, they were at a party in the home of Robert W. Kelly at 2820 Niles Road in the city of Warren, when they heard three gunshots outside. Butler came running inside the residence and told them appellant had shot him. One witness, Joseph Ellis, testified that he saw a bullet hole in Butler's chest.

Similarly, Patrolman Andre Leon of the Warren Police Department testified that, when he responded to a 9-1-1 call about a shooting at 2820 Niles Road, he found Butler lying on an interior stair of the residence with a large bullet hole in his chest. Michelle Allison, a nurse working in the intensive care unit of Trumbull Memorial Hospital, testified that Butler spent time in the intensive care unit after approximately seven hours of emergency surgery. He had tubes in his throat to help him breathe.

The Trumbull County Coroner, Dr. Theodore Soboslay, testified from Butler's hospital records that he died on May 2, 1995, twenty-five days after being shot. He stated that, according to the reports, the immediate cause of Butler's death was "hypovolemic shock, acute respiratory failure, multiple organ failure, [and] sepsis." He explained that Butler had died as a result of a number of problems. First, he lost a lot of blood. What was left in his system was insufficient to carry enough oxygen, so his cells and his organs died. Second, his lungs were filed with fluids so Butler could not breathe. Third, Butler contracted sepsis, which is an infection caused when bacteria enters the bloodstream. Dr. Soboslay was not permitted to testify as to what caused these problems. Because he had not yet rendered a formal verdict, Dr. Soboslay admitted on cross-examination that he could not officially say whether Butler died of suicide, homicide or in an accident.

Now we must determine whether this evidence produced at the first trial, when viewed in a light most favorable to the prosecution, was such that reasonable minds could have reached different conclusions as to whether the state proved beyond a reasonable doubt that the three bullets caused Butler's death.

A causal connection between the criminal agency and the cause of death is an essential element in a conviction for murder in the first or second degree. *State v. Cochrane* (1949), 151 Ohio St. 128, paragraph one of the syllabus. Causation must be both direct and proximate. As explained by one treatise:

> "Where the statute involves a specified result that is caused by conduct, it must be shown, as a minimal requirement, that the accused's conduct was an antecedent 'but for' which the result in question would not have occurred. This means that an accused's conduct must at least be a physical cause of the harmful result. But mere physical causation is not always enough; a particular physical cause is enough only when it is a cause of which the law will take cognizance. This idea has been implemented by requiring that the harmful result in question be the natural and probable consequence of the accused's conduct; if the physical causation is too remote, the law will not take cognizance of it." 1 Torcia, Wharton's Criminal Law (15 Ed. 1993) 146-48, Section 26.

There were a number of problems with the state's proof of direct causation.

First, there was no coroner's verdict. Under R.C. 313.19, the coroner's verdict constitutes the "legally accepted cause of death." It establishes the physiological cause of death and the immediate mechanical, chemical, or biological means by which the death was caused; it does not, however, assign criminal responsibility for the death. *State v. Cousin* (1982), 5 Ohio App. 3d 32. Although the coroner's verdict is entitled to much evidentiary weight on the issue of causation, *State v. Manago* (1974), 38 Ohio St. 2d 223, it is not indispensable in order to prove that an accused has committed murder, as the causal relationship between the acts of the accused and the victim's death may be proved by other evidence. See *id.* at 228.

There was other evidence that Butler died as a result of four ailments: blood loss, organ failure, fluid-filled lungs, and an infection. The link between these conditions and the death was adequately supported by Dr. Soboslay's testimony to that effect. Unfortunately, there was no expert medical testimony establishing the link between the shooting and these complications, which was the second problem with the state's proof.

The cases in this area are in agreement that the state must produce evidence to support each link in the chain of causation between the defendant's criminal act and the eventual death of the victim. For example, in *State v. Burke* (1995), 73 Ohio St. 3d 399, the court upheld a murder conviction against the defendant's challenge that the state failed to prove causation because the coroner clearly testified that the defendant's act of stabbing the victim twelve times caused an irregular heartbeat, which, in turn, caused the victim's death.

Contrast this case with *State v. Bynum* (1942), 69 Ohio App. 317, 24 O.O. 86, 43 N.E.2d 636, where the defendant was accused of first-degree manslaughter. The evidence showed that he smashed the victim over the head with a lead pipe on March 15, 1941. Thereafter, the victim apparently recovered to some degree. He continued to work at this job and died mysteriously some one hundred eighty-eight days after the assault. The coroner testified that the immediate cause of death was meningitis, which could possibly have been caused by bacteria entering the lining of the brain through the seams of an old skull fracture. He testified that the blow delivered by the defendant "might have been" or "could have been" the cause of death. On appeal, the Lucas County Court of Appeals reversed the conviction as being unsupported by the evidence, stating:

"That the cause of death was meningitis, in the absence of any other testimony on the subject, we assume; but that the meningitis causing death was the result of any blow suffered on March 15th or thereabouts is not supported by any competent evidence in the record. What 'might have resulted' or 'could have resulted' or a 'possible result' is quite too uncertain to support a verdict of conviction in a criminal case." *Id.* at 321, 24 O.O. at 88.

In the instant case, there was no direct evidence that the shooting caused the blood loss, organ failure, fluid in the lungs, and infection. For some reason, Dr. Soboslay was not permitted to testify that the one caused the others.

There was circumstantial evidence, however, upon which the jury could have inferred that the shooting caused these complications. Butler was shot three times, once in his chest, an extremely vital portion of his body. Expert medical evidence is not necessary in cases where the injuries are severe enough that the jury can infer that the injuries caused the death. *State v. Carter* (1992), 64 Ohio St. 3d 218. There was testimony that Butler underwent emergency surgery for seven hours immediately after the shooting, and that he had trouble breathing. Unlike the victim in *Bynum,* Butler never recovered, dying some three weeks after the shooting from complications that are easily understood as normally following such injuries, *e.g.,* shock, blood loss, and organ failure. A defendant is not relieved of culpability for the natural consequences of inflicting serious wounds on another merely because the victim later died of complications brought on by the injury. *State v. Tanner* (1993), 90 Ohio App. 3d 761.

There was enough circumstantial evidence presented in the first trial upon which the jury could rationally infer that the shooting caused the various complications. The judge's decision to send the case to the jury cannot be reversed on this ground. See *Cochrane, supra,* 151 Ohio St. at 130-131 (in an equally weak case, the court stated in dicta that the issue of causation was properly submitted to the jury); *State v. Swiger* (1966), 5 Ohio St. 2d 151 (evidence of causation, although weak, was sufficient to go to the jury).

The third problem with the state's proof of direct causation deals with Dr. Soboslay's comments about sepsis, the infection which he listed as one of the four immediate causes of Butler's death. Dr. Soboslay said the infection was a result of a "dirty surgery." After closely reading the transcript, we think he meant to say that when the emergency room physicians cut into his abdominal cavity to retrieve bullets, they found that his injuries had contaminated his abdominal cavity. In the second trial, there was evidence that the first bullet punctured Butler's large intestine, thereby spilling bacteria into the abdominal cavity as well as the bloodstream, but this fact was not revealed to the first jury. The state did not fully explain the cause of the infection, which probably confused the jury. Counsel for the defense suggested, on cross-examination of the coroner, that the infection could have been caused by the negligence of the surgeons, but there was no evidence to that effect. He repeated the suggestion during closing argument. We believe that, because of this misunderstanding, the first jury believed that there was reasonable doubt as to whether the shootings or the infection caused Butler's death and, therefore, acquitted appellant of murder.

Assuming *arguendo* that the infection was, in fact, caused by the negligence of the attending surgeons, this alone is not sufficient to break the chain of direct causation. The injuries inflicted by the defendant need not be the sole cause of death, as long as they constitute a substantial factor in the death. *State v. Johnson* (1977), 60 Ohio App. 2d 45, affirmed (1978), 56 Ohio St. 2d 35. "It is the general rule that one who inflicts injury upon another is criminally responsible for that person's death, regardless of whether different or more skillful medical treatment may have saved his life." *Id.,* 56 Ohio St. 2d at 40. Only gross negligence or willful maltreatment will relieve the defendant from liability. *Id.* Simple negligence is not enough.

Another weakness relates to the state's proof of proximate causation—the fact that there was a lapse of twenty-five days between the shooting and Butler's death. Of course, the case for proximate causation is strongest if the victim dies immediately or shortly after being injured by the defendant. But if the victim lingers for a substantial period of time, there may arise a question whether the death came at a time too remote from the injury to say for certain that the accused caused it. The common law adhered to a principle known as the "year and a day" rule, whereby an accused could not be convicted of murder if the victim lived for a year and one day after the injury. 3 Katz & Giannelli, Criminal Law (1996) 301, Chapter 96.3.

This rule is not followed in Ohio. See *State v. Sandridge* (C.P.1977), 5 O.O.3d 419, (indictment charging the defendant with murdering the victim, who died twenty-three months after the assault, would not be dismissed under the common-law rule). Today, the length of time between the act and the result is only one consideration in assessing the prosecution's showing of proximate cause. See *Swiger,* 5 Ohio St. 2d 151, 34 O.O.2d 270, (evidence sufficient to present a jury question as to proximate causation although, among other factors, victim's death occurred fifteen days after a beating administered by the accused).

In this case Butler died twenty-five days after the shooting. This evidence, when combined with other factors such as the severity of the wounds, the fact that Butler was in intensive care, and that he was never discharged from the hospital, is sufficient to say that reasonable minds may have reached different conclusions as to whether the shooting was the natural and proximate cause of the death.

In summary, none of the defects in the state's proof of causation was fatal to its case. The trial court committed no error in overruling appellant's motion for judgment of acquittal in the first trial. For these reasons, appellant's first assignment of error lacks merit.

The judgment of the trial court at issue here and appellant's conviction for felonious assault are hereby affirmed.

Judgment affirmed.

State v. Losey, 23 Ohio App. 3d 93 (1985)

PER CURIAM.

Defendant-appellant, Michael Desmar Losey, was indicted on December 23, 1983, for aggravated burglary in violation of R.C. 2911.01 and involuntary manslaughter in violation of R.C. 2903.04(A). The defendant waived a jury and the case proceeded to trial before the court in which the defendant admitted the aggravated burglary but denied liability for the involuntary manslaughter.

Defendant testified that he approached a house located at 616 Whitethorne Avenue shortly after 11:00 p.m. on November 25, 1983; that he knocked at the front door and, upon receiving no response, forced open the door and proceeded to attempt to remove a bicycle. His friend, who had been waiting outside, yelled that a car was slowly approaching. The defendant then placed the bicycle beside the front door and departed, leaving the front door open behind him. James Harper, the owner of 616 Whitethorne Avenue, testified that he heard a noise at approximately 1:00 a.m. Shortly thereafter, his mother, with whom he resided, appeared at his bedroom door inquiring about the noise. They proceeded together to the living room, whereupon they discovered the open front door and the bicycle standing near the door. James Harper stated that he then told his mother to go back to her bedroom while he went to check the rest of the house. After so checking, he returned to the living room and was calling the police when his mother appeared in the hallway looking very upset and then collapsed. He called an emergency squad, which had attempted to revive Mrs. Harper for almost an hour when the squadmen pronounced her dead. Prior to the burglary, Mrs. Harper had returned from bingo at approximately 10:00 p.m. that evening and had gone to bed. Based on these facts, the trial court found defendant guilty of aggravated burglary and involuntary manslaughter. Defendant appeals from the trial court's decision and asserts the following assignments of error:

> 1. The judgment of the trial court was against the manifest weight of the evidence, and should be reversed.
> A. The trial court erred in finding that the defendant's actions were the proximate cause of death, and therefore, the judgment should be reversed.***

The thrust of defendant's first assignment of error is that Mrs. Harper's death was not the proximate result of his conduct.

As relevant to our inquiry, involuntary manslaughter at common law was an unexcused, unintentional homicide resulting from the commission of a criminal act not amounting to a felony nor naturally tending to cause death or great bodily harm. Clark & Marshall, Crimes (1952) 353–354, Section 262. Essentially, that common-law unlawful act manslaughter concept was carried forward in Ohio's statutory treatment of involuntary manslaughter until the adoption of the new criminal code in 1974.

When the new criminal code was introduced in the Ohio General Assembly, it included a reckless homicide provision as a substitute for the former statute which had punished conduct without reference to a specific culpable mental state. However, as the result of the legislative process, the reckless homicide provision was dropped in favor of a section retaining traditional unlawful act manslaughter concepts, in the form of the present involuntary manslaughter statute. Goldsmith, *Involuntary Manslaughter: Review and Commentary on Ohio Law* (1979), 40 Ohio St. L. J. 569. The language of R.C. 2903.04 follows:

> (A) No person shall cause the death of another as a proximate result of the offender's committing or attempting to commit a felony.
>
> (B) No person shall cause the death of another as a proximate result of the offender's committing or attempting to commit a misdemeanor.
>
> ***

The result of the adoption of division (A) of the statute was a statute embodying a concept reminiscent of common-law felony murder. In addition, the General Assembly incorporated another form of felony murder into its definition of aggravated murder, obviating the necessity of proving prior calculation and design, where the actor purposely kills another while committing one of a list of specified felonies, R.C. 2903.01(B). Thus, if the defendant, in the course of committing armed robbery, purposely, but without prior calculation and design, kills the hold-up victim, he is guilty of aggravated murder, but, if the killing is accidental, then, he is guilty of involuntary manslaughter.

Prior to the adoption of the new criminal code, Ohio case law limited the class of unlawful acts which could serve as a predicate for involuntary manslaughter to those crimes whose nature was such that death was to be a reasonably anticipated result of their commission, and further limited criminal responsibility for a death resulting from the commission of those crimes to those instances where the death was the natural, logical and proximate result of the defendant's commission of the crime. *Black v. State (1921),* 103 Ohio St. 434, ***. Whether or not the first limitation survived the 1974 recodification and restricts the types of felonies which may serve as a predicate for involuntary manslaughter, is not at issue here since burglary is clearly such a felony. The second limitation, that the death must be the proximate result of the defendant's conduct in committing the crime, clearly survived in the language of R.C. 2903.04.

The term "proximate result" was used by the General Assembly to refine and limit the verb "cause." Thus, it is conceivable that defendant's conduct may have caused Mrs. Harper's death in the sense that he set in motion events which culminated in her death, which therefore would not have occurred in the absence of that conduct, but, nevertheless, that the death was not the proximate result of his conduct if it were not the natural, logical, and foreseeable result of his conduct. Under the statute, defendant cannot be held responsible for consequences no reasonable person could expect to follow from his conduct; he will be held responsible for consequences which are direct, normal, and reasonably inevitable—as opposed to extraordinary or surprising—when viewed in the light of ordinary experience. In this sense, then, "proximate result" bears a resemblance to the concept of "proximate cause" in that defendant will be held responsible for those foreseeable consequences which are known to be, or should be known to be, within the scope of the risk created by his conduct. *State v. Chambers (1977),* 53 Ohio App. 2d 266. Here, that means that death reasonably could be anticipated by an ordinarily prudent person as likely to result under these or similar circumstances. See *State v. Nosis* (1969), 22 Ohio App. 2d 16.

Consequences which are reasonably foreseeable from a burglary were aptly summarized by the Court of Appeals for Lorain County in its opinion in *State v. Chambers,* supra, 53 Ohio App .2d at 270-271, 373 N.E.2d 393:

> We conceive few dangers, faced by the law-abiding public, to be more extreme than the unlawful entrance of one person into a residence occupied by another. The risk of actual serious physical harm to a victim or wrongdoer, the threat of surprise of one by the other, the natural inclination of the victim, if present, to protect and defend his abode and his family are all factors too clear to discuss further. To imagine that the risk of physical harm is not foreseeable under the circumstances surrounding this case defies not only logic but also the characteristics of the human animal. ***

The evidence in this case does not describe a situation where the deceased was the victim of physical violence, or of fright or shock, resulting from a direct physical confrontation with a burglar. According to the evidence, Mrs. Harper heard a noise in the night and followed her son downstairs where he discovered that a door had been pried open.

The deputy coroner testified that, due to her existing condition, Mrs. Harper was a "prime candidate" to have a heart attack and that "[i]t would be more probable that an insult would have lethal consequence because of the already damaged heart." A hypothetical question posed to the deputy coroner by the prosecutor includes these facts:

> Q. *** Doctor, *** Hypothesize a 69-year-old woman who had severe generalized atherosclerosis to the head, brain, lower

extremities, and a mild case of cardiomegaly. She also has arterionephrosclerosis and has had three prior heart attacks in 1970, 1971, and in 1982.

She also has pleuritis and focal dense pulmonary lumphocytic infiltrate as well as a very high blood pressure.

Due to the atherosclerosis, she also has angina pectoris, and she has severe diabetes mellitus.

She would, however, normally stay away from things that upset her. On November the 25th, 1983 [the night of the incident], this woman played bingo, which her physician advised her against doing but which she had been doing for approximately 20 years. At approximately one o'clock in the morning *** her son heard a noise in the living room ***. His mother came to his room. They both went to investigate the noise.

Upon reaching the living room, both noticed that the front door was open and that a bicycle had been moved. Neither ever saw any intruder.

The woman went to her bedroom, returned to the living room, became very excited, and while her son was calling the police, collapsed on the living room floor by the hallway. ***

In the course of performing an autopsy on this person, there were some thrombi found near the area of the right ventricle in the artery.

Doctor, based upon the foregoing, do you have an opinion to a reasonable medical certainty as to the cause of that coronary thrombosis?

***

A. Yes, sir, I do.

Q. Would you state your opinion, please?

A. She died of an acute coronary thrombosis and that it was precipitated by the emotion.

The doctor's testimony established that defendant's conduct was a cause of Mrs. Harper's death in the sense that it set in motion events which culminated in her death. However, it still must be determined whether defendant was legally responsible for her death—whether the death was the proximate result of his conduct. It is not necessary that the accused be in a position to foresee the precise consequence of his conduct; only that the consequence be foreseeable in the sense that what actually transpired was natural and logical in that it was within the scope of the risk created by his conduct. That concept is well-illustrated by the facts of *State v. Chambers, supra,* where the defendant and a confederate broke into a residence, were confronted by the armed resident and, in the melee which ensued, defendant's confederate was mortally wounded by the resident. Determining that the companion's death was a foreseeable consequence of defendant's conduct, the court of appeals upheld his conviction for involuntary manslaughter.

By the same token, in this case, the causal relationship between defendant's criminal conduct and Mrs. Harper's death was not too improbable, remote, or speculative to form a basis for criminal responsibility. Although defendant did not engage in loud or violent conduct calculated to frighten or shock, his presence was nevertheless detected by Mrs. Harper.

There are numerous reported cases where criminal responsibility has attached to a death resulting from fright or shock where the defendant's criminal conduct was witnessed by the victim. See Annotation (1956), 47 A.L.R.2d 1072 and supplements. Most of those cases involved situations where the victim's health was fragile, even though the accused might not have been aware of that fact.

Although, in the context of a death precipitated by fright or shock attending the apparent commission of a burglary, we would be hesitant to stretch the concept of proximate result, with its component requirement of foreseeable consequences, to encompass a death resulting from events not triggered by contact or close contemporaneous physical proximity involving the accused and his victim, in this case, defendant and the victim were in the same house at the same time and the victim's fright was initially precipitated by her detection of defendant's presence.

Defendant also argues that the trial court's decision was impermissibly based upon an inference on an inference. This contention is not well-taken. There was direct evidence of Mrs. Harper's emotion. Her son testified that she was very upset upon discovering the burglary and that he had never seen her that upset. The cause of death, coronary thrombosis, was established by the direct evidence of the deputy coroner's testimony and the autopsy report. The only inference involved is whether the emotion caused the thrombosis. The coroner stated his opinion that, to a reasonable medical certainty, the emotion of discovering the burglary caused the attack. Dr. Murnane testified that stress could have caused the attack and would have done so within minutes of the stress.

The first assignment of error is overruled.

Notes and Questions

1. Historical Note. As mentioned in *State v. Beaver*, Ohio, like most jurisdictions, no longer follows the "year and a day" rule. *State v. Sandridge* provides historical background on the rule.

State v. Sandridge, 365 N.E.2d 898 (1977)

The term "year and a day" in the English common law has its historical roots in the Statute of Gloucester enacted in 1278. This statute allowed a year and a day from the time of the injury for a private appeal to be initiated. 65 Dickinson Law Review 166, 167. The "year and a day" rule of limitation on the right to prosecute an appeal seems by transition (and probably through ignorance and confusion) to have become a substantial element of the definition of criminal homicide. 19 Chicago Kent Law Review 181, 183.

Most American courts, with little thought given to either the antecedents or the validity of such a rule, follow the common-law principle that in order to constitute punishable homicide, death must accrue within a year and a day from the infliction of a mortal wound. 60 A.L.R.3d 1323, 1326. Nevertheless, courts of this state are not bound to hold that a common-law rule is the law of Ohio, but they are left to determine the question according to their best light and judgment, especially in view of the fact that all English statutes grew out of peculiar exigencies, many of which are foreign to our present conditions and habits. 9 0.Jur.2d Common Law 85, at 555.

The reason for the "year and a day" rule was announced by Lord Coke:

> "If he died after that time (a year and a day), it cannot be discerned, as the law presumes whether he died of the stroke or poison, etc., or a natural death; and in the case of life, the law ought to be certain." Coke, 3 Inst. 52.

Hence, this ancient rule was nothing more than an arbitrary settlement of what may have originally been a very difficult proof of physical cause. The difficulty of proof arose because: first, in the early English courts the jury reached the verdict upon their own knowledge, or expressed the community conviction on the issue; and second, medical technology had not progressed to the point where death could be precisely determined to have resulted from a particular cause. 65 Dickinson Law Review, at 170.

2. For those jurisdictions that do not adhere to the year and a day rule, do you think there should be any time limitations, outside of the Speedy Trial clock and statute of limitations, placed on when charges may be brought against a defendant? Before answering that question, consider the following.

Ian Urbina, *New Murder Charge in '66 Shooting*
NY Times (Sept. 19, 2007)

William J. Barnes shot and partly paralyzed a Philadelphia police officer in 1966, and he served 20 years for it and related offenses.

But last month, 41 years after the shooting, the district attorney filed new charges of murder after the officer, Walter T. Barclay Jr., died of an infection she says stems from the shooting. Mr. Barnes, now 71, was sent back to prison.

"The law is that when you set in motion a chain of events," District Attorney Lynne M. Abraham said, "a perpetrator of a crime is responsible for every single thing that flows from that chain of events, no matter how distant, as long as we can prove the chain is unbroken."

She plans to prove that the bullet that lodged near Mr. Barclay's spine in 1966 led to the urinary tract infection that led to his death last month.

The case has drawn national attention as most legal experts say they have never seen an attempt to stretch causation medically across four decades, and some say they worry about the precedent the case could set concerning double jeopardy.

Moreover, establishing an unbroken chain could be difficult in light of Mr. Barclay's medical history.

After his initial paralysis, his condition improved significantly and he regained motion in his legs, walking with braces and riding short distances on a stationary bicycle. But he reinjured his spine repeatedly, in two car accidents and in a fall from his wheelchair, according to interviews with relatives and news reports from the era.

While paralyzed, Mr. Barclay also contracted hepatitis, according to his family, which medical experts say could have weakened his ability later to fight off infections. The district attorney's office has also confirmed that although the coroner's office ruled his death a homicide, no autopsy was done on Mr. Barclay, who was buried last month.

Mr. Barclay himself even spoke of the role his own actions played in worsening his medical condition.

"The guy started spraying bullets around, and I caught two of them in the back," Mr. Barclay said in a 1978 interview about the night he was shot. "I got over that pretty much, but then I had a car accident and hurt my back again. Then I had another and hurt my back some more."

Allen M. Hornblum, an urban studies professor at Temple University who researched Mr. Barclay's history and invited Mr. Barnes to speak to his class about having turned his life around after a career in crime, said the new charges were "vindictive, pure and simple."

"Barnes served his time, but the police and the city want him to pay extra because he shot one of their own," he said, adding that even if the charge is dismissed, the case will probably take so long to get to that stage that Mr. Barnes, who has had two heart attacks in the last three years, will die waiting. Ms. Abraham has denied that the victim's being a police officer played any role in her decision to file new charges.

Ms. Abraham also argues that double jeopardy, which means a person cannot be charged twice for the same crime, does not apply in this case because the original crime was aggravated assault and the current crime — now that Mr. Barclay is dead — is murder. Mr. Barnes's court-appointed lawyer has not decided whether to challenge that view.

William Barclay, 59, the slain officer's brother, feels the prosecution is justified. "Barnes deserves to be back in prison," he said. "He is 71, and that's seven more years of life than my brother had."

"This was murder delayed," Mr. Barclay added, recounting his brother's bouts of pneumonia, painful and constant bedsores and the full-body muscle spasms that threw him from bed. "The length of time since the shooting shouldn't matter."

When asked about the car accidents, Mr. Barclay, who has lived in California since the 1970s, said he was not aware of them.

"Mr. Barnes is being held without bond, and he will not see a judge until his first court date in December," said his lawyer, Bobby Hoof.

In many states, the year and a day rule, a 19th-century common law rule, prevents new charges from being filed if a victim dies more than 366 days after the initial injury. But Paul Wright, editor of Prison Legal News, an independent monthly, said that as medical advancements have prolonged the lives of injured people; at least 20 states, including Pennsylvania, have eliminated the rule. Medical and forensic advancements, however, have also increased the burden of proof on prosecutors to clearly show how an injury led directly to a victim's later death, he said.

Such convictions, however, are not unprecedented. In Michigan, a man was convicted of assault with intent to murder in 1983 after shooting another man. Four years later, after sustaining head injuries in a fight, the shooting victim suffered seizures and died. Prosecutors filed new murder charges against the gunman, and using an autopsy were able to prove that the victim's death resulted from damage to his heart from the shooting, not the head injuries.

Jeffrey M. Lindy, a former federal prosecutor in Philadelphia, said he believed Ms. Abraham was pursuing the case against Mr. Barnes to please the police, but he predicted it would probably not make it to trial. "A judge will first have a hearing, and at that hearing a doctor is going to say, 'Look, the causation is not there,'" he said.

Sitting in a four-by-five-foot room at Graterford prison, 31 miles north of Philadelphia, Mr. Barnes said, "I was trying to start over."

Having spent 48 of his 71 years in prison on multiple offenses and parole violations, he was released in 2005 and had started meeting family who never knew he existed as he lived in a halfway house and worked as a janitor at a drugstore.

"Nothing shames me more than what happened that night," he said about the shooting. "I had a good family, a good life and bad morals. I'll have to answer to my maker for the suffering that man went through."

"But I'm an old man now," he said. "I paid my debt."

Mr. Barnes earned that debt one cold November morning in 1966 as he tried to pry open the back door of a beauty parlor. Responding to a call about a prowler, Officer Barclay, 23 at the time, arrived to find Mr. Barnes, who says he was drunk. Mr. Barnes shot Officer Barclay twice, once in the left thigh and once in the shoulder, the second shot lodging an inch from Officer Barclay's spine.

That bullet shattered his life, his family said. And yet he fought to recover. Within nine months, he was walking short distances with leg braces. He soon began driving a car with hand controls and moved into a ground-floor apartment to live on his own. He worked a desk job at police headquarters for a year or so.

Things took a turn for the worse, however. One morning while driving to work, Officer Barclay's car skidded off an icy road. He reinjured his spine, and the Police Department put him on permanent disability, according to court documents and news reports from the time. In the mid-1970s, he became a clerk at the information booth at 30th Street Station in Philadelphia.

But "age began to tell on him," said Rosalyn Barclay Harrison, Mr. Barclay's 68-year-old sister. There were also various injuries along the way. In 1975, he fell from his wheelchair, which left him without use of his left arm, according to a column written by Mr. Barclay's close friend Larry McMullen, a Philadelphia newspaper writer. In 1976, he was in a second car accident for which he underwent rehabilitation at Rolling Hill Hospital in Montgomery County, according to newspaper accounts.

Ms. Harrison said her brother's life was pure "agony."

She confirmed that Mr. Barclay was in at least one serious car accident and that in later years he got hepatitis. But she endorsed the new charges against Mr. Barnes. "In my own mind, I don't see this as double jeopardy," she said.

"I have no qualms about Barnes being recharged for murder," she added, with a pause, "because I do feel it that way."

3. In *State v. Losey*, the court attempts to put some limitations on its holding by writing the following:

> [W]e would be hesitant to stretch the concept of proximate result, with its component requirement of foreseeable consequences, to encompass a death resulting from events not

triggered by contact or close contemporaneous physical proximity involving the accused and his victim..[.]

Do you agree with these limitations? Can you think of a scenario where the defendant may be the proximate cause even though the defendant was not in close proximity to the victim?

4. Do you agree with the holding in *Losey*? Is it reasonably foreseeable that an unarmed burglar would cause such stress upon Mrs. Harper? What about Mrs. Harper's failing health, should that be taken into account? Does the court conclude that the offender takes his victim as he finds him or her, like the egg-shell skull doctrine found in torts?

B. Intervening Act

Certain intervening acts may break the proximate cause chain. In reading the following case, look to determine whether the actions of the victim were sufficient to break the causal chain.

United States v. Hamilton, 182 F. Supp. 548 (D.D.C. 1960)

HOLTZOFF, District Judge.

This is a trial of a charge of murder in the second degree. The trial is before the Court without a jury, as the defendant has waived his right to trial by jury.

The indictment avers that on or about December 2, 1959, within the District of Columbia, Benjamin E. Hamilton, with malice aforethought, murdered John W. Slye by means of striking him with his fists and stamping and kicking him with his shod feet. Specifically, the charge is that on the evening of December 2, 1959, the defendant and the deceased were in a fight on Lamont Street near Georgia Avenue in the City of Washington; that the deceased was knocked down in the course of the fight, and that then the defendant jumped on his face and kicked his face, inflicting wounds of which the deceased later died. The defense is that the wounds inflicted by the defendant on the deceased were not the cause of death.

The evidence in this case establishes the following salient facts. On the afternoon and evening of December 2, 1959, a number of men had gathered in a poolroom on Georgia Avenue near Lamont Street for the purpose of recreation. The defendant and the deceased were in that group. They played several games of pool. They imbibed intoxicating beverages in the rear of the establishment, and they also carried on desultory conversations. There was an exchange of banter between the deceased and the defendant, which developed into an argument, and finally into an acrimonious quarrel. The subject matter of the argument must have been trivial and inconsequential, because the defendant, although he narrated with a great degree of particularity the events of that evening, does not remember what the discussion was about. Both the deceased and the defendant were asked by the person in charge of the poolroom to leave, because it was undesirable that a fight should develop inside. Accordingly, both of them went outside and a fight started on Lamont Street. In the course of the fight, the deceased was knocked down by the defendant. While he was lying on the ground, the defendant apparently exploded in a fit of ungovernable rage and jumped on the face of the deceased and kicked him in the head as well.

The deceased was taken to the District of Columbia General Hospital, arriving there at 11:30 p.m. No useful purpose would be served by recounting the gory and harrowing details concerning the nature of the injuries sustained by the deceased to his face and head. Suffice it to say that he apparently was in a semi-comatose condition. He was violent and in shock. Blood was coming from his face.

Promptly upon arrival at the hospital, the deceased came into the competent hands of the Chief Resident of the Neurological Service, who impressed the Court as a completely dedicated and entirely devoted physician. He did everything possible that could be done for his patient. A blood transfusion was given to the deceased, his airways were cleansed, and tubes inserted into his nasal passages and trachea in order to maintain the breathing process. In view of the fact that he was violent, it was necessary to restrain the patient by fastening leather handcuffs on him. The doctor saw the patient several times during the night. In addition, the registered nurse in charge of the ward in which the deceased was placed, saw him at least every half hour or every thirty-five minutes. The deceased was in a room with only one other patient. A licensed practical nurse was constantly in attendance in that room. It is obvious that the patient received incessant and continuous care and treatment at the hands of both the medical and nursing staff of the hospital.

During the night it became desirable to change the bed clothes of the deceased, because they had become bloody. To accomplish this result, it was necessary to remove the restraints from the patient. They were not put back, because by that time, the patient was no longer violent and was resting better than when he arrived. About 6:30 in the morning, the patient had a convulsion, and immediately thereafter, he himself, with his own hands, pulled out the tubes. At 7:30 a.m., the patient died.

The Deputy Coroner, who performed the autopsy and who himself is an experienced physician, found the cause of death to be asphyxiation due to aspiration or inhalation of blood caused by severe injuries to the face, including multiple fractures of the nasal bones. The attending physician testified that the cause of death was asphyxia. In other words, the two physicians agree as to the cause of death. It should be said at this point that the purpose of the tubes was to assist in keeping the airways clear in order that the patient might breathe normally. It is claimed by able counsel for the defendant that the immediate cause of death was the fact that the patient pulled out the tubes, and that, therefore, he brought about his own death. This contention requires a consideration of the applicable principles of law.

It is well established that if a person strikes another and inflicts a blow that may not be mortal in and of itself but thereby starts a chain of causation that leads to death, he is guilty of homicide. This is true even if the deceased contributes to his own death or hastens it by failing to take proper treatment.

The principles of the common law on this subject are summarized in Hale's Pleas of the Crown, Volume 1, p. 427, in a passage that has been frequently quoted. He says:

> If a man give another a stroke, which it may be, is not in itself so mortal, but that with good care he might be cured, yet if he die of this wound within a year and a day, it is homicide or murder, as the case is, and so it hath been always ruled.

And, again, Hale says:

> But if a man receives a wound, which is not in itself mortal, but either for want of helpful applications, or neglect thereof, it turns to a gangrene, or a fever, and that gangrene or fever be the immediate cause of his death, yet, this is murder or manslaughter in him that gave the stroke or wound, for that wound, tho it were not the immediate cause of his death, yet, if it were the mediate cause thereof, and the fever or gangrene was the immediate cause of his death, yet the wound was the cause of the gangrene or fever, and so consequently is causa causati.

Judicial decisions applying this doctrine are too numerous to require a review. Suffice it to say that these principles have been adopted and applied in the District of Columbia, in *Hopkins v. United States*, 4 App. D.C. 430. In that case, the defendant had struck the deceased. Several weeks later the deceased died, and the autopsy showed that the death was caused by the blow that had been inflicted by the defendant. It was argued that the defendant was not guilty of homicide, because the deceased had neglected to take medical treatment after he was struck and that his failure to do so either caused or contributed to bringing about his death. This contention was overruled, and it was held that the mere fact that the deceased had neglected to procure proper treatment for the effects of the blow or wound did not relieve the defendant of his responsibility for the homicide.

Hawkins' Pleas of the Crown, Volume 1, Chapter 31, Section 10, summarizes this principle very succinctly. He says:

> But if a person hurt by another, die thereof within a year and a day, it is no excuse for the other that he might have recovered, i[f] he had not neglected to take care of himself.

It is urged by defense counsel, however, that this case should not be governed by the principles just discussed, because, in this instance, the deceased was not guilty merely of neglect, but took affirmative action which contributed to his death, namely, pulling out the tubes. The evidence is far from clear whether the action of the deceased in pulling out the tubes was a reflex action, or whether he was then only semi-conscious, or whether it was a conscious, deliberate act on his part. It is not necessary, however, to resolve this question of fact, because even if the act of the deceased in pulling out the tubes was conscious and deliberate, it would not help the defendant. First, there is not sufficient evidence to justify a finding that if the tubes had remained in the trachea and nasal passages of the deceased, he would have continued to live. Second, and quite irrespective of that consideration, even if it were to be assumed, arguendo, that the deceased might have lived if he had not pulled out the tubes, this circumstance would not have any effect on the liability and responsibility of the defendant for the death of the deceased.

In *People v. Lewis*, 124 Cal. 551 the facts were as follows. The defendant inflicted a gunshot wound on the deceased. This wound was mortal. The deceased, however, procured a knife and cut his throat, and thereby brought about his death sooner than would have been the case if it had resulted from the original wound. The defendant was convicted of manslaughter, and the conviction was affirmed by the highest court of California.

An even more extreme case is *Stephenson v. State*, 205 Ind. 141. There the defendant attempted to rape the deceased, and seriously, but not mortally, wounded her. She took poison and died as a result of the poisoning. The defendant was convicted of murder in the second degree, and the Supreme Court of Indiana affirmed the conviction. As against the argument in behalf of the defendant that there was no homicide, since the deceased took her own life by committing suicide, the Court held that the jury was justified in finding that the defendant by his acts or conduct rendered the deceased distracted and mentally irresponsible and that her taking poison was a natural and probable consequence of the unlawful and criminal treatment that the defendant had inflicted on the deceased.

Here the question before the Court is whether the defendant should be deemed guilty of homicide or guilty merely of assault with a dangerous weapon. As has been indicated by the Supreme Court, assault is a lesser included-offense in an indictment for murder, *Logan v. United States*, 144 U.S. 263. Further, the Court of Appeals for this Circuit has held that shoes on feet are dangerous weapons, at least when they inflict serious injuries, *Medlin v. United States*, 93 U.S. App. D.C. 64. The Court is of the opinion, however, that the injuries inflicted on the deceased by the defendant were the cause of death in the light of the principles of law heretofore discussed, and that, therefore, the defendant should be adjudged guilty of homicide.***

Accordingly, the Court finds the defendant guilty of manslaughter.

Notes and Questions

1. In *United States v. Hamilton*, why weren't the victim's actions sufficient to break the causal chain? What more must the victim do to break the causal chain? Are victims the only ones who can break the causal chain? What about acts of God or third parties?

2. *Hamilton* illustrates how a brutal assault or an attempted rape can cause the victim to end his or her life, resulting in a charge of homicide for the offender. Are there crimes for which this should not apply? Suppose in *State v. Losey* that the defendant was successful in stealing not only the bicycle but also family heirlooms, and Mrs. Harper was so distraught over the theft that she committed suicide. Would the defendant have been guilty of homicide?

C. Concurrence

The final requirement for a completed crime involves concurrence. With respect to concurrence, the defendant's actus reus and mens rea must occur at the same time. The next case illustrates what happens when they don't.

In re L.D., 63 Ohio Misc. 2d 303 (Ohio Ct. Com. P. 1993)

KENNETH A. ROCCO, Judge.

I. FACTS

On May 3, 1993, Lola D., age thirteen, was invited to spend the night at her friend Maria's house. As Lola accompanied her home, Maria decided to stop at the home of Angela France. Lola had no knowledge of the visit until the girls neared the France house. When nobody responded to their repeated knocking on the door of the France house, Lola opened the front door, which was unlocked, and called out. When no one answered, Lola went into the kitchen and stole a pack of cigarettes from the top of the refrigerator. Upon stealing the cigarettes, she left the Frances' house. The state has charged Lola with aggravated burglary, pursuant to R.C. 2911.11(A)(3), which makes it a felony of the first degree to trespass in a building occupied as a home, with the purpose of committing a theft offense therein. Maria was not charged with any offense in connection with the occurrence.

II. DISCUSSION

The issue in this case is whether the offense of aggravated burglary, pursuant to R.C. 2911.11(A)(3), requires that the intent to commit a theft offense exist at the time of the trespass. The child claims that she did not have the requisite intent at the time of her trespass to support the charge of aggravated burglary. The state argues that it is irrelevant whether Lola's intent to commit a theft offense was formed after she had already committed the trespass, because the act of trespassing is a continuing offense which at some point became simultaneous with her intention to steal the pack of cigarettes.

Although the language of R.C. 2911.11 appears to clearly require an intent to commit a theft offense or felony which is contemporaneous with the trespass, Ohio courts are inexplicably split in their resolution of this issue. See *State v. Clelland* (1992), 83 Ohio App. 3d 474, 487-488, 615 N.E.2d 276, 285-286, at fn. 3. Several Ohio appellate courts have determined that the purpose to commit a felony or theft offense must be formed either before or at the time of the initial trespass or entry. *Id.* Other Ohio appellate courts have held that the necessary felonious purpose may evolve during the course of the trespass. *Id.*

The state relies primarily on *State v. Steffen* (1987), 31 Ohio St. 3d 111, 31 OBR 273, 509 N.E.2d 383, in making its assertion that the intent to commit a theft offense may be formed after the initial trespass. However, this reliance is unfounded because the facts of *Steffen* are clearly distinguishable from the facts of this matter. The issue in *Steffen* was whether the defendant had in fact trespassed, because he had originally been invited into the victim's home as a salesman. The Supreme Court of Ohio affirmed the defendant's conviction for aggravated burglary, finding that the original invitation into the victim's home was vitiated when the defendant commenced his assault upon her. This rationale cannot be applied to the facts of this case. The issue here is not whether Lola committed a trespass, but whether she had the requisite intent at the time of the trespass to raise her offense to the level of aggravated burglary, a felony of the first degree.

The case most factually analogous to this one is *State v. Lewis* (1992), 78 Ohio App. 3d 518, 605 N.E.2d 451 (defendant entered house to purchase eggs, but when nobody was home he stole a checkbook). In *Lewis,* the Fourth District Court of Appeals declined to follow the line of cases holding that the requisite intent could be formed after the trespass had occurred, and instead held that the intent to commit a theft offense must be contemporaneous with the trespass.

The *Lewis* court based its decision on the express meaning of the language employed by the legislature in R.C. 2911.11. As the *Lewis* court stated:

> There is no question that the legislature could have included those situations where the intent is formed after the trespass. However, where the legislature says aggravated burglary shall be trespass with intent, a court may not, under the guise of construction, eliminate a distinction the legislature has created in the language of the statute.

Lewis, 78 Ohio App. 3d at 522, 605 N.E.2d at 454.

The distinction referred to by the *Lewis* court is critical, and will not be ignored by this court. It is based on the appellate court's thorough understanding of the five-hundred-year tradition of common law, which is the genesis of Ohio's current criminal statutes. This understanding is augmented by the Committee Comment to H.B. No. 511, which notes that the 1972 omnibus revisions, in large measure, reiterated Ohio's earlier analogous criminal statutes, which were themselves a reiteration of the common law. The 1972 revisions of the criminal statutes therefore reflect the common-law tradition that came before, and many structural differences are more apparent than real.

Even if there were not a common-law tradition and earlier analogous statutes on which to rely, logic and the legislative rationale for the differentiated penalties for aggravated burglary, lesser burglary offenses, and trespass would require this court to reach the conclusion that the state has inappropriately charged Lola.

The legislature clearly based its classification of the breaking and entering offenses on an assessment of the behavior's dangerousness. This measure of dangerousness is reflected in the elements of the offenses and the relative severity of the penalties, as well as in the Committee Comments to the statute. Of the historically related offenses, the charge of aggravated burglary carries with it the most severe penalty. According to the Committee Comment to H.B. No. 511, aggravated burglary is the most serious of the breaking and entering offenses because the "relative potential for harm to persons" is at a maximum. It would follow, then, that the lesser burglary offenses should apply to those instances of breaking and entering when the "relative potential for harm to persons" is moderate. Finally, trespass should apply to those types of related behaviors when there is minimal potential for harm to persons. The legislative intent that the charge of aggravated burglary be reserved for the most dangerous behaviors is very clear from the structure of the statute and the accompanying Comment.

As a society, we blur such distinctions in our criminal statutes at our own peril. The justice system does not operate in a vacuum, and the charges against an offender must reflect the reality of the offender's conduct. Presumably, the state has charged Lola with aggravated burglary, rather than with a lesser burglary offense or with trespass, because there was great "relative potential for harm to persons" inherent in her conduct. A juvenile who is adjudicated delinquent as an aggravated burglar is, by definition, a dangerous offender who is liable to be confined for a lengthy term in a secure juvenile correctional facility. Does the evidence in this matter indicate that Lola is a dangerous offender? According to the evidence presented, Lola does not appear to be a dangerous offender. To treat her as a dangerous offender for stealing a pack of cigarettes would, most certainly, provide grist for the literary mill of a Twenty-First-Century Victor Hugo. Of more immediate concern, if Lola were to be confined in a secure facility as a dangerous offender, who might be released on early parole to make room for her?

The severe overcrowding of Ohio's prisons and juvenile facilities is a fact of life with which we will contend during this decade and the next. It is common knowledge that there are many dangerous offenders in adult prisons and juvenile correctional facilities who, in the interest of public safety, ought to be securely confined for the maximum period allowed by law, if not longer. Likewise, it is common knowledge that if a nonviolent first offender, such as Lola, is committed to a secure facility, the pressures attendant to facility overcrowding would likely prompt the release of an offender who has served the minimum term allowed by law. As severe facility overcrowding tends to prompt the release of offenders such as Lola at the earliest opportunity allowed by law, those not released at the earliest opportunity are likely to be administratively classified as dangerous offenders. Hence, it is likely that a dangerous offender would be paroled early to make room for an offender such as Lola.

If any semblance of success in confronting crime is to be realized, the component parts of the justice system—police agencies, prosecuting agencies, the courts, and corrections—must formulate a strategic plan that sets goals and objectives and devises strategies to achieve those goals, including the rational allocations of justice resources. As there are precious few juvenile correctional cells because of institutional overcrowding, it would be folly to waste them on nonviolent first offenders. When a nonviolent first offender enters the front door of the institution, a dangerous offender is likely to exit the back door.

At the very minimum, a logical and rational justice policy would require that correctional cells, which are in short supply because of severe facility overcrowding, be allocated based on a dangerousness measure, such as the one implemented in by the legislature in its assessment of the "relative potential for harm to persons," at least until overcrowding is alleviated. Likewise, other justice resources in short supply, such as short-term detention cells, investigators, prosecutors, intensive behavior modification programming and courtrooms, ought to be allocated in accordance with a dangerousness measure. Such a policy would require that the "relative potential for harm" which distinguishes aggravated burglary, lesser burglary offenses and related trespass behaviors be scrupulously observed during investigation, at charging, during prosecution, at adjudication and disposition, and during corrections.

If a dangerous offender is paroled to make room for Lola, then we do blur the distinctions in our criminal statutes at our own peril. Such a haphazard approach to criminal justice is both mindless and dangerous to public safety. This court chooses not to blur the distinctions. The state's evidence is that Lola committed a trespass and a subsequent theft. There is no evidence that Lola harbored an intent to steal at the time she entered the home. If anything, the evidence indicates that when she opened the door and entered the home, it was her intention to call out to Angela.

III. CONCLUSION

It is this court's view that the relative potential for harm to persons was minimal as a result of Lola's conduct. The court finds that it is in the interest of justice, pursuant to Juv.R. 22, to amend the complaint to allege criminal trespass, pursuant to R.C. 2911.21, and petty theft, pursuant to R.C. 2913.02, both misdemeanors, which amended complaint conforms to the evidence at the trial.

The court further finds that the allegations of the amended complaint, alleging misdemeanor trespass and petty theft, have been proven by evidence beyond a reasonable doubt.

Notes and Questions

1. With respect to *In re L.D.*, where was the lack of concurrence?

2. At the time of *In re L.D.*, Ohio courts were split on whether the defendant had to formulate a plan to commit a felony prior to entering the dwelling in order to constitute burglary. Why do you think the judge decided to follow the common law rule with respect to this particular case? Do you think the judge thought that the prosecution overcharged this 13-year old? If you were the prosecutor, would you charge a 13-year old with aggravated burglary for stealing a pack of cigarettes from someone's home?

3. List the policy arguments made by the judge in *In re L.D.* Can you think of additional policy arguments? How much weight do you believe policy considerations should carry in individual criminal prosecutions?

PART III
Crimes Against the Person

Chapter 6
Homicide

A. Background

Some use the terms "homicide" and "murder" interchangeably. For the purposes of this book, "homicide" is the broader umbrella term that encompasses both "murder" and "manslaughter." Manslaughter, which includes both "voluntary" and "involuntary," will be discussed in depth immediately after the chapters on murder.

B. Malice Aforethought

Common law defines murder as the unlawful killing of another human being with malice aforethought. "Malice aforethought" is a legal term somewhat removed from the definitions traditionally associated with the words "malice" and "aforethought." It is best to think of "malice aforethought" as a legal term of art that serves as the mens rea for murder at common law.

The first method of proving malice aforethought is by demonstrating an intent to kill. However, this does not necessarily mean that the defendant has any ill-will towards the victim. The defendant only needs an intent to kill the victim. In this first method, malice aforethought is expressed. In contrast, malice aforethought is implied with the other three methods.

Infliction of serious bodily harm to the victim is the second way of proving malice aforethought. Here, the defendant need not want nor intend for the victim to die but the victim nonetheless does because the defendant inflicted serious bodily harm on the victim. An example of serious bodily harm is the intentional use of a deadly weapon. Generally speaking, the use of hands or feet in an attack on another will not be sufficient to imply malice aforethought. Exceptions to this rule may arise when a significant difference in age and size exists between the two parties or the defendant continuously assaults a helpless victim.

Depraved heart murder or reckless indifference to the value of human life is the third way of proving malice aforethought. Examples of the defendant acting with a depraved heart include playing Russian Roulette, firing a weapon into a room occupied with people, or driving a car at a very high speed on a crowded downtown street.

Felony murder is the fourth way of proving malice aforethought. Here, the victim dies while the defendant is carrying out a burglary, arson, rape, robbery, or kidnapping. Felony murder will be discussed in greater detail later in the book.

Fouts v. State, 8 Ohio St. 98 (1857)

***It is conceded, that *a purpose* or *design* to kill is not an essential ingredient in murder at common law. The crime at common law consists in the unlawful killing of a human being, under the king's peace, with malice prepense or aforethought, either *express* or *implied* by law. 1 Russ. on Cri. 482. This is the substance of the definition, or rather description, of murder given by Lord Coke, (3 Inst. 47, 50,) and sanctioned by Blackstone, (4 Bla. Com. 198,) and all the modern English authorities. The distinguishing feature in this definition is that of *malice prepense* or *aforethought*. By this *malice*, it is said, is meant, not simply a special malevolence to the individual slain, but a wicked, depraved and malignant spirit, a heart regardless of social duty, and deliberately bent on mischief. It is held, that there is *express malice* where one person kills another with a sedate, deliberate mind, and formed design, to take life; and that, where a person, not intending to take life, but designing to inflict a grievous bodily harm, or while perpetrating some other and collateral felony or misdemeanor, kills another, there *malice is implied* by law from the deliberate cruel act, or the depravity and criminal inclination of the perpetrator at the time. But, in England, murder is not classified into degrees, but every murder is of the same grade, and subject to the same penalty, whether *the malice* be *express* or *implied*. So that, *intention* or *formed purpose* to kill, is not essential to constitute murder at common law. An averment, therefore, of a purpose or intent to kill, is not requisite in an indictment for murder at common law.

But the common law in relation to murder, as well as other matters, is subject to modification and alteration by statute. In some of the states of this country, the law on the subject of murder differs materially from the common law of England. It is true, the statute enacted by Congress prescribes the punishment for murder without defining it, leaving the term murder, as used in the act, to be understood as defined at common law. Act 30, April, 1790, sec. 8. *United States* v. *Magill*, 1 Wash. C. C. Rep. 463. And in Massachusetts, it is simply provided by statute, that, "every person, who shall commit the crime of murder, shall suffer the punishment of death for the same," without describing what shall constitute murder. Under these statutes, of course, the form of the indictment for murder at common law would be proper, and altogether sufficient. In Pennsylvania, Virginia, New York, and other states, different degrees have been created in murder, affixing the punishment of death to murder with express malice, and other murder of the most aggravated character, and imprisonment as the punishment for the other and less aggravated kinds of murder. The statutes of these states, however, in making the different degrees in murder, have followed, as closely as practicable, the common law description of murder. So that, in many instances, the form of the indictment for murder at common law would seem to be sufficient in those states. In other states, however, murder is defined by statute essentially different from murder at common law in various and material matters. In Ohio, there are no crimes or misdemeanors by the common law, and the statute of this state, which defines murder with great precision and certainty, is recited by Wharton, in his Treatise on American Criminal Law, (page 510, third edition,) as an illustration of the essential difference between statutory murder and murder at common law. This statutory provision is as follows:

> That if any person shall *purposely*, and of deliberate and premeditated *malice*, or in the perpetration or attempt to perpetrate any rape, arson, robbery or burglary, or by administering poison, or causing the same to be done, kill another, every such person shall be deemed guilty of murder in the first degree, and, upon conviction thereof, shall suffer death.
>
> That if any person shall *purposely* and *maliciously*, but without deliberation and premeditation, kill another, every such person shall be deemed guilty of murder in the second degree, and, on conviction thereof, shall be imprisoned in the penitentiary, and kept at hard labor during life.

The Supreme Court of the state gave a construction to this statute, in a circuit decision, reported in Wright's Rep. 27, made as early as 1831, in the following language:

> Murder in the first degree is the *intentional, unlawful* killing, by one reasonable being of another, in the peace of the state, of *deliberate* and *premeditated* malice. Murder in the second degree, is the *intentional, malicious* and *unlawful* killing, by one reasonable being of another, in the peace of the state, *without deliberate* or *premeditated* malice. Manslaughter, under our statute, is the *unlawful* killing, by one reasonable being of another, in the peace of the state, *without malice*, either upon a

sudden quarrel, or *unintentionally*, while the slayer is in the commission of some unlawful act.

Malice and *a design to kill*, are essential ingredients in the crime of murder, in either degree, while the first ingredient is altogether excluded from the crime of manslaughter. The *intention* or *design to kill*, is also excluded from the crime of manslaughter, where the death result from an unlawful act, *designed* to effect another object; but if there arise a sudden quarrel, and one under great provocation, instantly kill another, *intentionally*, it would be manslaughter.

And in the same case, Judge Wright, in his instructions to the jury, said:

> To convict of *murder in the first degree*, you must, in addition to the points I have mentioned, be satisfied: 1. That the prisoner perpetrated the act *purposely;* 2. That he did it with *intent to kill;* 3. That he did it of deliberate and premeditated malice. . . .. If these things are *all* proven, and you find the defendant guilty of murder in the first degree, you need examine no farther. If not proven to your satisfaction, you will then examine further.
>
> To convict of *murder in the second degree*, you must be satisfied: 1. That the prisoner perpetrated the act *purposely* and MALICIOUSLY; 2. *With intent to kill;* and 3. *Without deliberation or premeditation*.

This interpretation of the statute relating to criminal homicide, has been substantially affirmed, in numerous subsequent decisions on the circuit; (*The State v. Gardner*, Wright's Rep. 392; and *The State v. Thompson*, Ibid. 617;) has been recognized by the supreme court in bank, in sundry cases, (*Shoemaker v. The State*, 12 Ohio Rep. 43; *Clark* v. *The State*, Ibid. 483,) and has been consistently followed as the settled law of Ohio for the last twenty-five years.

It may, therefore, be assumed as well settled, that murder, in Ohio, is different from murder by the common law of England, not simply in the fact of the two degrees into which it is divided, but especially and most essentially, in the fact that *a purpose or intent to kill* is made by the statute an essential and distinguishing feature in murder, both of the first and also of the second degree. It follows that an indictment for murder, under the statute of this State, must contain a direct averment of *a purpose* or *intent to kill*, in the description of the crime charged.***

Notes and Questions

1. As previously discussed, there are four ways to prove malice aforethought at common law. Did *Fouts v. State* discuss each method?

2. The *Fouts* court notes that Ohio, by the 1850s, had deviated from English Common Law with respect to murder. Can you identify Ohio's deviations as discussed in *Fouts*?

C. Degrees of Murder

The common law has no degrees of murder. They are a creature of statute. In 1794, Pennsylvania became the first state to categorize murder into degrees. Following Pennsylvania's lead, the majority of states classified murder as either first, second, and on the rare occasion, third degree. Ohio uses the terms aggravated murder and murder instead of first and second degree murder. One reason for categorizing murder into degrees is for sentencing purposes. For example, the death penalty is generally reserved only for crimes falling under first degree or aggravated murder.

O.R.C. 2903.01 Aggravated Murder

(A) No person shall purposely, and with prior calculation and design, cause the death of another or the unlawful termination of another's pregnancy.

(B) No person shall purposely cause the death of another or the unlawful termination of another's pregnancy while committing or attempting to commit, or while fleeing immediately after committing or attempting to commit, kidnapping, rape, aggravated arson, arson, aggravated robbery, robbery, aggravated burglary, burglary, trespass in a habitation when a person is present or likely to be present, terrorism, or escape.

(C) No person shall purposely cause the death of another who is under thirteen years of age at the time of the commission of the offense.

(D) No person who is under detention as a result of having been found guilty of or having pleaded guilty to a felony or who breaks that detention shall purposely cause the death of another.

(E) No person shall purposely cause the death of a law enforcement officer whom the offender knows or has reasonable cause to know is a law enforcement officer when either of the following applies:

   (1) The victim, at the time of the commission of the offense, is engaged in the victim's duties.

   (2) It is the offender's specific purpose to kill a law enforcement officer.

(F) Whoever violates this section is guilty of aggravated murder, and shall be punished as provided in section 2929.02 of the Revised Code.

(G) As used in this section:

    (1) "Detention" has the same meaning as in section 2921.01 of the Revised Code.

    (2) "Law enforcement officer" has the same meaning as in section 2911.01 of the Revised Code.

O.R.C. 2903.02 Murder

(A) No person shall purposely cause the death of another or the unlawful termination of another's pregnancy.

(B) No person shall cause the death of another as a proximate result of the offender's committing or attempting to commit an offense of violence that is a felony of the first or second degree and that is not a violation of section 2903.03 or 2903.04 of the Revised Code.

(C) Division (B) of this section does not apply to an offense that becomes a felony of the first or second degree only if the offender previously has been convicted of that offense or another specified offense.

(D) Whoever violates this section is guilty of murder, and shall be punished as provided in section 2929.02 of the Revised Code.

Notes and Questions

1. Most first degree or aggravated murder statutes around the country include, at a minimum, felony murder and premeditated murder. Many jurisdictions, like Ohio, include additional types of homicide. Look at the additional categories included in Ohio's aggravated murder statute. Do you agree or disagree with them? Also, do you think additions should be made? For example, would you include "murder for hire" or killing of a witness or juror in the aggravated murder statute? Before answering these questions, consider the following article.

Lawmaker Proposes Death Penalty for Murder of First Responders, Military Personnel Robert Higgs
Columbus Dispatch (Feb. 10, 2017)

COLUMBUS, Ohio—A Northeast Ohio lawmaker's first bill in the General Assembly would expand the state's aggravated murder laws to allow the death penalty when the victim is a first responder or military member.

A statehouse bill introduced by Rep. Dave Greenspan, a Republican from Westlake, would also expand penalties for felonious assault when the victim of the crime is a police officer, first responder, federal officer or military member.

"The intent is to really provide a strong deterrent," Greenspan said.

The bill, HB 38, is Greenspan's first as a legislator. Fourteen other lawmakers, including four from Northeast Ohio, signed on as co-sponsors.

Where did the idea come from?

The legislation grew from an idea Greenspan developed over the last few years as police, fire and military personnel were victims in attacks across the country.

Most recently was an ambush attack in December on firefighters in Youngstown when they responded to a call. One firefighter was wounded in the leg and another narrowly escaped injury when a bullet passed through his turnout coat but didn't hit him. The shooter was waiting across the street from the burning house when firefighters arrived.

What would the bill do?

Greenspan proposes amending Ohio's criminal laws dealing with aggravated murder and felonious assault.

Under current law, if the murder victim is a police officer, the defendant could face the death penalty if convicted. Greenspan's proposal would add first responders (firefighters and EMS personnel), military personnel (including ROTC, reserve forces and National Guard) and federal law enforcement officers to that section of law.

It would apply to current and former members of those groups.

In addition, it would add that group to laws applying to felonious assault, upping the crime to a first-degree felony and requiring that any sentences handed down are served consecutively, rather than concurrently.

How does it work?

The law requires that the victim either be engaged in their duty—such as a police officer on patrol—or that the offender specifically is looking to kill someone who is in the protected group.

So, for example, if an attacker strikes out against people in a VFW hall or veterans marching in a parade, it should be apparent, Greenspan said, that they are striking out against former military personnel.

What happens next?

The bill was assigned to the House Criminal Justice Committee.

It is scheduled to get its first hearing, along with testimony from

2. Why is murder committed with prior calculation and design classified as aggravated murder? Can you make an argument that all homicides should be treated equally? As a society, are we more concerned with murder that occurs on the spur of the moment or murder that is thought out and planned?

D. Prior Calculation and Design

State v. Walker, 2016-Ohio-8295

LANZINGER, J.

We accepted this discretionary appeal by the state of Ohio from a judgment of the Eighth District Court of Appeals that reversed a conviction of aggravated murder because it was not supported by sufficient evidence of prior calculation and design. During a bar fight, Dajhon Walker knowingly killed Antwon Shannon, and for that act Walker was properly convicted of felony murder under R.C. 2903.02(B). But the evidence did not show that this killing was done with prior calculation and design as required to sustain a conviction for aggravated murder. The elements of purpose and of prior calculation and design are distinct, and the state must prove both to support a conviction of aggravated murder under R.C. 2903.01.

We therefore affirm the judgment of the court of appeals.

RELEVANT FACTS

Trial Evidence

Antwon Shannon was killed during a bar fight that took place in the early morning hours of February 19, 2012, at the Tavo Martini Lounge, a Cleveland night club. Although the state presented witness testimony and the testimony of detectives and forensic experts at the jury trial, the primary evidence of the sequence of the events came from video footage recorded by 16 surveillance cameras located in and around the club.

The videos show that the victims, Antwon Shannon and Ivor Anderson, arrived at the club at approximately 12:27 a.m. and that they then began to drink and socialize. At 1:56 a.m., they were on the dance floor when Robert Steel, who also was dancing, began to twirl a glass of champagne in the air. Some of Steel's champagne spilled on Anderson, who responded with a remark. After dancing a bit longer and talking to a friend who was drinking champagne from a bottle, Steel began to talk to a group of people who were not identified at trial.

Meanwhile, Walker, Derrell Shabazz, and Otis Johnson were in a different area of the club, drinking and intermittently stopping to chat with one another in an outside hallway. At 2:01, Johnson made his way from the outside hallway onto the dance floor and over to Steel and the others, followed a minute later by Walker and Shabazz. The group talked on and off for the next nine minutes, repeatedly looking in the direction of Anderson and Shannon. The melee began at 2:11 a.m., when Steel ran at Anderson from behind and hit him with a champagne bottle that glanced off Anderson and hit Eunique Worley in the forehead. Once Steele started the fight, others became involved.

Walker joined in, hitting Shannon and throwing a bottle at him. Walker then hopped backwards, grabbing at his waistband, hunching over and moving to the side. Walker slipped and fell on Shannon, and Shabazz slipped and fell on Walker. All three recovered and stumbled in different directions: Shannon moved away from the fight, Walker went out of the cameras' view to the corner of the room behind a pillar, and Shabazz went over to Johnson, who apparently by mistake was hitting a member of their own group. A woman who had joined in the fight shoved Anderson backwards, propelling the group to the corner where Walker had gone. The video footage shows a gunshot flash a few seconds later with everyone in the club scattering. Walker appeared from the other side of the pillar fumbling with his waistband, and he and Shabazz hurried out of the area together.

Shannon was shot in the back from a distance of one to two feet by a .45 caliber bullet, which passed through his chest. Shannon died soon after.

Convictions and Appeal

A Cuyahoga County Grand Jury indicted Walker and Shabazz for aggravated murder, felony murder, having weapons while under a disability, and six counts of felonious assault (three pertaining to Shannon, one to Anderson, and two to Worley), along with firearm specifications. At a joint trial with Shabazz, the jury acquitted Walker of the felonious-assault counts against Worley but found him guilty of aggravated murder, felony murder, and four counts of felonious assault, and the trial court found him guilty of having a weapon while under a disability. Shabazz was sentenced to 22 years to life in prison, and Walker was sentenced to 25 years to life.

Walker appealed to the Eighth District Court of Appeals, arguing that his aggravated-murder conviction was not supported by sufficient evidence. The appellate court agreed and concluded that the state had failed to establish that Walker acted with prior calculation and design. 2014-Ohio-1827, 10 N.E.3d 200, ¶ 21 (8th Dist.). Relying on the standard set forth in *State v. Taylor,* 78 Ohio St. 3d 15, 676 N.E.2d 82 (1997), the court held that there was no evidence that Walker and Shannon knew one another, that the shooting occurred from a spontaneous eruption of events, or that Walker gave no thought to choosing the murder site beforehand. The court therefore reversed the conviction for aggravated murder but upheld the convictions for felony murder and the remaining offenses and remanded the matter to the trial court for resentencing. ***

Count One: Aggravated Murder

Under the aggravated-murder statute, the state was required to prove beyond a reasonable doubt that Walker "purposely, *and with prior calculation and design,* cause[d] the death" of Antwon Shannon. (Emphasis added.) R.C. 2903.01(A). The question raised by the state is whether sufficient evidence of prior calculation and design was presented to support Walker's conviction of aggravated murder.

When the Revised Code was adopted in 1953, the crime of murder in the first degree—the precursor to aggravated murder—prohibited purposeful killing with "deliberate and premeditated malice." Former R.C. 2901.01. Under this earlier standard, "a killing could be premeditated even though conceived and executed on the spur of the moment. The only requirement was that the malicious purpose be formed before the homicidal act, however short in time." *State v. Cotton,* 56 Ohio St. 2d 8, 11 (1978).

When it amended the aggravated-murder statute, R.C. 2903.01(A), to provide that "[n]o person shall purposely, and with priorcalculation and design, cause the death of another," the General Assembly explicitly rejected the notion that brief premeditation prior to a murder could establish prior calculation and design:

> [R.C. 2903.01(A) employs] the phrase, "prior calculation and design," to indicate an act of studied care in planning or analyzing the means of the crime, as well as a scheme compassing the death of the victim. Neither the degree of care nor the length of time the offender takes to ponder the crime beforehand are critical factors in themselves, but they must be sufficient to meet the proposed test of "prior calculation and design." In this context, *momentary deliberation is considered insufficient* to constitute a studied scheme to kill.

Ohio Legislative Service Commission, Proposed Ohio Criminal Code: Final Report of the Technical Committee to Study Ohio Criminal Laws and Procedures, at 71 (1971). See also State v. Taylor, 78 Ohio St. 3d 15 (1997). The General Assembly has defined the mens rea of purpose, stating that "[a] person acts purposely when it is the person's specific intention to cause a certain result." R.C. 2901.22(A). Evidence of purpose, however, does not automatically mean that the element of prior calculation anddesign also exists. State v. Campbell, 90 Ohio St. 3d 320 (2000) ("purpose to kill is not the same thing as priorcalculation and design and does not by itself satisfy the mens rea element of R.C. 2903.01(A)"). A purposeful killing committed with priorcalculation and design is aggravated murder: "No person shall purposely, and with prior calculation and design, cause the death of another ***." (Emphasis added.) R.C. 2903.01(A).

The phrase "prior calculation and design" by its own terms suggests advance reasoning to formulate the purpose to kill. Evidence of an act committed on the spur of the moment or after momentary consideration is not evidence of a premeditated decision or a studied consideration of the method and the means to cause a death. The General Assembly has determined that it is a greater offense to premeditate or to plan ahead to purposely kill someone. All prior-calculation-and-design offenses will necessarily include purposeful homicides; not all purposeful homicides have an element of prior calculation and design.

Since the enactment of R.C. 2903.01 in 1974, we have repeatedly emphasized that there is no "bright-line test that emphatically distinguishes between the presence or absence of 'prior calculation and design.' Instead, each case turns on the particular facts and evidence presented at trial." State v. Taylor, 78 Ohio St. 3d 15 (1997).

We traditionally consider three factors in determining whether a defendant acted with prior calculation and design: "(1) Did the accused and victim know each other, and if so, was that relationship strained? (2) Did the accused give thought or preparation to choosing the murder weapon or murder site? and (3) Was the act drawn out or 'an almost instantaneous eruption of events?' " State v. Taylor, 78 Ohio St. 3d 15 (1997).

We have upheld aggravated-murder convictions, holding that prior calculation and design existed when a defendant threatened to obtain a weapon and kill his victim and later carried out that plan. State v. Sowell, 39 Ohio St. 3d 322 (1988). See also State v. Toth, 52 Ohio St. 2d 206 (1977), and State v. Cassano, 96 Ohio St. 3d 94 (both upholding aggravated-murder convictions when the defendant had previously threatened to kill the victim). Shooting a person execution-style may also establish, at least in part, prior calculation and design. State v. Palmer, 80 Ohio St. 3d 543, 569-570 (1997).

The Taylor Case

The court of appeals decided Walker's case by applying the factors in *Taylor* at 19. In *Taylor,* another bar homicide, the circumstances surrounding the shooting show a scheme designed to implement the calculated decision to kill. Taylor knew his victim, who had previously dated Taylor's girlfriend. *Id.* at 21-22. And knowing that the victim frequently drank at a certain bar, Taylor chose to take a gun there. He, the girlfriend, and the victim had all been drinking at the bar for 20 to 30 minutes before he shot the victim after an argument. *Id.* at 22. As the victim lay wounded on the floor after several shots, Taylor approached and fired three or four more shots in the victim's back. *Id.* at 22. Pursuing and killing a fleeing or incapacitated victim after an initial confrontation strongly indicates prior calculation and design. *State v. Conway,* 108 Ohio St. 3d 214. *See also Palmer,* 80 Ohio St. 3d at 569-570, 687 N.E.2d 685 (after victim had fallen to the ground, defendant shot the victim in the head in an execution-style manner).

When examining the facts in Walker's case in light of the questions asked in *Taylor,* it appears from the evidence that Walker and Shannon did not know each other, that the killing resulted from a spontaneous eruption of events, and that Walker had not given thought to choosing the murder site. Additionally, Walker did not give thought or preparation to choosing the murder weapon: from his approach to the dance floor at approximately 2:02 a.m. until the fight began at 2:11 a.m., Walker did not move from the area, meaning that the weapon was already on his person before he was even aware of Steel's interaction with Anderson.

There is no evidence that Walker and his friends devised a scheme to shoot Shannon and then carried it out. The plan that existed among Walker's group that evening was a plan to commit felonious assault, not murder. The prosecutor understood this fact because he so characterized the reason behind the murder: Shannon "died because *the fight got so escalated* and the poor guy was so big that two little half pints couldn't take him over so what do you need? *Your fists aren't good enough. You take out a piece of metal ***.*" (Emphasis added.)

The video recordings of the incident show nothing that was carefully planned once the fight began. It quickly turned into a free-for-all with people outside Walker's original small group jumping in, two of Walker's original group fighting each other, and Shannon, Walker, and Shabazz slipping and falling on top of one another. In the middle of this fight, a single shot was fired in the presence of dozens of people.

Witnesses provided testimony to the jury of speculation as to what had happened, but the videos show an assault that quickly escalated into chaos. For approximately 20 seconds of that chaos, Walker was obscured from the security cameras by a pillar. A jury could reasonably infer that during that time, Walker decided to kill Shannon by shooting him, but it could not reasonably infer that he planned the murder beforehand with prior calculation and design. The element of prior calculation and design requires evidence that supports more than the inference of purpose. Inferring prior calculation and design from an inference of purpose is mere speculation. Accordingly, Walker's conviction for aggravated murder was not supported by sufficient evidence.

CONCLUSION

The evidence presented by the state in this case shows that Antwon Shannon was shot during a bar fight with Dajhon Walker and others. Neither the security cameras that recorded the fight nor the witnesses to the shooting were able to see who fired the shot. But the cameras did show that Walker moved away from the fight, and out of camera range, for approximately 20 seconds before the gunshot. Thus, there was insufficient evidence of prior calculation and design. We therefore affirm the judgment of the court of appeals vacating Walker's aggravated-murder conviction.

Aggravated murder is a purposeful killing that *also* requires proof of prior calculation and design: forethought, planning, choice of weapon, choice of means, and the execution of the plan. In this case, there is no evidence that Walker planned Shannon's murder beforehand. Walker knowingly killed Shannon and was properly convicted of felony murder, but he did not commit aggravated murder. We therefore affirm the judgment of the Eighth District Court of Appeals vacating the aggravated-murder conviction and remanding the cause to the Court of Common Pleas of Cuyahoga County for resentencing.

Judgment affirmed and cause remanded.

O'CONNOR, C.J., and PFEIFER and O'NEILL, JJ., concur.

O'DONNELL, J., dissenting.

Respectfully, I dissent.***

Notably, the state's brief cites five recent cases in which the Eighth District Court of Appeals has misapplied these standards in holding that the state presented insufficient evidence of prior calculation and design: *State v. Hill,* 8th Dist. Cuyahoga No. 98366, 2013-Ohio-578 (the appellate court rejected an inference of prior calculation and design when the accused and the victim argued about money over an extended period, the accused fired two shots, and then he fired a third shot while the victim was down on his knees); *State v. Woods,* 8th Dist. Cuyahoga No. 99630, 2014-Ohio-1722 (the appellate court rejected an inference of prior calculation and design when the accused lured the victim to his room and strangled her); *State v. Shabazz,* 8th Dist. Cuyahoga No. 100021, 2014-Ohio-1828 (the appellate court rejected the inference of prior calculation and design to support aggravated murder when Shabazz and his co-defendant were seen talking before an attack on Ivor Anderson and Antwon Shannon); *State v. Hicks,* 8th Dist. Cuyahoga No. 102206 (the appellate court rejected an inference that the accused planned to kill his estranged wife while on a date night after arguing with her earlier in the evening); *State v. Durham,* 2016-Ohio-691 (the appellate court rejected the inference that the accused had lured the victim behind a building before shooting him in the head).***

Prior to 1974, Ohio law "described 'deliberate and premeditated malice' as constituting first degree murder. *** [A] killing could be premeditated even though conceived and executed on the spur of the moment. The only requirement was that the malicious purpose be formed before the homicidal act, however short in time." *State v. Cotton,* 56 Ohio St. 2d 8 (1978).

Effective January 1, 1974, however, the General Assembly amended R.C. 2903.01(A) to define the offense of aggravated murder, providing that "[n]o person shall purposely, and with prior calculation and design, cause the death of another." Am. Sub. H.B. No. 511, 134 Ohio Laws, Part II, 1866, 1900. The term "prior calculation and design" is not defined by statute, but we have stated:

> The apparent intention of the General Assembly in employing this phrase was to require more than the few moments of deliberation permitted in common law interpretations of the former murder statute, and to require a scheme designed to implement the calculated decision to kill. Thus, instantaneous deliberation is not sufficient to constitute "prior calculation and design." *Cotton* at 11.

As we more recently explained in *State v. Maxwell,* 139 Ohio St. 3d 12:

> No bright-line test exists that "emphatically distinguishes between the presence or absence of 'prior calculation and design.' Instead, each case turns on the particular facts and evidence presented at trial." *State v. Taylor,* 78 Ohio St. 3d 15 (1997). However, when the evidence presented at trial "reveals the presence of sufficient time and opportunity for the planning of an act of homicide to constitute prior calculation, and the circumstances surrounding the homicide show a scheme designed to implement the calculated decision to kill, a finding by the trier of fact of prior calculation and design is justified." *State v. Cotton,* 56 Ohio St. 2d 8 (1978), paragraph three of the syllabus.

In *State v. Franklin,* 97 Ohio St. 3d 1, we reiterated three "pertinent" considerations in determining whether prior calculation and design existed: "(1) Did the accused and victim know each other, and if so, was that relationship strained? (2) Did the accused give thought or preparation to choosing the murder weapon or murder site? and (3) Was the act drawn out or 'an almost instantaneous eruption of events?'" *Id.* at ¶ 56, quoting *Taylor,* 78 Ohio St. 3d at 19, quoting *State v. Jenkins,* 48 Ohio App. 2d 99 (8th Dist. 1976). However "pertinent" they may be, we have never held that these are the *exclusive* factors to be applied in determining whether the accused acted with prior calculation and design.

Rather, we have recognized that "prior calculation and design can be found even when the killer quickly conceived and executed the plan to kill within a few minutes," *State v. Coley,* 93 Ohio St. 3d 253 (2001), as long as the killer's actions "went beyond a momentary impulse and show that he was determined to complete a specific course of action," *State v. Conway,* 108 Ohio St. 3d 214.

In *State v. Palmer,* 80 Ohio St. 3d 543 (1997), we explained that sufficient evidence of prior calculationand design existed when, after being involved in a minor accident with a pickup truck, Donald L. Palmer Jr. exited the vehicle with a loaded revolver that was cocked and ready to fire and shot the truck's driver, Charles Sponhaltz, twice in the head. *Id.* at 543. Although the killing took only moments, we concluded that "[t]he evidence, when viewed in a light most favorable to the state, was more than sufficient to show that [Palmer] had adopted a plan to kill Sponhaltz prior to exiting [the] vehicle and that, with a level of precision, [Palmer] followed through on his calculated decision to kill." *Id.* at 569.

Similarly, in *Taylor,* we explained that only a short time is needed to form prior calculation and design. In that case, Michael N. Taylor objected when Marion Alexander asked Taylor's girlfriend to play a song for him on the jukebox. 78 Ohio St. 3d at 16. Taylor told his girlfriend they were leaving and then walked up to Alexander and shot him multiple times, killing him. *Id.* at 16-17. We noted there that by bringing a firearm to a bar that he knew the victim frequented, the jury could infer that the accused intended to use it, *id.* at 22, and we concluded that "[e]ven though most of the evidence indicates that the time between the jukebox incident and the shooting was only two or three minutes, there was more than sufficient evidence for the jury to reasonably have found that [Taylor], with prior calculation and design, decided to shoot Alexander in that space of time," *id.*

The State Presented Sufficient Evidence of Prior Calculation and Design

Viewing the evidence in a light most favorable to the state, it is manifest that sufficient evidence of prior calculation and design exists to support Walker's conviction. Anderson testified that after he spoke to Steel, he suspected he might be attacked by Steel and his group, and the camera footage shows the group gesturing and looking toward him over an extended period of time. The video also reveals their preparations for the attack. Steel concealed an empty champagne bottle, Shabazz removed his glasses, and an unidentified accomplice zipped up his coat. Johnson also concealed a champagne bottle behind his forearm and walked across the dance floor, putting Anderson between himself and Steel. Steel then pointed toward Anderson as he danced, and the unidentified member of Steel's group stood close by.

Shabazz and Walker were watching Shannon when the fight started. Walker specifically targeted Shannon—circling the fight to reach him, punching him, and attempting to hit him with a champagne bottle. Based on this evidence, the jury could reasonably infer that the attack on Anderson and Shannon was preplanned and coordinated and it could also infer from the use of champagne bottles in the attack that there was an intent to cause serious injury or death.

Most importantly, the video reveals that Walker reached for his waistband and withdrew from the fight for approximately 20 seconds. From this evidence, the jury could reasonably infer that he was holding a firearm for that entire time, which gave him sufficient time and opportunity to reflect on whether to use it, and the jury could also reasonably conclude that within that 20 seconds Walker conceived a plan to kill either Shannon or Anderson, strategically placing himself behind the pillar and waiting for a clear shot. He then shot Shannon in the back at close range, and when the shot sounded, Shabazz showed no noticeable reaction, from which the jury could reasonably infer that Shabazz was not surprised by the shooting. And, after Walker emerged from behind the pillar, Shabazz is seen on the video tapping him on the chest in what the jury could reasonably view as a celebratory gesture.

Walker does not dispute that the evidence established that he murdered Shannon. And, based upon the evidence presented at trial, the jury reasonably concluded that he acted with prior calculation and design.

CONCLUSION

In this case, the court of appeals failed to view the evidence in a light most favorable to the state and further failed to draw all reasonable inferences in favor of the state; it therefore substituted its judgment for that of the jury in ruling that the state failed to present sufficient evidence that Walker murdered Shannon with prior calculation and design. The jury reasonably concluded that by participating in a coordinated and preplanned attack against Shannon and Anderson and by drawing a firearm, withdrawing from the attack, and waiting behind a pillar for 20 seconds before shooting Shannon in the back, Walker committed aggravated murder with prior calculation and design.

The pattern exhibited by the appellate court in failing to draw all reasonable inferences in favor of the state when considering a sufficiency challenge demonstrates a lack of understanding of the applicable legal standards and in my view results in a miscarriage of justice.

For these reasons, I would reverse the judgment of the court of appeals, reinstate the judgment of the trial court, and instruct the appellate court to adhere to the proper sufficiency analysis in all future cases.

KENNEDY and FRENCH, JJ., concur in the foregoing opinion.

Notes and Questions

1. Can prior calculation and design occur within seconds? If not, do you think there is a minimum amount of time necessary in order for a jury to find that the defendant completed the homicide with prior calculation and design?

2. In *State v. Walker*, the court states that "prior calculation and design" is not the same as "deliberate and premeditated malice." How would you explain the difference between the two?

3. The *Walker* court lists three factors to consider when determining whether a defendant has acted with prior calculation and design:

> (1) Did the accused and victim know each other, and if so, was that relationship strained? (2) Did the accused give thought or preparation to choosing the murder weapon or murder site? and (3) Was the act drawn out or "an almost spontaneous eruption of events"?

4. With respect to the third factor, what specifically is the "act" referenced by the court? Is the act the murder or the events leading up to the murder?

Chapter 7
Felony Murder and the Death Penalty

A. Introduction

Guyora Binder, *Making the Best of Felony Murder*
91 B.U.L. Rev. 403 (2011)

The felony murder doctrine, imposing murder liability for some unintended killings in the course of some felonies, is part of the law of almost every American jurisdiction. Yet it is also one of the most widely criticized features of American criminal law. Leading criminal law scholars have urged its abolition, condemning it as unprincipled and irrational. Critics charge that felony murder imposes undeserved strict liability for accidental death. Criminal law teachers impart this view to their students, and use felony murder to illustrate the perils of rigid rule formalism. Critics can point to examples like these eleven cases from ten different jurisdictions:

1. Seven months after stealing a car, James Colenburg, a Missouri man, was driving down a residential street when an unsupervised two-year-old suddenly darted in front of the stolen car. The toddler was struck and killed. Colenburg was convicted of felony murder predicated on theft.

2. Jonathan Miller, a fifteen-year-old Georgia youth, punched another boy in a schoolyard dispute. The second boy suffered a fatal brain hemorrhage. Miller was convicted of felony murder, predicated on the felonies of assault with a deadly weapon and battery with injury.

3. Suspecting Allison Jenkins of drug possession, an Illinois police officer chased him at gunpoint. As the officer caught him by the arm, Jenkins tried to shake free. The officer tackled Jenkins and fired the gun as they fell, killing his own partner. Jenkins was convicted of felony murder, predicated on battery of a police officer. No drugs were found.

4. Jonathan Earl Stamp robbed a California bank at gunpoint. Shortly thereafter, one of the bank employees had a fatal heart attack. Stamp was convicted of felony murder.

5. New York burglar William Ingram broke into a home, only to be met at the door by the homeowner, brandishing a pistol. The homeowner forced Ingram to lie down, bound him, and called the police. After police took Ingram away, the homeowner suffered a fatal heart attack. Ingram was convicted of felony murder.

6. Also in New York, Eddie Matos fled across rooftops at night after committing a robbery. A pursuing police officer fell down an airshaft to his death. Matos was convicted of felony murder.

7. John Earl Hickman was present when a companion overdosed on cocaine in Virginia. He was convicted of felony murder predicated on drug possession.

8. John William Malaske, a young Oklahoma man, got a bottle of vodka for his underage sister and her two friends. One of the friends died of alcohol poisoning. Malaske was convicted of felony murder predicated on the felony of supplying alcohol to a minor.

9. Ryan Holle, a young Florida man, routinely loaned his car to his housemate. At the end of a party, the housemate talked with guests about stealing a safe from a drug dealer's home, maybe by force. The housemate asked Holle for the car keys. Holle, tired, drunk, and unsure whether the housemate was serious, provided the keys and went to bed. The housemate and his friends stole the safe and one clubbed a resisting resident to death. Holle was convicted of felony murder and sentenced to life without parole.

10. Bernard Lambert, a Pennsylvania man who regularly gave rides to a friend, drove the friend to a home where he claimed someone owed him money. The friend broke in and shot a resident in the head. Lambert was convicted of felony murder predicated on burglary.

11. North Carolina college student Janet Danahey set fire to a bag of party decorations as a prank in front of the door of her ex-boyfriend's apartment in the exterior hallway of an apartment complex. To Danahey's surprise, the building caught fire and four people died in the blaze. Danahey pled guilty to four counts of felony murder.

These cases are indeed troubling. The New York Times featured the Holle case in a story portraying the felony murder doctrine as out of step with global standards of criminal justice. Many readers will recognize the Stamp case as one that criminal law textbooks use to illustrate the harshness of the felony murder rule. Janet Danahey's supporters present her case as a condemnation of the felony murder doctrine. Indeed, a doctrine designed to produce results like these would be hard to defend. Yet I will argue that such cases are anomalous rather than paradigmatic—misapplications of a rational doctrine rather than illustrations of an irrational one. Rather than agreeing with the academic consensus that felony murder liability should be abolished, I will argue that we should make the best of felony murder liability. By this, I mean two things.

First, in proposing reform rather than abolition, I acknowledge that many of my readers disapprove of felony murder liability. Like it or not, however, we are probably stuck with the felony murder doctrine. Legislatures have supported felony murder for decades in the teeth of academic scorn. Although most states revised their criminal codes in response to the American Law Institute's (ALI) Model Penal Code, only a few accepted the ALI's proposal to abolish felony murder. Today, criminal justice policy is less likely than ever to be influenced by academic criticism, as candidates for office find themselves competing to appear tougher on crime than their opponents. Moreover, in adhering to the felony murder doctrine, legislatures are likely following popular opinion. Opinion studies find that mock jurors are willing to punish negligent killers far more severely if they kill in the course of a serious felony like robbery. Felony murder liability is not going away and we are going to have to learn to live with it.

But we should also "make the best" of felony murder in a second way: we should try to make it "the best it can be," in Ronald Dworkin's sense. Of course those readers who believe the felony murder doctrine to be inherently unprincipled will find this aspiration of perfecting felony murder incoherent. Nevertheless, drawing on previous work, I will contend that felony murder liability is rationally justifiable on the basis of a plausible conception of desert. I limit this claim to murder punishable by incarceration: I do not maintain that felony murder alone justifies capital punishment. If felony murder liability is ever justifiable, however, felony murder rules can be improved by confining them to the limits of their justifying principles. Even readers who disagree with the felony murder doctrine's justifying principle should prefer that it be applied in a principled way rather than haphazardly. If the law of felony murder can be better or worse, we should make it the best it can be.***

By dismissing the felony murder doctrine as rationally indefensible, legal scholars deprive themselves of meaningful roles in reforming felony murder rules. Refusing to acknowledge any common ground with supporters of the felony murder doctrine, scholars offer legislators and voters little reason to listen to them. Moreover, by insisting that felony murder has no justifying purpose, legal scholars perversely encourage lawmakers to make the law of felony murder less rational and less just than it could be. Lectured that felony murder rules violate desert in principle, legislators may assume they must abandon considerations of justice in designing felony murder rules. Told that felony murder rules reflect cynical political pandering, courts will assume they are properly deferring to legislative intent when they impose undeserved punishment. Instructed by scholars that felony murder doctrine imposes strict liability, courts will more likely instruct juries to impose strict liability. In demanding abolition rather than reform, legal scholars make their narrow conception of the best the enemy of the good. The result is a self-fulfilling prophecy that encourages the arbitrariness and injustice it professes to condemn.

Because American felony murder rules rest on a widely supported and theoretically plausible moral principle, the most democratic approach to critiquing them is to test them against that principle. The most pragmatic strategy for improving the law of felony murder is to show lawmakers how to bring it into conformity with that principle. These are the aims of this Article. It pursues these aims by surveying and critiquing the current design of American felony murder rules in all felony murder states, as well as in the District of Columbia and the federal system. It finds that these rules roughly conform to the principle of dual culpability on most issues, in most jurisdictions. It reveals unjust results like the eleven cases summarized above to be anomalies, attributable to unusual rules or misapplications of enacted law. Finally, it offers guidelines for reforming felony murder law where necessary to avoid such results, while still convicting the surprised pedophile, the overconfident robber, and the myopic arsonist who deserve murder liability.

James J. Tomkovicz, *The Endurance of the Felony Murder Rule: A Study of the Forces that Shape Our Criminal Law* 51 Wash & Lee L. Rev. 1429 (1994)

The primary justification offered for the contemporary felony-murder rule is deterrence. The doctrine is allegedly designed to save lives by threatening potential killers with the serious sanction for first or second degree murder. One deterrent argument holds that the threat of a murder conviction for any killing in furtherance of a felony, even an accidental killing, might well induce a felon to forego committing the felony itself. Because it could lead to quite severe punishment, the risk averse might shy away from the entire felonious enterprise. Another argument, the more prevalent of the two main deterrent explanations of felony-murder, maintains that the rule is aimed at discouraging certain conduct during the felony, not the felony itself. The goal is to encourage greater care in the performance of felonious acts. Such care will lower the risks to human life and result in fewer deaths. Still another view suggests that felons who might kill intentionally in order to complete their felonies successfully will be discouraged by the rule's proclamation that the law will entertain no excuses for the homicide. Calculating felons will forego killing because of their awareness that the chance of constructing a defense that would eliminate or mitigate liability is virtually nonexistent and that, therefore, their likely fate is a murder conviction.

Undoubtedly, one purpose of felony-murder was to prevent future killings. That is true of every proscription of homicide. The history of the felony-murder rule, however, does not provide the sort of deterrent focus and emphasis that judges and scholars have found underlying the contemporary rule. The writings of Coke, Foster, Blackstone, and others do not justify the doctrine on deterrence grounds. It seems unlikely, at best, that the originators of the rule would have explained its rationales in the same way that modern courts and defenders do. At least no concrete evidence exists that the original perspective was the same as the contemporary perspective.

That does not, of course, make the deterrent explanation for today's versions erroneous or illogical. A rule that initially had one underlying understanding and rationale could survive today on different premises. The point is simply that the deterrent emphasis is a modern phenomenon.

It should not be surprising that this is so. The need to rationalize the felony-murder rule in deterrent terms arises only because of the rule's conflict with accepted culpability principles. There must be adequate justification to suspend the principles that mens rea is required for every element of an offense and that malice is required for the result element of murder. The protection of lives achieved through the enhanced deterrence that results from the felony-murder doctrine is thought to provide that justification.

When the felony-murder rule arose, the premises widely accepted today did not hold sway. The doctrine was not considered a departure from culpability norms, which were satisfied by the wrongfulness inherent in the felonious intent. Thus, while the rule did discourage life-endangering conduct, there was no necessity that it be sufficiently protective of human life to counterbalance an infringement of fundamental principles.

The use of strict liability--or lesser culpability than is the norm--as a means of preventing harm by maximizing deterrence and minimizing the possibilities of escaping liability is certainly not unknown in our modern criminal law. The growth of strict liability criminality has been a significant modern phenomenon. Lawmakers and other proponents of strict criminal liability believe that in a variety of ways strict liability can increase deterrence of behaviors that bring about particular social harms. As a result, these social harms are diminished.

First, strict liability can induce those who engage in the enterprises that engender the harms to exercise maximum care--even more than a reasonable person would--because they know that only prevention of the proscribed act or consequence can preclude liability. Second, some who fear they will not be able to avoid liability may refrain entirely from engaging in a risky enterprise. As a result, they will not create the occasions that bring about the social harm. Third, because many people engage in the enterprises that cause the harm, the availability of a "no mens rea" defense could clog the system and lead to lengthy delays in prosecution. The threat of a sanction, and thus the deterrent force of the law, could diminish. By eliminating the option of a no mens rea claim and by making the proof required for conviction simple, a higher volume of prosecutions can be handled, and the threat of prosecution and conviction can remain meaningful. Fourth, strict liability deprives defendants who cause harm culpably (that is, with negligence or a higher degree of fault) of the opportunity to deceive juries. Thus, the incentive to do wrong and escape under cover of false testimony is lessened, and deterrence is further enhanced.

The modern employment of strict liability is typically reserved for offenses of a "public welfare" or "regulatory" nature. There are two simple reasons for that limitation. First, strict liability--criminal responsibility without proof of moral fault--is thought acceptable only in cases in which the moral stigma is minor or limited and the sanction is not severe. Suspension of the fundamental principle that conviction and punishment are justifiable only when imposed on the morally blameworthy is not defensible unless the "imposition" on the individual is not great. Our respect for individuals and our sense of fair treatment leads us to eschew severe punishments and stigmata in the absence of proven moral fault.

Second, public welfare offenses generally address conduct that threatens a high volume of widespread harm to society. A high volume of prosecutions, or at least the threat thereof, is critical for achieving the preventive goals of the proscriptions. Strict liability is essential to maximizing the number of prosecutions and, thus, to achieving the very objects of the criminal prohibitions.

In sum, in the regulatory context, the gains to society are thought great, and the costs to the individual are considered tolerable. These two conditions make strict liability an important and acceptable tool. Both are essential to the balance that sustains modern strict liability legislation.

The deterrent reasoning underlying felony-murder tracks most of the reasoning underlying strict liability generally. Supporters claim that felony-murder induces felons to exercise maximum care during felonies, prompts potential felons to refrain from committing felonies in the first place, and warns prospective felons that they will not be able to hide behind false claims of accident or mere negligence. The problem, however, is that felony-murder does not fit the mold of crimes for which strict liability is considered appropriate and necessary. It is not a modern public welfare offense, but a *mala in se* common-law crime. The stigma could hardly be worse; the penalty could not be much higher. Moreover, there is no avalanche of felony killings. Strict liability is not essential to combat a widespread societal threat. Consequently, felony-murder does not fit the modern strict liability paradigm. Because the rule appears to infringe substantially upon accepted culpability principles without providing offsetting societal gains of sufficient magnitude, neither of the conditions that we properly consider essential to the acceptance of strict criminal liability exists. The balance that usually underlies and is thought to justify strict criminal liability is simply not struck in the felony-murder context.

Felony-murder stands apart from the body of public welfare crimes in another significant respect. Public welfare crimes do not ordinarily constitute alternative versions of an offense that otherwise requires mens rea. From their conception, they are strict liability crimes that do not require mens rea because that is their essence. The omission of the culpability element is inseparably linked to the reasons for their creation. Felony-murder, on the other hand, is a variety of murder, a stigmatizing common-law crime the essence of which is actual malice. Felony-murder is the no or lesser culpability branch of an offense that otherwise depends upon proof of serious subjective culpability. In that sense, it is somewhat unique and most unlike the range of strict liability offenses recently incorporated into the criminal law.

The problem with the modern felony-murder doctrine is not only that it seeks practical goals by prescribing severe punishments without proof of fault, but that it does so on the basis of unproven and highly questionable assumptions. While the felony-murder rule must save some lives, the odds are that the number is small indeed. The number of killings during felonies is relatively low. The subset of such killings that are nonculpable-- thus not already subject to the threat of a substantial sanction--is undoubtedly considerably smaller. Further, the addition of a small risk of a murder sanction for an unlikely event is probably not a major influence on some prospective felons' behavior, and a good number of those who are affected in some way probably would not have killed in any event. Moreover, some who are aware of and even sensitive to the threatened sanction will probably still kill negligently or accidentally.

Admittedly, it would be difficult, if not impossible, to prove that the felony-murder rule does not annually save a considerable number of lives. Nonetheless, in a world in which the evidence is uncertain (or nonexistent) and in which it seems unlikely that felons actually hear the rule's deterrent message in the ways that courts presume that they do, common sense would suggest putting the burden of proof upon those who contend that deterrent gains are sufficient to outweigh the infringement of our fundamental philosophy of fault and punishment.

One might contend that the suspicions about the efficacy of deterrence prove too much--that similar doubts about deterrent gains could be raised in all areas of criminal law. This argument misses the point. In most other areas there is no *need* to prove a countervailing deterrent gain because the culpability principle is not violated. Either culpability proportionate to liability is a part of the requisite proof, or the sanction is sufficiently small to be acceptable despite the absence of proven fault. Neither is true in the case of felony-murder. Proof of the level of culpability that ordinarily justifies a murder sanction is not required, and the available sanction is very severe.

I refer to the claim that the felony-murder rule actually results in substantial savings of human life--savings so substantial as to justify its infidelity to the conception of fault we usually hold dear--as the "deterrence delusion." Assertions that the doctrine exists to prevent killings that occur in the course of felonies *and* that it actually achieves its goal are rooted in blind faith or self-delusion. More should be required. If the rule is to stand upon deterrent premises, it is incumbent upon supporters to do more than speculate. They should have to justify the suspension of our normal insistence upon proof of blameworthiness. Without a credible foundation in established facts, deterrence is not a real justification, but is instead a poor excuse for our infidelity. We owe ourselves more honesty.

It is unclear whether the public and lawmakers actually believe the delusion or, instead, are aware of the spurious nature of the deterrent claim but, nonetheless, are content to rely upon it. There are probably members in each camp. What is clear is that while the delusion is the beginning of an explanation for felony-murder's survival, it is only the beginning. To get to the bottom of the felony-murder rule, it is necessary to explore the reasons that we would indulge such a delusion. On such an important matter, why have we been willing to rest on assumptions and not demand proof that the rule actually produces beneficial results? Why do we continue to sacrifice a fundamental principle on no more than unfounded faith in the deterrent efficacy of a doctrine with dubious parentage? Only forthright confrontation of these questions can bring us closer to understanding the felony-murder rule's remarkable persistence.

Notes and Questions

1. What is the purpose of having a law like felony murder? Why not just increase the penalties for committing the felony?

2. Felony murder has stood the test of time in America despite being abolished in England in 1958. Why do you think felony murder is still around? Do you think the law will still be around 20 years from now? As will be illustrated at the end of this section, some jurisdictions, like Ohio, are attempting to expand the reach of felony murder.

B. Felony Murder Proof Requirements

State v. Miller, 96 Ohio St. 3d 384 (2002)

LUNDBERG STRATTON, J.

On October 7, 1998, the Ashtabula County Grand Jury indicted Jeffrey Miller, defendant-appellee, on charges of aggravated murder in violation of R.C. 2903.01(A) and felony murder in violation of R.C. 2903.02(B). Both counts carried firearm specifications. The charges were in connection with the shooting death of defendant's wife, Lisa.

On September 4, 1998, Jeffrey Miller, defendant-appellee, stayed home while his wife, Lisa, went to work. Defendant spoke briefly with his neighbor, Ed

Capp, and mentioned that a couple of checks were missing and that he had asked Lisa about them earlier. Defendant told Capp that he planned to go over to his uncle's property that afternoon to go shooting.

Defendant arrived at his uncle Allen Massena's home around 12:30 p.m. and they left to look at a truck that defendant was considering purchasing. After being unable to find the truck, the two men returned to Massena's home to target practice. Defendant and Massena shot defendant's .357 Magnum. After the two finished target practice, defendant unloaded the gun, put the gun back into the holster, placed the remaining unfired ammunition in the back of his truck, and put the unloaded .357 in a separate place in his truck.***

Later that night, around 9:00 p.m., defendant went to the Iroquois Lounge and found Capp. Capp noticed that defendant had been drinking prior to entering the Iroquois. Capp bought defendant a beer, and the two men drank a shot. Defendant told Capp that Lisa did not come home and that he had left her a note stating that he was going to leave her. Defendant asked Capp if he would come over to his home and "get his hardware." Capp understood this to mean that defendant wanted Capp to help him remove his guns from his home. The two men left the bar in separate cars and met back at defendant's home.

After defendant and Capp tried unsuccessfully to light a bonfire, the two men entered defendant's house, and Capp sat down at the kitchen table while defendant went upstairs to bring down his guns. While Capp was seated at the kitchen table, he read a note that defendant had left there for Lisa. Capp testified that defendant stated in the note that he was leaving Lisa and that her crafts, her gambling, and her interests meant more than their marriage. According to Capp, defendant stated in the note that he was leaving to "pursue other interests or avenues." The note also indicated that defendant did not think that Lisa's work schedule, which included working weekends, was necessary.

Defendant came back downstairs carrying a .357 Magnum revolver in a holster. Capp told defendant that he did not want to bring defendant's guns into his own home unless they were unloaded. Defendant unloaded the .357 Magnum revolver and handed the gun to Capp. Capp took the revolver and checked to be certain that there were no bullets in the gun and then placed the gun back into its holster. Capp handed the gun back to defendant, who placed it on the kitchen table before going upstairs to retrieve his other guns.

Defendant returned with two shotguns that were both loaded. Capp watched as defendant unloaded the rifles and returned upstairs. Capp walked over to the stairs and saw defendant at the top of the stairs holding an ammunition box when Capp heard the sound of the automatic garage door opening.

Capp said, "Lisa's home," and he went back into the kitchen and picked up the revolver and the two shotguns. As Capp was leaving, he dropped one of the shotguns. Defendant told Capp, "Never mind. Leave them." Capp left without the guns.

Lisa's daughter-in-law, Karen Garside, later testified that she received a telephone call from the defendant at approximately 10:00 p.m. Defendant asked to speak to Karen's husband, Scott, Lisa's son. Karen informed defendant that Scott was not at home. Karen testified that defendant told her that he was looking for Lisa and wondered whether she knew where she was or whether she was with Scott. Karen told defendant that she did not know, and defendant asked Karen to have Scott call him when he returned. Defendant told Karen he was coming over to her home, but Karen asked him not to. Karen testified that defendant sounded drunk and upset.

Karen testified that she received another call from defendant around 10:20 p.m. in which he informed her that Lisa had returned, and he asked whether Scott had returned as well. Karen informed defendant that Scott had not returned, and defendant asked again that Karen have Scott call him when Scott returned. Karen again agreed to do so. Karen testified that she could hear Lisa in the background during this telephone call. Karen also testified that the tone of defendant's voice would stagger; he would be irritated one moment, anxious and worried the next, and she could tell once again that he had been drinking.

Melissa Garside, Lisa's daughter, testified that on September 4, 1998, she and Lisa had planned to meet at Lisa's home at 9:00 p.m. so Melissa could pick up a bed. Melissa called her mother's house at 8:55 p.m. to tell her that she was running late but received no answer, and the answering machine did not activate. Melissa tried again unsuccessfully to call her mother at 9:30 p.m. and 10:00 p.m. At approximately 10:20 p.m., Melissa reached her mother on the phone. Lisa informed her daughter that her husband, defendant, was "drunk off his ass and he's playing with all his guns." Immediately after that, defendant got on the phone and told Melissa, "Your mother is busy right now. You'll have to talk to her later." Defendant then hung up on Melissa.

Jason White, the Millers' other next-door neighbor, observed Lisa pull into her driveway and park in the garage. White heard the car door close and then heard defendant, who sounded angry, state, "If you don't shut up bitch, I'll kill you." White testified that an hour later, he heard a gunshot. He testified that he did not attempt to call 911 because he often heard gunshots coming from the Miller residence. White also testified that defendant drank a lot and had a beer in his hand every time White saw him.

Kimberly Cook, a dispatcher for the Ashtabula County Sheriff's Department, testified that defendant made two calls that night regarding an incident at his home. Defendant made the first call at 10:28 p.m. and claimed that the shooting was an accident. The second call was received at 10:30 p.m. Both calls were recorded by the 911 recording equipment and both calls were played for the jury.

Officer Ronald Kaydo of the Ashtabula Police Department was the first to arrive at the scene. Officer Kaydo testified that the revolver was lying on the kitchen table, about three feet from Lisa's body. He also observed a holster lying on the floor. Officer Kaydo testified that the holster had some damage to the end of it. Officer Kaydo observed Lisa slumped over the table and defendant with his left hand on the back of Lisa's neck, who stated that he was trying to stop the bleeding. Defendant said that "it was an accident, that he accidentally shot her." Officers conducted a safety sweep of the house. In the upstairs bedroom they found a large ammunition box, ammunition, and shotguns.

Richard Turbok, a firearms examiner with the Ohio Bureau of Criminal Identification and Investigation, testified that to a reasonable degree of certainty, the bullet found lodged in the wall stud of the kitchen in the Miller home was fired from defendant's .357 Magnum revolver. Turbok also testified as to the amount of force necessary to pull the trigger of the .357 Magnum revolver to make it fire. Turbok explained that the revolver could be discharged in single action or double action mode. He testified that the amount of weight it takes for the trigger to be pulled to fire the weapon was 6 pounds when the gun was in single action mode and 12½ pounds of pressure when the gun was in double action mode. Dr. Robert Challener, the Chief Deputy Coroner in Cleveland, performed the autopsy on Lisa Miller and determined that she had bled to death from having been shot once in the face from a distance of approximately 18 inches.

Defendant was indicted on charges of aggravated murder with a firearm specification in violation of R.C. 2903.01(A), and felony murder with a firearm specification in violation of R.C. 2903.02(B). A jury returned a verdict finding defendant not guilty of aggravated murder but guilty of murder while committing an offense of violence (felonious assault) and found that defendant had had a firearm while committing the offense of violence and had used it to facilitate the offense of murder while committing that offense. Defendant was sentenced to serve fifteen years to life in prison for felony murder and three years for the firearm specification with the two sentences to run consecutively.

In a split decision, the Ashtabula Court of Appeals reversed the judgment of the trial court and remanded the matter to the trial court for a new trial. The court of appeals held that because defendant had shot the victim in a vital portion of her body at a close range, the act had to be either intentional or accidental. Therefore, defendant could not have committed the underlying offense of felonious assault as a matter of law.***

FELONY MURDER

The newly enacted felony murder statute, R.C. 2903.02, became effective on June 30, 1998, well before the crimes occurred in this case. It provides:

(B) No person shall cause the death of another as a proximate result of the offender's committing or attempting to commit an offense of violence that is a felony of the first or second degree ***.

The underlying offense of violence for which defendant was charged in this case was felonious assault. Felonious assault, a second degree felony, is defined by R.C. 2903.11:

(A) No person shall *knowingly* ***:

(2) Cause or attempt to cause physical harm to another or to another's unborn by means of a deadly weapon or dangerous ordnance. (Emphasis added.)

R.C. 2901.22 defines the culpable mental states in Ohio and provides:

(B) A person acts *knowingly, regardless of his purpose,* when he is aware that his conduct will probably cause a certain result or will probably be of a certain nature. A person has knowledge of circumstances when he is aware that such circumstances probably exist (Emphasis added.)

The court of appeals appeared to have been troubled by the fact that the state charged the defendant with two crimes, thereby providing alternate theories of what occurred on September 4, 1998. "From the beginning, it was the state's contention that appellant intentionally shot his wife in the head. The defense, however, argued that the shooting was accidental. Clearly, one of those two choices represents the truth. Either appellant intended to shoot his wife, or it was accidental. If it was intentional, then appellant committed either aggravated murder or murder, depending on whether there was prior calculation and design. If it was unintentional, i.e., the gun was accidentally discharged while appellant was holding it or waiving it around, then such conduct would constitute negligent homicide. In either event, it was not a felonious assault."

The state readily acknowledges that it attempted to prove at trial that defendant purposely shot his wife. In fact, the state attempted to prove that defendant purposely shot his wife with prior calculation and design: aggravated murder. However, the prosecution is entitled to offer differing theories as to what actually transpired in the commission of an offense and is therefore entitled to use its discretion in deciding which charges to level against the defendant. See *State ex rel. Nagle v. Olin (1980),* 64 Ohio St. 2d 341. In this case, the prosecution believed that the facts could support a conviction for either aggravated murder (a purposeful killing with prior calculation and design) or felony murder (a killing as a proximate result of the offender's committing or attempting to commit an offense of violence that is a felony of the first or second degree, e.g., felonious assault). It was the jury's duty to assess which charge, if any, was supported by the facts presented.

In reversing the felony murder conviction, the court of appeals critically misconstrued the standard of mens rea necessary to commit felony murder. Felonious assault is defined as *knowingly* causing, or attempting to cause, physical harm to another by means of a deadly weapon. R.C. 2903.11(A). A person acts *knowingly, regardless of purpose,* when he is aware that his conduct will probably cause a certain result or will probably be of a certain nature. A person has knowledge of circumstances when he is aware that such circumstances probably exist. R.C. 2901.22(B).

The jury could certainly find that when the defendant placed a loaded gun within eighteen inches of his wife's head and shot it at her with such aim that he shot her in the cheek, he was aware that his conduct would probably cause a certain result, i.e., harm to his wife. The jury could reasonably believe that in an effort to injure his wife, defendant aimed the gun at a nonvital organ in an attempt to injure only, and one of them moved suddenly. The jury could reasonably believe that the shooting was not an accident. If the jury did not believe that the defendant intended to cause his wife's death, the evidence clearly supported the jury's conclusion that the defendant knew that physical harm to his wife was probable. The evidence was sufficient to support a conviction for felony murder based on felonious assault.

If defendant knowingly caused physical harm to his wife by firing the gun at her through a holster at close range, he is guilty of felonious assault. The fact that she died from her injuries makes him guilty of felony murder, regardless of his purpose.

The defendant contends that since felony murder has a lesser mens rea standard (knowingly) than murder (purposely), and since the two crimes carry the same punishment, prosecutors will now seek murder convictions under the felony murder statute based on felonious assault. However, prosecutors can still charge in the alternative and generally seek an indictment most aligned with the facts of the case. In addition, the General Assembly has chosen to define felony murder in this manner, and the General Assembly is presumed to know the consequences of its legislation.

CONCLUSION

Because we hold that felony murder as defined in R.C. 2903.02(B), with the underlying offense of violence being felonious assault, is supported by evidence that establishes that the defendant knowingly caused physical harm to the victim, we reverse the judgment of the court of appeals and reinstate the judgment of the trial court.

Notes and Questions

1. From the prosecutor's point of view, what is the benefit of proving felony murder as opposed to "purposely causing the death of another" or "purposely, and with prior calculation and design, cause the death of another"? Do you think it is easier to prove felony murder than other types of murder?

2. Is it possible to commit murder without also committing felony murder? In *State v. Miller*, it appears that the jury found that the defendant meant to shoot his wife, but not to kill her. Given the fact that the victim was shot in the face from 18 inches away, do you think the jury understood their verdict? Do you think the verdict was some kind of compromise among the jurors based on their doubts as to what really occurred? Should juries be allowed to do that? Suppose this had been an accident, and the defendant did not mean to fire the gun at all, should he be convicted?

C. Death of a Co-Felon

State v. Dixon, 2002 Ohio App. LEXIS 472 (Ohio Ct. App. 2002)

GLASSER, J. (By Assignment).

Defendant, Christopher Dixon, appeals from his conviction and sentence for felony murder and aggravated robbery.

On September 30, 1999, Dixon and his cousin Sherman Lightfoot made plans to rob the Jiffy Lube located at 3931 Salem Avenue in Dayton, Ohio. In preparation for the robbery, Dixon and Lightfoot obtained latex gloves and "Jason" masks, which were popularized in the movie, "Friday the 13th." At approximately 6:15 p.m., the two men drove a blue Camaro to the Jiffy Lube, parking it across the street. Dixon was wearing an orange-colored hooded sweatshirt, while Lightfoot was wearing a white hooded sweatshirt.

Dixon and Lightfoot entered the Jiffy Lube and Dixon grabbed one of the employees, Gregory Anderson. Lightfoot pointed a gun in Anderson's face, and the two robbers demanded to know where the money was located. Anderson told them it was in the office. Dixon and Lightfoot then took Anderson to the office. Anderson told them that only the manager had the key to the drawer where the money was kept. Lightfoot instructed Anderson to call for the manager. Anderson complied and the store manager, Michael McDonald, came to the office. At that point Lightfoot pointed the gun in McDonald's face.

McDonald began struggling with Lightfoot over the gun. During the struggle, the gun fired once. When Lightfoot momentarily stumbled and fell backward during the struggle, McDonald gained control over the gun. Lightfoot immediately regained his balance, and both he and Dixon ran out of the store. McDonald fired several shots in the direction of the fleeing suspects. Dixon ran back to the Camaro, got in and sped away. Lightfoot fell to the ground in the parking lot as a result of a gunshot wound to the head. Lightfoot subsequently died at Good Samaritan Hospital.

After being arrested, Dixon admitted to police his involvement in the Jiffy Lube robbery.

Dixon was indicted on one count of felony murder, R.C. 2903.02(B), and one count of aggravated robbery, R.C. 2911.01(A)(1). A firearm specification, R.C. 2941.145, accompanied each charge. Prior to trial Defendant moved to dismiss the felony murder charge, arguing that it violated his constitutional right to equal protection under the law. The trial court overruled Dixon's motion to dismiss. Dixon once again raised this same issue via his Crim. R. 29 motion, which the trial court also overruled.

Following a jury trial, Dixon was found guilty of both felony murder and aggravated robbery, and the accompanying firearm specifications. The trial court sentenced Dixon to fifteen years to life on the felony murder charge, and ten years on the aggravated robbery, said sentences to be served concurrently. The trial court also merged the two firearm specifications and imposed one additional and consecutive three year term of imprisonment for the use of a firearm.

From his conviction and sentence Dixon has timely appealed to this court.

FIRST ASSIGNMENT OF ERROR
DEFENDANT-APPELLANT'S CONSTITUTIONAL RIGHT TO EQUAL PROTECTION UNDER THE LAW WAS VIOLATED WHEN HE WAS CONVICTED OF FELONY MURDER PURSUANT TO R.C. 2903.02(B)

SECOND ASSIGNMENT OF ERROR
THE TRIAL COURT ERRED TO DEFENDANT-APPELLANT'S PREJUDICE WHEN IT OVERRULED HIS PRETRIAL MOTION TO DISMISS AND CRIMINAL RULE 29 MOTIONS FOR ACQUITTAL.

The issues raised in these two assignments of error are identical, and will be addressed together. Dixon argues that the State's decision to charge, convict and sentence him for felony murder violated his equal protection rights, because the felony murder statute, R.C. 2903.02(B), gives a prosecutor "unfettered discretion" to charge a person with felony murder without having to prove anything more than is required under the involuntary manslaughter statute, R.C. 2903.04(A). In other words, Dixon complains that the felony murder statute prohibits the same conduct as the involuntary manslaughter statute, yet those convicted of felony murder suffer a more severe punishment. In support of his argument, Dixon cites *State v. Wilson* (1979), 58 Ohio St. 2d 52, 388 N.E.2d 745, which held that if two criminal statutes "prohibit identical activity, require identical proof, and yet impose different penalties, then sentencing a person under the statute with the higher penalty violates the Equal Protection Clause."

R.C. 2903.02(B) provides:

> No person shall cause the death of another as a proximate result of the offender's committing or attempting to commit an offense of violence that is a felony of the first or second degree and that is not a violation of section 2903.03 or 2903.04 of the Revised Code.

Involuntary manslaughter is defined in R.C. 2903.04(A):

> No person shall cause the death of another or the unlawful termination of another's pregnancy as a proximate result of the offender's committing or attempting to commit a felony.

With respect to Dixon's equal protection argument, the issue is whether both statutes require the State to prove identical elements while prescribing different penalties. The test is "whether, if the defendant is charged with the elevated crime, the State has the burden of proving an additional element beyond that required by the lesser offense." *Wilson, supra*, at 55, 388 N.E.2d 745.

A comparison of the felony murder statute, R.C. 2903.02(B), and the involuntary manslaughter statute, R.C. 2903.04(A), reveals that they do not prohibit identical activity and require identical proof. Causing another's death as a proximate result of committing *any* felony, which is sufficient to prove involuntary manslaughter, is not always or necessarily sufficient to prove felony murder. In order to prove felony murder the State is required to prove more: that the underlying felony is an offense of violence, defined in R.C. 2901.01(A)(9), that is a felony of the first or second degree, and not a violation of R.C. 2903.03 or 2903.04.

While proof of felony murder, R.C. 2903.02(B), would always and necessarily prove involuntary manslaughter, R.C. 2903.04(A), the converse is not true. Proof of involuntary manslaughter is not sufficient to prove felony murder except in those particular cases where an additional requirement is met: the underlying felony is an offense of violence that is a felony of the first or second degree. Because felony murder requires proof of this additional requirement, Dixon's equal protection argument lacks merit. *Wilson, supra*. Felony murder carries a higher penalty than involuntary manslaughter because the harm involved in committing the underlying offense is greater; an offense of violence that is a felony of the first or second degree, versus any felony. Thus, R.C. 2903.02(B) bears a rational relationship to a legitimate governmental interest, protecting the safety of citizens. *State v. Bowes* (May 11, 2001), Lake App. No. 99-L-075, unreported.

In this particular case Dixon's underlying felony offense was aggravated robbery, R.C. 2911.01(A)(1), which is an offense of violence and a felony of the first degree. Thus, proof of involuntary manslaughter on the particular facts in this case would also prove felony murder.

Nevertheless, Dixon's equal protection argument still lacks merit.***

Dixon's other argument he makes in these assignments of error presents a more difficult question: whether a defendant can be convicted of felony murder for the death of his accomplice when that killing was committed by the intended victim of the underlying felony offense in the course of resisting that crime. Courts throughout the various states are divided on this issue, depending upon several variables including the specific language used in their respective felony murder statutes, the theory of criminal responsibility adhered to, and whether specific intent to cause death must be proved as an element of the offense. See 56 ALR.3d 239, 89 ALR.4th 683. In arguing that he cannot be convicted of felony murder as a result of the fatal shooting of his accomplice, Lightfoot, by the victim of the Jiffy Lube robbery, Dixon relies upon decisions from other states, and the common law understanding that felony murder involved a killing by either the defendant or one of his accomplices during the course of committing and in furtherance of the underlying felony.

At common law, murder was the unlawful killing of a human being with malice aforethought: an intentional killing with expressed malice. Katz & Gianelli, Criminal Law, Section 95.2 (1996). Over time, common law murder expanded to include situations involving "implied malice," one of which was a killing committed during the commission of a felony: felony murder. *Id.* Under the felony murder doctrine, the malice or intent involved in the underlying felony was transferred to the killing.

Limitations developed at common law on the felony murder doctrine. First, some courts required that the underlying felony be independent of the killing, which excluded manslaughter as the predicate offense. *Id.* Second, death had to be foreseeable, otherwise the underlying felony could not be considered the proximate cause of the death. *Id.* Third, there was a temporal limitation that the death had to occur during commission of the felony, during an attempt to commit the felony, or while fleeing immediately after attempting or committing the felony. *Id.* Fourth, the death of a co-felon was often not punishable as felony murder if the death was caused by some innocent third party, such as a victim, bystander or police officer. *Id.*

In Ohio all crimes are statutory, and there is a "felony murder" component in both the aggravated murder statute, R.C. 2903.01(B), and the murder statute, R.C. 2903.02(B). The felony murder component of the murder statute came into existence pursuant to the June 30, 1998, amendment to that statute. Unlike the felony murder component of the aggravated murder statute, R.C. 2903.01(B), the felony murder component of the murder statute, R.C. 2903.02(B), does not require any purpose or specific intent to cause death. The provision states:

> No person shall cause the death of another as a proximate result of the offender's committing or attempting to commit an offense of violence that is a felony of the first or second decree and that is not a violation of section 2903.03 or 2903.04 of the Revised Code.

The question presented in this case is whether Dixon can be convicted of felony murder when he and an accomplice, Lightfoot, joined together in the commission of an armed robbery, and during the commission of that offense the intended victim of that robbery shot and killed the accomplice, Lightfoot. Phrased in the language of R.C. 2903.02(B), the question is: did Dixon cause the death of Lightfoot as a proximate result of Dixon committing or attempting to commit aggravated robbery? To answer this question we must examine the specific wording used in R.C. 2903.02(B), and determine the intent of the General Assembly in writing it.

With respect to felony murder, two opposing theories of criminal responsibility exist. Under the "agency theory," the State must prove that either the defendant or someone acting in concert with him, an accomplice, killed the victim and that the killing occurred during the perpetration of and in furtherance of the underlying felony offense. *Moore v. Wyrick* (8th Cir., 1985), 766 F.2d 1253. Under the "proximate cause theory," it is irrelevant whether the killer was the defendant, an accomplice, or some third party such as the victim of the underlying felony or a police officer. Neither does the guilt or innocence of the person killed matter. Defendant can be held criminally responsible for the killing regardless of the identity of the person killed or the identity of the person whose act directly caused the death, so long as the death is the "proximate result" of Defendant's conduct in committing the underlying felony offense; that is, a direct, natural, reasonably foreseeable consequence, as opposed to an extraordinary or surprising consequence, when viewed in the light of ordinary experience. *Id; State v. Bumgardner* (August 21, 1998), Greene App. No. 97-CA-103.

Reviewing the precise wording used in the felony murder statute at issue, R.C. 2903.02(B), that provision states that "no person shall cause the death of another *as a proximate result of*" committing or attempting to commit an offense of violence that is a felony of the first or second degree. That wording clearly indicates an intent on the part of the Ohio legislature to adopt a proximate cause standard of criminal liability.

In *State v. Chambers, supra,* the Court of Appeals reviewed the involuntary manslaughter statute, R.C. 2903.04(A), the operative language of which is virtually identical to R.C. 2903.02(B) with respect to causation: "no person shall cause the death of another . . . *as a proximate result of*" committing or attempting to commit a felony. Upon facts nearly identical to those in the case before us, where defendant's accomplice was shot and killed by the victim of the underlying felony offense while resisting that crime, the Court of Appeals in *Chambers* concluded that defendant could be held criminally liable for involuntary manslaughter for the death of his accomplice. The *Chambers* Court reasoned that the Ohio legislature had manifested its intent, through the precise language used in the involuntary manslaughter statute, to follow the proximate cause theory, rather than agency, as the basis for criminal responsibility.

We conclude that the proper interpretation of the felony murder statute at issue in this case compels the same result as that reached in *Chambers,* because R.C. 2903.02(B) employs the exact same causation language, which demonstrates the legislature's intent to adopt proximate cause as the standard of criminal responsibility for R.C. 2903.02(B).

In *State v. Lovelace, supra,* the Court of Appeals stated:

> Generally, for a criminal defendant's conduct to be the proximate cause of a certain result, it must first be determined that the conduct was the cause in fact of the result, meaning that the result would not have occurred "but for" the conduct. Second, when the result varied from the harmed intended or hazarded, it must be determined that the result achieved was not so extraordinary or surprising that it would be simply unfair to hold the defendant criminally responsible for something so unforeseeable. LaFave & Scott, Criminal Law (1972).

Obviously, the death of Lightfoot would not have occurred when it did but for Dixon's conduct, acting in concert with Lightfoot, in robbing the Jiffy Lube at gunpoint. Moreover, the death of Lightfoot was foreseeable or should have been foreseeable to Dixon. Foreseeability is determined from the perspective of what the defendant knew or should have known, when viewed in light of ordinary experience. *Lovelace, supra.* It is not necessary that Dixon be able to foresee the precise consequences of his conduct; only that the consequences be foreseeable in the sense that what actually transpired was natural and logical in that it was within the scope of the risk created by Dixon. *Id; State v. Losey* (1985), 23 Ohio App. 3d 93.

In *State v. Bumgardner, supra,* this court observed:

> The term "proximate result" as it is used in the definition of involuntary manslaughter resembles the concept of "proximate cause" in that the defendant will be held responsible for those foreseeable consequences that are known to be, or should be known to be, within the scope of the risk created by his conduct. *Losey, supra,* citing *State v. Chambers* (1977), 53 Ohio App. 2d 266. "[A] defendant cannot be held responsible for consequences no reasonable person could expect to follow from his conduct; [but] he will be held responsible for consequences which are direct, normal, and reasonably inevitable—as opposed to extraordinary or surprising—when viewed in the light of ordinary experience." *Id.* Thus, if death could be reasonably anticipated by an ordinarily prudent person as likely to result from the circumstances created by the defendant in the commission of a felony, he may be convicted of involuntary manslaughter *regardless of whether he intended to cause a death.* (Emphasis added.)

Clearly, the shooting which killed Lightfoot was within the scope of the risk created by Dixon when he and Lightfoot robbed the Jiffy Lube at gunpoint. Dixon planned the robbery with Lightfoot, was an active participant during the robbery, and knew a deadly weapon was being employed to facilitate the robbery. The natural inclination of persons present during a robbery to forcibly defend themselves, their family and friends, and their property from theft and criminal aggression is a primal human instinct. *Chambers, supra.* Every robber or burglar knows when he attempts his crime that he is inviting dangerous resistance. *Id.* Add to this highly charged atmosphere the use of a firearm to facilitate the robbery, and the risk of serious physical harm or death to any person present, be it the intended victims, bystanders, or the wrongdoers themselves, becomes highly foreseeable. See *State v. Meek* (1978), 53 Ohio St. 2d 35.

The causal relationship between Dixon's criminal conduct and Lightfoot's death was not so remote or improbable as to be unforeseeable by any reasonable person. The death of Lightfoot was a natural, logical, and reasonably foreseeable consequence of the armed robbery that Dixon and Lightfoot were committing at the time, when viewed in the light of ordinary human experience. Accordingly, pursuant to the proximate cause standard of criminal responsibility adopted in R.C. 2903.02(B), Dixon may be held criminally liable for the death of his accomplice, Lightfoot, which he caused as a proximate result of committing or attempting to commit aggravated robbery. The trial court properly denied Dixon's motions to dismiss the felony murder charge.

The first and second assignments of error are overruled.

Notes and Questions

1. In *State v. Dixon*, how did the defendant cause Lightfoot's death? Wasn't McDonald the cause of Lightfoot's death? Also, wouldn't Lightfoot's independent and voluntary act (i.e., participating in the robbery) break any causal chain linking the defendant to Lightfoot's death?

2. What if Dixon was unaware of the fact that Lightfoot was armed during the robbery? Would it have made a difference in this case? What if neither Lightfoot nor Dixon went to the robbery armed, but Lightfoot was nonetheless killed because the manager was armed?

3. Some jurisdictions do not allow felony-murder prosecutions for the death of a co-felon or when the underlying death was caused by a third party. What arguments can be made for restricting felony murder in this fashion? What arguments can be made against having such a rule? If you were the prosecutor in this case, would you charge the defendant with felony murder? What about felony involuntary manslaughter? As *Dixon* illustrates, Ohio has a felony involuntary manslaughter rule. Not all states have a similar rule.

4. What policy arguments support adopting either the Agency or Proximate Result approach to felony murder as discussed in *Dixon*?

5. In what ways has Ohio modified the common law with respect to felony murder?

D. Attempted Felony Murder

State v. Nolan, 2013-Ohio-2829 (Ohio Ct. App. 2013)

THOMAS R. WRIGHT, J.

This appeal is from the final judgment in a criminal proceeding before the Portage County Court of Common Pleas. After a jury trial, appellant, Bobby D. Nolan, was found guilty of attempted felony murder, felonious assault, and possessing a firearm while under a disability. He maintains that his conviction must be reversed because he was denied proper discovery and the jury verdict was against the weight of the evidence.

The subject matter of this case concerns an altercation between appellant and the victim, Travis McPeak. The altercation happened in the yard of an apartment complex in Kent, Ohio, during the early morning hours of November 15, 2011. Prior to the incident, appellant and McPeak had met on only one occasion, approximately two years earlier when both men were incarcerated at the Portage County Jail.

Tiffany Burns was a resident of the apartment complex where the incident occurred. Prior to November 15, 2011, Tiffany had shared her apartment with Nicole David, who was appellant's girlfriend. Recently, Nicole had moved from the apartment and started to live with appellant. At that time, appellant was living with another friend, Joshua Tipton, in Stow, Ohio.

A few hours before the altercation, McPeak met Tiffany at a restaurant in Ravenna, Ohio. McPeak drove his own truck to the restaurant; however, at some point in the evening, he decided to "loan" his vehicle to Herschel Hill in exchange for illegal drugs.

After their initial rendezvous at the restaurant, McPeak and Tiffany went to the home of a female friend in Ravenna, where they used illegal drugs. Eventually, they decided to go to Tiffany's apartment in Kent. The female friend agreed to drive McPeak and Tiffany to Kent, and they arrived at the apartment at approximately 12:00 a.m.

Over the next two hours, McPeak and Tiffany watched a movie together. During this period, they had been alone in her apartment. At some point after the end of the movie, though, appellant came to the apartment. He was accompanied by Joshua Tipton and two other men. Prior to going to Tiffany's apartment, the four men had been at a local bar, where appellant had also engaged in illegal drug use.

Almost instantly after entering the apartment, appellant began to verbally harass McPeak, claiming that McPeak was a racist. At one point during the "harassing" stage of the altercation, appellant ordered McPeak to totally disrobe so that his clothes could be checked. Upon putting his garments back on, McPeak decided to leave and went out the sole outside door to Tiffany's apartment. He then proceeded to go toward the sidewalk that was located near the adjacent roadway. At that juncture, Tipton was seated in the vehicle he had used to drive appellant to the apartment. Tipton's vehicle was not parked directly in front of Tiffany's door, but instead was located a few yards down the roadway.

As McPeak got to the sidewalk and began to turn right, he saw a shadow coming toward him from behind. As McPeak turned to look, appellant attempted to hit him. However, McPeak was able to duck and avoid the intended blow. He then pushed appellant to the ground.

As appellant was standing up, he removed a firearm from the front pocket of his sweatshirt and immediately fired it in the general direction of McPeak. The bullet entered the outside edge of McPeak's left thigh, went across the entire width of the left thigh, and exited the inside edge of the thigh. The bullet did not hit the femur bone in the left thigh; nor did it hit the main artery for McPeak's left leg.

According to McPeak, he never saw appellant point the firearm at him, but only saw a flash of light. According to Joshua Tipton, who saw the altercation through the rearview mirror of his vehicle, appellant pointed the firearm downward, rather than at McPeak's torso or head. Pursuant to appellant's version of the events, he pointed the firearm downward because he was only attempting to intimidate McPeak.

Upon being shot, McPeak ran away from the apartment complex. While appellant yelled at McPeak as he was running, appellant did not fire the gun again and did not chase after him. Over the next thirty minutes, McPeak hid in two different locations and tried to contact Tiffany and his brother on his cell phone. When he was convinced that he was not being followed, McPeak walked into a local convenient store and asked to use the store phone. While he again tried to contact his brother, the store clerk called the police on her cell phone. After the police arrived and noticed McPeak's injury, he was transported to a local hospital.

When the Kent police tried to question McPeak about the shooting, he was initially evasive. In fact, at one point, he told an officer that he thought his truck had been stolen that night. However, after he was treated at the hospital, he explained the entire incident to the police and executed a written statement. In addition, McPeak was able to pick appellant out in a photo array.

The Kent police were never able to recover the firearm that appellant used in the shooting. In testifying for the state at trial, Joshua Tipton indicated that appellant threw the firearm into a local lake.

Within one week of the incident, the Portage County Grand jury returned a three-count indictment, charging appellant with two counts of attempted murder and one count of felonious assault. Each of the three counts had a firearm specification. While these charges were pending, the grand jury returned a supplemental indictment, under which appellant was charged with having a firearm while under a disability.

Pursuant to the first count of attempted murder, appellant was charged under R.C. 2923.02 and 2903.02(A), and essentially asserted that appellant purposely attempted to cause McPeak's death. The second attempted murder count was brought under R.C. 2923.02 and 2903.02(B), and asserted that appellant knowingly engaged in behavior that, if successful, would have caused McPeak's death as a proximate cause of his commission of the underlying offense of felonious assault.***

At the conclusion of the trial, the jury found appellant not guilty on the first count of attempted murder. However, the jury returned a guilty verdict on the remaining three counts. At the subsequent sentencing hearing, the trial court held that the second attempted murder count and the felonious assault count would be merged because they were allied offenses of similar import.***

In appealing his conviction, appellant has asserted three assignments of error for review:***

Under his final assignment, appellant maintains his conviction should be reversed as being against the manifest weight of the evidence. As with his previous two assignments, appellant's argument focuses upon whether the facts of this case justified a finding that he acted purposefully when he fired the gun toward McPeak. According to him, the evidence could only be interpreted to demonstrate that he acted recklessly or negligently.

In relation to the infliction of the wound to McPeak's thigh, appellant was only found guilty of attempted felony murder and felonious assault. Prior to discussing the substance of appellant's evidentiary challenge, this court is compelled to address a separate question pertaining solely to the validity of his conviction for attempted felony murder. After oral arguments, we ordered the parties to submit supplemental briefing on the legal issue of whether attempted felony murder is a viable criminal offense under Ohio law. Specifically, the parties were instructed to consider our prior analysis on the issue in *State v. Hendrix*, 11th Dist. No. 2011–L–043. In conjunction with his new submission, appellant has asserted a supplemental assignment of error for review:

> Whether as a matter of law, the appellant can be convicted of attempted felony murder when there was no resultant death.

Appellant now contends that his conviction for attempted felony murder must be declared void because, since the death of another person is a required element for felony murder, the offense has no application in situations where the victim survives the incident. In response, the state argues that attempted felony murder is a recognized criminal offense because the Supreme Court of Ohio has expressly upheld convictions for this crime.

In responding to appellant's supplemental assignment in this case, the state has not tried to directly refute this court's legal analysis in *Hendrix*. Instead, the state argues that *Hendrix* conflicts with the Ohio Supreme Court's decision in *State v. Williams,* 124 Ohio St. 3d 381. According to the state, *Williams* stands for the proposition that a criminal defendant can be charged and convicted of attempted felony murder in Ohio.

The basic offense of felony murder is defined in R.C. 2903.02(B):

> (B) No person shall cause the death of another as a proximate result of the offender's committing or attempting to commit an offense of violence that is a felony of the first or second degree ***

Under the plain and unambiguous elements for felony murder, the state is not required to prove that the perpetrator acted with a specific mens rea in regard to causing the death of another person. Instead, the state is only obligated to show that the perpetrator had the necessary mens rea to commit the underlying violent offense. In contrast, Ohio's "attempt" statute, R.C. 2923.02(A), contains an express mens rea requirement: "No person, purposely or knowingly, *** shall engage in conduct that, if successful, would constitute or result in the offense."

In light of the respective elements under R.C. 2903.02(B) and 2923.02(A), a charge of "attempted felony murder" creates a purported offense that has conflicting elements. Although an accused must act purposely or knowingly in order to be found guilty of an "attempted" offense, such a state of mind is not needed in causing the death of another under felony murder. The import of this obvious conflict was addressed by this court in *Hendrix*, 2012-Ohio-2832:

> An "attempt" is typically referred to as an inchoate crime. *See e.g. In re Phillips*, 5th Dist. No. CT2001–005. In other words, the crime of "attempt" is committed prior to and in preparation for an additional offense. An attempt requires the specific intent to bring about a criminal result as well as a significant overt act in furtherance of that intent. *See State v. Williams*, 8th Dist. No. 72659. Although an attempt is a complete offense in itself, it presumes the underlying crime for which the offender has prepared has not been completed.
>
> Felony murder, alternatively, involves an inadvertent homicide resulting from the commission of a felony of violence. *See e.g. State v. Mays*, 2d Dist. No. 24168. By definition, therefore, felony murder charge requires both a felony of violence *and* an unintended death. The victim, in this case, however, survived. Not only is it impossible to attempt to cause an unintended result, one cannot specifically intend to commit a crime that statutorily requires a homicide where no death occurs. We therefore hold the trial court should have dismissed the counts of attempted felony murder and complicity to attempted felony murder as both counts charge crimes which are logically impossible. (Emphasis sic.)

In responding to appellant's supplemental assignment in this case, the state has not tried to directly refute this court's legal analysis in *Hendrix*. Instead, the state argues that *Hendrix* conflicts with the Ohio Supreme Court's decision in *State v. Williams*, 124 Ohio St. 3d 381. According to the state, *Williams* stands for the proposition that a criminal defendant can be charged and convicted of attempted felony murder in Ohio.

In *Williams,* the defendant fired two gunshots in the general vicinity of the victim. Although one of the bullets struck the victim's spine and paralyzed him, he did not die from his injuries. The *Williams* defendant was then indicted on two counts of felonious assault and two counts of attempted murder, including one count of attempted felony murder under R.C. 2903.02(B). After the jury found the defendant guilty on all four counts, the trial court imposed a separate sentence for each offense. On appeal, the Eighth Appellate District held that the two counts of felonious assault should have been merged into the two counts of attempted murder, and that the two attempted murders should have then been merged for a single conviction and sentence.

In accepting the state's appeal in *Williams,* the Ohio Supreme Court only reviewed two issues: (1) are attempted felony murder and felonious assault under R.C. 2903.11(A)(1) allied offenses of similar import; and (2) are attempted "purposeful" murder and felonious assault under R.C. 2903.11(A)(2) allied offenses of similar import? *Id.* at ¶ 2. In resolving the first issue, the Supreme Court never addressed the question of whether attempted felony murder is a viable criminal offense in Ohio. In fact, there is no indication in the *Williams* opinion that the legal propriety of the attempted felony murder charge was ever challenged by the defendant. Hence, even though the Supreme Court implicitly assumed for the purposes of its limited discussion that the conviction for attempted felony murder was proper, the *Williams* decision is not dispositive of whether attempted felony murder constitutes a valid crime for which a defendant can be tried and convicted.

To the foregoing extent, the state has failed to demonstrate that our *Hendrix* holding is inconsistent with any prior Ohio Supreme Court decision. In addition, the state has not cited any other Ohio appellate opinion reaching a different conclusion on the issue. Moreover, our review of various decisions in other states establishes that *Hendrix* is consistent with the majority view. This point was recently discussed by an Arizona state appellate court in *State v. Moore,* 218 Ariz. 534:

> Finally, the overwhelming majority of state courts that have addressed whether attempted felony murder is a cognizable crime have reached the same conclusion. *See* [People v.] Patterson [209 Cal. App. 3d 610]; *State v. Gray,* 654 So.2d 552 (Fla. 1995); *State v. Pratt,* 125 Idaho 546, ("*Attempted* felony murder is not a crime in Idaho. Instead, there is either the crime of murder, or the crime of attempt to commit a crime, in which case the state bears the burden of proving that the defendant *intended* to commit the crime."); *People v. Viser,* 62 Ill.2d 568,

("(T)he offense of attempt requires an 'intent to commit a specific offense', while the distinct characteristic of felony murder is that it does not involve an intention to kill. There is no such criminal offense as an attempt to achieve an unintended result.") (citations omitted); *Head [v. State]*, 443 N.E.2d [44] at 50 [(Ind. 1982)]; *[State v.] Robinson*, [256 Kan. 133], 883 P.2d; *Bruce v. State*, 317 Md. 642, ("Because a conviction for felony murder requires no specific intent to kill, it follows that because a criminal attempt is a specific intent crime, attempted felony murder is not a crime in Maryland") *State v. Dahlstrom*, 276 Minn. 301, (Minn. 1967); *State v. Darby*, 200 N.J. Super. 327, (N.J. Super. Ct. App. Div. 1984) *(" 'Attempted felony murder' is a self-contradiction, for one does not 'attempt' an unintended result.");* *State v. Price*, 104 N.M. 703, (N.M. Ct. App. 1986) ("Thus, the result-oriented nature of the doctrine and the unpopularity of felony murder are among the concerns which persuade us not to recognize the crime of attempted felony murder."); *State v. Kimbrough*, 924 S.W.2d 888 (Tenn. 1996); *Goodson v. Virginia*, 467 S.E.2d 848, (Va. Ct. App. 1996) ("We join the majority of states and hold that, in order for a felony murder analysis to be applicable, a homicide must occur."); *In re Richey*, 175 P.3d 585, (Wash. 2008). *But see White v. State*, 266 Ark. 499, (Ark. 1979) (finding that attempted felony murder is a cognizable offense in Arkansas).

Given the lack of any conflicting authority in Ohio and the nature of the analysis followed by the vast majority of courts in other states, this court concludes that the *Hendrix* holding shall continue to be binding authority in this jurisdiction. That is, attempted felony murder is not a viable criminal offense. When the victim of a violent felony offense does not die as a result of his injuries, the defendant can be charged with attempted murder only if he purposely intended to cause the victim's death. If such a mens rea cannot be proven, the defendant can only be indicted on whatever underlying "assault" offense is applicable under the facts of the case.

In this case, McPeak was able to survive the injury to his thigh. As a result, the jury should have only been allowed to consider the "purposeful" attempted murder count under R.C. 2903.02(A). Because attempted felony murder constitutes a logical impossibility which cannot be charged as a criminal offense, it was plain error for the trial court to permit the state to go forward on that count. As the count of attempted felony murder should have been dismissed, appellant's supplemental assignment has merit.

Notes and Questions

1. Why did the court in *State v. Nolan* find attempted felony murder to be a logical impossibility? Why do you suppose other states, like Arkansas, recognize attempted felony murder? Can you make the case for why Ohio should recognize attempted felony murder?

E. Independent Merger Doctrine

State v. Cherry, 2002-Ohio-3738 (Ohio Ct. App. 2002)

WHITMORE, Judge.

Defendant-Appellant Elliott Cherry has appealed from a judgment order of conviction and sentence from the Summit County Court of Common Pleas finding him guilty of child endangering in violation of R.C. 2919.22(B)(1) and murder in violation of R.C. 2903.02(B). This Court affirms.

I

On the evening of May 1, 2001, Appellant was at the apartment of his girlfriend, Jocola Martin. Appellant was alone at the apartment with Ms. Martin's thirteen-month-old son Elijah Kimbrough and Appellant's one and one-half-year-old daughter Zorrie; Ms. Martin had gone to work earlier in the evening.

At approximately 10:21 p.m., 911 dispatchers received a call from Appellant. Appellant told the dispatchers that Elijah had fallen down a stairway and had stopped breathing. Emergency medical technicians and police officers responding to the call converged at the apartment. Elijah was rushed to Children's Hospital, where he was pronounced dead at 11:10 p.m.

Two days later Appellant was indicted on one count of murder, in violation of R.C. 2903.02(B) with the predicate offense of felonious assault; felonious assault, in violation of R.C. 2903.11(A)(1); and endangering children, in violation of R.C. 2919.22(A). A supplemental indictment was filed three months later charging Appellant with murder, in violation of R.C. 2903.02(B) with the predicate offense endangering children; and endangering children, in violation of R.C. 2919.22(B)(1).***

At trial, Officer Aey testified that he was one of the officers who was dispatched to the apartment from which Appellant had placed the 911 call. Officer Aey stated that he spoke with Appellant after the medical personnel had taken Elijah to the hospital, and that at that time Appellant related to him the following sequence of events: Appellant was doing laundry in the lower level of the apartment when he heard a "thud." Appellant went to the stairway, and found Elijah at the second or third step from the bottom. The infant gasped as Appellant took Elijah in his arms and carried him up the stairs, and Appellant told him to breathe. When they reached the top of the stairs, Appellant set the child down and telephoned his mother and 911. According to Officer Aey, Appellant reported that Elijah had a history of falling down steps, and had fallen down the steps of the third level stairway earlier in the day.

Sergeant Hudnall of the Akron Police Department also testified at Appellant's trial. Sergeant Hudnall stated that he was another of the officers who responded to Appellant's 911 call, and interviewed Appellant at the apartment. The Sergeant testified that Appellant told him that Elijah had fallen down the steps of the basement stairway while he was doing laundry.

The state also presented testimony from Detective Hamas of the Akron Police Department. Detective Hamas testified that he arrived at the apartment while Sergeant Hudnall was talking to Appellant. Detective Hamas stated that Appellant voluntarily agreed to accompany him to the police station to give a statement to the police. The Detective testified that he and Detective Vincent Benson questioned Appellant in an interview room at the detective bureau, where Appellant repeated his account of Elijah's fall down the basement steps. After the interview, Detective Benson took Appellant home.

Detective Benson was the state's next witness at the trial. Detective Benson's description of what Appellant told the detectives during the interview at the detective bureau matched the account given by Detective Hamas. In addition, Detective Benson stated that Appellant agreed to return to the police station with Ms. Martin the following day at noon.

The next day, Appellant and Ms. Martin came back to the police station for further questioning. After the detectives interviewed Ms. Martin, Appellant was brought to the interview room. Detective Benson testified that Appellant was voluntarily in the interview room, and was free to leave. Present in the interview room with Appellant was Detective Benson, Detective Dalvin Horton, and assistant city prosecutor Tom Dicaudo. Detective Benson then testified to the following sequence of events: After Appellant repeated his account of Elijah's fall down the stairs, one of the interviewers interjected that the coroner had informed them that Elijah's injuries were not caused by a fall down the stairs, but by a blunt force trauma to the abdomen. At some point during the questioning, the interviewers placed in front of Appellant a picture of Elijah's open abdominal cavity taken during the child's autopsy. The picture showed multiple tears in the infant's liver. Upon seeing the photograph, Appellant dropped his head and said that "his life was over." Appellant admitted that the children had been irritating him, and that he had "backhanded Elijah in the stomach" one time. The detectives then told Appellant he was under arrest, and Detective Horton was asked to read Appellant his *Miranda* rights.***

Dr. Lisa Kohler, Chief Medical Examiner of Summit County, also testified at the trial. Dr. Kohler stated that she performed an autopsy on Elijah's body, which revealed two large tears in the infant's liver, lacerations in the membrane holding the bowels in place, and subdural bleeding. According to Dr. Kohler, the tears in the liver were the result of a deeply penetrating blow administered with significant force from an object with a small surface area, such as a fist or a heel. Dr. Kohler testified that the cause of Elijah's death was blood loss due to blunt force injury to the abdomen. The doctor stated that the child's fatal injuries could not have been caused by a fall down the steps.

The jury found Appellant not guilty of felonious assault and not guilty of murder with the predicate offense of felonious assault, but guilty of child endangering and guilty of murder with child endangering as the predicate offense. The trial court sentenced Appellant to serve eight years in prison for child endangering and fifteen years to life for murder. Appellant has timely appealed from his convictions and sentence, asserting four assignments of error.

II

Assignment of Error Number One

In his first assignment of error, Appellant has argued that his conviction for felony murder violated his federal and state constitutional guarantees of due process and equal protection of the laws. Appellant has purported to attack the constitutionality of Ohio's felony murder statute both on its face and as applied to his case. "If a statute is unconstitutional as applied, the State may continue to enforce the statute in different circumstances where it is not unconstitutional, but if a statute is unconstitutional on its face, the State may not enforce the statute under any circumstances." *Holeton v. Crouse Cartage Co.*, 92 Ohio St. 3d 115.***

Appellant's attack on the constitutionality of R.C. 2903.02(B) consists of four components. This Court will address each in turn.

A. "R.C. 2903.02(B) *is unconstitutional because it fails to require that the underlying felony in a murder conviction be independent from the conduct which kills.*"

Appellant has first argued that R.C. 2903.02(B) is unconstitutional because it fails to adopt the independent felony, or merger, doctrine recognized by some courts, legislatures, and scholars. According to this doctrine, only crimes that are independent of the conduct which kills can serve as the predicate offenses for felony murder. Appellant has argued that in his case, the acts constituting child endangering were the same acts that constituted a necessary part of the homicide—to wit, Elijah's death. Consequently, Appellant has contended, the charge of child endangering should have merged into the homicide and precluded the state's prosecution of Appellant for felony murder. Appellant has argued that the Ohio statute's failure to recognize the merger doctrine resulted in the capricious, unreasonable, and arbitrary elevation of the charge against him to murder for alleged conduct that historically would have been prosecuted as involuntary manslaughter.

Appellant was convicted of felony murder pursuant to R.C. 2903.02(B), with a conviction for child endangering in violation of R.C. 2919.22(B)(1) as the predicate felony offense. R.C. 2903.02(B), which became effective June 30, 1998, provides: "No person shall cause the death of another as a proximate result of the offender's committing or attempting to commit an offense of violence that is a felony of the first or second degree[.]" R.C. 2919.22(B) provides:

> No person shall do any of the following to a child under eighteen years of age or a mentally or physically handicapped child under twenty-one years of age:
> (1) Abuse the child[.]

R.C. 2919.22(E)(2)(d) states that a violation of R.C. 2919.22(B)(1) which results in serious physical harm to the victim is a felony of the second degree. R.C. 2901.01(A)(9) provides that a violation of R.C. 2919.22(B)(1) is an offense of violence.

This Court agrees that in adopting R.C. 2903.02(B), the General Assembly rejected the independent felony/merger doctrine. Appellant has failed to demonstrate, however, that this legislative decision does not bear a rational relationship to a legitimate state interest.

In rejecting an argument identical to the one raised by Appellant, the First District Court of Appeals noted the limitations on the offenses that can serve as predicate felonies under R.C. 2903.02(B) and stated:

> The General Assembly has thus narrowly defined the scope of felony murder under R.C. 2903.02(B), and related it to the legitimate purpose of punishing the taking of human life while committing a separate offense of violence. Only eleven first- and second-degree offenses may serve as predicate offenses under this statute. Voluntary and involuntary manslaughter may not. *State v. Pickett,* 1st Dist. No. C–000424, 2001-Ohio-4022.

The Eleventh District Court of Appeals also found R.C. 2903.02(B) constitutional in spite of the statute's failure to incorporate the merger doctrine, concluding that "it is a legislative prerogative to provide what form or forms of the felony-murder rule it wishes to implement as long as the statutes enacted are otherwise within constitutional parameters." *State v. Hayden* (July 14, 2000), 11th Dist. No. 99-L-037.

This Court agrees with the reasoning of *Pickett* and *Hayden,* and finds that neither R.C. 2903.02(B) nor Appellant's conviction for felony murder where the predicate offense was not independent of the conduct that killed Elijah are in violation of equal protection or due process guarantees. Appellant's first argument is without merit.

B. "R.C. 2903.02(B) is unconstitutional because felonies which are not inherently dangerous to human life can be used as the underlying felony in a murder conviction."

In his second argument, Appellant has contended that R.C. 2903.02(B) is unconstitutional because it permits felonies that are not "inherently dangerous to human life" to serve as predicate felony offenses. After carefully reviewing the record, however, this Court finds that Appellant failed to raise this argument in the court below. "Failure to raise at the trial court level the issue of the constitutionality of a statute or its application, which is apparent at the time of trial, constitutes a waiver of such issue *** and therefore need not be heard for the first time on appeal." *State v. Awan* (1986), 22 Ohio St. 3d 120. Accordingly, we decline to address further the second component of Appellant's first assignment of error.

C. "R.C. 2903.02(B) is unconstitutional because it relieves the State of the burden of proving the offender 'purposely' took the life of the victim."

In his third argument, Appellant has averred that R.C. 2903.02(B) is unconstitutional because it allows the state to obtain a conviction for felony murder without having to prove a purposeful intent to kill. According to Appellant, the lack of a mens rea element in Ohio's felony murder statute permits a defendant to be charged with murder for conduct which would have traditionally been prosecuted as involuntary manslaughter.

Ohio courts addressing this argument have rejected Appellant's reasoning on the basis that the state still must prove the mens rea element by proving intent to commit the predicate felony. In *Hayden,* supra, the Eighth District Court of Appeals concluded:

> Under the common law approach, R.C. 2903.02(B) does not relieve the state of the burden of proving *mens rea* simply because the intent to kill is conclusively presumed so long as the state proves the required intent to commit the underlying felony. At common law, "malice aforethought" was ascribed to a felon who killed another in the perpetration of an inherently dangerous felony such as rape, robbery, or burglary. Specifically, under the common law rule, the United States Supreme Court recognized that "prosecutors do not need to prove a culpable

mental state with respect to the murder because intent to kill is conclusively presumed if the state proves intent to commit the underlying felony." *Hopkins v. Reeves* (1998), 524 U.S. 88. Thus, several states have found that felony-murder statutes pass constitutional muster regarding the *mens rea* issue because those statutes require the state prove the intent of the underlying felony.

This Court has specifically adopted the foregoing rationale in *State v. Smathers* (Dec. 20, 2000), 9th Dist. No. 19945, at 5-6, appeal not allowed. Appellant has urged us to find that *Smathers* is not controlling in the instant case because Appellant was convicted of child endangering, for which the mens rea element is "recklessly." See R.C. 2901.22(B). The appellant in *Smathers,* by contrast, was convicted of felonious assault in violation of R.C. 2903.11(A)(1), which includes a mens rea element of "knowingly."

This Court is not aware of any appellate cases addressing a defendant's conviction for murder under the current version of R.C. 2903.02(B) based solely upon a predicate offense with a mens rea of "recklessly." After careful review of the statutory provisions at issue, however, we conclude that Appellant's conviction for murder based on a predicate felony with a mens rea of "recklessly" did not violate his constitutional rights.

In the instant case, the trial court instructed the jury on the following definition of "recklessly:"

> A person acts recklessly when, with heedless indifference to the consequences, he perversely disregards a known risk that his conduct is likely to cause a certain result or be of a certain nature. A person is reckless with respect to circumstances when with heedless indifference to the consequences, he perversely disregards a known risk that such circumstances are likely to exist.

[handwritten margin note: Child endangerment requirement]

The trial court's instruction with respect to the count of child endangering charged the jury that in order to find Appellant guilty, it must find that Appellant "did recklessly abuse the child resulting in serious physical harm to a child."

R.C. 2903.02(B) evidences a clear legislative intent to subject those who commit the most serious felonies to liability for murder, where commission of those felonies results in death. Where commission of child endangering in violation of R.C. 2919.22(B)(1) results in serious physical harm to the child victim, the violation is a felony of the second degree and thereby becomes included in the class of eligible R.C. 2903.02(B) predicate felonies. R.C. 2919.22(E)(2)(d); R.C. 2903.02(B). The consequence of this statutory scheme is to subject one who causes serious physical harm to a child through an act of reckless abuse to prosecution for murder, where the death of the child is a proximate result of such abuse.

In light of the legislature's clear desire to punish under R.C. 2903.02(B) those who proximately cause the death of children by acts of reckless abuse, we find no merit to Appellant's argument that his constitutional rights were violated by predicating his conviction on a felony with a mens rea of "recklessly." The state was still required to prove that Appellant perversely disregarded a known risk that his conduct was likely to cause a certain result or be of a certain nature when he abused Elijah, and that Elijah died as a proximate result of the abuse. Giving due deference to the legislature's evident solicitude for the protection of children, we conclude that proof that Appellant "recklessly" abused Elijah was sufficient to establish the requisite culpable mental state to convict Appellant of murder as proscribed by R.C. 2903.02(B). See *Hayden* and *Smathers,* supra. Appellant's third argument is without merit.

D. "R.C. 2903.02(B) is unconstitutional because it violates equal protection by giving prosecutors' [sic] undue discretion in charging since murder under R.C. 2903.02(B) and involuntary manslaughter under R.C. 2903.04 prohibit identical activity and subject offenders to different punishment."

In his fourth argument, Appellant has contended that his conviction for murder violates his constitutional right to equal protection of the laws because R.C. 2903.02(B) and R.C. 2903.04 (involuntary manslaughter) prohibit identical conduct, yet subject offenders to different penalties. Appellant has argued that the offenders prosecuted under each statute constitute classes of similarly situated defendants who are treated differently based on distinctions that are not rationally related to a legitimate government interest.

Appellant has directed us to *State v. Wilson* (1979), 58 Ohio St. 2d 52, in which the Ohio Supreme Court stated that the issue under such an equal protection challenge is "whether both statutes require the state to prove identical elements while prescribing different penalties." *Id.* at 55, 388 N.E.2d 745. According to *Wilson,* "if the statutes prohibit identical activity, require identical proof, and yet impose different penalties, then sentencing a person under the statute with the higher penalty violates the Equal Protection Clause." *Id.,* at 55-56, 388 N.E.2d 745.

Appellant's equal protection argument has been rejected by numerous Ohio appellate districts on the ground that additional elements must be proven to obtain a conviction for felony murder. Specifically, it has been held that:

> [T]o be convicted of felony-murder, one must have committed or attempted to commit an offense *of violence* that is a felony of the *first or second degree* whereas the involuntary

manslaughter statute only requires that the offender have committed or attempted to commit *any* felony. There is no requirement [for an involuntary manslaughter conviction] that the felony was one of violence or that it was of the first or second degree." (Emphasis sic.) *State v. Miller* (June 29, 2001), 11th Dist. No. 99–CA–0078, appeal not allowed (2001), 93 Ohio St. 3d 1476.

In addition, it has been determined that:

Felony murder carries a higher penalty than involuntary manslaughter because the harm involved in committing the underlying offense is greater; an offense of violence that is a felony of the first or second degree, versus any felony. Thus, R.C.2903.02(B) bears a rational relationship to a legitimate governmental interest, protecting the safety of citizens."*** Accordingly, Appellant's fourth argument is not well taken.

Notes and Questions

1. As noted in *State v. Cherry*, some states recognize the independent merger doctrine. Why do you think those states do? What justifications did the *Cherry* court offer for not recognizing the independent merger doctrine?

2. In *Cherry,* why didn't the prosecutor charge the defendant with "purposely caus[ing] the death of another" as opposed to felony murder? What benefits did the prosecution obtain by using felony murder?

3. Are you concerned with the prosecution's ability to obtain a felony murder conviction with a lower mens rea? Here, the prosecution only had to prove that the defendant acted recklessly.

F. Temporal Proximity

Dana K. Cole, *Expanding Felony-Murder in Ohio: Felony-Murder or Murder Felony?*
63 Ohio St. L.J. 15 (2002)

The common law felony-murder rule provides that a person will be held criminally responsible for a death that occurs "in the commission or attempted commission of" a felony. Modern statutes use similar words or phrases such as "while," "during," "in perpetration of," "in the commission of," "in furtherance of," and "in the course of."

In what way do these phrases define the scope of the felony-murder rule? Certainly, temporal proximity is required. Temporal proximity is not limited to deaths occurring at the exact moment of the felony, but includes a period before and after the completion of the felony. This period begins with the initiation of an attempt to commit the underlying felony, and ends when the defendant reaches "a place of temporary safety." If the death occurs before the initiation of an attempt to commit the underlying felony, the felony-murder rule does not apply. Similarly, deaths occurring after the accused has retreated to a place of temporary safety are not within the scope of the felony-murder rule.

Although temporal proximity is required, the law generally demands more of a nexus between the underlying felony and the death than the "mere coincidence of time and place." Typically, a causal connection between the underlying felony and the death is also required. Most jurisdictions go beyond mere cause-in-fact or but-for causation and require that the death must be a natural and foreseeable consequence of the felony.

In a line of cases beginning with *State v. Williams*, the Ohio Supreme Court broadly interpreted the "while committing or attempting to commit" language found in Ohio's aggravated felony-murder rule and felony-murder death penalty specification statute. The court essentially replaced the statutory term "while" with the judicially created phrase "part of one continuous occurrence." The court then defined this phrase as essentially requiring only an overly broad form of temporal proximity between the underlying felony and the death. As long as the death and the underlying felony occur within the same general time frame, the felony-murder rule applies without regard to whether the death and the underlying felony were otherwise related. Even if the intent to commit the underlying felony was formed subsequent to the death, as a complete afterthought, the Ohio Supreme Court will permit the state to seek an aggravated murder conviction, and even the death penalty, under its felony-murder doctrine.

Notes and Questions

1. The majority of jurisdictions follow the prevailing view that there can be no felony-murder (and/or felony murder aggravating circumstance) where the felony occurs as an afterthought to the killing. These include Alabama, Arkansas, California, District of Columbia, Idaho, Maryland, Massachusetts, Michigan, Missouri, Nebraska, New York, Pennsylvania, Tennessee, Texas, and Wyoming.

Jurisdictions following the minority view that felony-murder (and/or felony-murder aggravating circumstances) does not require that the intent to commit the underlying felony be formed prior to the act causing death include Illinois, New Mexico, North Carolina, Ohio, Oklahoma, and Washington.

Why do you think Ohio became one of the minority jurisdictions? Before answering that question, re-read Ohio's aggravated murder statute. Unlike many traditional felony murder statutes, Ohio has a mens rea requirement. Do you think this mens rea requirement makes the court more comfortable with expanding the law here? What is Ohio's felony murder rule seeking to deter?

G. Death Penalty

Furman v. Georgia, 408 U.S. 238 (1972)

Certiorari was granted to review decisions of the Supreme Court of Georgia, 225 Ga. 253, affirming imposition of death penalty on defendants convicted of murder and rape, and to review judgment of the Court of Criminal Appeals of Texas, 447 S.W.2d 932, affirming imposition of death penalty on defendant convicted of rape. The Supreme Court held that imposition and carrying out of death penalty in cases before court would constitute cruel and unusual punishment in violation of Eighth and Fourteenth Amendments.

Judgment in each case reversed in part and cases remanded.

Mr. Justice DOUGLAS, Mr. Justice BRENNAN, Mr. Justice STEWART, Mr. Justice WHITE and Mr. Justice MARSHALL filed separate opinions in support of judgments.

Mr. Chief JUSTICE BURGER, Mr. Justice BLACKMUM, Mr. Justice POWELL and Mr. Justice REHNQUIST filed separate dissenting opinions.

Gregg v. Georgia, 428 U.S. 153 (1976)

Judgment of the Court, and opinion of Mr. Justice STEWART, Mr. Justice POWELL, and Mr. Justice STEVENS, announced by Mr. Justice STEWART.

The issue in this case is whether the imposition of the sentence of death for the crime of murder under the law of Georgia violates the Eighth and Fourteenth Amendments.

I

The petitioner, Troy Gregg, was charged with committing armed robbery and murder. In accordance with Georgia procedure in capital cases, the trial was in two stages, a guilt stage and a sentencing stage. The evidence at the guilt trial established that on November 21, 1973, the petitioner and a traveling companion, Floyd Allen, while hitchhiking north in Florida were picked up by Fred Simmons and Bob Moore. Their car broke down, but they continued north after Simmons purchased another vehicle with some of the cash he was carrying. While still in Florida, they picked up another hitchhiker, Dennis Weaver, who rode with them to Atlanta, where he was let out about 11 p. m. A short time later the four men interrupted their journey for a rest stop along the highway. The next morning the bodies of Simmons and Moore were discovered in a ditch nearby.

On November 23, after reading about the shootings in an Atlanta newspaper, Weaver communicated with the Gwinnett County police and related information concerning the journey with the victims, including a description of the car. The next afternoon, the petitioner and Allen, while in Simmons' car, were arrested in Asheville, N. C. In the search incident to the arrest a .25-caliber pistol, later shown to be that used to kill Simmons and Moore, was found in the petitioner's pocket. After receiving the warnings required by *Miranda v. Arizona*, 384 U.S. 436 (1966), and signing a written waiver of his rights, the petitioner signed a statement in which he admitted shooting, then robbing Simmons and Moore. He justified the slayings on grounds of self-defense. The next day, while being transferred to Lawrenceville, Ga., the petitioner and Allen were taken to the scene of the shootings. Upon arriving there, Allen recounted the events leading to the slayings. His version of these events was as follows: After Simmons and Moore left the car, the petitioner stated that he intended to rob them. The petitioner then took his pistol in hand and positioned himself on the car to improve his aim. As Simmons and Moore came up an embankment toward the car, the petitioner fired three shots and the two men fell near a ditch. The petitioner, at close range, then fired a shot into the head of each. He robbed them of valuables and drove away with Allen.***

The trial judge submitted the murder charges to the jury on both felony-murder and nonfelony-murder theories. He also instructed on the issue of self-defense but declined to instruct on manslaughter. He submitted the robbery case to the jury on both an armed-robbery theory and on the lesser included offense of robbery by intimidation. The jury found the petitioner guilty of two counts of armed robbery and two counts of murder.

At the penalty stage, which took place before the same jury, neither the prosecutor nor the petitioner's lawyer offered any additional evidence. Both counsel, however, made lengthy arguments dealing generally with the propriety of capital punishment under the circumstances and with the weight of the evidence of guilt. The trial judge instructed the jury that it could recommend either a death sentence or a life prison sentence on each count. The judge further charged the jury that in determining what sentence was appropriate the jury was free to consider the facts and circumstances, if any, presented by the parties in mitigation or aggravation.

Finally, the judge instructed the jury that it "would not be authorized to consider (imposing) the penalty of death" unless it first found beyond a reasonable doubt one of these aggravating circumstances:

"One That the offense of murder was committed while the offender was engaged in the commission of two other capital felonies, to-wit the armed robbery of (Simmons and Moore).

"Two That the offender committed the offense of murder for the purpose of receiving money and the automobile described in the indictment.

"Three The offense of murder was outrageously and wantonly vile, horrible and inhuman, in that they (Sic) involved the depravity of (the) mind of the defendant." Tr. 476-477.

Finding the first and second of these circumstances, the jury returned verdicts of death on each count.***

III

The Court on a number of occasions has both assumed and asserted the constitutionality of capital punishment. In several cases that assumption provided a necessary foundation for the decision, as the Court was asked to decide whether a particular method of carrying out a capital sentence would be allowed to stand under the Eighth Amendment. But until *Furman v. Georgia*, 408 U.S. 238 (1972), the Court never confronted squarely the fundamental claim that the punishment of death always, regardless of the enormity of the offense or the procedure followed in imposing the sentence, is cruel and unusual punishment in violation of the Constitution. Although this issue was presented and addressed in *Furman*, it was not resolved by the Court. Four Justices would have held that capital punishment is not unconstitutional *per se*; two Justices would have reached the opposite conclusion; and three Justices, while agreeing that the statutes then before the Court were invalid as applied, left open the question whether such punishment may ever be imposed. We now hold that the punishment of death does not invariably violate the Constitution.***

The imposition of the death penalty for the crime of murder has a long history of acceptance both in the United States and in England. The common-law rule imposed a mandatory death sentence on all convicted murderers. *McGautha v. California*, 402 U.S. 183 (1971). And the penalty continued to be used into the 20th century by most American States, although the breadth of the common-law rule was diminished, initially by narrowing the class of murders to be punished by death and subsequently by widespread adoption of laws expressly granting juries the discretion to recommend mercy. Id., at 199-200.

It is apparent from the text of the Constitution itself that the existence of capital punishment was accepted by the Framers. At the time the Eighth Amendment was ratified, capital punishment was a common sanction in every State. Indeed, the First Congress of the United States enacted legislation providing death as the penalty for specified crimes. C. 9, 1 Stat. 112 (1790). The Fifth Amendment, adopted at the same time as the Eighth, contemplated the continued existence of the capital sanction by imposing certain limits on the prosecution of capital cases:

"No person shall be held to answer for a capital, or otherwise infamous crime, unless on a presentment or indictment of a Grand Jury . . .; nor shall any person be subject for the same offense to be twice put in jeopardy of life or limb; . . . nor be deprived of life, liberty, or property, without due process of law . . . ."

And the Fourteenth Amendment, adopted over three-quarters of a century later, similarly contemplates the existence of the capital sanction in providing that no State shall deprive any person of "life, liberty, or property" without due process of law.

For nearly two centuries, this Court, repeatedly and often expressly, has recognized that capital punishment is not invalid *per se*. In Wilkerson v. Utah, where the Court found no constitutional violation in inflicting death by public shooting, it said:

"Cruel and unusual punishments are forbidden by the Constitution, but the authorities referred to are quite sufficient to show that the punishment of shooting as a mode of executing the death penalty for the crime of murder in the first degree is not included in that category, within the meaning of the eighth amendment."

Rejecting the contention that death by electrocution was "cruel and unusual," the Court in *In re Kemmler* reiterated:

> "(T)he punishment of death is not cruel, within the meaning
> of that word as used in the Constitution. It implies there
> something inhuman and barbarous, something more than the
> mere extinguishment of life."

Again, in *Louisiana ex rel. Francis v. Resweber*, the Court remarked: "The cruelty against which the Constitution protects a convicted man is cruelty inherent in the method of punishment, not the necessary suffering involved in any method employed to extinguish life humanely." And in *Trop v. Dulles*, Mr. Chief Justice Warren, for himself and three other Justices, wrote:

"Whatever the arguments may be against capital punishment, both on moral grounds and in terms of accomplishing the purposes of punishment . . . the death penalty has been employed throughout our history, and, in a day when it is still widely accepted, it cannot be said to violate the constitutional concept of cruelty."

Four years ago, the petitioners in Furman and its companion cases predicated their argument primarily upon the asserted proposition that standards of decency had evolved to the point where capital punishment no longer could be tolerated. The petitioners in those cases said, in effect, that the evolutionary process had come to an end, and that standards of decency required that the Eighth Amendment be construed finally as prohibiting capital punishment for any crime regardless of its depravity and impact on society. This view was accepted by two Justices. Three other Justices were unwilling to go so far; focusing on the procedures by which convicted defendants were selected for the death penalty rather than on the actual punishment inflicted, they joined in the conclusion that the statutes before the Court were constitutionally invalid.

The petitioners in the capital cases before the Court today renew the "standards of decency" argument, but developments during the four years since Furman have undercut substantially the assumptions upon which their argument rested. Despite the continuing debate, dating back to the 19th century, over the morality and utility of capital punishment, it is now evident that a large proportion of American society continues to regard it as an appropriate and necessary criminal sanction.

The most marked indication of society's endorsement of the death penalty for murder is the legislative response to Furman. The legislatures of at least 35 States have enacted new statutes that provide for the death penalty for at least some crimes that result in the death of another person. And the Congress of the United States, in 1974, enacted a statute providing the death penalty for aircraft piracy that results in death. These recently adopted statutes have attempted to address the concerns expressed by the Court in Furman Primarily (i) by specifying the factors to be weighed and the procedures to be followed in deciding when to impose a capital sentence, or (ii) by making the death penalty mandatory for specified crimes. But all of the post-Furman Statutes make clear that capital punishment itself has not been rejected by the elected representatives of the people.

In the only statewide referendum occurring since Furman And brought to our attention, the people of California adopted a constitutional amendment that authorized capital punishment, in effect negating a prior ruling by the Supreme Court of California in *People v. Anderson*, 6 Cal. 3d 628.

The jury also is a significant and reliable objective index of contemporary values because it is so directly involved. See Furman v. Georgia. The Court has said that "one of the most important functions any jury can perform in making . . . a selection (between life imprisonment and death for a defendant convicted in a capital case) is to maintain a link between contemporary community values and the penal system." *Witherspoon v. Illinois*, 391 U.S. 510 (1968). It may be true that evolving standards ave influenced juries in recent decades to be more discriminating in imposing the sentence of death. But the relative infrequency of jury verdicts imposing the death sentence does not indicate rejection of capital punishment Per se. Rather, the reluctance of juries in many cases to impose the sentence may well reflect the humane feeling that this most irrevocable of sanctions should be reserved for a small number of extreme cases. See Furman v. Georgia,. Indeed, the actions of juries in many States since Furman are fully compatible with the legislative judgments, reflected in the new statutes, as to the continued utility and necessity of capital punishment in appropriate cases. At the close of 1974 at least 254 persons had been sentenced to death since *Furman*, and by the end of March 1976, more than 460 persons were subject to death sentences.

As we have seen, however, the Eighth Amendment demands more than that a challenged punishment be acceptable to contemporary society. The Court also must ask whether it comports with the basic concept of human dignity at the core of the Amendment. *Trop v. Dulles*, 356 U.S., at 100. Although we cannot "invalidate a category of penalties because we deem less severe penalties adequate to serve the ends of penology," Furman v. Georgia, the sanction imposed cannot be so totally without penological justification that it results in the gratuitous infliction of suffering.

The death penalty is said to serve two principal social purposes: retribution and deterrence of capital crimes by prospective offenders.

In part, capital punishment is an expression of society's moral outrage at particularly offensive conduct. This function may be unappealing to many, but it is essential in an ordered society that asks its citizens to rely on legal processes rather than self-help to vindicate their wrongs.

"The instinct for retribution is part of the nature of man, and channeling that instinct in the administration of criminal justice serves an important purpose in promoting the stability of a society governed by law. When people begin to believe that organized society is unwilling or unable to impose upon criminal offenders the punishment they 'deserve,' then there are sown the seeds of anarchy of self-help, vigilante justice, and lynch law." *Furman v. Georgia*, supra, 408 U.S., at 308.***

Statistical attempts to evaluate the worth of the death penalty as a deterrent to crimes by potential offenders have occasioned a great deal of debate. The results simply have been inconclusive. As one opponent of capital punishment has said:

"(A)fter all possible inquiry, including the probing of all possible methods of inquiry, we do not know, and for systematic and easily visible reasons cannot know, what the truth about this 'deterrent' effect may be . . . .

"The inescapable flaw is . . . that social conditions in any state are not constant through time, and that social conditions are not the same in any two states. If an effect were observed (and the observed effects, one way or another, are not large) then one could not at all tell whether any of this effect is attributable to the presence or absence of capital punishment. A 'scientific' that is to say, a soundly based conclusion is simply impossible, and no methodological path out of this tangle suggests itself." C. Black, Capital Punishment: The Inevitability of Caprice and Mistake 25-26 (1974).

Although some of the studies suggest that the death penalty may not function as a significantly greater deterrent than lesser penalties, there is no convincing empirical evidence either supporting or refuting this view. We may nevertheless assume safely that there are murderers, such as those who act in passion, for whom the threat of death has little or no deterrent effect. But for many others, the death penalty undoubtedly is a significant deterrent. There are carefully contemplated murders, such as murder for hire, where the possible penalty of death may well enter into the cold calculus that precedes the decision to act. And there are some categories of murder, such as murder by a life prisoner, where other sanctions may not be adequate.

The value of capital punishment as a deterrent of crime is a complex factual issue the resolution of which properly rests with the legislatures, which can evaluate the results of statistical studies in terms of their own local conditions and with a flexibility of approach that is not available to the courts. *Furman* v. *Georgia,* supra, 408 U.S., at 403-405. Indeed, many of the post-Furman statutes reflect just such a responsible effort to define those crimes and those criminals for which capital punishment is most probably an effective deterrent.

In sum, we cannot say that the judgment of the Georgia Legislature that capital punishment may be necessary in some cases is clearly wrong. Considerations of federalism, as well as respect for the ability of a legislature to evaluate, in terms of its particular State, the moral consensus concerning the death penalty and its social utility as a sanction, require us to conclude, in the absence of more convincing evidence, that the infliction of death as a punishment for murder is not without justification and thus is not unconstitutionally severe.

Finally, we must consider whether the punishment of death is disproportionate in relation to the crime for which it is imposed. *** But we are concerned here only with the imposition of capital punishment for the crime of murder, and when a life has been taken deliberately by the offender, we cannot say that the punishment is invariably disproportionate to the crime. It is an extreme sanction, suitable to the most extreme of crimes.

We hold that the death penalty is not a form of punishment that may never be imposed, regardless of the circumstances of the offense, regardless of the character of the offender, and regardless of the procedure followed in reaching the decision to impose it.

Justice WHITE with THE CHIEF JUSTICE and justice REHNQUIST (concurring)

III

The threshold question in this case in whether the death penalty may be carried out for murder under the Georgia legislative scheme consistent with the decision in Furman v. Georgia, supra. In Furman, this Court held that as a result of giving the sentencer unguided discretion to impose or not to impose the death penalty for murder, the penalty was being imposed discriminatorily, wantonly and freakishly, and so infrequently that any given death sentence was cruel and unusual. Petitioner argues that, as in *Furman*, the jury still the sentencer; that the statutory criteria to be considered by the jury on the issue of sentence under Georgia's new statutory scheme are vague and do not purport to be all-inclusive; and that, in any event, there are No circumstances under which the jury is required to impose the death penalty. Consequently, the petitioner argues that the death penalty will inexorably be imposed in as discriminatory, standardless, and rare a manner as it was imposed under the scheme declared invalid in Furman.

The argument is considerably overstated. The Georgia Legislature has made an effort to identify those aggravating factors which it considers necessary and relevant to the question whether a defendant convicted of capital murder should be sentenced to death. The jury which imposes sentence is instructed on all statutory aggravating factors which are supported by the evidence, and is told that it may not impose the death penalty unless it unanimously finds at least one of those factors to have been established beyond a reasonable doubt. The Georgia Legislature has plainly made an effort to guide the jury in the exercise of its discretion, while at the same time permitting the jury to dispense mercy on the basis of factors too intangible to write into a statute, and I cannot accept the naked assertion that the effort is bound to fail. As the types of murders for which the death penalty may be imposed become more narrowly defined and are limited to those which are particularly serious or for which the death penalty is peculiarly appropriate as they are in Georgia by reason of the aggravating-circumstance requirement, it becomes reasonable to expect that juries even given discretion Not to impose the death penalty will impose the death penalty in a substantial portion of the cases so defined. If they do, it can no longer be said that the penalty is being imposed wantonly and freakishly or so infrequently that it loses its usefulness as a sentencing device. There is, therefore, reason to expect that Georgia's current system would escape the infirmities which invalidated its previous system under Furman. However, the Georgia Legislature was not satisfied with a system which might, but also might not, turn out in practice to result in death sentences being imposed with reasonable consistency for certain serious murders. Instead, it gave the Georgia Supreme Court the power and the obligation to perform precisely the task which three Justices of this Court, whose opinions were necessary to the result, performed in *Furman*: namely, the task of deciding whether *in fact* the death penalty was being administered for any given class of crime in a discriminatory, standardless, or rare fashion.

In considering any given death sentence on appeal the Georgia Supreme Court is to determine whether the sentence imposed was consistent with the relevant statutes I. e., whether there was sufficient evidence to support the finding of an aggravating circumstance. Ga. Code Ann. s 27-2537(c)(2) (Supp.1975). However it must do much more than determine whether the penalty was lawfully imposed. It must go on to decide after reviewing the penalties imposed in "similar cases" whether the penalty is "excessive or disproportionate" considering both the crime and the defendant. s 27-2537(c)(3) (Supp. 1975). The new Assistant to the Supreme Court is to assist the court in collecting the records of "all capital felony cases" in the State of Georgia in which sentence was imposed after January 1, 1970. s 27-2537(f) (Supp. 1975). The court also has the obligation of determining whether the penalty was "imposed under the influence of passion, prejudice or any other arbitrary factor." s 27-2537(c)(1) (Supp. 1975). The Georgia Supreme Court has interpreted the appellate review statute to require it to set aside the death sentence whenever juries across the State impose it only rarely for the type of crime in question; but to require it to affirm death sentences whenever juries across the State generally impose it for the crime in question. Thus in this case the Georgia Supreme Court concluded that the death penalty was so rarely imposed for the crime of robbery that it set aside the sentences on the robbery counts and effectively foreclosed that penalty from being imposed for that crime in the future under the legislative scheme now in existence. Similarly the Georgia Supreme Court has determined that juries impose the death sentence too rarely with respect to certain classes of rape. However it concluded that juries "generally throughout the state" have imposed the death penalty for those who murder witnesses to armed robberies. *Jarrell v. State*, 234 Ga. 410 (1975). Consequently it affirmed the sentences in this case on the murder counts. If the Georgia Supreme Court is correct with respect to this factual judgment imposition of the death penalty in this and similar cases is consistent with Furman. Indeed, if the Georgia Supreme Court properly performs the task assigned to it under the Georgia statutes, death sentences imposed for discriminatory reasons or wantonly or freakishly for any given category of crime will be set aside. Petitioner has wholly failed to establish, and has not even attempted to establish, that the Georgia Supreme Court failed properly to perform its task in this case or that it is incapable of performing its task adequately in all cases; and this Court should not assume that it did not do so.

Mr. Justice BRENNAN, dissenting.

The Cruel and Unusual Punishments Clause "must draw its meaning from the evolving standards of decency that mark the progress of a maturing society." The opinions of Mr. Justice Stewart, Mr. Justice Powell, and Mr. Justice Stevens today hold that "evolving standards of decency" require focus not on the essence of the death penalty itself but primarily upon the procedures employed by the State to single out persons to suffer the penalty of death. Those opinions hold further that, so viewed, the Clause invalidates the mandatory infliction of the death penalty but not its infliction under sentencing procedures that Mr. Justice Stewart, Mr. Justice Powell, and Mr. Justice Stevens conclude adequately safeguard against the risk that the death penalty was imposed in an arbitrary and capricious manner.

In *Furman v. Georgia*, 408 U.S. 238, 257 (1972) (concurring opinion), I read "evolving standards of decency" as requiring focus upon the essence of the death penalty itself and not primarily or solely upon the procedures under which the determination to inflict the penalty upon a particular person was made. I there said:

> "From the beginning of our Nation, the punishment of death has stirred acute public controversy. Although pragmatic arguments for and against the punishment have been frequently advanced, this longstanding and heated controversy cannot be explained solely as the result of differences over the practical wisdom of a particular government policy. At bottom, the battle has been waged on moral grounds. The country has debated whether a society for which the dignity of the individual is the supreme value can, without a fundamental inconsistency, follow the practice of deliberately putting some of its members to death. In the United States, as in other nations of the western world, `the struggle about this punishment has been one between ancient and deeply rooted beliefs in retribution, atonement or vengeance on the one hand, and, on the other, beliefs in the personal value and dignity of the common man that were born of the democratic movement of the eighteenth century, as well as beliefs in the scientific approach to an understanding of the motive forces of human conduct, which are the result of the growth of the sciences of behavior during the nineteenth and twentieth centuries.' It is this essentially moral conflict that forms the backdrop for the past changes in and the present operation of our system of imposing death as a punishment for crime." Id., at 296.

That continues to be my view. For the Clause forbidding cruel and unusual punishments under our constitutional system of government embodies in unique degree moral principles restraining the punishments that our civilized society may impose on those persons who transgress its laws. Thus, I too say: "For myself, I do not hesitate to assert the proposition that the only way the law has progressed from the days of the rack, the screw and the wheel is the development of moral concepts, or, as stated by the Supreme Court . . . the application of `evolving standards of decency' . . . ."

This Court inescapably has the duty, as the ultimate arbiter of the meaning of our Constitution, to say whether, when individuals condemned to death stand before our Bar, "moral concepts" require us to hold that the law has progressed to the point where we should declare that the punishment of death, like punishments on the rack, the screw, and the wheel, is no longer morally tolerable in our civilized society. My opinion in *Furman v. Georgia* concluded that our civilization and the law had progressed to this point and that therefore the punishment of death, for whatever crime and under all circumstances, is "cruel and unusual" in violation of the Eighth and Fourteenth Amendments of the Constitution. I shall not again canvass the reasons that led to that conclusion. I emphasize only that foremost among the "moral concepts" recognized in our cases and inherent in the Clause is the primary moral principle that the State, even as it punishes, must treat its citizens in a manner consistent with their intrinsic worth as human beings - a punishment must not be so severe as to be degrading to human dignity. A judicial determination whether the punishment of death comports with human dignity is therefore not only permitted but compelled by the Clause.

I do not understand that the Court disagrees that "[i]n comparison to all other punishments today . . . the deliberate extinguishment of human life by the State is uniquely degrading to human dignity." Id., at 291. For three of my Brethren hold today that mandatory infliction of the death penalty constitutes the penalty cruel and unusual punishment. I perceive no principled basis for this limitation. Death for whatever crime and under all circumstances "is truly an awesome punishment. The calculated killing of a human being by the State involves, by its very nature, a denial of the executed person's humanity. . . . An executed person has indeed `lost the right to have rights.'" Id., at 290. Death is not only an unusually severe punishment, unusual in its pain, in its finality, and in its enormity, but it serves no penal purpose more effectively than a less severe punishment; therefore the principle inherent in the Clause that prohibits pointless infliction of excessive punishment when less severe punishment can adequately achieve the same purposes invalidates the punishment. Id., at 279.

The fatal constitutional infirmity in the punishment of death is that it treats "members of the human race as nonhumans, as objects to be toyed with and discarded. [It is] thus inconsistent with the fundamental premise of the Clause that even the vilest criminal remains a human being possessed of common human dignity." Id., at 273. As such it is a penalty that "subjects the individual to a fate forbidden by the principle of civilized treatment guaranteed by the [Clause]." I therefore would hold, on that ground alone, that death is today a cruel and unusual punishment prohibited by the Clause. "Justice of this kind is obviously no less shocking than the crime itself, and the new `official' murder, far from offering redress for the offense committed against society, adds instead a second defilement to the first."

Mr. Justice MARSHALL, dissenting.

In *Furman v. Georgia*, I set forth at some length my views on the basic issue presented to the Court in these cases. The death penalty, I concluded, is a cruel and unusual punishment prohibited by the Eighth and Fourteenth Amendments. That continues to be my view.

I have no intention of retracing the "long and tedious journey," id., at 370, that led to my conclusion in Furman. My sole purposes here are to consider the suggestion that my conclusion in Furman has been undercut by developments since then, and briefly to evaluate the basis for my Brethren's holding that the extinction of life is a permissible form of punishment under the Cruel and Unusual Punishments Clause.

In Furman I concluded that the death penalty is constitutionally invalid for two reasons. First, the death penalty is excessive. Id., at 331-332; 342-359. And second, the American people, fully informed as to the purposes of the death penalty and its liabilities, would in my view reject it as morally unacceptable. Id., at 360-369.

Since the decision in Furman, the legislatures of 35 States have enacted new statutes authorizing the imposition of the death sentence for certain crimes, and Congress has enacted a law providing the death penalty for air piracy resulting in death. 49 U.S.C. 1472 (i), (n) (1970 ed., Supp. IV). I would be less than candid if I did not acknowledge that these developments have a significant bearing on a realistic assessment of the moral acceptability of the death penalty to the American people. But if the constitutionality of the death penalty turns, as I have urged, on the opinion of an informed citizenry, then even the enactment of new death statutes cannot be viewed as conclusive. In Furman, I observed that the American people are largely unaware of the information critical to a judgment on the morality of the death penalty, and concluded that if they were better informed they would consider it shocking, unjust, and unacceptable. A recent study, conducted after the enactment of the post-Furman statutes, has confirmed that the American people know little about the death penalty, and that the opinions of an informed public would differ significantly from those of a public unaware of the consequences and effects of the death penalty.

Even assuming, however, that the post-Furman enactment of statutes authorizing the death penalty renders the prediction of the views of an informed citizenry an uncertain basis for a constitutional decision, the enactment of those statutes has no bearing whatsoever on the conclusion that the death penalty is unconstitutional because it is excessive. An excessive penalty is invalid under the Cruel and Unusual Punishments Clause "even though popular sentiment may favor" it. Id., at 331. The inquiry here, then, is simply whether the death penalty is necessary to accomplish the legitimate legislative purposes in punishment, or whether a less severe penalty - life imprisonment - would do as well.

The two purposes that sustain the death penalty as nonexcessive in the Court's view are general deterrence and retribution. In Furman, I canvassed the relevant data on the deterrent effect of capital punishment. The state of knowledge at that point, after literally centuries of debate, was summarized as follows by a United Nations Committee:

> "It is generally agreed between the retentionists and abolitionists, whatever their opinions about the validity of comparative studies of deterrence, that the data which now exist show no correlation between the existence of capital punishment and lower rates of capital crime."
>
> The available evidence, I concluded in Furman, was convincing that "capital punishment is not necessary as a deterrent to crime in our society." Id., at 353.

The Solicitor General in his amicus brief in these cases relies heavily on a study by Isaac Ehrlich, reported a year after Furman, to support the contention that the death penalty does deter murder. Since the Ehrlich study was not available at the time of Furman and since it is the first scientific study to suggest that the death penalty may have a deterrent effect, I will briefly consider its import.

The Ehrlich study focused on the relationship in the Nation as a whole between the homicide rate and "execution risk" - the fraction of persons convicted of murder who were actually executed. Comparing the differences in homicide rate and execution risk for the years 1933 to 1969, Ehrlich found that increases in execution risk were associated with increases in the homicide rate. But when he employed the statistical technique of multiple regression analysis to control for the influence of other variables posited to have an impact on the homicide rate, 6 Ehrlich found a negative correlation between changes in the homicide rate and changes in execution risk. His tentative conclusion was that for the period from 1933 to 1967 each additional execution in the United States might have saved eight lives.

The methods and conclusions of the Ehrlich study have been severely criticized on a number of grounds. It has been suggested, for example, that the study is defective because it compares execution and homicide rates on a nationwide, rather than a state-by-state, basis. The aggregation of data from all States - including those that have abolished the death penalty - obscures the relationship between murder and execution rates. Under Ehrlich's methodology, a decrease in the execution risk in one State combined with an increase in the murder rate in another State would, all other things being equal, suggest a deterrent effect that quite obviously would not exist. Indeed, a deterrent effect would be suggested if, once again all other things being equal, one State abolished the death penalty and experienced no change in the murder rate, while another State experienced an increase in the murder rate.

The most compelling criticism of the Ehrlich study is that its conclusions are extremely sensitive to the choice of the time period included in the regression analysis. Analysis of Ehrlich's data reveals that all empirical support for the deterrent effect of capital punishment disappears when the five most recent years are removed from his time series - that is to say, whether a decrease in the execution risk corresponds to an increase or a decrease in the murder rate depends on the ending point of the sample period. 10 This finding has cast severe doubts on the reliability of Ehrlich's tentative conclusions. Indeed, a recent regression study, based on Ehrlich's theoretical model but using cross-section state data for the years 1950 and 1960, found no support for the conclusion that executions act as a deterrent.

The Ehrlich study, in short, is of little, if any, assistance in assessing the deterrent impact of the death penalty. Accord, *Commonwealth v. O'Neal*, ___ Mass. ___, ___, 339 N. E. 2d 676, 684 (1975). The evidence I reviewed in Furman remains convincing, in my view, that "capital punishment is not necessary as a deterrent to crime in our society." 408 U.S., at 353 . The justification for the death penalty must be found elsewhere.

The other principal purpose said to be served by the death penalty is retribution. The notion that retribution can serve as a moral justification for the sanction of death finds credence in the opinion of my Brothers Stewart, Powell, and Stevens, and that of my Brother White in *Roberts v. Louisiana*, post, p. 337. See also Furman v. Georgia, 408 U.S., at 394 -395 (Burger, C.J., dissenting). It is this notion that I find to be the most disturbing aspect of today's unfortunate decisions.

The concept of retribution is a multifaceted one, and any discussion of its role in the criminal law must be undertaken with caution. On one level, it can be said that the notion of retribution or reprobation is the basis of our insistence that only those who have broken the law be punished, and in this sense the notion is quite obviously central to a just system of criminal sanctions. But our recognition that retribution plays a crucial role in determining who may be punished by no means requires approval of retribution as a general justification for punishment. It is the question whether retribution can provide a moral justification for punishment - in particular, capital punishment - that we must consider.

My Brothers Stewart, Powell, and Stevens offer the following explanation of the retributive justification for capital punishment:

> "'The instinct for retribution is part of the nature of man, and channeling that instinct in the administration of criminal justice serves an important purpose in promoting the stability of a society governed by law. When people begin to believe that organized society is unwilling or unable to impose upon criminal offenders the punishment they "deserve," then there are sown the seeds of anarchy—of self-help, vigilante justice, and lynch law.'" Ante, at 183, quoting from Furman v. Georgia, supra, at 308 (Stewart, J., concurring).

This statement is wholly inadequate to justify the death penalty. As my Brother Brennan stated in Furman, "[t]here is no evidence whatever that utilization of imprisonment rather than death encourages private blood feuds and other disorders." 408 U.S., at 303 (concurring opinion). It simply defies belief to suggest that the death penalty is necessary to prevent the American people from taking the law into their own hands.

In a related vein, it may be suggested that the expression of moral outrage through the imposition of the death penalty serves to reinforce basic moral values - that it marks some crimes as particularly offensive and therefore to be avoided. The argument is akin to a deterrence argument, but differs in that it contemplates the individual's shrinking from antisocial conduct, not because he fears punishment, but because he has been told in the strongest possible way that the conduct is wrong. This contention, like the previous one, provides no support for the death penalty. It is inconceivable that any individual concerned about conforming his conduct to what society says is "right" would fail to realize that murder is "wrong" if the penalty were simply life imprisonment.

The foregoing contentions - that society's expression of moral outrage through the imposition of the death penalty pre-empts the citizenry from taking the law into its own hands and reinforces moral values - are not retributive in the purest sense. They are essentially utilitarian in that they portray the death penalty as valuable because of its beneficial results. These justifications for the death penalty are inadequate because the penalty is, quite clearly I think, not necessary to the accomplishment of those results.

There remains for consideration, however, what might be termed the purely retributive justification for the death penalty - that the death penalty is appropriate, not because of its beneficial effect on society, but because the taking of the murderer's life is itself morally good. Some of the language of the opinion of my Brothers Stewart, Powell, and Stevens in No. 74-6257 appears positively to embrace this notion of retribution for its own sake as a justification for capital punishment. They state:

> "[T]he decision that capital punishment may be the appropriate sanction in extreme cases is an expression of the community's belief that certain crimes are themselves so grievous an affront to humanity that the only adequate response may be the penalty of death." Ante, at 184 (footnote omitted).

They then quote with approval from Lord Justice Denning's remarks before the British Royal Commission on Capital Punishment:

> "'The truth is that some crimes are so outrageous that society insists on adequate punishment, because the wrong-doer deserves it, irrespective of whether it is a deterrent or not.'"
> Ante, at 184 n. 30.

Of course, it may be that these statements are intended as no more than observations as to the popular demands that it is thought must be responded to in order to prevent anarchy. But the implication of the statements appears to me to be quite different—namely, that society's judgment that the murderer "deserves" death must be respected not simply because the preservation of order requires it, but because it is appropriate that society make the judgment and carry it out. It is this latter notion, in particular, that I consider to be fundamentally at odds with the Eighth Amendment. The mere fact that the community demands the murderer's life in return for the evil he has done cannot sustain the death penalty, for as Justices Stewart, Powell, and Stevens remind us, "the Eighth Amendment demands more than that a challenged punishment be acceptable to contemporary society." Ante, at 182. To be sustained under the Eighth Amendment, the death penalty must "compor[t] with the basic concept of human dignity at the core of the Amendment," ibid.; the objective in imposing it must be "[consistent] with our respect for the dignity of [other] men." Ante, at 183. Under these standards, the taking of life "because the wrongdoer deserves it" surely must fall, for such a punishment has as its very basis the total denial of the wrongdoer's dignity and worth.

The death penalty, unnecessary to promote the goal of deterrence or to further any legitimate notion of retribution, is an excessive penalty forbidden by the Eighth and Fourteenth Amendments. I respectfully dissent from the Court's judgment upholding the sentences of death imposed upon the petitioners in these cases.

Notes and Questions

1. As discussed in *Gregg v. Georgia*, the Supreme Court determined, at least initially in *Furman v. Georgia*, that the death penalty as imposed by the states violated the Eighth Amendment because of its arbitrariness and discriminatory effect. As a result, states that wanted to impose capital punishment post-Furman had to rewrite their laws to comply with the Eighth Amendment.

The crimes and circumstances under which a defendant may be charged with a capital offense arise under O.R.C. 2924.04. After reading this statute, ask yourself two questions. First, does this statute provide sufficient guidance to remove the arbitrariness and discriminatory effect of the death penalty? Second, what additional aggravating and mitigating factors would you want the jury to consider prior to imposing death on the defendant?

O.R.C. 2929.04 Death Penalty or Imprisonment—
Aggravating and Mitigating Factors

(A) Imposition of the death penalty for aggravated murder is precluded unless one or more of the following is specified in the indictment or count in the indictment pursuant to section 2941.14 of the Revised Code and proved beyond a reasonable doubt:

(1) The offense was the assassination of the president of the United States or a person in line of succession to the presidency, the governor or lieutenant governor of this state, the president-elect or vice president-elect of the United States, the governor-elect or lieutenant governor-elect of this state, or a candidate for any of the offices described in this division. For purposes of this division, a person is a candidate if the person has been nominated for election according to law, if the person has filed a petition or petitions

according to law to have the person's name placed on the ballot in a primary or general election, or if the person campaigns as a write-in candidate in a primary or general election.

(2) The offense was committed for hire.

(3) The offense was committed for the purpose of escaping detection, apprehension, trial, or punishment for another offense committed by the offender.

(4) The offense was committed while the offender was under detention or while the offender was at large after having broken detention. As used in division (A)(4) of this section, "detention" has the same meaning as in section 2921.01 of the Revised Code, except that detention does not include hospitalization, institutionalization, or confinement in a mental health facility or mental retardation and developmentally disabled facility unless at the time of the commission of the offense either of the following circumstances apply:

> (a) The offender was in the facility as a result of being charged with a violation of a section of the Revised Code.

> (b) The offender was under detention as a result of being convicted of or pleading guilty to a violation of a section of the Revised Code.

(5) Prior to the offense at bar, the offender was convicted of an offense an essential element of which was the purposeful killing of or attempt to kill another, or the offense at bar was part of a course of conduct involving the purposeful killing of or attempt to kill two or more persons by the offender.

(6) The victim of the offense was a law enforcement officer, as defined in section 2911.01 of the Revised Code, whom the offender had reasonable cause to know or knew to be a law enforcement officer as so defined, and either the victim, at the time of the commission of the offense, was engaged in the victim's duties, or it was the offender's specific purpose to kill a law enforcement officer as so defined.

(7) The offense was committed while the offender was committing, attempting to commit, or fleeing immediately after committing or attempting to commit kidnapping, rape, aggravated arson, aggravated robbery, or aggravated burglary, and either the offender was the principal offender in the commission of the aggravated murder or, if not the principal offender, committed the aggravated murder with prior calculation and design.

(8) The victim of the aggravated murder was a witness to an offense who was purposely killed to prevent the victim's testimony in any criminal proceeding and the aggravated murder was not committed during the commission, attempted commission, or flight immediately after the commission or attempted commission of the offense to which the victim was a witness, or the victim of the aggravated murder was a witness to an offense and was purposely killed in retaliation for the victim's testimony in any criminal proceeding.

(9) The offender, in the commission of the offense, purposefully caused the death of another who was under thirteen years of age at the time of the commission of the offense, and either the offender was the principal offender in the commission of the offense or, if not the principal offender, committed the offense with prior calculation and design.

(10) The offense was committed while the offender was committing, attempting to commit, or fleeing immediately after committing or attempting to commit terrorism.

(B) If one or more of the aggravating circumstances listed in division (A) of this section is specified in the indictment or count in the indictment and proved beyond a reasonable doubt, and if the offender did not raise the matter of age pursuant to section 2929.023 of the Revised Code or if the offender, after raising the matter of age, was found at trial to have been eighteen years of age or older at the time of the commission of the offense, the court, trial jury, or panel of three judges shall consider, and weigh against the aggravating circumstances proved beyond a reasonable doubt, the nature and circumstances of the offense, the history, character, and background of the offender, and all of the following factors:

(1) Whether the victim of the offense induced or facilitated it;

(2) Whether it is unlikely that the offense would have been committed, but for the fact that the offender was under duress, coercion, or strong provocation;

(3) Whether, at the time of committing the offense, the offender, because of a mental disease or defect, lacked substantial capacity to appreciate the criminality of the offender's conduct or to conform the offender's conduct to the requirements of the law;

(4) The youth of the offender;

(5) The offender's lack of a significant history of prior criminal convictions and delinquency adjudications;

(6) If the offender was a participant in the offense but not the principal offender, the degree of the offender's participation in the offense and the degree of the offender's participation in the acts that led to the death of the victim;

(7) Any other factors that are relevant to the issue of whether the offender should be sentenced to death.

(C) The defendant shall be given great latitude in the presentation of evidence of the factors listed in division (B) of this section and of any other factors in mitigation of the imposition of the sentence of death.

The existence of any of the mitigating factors listed in division (B) of this section does not preclude the imposition of a sentence of death on the offender but shall be weighed pursuant to divisions (D)(2) and (3) of section 2929.03 of the

Revised Code by the trial court, trial jury, or the panel of three judges against the aggravating circumstances the offender was found guilty of committing.

2. Another unique aspect of a death penalty case is the trial process. Jurisdictions to include Ohio use a bifurcated system to adjudicate both the defendant's guilt and, if necessary, the sentence. The following is an excerpt discussing Ohio's bifurcated process.

Taken from S. Adele Shank, *The Death Penalty in Ohio: Fairness, Reliability, and Justice at Risk—A Report on Reforms in Ohio's Use of the Death Penalty Since the 1997 Ohio State Bar Association Recommendations Were Made* 63 Ohio St. L.J. 371 (2002)

II. OHIO'S COMPLEX DEATH PENALTY PROCESS

Sadly, there are still attorneys and judges who say that a capital case is no different than an "ordinary" felony—only that the possible penalty is greater. This simplistic view of the state's use of the ultimate penalty known to humankind is unfortunately shared by many members of the public and contributes greatly to the false perception that capital cases are fraught with unnecessary delay. In fact, many capital cases are pushed through the legal system at a pace and under circumstances that make it difficult for even experts in capital litigation to provide effective assistance. Capital litigation is complex, time consuming, and intellectually and emotionally demanding legal work. The failure to understand this underlies many of the defects in Ohio's capital sentencing system, including the underfunding of indigent defense and the imposition of unreasonably short time limits at various points in the legal process.

Experts around the country report that an average capital defense at the trial level, done reasonably well, requires between 400 and 1,500 hours of attorney time. Capital cases also significantly increase the expenditure of court time as compared to non-capital trials. If any difference exists between Ohio's capital sentencing scheme and those in other states, it is that Ohio has devised a more complex death penalty structure that requires an even greater attention to detail and thus more time.

A. The Bifurcated Trial

Capital cases, in Ohio and throughout the country, are handled through a bifurcated trial process in which innocence or guilt is determined in the first stage and, assuming a guilty verdict, penalty is determined in the second stage. This bifurcated system alone, while constitutionally mandated, makes capital trials more difficult to prepare than even a non-capital murder case. Defense counsel must plan for two separate proceedings—a defense on guilt and a mitigation strategy should the defense fail.

This bifurcated process significantly impacts jury selection. It necessarily includes a process known as death qualification that excludes from jury service all those whose moral qualms about the death penalty preclude them from voting for a capital sentence. This part of the voir dire process is routinely done with each juror individually, in order to allow the potential juror to freely express his or her private thoughts and to avoid having the juror's qualms or, sometimes, religious arguments sway the other jurors. Although time consuming, this aspect of voir dire is as important to the judge and prosecutor as it is to the defendant. A single juror tainted by bias requires reversal of the case should there be a conviction.

The bifurcated trial uses the same jury for the guilt/innocence determination and the penalty decision. This requires defense counsel to know on the day voir dire begins what his or her mitigation strategy will be. The jurors must be able to fairly consider all evidence that weighs against a capital sentence should the case proceed to a penalty determination. Effective voir dire must address this issue. Because counsel must be prepared before trial for a penalty phase that may not take place, the pre-trial preparation for a capital case is necessarily more time consuming than for a non-capital felony case.

Publicity is frequently an issue in capital cases. That, too, contributes to the complexity of proceedings. Often hearings are held to determine if and to what extent media coverage will be allowed. These can place a great burden on the court. Rarely does publicity become an issue in non-capital felony cases. When pre-trial publicity is extensive, it impacts the length of the voir dire process. Veniremen must be questioned privately about such matters in order not to spread media accounts to the entire pool of potential jurors. While critical to insuring that the jury is impartial, this process greatly increases the in-court time spent by the judge, prosecutor, and defense counsel.

The bifurcated trial also increases the volume of motion practice in capital cases. Issues of all sorts must be addressed for both phases of trial—from the use of confessions and statements made in the course of psychiatric examinations, through the legality of jail house snitch testimony, to the granting and denying of prosecutorial immunity in order to shape the trial testimony, requests for experts, and constitutional challenges—before trial begins.

Jury instructions must be analyzed and drafted for two proceedings. Ohio standards for proper instructions have changed repeatedly. Counsel who is not familiar with capital jury issues will inevitably fail to preserve his client's rights. The Ohio Supreme Court has held that several often given instructions are improper in capital cases but, rather than placing the burden on the courts to instruct properly, the Court finds the errors waived when trial counsel fails to object.

In addition to increased preparation of pleadings and in-court work that falls on all participants, capital litigation requires increased investigation, which must be done by the defense. Counsel must investigate the prosecution's guilt phase case and investigate his client's life and mental health for mitigation. When a client presents mental health issues that may provide a defense, the equation for the investigation and presentation of evidence is extremely complex.***

Notes and Questions

1. What benefits are there to the constitutionally mandated bifurcated process?

2. In our modern society of 24-hour news and pervasive social media, is it ever possible to find 12 truly impartial death penalty jurors?

H. Race, Gender, and the Death Penalty

McCleskey v. Kemp, 481 U.S. 279 (1987)

This case presents the question whether a complex statistical study that indicates a risk that racial considerations enter into capital sentencing determinations proves that petitioner McCleskey's capital sentence is unconstitutional under the Eighth or Fourteenth Amendment.

I

McCleskey, a black man, was convicted of two counts of armed robbery and one count of murder in the Superior Court of Fulton County, Georgia, on October 12, 1978. McCleskey's convictions arose out of the robbery of a furniture store and the killing of a white police officer during the course of the robbery. The evidence at trial indicated that McCleskey and three accomplices planned and carried out the robbery. All four were armed. McCleskey entered the front of the store while the other three entered the rear. McCleskey secured the front of the store by rounding up the customers and forcing them to lie face down on the floor. The other three rounded up the employees in the rear and tied them up with tape. The manager was forced at gunpoint to turn over the store receipts, his watch, and $6. During the course of the robbery, a police officer, answering a silent alarm, entered the store through the front door. As he was walking down the center aisle of the store, two shots were fired. Both struck the officer. One hit him in the face and killed him.

Several weeks later, McCleskey was arrested in connection with an unrelated offense. He confessed that he had participated in the furniture store robbery, but denied that he had shot the police officer. At trial, the State introduced evidence that at least one of the bullets that struck the officer was fired from a .38 caliber Rossi revolver. This description matched the description of the gun that McCleskey had carried during the robbery. The State also introduced the testimony of two witnesses who had heard McCleskey admit to the shooting.

McCleskey next filed a petition for a writ of habeas corpus in the Federal District Court for the Northern District of Georgia. His petition raised 18 claims, one of which was that the Georgia capital sentencing process is administered in a racially discriminatory manner in violation of the Eighth and Fourteenth Amendments to the United States Constitution. In support of his claim, McCleskey proffered a statistical study performed by Professors David C. Baldus, Charles Pulaski, and George Woodworth, and (the Baldus study) that purports to show a disparity in the imposition of the death sentence in Georgia based on the race of the murder victim and, to a lesser extent, the race of the defendant. The Baldus study is actually two sophisticated statistical studies that examine over 2,000 murder cases that occurred in Georgia during the 1970's. The raw numbers collected by Professor Baldus indicate that defendants charged with killing white persons received the death penalty in 11% of the cases, but defendants charged with killing blacks received the death penalty in only 1% of the cases. The raw numbers also indicate a reverse racial disparity according to the race of the defendant: 4% of the black defendants received the death penalty, as opposed to 7% of the white defendants.

Baldus also divided the cases according to the combination of the race of the defendant and the race of the victim. He found that the death penalty was assessed in 22% of the cases involving black defendants and white victims; 8% of the cases involving white defendants and white victims; 1% of the cases involving black defendants and black victims; and 3% of the cases involving white defendants and black victims. Similarly, Baldus found that prosecutors sought the death penalty in 70% of the cases involving black defendants and white victims; 32% of the cases involving white defendants and white victims; 15% of the cases involving black defendants and black victims; and 19% of the cases involving white defendants and black victims.

Baldus subjected his data to an extensive analysis, taking account of 230 variables that could have explained the disparities on nonracial grounds. One of his models concludes that, even after taking account of 39 nonracial variables, defendants charged with killing white victims were 4.3 times as likely to receive a death sentence as defendants charged with killing blacks. According to this model, black defendants were 1.1 times as likely to receive a death sentence as other defendants. Thus, the Baldus study indicates that black defendants, such as McCleskey, who kill white victims have the greatest likelihood of receiving the death penalty.***

McCleskey's first claim is that the Georgia capital punishment statute violates the Equal Protection Clause of the Fourteenth Amendment. He argues that race has infected the administration of Georgia's statute in two ways:

persons who murder whites are more likely to be sentenced to death than persons who murder blacks, and black murderers are more likely to be sentenced to death than white murderers. As a black defendant who killed a white victim, McCleskey claims that the Baldus study demonstrates that he was discriminated against because of his race and because of the race of his victim. In its broadest form, McCleskey's claim of discrimination extends to every actor in the Georgia capital sentencing process, from the prosecutor who sought the death penalty and the jury that imposed the sentence, to the State itself that enacted the capital punishment statute and allows it to remain in effect despite its allegedly discriminatory application. We agree with the Court of Appeals, and every other court that has considered such a challenge, that this claim must fail.

A

***Thus, to prevail under the Equal Protection Clause, McCleskey must prove that the decisionmakers in *his* case acted with discriminatory purpose. He offers no evidence specific to his own case that would support an inference that racial considerations played a part in his sentence. Instead, he relies solely on the Baldus study. McCleskey argues that the Baldus study compels an inference that his sentence rests on purposeful discrimination. McCleskey's claim that these statistics are sufficient proof of discrimination, without regard to the facts of a particular case, would extend to all capital cases in Georgia, at least where the victim was white and the defendant is black.

The Court has accepted statistics as proof of intent to discriminate in certain limited contexts. First, this Court has accepted statistical disparities as proof of an equal protection violation in the selection of the jury venire in a particular district. Although statistical proof normally must present a "stark" pattern to be accepted as the sole proof of discriminatory intent under the Constitution, *Arlington Heights Metropolitan Housing Dev. Corp.,* 429 U.S. 252 (1977)***

But the nature of the capital sentencing decision, and the relationship of the statistics to that decision, are fundamentally different from the corresponding elements in the venire-selection or Title VII cases. Most importantly, each particular decision to impose the death penalty is made by a petit jury selected from a properly constituted venire. Each jury is unique in its composition, and the Constitution requires that its decision rest on consideration of innumerable factors that vary according to the characteristics of the individual defendant and the facts of the particular capital offense. Thus, the application of an inference drawn from the general statistics to a specific decision in a trial and sentencing simply is not comparable to the application of an inference drawn from general statistics to a specific venire-selection or Title VII case. In those cases, the statistics relate to fewer entities, and fewer variables are relevant to the challenged decisions.

Another important difference between the cases in which we have accepted statistics as proof of discriminatory intent and this case is that, in the venire-selection and Title VII contexts, the decisionmaker has an opportunity to explain the statistical disparity.*** Moreover, absent far stronger proof, it is unnecessary to seek such a rebuttal, because a legitimate and unchallenged explanation for the decision is apparent from the record: McCleskey committed an act for which the United States Constitution and Georgia laws permit imposition of the death penalty.

Finally, McCleskey's statistical proffer must be viewed in the context of his challenge. McCleskey challenges decisions at the heart of the State's criminal justice system. "[O]ne of society's most basic tasks is that of protecting the lives of its citizens and one of the most basic ways in which it achieves the task is through criminal laws against murder." *Gregg v. Georgia,* 428 U.S. 153, 226 (1976) (WHITE, J., concurring). Implementation of these laws necessarily requires discretionary judgments. Because discretion is essential to the criminal justice process, we would demand exceptionally clear proof before we would infer that the discretion has been abused. The unique nature of the decisions at issue in this case also counsels against adopting such an inference from the disparities indicated by the Baldus study. Accordingly, we hold that the Baldus study is clearly insufficient to support an inference that any of the decisionmakers in McCleskey's case acted with discriminatory purpose.

B

McCleskey also suggests that the Baldus study proves that the State as a whole has acted with a discriminatory purpose. He appears to argue that the State has violated the Equal Protection Clause by adopting the capital punishment statute and allowing it to remain in force despite its allegedly discriminatory application. But "'[d]iscriminatory purpose' . . . implies more than intent as volition or intent as awareness of consequences. It implies that the decisionmaker, in this case a state legislature, selected or reaffirmed a particular course of action at least in part 'because of,' not merely 'in spite of,' its adverse effects upon an identifiable group." *Personnel Administrator of Massachusetts v. Feeney,* 442 U.S. 256 (1979) (footnote and citation omitted). For this claim to prevail, McCleskey would have to prove that the Georgia Legislature enacted or maintained the death penalty statute *because of* an anticipated racially discriminatory effect. In *Gregg v. Georgia, supra,* this Court found that the Georgia capital sentencing system could operate in a fair and neutral manner. There was no evidence then, and there is none now, that the Georgia Legislature enacted the capital punishment statute to further a racially discriminatory purpose.

Nor has McCleskey demonstrated that the legislature maintains the capital punishment statute because of the racially disproportionate impact suggested by the Baldus study. As legislatures necessarily have wide discretion in the choice of criminal laws and penalties, and as there were legitimate reasons for the Georgia Legislature to adopt and maintain capital punishment, see *Gregg v. Georgia, supra,* at 183-187 (joint opinion of Stewart, Powell, and Stevens, JJ.), we will not infer a discriminatory purpose on the part of the State of Georgia. Accordingly, we reject McCleskey's equal protection claims.***

III

McCleskey also argues that the Baldus study demonstrates that the Georgia capital sentencing system violates the Eighth Amendment. We begin our analysis of this claim by reviewing the restrictions on death sentences established by our prior decisions under that Amendment.***

To evaluate McCleskey's challenge, we must examine exactly what the Baldus study may show. Even Professor Baldus does not contend that his statistics *prove* that race enters into any capital sentencing decisions or that race was a factor in McCleskey's particular case. Statistics at most may show only a likelihood that a particular factor entered into some decisions. There is, of course, some risk of racial prejudice influencing a jury's decision in a criminal case. There are similar risks that other kinds of prejudice will influence other criminal trials. *** McCleskey asks us to accept the likelihood allegedly shown by the Baldus study as the constitutional measure of an unacceptable risk of racial prejudice influencing capital sentencing decisions. This we decline to do.***

McCleskey's argument that the Constitution condemns the discretion allowed decisionmakers in the Georgia capital sentencing system is antithetical to the fundamental role of discretion in our criminal justice system. Discretion in the criminal justice system offers substantial benefits to the criminal defendant. Not only can a jury decline to impose the death sentence, it can decline to convict or choose to convict of a lesser offense. Whereas decisions against a defendant's interest may be reversed by the trial judge or on appeal, these discretionary exercises of leniency are final and unreviewable. Similarly, the capacity of prosecutorial discretion to provide individualized justice is "firmly entrenched in American law." 2 W. LaFave & D. Israel, Criminal Procedure § 13.2(a), p. 160 (1984). As we have noted, a prosecutor can decline to charge, offer a plea bargain, or decline to seek a death sentence in any particular case. See n. 28, *supra.* Of course, "the power to be lenient [also] is the power to discriminate," K. Davis, Discretionary Justice 170 (1973), but a capital punishment system that did not allow for discretionary acts of leniency "would be totally alien to our notions of criminal justice." *Gregg v. Georgia,* 428 U.S., at 200.

C

At most, the Baldus study indicates a discrepancy that appears to correlate with race. Apparent disparities in sentencing are an inevitable part of our criminal justice system. The discrepancy indicated by the Baldus study is "a far cry from the major systemic defects identified in *Furman*," *Pulley v. Harris,* 465 U.S., at 54.[***] Where the discretion that is fundamental to our criminal process is involved, we decline to assume that what is unexplained is invidious. In light of the safeguards designed to minimize racial bias in the process, the fundamental value of jury trial in our criminal justice system, and the benefits that discretion provides to criminal defendants, we hold that the Baldus study does not demonstrate a constitutionally significant risk of racial bias affecting the Georgia capital sentencing process.

V

Two additional concerns inform our decision in this case. First, McCleskey's claim, taken to its logical conclusion, throws into serious question the principles that underlie our entire criminal justice system. The Eighth Amendment is not limited in application to capital punishment, but applies to all penalties. *Solem v. Helm,* 463 U.S. 277, 289-290 (1983). Thus, if we accepted McCleskey's claim that racial bias has impermissibly tainted the capital sentencing decision, we could soon be faced with similar claims as to other types of penalty. Moreover, the claim that his sentence rests on the irrelevant factor of race easily could be extended to apply to claims based on unexplained discrepancies that correlate to membership in other minority groups, and even to gender. Similarly, since McCleskey's claim relates to the race of his victim, other claims could apply with equally logical force to statistical disparities that correlate with the race or sex of other actors in the criminal justice system, such as defense attorneys, or judges. Also, there is no logical reason that such a claim need be limited to racial or sexual bias. If arbitrary and capricious punishment is the touchstone under the Eighth Amendment, such a claim could—at least in theory—be based upon any arbitrary variable, such as the defendant's facial characteristics, or the physical attractiveness of the defendant or the victim, that some statistical study indicates may be influential in jury decisionmaking. As these examples illustrate, there is no limiting principle to the type of challenge brought by McCleskey. The Constitution does not require that a State eliminate any demonstrable disparity that correlates with a potentially irrelevant factor in order to operate a criminal justice system that includes capital punishment. As we have stated specifically in the context of capital punishment, the Constitution does not "plac[e] totally unrealistic conditions on its use." *Gregg v. Georgia,* 428 U.S., at 199.

Second, McCleskey's arguments are best presented to the legislative bodies. It is not the responsibility—or indeed even the right—of this Court to determine the appropriate punishment for particular crimes. It is the legislatures, the elected representatives of the people, that are "constituted to respond to the will and consequently the moral values of the people." *Furman v. Georgia,* 408 U.S., at 383 (Burger, C.J., dissenting). Legislatures also are better qualified to weigh and "evaluate the results of statistical studies in terms of their own local conditions and with a flexibility of approach that is not available to the courts," *Gregg v. Georgia, supra,* 428 U.S., at 186. Capital punishment is now the law in more than two-thirds of our States. It is the ultimate duty of courts to determine on a case-by-case basis whether these laws are applied consistently with the Constitution. Despite McCleskey's wide-ranging arguments that basically challenge the validity of capital punishment in our multiracial society, the only question before us is whether in his case, see *supra,* at 1761-1762, the law of Georgia was properly applied. We agree with the District Court and the Court of Appeals for the Eleventh Circuit that this was carefully and correctly done in this case.

VI

Accordingly, we affirm the judgment of the Court of Appeals for the Eleventh Circuit.

Justice BRENNAN, with whom Justice MARSHALL joins, and with whom Justice BLACKMUN and Justice STEVENS join in all but Part I, dissenting

I

Adhering to my view that the death penalty is in all circumstances cruel and unusual punishment forbidden by the Eighth and Fourteenth Amendments, I would vacate the decision below insofar as it left undisturbed the death sentence imposed in this case. *Gregg v. Georgia,* 428 U.S. 153 (1976) (Brennan, J., dissenting). The Court observes that "[t]he *Gregg*-type statute imposes unprecedented safeguards in the special context of capital punishment," which "ensure a degree of care in the imposition of the death penalty that can be described only as unique." *Ante,* at 1778, n.37. Notwithstanding these efforts, murder defendants in Georgia with white victims are more than four times as likely to receive the death sentence as are defendants with black victims. Petitioner's Exhibit DB 82. Nothing could convey more powerfully the intractable reality of the death penalty: "that the effort to eliminate arbitrariness in the infliction of that ultimate sanction is so plainly doomed to failure that it—and the death penalty—must be abandoned altogether." *Godfrey v. Georgia,* 446 U.S. 420, 442(1980) (MARSHALL, J., concurring in judgment).***

II

At some point in this case, Warren McCleskey doubtless asked his lawyer whether a jury was likely to sentence him to die. A candid reply to this question would have been disturbing. First, counsel would have to tell McCleskey that few of the details of the crime or of McCleskey's past criminal conduct were more important than the fact that his victim was white. Petitioner's Supplemental Exhibits (Supp. Exh.) 50. Furthermore, counsel would feel bound to tell McCleskey that defendants charged with killing white victims in Georgia are 4.3 times as likely to be sentenced to death as defendants charged with killing blacks. Petitioner's Exhibit DB 82. In addition, frankness would compel the disclosure that it was more likely than not that the race of McCleskey's victim would determine whether he received a death sentence: 6 of every 11 defendants convicted of killing a white person would not have received the death penalty if their victims had been black, Supp. Exh. 51, while, among defendants with aggravating and mitigating factors comparable to McCleskey's, 20 of every 34 would not have been sentenced to die if their victims had been black. *Id.,* at 54. Finally, the assessment would not be complete without the information that cases involving black defendants and white victims are more likely to result in a death sentence than cases featuring any other racial combination of defendant and victim. *Ibid.* The story could be told in a variety of ways, but McCleskey could not fail to grasp its essential narrative line: there was a significant chance that race would play a prominent role in determining if he lived or died.

The Court today holds that Warren McCleskey's sentence was constitutionally imposed. It finds no fault in a system in which lawyers must tell their clients that race casts a large shadow on the capital sentencing process. The Court arrives at this conclusion by stating that the Baldus study cannot *"prove that race enters into any capital sentencing decisions or that race was a factor in McCleskey's particular case." Ante,* at 1775 (emphasis in original). Since, according to Professor Baldus, we cannot say "to a moral certainty" that race influenced a decision, *ante,* at 1771, n.29, we can identify only "a likelihood that a particular factor entered into some decisions," *ante,* at 1775, and "a discrepancy that appears to correlate with race." *Ante,* at 1777. This "likelihood" and "discrepancy," holds the Court, is insufficient to establish a constitutional violation. The Court reaches this conclusion by placing four factors on the scales opposite McCleskey's evidence: the desire to encourage sentencing discretion, the existence of "statutory safeguards" in the Georgia scheme, the fear of encouraging widespread challenges to other sentencing decisions, and the limits of the judicial role. The Court's evaluation of the significance of petitioner's evidence is fundamentally at odds with our consistent concern for rationality in capital sentencing, and the considerations that the majority invokes to discount that evidence cannot justify ignoring its force.

*** For the Georgia system as a whole, race accounts for a six percentage point difference in the rate at which capital punishment is imposed. Since death is imposed in 11% of all white-victim cases, the rate in comparably aggravated black-victim cases is 5%. The rate of capital sentencing in a white-victim case is thus 120% greater than the rate in a black-victim case. Put another way, over half—55%—of defendants in white-victim crimes in Georgia would not have been sentenced to die if their victims had been black. Of the more than 200 variables potentially relevant to a sentencing decision, race of the victim is a powerful explanation for variation in death sentence rates—as powerful as nonracial aggravating factors such as a prior murder conviction or acting as the principal planner of the homicide.

These adjusted figures are only the most conservative indication of the risk that race will influence the death sentences of defendants in Georgia. Data unadjusted for the mitigating or aggravating effect of other factors show an even more pronounced disparity by race. The capital sentencing rate for all white-victim cases was almost *11 times* greater than the rate for black-victim cases. Supp. Exh. 47. Furthermore, blacks who kill whites are sentenced to death at nearly *22 times* the rate of blacks who kill blacks, and more than *7 times* the rate of whites who kill blacks. *Ibid.* In addition, prosecutors seek the death penalty for 70% of black defendants with white victims, but for only 15% of black defendants with black victims, and only 19% of white defendants with black victims. *Id.,* at 56. Since our decision upholding the Georgia capital sentencing system in *Gregg,* the State has executed seven persons. All of the seven were convicted of killing whites, and six of the seven executed were black. Such execution figures are especially striking in light of the fact that, during the period encompassed by the Baldus study, only 9.2% of Georgia homicides involved black defendants and white victims, while 60.7% involved black victims.

McCleskey's statistics have particular force because most of them are the product of sophisticated multiple-regression analysis. Such analysis is designed precisely to identify patterns in the aggregate, even though we may not be able to reconstitute with certainty any individual decision that goes to make up that pattern. Multiple-regression analysis is particularly well suited to identify the influence of impermissible considerations in sentencing, since it is able to control for permissible factors that may explain an apparent arbitrary pattern. While the decisionmaking process of a body such as a jury may be complex, the Baldus study provides a massive compilation of the details that are most relevant to that decision.***

The statistical evidence in this case thus relentlessly documents the risk that McCleskey's sentence was influenced by racial considerations. This evidence shows that there is a better than even chance in Georgia that race will influence the decision to impose the death penalty: a majority of defendants in white-victim crimes would not have been sentenced to die if their victims had been black. In determining whether this risk is acceptable, our judgment must be shaped by the awareness that "[t]he risk of racial prejudice infecting a capital sentencing proceeding is especially serious in light of the complete finality of the death sentence," *Turner v. Murray,* 476 U.S. 28 (1986), and that "[i]t is of vital importance to the defendant and to the community that any decision to impose the death sentence be, and appear to be, based on reason rather than caprice or emotion," *Gardner v. Florida,* 430 U.S. 349 (1977). In determining the guilt of a defendant, a State must prove its case beyond a reasonable doubt. That is, we refuse to convict if the chance of error is simply less likely than not. Surely, we should not be willing to take a person's life if the chance that his death sentence was irrationally imposed is *more* likely than not. In light of the gravity of the interest at stake, petitioner's statistics on their face are a powerful demonstration of the type of risk that our Eighth Amendment jurisprudence has consistently condemned.***

Frank R. Baumgartner, *The Impact of Race, Gender, and Geography on Ohio Executions*

Ohio's use of the death penalty in the modern era has been marked by substantial disparities by the race and gender of the victim of the crime, and by geography.[12] These disparities are so great that they call in to question the equity of the application of the harshest penalty, adding to growing concerns that the death penalty is applied in an unfair, capricious, and arbitrary manner.

Between 1976 and 2014, the state of Ohio executed 53 men. Here are a few key findings of this research:

- Sixty-five percent of all executions carried out in Ohio between 1976 and 2014 were for crimes involving White victims despite the fact that 43% of all homicide victims are White.
- Only 27% of all homicide victims are female, but 52% of all executions carried out in Ohio were for homicides involving female victims.
- Homicides involving White female victims are six times more likely to result in an execution than homicides involving Black male victims.
- In cases where Black inmates were executed, 26% of all of the victims

---

[12] A more complete analysis is available in the following article, which is based on the same dataset as used here. That published and peer-reviewed article contains a full bibliography of relevant studies on the issue of race-of-victim effects. See Baumgartner, Grigg and Mastro 2015. Homicide victims data stem from a U.S. Department of Justice report that covers 1976 through 1999. Homicide data by county stem from annual BJS reports from 1984 through 2012, the most recent year available. These reports do not allow separation by race and gender of the victim, however. In any case, the two homicide datasets show very similar results, though they cover slightly different time periods. Executions carried out in 2014 are typically for crimes committed between 10 and 30 years earlier. The crimes for which Ohio inmates were executed through the end of 2014 were committed between 1982 and 2003.

were White. In cases where White inmates were executed, just 8% of the victims were Black.

- Just four out of Ohio's 88 counties (Lucas, Summit, Cuyahoga, and Hamilton)—or just 5%—are responsible for more than half of the state's 53 executions.

- Only three counties (Summit, Cuyahoga, and Hamilton) have produced more than five executions each. More than three-quarters of all Ohio counties (69) have never produced an execution.

- Lake County has an execution rate that is 11 times the state's average execution rate of .36 executions per 100 homicides. Belmont County's rate is more than eight times the state average.

- The three most populous counties (Cuyahoga, Franklin, and Hamilton) have very different execution rates, even though their homicide rates are relatively similar. Hamilton has the highest execution rate at .60 executions per 100 homicides: this is more than double the execution rate in Cuyahoga, and nearly nine times the rate in Franklin County.

- The homicide rate in counties that have produced no executions (.47 homicides per 1,000 population) is dramatically lower than the homicide rate in counties that have produced executions (1.79 homicides per 1,000 population).

With 53 executions in the modern period, but nearly 16,000 homicides between 1976 and 1999, the average likelihood that a homicide will lead to an execution is just .53 percent. However, Table 1 shows that the likelihood that a homicide with result in an execution is .81 percent when the victim is White, but only .29 when the victim is Black. The percent is .35 when the victim is male, and 1.05 when the victim is female. The greatest disparity occurs when combining race and gender, as the likelihood that the crime will result in an execution increases to 1.55 when the victim is a White female, but decreases to just .25 percent when the victim is a Black male. The likelihood that a homicide will result in an execution is nearly identical when the victim is a White male or a Black female.

Table 1. Ohio Executions and Homicides by Race and Gender of Victims.

Victim Characteristic	Homicides		Executions		Executions Per 100 Homicides
	Number	Percent	Number	Percent	
Whites	6,763	42.98	55	65.48	0.81
Blacks	8,832	56.14	26	30.95	0.29
Other, Unknown	139	0.89	3	3.57	-
Total	15,734	100.00	84	100.00	0.53

Males	11,527	73.26	40	47.62	0.35
Females	4,204	26.72	44	52.38	1.05
Unknown	3	0.01	-	-	-
Total	15,734	100.00	84	100.00	0.53
White Female	2,264	14.39	35	41.67	1.55
White Male	4,499	28.60	20	23.81	0.44
Black Female	1,903	12.10	9	10.71	0.47
Black Male	6,929	44.04	17	20.24	0.25
Other, Unknown	139	0.89	3	3.57	-
Total	15,734	100.00	84	100.00	0.53

Note: Numbers refer to victims, not inmates executed. Ohio executed 53 inmates from 1976 through 2014 for crimes involving 84 victims. Ratios not calculated for other or unknown categories because these are not compatible across the two data sources.

Figure 1 illustrates these stark comparisons.

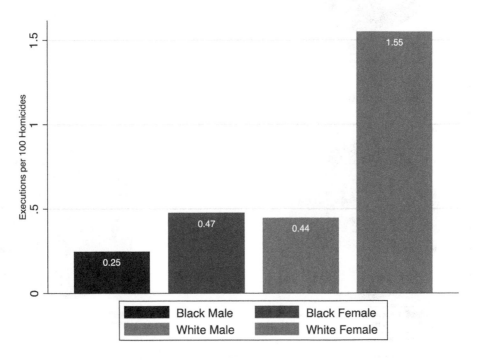

Note: Figure 1 shows the percentage of homicides that eventually result in an execution.

Figures 2, 3, and 4 show how homicides (on the left side) and executions (right) compare. Each is a simple pie chart. Figure 2, for example, shows that homicides are largely focused on men, who constitute 73.3 percent of the victims. Among execution cases, however, men are a lower percent of the victims: 47.6 percent. Figure 3 shows the equivalent data for race, and Figure 4 shows race and gender combined. Figure 4 makes clear that Black males are severely underrepresented among victims in execution cases, considering that they constitute 44.1 percent of all homicide victims statewide.

Figure 2. Gender of Victims

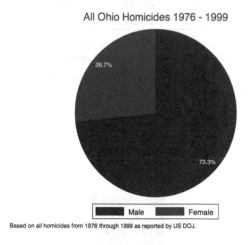

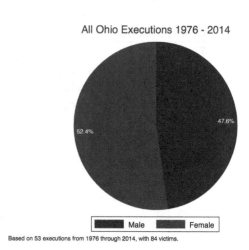

Based on all homicides from 1976 through 1999 as reported by US DOJ.

Based on 53 executions from 1976 through 2014, with 84 victims.

Figure 3. Race of Victims

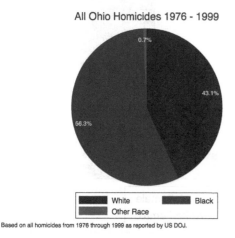

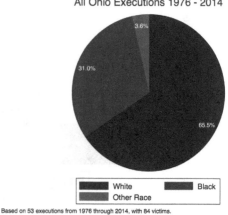

Based on all homicides from 1976 through 1999 as reported by US DOJ.

Based on 53 executions from 1976 through 2014, with 84 victims.

Figure 4. Race and Gender of Victims

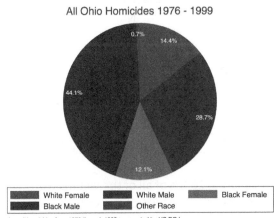

All Ohio Homicides 1976 - 1999

Based on all homicides from 1976 through 1999 as reported by US DOJ.

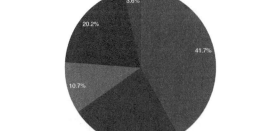

All Ohio Executions 1976 - 2014

Based on 53 executions from 1976 through 2014, with 84 victims.

Figure 5 compares the race and gender of victims with the race of the executed offender. Of the 53 men who have been executed by the state of Ohio between 1976 and 2014, 34 were White males and 19 were Black males. Table 2 shows the race of the victims for both the White and Black male inmates who have been executed.

Figure 5. Race and Gender of Victims for White and Black Inmates Executed
a. White Inmates   b. Black Inmates

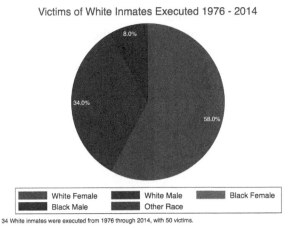

Victims of White Inmates Executed 1976 - 2014

34 White inmates were executed from 1976 through 2014, with 50 victims.

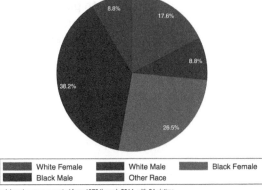

Victims of Black Inmates Executed 1976 - 2014

19 Black inmates were executed from 1976 through 2014, with 34 victims.

Table OH 2. Victims of White and Black Male Inmates Executed

Victims	White Inmates		Black Inmates	
	N	%	N	%
White Female	29	58.0	6	17.6
White Male	17	34.0	3	8.8
Black Female	0	0.0	9	26.5
Black Male	4	8.0	13	38.2
Other Race	0	0.0	3	8.8
Total	50	100.0	34	100.0

In cases where Black inmates were executed, 26.5% of all of the victims were White. In cases where White inmates were executed, just 8% of the victims were Black. The vast majority of homicides involve perpetrators and victims of the same race.

Nationally, the Bureau of Justice Statistics reports that between 1980 and 2008, 84 percent of the victims of White perpetrators were also White. Similarly, Black perpetrators killed Black victims 93 percent of the time. Further, this tendency for crimes to be within racial group remains true even among "stranger homicides" – where the victim does not know the offender. Just 26.7 percent of stranger homicides were cross-racial (as were just 9.7 percent of homicides involving friends or acquaintances) (BJS 2011). The importance of the victims' race in the application of the death penalty has created a system where Whites are likely to face the death penalty only for within-race crimes, and Blacks for within-race and cross-race crimes. In other words, the race and gender of the victim is a determining factor in deciding who faces execution in Ohio.

Ohio's death penalty system is arbitrary not only on the basis of the race and gender characteristics of the victims, but it also shows dramatic disparities by geography. Figure 6 below shows the number of executions across the state's 88 counties.

Figure 6. Executions by County

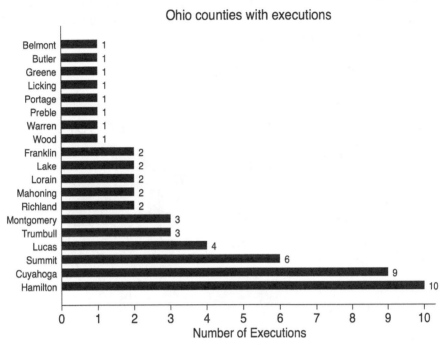

Ohio counties with executions

Ohio carried out 53 executions from 1976 through 2014.

As Figure 7 below makes clear, 69 counties have had no executions. Just four out of Ohio's 88 counties (Lucas, Summit, Cuyahoga, and Hamilton) are responsible for more than half of the state's 53 executions. Only three counties have produced more than five executions. More than three-quarters of all Ohio counties have never produced an execution.

Figure 7. Map of Ohio Executions by County

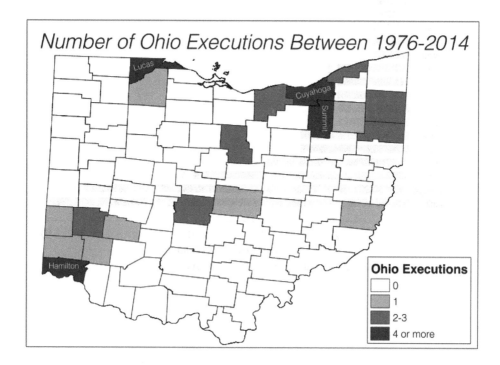

Table 3 below shows the 2010 population, the total number of homicides reported by the U.S. Bureau of Justice Statistics for the period of 1984 through 2012, the number of homicides, and the rate of homicides per 1,000 population, and the number of executions per 100 homicides for each county in Ohio.

Table 3. Ohio Counties with Executions, by Homicides and Population

County	Population (2010)	Homicides (1984-2012)	Executions (1976-2014)	Homicides Per 1,000 Population	Executions Per 100 Homicides
Hamilton	802,374	1,676	10	2.09	0.60
Cuyahoga	1,280,122	3,581	9	2.80	0.25
Summit	541,781	636	6	1.17	0.94
Lucas	441,815	838	4	1.90	0.48
Montgomery	535,153	1,308	3	2.44	0.23
Trumbull	210,312	172	3	0.82	1.74
Franklin	1,163,414	2,745	2	2.36	0.07
Lake	230,041	50	2	0.22	4.00
Lorain	301,356	180	2	0.60	1.11
Mahoning	238,823	1,019	2	4.27	0.20
Richland	124,475	101	2	0.81	1.98
Belmont	70,400	33	1	0.47	3.03
Butler	368,130	269	1	0.73	0.37
Greene	161,573	61	1	0.38	1.64
Licking	166,492	40	1	0.24	2.50
Portage	161,419	56	1	0.35	1.79
Preble	42,270	35	1	0.83	2.86
Warren	212,693	54	1	0.25	1.85
Wood	125,488	41	1	0.33	2.44
Counties with No Executions	4,358,373	2,029	-	0.47	-
Total	11,563,504	12,924	53	1.29	0.36

Note: Sixty-nine counties in Ohio had no executions. Their combined population and homicide numbers are shown in the second to last row above. Table 3 refers to the numbers of inmates executed and the total number of homicides by county, whereas Table 1 referred to the number of victims.

Figure 8. Map of Ohio Counties by Execution Rate

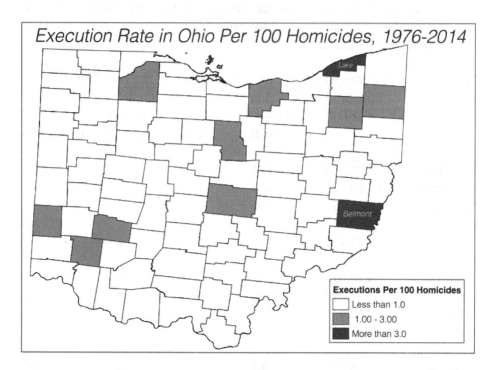

Perhaps the most relevant demonstration of the great disparity in the use of the death penalty is in comparing executions per 100 homicides by county. Whereas the overall average for the state is approximately 0.36 executions per 100 homicides, Lake County has an execution rate that is 11 times the state's average execution rate, and Belmont County's rate is more than eight times the state average. The three most populous counties (Cuyahoga, Franklin, and Hamilton) have very different execution rates, even though their homicide rates are relatively similar. Hamilton has the highest execution rate at .60 executions per 100 homicides: this is more than double the execution rate in Cuyahoga, and nearly nine times the rate in Franklin County.

The homicide rate in counties that have produced no executions (.47 homicides per 1,000 population) is dramatically lower than the homicide rate in counties that have produced executions (1.79 homicides per 1,000 population). There is no correlation between the homicide rate in a given county and the execution rate.

Conclusion:

The findings of this research indicate that factors such as the victims' race and gender, as well as the county in which the offender was convicted, inappropriately influence who is executed in Ohio. At the very least, this data should give prosecutors pause when determining whether to seek the death penalty. If left unaddressed, these racial, gender, and geographic disparities may erode judicial and public confidence in the state's ability to fairly administer the ultimate punishment. A punishment that is so arbitrarily and unfairly administered could reasonably be deemed unconstitutional. As the nation considers so many elements of the debate surrounding capital punishment, we should look closely at the recent history of how it has actually been administered. This review of simple statistics associated with Ohio's modern experience with the punishment shows clearly that it is geographically arbitrary and that the race and gender of the victim of the crime are associated with dramatic disparities in the likelihood of execution for the offender. These disparities are not measured by a few percentage points of difference. Rather, they differ by orders of magnitude, clearly demonstrating that vast inequities characterize the implementation of capital punishment in Ohio.

References and Credits:

Frank R. Baumgartner, Amanda Grigg, and Alisa Mastro. 2015. #BlackLivesDon'tMatter: Race- of-Victim Effects in US Executions, 1977-2013. *Politics, Groups, and Identities* 3, 2: 209-21.

U.S. Bureau of Justice Statistics. 2011. Homicide Trends in the United States, 1980-2008. Washington, DC: US DOJ, NCJ236018, November.

Maps created by Policy Analyst and Urban Historian Adam Gosney.

Thanks to UNC student Colin Wilson for research assistance.

Notes and Questions

1. Were you surprised to learn that homicide victims and their assailants in the far majority of cases are from the same race? With that said, why do you think African-American males who kill white females face the greatest likelihood of the death penalty?

2. Looking back at the principles of punishment discussed earlier in this book, what principle(s) support imposition of the death penalty?

Chapter 8
Voluntary Manslaughter

A. Background

At common law, voluntary manslaughter is the intentional killing of another in the heat of passion. With voluntary manslaughter, the killing is not excused but mitigated because the defendant had been adequately provoked. *State v. Shane,* discussed next, examines the type of conduct that may provoke a reasonable person to take the life of another human being.

B. Provocation

State v. Shane, 63 Ohio St. 3d 630 (1992)

ALICE ROBIE RESNICK, Justice.

The issue certified for our review is the proper allocation of the burden of proof when a judge gives an instruction on voluntary manslaughter in a murder prosecution. However, for the reasons which follow, we do not reach the certified issue, but affirm the judgment of the court of appeals on different grounds.

The trial judge instructed the jury on voluntary manslaughter prior to its deliberations.

Because we determine that the evidence of provocation presented by Shane was insufficient, as a matter of law, to warrant an instruction on voluntary manslaughter, we find that the trial judge should have refused to give the jury an instruction on that offense. The fact that the trial judge did give the instruction was harmless error, particularly in light of this court's determination today in *State v. Rhodes* (1992), 63 Ohio St. 3d 613, that a similar jury instruction was proper.

I

Voluntary manslaughter is an inferior degree of murder, for " 'its elements are *** contained within the indicted offense, except for one or more additional mitigating elements ***.' " *State v. Tyler* (1990), 50 Ohio St. 3d 24. Even though voluntary manslaughter is not a lesser included offense of murder, the test for whether a judge should give a jury an instruction on voluntary manslaughter when a defendant is charged with murder is the same test to be applied as when an instruction on a lesser included offense is sought. *Tyler, supra,* 50 Ohio St. 3d at 37.***

Ohio's voluntary manslaughter statute, R.C. 2903.03, reads:

> (A) No person, while under the influence of sudden passion or in a sudden fit of rage, *either of which is brought on by serious provocation occasioned by the victim that is reasonably sufficient to incite the person into using deadly force,* shall knowingly cause the death of another.
>
> (B) Whoever violates this section is guilty of voluntary manslaughter, an aggravated felony of the first degree. (Emphasis added.)

The statute makes clear that the sudden passion or sudden fit of rage must be "brought on by serious provocation occasioned by the victim that is reasonably sufficient to incite the person into using deadly force ***." The question which must be answered in each case is: How much provocation is "reasonably sufficient" provocation?

An inquiry into the mitigating circumstances of provocation must be broken down into both objective and subjective components.[13] In determining whether the provocation is reasonably sufficient to bring on sudden passion or a sudden fit of rage, an objective standard must be applied. Then, if that standard is met, the inquiry shifts to the subjective component of whether this actor, in this particular case, actually was under the influence of sudden passion or in a sudden fit of rage. It is only at that point that the " *** emotional and mental state of the defendant and the conditions and circumstances that surrounded him at the time *** " must be considered. *Deem, supra,* paragraph five of the syllabus. If

---

[13] "There are four obstacles for the defendant to overcome before he can have his intentional killing reduced from murder to voluntary manslaughter: (1) There must have been a reasonable provocation. (2) The defendant must have been in fact provoked. (3) A reasonable man so provoked would not have cooled off in the interval of time between the provocation and the delivery of the fatal blow. And (4), the defendant must not in fact have cooled off during that interval." 2 LaFave & Scott, Substantive Criminal Law (1986) 255, Section 7.10.

Factors (1) and (3) are objective; factors (2) and (4) are subjective. For purposes of this discussion, we assume that factors (3) and (4) are present. We also accept factor (2) as true, in part because we must consider the evidence in the light most favorable to the defendant. Therefore, we focus our inquiry on factor (1).

insufficient evidence of provocation is presented, so that no reasonable jury would decide that an actor was reasonably provoked by the victim, the trial judge must, as a matter of law, refuse to give a voluntary manslaughter instruction. In that event, the objective portion of the consideration is not met, and no subsequent inquiry into the subjective portion, when the defendant's own situation would be at issue, should be conducted.

The provocation must be *reasonably sufficient* to incite the defendant to use deadly force. For provocation to be reasonably sufficient, it must be sufficient to arouse the passions of an ordinary person beyond the power of his or her control. Once the defendant has been sufficiently provoked by the victim, it may be proper to label the conduct from that point onward "understandable." See 2 LaFave & Scott, Substantive Criminal Law (1986) 256, Section 7.10. Our criminal law recognizes that the provoked defendant is less worthy of blame than the unprovoked defendant, but the law is unwilling to allow the provoked defendant to totally escape punishment.[14] The jury, because it has the ability to find the sufficiently provoked defendant guilty of voluntary manslaughter, rather than murder, is able to exercise the value judgment provided by the law in these circumstances.

There are certain types of situations that have been regarded as particularly appropriate cases in which voluntary manslaughter instructions are often given when murder charges are brought. For example, assault and battery, mutual combat, illegal arrest and discovering a spouse in the act of adultery are some of the classic voluntary manslaughter situations. Because the present case involves none of those situations, we make no comment on the appropriateness of a voluntary manslaughter instruction in a murder prosecution involving one of those categories of cases. The case before us involves a defendant who allegedly was provoked to act under the influence of sudden passion or in a sudden fit of rage by his fiancee's words informing him of her sexual infidelity. Therefore, we consider only whether the provocation alleged in such a situation is reasonably sufficient so that a voluntary manslaughter instruction should have been given.

Many courts have adopted a rule that "mere words" cannot be sufficient provocation to reduce a murder charge to voluntary manslaughter, no matter how insulting or inciteful. This general rule usually applies even if the spoken words have the effect of informing the defendant of some provocative event that has taken place. But, see, *e.g., Commonwealth v. Berry* (1975), 461 Pa. 233 (manslaughter instruction approved when defendant killed victim after defendant was told by his mother that victim had assaulted her). It appears, however, that courts are generally more inclined to give a manslaughter instruction when the alleged provocation is a victim-spouse's confession of

---

[14] The act of killing while under the influence of sudden passion or in a sudden fit of rage is not so easily excused as is, for example, a killing in self-defense, for which a defendant is allowed to escape punishment.

adultery. The typical scenario is a wife's confession of adultery which allegedly so provokes a husband that he kills her in a sudden fit of rage. Some courts have limited this infidelity exception to the acts between spouses, but have not applied it when the parties are romantically involved but are not married, even when the relationship is similar to a marriage. See, generally, *People v. McCarthy* (1989), 132 Ill.2d 331. This adultery exception has been totally rejected by some courts, unless the situation is where the spouse discovers the other spouse in the act of adultery itself, or immediately thereafter. See, *e.g., People v. Chevalier, supra.* Finally, a few courts have not followed a "mere words" rule, but, instead, have approved a manslaughter jury instruction when words alone were the only provocation alleged, and no relationship existed between victim and assailant. See, *e.g., State v. Harwood* (1974), 110 Ariz. 375; *State v. Boyd* (1975), 216 Kan. 373.

While the "mere words" rule is attractive—it has the advantage of offering a bright line test which eliminates an entire class of cases—the rule has been criticized as imposing an "unnecessary limitation on the use of voluntary manslaughter as a mitigating defense." Romero, Sufficiency of Provocation for Voluntary Manslaughter in New Mexico: Problems in Theory and Practice (1982), 12 New Mex. L. Rev. 747, 776. It is argued that such a rule ignores the fact that sometimes words may be even more inflammatory than aggressive actions, and that the rule keeps from the jury some situations that should qualify for a manslaughter instruction. Nevertheless, we do not believe that words alone are generally as inflammatory as aggressive actions. Further, it is only when a jury could reasonably find that the defendant was incited by sufficient provocation brought on by the victim that an instruction on voluntary manslaughter should be given in a murder prosecution.

We disapprove of a rule which does not allow "mere words" to be sufficient provocation to reduce murder to manslaughter generally, but which makes a specific exception where the provocation consists of mere words by one spouse informing the other spouse of infidelity. This exception to the general rule has its foundation in the ancient common-law concept that the wife is the property of the husband. See *Regina v. Mawgridge* (1707), Kelyng, J. 119, 137, 84 Eng.Rep. 1107, 1115: "[W]hen a man is taken in adultery with another man's wife, if the husband shall stab the adulterer, or knock out his brains, that is bare manslaughter: for jealousy is the rage of a man, and adultery is the highest invasion of property ***." (Citations omitted.) This archaic rule has no place in modern society. Words informing another of infidelity should not be given special treatment by courts trying to determine what provocation is reasonably sufficient provocation. The killing of a spouse (usually a wife) by a spouse (usually a husband) who has just been made aware of the victim spouse's adultery simply is not an acceptable response to the confession of infidelity. See Comment,

Provoked Reason in Men and Women: Heat-of-Passion Manslaughter and Imperfect Self–Defense (1986), 33 U.C.L.A. L. Rev. 1679, 1696–1697.

We hold that words alone will not constitute reasonably sufficient provocation to incite the use of deadly force in most situations. Rather, in each case, the trial judge must determine whether evidence of reasonably sufficient provocation occasioned by the victim has been presented to warrant a voluntary manslaughter instruction. The trial judge is required to decide this issue as a matter of law, in view of the specific facts of the individual case. The trial judge should evaluate the evidence in the light most favorable to the defendant, without weighing the persuasiveness of the evidence. *State v. Wilkins* (1980), 64 Ohio St. 2d 382.

II

Bearing in mind that to be reasonably sufficient provocation the provocation must be *occasioned by the victim,* we will now proceed to consider the facts of this case in light of the foregoing principles. We find that Tina Wagner did very little to provoke Shane into a sudden fit of rage. It was Shane who woke her up when he returned to the apartment that night. When they went into the bedroom, he repeatedly asked her questions in an attempt to get her to confess her infidelity to him. When Wagner initially denied that she had been involved with other men, Shane called her a liar. When Wagner finally did admit her infidelity, Shane then lost control. From the evidence presented it would appear that the anger built up in Shane's own mind, and he manufactured much of it himself by provoking Wagner to give the responses she did.

Provocation, to be reasonably sufficient, must be *serious.* But it was only Wagner's statements to Shane that caused him to become enraged. It was revealed at trial that Wagner's urine alcohol content was 0.27 grams per deciliter. Several witnesses, including Shane himself, testified at trial that Wagner was intoxicated.

An expert testified at trial that the strangulation of Wagner took from between one to five minutes to complete. Because we must view the evidence favorably to Shane, we do not take into account the testimony of another expert that a minimum of four or five minutes probably elapsed from the time Shane started to strangle Wagner until she was actually dead. A strangulation is not like a gunshot, which happens fast and could be immediately regretted. Rather, the passion or rage had to be sustained for at least one minute before the act was completed.

A psychologist who testified at trial offered his opinions about Shane's personal propensity to be provoked in the situation as it developed. However, even assuming that Shane subjectively could be easily provoked by Wagner to act under the influence of sudden passion or in a sudden fit of rage, there still must be sufficient provocation by the victim so that a reasonable person would be so provoked. Accepting as fact that Shane was actually provoked only satisfies one part of the provocation inquiry. Because we find that the provocation by the victim in this case was not reasonably sufficient provocation, we hold that the objective portion of the inquiry has not been satisfied. Thus, a reasonable person would not have been provoked in the circumstances of this case.

Hence, we find that the totality of the evidence in this case, even when viewed in a light most favorable to the defendant, did not raise a possibility of serious provocation. Shane alleges that it was only mere words that provoked him. Considering this fact, together with the surrounding circumstances of the case, we conclude that no reasonable jury could have decided that Shane was sufficiently provoked by the victim so that a conviction on the inferior-degree offense of voluntary manslaughter could have been forthcoming.

CONCLUSION

When reasonably sufficient evidence of provocation has not been presented, no jury instruction on voluntary manslaughter should be given. In this case, the provocation that allegedly caused Shane to act under the influence of sudden passion or in a sudden fit of rage was not reasonably sufficient, as a matter of law, to incite him to use deadly force. We find that no reasonable jury could have found Shane not guilty of murder, but guilty of voluntary manslaughter. Accordingly, the judgment of the court of appeals upholding defendant's murder conviction is affirmed.
Judgment affirmed.

Notes and Questions

1. Some have referred to voluntary manslaughter as a crime created by men for men. Do you agree? If voluntary manslaughter was created by men for men how has *State v. Shane* cut into this belief?

2. In *Shane*, the court says, "words alone will not constitute reasonably sufficient provocation to incite the use of deadly force in most situations." Can you think of a situation where words alone might be sufficient? Remember, the standard here is objective, not subjective. Thus, the words must be sufficient to cause a reasonable person to lose self-control.

3. *Shane* listed four requirements for reducing murder to manslaughter: (1) There must have been a reasonable provocation; (2) the defendant must have been in fact provoked; (3) a reasonable man so provoked would not have cooled off in the interval of time between the provocation and the delivery of the fatal blow; and (4) the defendant must not in fact have cooled off during that interval.

If the defendant fails to meet either (1) or (3), would the defendant most likely face murder or aggravated murder? Similarly, if the defendant failed to meet either (2) or (4), would the defendant most likely face murder or aggravated murder?

4. The court uses the term "objective reasonable person" in discussing voluntary manslaughter. Is this phrase accurate? If someone unlawfully takes the life of another, can they ever be deemed a reasonable person? Arguably, reasonable people do not kill each other absent facing some type of imminent threat of harm.

5. *State v. Torres*, 2002-Ohio-1203, excerpted below, provides examples of actions that are sufficient and insufficient provocation for voluntary manslaughter.

> [I]t will be not sufficient provocation where a victim merely throws a phone book at a defendant. *State v. Kent* (June 14, 1999), Warren County App. No. CA98-08-094. Fear alone is not adequate provocation. *State v. Stubblefield* (May 31, 2001), Cuyahoga County, App. No. 78361, *unreported.* Provocative language alone is not sufficient provocation. *State v. Moore* (May 31, 2001), Cuyahoga County App. No. 78085, *unreported.* The act of holding a heavy object, such as a hammer or a baseball bat, will not be sufficient provocation. *State v. Beranek* (Dec. 14, 2000), Cuyahoga County App. No. 76260.
>
> Comparatively, the First District Court of Appeals found sufficient provocation in *State v. Napier* (1995) 105 Ohio App. 3d 713, where the defendant-appellant shot her neighbor with whom she was having a property dispute. In *Napier* the shooting occurred during an argument and after the victim threw a large metal sign at the defendant-appellant. In that case the court found:
>
> > "Given the emotionally charged atmosphere that preceded the assault and the fact that [the victim] did strike [the appellant] on the arm with the sign, the jury could have reasonably concluded that the mitigating element of serious provocation was established in this case which caused [the appellant] to respond with deadly force."

In *State v. Koliser* (March 15, 2000), Columbiana County App. No.97-CO-16, *unreported* the Seventh District Court of Appeals found sufficient provocation in the following situation:

> Appellant testified that he was facing the mantle in the living room of the apartment and that, " ***as I turn around [the victim] was in my face saying, 'Why did you bite me?' At the same time grabbing me, picking me up like a bear hug. He was picking me up, and bending me backwards, and we went into the stereo. At the same time, he got cut." An attack as Appellant described is sufficient to arouse the passions of an ordinary person beyond the power of his or her control. Moreover, as the trial court stated at sentencing, " *** to some extent the victim induced, or put himself in a position where this crime happened." Appellant has satisfied the objective portion of the test***. (citations omitted)

6. Does voluntary manslaughter create "victim-blaming" to some extent? Is that fair considering the accused has committed a homicide which society abhors? In contrast, if even a reasonable person would have been incited to use deadly force, should this be a crime at all? After all, the person is acting reasonably. What more should society require?

C. Burden of Proof

State v. Rhodes, 63 Ohio St. 3d 613 (1992)

WRIGHT, Justice.

Wright, J. This case requires us to decide whether a defendant on trial for murder bears the burden of establishing by a preponderance of the evidence that he was "under the influence of sudden passion or in a sudden fit of rage, either of which was brought on by serious provocation occasioned by the victim that *** [was] reasonably sufficient to incite the *** [defendant] into using deadly force *** "—the mitigating circumstances of R.C. 2903.03(A)—, in order for a jury to find the defendant guilty of voluntary manslaughter rather than murder. In order to understand the import of the issue before us, a review of the law of voluntary manslaughter is necessary. The text of the relevant portion of the voluntary manslaughter statute, R.C. 2903.03(A), reads as follows:

No person, while under the influence of sudden passion or in a sudden fit of rage, either of which is brought on by serious provocation occasioned by the victim that is reasonably sufficient to incite the person into using deadly force, shall knowingly cause the death of another.

R.C. 2903.03 defines voluntary manslaughter as a single offense that, under certain circumstances, permits a defendant to mitigate a charge of murder to manslaughter. The crime comprises elements that must be proven by the prosecution and mitigating circumstances that must be established by the defendant. Under the statute, the jury must find a defendant guilty of voluntary manslaughter rather than murder if the prosecution has proven, beyond a reasonable doubt, that the defendant knowingly caused the victim's death, and if the defendant has established by a preponderance of the evidence the existence of one or both of the mitigating circumstances.

Voluntary manslaughter is, by our prior definition, an inferior degree of murder. *State v. Tyler* (1990), 50 Ohio St. 3d 24. Thus, if a defendant on trial for murder or aggravated murder (or the prosecution in such trial) produces evidence of one or both of the mitigating circumstances set forth in R.C. 2903.03, that evidence will be sufficient to entitle a defendant to an instruction on voluntary manslaughter as an inferior degree of murder if under any reasonable view of the evidence, and when all of the evidence is construed in a light most favorable to the defendant, a reasonable jury could find that the defendant had established by a preponderance of the evidence the existence of one or both of the mitigating circumstances. *State v. Wilkins* (1980), 64 Ohio St. 2d 382.

If a defendant is not charged with murder or aggravated murder, but rather is on trial for voluntary manslaughter, neither party is required to establish either of the mitigating circumstances. Rather, the court presumes (to the benefit of the defendant) the existence of one or both of the mitigating circumstances as a result of the prosecutor's decision to try the defendant on the charge of voluntary manslaughter rather than murder. In that situation, the prosecution needs to prove, beyond a reasonable doubt, only that the defendant knowingly caused the death of another, and it is not a defense to voluntary manslaughter that neither party is able to demonstrate the existence of a mitigating circumstance. *State v. Calhoun* (1983), 10 Ohio App. 3d 23, motion for leave to appeal overruled (1983).

We now turn our attention to the central issue in this matter: whether the trial court's instruction to the jury on the burden of establishing either of the mitigating circumstances of R.C. 2903.03 was proper. Because the instruction at issue was not objected to at trial, and because the record does not reflect that the court rejected a defense-proposed alternative to the instruction given, we review the instruction for plain error. *State v. Underwood* (1983), 3 Ohio St. 3d 12.

In its instructions to the jury, the court placed upon the defendant the burden of establishing by a preponderance of the evidence either of the mitigating circumstances of R.C. 2903.03(A). In *State v. Muscatello* (1978), 55 Ohio St .2d 201, we analyzed the predecessor manslaughter statute and determined that the "mitigating circumstance" of "extreme emotional stress" was not an element of the crime of voluntary manslaughter. *Id.* at paragraph one of the syllabus. We also determined that the defendant was not required to establish the mitigating circumstance of extreme emotional stress by either a preponderance of the evidence or beyond a reasonable doubt "in order for the jury to consider the *** [inferior degree] offense of voluntary manslaughter." *Id.* at paragraph three of the syllabus. At the time the defendant in *Muscatello* originally went to trial, former R.C. 2901.05(A) placed only the burden of production, and not the burden of persuasion, upon the defendant asserting an affirmative defense. *State v. Robinson* (1976), 47 Ohio St. 2d 103.

Muscatello is as instructive for what it does not say as it is for what it does. Although some would suggest that *Muscatello* stands for the proposition that the mitigating circumstance "extreme emotional stress" is not an element of an affirmative defense, and thus its equivalent under the current statute, "sudden passion or sudden fit of rage," also does not need to be proven as an element of an affirmative defense, we find no such language in the court's opinion. Indeed, an examination of the court of appeals' decision affirmed in *Muscatello* substantially contradicts that suggestion: "Emotional stress as a mitigating circumstance is similar to an affirmative defense since it operates as a defense to the higher offenses of aggravated murder and murder. As such, the law in Ohio applicable to affirmative defenses is also clearly applicable to the mitigating factor of emotional stress." *State v. Muscatello* (1977), 57 Ohio App. 2d 231. Clearly, the court of appeals directly, and this court by implication, in the respective *Muscatello* opinions, viewed the law relating to affirmative defenses as applicable to the mitigation of a charge of murder to voluntary manslaughter, and, for that reason, both courts chose not to place the burden of persuasion upon the defendant who sets forth a mitigating circumstance.

In 1978, the General Assembly amended former R.C. 2901.05(A) and changed the burden imposed upon a defendant asserting an affirmative defense (137 Ohio Laws, Part II, 3895, 3896). Currently, a defendant bears the burden of production, as before, as well as the burden by a preponderance of the evidence to prove an affirmative defense. R.C. 2901.05(A). In view of that statutory change, our decision now whether the implicit rationale underlying *Muscatello* should stand will determine whether a court may require a defendant to prove either of the mitigating circumstances by a preponderance of the evidence.

We see no reason to alter the course set forth in *Muscatello,* and we thus continue to view the law regarding affirmative defenses to be applicable to the proof of mitigation to reduce a charge of murder to manslaughter. As before, the defendant bears the burden of producing evidence of a mitigating circumstance "in order for a jury to consider *** [as an inferior degree of murder,] voluntary manslaughter." *Muscatello,* 55 Ohio St. 2d at 203. The jury now, however, must weigh the evidence in mitigation in light of defendant's burden to establish the existence of either of the mitigating circumstances by a preponderance of the evidence. To that extent, we apply the current statute concerning affirmative defenses to our prior decision in *Muscatello* and modify it accordingly.

The result here is consistent with the practice approved by the United States Supreme Court in *Patterson v. New York* (1977), 432 U.S. 197. In *Patterson,* the court upheld a New York law that placed the burden of persuasion upon the defendant to prove by a preponderance of the evidence that he acted under the influence of extreme emotional stress to reduce the crime of second-degree murder to manslaughter. Because placing the burden to prove mitigation upon the defendant does not require him to disprove an element of the offense of murder, we similarly find the practice to be acceptable under both the Ohio and United States Constitutions.

Thus, we hold that a defendant on trial for murder or aggravated murder bears the burden of persuading the fact finder, by a preponderance of the evidence, that he or she acted under the influence of sudden passion or in a sudden fit of rage, either of which was brought on by serious provocation occasioned by the victim that was reasonably sufficient to incite the defendant into using deadly force, R.C. 2903.03(A), in order for the defendant to be convicted of voluntary manslaughter rather than murder or aggravated murder. The court shall instruct the jury on the offense of voluntary manslaughter if the defendant meets his burden of production with respect to evidence of one or both of the mitigating circumstances of R.C. 2903.03(A).

In this case, the trial court properly placed the burden of proof upon the defendant to prove the mitigating circumstances of R.C. 2903.03(A) by a preponderance of the evidence. The judgment of the court of appeals is reversed.

Judgment reversed.

Notes and Questions

1. In criminal law, the prosecution must prove each and every element of the crime beyond a reasonable doubt. The defendant is not required to prove his or her innocence. To do otherwise is so-called "burden shifting" and runs afoul of the constitution. Did burden shifting occur in *State v. Rhodes?*

2. The court in *Rhodes* states that neither the prosecution nor defense need to prove the mitigating factors of voluntary manslaughter if that is the only crime charged. Do you see why this is? If you were a prosecutor, in what circumstances would you charge a defendant with voluntary manslaughter instead of

murder? Would the determining factor be the defendant's mens rea since in Ohio voluntary manslaughter requires the defendant to commit the homicide "knowingly" while murder requires "purposely"?

D. Imperfect Self-Defense

As discussed previously in this chapter, defendants may attempt to reduce murder to manslaughter for an intentional killing that arises in the "heat of passion." In certain jurisdictions, defendants may also get murder reduced to manslaughter under the "imperfect self-defense" doctrine. This doctrine arises when the defendant, who is not the aggressor, honestly but unreasonably believes that he has to use lethal force to defend himself. As illustrated by *State v. Goff*, not all states recognize the imperfect self-defense doctrine.

State v. Goff, 2013-Ohio-42 (Ohio Ct. App. 2013)

***The imperfect self-defense doctrine would have allowed Megan to mitigate her murder conviction to a voluntary manslaughter conviction if she had an honest, *but unreasonable,* belief that she was in danger of death or great bodily harm from William. *See Dykes v. State*, 319 Md. 206, (1990). As Megan acknowledges, Ohio does not recognize the imperfect self-defense doctrine. Megan, however, argues that "[t]he doctrine of imperfect self-defense as a means of mitigating an intentional, but not premeditated, killing to voluntary manslaughter has a long history in the criminal law." Megan notes that thirteen jurisdictions have adopted the imperfect self-defense doctrine. She asserts that the trial court should have given the jury her proposed imperfect-self-defense instruction.

As stated, a trial court has discretion to determine whether the evidence is sufficient to require a jury instruction. And here, the trial court did not abuse its discretion by refusing to instruct the jury on a doctrine that Ohio law does not recognize. Thus, the trial court did not err when it refused to instruct the jury on the imperfect self-defense doctrine.***

Chapter 9
Involuntary Manslaughter

A. Background

At common law, involuntary manslaughter was the unintentional death of another that occurs because of the gross negligence or recklessness of the defendant or while the defendant commits an unlawful act, such as a misdemeanor. The defendant may be convicted of involuntary manslaughter even if he did not intend to inflict serious bodily harm or kill the victim.

Many jurisdictions, including Ohio, have modified involuntary manslaughter by statute. In Ohio, death by the defendant's negligence (O.R.C. 2903.05) or recklessness (O.R.C. 2903.041) is covered by separate statutes. Involuntary manslaughter (O.R.C. 2903.04) is solely limited to instances where the death of the victim occurs during a felony or misdemeanor. Committing the felony or misdemeanor serves as a substitute for criminal negligence. One question that arises here is how minor or insignificant can the misdemeanor be without violating the Eighth Amendment's prohibition on cruel and unusual punishment. This question is addressed in *State v. Weitbrecht*.

The second case to be examined in this chapter is *State v. Hill*, which explores Ohio's Negligent Homicide statute. The final case, *State v. English*, looks at reckless homicide.

1. Unlawful-Act Involuntary Manslaughter

State v. Weitbrecht, 86 Ohio St. 3d 368 (1999)

FRANCIS E. SWEENEY, SR., J.

The issue certified for our review is, "Does Ohio's involuntary manslaughter statute [R.C. 2903.04(B)] as applied to a minor misdemeanor traffic offense which results in a vehicular homicide violate the Eighth Amendment to the United States

Constitution and Section 9, Article [I] of the Ohio Constitution?" For the reasons that follow, we answer the certified question in the negative.

R.C. 2903.04 provides, in relevant part:

> (B) No person shall cause the death of another *** as a proximate result of the offender's committing or attempting to commit a misdemeanor of the first, second, third, or fourth degree or a minor misdemeanor.
>
> (C) Whoever violates this section is guilty of involuntary manslaughter. *** Violation of division (B) of this section is a felony of the third degree.

A third degree felony carries the potential penalty of one to five years in prison and a fine of up to $10,000. (R.C. 2929.14[A][4]; 2929.18[A][3] [c].)

Appellee successfully argued to the lower courts that the potential penalty imposed for a violation of R.C. 2903.04(B) is disproportionate to the crime committed (a minor misdemeanor), and is violative of the constitutional prohibition against cruel and unusual punishments. We are now asked to decide whether the lower courts were correct in finding that R.C. 2903.04(B) violates the Eighth Amendment to the United States Constitution and Section 9, Article I of the Ohio Constitution. In resolving this issue, we are mindful that legislative enactments are to be afforded a strong presumption of constitutionality. *State v. McDonald* (1987), 31 Ohio St. 3d 47. Any reasonable doubt regarding the constitutionality of a statute must be resolved in favor of the legislature's power to enact the law. *Id.* Thus, the legislation will not be struck down unless the challenger establishes that it is unconstitutional beyond a reasonable doubt. *State v. Thompkins* (1996), 75 Ohio St. 3d 558.

The Eighth Amendment to the Constitution of the United States provides: "Excessive bail shall not be required, nor excessive fines imposed, nor cruel and unusual punishments inflicted." Section 9, Article I of the Ohio Constitution is couched in identical language. Historically, the Eighth Amendment has been invoked in extremely rare cases, where it has been necessary to protect individuals from inhumane punishment such as torture or other barbarous acts. *Robinson v. California* (1962), 370 U.S. 660. Over the years, it has also been used to prohibit punishments that were found to be disproportionate to the crimes committed. In *McDougle v. Maxwell* (1964), 1 Ohio St. 2d 68, this court stressed that Eighth Amendment violations are rare.

We stated that "[c]ases in which cruel and unusual punishments have been found are limited to those involving sanctions which under the circumstances would be considered shocking to any reasonable person." *Id.* at 70, 30 O.O.2d at 39, 203 N.E.2d at 336. Furthermore, "the penalty must be so greatly disproportionate to the offense as to shock the sense of justice of the community." *Id.* See, also, *State v. Chaffin* (1972), 30 Ohio St. 2d 13, paragraph three of the syllabus.

The United States Supreme Court has also discussed the concept of whether the Eighth Amendment requires that sentences be proportionate to the offenses committed. An Eighth Amendment challenge on these grounds was initially applied only in cases involving the death penalty or unusual forms of imprisonment. *Enmund v. Florida* (1982), 458 U.S. 782. Then, in *Solem v. Helm* (1983), 463 U.S. 277, the court applied the Eighth Amendment to reverse a felony sentence on proportionality grounds, finding that "a criminal sentence must be proportionate to the crime for which the defendant has been convicted." In so holding, the *Solem* court set forth the following tripartite test to review sentences under the Eighth Amendment:

> First, we look to the gravity of the offense and the harshness of the penalty. *** Second, it may be helpful to compare the sentences imposed on other criminals in the same jurisdiction. If more serious crimes are subject to the same penalty, or to less serious penalties, that is some indication that the punishment at issue may be excessive. *** Third, courts may find it useful to compare the sentences imposed for commission of the same crime in other jurisdictions.

More recently, in *Harmelin v. Michigan* (1991), 501 U.S. 957, the United States Supreme Court revisited the issue of proportionality as it relates to the Eighth Amendment. In *Harmelin,* the court was asked to decide whether a mandatory term of life imprisonment without possibility of parole for possession of six hundred seventy-two grams of cocaine violated the prohibition against cruel and unusual punishments. In finding no constitutional violation, the lead opinion rejected earlier statements made in *Solem v. Helm* and stated that the Eighth Amendment contains no proportionality guarantee. However, this statement failed to garner a majority. The three Justices who concurred in part would refine the *Solem* decision to an analysis of "gross disproportionality" between sentence and crime. As stated by Justice Kennedy in his opinion concurring in part, "The Eighth Amendment does not require strict proportionality between crime and sentence. Rather, it forbids only extreme sentences that are 'grossly disproportionate' to the crime." *Id.* at 1001.

With these principles in mind, we now turn to the case at hand. Appellant contends that R.C. 2903.04(B), as applied to a minor misdemeanor traffic offense, does not constitute cruel and unusual punishment because its potential penalty for causing the death of another is not disproportionate to the offense committed and does not shock the community's sense of justice. Appellant relies on *State v.*

Stanford (Sept. 23, 1996), Trumbull App. No. 95-T-5358, to support its position. The *Stanford* decision is of little value in helping us resolve this issue because the court was without a sufficient basis to review the issue. However, the *Garland* court did fully consider the issue. In *Garland,* the defendant was convicted of involuntary manslaughter with the underlying minor misdemeanor of failure to stop at a stop sign and was sentenced to a term of five to ten years. The court held that "[t]he sentence imposed by the trial court falls within the range of punishments contained within the sentencing statute for this offense. There is no evidence to suggest that appellant's sentence would shock the conscience of the community. *** Accordingly, the punishment imposed cannot be deemed cruel and unusual." *Id.* at 466.

In contrast, appellee argues that the court of appeals' decision was correct and urges us to follow the appellate decisions of *State v. Campbell* (1997), 117 Ohio App. 3d 762, and *State v. Shy* (June 30, 1997), Pike App. No. 96 CA 587, which used the tripartite test set forth in *Solem* to find that R.C. 2903.04(B) violates the Cruel and Unusual Punishment Clauses of the United States and Ohio Constitutions. In these decisions, the courts found that the potential punishment for committing a minor misdemeanor traffic offense is grossly disproportionate to the crime. Furthermore, the courts found that the potential sentence under R.C. 2903.04(B) was excessive when compared to similar related Ohio crimes that require a greater degree of culpability (such as negligent homicide, vehicular homicide, and aggravated vehicular homicide), and when compared with other jurisdictions. These decisions also relied, in part, on dictum from our decision in *State v. Collins* (1993), 67 Ohio St. 3d 115, which questioned the policy behind applying the involuntary manslaughter statute to include minor misdemeanors as predicate offenses.

At the outset, we reject appellee's reliance on the *Collins* decision. In *Collins,* we interpreted the statutory language of former R.C. 2903.04(B), which stated that it applied to "misdemeanors." Under the principles of statutory construction, and in reviewing various sections of R.C. Title 29 that differentiate between misdemeanors and minor misdemeanors, we found that the statute as written did not include minor misdemeanors. Thus, we held that offenses classified as minor misdemeanors could not serve as a predicate offense for a charge of involuntary manslaughter. Since the General Assembly has amended R.C. 2903.04 so that Ohio's involuntary manslaughter statute now encompasses minor misdemeanors as predicate offenses, the current version of R.C. 2903.04 differs from that which we interpreted in *Collins.* Thus, our decision in *Collins* has no bearing on our decision today.

We also reject the reasoning employed by those courts, which found that R.C. 2903.04(B) violates the prohibition against cruel and unusual punishments. Although the potential maximum penalty of five years' imprisonment may be somewhat severe, it is not tantamount to cruel and unusual punishment.

Unfortunately, lives were lost as a result of the traffic accident. Where human lives are lost, the gravity of the crime is serious and is not lessened by the fact that the underlying crime consists of a minor misdemeanor. Furthermore, we note that the trial court has the option of imposing a less stringent punishment than actual incarceration. For instance, an offender can be sentenced to a term of probation (R.C. 2929.15 to R.C. 2929.17) or, if incarcerated, can file an application for judicial release after six months (R.C. 2929.20[A]; [B][2]). Under these circumstances, we cannot say that the potential penalty for violating R.C. 2903.04(B) is "so greatly disproportionate to the offense as to shock the sense of justice of the community." *McDougle v. Maxwell,* 1 Ohio St. 2d at 70, 30 O.O.2d at 39, 203 N.E.2d at 336; *cf. Harmelin v. Michigan,* 501 U.S. at 995, where the court held that severe, mandatory penalties may be cruel, but they are not unusual in the constitutional sense, and do not violate the Eighth Amendment.

In reaching this decision, we are cognizant of the fact that reviewing courts should grant substantial deference to the broad authority that legislatures possess in determining the types and limits of punishments for crimes. *Solem,* 463 U.S. at 290. We find that the General Assembly acted within its discretion in setting forth the penalties it did when the commission of minor misdemeanors results in the deaths of individuals.

Accordingly, we hold that R.C. 2903.04(B), as applied to a minor misdemeanor traffic offense which results in a vehicular homicide, does not violate the Eighth Amendment to the United States Constitution or Section 9, Article I of the Ohio Constitution.

The judgment of the court of appeals is reversed, and the cause is remanded to the trial court.

Judgment reversed and cause remanded.

PFEIFER, J., dissenting.

Dispassionate dissection of a legal conundrum is often required to achieve the correct result in matters that come before this court. In those instances, the facts of the case are secondary to the legal analysis. Here, where we are considering whether the sentence at issue would "shock the sense of justice of the community," the facts must stand at the center of our consideration. The facts in this case tell the whole story.

While driving on Highway 62 on April 27, 1997, Nancy Weitbrecht apparently suffered a cardiac event, lost consciousness, crossed left of center, and collided with the Carroll vehicle. She lost her husband and a friend in the accident, and must live with the fact that she also caused the death of Vera Carroll. The state stipulated that there was no evidence of criminal recklessness or criminal negligence on her part. Nancy Weitbrecht now faces a potential five-year prison term. It would be hard to conjure up a situation more shocking to the community's sense of justice, or a more inappropriate exercise of prosecutorial discretion. I accordingly dissent.

Notes and Questions

1. Based on the facts of *State v. Weitbrecht*, would a five-year sentence for the appellee "shock the sense of justice of the community"?

2. If you were the prosecutor in *Weitbrecht*, would you have pursued a charge of involuntary manslaughter? Do you suppose a jury will find the defendant in *Weitbrecht* guilty given the facts indicated by the dissent? What about the fact that the defendant lost consciousness, doesn't that remove the actus reus?

3. Setting aside the facts of *Weitbrecht,* do you agree that applying involuntary manslaughter to minor misdemeanors is constitutional? Why do you suppose the legislature chose to amend the statute to include minor misdemeanors? If you were a state legislator, would you have voted for or against the amendment?

2. Criminal-Negligence Involuntary Manslaughter

a. Negligent Homicide

State v. Hill, 31 Ohio App. 3d 65 (1987)

PER CURIAM.

This cause came on to be heard upon the appeal from the Court of Common Pleas of Hamilton County.

The question raised by the assignment of error is whether the trial court erred in refusing to instruct the jury on the lesser included offenses of involuntary manslaughter and negligent homicide. Defendant, Raymond D. Hill, was indicted for, and found guilty of, murder in violation of R.C. 2903.02. We hold the court did not err.

Defendant shot his mother with a Remington 30.06 bolt-action rifle (model 700), a high-powered weapon he used for hunting deer. The prosecution's evidence disclosed that Mrs. Hill's body was found sitting in a chair at the foot of her bed, slumped to her right, with the right portions of her jaw, throat, shoulder and upper chest destroyed by the blast. The projectile had a lead core and an open-nosed copper jacket; it "exploded" on contact with the body. Parts of the projectile were found on the closet floor behind the body. The stippling of powder on the body indicated the muzzle was six to forty-two inches from the victim's face. The rifle was found on the top of a sewing machine in the adjoining living room; it had an average "pull" on the trigger which was fitted with a "saddle" that made it easier to grip. Boxes of ammunition and loose rounds were found around the house and in defendant's bedroom. There was a bullet hole in the living room floor, and two empty casings were found, one in the bedroom and one in the living room.

There were no third-party witnesses to the shooting. After the shooting, defendant drove several city blocks to the municipal police station in Fairfax and reported the shooting to an officer, saying among other things, "I got my high-powered rifle and shot her in the head."

The prosecution argued that the shooting was purposeful, either to acquire Mrs. Hill's modest house and car, or to stop his mother's harassment of him, perhaps combined with the frustration from his bankruptcy, loss of his house, and separation from his wife. He had been consuming alcohol for several hours before the event. The prosecution argued that Mrs. Hill was shot while she was dozing in her chair. One of Mrs. Hill's sisters thought the defendant "mistreated" his mother. There were unexplained bruises on her body.

Defendant's testimony was that his mother was undergoing chemotherapy for inoperable cancer and drank to excess. He claimed she was too drunk that afternoon to go to the hospital for another treatment, and that in frustration he searched the kitchen and other parts of the house for the bottle of liquor she had hidden. He never found it. He got his rifle and shot a round into the living room floor to scare her into telling him where the whiskey was, without avail. Inadvertently, he reloaded the rifle but failed to put it on "safe." She went to the chair in her bedroom, and he followed, arguing with her about giving up alcohol and pursuing the chemotherapy. He sat on a bed, across from her as they talked. When he began to stand up, the rifle discharged by mistake. He left the house in a panic and became distraught at the police station, asking the police to arrange to turn him loose so as to shoot him as he ran away.

In defense counsel's opening statement and closing argument, the defense admitted the shooting but claimed that the only question was whether it was accidental or purposeful. The jury was properly instructed on purposeful homicide and accident. Defense counsel, however, duly requested the court to instruct the jury on involuntary manslaughter in violation of R.C. 2903.04(B) and negligent homicide in violation of R.C. 2903.05. The court refused. We find no error.

Defendant was not entitled to a jury instruction on involuntary manslaughter because defendant's own testimony fails to prove the misdemeanor of aggravated menacing or any other misdemeanor that could form the underlying (or "causative") offense for involuntary manslaughter. Involuntary manslaughter may, on the proper evidence, be a lesser included offense of murder. *State v. Rohdes* (1986), 23 Ohio St. 3d 225, unreported. But the evidence in the instant case does not disclose that an aggravated menacing or any other misdemeanor was being committed at the moment the fatal shot was discharged. Defendant said he was arising from his seated position when the rifle discharged, and while he had earlier blasted the living room floor, he was not menacing his mother at the moment of the fatal shot.

Nor was defendant entitled to a jury instruction on negligent homicide, for three reasons.

First, we decided in *State v. Jenkins* (1983), 13 Ohio App. 3d 122, that negligent homicide is not a lesser included offense of murder regardless of whether the offense is committed with a deadly weapon. Second, assuming *arguendo* that negligent homicide is a lesser included offense of murder, from the outset of the trial defendant argued that the shooting was accidental and he did not assert negligent homicide until he asked for a jury instruction. *State v. King* (1984), 20 Ohio App. 3d 62. Third, making the same assumption about negligent homicide as a lesser included offense, the evidence was not sufficient for a trier of fact reasonably to find defendant was negligent, using the definition of negligence found in R.C. 2901.22(D). *State v. Rohdes, supra,* held that slipping or tripping in the snow while holding a loaded handgun (which discharged one shot that killed the victim) is an accident and not the "substantial lapse from due care" required by R.C. 2903.05, as set forth in R.C. 2901.22(D). We perceive no difference of substance between that case and the instant case.

We affirm.

BLACK, J., dissents.

I respectfully dissent because the defendant was entitled, in my judgment, to have the jury instructed that negligent homicide was a lesser included offense of murder in this case. I agree with the majority that he was not entitled to an instruction on involuntary manslaughter as a lesser included offense because the evidence failed to establish any underlying (or "causative") misdemeanor, such as aggravated menacing.

I am not persuaded by any of the three reasons cited by the majority as justification for the trial court's refusal to instruct on negligent homicide as a lesser included offense in this case. First, the decision in *State v. Jenkins* (1983), 13 Ohio App. 3d 122, has been overruled, in effect, by *State v. Rohdes* (1986), 23 Ohio St. 3d 225. The Supreme Court concluded that Rohdes was not entitled to the requested instruction on negligent homicide, not because it could never be a lesser included offense of murder as a matter of law, but because the evidence was not sufficient to establish Rohdes' criminal negligence. Thus, by implication if not by express statement, the Supreme Court held that given the appropriate evidence, the instruction would be required.

Second, I find in the record a sufficient basis for entitlement by the defendant to an instruction on negligent homicide. Defense counsel made no claim to it in the opening statement, but defendant's own testimony was amply sufficient to raise the issue of criminal negligence. He testified that as he rose from a sitting position, the loaded and cocked rifle in his hands, without a safety on, discharged without his conscious intent.

He conceded that while hunting he never carried a loaded and cocked gun without a safety on, and that a gun should never be pointed at a person at any time. A trier of fact could reasonably conclude that defendant's conduct was negligent. In brief, the evidence of negligence is patent on the record. This fact distinguishes the instant case from *State v. King* (1984), 20 Ohio App. 3d 62, because in that case, the evidence was that the homicide was justified as an intentional killing in self-defense.

Third, I am convinced that the evidence of defendant's conduct in handling a high-powered hunting rifle in the narrow confines of his mother's bedroom, and in her presence, raised the issue of criminal negligence, and that a reasonable trier of fact could find beyond a reasonable doubt that defendant had acted with a substantial lack of due care in failing to perceive or avoid the risk that his handling of the rifle might cause serious injury or death to his mother. R.C. 2901.22(A). Otherwise stated, the evidence was such that reasonable minds had to determine beyond a reasonable doubt whether defendant acted purposely, or negligently, or without culpability (that is, by accident).

I would reverse the judgment below and remand the case for further proceedings.

Notes and Questions

1. In *State v. Hill*, who has the better argument—the majority or the dissent? Do you think your view is influenced by your knowledge and familiarity with weapons or how accustomed you are to being around firearms?

2. Are "accident" and "negligence" distinguishable in Ohio criminal law? If yes, how would you define each term? If you were the defense attorney, how would your negligence argument differ from your accident argument? Could you make both arguments as alternative defenses?

b. Reckless Homicide

State v. English, 2014-Ohio-89 (Ohio Ct. App. 2014)

DORRIAN, J.

Defendant-appellant, Quayjuan A. English ("appellant"), appeals from his convictions in the Franklin County Court of Common Pleas of reckless homicide with a firearm specification and tampering with evidence. Because we conclude that the convictions were supported by sufficient evidence and were not against the manifest weight of the evidence, and because appellant was not entitled to a jury instruction on negligent homicide, we affirm.

This conviction from which this appeal is taken resulted from an unintentional shooting that occurred on the afternoon of July 5, 2011. On that date, appellant and David Rivers ("Rivers"), were among a group of individuals gathered in and around Rivers' car, which was parked in the backyard of Rivers' residence. At one point, while appellant was sitting in the right-side backseat of the car, he was handed a shotgun. There were two individuals seated in the left and right-side front seats of the car, while Rivers stood near the left-side rear door area and another individual stood near the right-side rear door area. Appellant later testified at trial that, after being handed the shotgun, he began to "mess with" or "flick" the shotgun's hammer. Other witnesses indicated at trial that appellant was swinging the shotgun around while flicking the hammer. While appellant was manipulating the hammer, the shotgun discharged, firing a single shot that struck Rivers in the upper right chest from a distance of approximately two to four feet away. After the shooting, the police were called and medical personnel responded, but Rivers was pronounced dead at the scene.

When the police arrived, appellant admitted that he was holding a gun and "pulled back the thing on the top," but claimed that he did not pull the trigger, did not know the gun was loaded, and did not see where Rivers was standing. An individual retrieved a .22 caliber rifle from under the porch of the residence and gave it to one of the officers. Based on the appearance of Rivers' wound, the police doubted that the rifle fired the fatal shot, but they could not locate any other weapons at the time. A neighbor, Thomas Christian ("Christian") told police that he saw an individual throw a gun into his yard. Christian later testified at trial that he told the individual to get the gun out of his yard and that the same person then grabbed the shotgun and ran to the side of his house. Ten days after the shooting, Christian found a shotgun in his cellar area and reported it to the police. At trial, appellant identified the shotgun recovered from Christian's cellar area as the same one that he held while sitting in Rivers' car. An autopsy report indicated that Rivers died as a result of a shotgun wound to his right upper chest area and that shotgun pellets and wadding were recovered from his body near the area of the wound.

Appellant was indicted on four charges related to the events of July 5, 2011: involuntary manslaughter (a first-degree felony) with a firearm specification, reckless homicide (a third-degree felony) with a firearm specification, improperly handling firearms in a motor vehicle (a fourth-degree felony), and tampering with evidence (a third-degree felony). Following a jury trial, appellant was convicted of reckless homicide with a firearm specification and tampering with evidence, and found not guilty on the other two charges in the indictment.

In appellant's first assignment of error, he argues that the trial court erred in denying his motion under Crim. R. 29 for acquittal on the charge of reckless homicide. He also asserts that his conviction for reckless homicide was against the manifest weight of the evidence.***

Appellant's Crim. R. 29 motion related to the charge of reckless homicide in violation of R.C. 2903.041. That statute provides, in relevant part, that "[n]o person shall recklessly cause the death of another." "A person acts recklessly when, with heedless indifference to the consequences, he perversely disregards a known risk that his conduct is likely to cause a certain result or is likely to be of a certain nature. A person is reckless with respect to circumstances when, with heedless indifference to the consequences, he perversely disregards a known risk that such circumstances are likely to exist." R.C. 2901.22(C).

Appellant argues that no rational trier of fact could conclude that he acted recklessly. Although he concedes that he held the shotgun while sitting in the backseat of the car and that he repeatedly "flicked" the shotgun's hammer, he denies that he pulled the trigger. Appellant denies that he acted recklessly because he did not perversely disregard a known risk that flicking the hammer without pulling the trigger would cause the shotgun to fire. At trial, Amy Amstutz ("Amstutz"), a forensic scientist from the Columbus division of police, testified regarding operability tests she performed on the shotgun. Amstutz testified that she tested what would occur if the hammer was flicked or pulled back and allowed to fall forward before reaching the fully cocked position, without applying pressure to the trigger. She stated that, on two of twenty-five occasions, this caused the shotgun to discharge. Amstutz explained that this was possibly due to worn parts inside the shotgun. Based on these and other tests, Amstutz described the shotgun as having a "sometimes operable hammer safety." (Tr. 348.)

Appellant asserts that the state needed to prove that he perversely disregarded a specific, known risk, rather than a general risk that a shotgun could be dangerous. Appellant argues that, without knowledge that this specific shotgun could discharge while manipulating the hammer, but not applying any pressure to the trigger, he could not have disregarded the specific risk the gun posed to those who surrounded him. He argues that no reasonable juror could have concluded that he was aware of the specific risk posed by the "sometimes operable hammer safety" on the shotgun. In support of this argument, appellant cites *State v. Peck,* 172 Ohio App. 3d 25, 2007-Ohio-2730 (10th Dist.). However, we find these decisions to be distinguishable from the present appeal.

In *Peck,* this court overturned a reckless homicide conviction, concluding that it was not supported by sufficient evidence. *Peck* at ¶ 26. The defendant in *Peck* was a tow truck driver who failed to inspect a "snatch block," used to tow heavy equipment, for its weight capacity before attempting to remove a heavy truck stuck in mud near a freeway. *Id .* at ¶ 4. When he attempted to pull the truck from the mud, the snatch block broke, causing it to crash through the windshield of a passing car and killing the driver. *Id.* at ¶ 5. This court concluded that because the tow truck driver "did not know the [weight capacity] rating of the snatch block, and because he was unaware of the risk associated with using a snatch block without checking its rating, he was ignorant of the risk that the snatch block would fail" and, therefore, had not acted recklessly. *Id.* at ¶ 23. Thus, because the tow truck driver did not know of the specific risk that caused the decedent's death, he was not aware of the risk his conduct created and did not act recklessly. *Id.* at ¶ 25.

The facts in *Peck* were quite different from the facts of this case. As discussed below, there was some testimony suggesting that appellant may have had his finger on or near the shotgun's trigger. However, even if appellant is correct that he was only flicking the hammer, we conclude that the evidence was sufficient to establish that he perversely disregarded a known risk that his conduct was likely to cause harm. The Supreme Court of Ohio has recognized that "a firearm is an inherently dangerous instrumentality, the use of which is reasonably likely to produce death" when fired at an individual. *State v. Widner,* 69 Ohio St. 2d 267, 270 (1982). Appellant testified that he did not have any experience with shotguns or any other firearms. He admitted that he did not know whether the shotgun was loaded and did not know how to open it or otherwise determine whether it was loaded. Appellant even testified that, when he was handed the shotgun, he thought "what are they giving me the gun for?" (Tr. 686). Despite this lack of knowledge, appellant admitted that he began "messing with" the hammer of the shotgun. The hammer is part of the firing mechanism of the shotgun.

At the time that appellant was holding the shotgun, he was sitting in the backseat of the car, and there were two individuals sitting in the front seats, with Rivers standing near the rear of the vehicle on the driver's side and another individual standing near the rear on the passenger's side. Thus, appellant was in close proximity to several other people while he sat flicking the shotgun's hammer. There was also testimony that one of the individuals standing near the car told appellant to move the gun away from him, which should have further alerted appellant to the risk associated with playing with the shotgun. Under these circumstances, while appellant may not have specifically known that the shotgun in his hands had a "sometimes operable hammer safety," it was clear that his actions created a risk of harm to nearby individuals and that appellant perversely disregarded that risk by continuing to play with the shotgun's hammer mechanism. *See State v. G.G.,* 10th Dist. No. 12AP-188, 2012-Ohio-5902, ¶ 14 ("A known risk of handling and manipulating a gun while standing in very close proximity to a child and while pointing it in the direction of that child, without checking the chamber to see if a bullet is still in the firearm, is that the firearm will discharge in the direction of the child, and the bullet will narrowly miss that child.").

Appellant also cites *Martin* in support of his argument that the state was required to prove that he cocked the shotgun's hammer and pulled the trigger.

However, *Martin* involved a very different factual scenario. The defendant in *Martin* was convicted of reckless homicide after his girlfriend was fatally shot. The defendant claimed that the victim had a gun and that it discharged as he tried to take it away from her. *Martin* at ¶ 37. On appeal, this court held that there was sufficient evidence to support the conviction, in part because there was evidence that the gun could not be fired any other way than through application of pressure on the trigger, and it was not more likely than other firearms to discharge unintentionally. *Id.* at ¶ 63. There was also testimony from a forensic pathologist that, based on the fact that the victim was right-handed and the location of her wounds, it was unlikely that the fatal wound was self-inflicted. *Id.* In the present appeal, by contrast, there is no dispute regarding the fact that appellant was holding the shotgun when it discharged. There is also no dispute that appellant was manipulating the shotgun's hammer, which is part of the firing mechanism. Under these circumstances, we conclude that the evidence was sufficient to support a reckless homicide conviction because a rational trier of fact could have found that appellant acted recklessly by perversely disregarding a known risk that manipulating part of the firing mechanism of a possibly loaded firearm posed to those individuals near him. Therefore, the trial court did not err by denying appellant's Crim. R. 29 motion on the reckless homicide charge.

Appellant's first assignment of error also asserts that his reckless homicide conviction was against the manifest weight of the evidence.***

Although there was conflicting testimony regarding appellant's handling of the shotgun, we cannot conclude that the jury lost its way in finding appellant guilty of reckless homicide. Appellant admitted that he had no prior experience with guns and did not know if the shotgun was loaded. He testified that he held the shotgun stationary in his lap and merely flicked the hammer, without placing his finger anywhere near the trigger. LaQuan Stepherson ("Stepherson"), who was in the left-side front seat of the car when the shotgun discharged, also testified that appellant was just holding the shotgun and did not have his hand on the trigger.

However, Stepherson admitted that he was looking forward when the shotgun discharged and did not see what happened. Additionally, there was other testimony suggesting that appellant was much more careless with the shotgun and disregarded the risk to those around him. Nyrere Pullins ("Pullins"), who was standing near the rear door on the right side of the car when the shotgun discharged, testified that appellant was swinging the shotgun around while holding it. Pullins testified that appellant swung the shotgun in his direction and he told appellant to move it. Pullins stated that appellant then swung the gun in the other direction, where Rivers was standing, and it discharged. Pullins also testified that, while appellant was playing with the shotgun's hammer, he had his finger on the trigger. Pullins described appellant as "playing with the trigger and the hammer, like he didn't—like he was trying to figure out how to shoot it." (Tr.

424 .) Tarann Young ("Young"), who was sitting in the right-side front seat of the car when the shotgun discharged, also testified that he heard Pullins tell appellant to watch out or move the shotgun just before it discharged. The autopsy report indicated that Rivers was killed by a shot fired into his right upper chest area from a distance of approximately two to four feet away, suggesting that he likely would have been visible to appellant just beyond the end of the shotgun.

After reviewing the testimony and evidence presented at trial, we conclude that the jury did not clearly lose its way in finding appellant guilty of the charge of reckless homicide. As explained above, the evidence was sufficient to establish all of the elements of the crime. The jury was able to weigh the evidence and evaluate the credibility of all witnesses, including appellant and Pullins, in reaching its decision. While there was evidence supporting both the state's theory and appellant's theory, this is not an exceptional case where the evidence weighs heavily against conviction.

Accordingly, we overrule appellant's first assignment of error.

Notes and Questions

1. Do you think the dissenting judge in *State v. Hill* would have found that the criminal defendant in *State v. English* was entitled to a jury instruction on negligent homicide?

2. What are the differences among involuntary manslaughter, negligent homicide, and reckless homicide? Could the defendant's behavior in *English* be characterized as any other type of homicide offense (e.g., could this be depraved heart murder at common law)?

Chapter 10
Assault and Battery

A. Background

At common law, assault and battery were misdemeanors. Battery, a general intent crime, consists of either a bodily injury or an offensive touching. Assault, a specific intent crime, occurs when the criminal defendant attempts to commit a battery. It should be noted, however, there is no universally accepted definition of assault.

Today, many jurisdictions consolidate the two crimes and categorize them as either assault or assault and battery. Also, some jurisdictions have expanded the definition of assault to include the civil-assault situation of intentionally causing apprehension. Ohio has created additional laws like aggravated menacing to cover conduct such as placing another in fear of imminent harm.

This chapter explores the connection assault has with disorderly conduct and attempted murder by looking at *State v. Williams*. This chapter also examines *State v. Deem,* which discusses the difference between felonious assault and aggravated assault. Many states like Ohio have created different forms of assault to reflect the level of harm caused to the victim and the defendant's state of mind.

State v. Williams, 1990 WL 47451 (Ohio Ct. App. 1990)

On March 27, 1988, appellant, Joseph Williams, became involved in a fight at the Middlefield Tavern. The police cited appellant for disorderly conduct in violation of Middlefield Ordinance 509.03(a)(1) which states:

> (a) No person shall recklessly cause inconvenience, annoyance or alarm to another, by doing any of the following:
> (1) Engaging in fighting, in threatening harm to persons or property, or in violent or turbulent behavior; ***.

On March 31, 1988, a complaint was filed by Sgt. Malliski of the Middlefield Police Department against appellant for attempted aggravated murder in connection with the incident at the Middlefield Tavern on March 27, 1988. Appellant was arrested, posted bail, and was released.

On April 11, 1988, appellant made his initial appearance before the Chardon Municipal Court on the disorderly conduct charge. He pled no contest, was found guilty, and fined. He paid the fine.

On April 27, 1988, appellant was indicted for attempted murder by the Geauga County Grand Jury for his participation in the fight at the Middlefield Tavern. He subsequently pled not guilty.

On July 27, 1988, appellant filed a motion to dismiss based on double jeopardy. He asserted that disorderly conduct is a lesser included offense of attempted murder and, therefore, his conviction for disorderly conduct was a bar, based on double jeopardy, to further prosecution.

Following a hearing, the trial court denied appellant's motion to dismiss based on the authority of *Ohio v. Johnson* (1984), 467 U.S. 493, and it specifically found that disorderly conduct is not a lesser included offense of attempted murder.

Appellant timely filed a notice of appeal from that decision, assigning the following as error: "The trial court erred in overruling the defendant's motion to dismiss founded on a claim of double jeopardy."

Appellant argues that his motion to dismiss the attempted murder charge should have been granted based on double jeopardy. He claims that disorderly conduct is a lesser included offense of attempted murder and, therefore, his plea to disorderly conduct barred the subsequent indictment for attempted murder.

Appellant is correct in his assertion that a conviction of a lesser included offense prohibits prosecution of the greater offense. *Brown v. Ohio* (1977), 432 U.S. 161. The critical issue in the present case, therefore, is whether disorderly conduct is a lesser included offense of attempted murder.

The test to determine if an offense is a lesser included offense was set forth by the Ohio Supreme Court in *State v. Kidder* (1987), 32 Ohio St. 3d 279. The court held that an offense could only be lesser included if:

> *** (i) the offense is a crime of lesser degree than the other, (ii) the offense of the greater degree cannot, as statutorily defined, ever be committed without the offense of the lesser degree also being committed, and (iii) some element of the greater offense is not required to prove the commission of the lesser offense.***

Id. at 282.

It is clear that the first and third prongs of the test are met in the case sub judice. Disorderly conduct is a minor misdemeanor whereas attempted murder is a first degree felony. In addition, it is necessary to prove that a person had engaged in conduct which, if successful, would have caused the death of another in order to find that person guilty of attempted murder. See R.C. 2903.02 and 2923.02. The element of conduct which, if successful, would cause death is not present in the disorderly conduct ordinance in question.

The second prong of the test, however, is not met by the offenses in question in the instant cause. The second prong would require that attempted murder, as statutorily defined, could not be committed without disorderly conduct also being committed. This is clearly not the case. To be guilty of annoyance, or alarm to others. It is not a prerequisite to attempted murder for the potential victim to even know that he or she is in danger. The statute focuses on the intent and actions of the perpetrator, not the victim. The second prong of the Kidder test is not met and, therefore, disorderly conduct is not a lesser included offense of attempted murder.

Appellant's assignment of error is without merit.

The judgment of the trial court is affirmed.

FORD, J., concurs with concurring opinion.

***Appellant, in the case sub judice, argues that, pursuant to Roberts, if disorderly conduct is a lesser included offense of assault, and assault is a lesser included offense of murder (and, presumably, attempted murder), then disorderly conduct should, by extension, be found to be a lesser included offense of attempted murder. Appellant's argument is creative, but ultimately unavailing. The reason that appellant's argument is not convincing lies in the subsuming, in the statutory crime of assault, of two different common law crimes: assault and battery.

Although, under Ohio law, the only recognized crimes are statutory, the intent of the drafters of R.C. 2903.13 was to "[prohibit] simple assault and simple battery in the traditional [common law] sense." Committee note to R.C. 2903.13. At common law, criminal assault was a display of force that would give the victim reason to fear or expect immediate bodily harm. This crime is different from the crime of battery, in that battery, technically defined, requires physical contact of some sort, whereas assault does not.

Consequently, when considering the issue of whether disorderly conduct is a lesser included offense of attempted murder, this court must consider whether disorderly conduct is a crime of lesser degree than attempted murder; whether attempted murder can be committed without committing disorderly conduct; and whether there is an element of attempted murder which is not required to prove the commission of disorderly conduct. As the majority notes, clearly disorderly conduct, a minor misdemeanor, is a crime of a lesser degree than attempted murder, a first degree felony. Further, the state can prove disorderly conduct without demonstrating that the perpetrator attempted to kill the victim.

The analytical difficulty that lies in construing disorderly conduct as a lesser included offense of attempted murder comes in construction of the second tenet of the Kidder test. Under Kidder, disorderly conduct can only be considered a lesser included offense of attempted murder if, using the statutory constructions of both crimes, one could not commit attempted murder without also committing disorderly conduct. The phrase "as statutorily defined" implies that the elements of the crimes in question are not merely similar but are substantially identical.

In order to show that a defendant is guilty of attempted murder, the state must show that the defendant purposely or knowingly engaged in conduct which, if successful, would constitute murder. R.C. 2923.02(A). Disorderly conduct, as defined in the Middlefield ordinance, is engaging in fighting, threatening harm to persons or property, or in violent or turbulent behavior which would cause the victim, upon apprehending such behavior, to be inconvenienced, annoyed or alarmed. In the disorderly conduct ordinance, the state must not only prove that the defendant acted offensively, but also that the victim witnessed the behavior and was inconvenienced, annoyed, or alarmed by it. There is no concomitant necessity to show that the victim was aware of the crime being committed in the statutory murder statute and, in fact, the victim may be totally unaware that someone is trying to kill him/her.

Applying the rationale of Kidder by analogy, it would appear that there is a requirement that the victim be aware of the impending danger of physical attack in the crime of technical assault. Consequently, someone who is committing the crime of technical assault must also, by extension, commit the crime of disorderly conduct. In a completed assault (common law battery), the victim does not have to be aware of the offensive touching in order for the crime of battery to be committed. However, the assault, once completed, would not be a greater offense, under the Kidder test, of disorderly conduct.

The Ohio Supreme Court, in Kidder, utilized analysis similar to the case at bar in holding that aggravated menacing, R.C. 2903.21, is not a lesser included offense of attempted murder. The court stated:

> *** [M]urder can be committed without the victim's being aware of impending serious physical harm [as opposed to aggravated menacing, which requires that the victim be aware that the perpetrator intend to cause harm to the victim, the victim's property, or the victim's immediate family]. Thus, the second prong of the statutory-elements test is not met, and no set of facts adduced at trial would have warranted a charge to the jury on the lesser, but not included, offense of aggravated menacing. ***

Kidder at 283.

The absence of an awareness element in the statutory crime of attempted murder similarly bars this court from finding that disorderly conduct is a lesser included offense of attempted murder. It is for this reason that the holding in this case must be explicitly distinguished from Roberts. As a result, the appellant may be tried for attempted murder irrespective of having previously been convicted of disorderly conduct.

Therefore, for the foregoing reasons, I concur.

Notes and Questions

1. In Ohio, assault is defined by ORC 2903.13 as:

> A. No person shall knowingly cause or attempt to cause physical harm to another or to another's unborn.
> B. No person shall recklessly cause physical harm to another or another's unborn.

Besides mens rea, what distinguishes Section A and B? Can you attempt a reckless crime? Prior to answering that question briefly review the chapter on attempt.

2. Does Ohio's assault statute encompass both of the common law crimes of assault and battery as discussed by Judge Ford in *State v. Williams*? What if an offender has only an intent to place the victim in fear of imminent harm? The answer to the aforementioned questions may be found in Ohio's menacing statute (ORC 2903.21) which reads as follows:

> (A) No person shall knowingly cause another to believe that the offender will cause physical harm to the person or property of the other person, the other person's unborn, or a member of the other person's immediate family. In addition to any other basis for the other person's belief that the offender will cause physical harm to the person or property of the other person, the other person's unborn, or a member of the other person's immediate family, the other person's belief may be based on words or conduct of the offender that are directed at or identify a corporation, association, or other organization that employs the other person or to which the other person belongs.

B. Felonious Assault and Aggravated Assault

State v. Deem, 40 Ohio St. 3d 205 (1988)

Since 1983, defendant-appellee, Robert Deem, and Kandace Shauck had maintained a close relationship. They lived together for approximately one and one-half years, but separated in 1985. In 1986, they began meeting again. In May of that year, each filed criminal charges against the other in either or both Hamilton and Clermont Counties.

According to appellee, on May 27, 1986, he waited in his car at a roadside park on State Route 125, near Bethel, Ohio, for Shauck to pass by in her car on her way to work. After Shauck drove by, appellee followed her in his car. Appellee pulled alongside Shauck's car and motioned for her to pull over to the side of the road. Shauck responded only by shaking her head. At some point, the cars bumped. There is disagreement as to which car first bumped the other but eventually appellee forced Shauck's car off the road and into a ditch. Appellee stopped his car in front of Shauck's. Appellee then went to Shauck's car and attempted to convince Shauck to open her window. When Shauck refused, appellee went back to his car, obtained a hammer, walked back to Shauck's car and broke the driver's side window. According to appellee, he then fled as others approached. However, other testimony established that appellee reached through the broken window and stabbed Shauck numerous times, causing about thirty wounds. Shauck was subsequently hospitalized. Appellee fled into the woods and turned himself in to the authorities two days later.

Appellee was charged with felonious assault (R.C. 2903.11) and tried by a jury for the stabbing of Shauck. Just prior to the close of evidence, defense counsel requested a jury instruction on aggravated assault (R.C. 2903.12) as a lesser included offense of felonious assault. Defense counsel requested the aggravated assault instruction based on appellee's testimony that appellee was provoked and confused as to why Shauck bumped her car into his and that he wanted answers as to who had filed criminal charges against him in Clermont County. The trial court rejected the requested instruction. Despite appellee's claim that he did not stab Shauck, appellee was convicted of felonious assault with a specification of a prior kidnapping conviction. Appellee was sentenced to not less than twelve but not more than fifteen years in the state penitentiary.

Appellee appealed, contending that regardless of whether aggravated assault is a lesser included offense of felonious assault, the trial court should have instructed the jury on mitigating evidence that would require a finding of guilty only as to aggravated assault. The court of appeals found aggravated assault to be a lesser included offense of felonious assault and reversed appellee's conviction and ordered a new trial.

The cause is now before this court pursuant to the allowance of a motion for leave to appeal.***

HOLMES, Justice.

This case presents us with the recurring issue of whether the jury in a criminal trial should be instructed on a particular offense for which the defendant was not indicted as a lesser offense of the crime for which the defendant was indicted, pursuant to R.C. 2945.74 and Crim. R. 31(C). Specifically, appellee insists that he was entitled to a jury instruction on aggravated assault as a lesser included offense of felonious assault, based on the evidence of provocation which he presented at trial. We disagree and thus reverse the court of appeals since, in the final analysis, the evidence of provocation presented by appellee was insufficient, as a matter of law, to support a conviction on aggravated assault.***

This case does not involve an attempted felonious assault. Neither is aggravated assault, on which a jury charge was requested, a lesser *included* offense of felonious assault. "Felonious assault" is defined in R.C. 2903.11 as follows:

(A) No person shall knowingly:
(1) Cause serious physical harm to another;
(2) Cause or attempt to cause physical harm to another by means of a deadly weapon or dangerous ordnance, as defined in section 2923.11 of the Revised Code.
(B) Whoever violates this section is guilty of felonious assault, an aggravated felony of the second degree. If the victim of the offense is a peace officer, as defined in section 2935.01 of the Revised Code, felonious assault is an aggravated felony of the first degree.

"Aggravated assault" is defined in R.C. 2903.12 as follows:

(A) No person, while under the influence of sudden passion or in a sudden fit of rage, either of which is brought on by serious provocation occasioned by the victim that is reasonably sufficient to incite the person into using deadly force, shall knowingly:
(1) Cause serious physical harm to another;
(2) Cause or attempt to cause physical harm to another by means of a deadly weapon or dangerous ordnance, as defined in section 2923.11 of the Revised Code.
(B) Whoever violates this section is guilty of aggravated assault, a felony of the fourth degree. If the victim of the offense is a

peace officer, as defined in section 2935.01 of the Revised Code, aggravated assault is a felony of the third degree.

Applying the three-prong lesser included offense test as modified above, although aggravated assault carries a lesser penalty than felonious assault (either a third or fourth degree felony), felonious assault, as statutorily defined, *can* be committed without an aggravated assault also being committed, since the provocation element is lacking in felonious assault. In addition, the third prong of the lesser included offense test is not satisfied because *all* the elements required to prove the greater offense (felonious assault) are required to prove the commission of the lesser offense.

However, as statutorily defined, the offense of aggravated assault is an inferior degree of the indicted offense—felonious assault—since its elements are identical to those of felonious assault, except for the additional mitigating element of serious provocation. In fact, these two offenses contain four possible degrees of decreasing severity. If a peace officer is the victim of felonious assault, the crime is an aggravated felony of the first degree. If the victim is not a peace officer, the crime is an aggravated felony of the second degree. If the elements comprising felonious assault result from serious provocation, and the victim is a peace officer, the crime is a felony of the third degree (and is called aggravated assault). If the elements comprising felonious assault result from serious provocation, and the victim is not a peace officer, the crime is a felony of the fourth degree (and again is called aggravated assault). Thus, in a trial for felonious assault, where the defendant presents sufficient evidence of serious provocation (such that a jury could both reasonably acquit defendant of felonious assault and convict defendant of aggravated assault), an instruction on aggravated assault (as a different degree of felonious assault) *must* be given.

Here, since appellee Deem did not present sufficient evidence of provocation, the instruction on aggravated assault was properly refused. "Provocation, to be serious, must be reasonably sufficient to bring on extreme stress and the provocation must be reasonably sufficient to incite or to arouse the defendant into using deadly force. In determining whether the provocation was reasonably sufficient to incite the defendant into using deadly force, the court must consider the emotional and mental state of the defendant and the conditions and circumstances that surrounded him at the time." *State v. Mabry* (1982), 5 Ohio App. 3d. The only evidence presented at trial of provocation of appellee Deem by the victim was the historically stormy relationship between the two and the alleged "bumping" of Deem's car by the victim with her car. Neither of these remote and minor incidents was reasonably sufficient, as a matter of law, to incite or arouse appellee into repeatedly stabbing the victim, particularly given the time for reflection between the "bumping" and the stabbing, and given the circumstances of appellee's lying in wait for the victim to pass by in her car. Thus, even though aggravated assault is an offense of inferior degree to the indicted crime, an instruction thereon was not supported by the evidence presented in this case, and was properly refused.

Therefore, we reverse the judgment of the court of appeals and reinstate appellee's conviction of felonious assault with a specification of a prior kidnapping conviction.

Judgment Reversed.

SWEENEY, Justice, concurring in syllabus but dissenting from judgment.

I concur in the majority's syllabus law and much of the discussion related thereto in this cause since it clarifies the instances when a charge on a lesser included or inferior degree offense must be given. However, I dissent from the majority's judgment that such instruction was not warranted here on the grounds that appellee did not present sufficient evidence of provocation.

In my view, since the evidence appeared to be conflicting, an instruction on the lesser included or inferior degree offense of aggravated assault should have been given. As this court stated in *State v. Wilkins* (1980), 64 Ohio St. 2d 382, with respect to lesser included offense instructions:

> The persuasiveness of the evidence regarding the lesser included offense is irrelevant. If under any reasonable view of the evidence it is possible for the trier of fact to find the defendant not guilty of the greater offense and guilty of the lesser offense, the instruction on the lesser included offense must be given. The evidence must be considered in the light most favorable to defendant.

Accord *State v. Davis* (1983), 6 Ohio St. 3d 91. I believe that such a guideline is appropriate and is applicable to the cause *sub judice*. Therefore, I would affirm the decision of the court of appeals below.

It should be pointed out that the defendant's expert witness was not permitted to testify before the jury because the trial court found that defendant's assertion of a "complete defense" precluded the expert testimony since it was designed to provide the basis upon which the jury could find the mitigating element of provocation. Hence, the majority's conclusion that the instruction on aggravated assault was properly refused since Deem did not present sufficient evidence of provocation is patently erroneous. Deem was ready, willing and able to present evidence of provocation by way of expert testimony. However, the trial court erroneously prevented the expert evidence of provocation from being submitted to the jury. To deny Deem the benefit of a new trial because he did not present sufficient evidence of provocation to the jury merely compounds the error committed by the trial court, and paints a misleading picture of the proceedings that took place below. One cannot proffer evidence to a jury that one is erroneously prevented from proffering in the first place.

Based on the foregoing, I would affirm the judgment of the court of appeals, and remand the cause for a new trial.

Notes and Questions

1. As the dissent notes in *State v. Deem*, the defendant asserted a "complete defense" claiming that he fled the scene after breaking the victim's window and did not stab her. Do you agree with the trial court's holding that such a defense necessarily precludes the defendant from offering any evidence of adequate provocation? If you were Deem's defense counsel, how would you formulate an argument that reasonably included both defenses?

2. *State v. Torres*, 2002-Ohio-1203, excerpted below, provides examples of conduct that has been found to be sufficient and insufficient provocation for aggravated assault.

> This court has had limited opportunities to examine the issue of reasonable provocation with respect to the mitigating instruction of aggravated assault. One such opportunity occurred in *State v. Gutierrez* (Sept. 21, 1995), Hancock County App. No. 5-95-10, *unreported* where we determined that the defendant did not present sufficient evidence of provocation to warrant an instruction on aggravated assault. In *Gutierrez,* the only evidence of provocation presented at trial was that victim kicked the appellant in the head as the appellant was punching a non-responsive friend of the victim's and only after the appellant did not respond to the victim's requests to stop the punching.
>
> In *State v. Simon* (Oct. 21, 1998), Hancock County App. No. 5-98-14, *unreported* this court affirmed the denial of an instruction on aggravated assault where the defendant-appellant pointed a loaded shotgun at a peace officer who was attempting to execute a valid warrant to remove the defendant-appellant from his ex-wife's home. Not surprisingly, we held that a police officer entering a home with a valid warrant was not sufficient provocation.
>
> In *State v. Coldiron* (March 31, 1993), Auglaize County App. No. 2-92-20, *unreported* the appellant tried to establish serious provocation to mitigate the felonious assault charge to aggravated assault with facts that: (1) the victim had punched him in the jaw almost 5 hours earlier; (2) the victim called him a

punk and shut the door; (3) that he was fearful of the victim's violent propensities; (4) that both he and the victim were intoxicated; (5) the victim had a bottle in his hand when appellant entered into his dark room; and (6) that [] he struck the victim first out of fear that the victim would strike him first. In this case the appellant knocked on door, victim opened then slammed it. Appellant knocked again, victim opened again and this time when the victim opened it the appellant went in swinging. This court held on these facts that there was not sufficient evidence of adequate provocation.***

Our inquiry warrants the examination of cases in which trial courts deemed that there *was* sufficient provocation to warrant an instruction on aggravated assault. In *State v. Farley* (Aug. 25, 1995), Auglaize County App. No. 2-95-8, *unreported* the appellant was charged with felonious assault but convicted of aggravated assault. There, the appellant and the victim were involved in two work place disputes over missing equipment. The second confrontation turned violent after the victim and others taunted the appellant by calling him a "cry baby" and "dumb hillbilly." Further insults were exchanged between the parties until the victim pulled the appellant off of his forklift and the two began physically fighting. Eventually the two men were separated momentarily until the victim charged the appellant again. The co-worker broke the men up for a second time. At this time, the appellant retrieved a knife from his forklift and cut the victim on the forearm. In *Farley* the victim came after the defendant twice before the defendant resorted to deadly force. That was enough for the trial court to allow the instruction on aggravated assault.

3. In light of the previous examples of conduct found to be adequate provocation, do you agree with the majority in *Deem* that the defendant was not entitled to an instruction on aggravated assault?

Chapter 11
Sexual Assault

A. Background

At common law, rape was both a general intent crime and a capital offense. Rape was defined as unlawful sexual intercourse with a female, not one's wife, forcibly and without her consent. Not surprisingly, modern day statutes have dramatically altered the common law definition of rape. First, the marital rape exception has either been eliminated or dramatically altered. Second, males, as well as females, can be victims of rape. Third, the physical resistance requirement, which arose from the "without her consent" element, was removed. Fourth, in addition to covering genital copulation, most rape or sexual assault statutes also cover anal and oral copulation and, in some instances, other methods of penetration. These changes, among other things, have led states to categorize rape or sexual assault into degrees or separate crimes depending on the conduct of the criminal defendant. For example, in addition to rape, Ohio has crimes such as sexual battery, unlawful sexual conduct with a minor, gross sexual imposition, and sexual imposition.

Besides the modifications to criminal statutes, evidentiary changes were also made. The common law rule requiring corroboration of the victim's testimony has been eliminated. In addition, most states have created rape shield statutes that dramatically limit the introduction of evidence about the victim's prior sexual history. *Lewis v. Wilkinson,* discussed at the end of this chapter, examines Ohio's rape shield statute. Rape shield laws were passed because defense attorneys would routinely attempt to offer evidence of the victim's sexual reputation and prior sexual experiences to suggest that the victim consented to the sex act or was merely fabricating a claim of rape.

Two elements that are routinely challenged in sexual assault cases are "force" and "consent". *State v. El-Berri* directly addresses the question of consent and also examines how force relates to consent. The chapter then examines affirmative consent and the marital rape exception. The third case in this chapter, *In re D.B.,* explores the constitutional issues that may arise with statutory rape.

B. Force

State v. El-Berri, 2008 WL 2764873 (Ohio Ct. App. 2008)

MARY EILEEN KILBANE, J.

Defendant-appellant Tamer El-Berri (El-Berri) appeals his convictions for rape and kidnapping. For the following reasons, we affirm in part, reverse in part and remand.

On January 4, 2006, a Cuyahoga County Grand Jury indicted El-Berri on one count of kidnapping with a sexual motivation specification attached and one count of rape.

The facts giving rise to the instant case occurred in the late evening on December 22, 2004. The sixteen-year-old victim worked at El-Berri's cellular phone business located at Great Northern Mall. There was a heavy snowfall that night and, at the close of the victim's shift, El-Berri offered to drive the victim home as she lacked experience driving in snow storms. Brenda Carmak (Carmak), the victim's mother, consented because El-Berri and his girlfriend, Nicolet Arcuri (Arcuri), were family friends.

On the night in question, instead of taking the victim directly home, El-Berri drove past her exit and went to his home. While there, El-Berri proceeded to remove the victim's clothes, forced her over the couch, and engaged in vaginal intercourse with her against her will.

The victim arrived home later that evening via taxi cab because El-Berri's motor vehicle became stuck in the snow. Carmak described the victim as looking "white as a ghost, scared to death." The victim told Carmak that El-Berri raped her. Carmak took the victim to the hospital where vaginal swabs confirmed the presence of seminal fluid, although testing was unable to produce a male DNA profile.

On January 2, 2007, the case proceeded to jury trial. On January 11, 2007, the jury returned its verdict and found El-Berri guilty of kidnapping with a sexual motivation specification and guilty of rape.

On February 1, 2007, the trial court sentenced El-Berri to seven years of imprisonment for kidnapping and seven years of imprisonment for rape, counts to be served concurrently. The trial court also conducted a House Bill 180 hearing and designated El-Berri a sexually oriented offender.

On February 26, 2007, El-Berri filed a notice of appeal and asserted four assignments of error for our review.***

Pursuant to R.C. 2907.02(A)(2), there is *sufficient* evidence that El-Berri purposely compelled the victim to submit by force. The victim's testimony included: she did not consent to having sexual intercourse with El-Berri; El-Berri removed her clothes; he forced her onto the couch; and El-Berri engaged in vaginal intercourse with her against her will. Force "need not be overt and physically brutal, but can be subtle and psychological" depending on the age of the victim and relationship to the parties. *State v. Eskridge* (1988), 38 Ohio St. 3d 56. (Further holding that, "as long as it can be shown that the rape victim's will was overcome by fear or duress, the forcible element of rape can be established.") *Id.* at 59. Other witnesses, who observed the victim shortly after the incident, described that "[s]he looked white as a ghost, scared to death."

At the time of the offense, the victim was a sixteen-year-old minor child, while El-Berri was fifteen years her senior. In addition, El-Berri was the victim's employer and a family friend, whereby a factfinder could determine that he occupied a position of authority over the victim. Indeed, the evidence shows that the victim (and her mother) entrusted El-Berri to drive her home because of a heavy snow storm and her lack of experience with driving. Instead of taking her home, El-Berri took the victim to his house, where he subjected her to sexual intercourse and then sent her home in a taxicab.

The victim also stated that she was very scared and that she didn't know what El-Berri was going to do to her. She clearly testified that she did not want to have any kind of sexual relations with El-Berri that night. Under the sufficiency standard, we are bound to accept that testimony as true and simply cannot reverse a conviction for insufficiency by disregarding or disbelieving evidence. The weight and credibility of that testimony was for the trier of fact to decide.

The dissent's comprehensive survey of the record and weighing of the evidence reflects a manifest weight analysis, rather than one of sufficiency. In essence, the dissent concludes that absent some overt evidence of resistance a rape could not have occurred between a thirty-one-year-old employer and his sixteen-year-old employee. But to reach this conclusion, the dissent rejects the reasonable inference that the victim submitted because she was, as she said, "scared." El-Berri's position of authority as her boss and the disparity in their ages cannot be discounted where the law is that the "force and violence necessary to commit the crime of rape depends on the age, size, and strength of the parties and their relation to each other." *Eskridge,* at paragraph one of the syllabus. While the dissent advances a strong argument for reaching a different conclusion on these points than the jury did, it is not within our province to weigh and resolve these facts when conducting a sufficiency analysis. The record also supports El-Berri's conviction for kidnapping under R.C. 2905.01(A)(4) with a sufficiency of the evidence, which provides that no person, "by force, threat, or deception," shall "remove another from the place where the other person is found or restrain the liberty of the other person" to engage in sexual activity against the victim's will.

The dissent finds insufficient evidence in that the victim's initial agreement to the detour and that he asked her permission to stop at his home as being dispositive of the kidnapping by deception charge. It seems unlikely there would be a case where a person accused of kidnapping someone by deception would have explicitly advised the victim of such an intent, nor would the unwitting victim's initial agreement to the detour alter an undisclosed, subjective ill-intent. Although the victim willingly allowed El-Berri to drive her home, he did not do so. Instead, he took her to his house for the alleged purpose of getting "something." Given the course of events that ensued, *a rational trier of fact could glean from the evidence* that El-Berri's true purpose was not to get anything, but to lure the victim to his house in order to engage in sexual activity with the victim against her will. See, e.g., *State v. Ware* (1980), 63 Ohio St. 2d 84. Accordingly, there is evidence from which a rational trier of fact could conclude that El-Berri committed kidnapping by deception. There is also evidence that El-Berri used force to restrain the victim when he bent her over the couch in order to engage in sexual intercourse with her. Further, in viewing the evidence in a light most favorable to the State, there is sufficient evidence to sustain El-Berri's conviction for rape and kidnapping. Thus, the trial court did not err when it denied El-Berri's Crim. R. 29 motion for acquittal.

El-Berri's first assignment of error is overruled.

MELODY J. STEWART, J., Dissenting.

I respectfully dissent from the majority decision affirming El-Berri's convictions for rape and kidnapping. The facts do not show that he compelled the victim to submit by force or threat of force, neither do they show that he restrained her liberty in any manner. Although El-Berri's conduct with a minor whom he employed was wholly inappropriate and distasteful to say the least, it did not support a finding of guilt on the charged offenses.

A more complete recitation of the facts shows that at trial, the victim's mother testified that her boyfriend owned a store where she and her daughter, the victim, worked. The boyfriend leased a portion of the store to a cell phone company owned and operated by El-Berri and his girlfriend. The victim's mother said that she and the girlfriend became friendly, and that she would sometimes fill in at the cell phone store for the girlfriend. The mother said that El-Berri had trained the victim in the cell phone business and that he employed her at the boyfriend's store.

In December 2004, El-Berri assigned the victim to work at one of his stores located in a shopping mall. On the night of the incident, El-Berri scheduled the victim to work until 11:00 p.m. A heavy snow was falling that night and the victim's mother became concerned about the victim's ability to drive in poor weather. In its recitation of the facts, the majority states that "El-Berri offered to drive the victim home as she lacked experience driving in snow storms." This statement is not exactly correct. It is undisputed that the mother called the victim to see if she wanted to be picked up. The mother testified that the victim told her El-Berri would give her a ride home; the victim testified that her mother asked her if El-Berri would give her a ride.

As they traveled on the interstate, El-Berri told the victim that he needed to stop by his house to get something. The victim testified that El-Berri asked her if he could make a detour to his house in order to get something, and that she told El-Berri it was "okay."

When he pulled up to the house, El-Berri asked the victim if she wanted to come in with him. She agreed to do so. When they entered the house, El-Berri went into another room while the victim remained in the kitchen. El-Berri called for the victim to join him. She went into the living room and El-Berri started to rub her back. She did not say anything while he did this. He then bent her over the couch and started to unbutton her pants. During her testimony, she said that she was "scared" when asked what her thoughts were at the time, but she did not say anything to El-Berri. She testified that El-Berri pulled down her pants and underwear and then "put his penis in [her] vagina." She did not recall how long his penis was in her vagina, but when he removed his penis, El-Berri asked her if she was ready to go. She replied that she was, pulled her clothes up and left with him. The victim testified that as they were leaving, El-Berri's car became stuck in the snow. Unable to move the car, he called for a cab and both she and El-Berri went back in the house to wait. The victim stated that it took awhile for the cab to arrive, and neither she nor El-Berri said anything to each other during the wait.

When the cab arrived, El-Berri gave the victim money to pay the fare. The victim entered the cab and gave the driver directions to her house. At the same time, the mother, having grown concerned because the victim had not arrived home, called the victim's cell phone and asked where she was. The victim told her she was on her way home in a cab. When asked, "Did your mom want to know why you were in a cab," the victim responded, "I told her I would talk to her when I get home."

When the victim arrived home, she learned that her mother was talking on the telephone with El-Berri's girlfriend. The victim went into a bedroom and her mother handed the telephone to her. The victim briefly spoke with the girlfriend. The mother testified that the two argued on the phone. However, during cross-examination, the victim indicated that she and the girlfriend did not argue at all. Furthermore, when asked, "It was just a pleasant conversation, you told her you are with Tamer and that was that, right?" The victim answered, "yes." When she concluded the telephone call, the victim stated that she told her mother "what happened" with El-Berri.

The direct examination went as follows:

Q. Did you tell your mom, once the phone conversation stopped—when you got home your mom was on the phone. Then there came a time when your mom was no longer on the phone. Okay?

> After your mom was no longer on the phone did you tell your mom what happened?
>
> A. Yes.
>
> Q. How did that come about?
>
> A. I don't remember. I just remember telling her.
>
> Q. Do you remember what you told your mom?
>
> A. I told her what happened.
>
> Q. Back at Tamer's house?
>
> A. Yes.

The mother and her boyfriend then drove to El-Berri's house to confront him. The mother testified that the girlfriend answered the door and said to her, "you better not have your f***ing daughter with you." The mother angrily confronted El-Berri as he stood in the doorway and asked him "how could he betray me." The mother testified that her boyfriend said something, however, what was said is not in the record. Whatever the boyfriend stated, the mother testified that El-Berri said, "it is not like he was the first one." The mother stated that El-Berri invited them in to talk, but she refused.

The mother and her boyfriend returned home and the mother took the victim to the hospital emergency room. Results from a rape kit revealed the presence of seminal fluid on vaginal swabs, rectal swabs and the victim's underwear, but no semen was found on the vaginal smear slide, the rectal smear slide, the oral smear slide, the oral swabs, or the skin swabs. The source of the seminal fluid could not be determined as testing was unable to produce a male DNA profile. A record from the hospital emergency room contained an account of events that stated, "when the boss's [girlfriend] asked [the victim] if the patient had 'slept with Tamer' the patient said yes."

For his defense, El-Berri offered the testimony of the girlfriend who also lived with El-Berri. She stated that she ended her relationship with El-Berri immediately after the incident. She said that she had developed a close relationship with both the victim and her mother, and thought of herself and the victim as "almost best friends" and that the victim would tell others that they were "sisters" because they looked so much alike. The girlfriend testified that during the week before the incident occurred, and apparently coinciding with the victim's assignment to the mall location, she noticed El-Berri acting "a little weird" and staying longer at work than normal. While at her mother's house on the night in question, the girlfriend became concerned when El-Berri was not home by midnight, so she called the victim's mother to inquire into the victim's whereabouts. The victim's mother told the girlfriend that the victim was working with El-Berri.

The girlfriend said that this was when she first learned that the victim had been working at the mall with El-Berri, and it aroused her suspicions. Later that evening, she again called the mother to find out if the victim had come home, thinking that if the victim had arrived home, it meant that El-Berri likewise should be home. The girlfriend and the victim's mother were on the telephone when the victim's cab arrived. The girlfriend asked the mother to go to the cab driver and ask him where he had picked up the victim. When told that the cab had come from El-Berri's house, it confirmed the girlfriend's suspicions that El-Berri and the victim were having an affair. At that point, the girlfriend asked to speak with the victim and told her to admit that she was having an affair with El-Berri. The victim admitted to the girlfriend that she had an affair with El-Berri, but said that they only had sex one time.

I

At common law, the crime of rape was defined as "the unlawful carnal knowledge, by a man, of a woman, forcibly and against her will." *Smith v. State* (1861), 12 Ohio St. 466, 470. The courts interpreted rape as requiring proof of certain conduct by both the accused and the victim.

"Because 'against her will' is synonymous with 'without her consent,' many jurisdictions substituted the latter term. The prosecution, therefore, in order to satisfy its burden of proving all of the elements of the crime charged, had to establish both the victim's lack of consent and the defendant's use of force. The focus on the conduct of both the victim and the defendant resulted in the rule that the victim had to prove 'resistance to the utmost' to establish rape. Absent such resistance, rape was not established, notwithstanding evidence of the use of force." Wilk, Expert Testimony on Rape Trauma Syndrome: Admissibility and Effective Use in Criminal Rape Prosecution (1984), 33 Am. U. L. Rev. 417, 420-421. See, also, *State v. Driscoll* (1922), 106 Ohio St. 33, 40.

A drawback of the "consent" requirement was that it tended to encourage a focus on the complainant's state of mind, and evidence of her prior sexual experience was often used to insinuate that she wanted to have sex. Abrams, Hearing the Call of Stories (1991), 79 Cal. L. Rev. 971, 1033-1034. To prevent such tactics, many modern statutes, guided by the Modern Penal Code, eliminated the express requirements of unwillingness or nonconsent. The drafters explained that the Code's approach was not that "consent by the victim is irrelevant or that inquiry into the level of resistance by the victim cannot or should not be made. Compulsion plainly implies non-consent ***." Model Penal Code, Section 213.1, comment, at 301-306. One commentator has stated that under the Model Penal Code approach:

> The resistance standard is rejected where force is proved, but "resistance by a woman of ordinary resolution" is the statutory standard used to define Gross Sexual Imposition, where the force exerted by the defendant is not an element. Thus, while

the drafters intended to focus primarily on the actions of the defendant, they continued to stress the importance of the victim's non-consent. The drafters noted that "the possibility of consent by the victim, even in the face of conduct that may give some evidence of overreaching, cannot be ignored," and echoed the concern of other commentators concerning the ambivalence of women toward forceful sexual intercourse. It was therefore *clearly intended* that the language *"compels [the victim] to submit by force" includes proof of the victim's non-consent.* (Emphasis added.)

Ohio modeled its rape statute on the Model Penal Code. As applicable to this case, R.C. 2907.02(A)(2) states that no person shall engage in sexual conduct with another when "the offender purposely compels the other person to submit by force or threat of force." A defendant purposely compels a victim to submit by force or threat of force when the defendant uses physical force against the victim, or creates the belief that physical force will be used if the victim does not submit. *State v. Schaim,* 65 Ohio St. 3d 51. Depending on age and relationship, force "need not be overt and physically brutal, but can be subtle and psychological." *State v. Eskridge* (1988), 38 Ohio St. 3d 56. Physical resistance must no longer be shown by the victim. See R.C. 2907.02(C) ("A victim need not prove physical resistance to the offender in prosecutions under this section.").

Lack of consent is no longer an express element of rape. Nevertheless, there is an undeniable interplay between the concepts of resistance and consent. R.C. 2907.03(C) states only that the victim does not have to prove "physical" resistance to the defendant. This is not the same as saying that no resistance of any kind is required. With certain exceptions addressed shortly, if the use of force or threat of force is not apparent from the defendant's conduct, there must be some evidence of lack of consent or resistance to show that the defendant "purposely compel[led]" the other person to submit. See R.C. 2907.02(A)(2). Absent this showing, there would be no evidence that the defendant had the mens rea to cause the victim to capitulate. If the victim does nothing to communicate, either verbally or nonverbally, a lack of consent, a defendant cannot be found to have compelled the victim to submit to the sexual conduct. A victim must affirmatively convey some indicia of non-consent as a predicate to a finding that the victim had been, in the absence of any force or threat of force, compelled to submit to the sexual conduct.

I am aware that there are proponents of the concept of "affirmative consent." These advocates suggest that in the absence of express words of consent, the victim must be deemed to be non-consenting. See, generally, Note, Addressing Acquaintance Rape: The New Direction of the Rape Law Reform Movement (1995), 69 St. John's L. Rev. 291, 310-312. This standard, however, is inconsistent with R.C. 2907.02(A)(2), which requires the offender to have purpose to compel the other person to submit to sexual conduct by force or threat of force. A standard that would, in the absence of force or threat of force, allow a victim to say nothing or manifest no form of resistance during the act but later voice her lack of consent, would fail as a matter of law under circumstances like those presented here because the defendant could not know that compulsion had been used against the victim.

II

The dispositive question is whether, in the absence of any evidence relating to force or the threat of force, El-Berri compelled the victim to engage in sexual conduct with him. The majority's discussion of the facts going to the elements of the offense is incomplete and belies the victim's own testimony. It offers no facts to show any force or threat of force used against the victim, and ignores significant testimony by the victim which showed that at all events she never communicated, in any manner whatsoever, that she did not consent to El-Berri's advances.

During direct examination by the state, the victim said that she asked El-Berri for a ride home, agreed to detour to his house, and further accepted his invitation to enter his house. When asked whether she said anything to El-Berri as he rubbed her back, the victim at first said, "I don't remember," and when asked again, she said "no." When asked whether she said anything to El-Berri as he began to remove her pants and underwear, she said "no." Although she testified that she was "scared" as El-Berri did these things, when asked if there was any reason why she did not say anything at the time, the victim replied, "No. I don't know." Even though she claimed that she did not voluntarily bend over the couch, she continued to remain silent throughout. After referencing the specific act of penetration, the state asked the victim, "[i]s there any reason why you didn't say anything to him?" She replied, "I don't know." The testimony shows that her only word to him during and after the incident was "yes" when asked "if she was ready to go."

The victim's cross-examination further confirmed her lack of communication throughout the incident:

> Q. And you told the prosecutor that he began rubbing your back, correct?
> A. Yes.
> Q. And you didn't say anything, right?
> A. Right.
> Q. And then he basically started removing your pants?
> A. Yes.

> Q. And, again, you indicated to the prosecutor that you didn't say anything?
> A. Right.

After questioning the victim regarding how El-Berri penetrated her, the defense asked the following:

> Q. Again, you never said anything to him while he was doing this, correct?
> A. Right.
> Q. And you knew Tamer, right?
> A. Yes.
> Q. You have known him for a while, right?
> A. Right.
> Q. Yet you never said Tamer, what are you doing?
> A. No, I didn't.
> Q. Never said Tamer, I don't want to do this?
> A. No.
> Q. Never said Tamer, hey, [your girlfriend] and I are friends and if she finds out we are all going to be in trouble. Do you ever say that?
> A. No.
> Q. Did it ever occur to you?
> A. Yes.

At no point in any of the victim's testimony does it show that El-Berri used physical force of any kind to engage in sexual conduct. Neither is there any evidence from which a reasonable trier of fact could find that El-Berri compelled the victim through nonphysical means or by the threat of force. The victim gave no verbal objection to his actions, nor did she engage in any form of nonverbal conduct, hesitation, or resistance to indicate that she did not consent to El-Berri's actions. Likewise, the state offered no evidence to show that El-Berri said anything coercive or threatening to the victim in the moments leading up to the sexual conduct.

While testifying, the victim stated that she was "scared" during the incident. However, her testimony does not indicate what she was afraid of or why she was scared. Unlike her earlier testimony where she specifically explains how she "was scared to drive in the snow," she did not testify that she was scared of El-Berri, scared that he might harm her or of what he might do to her, scared of losing her job, or scared of his retaliating against her. She may very well have been scared of having intercourse or scared of El-Berri's girlfriend coming home or scared of the unknown. All of these possibilities are plausible based on the evidence. The majority erroneously concludes that the victim's acknowledgment that she had been scared during the incident was sufficient to show that El-Berri used force or the threat of force to compel her to submit. The majority's conclusion is a non sequitur because it does not necessarily follow that a person is being forced or compelled to do anything just because she is scared. Furthermore, the victim did not testify in any manner which would indicate that El-Berri knew she was afraid. If there had been any testimony to the effect that the victim's fear was manifest in any form or fashion, that evidence could be deemed sufficient to communicate to El-Berri that he was compelling the victim's submission to his advances. But the victim's testimony did not indicate that her fear, whatever its origin, was apparent or obvious to El-Berri. By her own admission, she wordlessly allowed him to escalate the encounter and engage in sex with her.

This analysis is not to suggest what the victim should or should not have done under the circumstances. But accepting her testimony as true, no reasonable trier of fact could conclude that there was evidence to show El-Berri knew that the victim did not consent to his actions. A defendant cannot be found to have compelled another to submit by force or threat of force when the evidence fails to show that the victim gave the defendant reason to know that she was being compelled. Under the circumstances of a case like this one, without any affirmative evidence showing lack of consent, a defendant will have no reason to know that his advances are unwelcome and therefore non-consensual.

The majority finds compelling as evidence of the element of force the victim's statement that El-Berri "bent" her over the couch to have sex with her. The victim's use of the word "bent," standing alone, does not establish that El-Berri used force. Indeed, the most detailed account of his actions is given by the victim's testimony in response to being asked to describe the scenario where she states, "Like he put my arms on the couch and bent me over." A fair reading of the testimony shows that El-Berri positioned her over the couch rather than forced her over it against her will as the majority. This conclusion is consistent with the absence of any other testimony to show that El-Berri used force of any kind during this part of their encounter. For each action he made, whether rubbing her back, removing her clothes or bending her over the couch, the victim made no outward manifestation whatsoever that any of these actions were unwanted or that she was scared. A mere reference to being bent over the couch does not amount to force under these circumstances.

The majority likewise errs by accepting the argument that the victim was only 16 and one-half years old at the time and could not be expected to have the emotional or practical experience necessary to deal with the situation that was presented in this case.

In *State v. Eskridge* (1988), 38 Ohio St. 3d 56, Eskridge was convicted of raping his four-year-old daughter and sentenced to life imprisonment on a finding that he used force during the commission of the rape. This court reversed the life sentence because it concluded that the state failed to present any evidence that Eskridge used force. The supreme court reversed this court, stating in paragraph one of the syllabus that "[t]he force and violence necessary to commit the crime of rape depends upon the age, size and strength of the parties and their relation to each other. With the filial obligation of obedience to a parent, the same degree of force and violence may not be required upon a person of tender years, as would be required were the parties more nearly equal in age, size and strength." In reaching this conclusion, the supreme court noted that the element of force as charged in a rape case "need not be overt and physically brutal, but can be subtle and psychological." *Id.* at 58-59.

In *State v. Schaim,* 65 Ohio St. 3d 5, the supreme court considered an appeal in which Schaim had been convicted of repeatedly demanding sex from his 19-year-old daughter in exchange for granting her certain privileges, even though there had been no proof of force. The state argued that a pattern of incest could suffice to establish the force element. The supreme court rejected this argument, explaining that:

> *State v. Eskridge* is based solely on the recognition of the amount of control that parents have over their children, particularly young children. Every detail of a child's life is controlled by a parent, and a four-year-old child knows that disobedience will be punished, whether by corporal punishment or an alternative form of discipline. Because of the child's dependence on his or her parents, a child of tender years has no real power to resist his or her parent's command, and every command contains an implicit threat of punishment for failure to obey. Under these circumstances, a minimal degree of force will satisfy the elements of forcible rape.

Id., paragraph one of the syllabus.

> The same rationale does not apply to an adult. No matter how reprehensible the defendant's alleged conduct, a woman over the age of majority is not compelled to submit to her father in the same manner as is a four-year-old girl. She is no longer completely dependent on her parents, and is more nearly their equal in size, strength, and mental resources. Although we are aware of the devastating effects of incest on its victims, and are sympathetic to the victim whose will to resist has been overcome by a prolonged pattern of abuse, we reluctantly conclude that a pattern of incest is not always a substitute for the element of force required by R.C. 2907.02(A)(2). A defendant purposely

compels another to submit to sexual conduct by force or threat of force if the defendant uses physical force against that person, or creates the belief that physical force will be used if the victim does not submit. A threat of force can be inferred from the circumstances surrounding sexual conduct, but a pattern of incest will not substitute for the element of force where the state introduces no evidence that an adult victim believed that the defendant might use physical force against her.

Id. at 55.

The victim in this appeal was 16 and one-half years old at the time of the incident, falling between the *Eskridge* "child of tender years" and the *Schaim* "woman over the age of majority." She was a sophomore in high school, had obtained her driver's license five months before the events in this case, worked, and at all times during the night of the incident had her cellular telephone with her. The victim had no filial relationship with El-Berri. She met El-Berri because he leased retail space in a store owned by her parents. She developed a close friendship with El-Berri's girlfriend and, on one or two occasions, even socialized with the girlfriend and El-Berri. When the girlfriend worked at the store owned by the victim's parents, the victim spent so much time with her that she became knowledgeable about El-Berri's business. He then hired her to work at his retail space located inside the store owned by the victim's parents, although that arrangement appeared to be informal. The victim testified that she earned a commission on each cell phone that she sold and El-Berri paid her in cash. The victim was unclear as to exactly how long she had worked at El-Berri's mall location, saying that it was "more than a week."

Unlike the four-year-old victim of incest in *Eskridge,* there is no evidence in this case to show or suggest that El-Berri had any type of control over the victim. Likewise, there was no evidence to show that the victim's age caused her to be so dependent on El-Berri that she capitulated to his advances because of fear or duress. The evidence shows that the victim was very friendly with El-Berri and his girlfriend and apparently comfortable enough around El-Berri to 1) ask him to drive her home, 2) consent to stopping at his house, 3) agree to go inside with him, and 4) go back inside the house with him to wait for a cab after the sexual encounter had occurred. Throughout all of the events in his house that led to the sexual encounter, the victim's only response to why she did not object to El-Berri's advances was "I don't know." This testimony was insufficient to show the kind of subtle coercion addressed in *Eskridge.* The victim gave no outward indication of her state of mind, and admitted that she said nothing to El-Berri. She gave no nonverbal communication, either by hesitating, resisting or showing her fear, to communicate her lack of consent. Importantly, at no point in her testimony did the victim attribute her silence to being "scared." As events escalated, the victim remained silent, giving El-Berri no indication that his actions were unwanted. With the absence of force or subtle coercion, El-Berri could not know that his advances were unwelcome. To find otherwise would make the actions of any initiator in a sexual encounter no different from those of a rapist.

III

With regard to the kidnapping count, I find no evidence to support the majority's assertion that El-Berri's "true purpose" was to "lure the victim to his house in order to engage in sexual activity with the victim against her will." Ante at 5.

Viewing the evidence in a light most favorable to the state shows that the victim, or her mother, asked El-Berri to give her a ride home. He drove past her exit on the freeway, and told her that he was "going to stop at his house and get something." When asked if that was "okay" with her, the victim said "yes." When they arrived at his house, El-Berri "asked me if I was going to come in. I said sure." They entered through the kitchen door. El-Berri walked through the kitchen and entered a different room—either the bedroom or the living room. The victim remained in the kitchen until he called for her to join him. The victim walked into the living room and El-Berri said something to her, but she could not recall what he said. He then began rubbing her back.

None of this evidence shows that El-Berri restrained the victim's liberty. As noted in the discussion of the rape count, El-Berri did not use any physical force or restraint against the victim. To the contrary, he asked for the victim's permission to stop at the house and she consented to enter. There is simply no evidence to show that El-Berri restrained the victim's liberty at any point in time.

The majority appears to conclude that El-Berri deceived the victim by bringing her to his house under pretense while all along intending to sexually assault her.

The word "deception" is not defined in R.C. Chapter 2905. However, R.C. 2913.01(A) defines "deception" as "knowingly deceiving another or causing another to be deceived by any false or misleading representation, *** or by any other conduct, act, or omission that creates, confirms, or perpetuates a false impression in another, including a false impression as to law, value, state of mind, or other objective or subjective fact." Although this definition does not expressly apply to R.C. Chapter 2905, it nonetheless conforms to the generally-accepted meaning of the word "deception," so I apply it here. See R.C. 1.42; *State v. Young* (July 28, 1992), Meigs App. No. 458.

The majority's assertion that El-Berri "lured" the victim to his house in order to engage in "sexual activity with the victim against her will" finds absolutely no support in the record. There is no evidence of any kind to show what El-Berri's intentions were as they drove from the mall. Even if one assumes that he did hope to engage in sexual activity with the victim, the trial testimony did not show that he intended to do so against her will. To the contrary, he asked for and received the victim's permission to stop at his house. Once at the house, he asked her if she wanted to come inside without any threat or hint of force or duress. Whatever El-Berri's intentions may have been, there is no evidence to show that he deceived the victim into entering his house.

The only evidence to show El-Berri's purpose in going to his house was the victim's testimony that he needed to stop by his house to get something. The victim did not know or did not say what El-Berri needed to retrieve from the house, but there is no question that he entered a least one other room of the house while she remained standing in the kitchen. This conduct at least supports the possibility that he accomplished his purpose of retrieving something from his house. At all events, El-Berri made no demonstrably false statements to the victim, and she willingly agreed to accompany him regardless of any unstated ulterior motive he may have had.

IV

Having reviewed all the evidence in a light most favorable to the state, I find as a matter of law that the state failed to prove all the elements of rape and kidnapping beyond a reasonable doubt. Although there are jurisdictions that make it unlawful for someone of El-Berri's age to have sexual intercourse with a 16-year-old, Ohio is not one of those jurisdictions. With the absence of force or threat of force, the state could only prove that a rape occurred by offering evidence that the victim did not consent to engaging in sexual conduct with El-Berri and that she communicated her lack of consent to him. The state failed to elicit any testimony from the victim showing that she communicated her lack of consent to El-Berri. As despicable as El-Berri's conduct on the night of this incident may be viewed, I find the evidence legally insufficient to establish the rape and kidnapping counts. I therefore dissent.

Notes and Questions

1. Is the dissent in *State v. El-Berri* attempting to resurrect the resistance standard? In the absence of any evidence relating to force or the threat of force, should the prosecution be required to show that the victim did not consent?

2. Was it sufficient in *El-Berri* that the victim was "scared"? Why or why not? Does it surprise you that neither the prosecution nor the defense asked the victim what she was scared of? It may go back to the old adage that a lawyer should never ask a question that she doesn't know the answer to.

3. Why did the dissent in *El-Berri* feel the need to offer "a more complete recitation of the facts"? What facts, if any, presented by the dissent did you find compelling with respect to determining El-Berri's guilt or innocence?

4. Pursuant to R.C. 2907.02, "[n]o person shall engage in sexual conduct with another when the offender purposely compels the other person to submit by force or threat of force." The Ohio Supreme Court has gone on to say, "force and violence necessary to commit the crime of rape depends on the age, size, and strength of the parties and their relation to each other." *State v. Eskridge*, 38 Ohio St. 3d 56 (1988). With this said, do you think it would matter if the victim in *El Berri* was 17 rather than 16 and a half? What about 18?

5. In order to convict El-Berri, the prosecution had to prove that the defendant compelled the victim to engage in sexual conduct by force or threat of force. If you had to prove the "force" element, what evidence would you offer?

6. In addition to engaging in sexual conduct through force or threat of force, a criminal defendant may not use fraud to obtain consent. Generally speaking, fraud in factum will remove or vitiate the victim's consent. For example, a doctor informs his patient that he is performing a medical procedure but in reality engages in sexual intercourse with the patient. In contrast, fraud in the inducement will not vitiate consent because the victim knows that she is consenting to the act and is only misled as to the identity of her sexual partner. For example, the defendant lies about himself or his identity in order to obtain consent from the victim.

C. Affirmative Consent

Jonathan Witmer-Rich, *Unpacking Affirmative Consent: Not as Great as You Hope, Not as Bad as You Fear*, 49 Tex. Tech. L. Rev 57 (2016)

The main difficulty in many contested cases of rape or sexual assault is how to interpret various signals—verbal and nonverbal—sent between the parties to the encounter. The dispute is not over whether a signal was sent at all, and thus, requiring affirmative consent does not assist with or change that difficult task. That is because the problem is not in determining whether *some* affirmative signal was sent but in determining whether the combination of words and conduct, on balance and in context, indicated agreement to sex.

Definitions of affirmative consent vary somewhat, but they can be categorized conceptually into two main groups: those that require some affirmative signal of consent and those that additionally require that consent be unambiguous or clearly expressed.***

The American Law Institute (ALI) is currently considering revisions to the rape and sexual assault provisions of the Model Penal Code. The discussion draft dated April 28, 2015 included an affirmative consent provision defined as follows: "'Consent' means a person's positive agreement, communicated by either words or actions, to engage in a specific act of sexual penetration or sexual contact."***

A number of university policies go further than the standards set forth above and also include language requiring that affirmative consent be unambiguous or clear.***

For example, the University of Minnesota's policy defines affirmative consent as "informed, freely and affirmatively communicated willingness to participate in sexual activity that is expressed by clear and unambiguous words or actions." The Yale University policy requires a "positive, unambiguous, and voluntary agreement to engage in specific sexual activity throughout a sexual encounter. Consent cannot be inferred from the absence of a 'no'; a clear 'yes,' verbal or otherwise, is necessary." Other universities similarly use language requiring unambiguous consent.

A. "YES MEANS YES" IS A SLOGAN, NOT A LEGAL STANDARD

The catchphrase of affirmative consent is "yes means yes." This is a slogan, not a legal standard.

Commentators regularly affiliate the concept of affirmative consent with the phrase "yes means yes." Janet Napolitano, the president of the University of California system, summed up her adoption of an affirmative consent policy for the University of California by explaining, "Put simply, only yes means yes."

Taken as a slogan, "yes means yes" seems a worthwhile and valuable educational tool. The "yes means yes" slogan is designed to encourage all parties to a sexual encounter (particularly college students, at whom much of the advocacy is aimed) to make sure that their partner has freely indicated that he or she wants to have sex. It is designed to discourage persons from assuming that consent is present unless their partner objects and instead to encourage them to get an affirmative signal of agreement.

An educational slogan is not the same thing as a legal standard, however, and "yes means yes" is the former, not the latter. First, none of the affirmative consent policies actually define affirmative consent as "only yes means yes."

If it were a legal standard, the claim that "only yes means yes" could not be taken literally. None of the existing affirmative consent standards require participants in sexual activity to use the word "yes." Thus, the claim that "only yes means yes" does not mean that consent can be signaled only by using the term "yes."

Another possible interpretation of "yes means yes" is that an agreement to sex must be signaled by some words or conduct that are the equivalent of a "yes." Not many affirmative consent policies actually state this, but a few do. Yale's policy states that "a clear 'yes,' verbal or otherwise, is necessary."

Here, it is important to separate the following two ideas, discussed at greater length in Section III.C: an *affirmative* indication of agreement versus an *unambiguous* indication of agreement. The Yale policy requires both; many policies only require the former. "Yes means yes," as a legal standard, would not require that the indication of agreement be unambiguous, only that it be present.

Finally, as noted in the following Section, affirmative consent policies recognize that the affirmative signal of agreement to sex does not have to be verbal but can be expressed through conduct or words.

The point here is not to criticize the phrase "yes means yes" but to clarify what purpose it serves. It is a slogan and may be an effective slogan and public relations tool. It is not, however, the actual legal standard or legal definition of affirmative consent. Discussions of affirmative consent would benefit from clarity on this point.

B. AFFIRMATIVE CONSENT DOES NOT MEAN "EXPRESS VERBAL AGREEMENT"

Most legal commentators recognize that an affirmative consent standard does not require an express verbal agreement. Michelle Anderson, defending the concept, has noted that affirmative consent can include "verbal or nonverbal agreement." Janet Halley, criticizing the concept, has likewise recognized that California's standard "does not require *express* consent, consent in words" but presumably includes consent "given by conduct." A recent ALI draft of an affirmative consent proposal provided that consent constituted a "positive agreement, communicated by either words or actions." The commentary noted that "[s]ome scholars have urged a requirement of explicit *verbal* assent," but it concluded that this standard "finds no support in existing law and departs too far from current social practice."51 The draft thus "recognizes the social reality that consensual sexual encounters quite frequently are not preceded by an explicit verbal 'yes.'" New Jersey's *M.T.S.* decision, one of the earliest legal sources of an affirmative consent standard, noted that affirmative consent "can be indicated either through words or through actions."

While legal commentators appear to appreciate this point, some journalists and advocates state or strongly imply that affirmative consent requires express verbal agreement. A *New York Magazine* feature on the sex lives of college students claimed affirmative consent meant "every step toward sex being explicitly agreed to with a 'yes.'" One of the California law's cosponsors stated that the California bill means that individuals "must say 'yes.'"

It is easy enough to require express verbal consent if that is the goal— sexual assault can simply be defined as engaging in sexual conduct without express verbal consent. Antioch College received considerable attention in the early 1990s for adopting a policy that did, in fact, require express verbal consent at each stage of a sexual encounter. This approach was heavily criticized and was not adopted by many other schools or jurisdictions. None of the current affirmative consent policies contain this requirement.

C. AFFIRMATIVE CONSENT IS DIFFERENT FROM "UNAMBIGUOUS CONSENT"

The most pervasive misunderstanding of affirmative consent is the notion that affirmative consent necessarily means "unambiguous consent." This is mistaken. Affirmative does not mean unambiguous.

Most affirmative consent policies do not require clear and unambiguous consent, but some of them do. This is a major difference, which has gone largely unnoticed in the literature. Requiring unambiguous consent represents a major change to existing sexual assault law or university policies. Simply requiring affirmative consent does not.

Dictionary definitions of "affirmative" do not support interpreting that word to mean "unambiguous" or "unequivocal." *Random House*'s definitions of affirmative as an adjective include:

> 1. affirming or asserting the truth, validity, or fact of something
> 2. expressing agreement or consent . . . .
> 3. positive; not negative
>
> . . . .
>
> 7. a manner or mode that indicates assent . . . .

Webster's Third New International Dictionary defines affirmative (adjective) as follows:

> [1.] CONFIRMATIVE, RATIFYING
> [2.] asserting a predicate of a subject or of a part of a subject *also*: asserting the truth or validity of a statement . . . contrasted with *negative*
> [3.a.] asserting that the fact is so: declaratory of what exists
>
> . . . .

None of the various definitions indicate that affirmative means unambiguous or unequivocal.

348 | Part III: Crimes Against the Person

In the context of affirmative consent, the term affirmative seems to require some active signal of agreement rather than the absence of an express "no." Thus, Michelle Anderson explained that

> [a]ffirmative consent is the notion that mere passivity or acquiescence to the will of another does not constitute meaningful permission to engage in sexual penetration. Meaningful consent must be active, and a person should have to communicate positive, verbal or nonverbal agreement to engage in penetration before someone else should be allowed to penetrate them.

The contrast here is between some affirmative (or positive) signal versus inferring consent from the absence of any signal (or passivity). This is not the same thing as requiring the affirmative signal also be unequivocal or very clear.

Wisconsin law requires that consent be affirmative—"an affirmative indication of willingness"—but there is no language in the statute or the case law suggesting that affirmative consent must be clear or unambiguous. The same is true in New Jersey—consent must be expressed affirmatively, but there is no case law suggesting that affirmative consent must be clear or unambiguous.

Canada likewise has an affirmative consent standard for sexual assault cases requiring "that the complainant had affirmatively communicated by words or conduct her agreement to engage in sexual activity." At least one commentator characterized this as requiring communication that is "express, explicit, and unambiguous." But the Canadian case law, like that of Wisconsin and New Jersey, does not appear to contain this additional requirement that the consent be unambiguous.***

The failure to be clear about the difference between affirmative and unambiguous consent has resulted in confusion in university affirmative consent policies. Most commentary on the recent trend of affirmative consent policies at colleges and universities is either generally positive or generally negative. These commentators fail to appreciate what appears to be a very considerable difference: some university policies require that consent be affirmative but say nothing about consent being unambiguous, whereas other policies require that consent be both affirmative and unambiguous. Finally, some university policies blend the two approaches in a particularly confusing way.

D. AFFIRMATIVE CONSENT AND THE ONGOING SHIFT FROM "NO" TO "YES"

Advocates of affirmative consent routinely state that under existing law, the complainant must prove some clear act of disagreement ("no"), whereas under an affirmative consent standard, the focus "shifts" to whether the defendant received an affirmative signal of agreement ("yes"). This seems to be another major concern behind the drive for affirmative consent policies.

Several significant clarifications are needed to understand this shift— and to what degree it represents a shift at all.

The first clarification involves distinguishing practice from doctrine. In practice, it may be true that some prosecutors, judges, and juries are reluctant to find guilt in cases involving a complainant who is silent or passive rather than one who affirmatively expresses her nonconsent. This practice question is different, however, from the substance of the existing legal doctrine.

The second clarification is understanding the actual state of the doctrine. Doctrinally, it is no longer generally true to state that the law requires an affirmative expression of nonconsent ("no"). The shift from "no" to "yes" has mostly already occurred, regardless of whether jurisdictions use the phrase "affirmative consent." The change from "no" to "yes" in rape and sexual assault law has been underway for decades as courts have steadily abandoned and rejected any rule that requires the complainant to express a "no" or offer "verbal resistance."

On the first point, it may be true that the criminal justice system sometimes requires the complainant to prove some clear act of disagreement ("no") to proceed with a rape prosecution or conviction. It is difficult to assess how often, as a matter of practice, police, prosecutors, judges, or juries require clear evidence of a "no" from the complainant.

If a complainant explains to police or prosecutors that she did not say anything (and thus did not say "no") during a sexual encounter, then the police or prosecutor may use that fact as a reason not to prosecute the case. Some may refuse to prosecute because they believe that a failure to say "no" means the complainant actually wanted to have sex at the time and only later felt regret. Some may refuse to prosecute because even though they believe the complainant did not consent, they believe (falsely) that the law requires affirmative nonconsent. Some may refuse to prosecute because even though they know that the law does not require affirmative nonconsent, they nonetheless believe that a factfinder (judge or jury) will refuse to convict without clear evidence of nonconsent.

In addition to the role of the police and prosecutor, factfinders (judges or juries) may refuse to convict in a rape or sexual assault case in which the victim does not clearly express her disagreement ("no"). In part, this may stem from confusion about the legal standard because jury instructions in rape and sexual assault cases often do not offer much explanation of what constitutes consent.

A final confounding factor is that in many American jurisdictions, sex without consent *simpliciter* is not a crime. Instead, the prosecution must prove an additional element, such as force or threat of force. Thus, in many cases in which the complainant was passive, the most difficult problem in obtaining a conviction is not the consent requirement but the force or threat of force requirement.

In short, as a description of how the legal process sometimes works, it is no doubt true that in some cases, the complainant must prove some clear act of disagreement for the prosecutor to prosecute the case and obtain a conviction.

In another sense, however, the claim that the law requires an affirmative "no" is false in many jurisdictions—false as a description of the doctrinal law. Some of this is a chronological issue. Traditionally, the law was clear that the prosecution in a rape case had to prove affirmative nonconsent ("no"). The older the case, the more likely for it to reflect this view; more recent decisions have repudiated many of those older cases. A few jurisdictions, such as Idaho, still explicitly require some express verbal or physical resistance to prove forcible rape. And there are a few recent cases suggesting that evidence of the complainant remaining passive and silent as well as failing to resist or manifest nonconsent is insufficient to show nonconsent.

But in recent years, there are many more cases—including cases in jurisdictions that have not adopted affirmative consent standards and that still require both force and nonconsent—in which rape or sexual assault convictions are affirmed on evidence of a purely passive complainant who did not affirmatively register her disagreement. For example, in *People v. Iniguez*, a 1994 case, the Supreme Court of California affirmed a conviction for forcible rape when the complainant was awoken by the defendant soon before he began having sex with her. The court found sufficient evidence of nonconsent even though the complainant remained entirely silent and passive throughout.

There are quite a few cases—from a variety of jurisdictions that have not claimed to adopt affirmative consent definitions—demonstrating successful prosecutions of rape and sexual assault charges in cases in which the victim remained silent and passive and did not affirmatively state or indicate "no."***

E. THE ROLE OF SILENCE IN AFFIRMATIVE CONSENT: AN AMBIGUOUS STANDARD

***This leaves the first interpretation: silence standing alone is not sufficient to demonstrate consent, but silence or passivity after active signals of agreement may be one way to infer ongoing agreement.

This interpretation is both reasonable and plausible and, for some of the affirmative consent policies, clearly stated by the text. It is not, however, a meaningful change from existing law. At most, this interpretation is a modest clarification. As such, it is valuable insofar as it may assist juries who are confused on this point. But it does not significantly change the existing law of rape and sexual assault because existing doctrinal law, for the most part, already incorporates this insight that silence standing alone does not constitute consent.***

In many cases, however, the dispute is not over silence alone but over the complainant's silence or passivity when viewed in combination with earlier words or conduct that the defendant claims indicated affirmative agreement.

Michelle Anderson recognized this problem in her critical assessment of the "no means no" versus "yes means yes" debate. In particular, Anderson highlighted the role of silence under the "yes means yes" model and noted how similar it is, in many contexts, to the role of silence under the "no means no" model.

During a sexual encounter, once there are affirmative signals of agreement, silence is then often used to infer ongoing consent. For example, Anderson cited Stephen Schulhofer, the "architect of the Yes Model," who notes that "sexual petting" can indicate agreement to sexual penetration. Schulhofer stated, "If she doesn't say 'no,' and if her silence is combined with passionate kissing, hugging, and sexual touching, it is usually sensible to infer actual willingness." Anderson thus observed that "[w]hen things heat up, . . . the Yes Model melts into the No Model, in which silence constitutes consent." She argued that this mode of analysis is really no different from the "no means no" model:

> If the woman is silent and fails to say "no," one may presume she consents to penetration. What happened to "actual permission" for penetration? Passionate kissing, hugging, and sexual touching supply it. Once she engages in kissing and petting, the No Model supplants the Yes Model, and verbal resistance is again required.

Anderson's criticism here led her to propose a new standard for consent— the "negotiation model." Discussion of that proposal is beyond the scope of this Article, which focuses on affirmative consent. For present purposes, the importance is Anderson's recognition of the substantial overlap, in many circumstances, between the No Model and the Yes Model.

In sum, affirmative consent policies suffer from a critical ambiguity related to the roles of silence or passivity. Whether the affirmative consent standard claims that "silence is irrelevant to consent" rather than "silence alone does not equal consent" is often unclear. The former approach would be radical and unworkable, and perhaps for those reasons, supporters of affirmative consent policies do not seem to advocate for it. The latter approach is reasonable but does not represent more than a modest clarification of most existing doctrines.

In any event, clarity on this point—on the part of both critics and advocates—would advance the debate over affirmative consent.***

The basic concept of affirmative consent simply means that some signal of agreement must be sent by each party to a sexual encounter. This is a modest requirement and is largely a *fait accompli* because it appears to reflect the practice of most American jurisdictions in rape and sexual assault cases.

The concept of unambiguous consent is different from that of affirmative consent, and this seems to be the source of much of the uncertainty, unease, and confusion over adopting affirmative consent policies. Advocates should be clear about whether they propose only affirmative consent or the additional, more radical requirement of unambiguous consent, and likewise, critics should separate the two concepts.

Notes and Questions

1. After reading this section, do you agree or disagree with the affirmative consent model. If you agree with this model which form of affirmative consent do you support?

2. After reading *State v. El Berri*, do you think "the shift" from "no" to "yes," as described by Professor Jonathan Witmer-Rich in his article, has already occurred in Ohio?

D. Marital Exception

Patricia J. Falk, *Husbands Who Drug Their Wives: The Injustice of the Marital Exception in Ohio's Sexual Offenses*, 36 Women's Rts. L. Rep. 265 (2015)

Ohio's rape and other sexual offense provisions encapsulate almost the entire evolution of the marital exemption in rape law. The statutes include the marital exemption as the baseline or background rule in accordance with the practice of every jurisdiction in the United States, until fairly recently. For instance, the rape statute begins "No person shall engage in sexual conduct with another who is not the *spouse* of the offender. . . ." Similarly, the sexual battery statute provides: "No person shall engage in sexual conduct with another, *not the spouse of the offender,* when any of the following apply: . . ." The gross sexual imposition statute provides: "No person shall have sexual contact with another, *not the spouse of the offender;* cause another, *not the spouse of the offender,* to have sexual contact with the offender; or cause two or more other persons to have sexual contact when any of the following applies: . . ." Finally, the sexual imposition statute provides: "No person shall have sexual contact with another, *not the spouse of the offender,* cause another, *not the spouse of the offender,* to have sexual contact with the offender; or cause two or more other persons to have sexual contact when any of the following applies: . . ." This language, reminiscent of the full marital rape exemption as it existed in England and, subsequently, in all American jurisdictions, provides that criminal liability will attach only if the offender engages in the prohibited activities with someone other than his spouse.

Juxtaposed against this background rule, Ohio's sexual offenses contain three separate exceptions to the marital immunity. These exceptions can be understood as partially lifting or nullifying the marital exemption under specified circumstances, thereby permitting the criminal prosecution of offenders despite their marital relationship to the victim. More specifically, Ohio's sexual offense provisions contain three discrete exceptions to the application of the marital exemption: (1) through the operation of the definition of a "spouse," (2) in the factual circumstance of the offender and victim living separate and apart under the rape statute, and (3) when the offender compels the victim to submit by force or threat of force under the rape statute.***

In summary, spouses in Ohio are protected from all forms of nonconsensual sexual conduct and sexual contact if they are in the process of altering their legal relationship, i.e., by getting an annulment, divorce, dissolution, or legally separating. If the spouses are living separate and apart, they are also protected from various types of rape, those that do and do not include "forcible compulsion," such as being drugged as a prelude to the sexual assault; none of the other sexual offenses include this language. Finally, if the offender used force to compel his spouse to submit to sexual intercourse (forcible rape), then Ohio spouses receive the full measure of protection against rape—even if they are cohabiting with the offender. However, cohabiting spouses would not be protected from other types of "non-forcible" rape, such as being drugged and sexually assaulted, or less serious types of sexual offenses. Thus, Ohio's rape and sexual offense provisions contain a complex, multi-tiered partial lifting of the marital exemption, possibly graded by the perceived seriousness of the completed offense, but lacking any other organizational structure.***

[T]he problem of the marital immunity barring prosecution of husbands who drug and sexually assault their wives cannot be solved by trying to subsume this behavior under the forcible

compulsion subsection of the rape statute. Even if it could be solved by doing so, other types of rape—sexual penetration of a person who is mentally or physically incapacitated—and other sexual offenses like sexual battery would still fall outside the realm of punishment. The solution must come in terms of legislative enactment rather than judicial expansion of the scope of existing statutory provisions.***

More than 1 in every 7 women who have ever been married have been raped in marriage!

> "I believed my husband loved and respected me and would have protected me from harm. . . . Instead he violated and betrayed my trust (and) treated my body with total disregard and contempt."

*** Beginning more than forty years ago in 1975 and most recently in 1986, the Ohio legislature has lifted the marital immunity for certain categories of spouses *(e.g.,* those who are legally separated, getting divorced, living separate and apart, or forcibly violated), but not for other spouses *(e.g.,* those who are drugged then raped or those who are substantially incapacitated and incapable of consenting). This statutory scheme defies logic in terms of both the historical and modern legal and public policy justifications for the exemption, undervalues the quantum of harm experienced by victims of these offenses, violates the prevailing legal norms in the treatment of women, and defies the values of statutory clarity and comprehensibility in criminal statutes. The partial lifting of the marital immunity has created an indefensible no-man's land, uncomfortably suspended between the traditional rule and the strong modern trend toward complete abolition.

The reasons that the marital immunity should be abolished in a prosecution for forcible rape apply with equal or greater force to other types of rape and to other sexual offense categories. The grave injustice of failing to protect women who are married to the same extent as women who are not married exists whether the rape is accomplished by forcible compulsion or by drugging. As a factual matter, men who batter women are not limited to using their fists, but also render their victims unconscious by drugging or other means. 12 2 To allow prosecution only in cases involving physical force privileges certain battering conduct, based on little more than the fortuitous choice of criminal means.***

A. THE TRADITIONAL LEGAL AND POLICY JUSTIFICATIONS FOR THE MARITAL EXEMPTION ARE OUTMODED AND UNTENABLE

> "Rape entered the law through the back door, as it were, as a property crime of man against man. Woman, of course, was viewed as the property."

> By marriage, the husband and wife are one person in law: that is, the very being or legal existence of the woman is suspended during the marriage, or at least is incorporated and

consolidated into that of the husband; under whose wing, protection and cover, she performs everything. . . .

Three hundred years ago, Matthew Hale published an extra-judicial statement about the relationship between marriage and the crime of rape that has continued to affect the prosecution of modern rape cases into 21st century America: "[T]he husband cannot be guilty of a rape committed by himself upon his lawful wife, for by their mutual matrimonial consent and contract the wife hath given herself in this kind unto her husband, which she cannot retract." Another English jurist, William Blackstone contributed this conceptualization of the relationship between husbands and wives: "This doctrine contends that 'the husband and wife are one person in law,' with the 'legal existence of the woman . . . suspended during the marriage."

Over the ensuing centuries, legal commentators have derived four related rationales for the marital exemption from these statements by Hale and Blackstone, namely that upon marriage: (1) the woman became the chattel or property of her husband, (2) the woman and man became one legal entity - the man, (3) a contract existed between the couple such that the wife could not deny her husband any form of sexual activity, and (4) the woman irrevocably consented to all types of sexual activity. In the modern era, courts, commentators, and legislators have reacted to these justifications for the marital exemption with understandable derision. Wayne LaFave simply states: "None of the historical justifications for the marital rape exemption have any validity today."' As John F. Decker and Peter G. Baroni, note in their recent survey of rape law:

> The exemption is rooted in a centuries-old extrajudicial statement and has persisted in the common law tradition ever since. The cases that have dealt with the marital exemption at length have exposed it as irrational and ungrounded, and have provided a blueprint for eliminating the marital exemption altogether.

It is now universally agreed that women are not the property of their husbands and that women have a separate legal existence from their husbands. In an era when divorce rates are about 50 per cent, the notion of an irrevocable contract between husband and wife may be similarly disputed. Finally, rape law has evolved to the extent of recognizing that consent may be withdrawn at any time up to sexual penetration, and even post-penetration, rendering any notion of longterm, irrevocable consent as simply untenable.

Turning to Ohio law, reconsider the comments attached to the pattern Ohio Jury Instructions for forcible rape:

The Committee believes that with the enactment of R.C. 2907.02(A)(2), forcible sexual conduct with a spouse is rape. The common law (and statutory) defenses of implied consent and "the wife is a man's chattel" no longer exist.

On its face, the logic of this comment is unassailable. The problem is that the repudiation of these ancient justifications does not go far enough in Ohio. Why is it only limited to cases involving forcible rape, when it should be applied much more broadly to encompass the other types of rape as well as the other sexual offenses? Could one seriously contend that women do not impliedly consent to forcible rape by their husbands, but they do impliedly consent to being drugged and then raped by their husbands? Similarly, could one argue the notion that "the wife is a man's chattel" does not apply in the circumstance when a husband forcibly rapes his wife, but that it *does* apply in the situation when he uses drugs to subdue her so she cannot express lack of consent? To ask these questions is to answer them.

Despite the broad-reaching language of the comment to the jury instructions, Ohio's sexual offenses continue to protect those who engage in sexual assaults that cannot be classified as "forcible," such as when the assailant subdues his marital partner by drugging her or when he takes advantage of a marital partner with significant mental or physical impairments. Similarly, the repudiation of the marital unities theory and the marriage contract theory cannot be confined to a partial lifting of the marital exemption. These justifications do not furnish support for any type of marital immunity.

B. MODERN LEGAL AND POLICY JUSTIFICATIONS CANNOT SUPPORT THE MARITAL EXEMPTION

"All of *the* prominent reasons used to justify marital rape rules, such as privacy and family harmony, fear of vindictive complaints, and problems of proof, have fared poorly in the face of equal protection and statutory challenges."[']

The modem defenders of the marital rape exemption, in contrast, submerge and deny the harm that the rule causes women. This has been good strategy for a reason. It is much more difficult to justify the harm that marital rape inflicts upon wives, and explain the absence of legal remediation, in a nation now formally committed to women's legal equality and the undoing of women's subjection at common law.

A second, more modem set of rationales or justifications for the marital exemption have taken the place of the traditional or historical ones. These rationales are as flawed as the ones they replaced. The most common modern justifications are: (1) marital unity should be protected against the intrusion of the state, (2) greater proof problems will arise with respect to rape in marriage, (3) women may lie about the fact of rape within marriage, and (4) martial rape is not as serious an offense as other forms of sexual assault. None of these rationales have held up on closer scrutiny; they have been sharply disputed by commentators, researchers, and courts.

Perhaps the most important modem justification of the marital exemption is that rape within marriage is less serious, damaging, or harmful than other forms of sexual violation - after all, the parties are married to each other and the woman has presumably had sexual intercourse with her husband on numerous occasions. Joshua Dressler explains: "When intercourse is coerced on a given occasion in the marital relationship, the argument proceeds, the wife's autonomy is less seriously violated than if the perpetrator were a stranger or someone with whom the victim had not indicated a general willingness to have sexual relations."

Empirical data support the opposite conclusion. The victims of marital rape do experience multiple physical, psychological, and emotional harms. The bodily consequences of victimization include physical injuries, unwanted pregnancy, sexually transmitted diseases, and exposure to HIV and AIDS. As one commentator states: One of the biggest myths about marital rape is that "it's no big deal"—that the woman says she's tired and wants to go to bed, and the husband misunderstands. That's not reality. A rape or sexual assault is a horrifying experience that is used as a means to degrade, humiliate and control. There is no way the crime can be rationalized or excused whether it happened between strangers or intimate partners.

In fact, compelling evidence supports the conclusion that marital rape is *more* harmful than rape outside of marriage.

Research indicates that wife rape victims are more likely to be raped multiple times compared with stranger and acquaintance rape victims. In research with wife rape victims, most report being raped more than once, with at least 1/3 of the women reporting being raped more than 20 times
over the course of their relationship (citations omitted). Women who experience wife rape suffer long lasting physical and psychological injuries as severe or more severe than stranger rape victims.

Similarly, Jill Elaine Hasday reports: "[T]he best available empirical studies report that marital rape is both widespread and extremely damaging, frequently causing even more trauma than rape outside of marriage."

The psychological consequences of rape can be debilitating: "Despite commonly held views, the psychological reactions of victims of intimate partner rape can be far more severe than the response of those who have suffered rape by a stranger, because in addition to all the other horrors, there is the sense of betrayal and destruction of any trust that once existed." Anderson points out: "[C]ontrary to popular belief, wife rape tends to be more violent and psychologically damaging than stranger rape."The sense of betrayal suffered by marital partners is considerable.

Research also confirms that sexual assault in marriage may be a precursor to homicide, and that sexual assault within marriage must be understood as simply one category of spousal abuse and battering. Rather than viewing rape as a single isolated event in a marriage, sexual assault is part of the pattern of abuse that occurs in battering relationships.

> Every day, three women in the U.S. are murdered by their current or former husbands or boyfriends, and a leading indicator of their deaths is sexual assault. David Adams, in his book "Why Do They Kill?," found that three quarters of women he interviewed who survived nearly fatal attacks said their abusive partner had raped them.

Thus, the legal argument or public policy rationale that rape or other sexual assaults are less serious offenses when they occur in marriage rather than outside of it cannot be supported by either theory or fact.

Notes and Questions

1. Professor Falk makes a very compelling argument for removing the common law's marital exemption for sexual assault crimes. Do you agree or disagree with her assertions? Before answering that question, consider the following real life case.

Jessica Foxx, *Dementia Sex Culture: Out with the Old, in with the New,* 9 J. Am. Acad. Matrim. Law. 187 (2016)

[Henry Rayhons and Donna Lou Young] both in their seventies, grew smitten with each other in their church choir. Both were widowed after the deaths of their longtime spouses. Henry had four adult children and was the Iowa Republican State Representative for the Eighth District. Donna had three adult children, was an avid beekeeper, and sold honey. On December 15, 2007, the pair married in their church, surrounded by children and grandchildren. A few years into the marriage, Donna received a diagnosis of early-onset Alzheimer's. She suffered headaches and forgetfulness, and drove on the wrong side of the road. Donna's daughter, Linda, took her to lunch in March 2014 and noticed that under her coat, Donna was wearing only a night teddy, which left her breasts exposed. While in the restaurant bathroom, she put her hands in the toilet bowl. In late March, Donna's children moved her out of the marital home and into Concord Care Center, a nursing facility, approximately five minutes from Henry. Henry began to quarrel with Donna's family, because he objected to Donna's move and disagreed with the kind of care she received at the nursing home.

Donna quickly reached a point where she could not repeat the words "sock" and "blue." On May 15, 2014, during a care plan meeting between Donna's family and nursing home staff . . . Henry was informed that Donna no longer had the cognitive ability to consent to sexual activity. . . . On May 23, 2014, Donna's roommate, Polly Schoneman, reported to nursing home staff that Henry came to visit and pulled the curtains shut, whereupon Mrs. Schoneman heard noises indicating that the couple was engaging in sexual intercourse. The staff contacted the Garner Police Department. Upon reviewing surveillance video, they discovered that Henry had been in Donna's room for approximately thirty minutes, and on his way out, had discarded Donna's underwear in the hallway laundry hamper. Soon after, during an interview between Henry and a special agent with the Division of Criminal Investigation (DCI), Henry stated that he had sexual contact with Donna on the day in question and also that he possessed a copy of the care plan stating Donna was no longer able to give cognitive consent to sexual activities. It was not until June 17, 2014 that a judge ordered Donna's daughter temporary guardian of her mother. A final hearing to appoint her full guardian of her mother and conservator of her estate was set for August 12, 2014. However, Donna succumbed to Alzheimer's and passed away on August 8, 2014. Officers arrested Henry just a week after his wife's death and charged him with sexual abuse in the third degree, a felony, for the alleged sexual activities of May 23, 2014.

Henry pled not guilty to the charges, testifying that the couple merely held hands and kissed on the night in question. His attorney stated that Henry's former confession to the DCI agent was coerced. The hospital examination and rape kit completed the evening of the alleged sexual encounter were inconclusive as to whether Donna even had sex that evening. Though a semen stain found on her sheets matched Henry's DNA, the lab technician testified that the age of that sample could not be determined. A juror who participated in the case, Angela Nelson, said that the judge instructed the jury to answer three questions: Did Henry have sexual contact with Donna on the night of May 23, 2014; did Henry commit the sexual act while Donna was incapable of consent; and did this act occur while Henry and Donna were no longer living together?

Ms. Nelson said the jury based its not guilty verdict on several points. For many jurors, a fitted sheet taken from Donna's bed was the most important piece of evidence. Out of thirty stains found on that sheet, there was only one semen stain that matched Henry's DNA. Strangely, investigators found none of Donna's DNA on the sheet, though she had been sleeping on it for an unknown amount of time. Further, no witness could conclusively say whether the sheet originated from Concord Care Center or the condo the couple shared as their marital home. There was no witness called to testify as to the laundry schedule or the last time that particular sheet had been washed. This meant that the semen stain could possibly have dated back to when the couple was living in the marital home.

Moreover, Polly, Donna's roommate, testified that she saw nothing on the night in question, but heard whispers, and felt as though she was intruding. When examined by defense counsel, Polly said the noises she heard were not sexual. However, when cross-examined by the prosecution, she said those noises were sexual. Moreover, she stated that in her opinion, Donna was capable of caring for herself, making her own decisions, and communicating with others. Henry testified that Donna had a continued interest in sexual activity, sometimes initiating it. There was no testimony that Donna resisted intimacy from Henry. This forced the jury consider the possibility that Donna possessed capacity to understand and desire the sexual contact.

The Iowa state statute said that a person is guilty of sexual abuse, in part, if "the other person is suffering from a mental defect or incapacity which precludes giving consent." However, the statute offered no definition of mental defect or incapacity. The Iowa statutes left unclear whether dementia qualified as a mental defect or incapacity which precludes giving consent. The jury found Henry not guilty. . . . This is not the first case involving sexual abuse in a nursing home. However, this circumstance, in which the state charged a spouse of an Alzheimer's patient with sexual abuse, appears to be the first of its kind in the United States. It raised serious issues into the public spotlight. The first is that there is no clear cut point at which a dementia patient can no longer consent to sexual activity...Further, many state statutes fall short of encompassing a non-consenting dementia patient in their sexual assault statutes by omitting any formal definition of mental defect.

E. Statutory Rape

All states have an age at which a person can consent to intercourse. Sexual contact with a minor below the age of consent can be broadly defined as statutory rape. In many jurisdictions, statutory rape is a strict liability crime. *In re D.B.* explores the constitutional issues that arise when both parties are underage.

In re D.B., 129 Ohio St. 3d 104 (2011)

LANZINGER, J.

This appeal challenges the constitutionality of applying to a child under the age of 13 the statute that defines sexual activity with a child under 13 as rape, a first-degree felony. R.C. 2907.02(A)(1)(b). The case arises from incidents in which two boys under 13 years of age engaged in sexual activity. Because we hold that the statute is unconstitutional as applied in these circumstances, we reverse.

I. CASE BACKGROUND

On August 1, 2007, appellee, the state of Ohio, filed a complaint in the Juvenile Division of the Court of Common Pleas of Licking County against D.B., who was then 12 years old, charging him with nine counts of rape in violation of R.C. 2907.02(A)(1)(b) arising from conduct occurring between him and an 11-year-old boy, M.G. The complaint also charged D.B. with one count of rape in violation of R.C. 2907.02(A)(1)(b) arising from conduct occurring with A.W., also 12 years old. All the counts alleged that D.B. was a delinquent child under R.C. 2152.02(F).

D.B. filed a motion to dismiss the complaint, alleging that the state could not establish sufficient evidence that he was guilty of rape and that application of R.C. 2907.02(A)(1)(b) in this case violates his federal and state rights to due process and equal protection because the statute is vague and overbroad. The state subsequently filed an amended complaint, which dropped the count related to A.W. and amended multiple counts to allege that D.B. had engaged in forcible sexual conduct with M.G. or had used verbal threats to get him to comply, in violation of R.C. 2907.02(A)(2). The first count of the amended complaint alleged only that D.B. had engaged in sexual conduct with a person less than 13 years of age in violation of R.C. 2907.02(A)(1)(b). The remaining eight counts alleged that D.B. had engaged in conduct with M.G. in violation of R.C. 2907.02(A)(1)(b) or R.C. 2907.02(A)(2) (forcible sexual conduct). Each count also alleged that D.B. was a delinquent child under R.C. 2152.02(F).***

A.W. testified that he had observed D.B. and M.G. engage in anal sex. A.W. testified that D.B. "bribed" M.G. with video games to engage in sexual conduct. Both A.W. and M.G. stated that the sexual conduct was always initiated by D.B. and that D.B. would either bargain with, or use physical force on, M.G. to convince M.G. to engage in sexual conduct.

According to A.W., D.B. and M.G. did not engage in sexual conduct until M.G. himself agreed to the activity. D.B.'s father testified that while D.B. was significantly bigger than other children his age, he was not an aggressive child and he never used his size to bully or intimidate other children.

Defense counsel moved for acquittal at the conclusion of the state's case. The court dismissed counts 3, 4, 5, and 6 after finding that no specific evidence existed to support them. Determining that there was no basis for finding that D.B. had engaged in forcible sexual conduct, the court also dismissed those portions of counts 2, 7, and 9 that alleged forcible rape. D.B.'s motion to dismiss the counts alleging a violation of R.C. 2907.02(A)(1)(b) was denied.

The hearing resumed on March 4, 2008. Count 1, count 8, and the allegations of violations of R.C. 2907.02(A)(1)(b) in counts 2, 7, and 9 remained from the amended complaint. Following the presentation of the defense's case, the court stated that while there was "no question whatsoever" that the sexual acts detailed in the remaining counts took place, it could not find that D.B. used force during any of the acts. The court therefore adjudicated D.B. delinquent based on the violation of R.C. 2907.02(A)(1)(b) alleged in counts 1, 2, 7, 8, and 9.

At the dispositional hearing, the court committed D.B. to the Department of Youth Services for a minimum of five years to the maximum period of his 21st birthday, suspended the commitment, and placed D.B. on probation for an indefinite period of time. The court further ordered D.B. to attend counseling and group therapy.

On appeal to the Fifth District Court of Appeals, D.B. argued that application of R.C. 2907.02(A)(1)(b) violated his federal rights to due process and equal protection, that the juvenile court abused its discretion in adjudicating him delinquent for rape, and that the juvenile court erred in overruling a motion to suppress statements he had made to law enforcement when he was questioned in his bedroom and at the sheriff's office. *In re D.B.,* Licking App. No. 2009 CA 000242. The court of appeals upheld the constitutionality of R.C. 2907.02(A)(1)(b) as applied and held that the trial court did not abuse its discretion in adjudicating D.B. delinquent for rape for engaging in sexual conduct with an 11-year-old child. Id. at ¶ 23, 28.***

II. ANALYSIS

D.B. does not assert that R.C. 2907.02(A)(1)(b) is unconstitutional on its face, meaning that it can never be applied without violating constitutional rights, but asserts that it is unconstitutional as applied to him. "A statute may be challenged as unconstitutional on the basis that it is invalid on its face or as applied to a particular set of facts. See, e.g., *United States v. Eichman* (1990), 496 U.S. 310. In an as-applied challenge, the challenger 'contends that application of the statute in the particular context in which he has acted, or in which he proposes to act, [is] unconstitutional.' *Ada v. Guam Soc. of Obstetricians & Gynecologists* (1992), 506 U.S. 1011. Thus, we focus on the statute and its particular application in an as-applied challenge.

R.C. 2907.02(A)(1)(b) criminalizes what is commonly known as "statutory rape." The statute holds offenders strictly liable for engaging in sexual conduct with children under the age of 13—force is not an element of the offense because a child under the age of 13 is legally presumed to be incapable of consenting to sexual conduct.

R.C. 2907.02(A)(1) provides:

> No person shall engage in sexual conduct with another who is not the spouse of the offender or who is the spouse of the offender but is living separate and apart from the offender, when any of the following applies:
> ***

(b) The other person is less than 13 years of age, whether or
not the offender knows the age of the other person.

The statute furthers the state's interest in protecting young children. Indeed, the Legislature Service Commission stated that R.C. 2907.02(A)(1)(b) was created to protect a prepubescent child from the sexual advances of another because "engaging in sexual conduct with such a person indicates vicious behavior on the part of the offender." 1973 Legislative Service Commission comments to Am. Sub. H.B. No. 511, 134 Ohio Laws, Part II, 1866.

D.B. argues that R.C. 2907.02(A)(1)(b) is unconstitutional in two ways. First, he argues that the statute is vague as applied to children under the age of 13 and thus violates his right to due process. Second, he argues that the statute was applied in an arbitrary manner in this case in contravention of his constitutional right to equal protection. This case thus asks whether a child's federal constitutional rights are violated when, as a member of the class protected under R.C. 2907.02(A)(1)(b), he or she is adjudicated delinquent based upon a violation of this statute.

A. Due Process

D.B. argues that R.C. 2907.02(A)(1)(b) is unconstitutional as applied to him because it fails to provide guidelines that designate which actor is the victim and which is the offender, resulting in arbitrary and discriminatory enforcement.***

As applied to children under the age of 13 who engage in sexual conduct with other children under the age of 13, R.C. 2907.02(A)(1)(b) is unconstitutionally vague because the statute authorizes and encourages arbitrary and discriminatory enforcement. When an adult engages in sexual conduct with a child under the age of 13, it is clear which party is the offender and which is the victim. But when two children under the age of 13 engage in sexual conduct with each other, each child is both an offender and a victim, and the distinction between those two terms breaks down.

The facts of this case provide an example of the temptation for prosecutors to label one child as the offender and the other child as the victim. Based apparently upon the theory that D.B. forced M.G. to engage in sexual conduct, the state alleged that D.B., but not M.G., had engaged in conduct that constituted statutory rape. However, while the theory of D.B. as the aggressor was consistent with the counts alleging a violation of R.C. 2907.02(A)(2), which proscribes rape by force, this theory is incompatible with the counts alleging a violation of statutory rape because anyone who engages in sexual conduct with a minor under the age of 13 commits statutory rape regardless of whether force was used. Thus, if the facts alleged in the complaint were true, D.B. and M.G. would both be in violation of R.C. 2907.02(A)(1)(b).

The prosecutor's choice to charge D.B. but not M.G. is the very definition of discriminatory enforcement. D.B. and M.G. engaged in sexual conduct with each other, yet only D.B. was charged. The facts of this case demonstrate that R.C. 2907.02(A)(1)(b) authorizes and encourages arbitrary and discriminatory enforcement when applied to offenders under the age of 13. The statute is thus unconstitutionally vague as applied to this situation.

It must be emphasized that the concept of consent plays no role in whether a person violates R.C. 2907.02(A)(1)(b): children under the age of 13 are legally incapable of consenting to sexual conduct. Furthermore, whether D.B. used force to engage in sexual conduct does not play a role in our consideration of R.C. 2907.02(A)(1)(b). The trial court found that D.B. did not use force. Whether an offender used force is irrelevant to the determination whether the offender committed rape under R.C. 2907.02(A)(1)(b).

We note that while we hold that R.C. 2907.02(A)(1)(b) is unconstitutional as applied to a child under the age of 13 who engages in sexual conduct with another child under the age of 13, a child under the age of 13 may be found guilty of rape if additional elements are shown: the offender substantially impairs the other person's judgment or control, R.C. 2907.02(A)(1)(a); the other person's ability to resist or consent is substantially impaired because of a mental or physical condition, R.C. 2907.02(A)(1)(c); or the offender compels the other person to submit by force or threat of force, R.C. 2907.02(A)(2). None of those additional elements was present here.

B. Equal Protection

Application of R.C. 2907.02(A)(1)(b) in this case also violates D.B.'s federal right to equal protection. "The Equal Protection Clause directs that 'all persons similarly circumstanced shall be treated alike.' " *F.S. Royster Guano Co. v. Virginia,* 253 U.S. 412.

The plain language of the statute makes it clear that every person who engages in sexual conduct with a child under the age of 13 is strictly liable for statutory rape, and the statute must be enforced equally and without regard to the particular circumstances of an individual's situation. R.C. 2907.02(A)(1)(b) offers no prosecutorial exception to charging an offense when every party involved in the sexual conduct is under the age of 13; conceivably, the principle of equal protection suggests that both parties could be prosecuted as identically situated. Because D.B. and M.G. were both under the age of 13 at the time the events in this case occurred, they were both members of the class protected by the statute, and both could have been charged under the offense. Application of the statute in this case to a single party violates the Equal Protection Clause's mandate that persons similarly circumstanced shall be treated alike.

All three boys allegedly engaged in sexual conduct with a person under the age of 13; however, only D.B. was charged with a violation of R.C.

2907.02(A)(1)(b). This arbitrary enforcement of the statute violates D.B.'s right to equal protection. We accordingly hold that application of the statute in this case violated D.B.'s federal equal-protection rights. The statute is unconstitutional as applied to him.

III. CONCLUSION

R.C. 2907.02(A)(1)(b) prohibits one from engaging in sexual conduct with a person under the age of 13. As applied to offenders who are under the age of 13 themselves, the statute is unconstitutionally vague in violation of the Due Process Clause of the United States Constitution because arbitrary and discriminatory enforcement is encouraged. Application of the statute in this case also violates the Equal Protection Clause of the United States Constitution because only one child was charged with being delinquent, while others similarly situated were not.

We thus hold that R.C. 2907.02(A)(1)(b) is unconstitutional as applied to a child under the age of 13 who engages in sexual conduct with another child under 13.

Judgment reversed and cause remanded

Notes and Questions

1. Consider the following hypothetical: A 13-year-old and a child of 12 years and 11 months engage in sexual intercourse. Is it clear which party is the offender and which is the victim? What public policy arguments are there for applying the statutory rape statute to this situation? For not applying it?

2. Why is the court in *In re D.B.* unconcerned about whether D.B. used force or if M.G. consented to sex?

3. Ohio's statutory rape statute applies "whether or not the offender knows the age of the other person," and the *In re D.B.* court emphasizes that this is a strict liability offense. Are there any defenses to a statutory rape charge?

4. The court in *In re D.B.* found Ohio's statutory rape law unconstitutional as applied to the defendant. Specifically, the court found the law to be vague. To avoid being found unconstitutionally vague, a criminal law must: (1) provide the kind of notice to allow ordinary people to understand what conduct it prohibits, and (2) not be susceptible to arbitrary and discriminatory enforcement. Of these two requirements, which one was not met in *In re D.B.*?

F . Rape Shield Statute

Lewis v. Wilkinson, 307 F. 3d 413 (6th Cir. 2002)

STEEH, District Judge.

In this habeas corpus petition, Petitioner Nathaniel M. Lewis argues that the trial court's exclusion of certain evidence in his rape trial prevented him from conducting appropriate cross-examination, thus violating his Sixth Amendment right of confrontation. Because we find that the excluded evidence reasonably goes to the issue of the victim's consent, as well as her motive in pursuing charges against Lewis, Petitioner's constitutional right of confrontation has been violated. Therefore, the district court's denial of habeas relief is REVERSED in accordance with this court's opinion.

I

Appellant Nathaniel M. Lewis was indicted on November 6, 1996 by a Summit County Grand Jury on the charge of Rape, a violation of Ohio Revised Code § 2907.02(A)(2). The case proceeded to jury trial before the Court of Common Pleas on June 2, 1997. The jury returned a guilty verdict on June 6, 1997. On July 16, 1997, Lewis was sentenced to the Ohio Department of Rehabilitation and Correction for a term of eight years and is presently serving his sentence. Lewis filed a motion for new trial, which was denied by the trial court on July 16, 1997.***

II

Nathaniel Lewis and Christina Heaslet were friends who met during their first year at the University of Akron. Heaslet testified that Lewis was a joker and a flirt who was interested in her sexually. She responded to Lewis's advances by explaining she "wasn't that kind of person that started having sex with anybody that she just met." She testified she was physically attracted to Lewis, but he "tried to hook up with everybody" and was not interested in the kind of relationship that she was.

On the evening of October 12, 1996, at 8:45 p.m., Heaslet called Lewis and invited him to her dormitory room. Lewis arrived at approximately 8:50 p.m. They made plans earlier in the day for him to come to her room to borrow some music compact discs. Heaslet and Lewis watched television, listened to music, and talked with Keryn Mayback, while Heaslet drank wine coolers. Ms. Mayback left at approximately 9:30 or 9:45, and Heaslet and Lewis were alone in Heaslet's room. Shortly after Mayback left, while Heaslet and Lewis were listening to music, Lewis got up and turned off the light. According to Heaslet's testimony, Lewis grabbed her, threw her on the bed, and took off all her clothes. Lewis then completely disrobed, stood up, pulled out a condom, and placed it on his penis. Heaslet testified she was repeatedly pushed down by Lewis, and her legs were forced apart, while she continued to cry "don't do this." Lewis then penetrated her.

Lewis's testimony was that after he turned the lights off he told Heaslet to come and find him. Heaslet found him on the bed, and he put his hand up her shirt. Heaslet removed her bra, and they started kissing. Together they removed Heaslet's sweatshirt, and then Lewis disrobed and put on a condom. Meanwhile, Heaslet took off the rest of her clothes. According to Lewis, Heaslet did not say anything during the time they had intercourse.

Lewis then turned on the lights, wrapped the condom in a tissue and threw it in the trash. Heaslet picked up the condom wrapper, threw it in the trash, and told Lewis he had to leave. Heaslet left the room with Lewis. Lewis stopped a couple of doors down the hall to write a note on another girl's door. Heaslet rode down the elevator with Lewis and signed him out at the front desk.

Heaslet then went to see Alison Legitt, the Resident Coordinator for the dormitory, who called the police. Heaslet did not want to speak to the police initially. She was taken to the hospital, but did not want to see a rape counselor, and for the first several hours did not wish to file any charges. Heaslet eventually agreed to see a counselor on October 14, and was encouraged by her counselor to keep a diary. Lewis was arrested in his dormitory room in the early hours of October 13. He waived his *Miranda* rights and gave a statement explaining that he and Heaslet had consensual sex.

Several weeks prior to the scheduled trial date, Lewis received in the mail an envelope that had been sent anonymously to his home address. The envelope contained xeroxed excerpts of Heaslet's diary. Lewis gave the envelope to his trial counsel, who disclosed the contents to the assistant prosecutor and the trial judge. Lewis's counsel requested the production of the entire diary. The State acquired Heaslet's complete diary and provided it to the court for *in camera* review. The State moved the court *in limine* to exclude reference to the diary except for certain limited portions. The court marked the entire diary as Exhibit "E". The portions anonymously sent to Lewis were marked Exhibits "A", "B", "C" and "D". Defense counsel argued for permission to cross-examine Heaslet on excerpts "A", "B", "C" and "D", arguing they were relevant to Heaslet's veracity and motive to lie and spoke directly to the issue of consent. Defense counsel was particularly interested in excerpt "B" contained in the entry dated April 20, 1997:

> I can't believe the trial's only a week away. I feel guilty (sort
> of) for trying to get Nate locked up, but his lack of respect for
> women is terrible. I remember how disrespectful he always was
> to all of us girls in the courtyard . . . he thinks females are a bunch
> of sex objects! And he's such a player! He was trying to get with

Holly and me, and all the while he had a girlfriend. I think I pounced on Nate because he was the last straw. That, and because I've always seemed to need some drama in my life. Otherwise I get bored. That definitely needs to change. I'm sick of men taking advantage of me . . . and I'm sick of myself for giving in to them. I'm not a nympho like all those guys think. I'm just not strong enough to say no to them. I'm tired of being a whore. This is where it ends.

Citing the rape shield law, Ohio Revised Code § 2907.02(D), the trial court prohibited the defense from introducing the following language from Exhibit "B":

> . . . and I'm sick of myself for giving in to them. I'm not a nympho like all those guys think. I'm just not strong enough to say no to them. I'm tired of being a whore. This is where it ends.

The defense had argued that this provision, when read in context, was vital because it stated, or at least implied, that Heaslet had not said "no" to Lewis, and it could be construed as an admission that she had consented to intercourse with Lewis. It also provided an apparent motive as to why she would falsely claim she was raped—she was upset with herself for giving in to men. The State had argued that the language at issue constituted opinion and reputation evidence of the victim's past sexual activity and was therefore protected under the rape shield law. The trial court agreed with the State, holding that any probative value of the evidence was outweighed by its prejudicial effect.***

IV

The Sixth Amendment guarantees a defendant the right to be confronted with the witnesses against him. U.S. Const. amend. VI. The right to confrontation includes the right to conduct reasonable cross-examination. *Davis v. Alaska*, 415 U.S. 308, 315-16, 94 S. Ct. 1105, 39 L. Ed. 2d 347 (1974). Cross-examination is the "principal means by which the believability of a witness and the truth of his testimony are tested." *Id.* at 316, 94 S. Ct. 1105. The exposure of a witness's motivation in testifying is a proper and important function of the constitutionally protected right of cross-examination. *Id.* at 316-17, 94 S. Ct. 1105. In this vein, the Supreme Court has "distinguished between a 'general attack' on the credibility of a witness—in which the cross-examiner 'intends to afford the jury a basis to infer that the witness's character is such that he would be less likely than the average trustworthy citizen to be truthful in his testimony'—and a more particular attack on credibility 'directed toward revealing possible biases, prejudices, or ulterior motives as they may relate directly to issues or personalities in the case at hand.' " *Boggs v. Collins,* 226 F.3d 728, 736 (6th Cir. 2000).

The *Boggs* case involved the trial court's exclusion of evidence in a rape trial of an alleged prior false accusation of rape. The defense sought to introduce such evidence so that the jury could infer that if the victim lied or fabricated once, she would do so again. *Id.* at 739. The court found this to be an attack on the witness's general credibility. "Under *Davis* and its progeny, the Sixth Amendment only compels cross-examination if that examination aims to reveal the motive, bias or prejudice of a witness/accuser." *Id.* at 740. The court was unable to find a plausible theory of motive or bias for allowing such evidence to be presented, and concluded that Boggs did not demonstrate a Confrontation Clause infraction. *Id.*

The trial court has discretion to impose limits on cross-examination based on concerns about harassment, prejudice, confusion of the issues, witness safety, or interrogation that is repetitive or only marginally relevant. *Id.* at 736. The Confrontation Clause "guarantees an *opportunity* for effective cross-examination, not cross-examination that is effective in whatever way, and to whatever extent, the defense might wish." *Id.*

Petitioner's prayer for relief concerns the evidentiary rulings made by the trial court under Ohio Revised Code Section 2907.02(D), Ohio's rape shield law. That section provides:

> Evidence of specific instances of the victim's sexual activity, opinion evidence of the victim's sexual activity, and reputation evidence of the victim's sexual activity shall not be admitted under this section unless it involves evidence of the origin of semen, pregnancy, or disease, or the victim's past sexual activity with the offender, and only to the extent that the court finds that the evidence is material to a fact at issue in the case and that its inflammatory or prejudicial nature does not outweigh its probative value.

Evidence of specific instances of the defendant's sexual activity, opinion evidence of the defendant's sexual activity, and reputation evidence of the defendant's sexual activity shall not be admitted under this section unless it involves evidence of the origin of semen, pregnancy, or disease, the defendant's past sexual activity with the victim, or is admissible against the defendant under section 2945.59 of the Revised Code, and only to the extent that the court finds that the evidence is material to a fact at issue in the case and that its inflammatory or prejudicial nature does not outweigh its probative value.

Specifically, petitioner takes issue with the trial court's exclusion of the portion of Exhibit "B" which reads:

> . . . and I'm sick of myself for giving in to them. I'm not a nympho like all those guys think. I'm just not strong enough to say no to them. I'm tired of being a whore. This is where it ends.

Appellant argues that the trial court's ruling to exclude a portion of the victim's diary goes against the Supreme Court's clearly established precedent that cross-examination regarding motive is constitutionally protected. In support, appellant cites to *Olden v. Kentucky,* 488 U.S. 227, wherein defendant Olden was charged with the rape and kidnap of the victim. Olden's defense was consent, and he sought to confront the victim with evidence of her cohabitation with another man. Olden's theory was that the victim had concocted a story to protect her relationship with the other man. The trial court excluded this evidence because while the victim was white, her boyfriend was black and so was Olden, and the court believed this fact would have created prejudice against the victim. The Supreme Court concluded that the prejudicial effect of any testimony could not "justify the exclusion of cross-examination with such strong potential to demonstrate the falsity of [the victim's] testimony." *Id.* at 232, 109 S. Ct. 480.

In this case, the trial court stated its reason for excluding the portion of the diary as follows:

> The court finds that the evidence at issue does not fall within the exceptions to the rape shield law set forth in 2907, subsection D, that the introduction of that evidence will directly elicit information about the opinion of this victim's sexual activity, all of which is excluded under the rape shield statute; that even if this were to be construed as admissible somehow, it would be misleading to the jury and unduly prejudicial and inflammatory, would outweigh any possible probative value in this case, in particular, the court notes that where the victim meant to describe the defendant Nate, she did use his name in particular, the generic references to them are too misleading, too ambiguous in this case to generate a true probative issue as far as the court is concerned.

This court's duty "is not to determine whether the exclusion of the evidence by the trial judge was correct or incorrect under state law, but rather whether such exclusion rendered petitioner's trial so fundamentally unfair as to constitute a denial of federal constitutional rights." *Logan v. Marshall,* 680 F.2d 1121 (6th Cir. 1982). On motion for reconsideration, the district court concluded that the excluded diary excerpts went to the victim's general credibility, and were therefore properly excluded pursuant to *Williams* and *Boggs.*

In this court's view, the excluded excerpts are evidence of consent and motive, as argued by appellant. For example, the excluded statements: "I'm just not strong enough to say no to them" and "this is where it ends," when read together with the admitted statements: "I'm sick of men taking advantage of me" and "I think I pounced on Nate because he was the last straw," could reasonably be read as Heaslet pursuing rape charges against Lewis as a way of taking a stand against all the men who previously took advantage of her. The excluded statement: "I'm just not strong enough to say no to them" may be construed as evidence that Heaslet consented to have intercourse with Lewis. The trial court concluded that the references to "them" in the excluded statements, as opposed to the specific references to "Nate" used previously in the same diary entry, render the later statements generic, misleading, and ambiguous. However, this court believes the statements can reasonably be taken to infer consent and motive, and should have been given to the jury to make the ultimate determination.

The decisions in *Davis* and *Boggs* dictate that the issue of a witness's motivation in testifying carries with it the constitutionally protected right of cross-examination. This court disagrees with the district court's characterization of the excluded diary entries as going solely to general credibility of the witness. When a trial court has limited cross-examination from which a jury could have assessed a witness's motive to testify, a court must take two additional steps:

> First, a reviewing court must assess whether the jury had enough information, despite the limits placed on otherwise permitted cross-examination, to assess the defense theory of . . . improper motive. Second, if this is not the case, and there is indeed a denial or significant diminution of cross-examination that implicates the Confrontation Clause, the Court applies a balancing test, weighing the violation against the competing interests at stake. *Boggs,* 226 F.3d at 739 (citations omitted).

Turning to the first inquiry, the court must determine whether the jury had enough information to assess the defense theory of improper motive. The Ohio Court of Appeals held "[i]n the instant case, defense counsel conducted a thorough examination of Ms. Heaslet regarding her prior statements. The probative value of introducing the actual written statements was substantially outweighed due to its cumulative nature." The Magistrate Judge also looked at the cross-examination of Heaslet and determined that it "served the same purpose that Mr. Lewis sought to be accomplished by the statements excluded from evidence: to show that Ms. Heaslet may have fabricated the charge against Mr. Lewis and consented to sexual relations." However, the evidence referred to by the Magistrate Judge went to Ms. Heaslet's feelings of guilt over pressing charges; and about her financial difficulties at the time of the incident and her subsequent diary entry that she was suing Mr. Lewis civilly as a way of getting out of debt.

Appellant argues that the excluded portion was not cumulative, because it contained Heaslet's own words and was more direct on the issue of motive and consent than the admitted portion of the April 20 entry. When the excluded portion is read together with the rest of the diary entry, the fact finder could reasonably infer an admission of consent and an improper motive. The court agrees with appellant that, without the excluded statements, the jury did not have adequate information to assess the defense theories of consent and improper motive.

A finding that the Confrontation Clause is implicated requires the court to weigh such violation against the competing interests at stake—in this case the protections offered by Ohio's rape shield law. The state interests advanced by the rape shield law have been identified by the Ohio Supreme Court as follows:

> First, by guarding the complainant's sexual privacy and protecting her from undue harassment, the law discourages the tendency in rape cases to try the victim rather than the defendant. In line with this, the law may encourage the reporting of rape, thus aiding crime prevention. Finally, by excluding evidence that is unduly inflammatory and prejudicial, while being only marginally probative, the statute is intended to aid in the truth-finding process. *State v. Gardner,* 59 Ohio St. 2d 14, (1979).

The excluded statements unquestionably go to the alleged victim's reputation for "giving in" to men, for not being "strong enough to say no" and for "being a whore," as she characterizes herself in her diary. To permit cross-examination on these statements could lead to a trial of the victim's sexual history with other men. However, the court could minimize any danger of undue prejudice by admitting the evidence with a cautionary instruction and strictly limiting the scope of cross-examination. The statements have substantial probative value as to both consent and the victim's motive in pressing charges against appellant. The constitutional violations in this case are significant enough to outweigh any violation of the rape shield law, whose purposes can be served by the instructions of the trial court.

Appellee argues that, assuming *arguendo* the trial court did err in not allowing defense counsel to use the particular excerpts at issue, such error was harmless. The test for harmless error, for purposes of determining habeas corpus relief, is whether the error made at trial "had a substantial and injurious effect or influence in determining the jury's verdict, rather than whether the error was harmless beyond a reasonable doubt." *Brecht v. Abrahamson,* 507 U.S. 619, (1993).

While the jury was exposed to other excerpts of Heaslet's diary, and the attorneys engaged in cross-examination as to those excerpts, the excluded excerpt "B" would not have been cumulative. The excluded diary excerpt went to a different type of motive than that implied by the other evidence, which went mostly to Heaslet's pecuniary interests. The excluded evidence was in fact the strongest evidence of Heaslet's motive to take a stand against all of the men who had wronged her, and at the same time to protect her reputation. More importantly, the excluded evidence permitted the jury the reasonable inference that Heaslet consented to have intercourse with Lewis. The trial court's decision to exclude excerpt "B" had a "substantial and injurious influence in determining the jury's verdict." As such, the evidentiary decision was not harmless error.

V

Appellant was denied his Sixth Amendment right to confrontation when the trial court excluded several statements from the alleged victim's diary. The statements at issue, especially when read with the diary entry in its entirety, can reasonably be said to form a particularized attack on the witness's credibility directed toward revealing possible ulterior motives, as well as implying her consent. This court recognizes the difficulty a trial judge faces in making an evidentiary decision with the urgency that surrounds the wrapping up of pretrial loose ends prior to the start of jury selection. The trial court took the state's interests in protecting rape victims into account in excluding the statements, but did not adequately consider the defendant's constitutional right to confrontation. The jury should have been given the opportunity to hear the excluded diary statements and some cross examination, from which they could have inferred, if they chose, that the alleged victim consented to have sex with the appellant and/or that the alleged victim pursued charges against the appellant as a way of getting back at other men who previously took advantage of her. The trial court can reduce the prejudicial effect of such evidence by limiting the scope of cross-examination as to the victim's prior sexual activity and her reputation.

For the foregoing reasons, we REVERSE the district court's denial of habeas relief and REMAND with directions to issue a conditional writ of habeas corpus releasing Lewis from custody, unless he is retried within a reasonable period of time to be determined by the district court.

Notes and Questions

1. If you were a juror in the Nathaniel Lewis rape trial, would you want to know about the victim's diary entries? Why or why not? What policy reasons exist for keeping the diary entries out of evidence?

2. Follow up on *Lewis v. Wilkinson*: Once the 6th Circuit Court of Appeals ruled in favor of Nathaniel M. Lewis, the prosecution decided not to retry the case. Mr. Lewis spent approximately five years in prison while appealing his case. Subsequent to his release, Mr. Lewis brought a successful civil suit against the state of Ohio for wrongful imprisonment.

3. Historical Note: Lord Chief Justice Matthew Hale once wrote, "rape . . . is an accusation easily to be made and harder to be proved, and harder to be defended by the party accused, tho never so innocent." After reading this chapter on sexual assault, do you agree or disagree with the aforementioned statement?

Chapter 12
Kidnapping and Robbery

A. Kidnapping, Abduction, and Unlawful Restraint

At common law, kidnapping was the forcible abduction of a person from his own country to another country. This definition has been expanded by all jurisdictions. Ohio has three separate statutes addressing the movement or restraint of individuals against their will. These statutes are kidnapping (O.R.C. 2905.01), abduction (O.R.C. 2905.02), and unlawful restraint (O.R.C. 2905.03). In some jurisdictions, unlawful restraint or false imprisonment is a lesser offense of kidnapping. To be convicted of unlawful restraint the defendant must unlawfully and without valid consent restrain the victim's liberty. The first case in this chapter examines the differences among kidnapping, abduction, and unlawful restraint.

State v. Kroesen, 2000 WL 1715764 (Ohio Ct. App. 2000)

BOWMAN, P.J.

Defendant-appellant, Jason M. Kroesen, was indicted on one count of attempted murder in violation of R.C. 2923.02, one count of felonious assault in violation of R.C. 2903.11, and two counts of kidnapping in violation of R.C. 2905.01. The indictments arose out of an incident which occurred in the early hours of August 29, 1999.

Ron Groves testified that he and appellant drove to Columbus from their homes in St. Clairsville to spend time with friends of Groves and to watch the Ohio State football game. Groves testified that they arrived in Columbus in the early afternoon on Saturday, August 28, 1999. They were staying with Groves' friends, Jamal Smith, Greg Potney and Smith's girlfriend, Carrie Weinmiller, who lived at 1543 Summit Street. In the afternoon, Smith went to work. During the afternoon and evening hours, appellant, Groves and Weinmiller were ingesting crack cocaine and marijuana. Appellant and Groves left 1543 Summit and went to another friend's house and then to a bar, where they consumed some alcohol and eventually returned to 1543 Summit. Groves testified that they returned after last call, around midnight. Weinmiller was on the porch drinking a beer. Weinmiller went inside to watch television and appellant and Groves went upstairs. The telephone rang and a woman asked for Smith, who still was not home from work, then asked for Groves. Groves testified that, after he talked on the phone, appellant believed that Groves had been talking to appellant's ex-girlfriend. Groves tried to explain that the telephone call was from a woman that Smith had met on the internet but appellant did not believe him. Appellant pulled a knife and forced Groves downstairs to check the caller ID machine in an effort to reach the woman who had called. The caller ID indicated the call had come from a Super 8 motel. Groves testified that appellant then attempted to call the woman several times but was unsuccessful.

According to Groves, appellant then forced Weinmiller and Groves back upstairs. He was threatening both of them. Groves testified appellant threatened to beat him with an ashtray and cut off his fingers. Groves stated that appellant punched him. Groves then gave appellant a bear hug in an attempt to stop him. They struggled and appellant stabbed Groves several times. Eventually, Groves and appellant ran out of the room. Groves testified that the whole incident took approximately three hours.

Weinmiller's testimony was substantially the same as Groves, except that she testified Groves and appellant did not return until after 2:30 a.m., and the entire incident only took approximately twenty minutes. She testified that the three were ingesting cocaine and marijuana in the afternoon. Groves and appellant left the house at approximately 10:30 p.m. When they returned, she was sitting on the porch and then went inside to watch television, and Groves and appellant went upstairs. Weinmiller testified that after Groves talked on the phone, both Groves and appellant came downstairs to check the caller ID. Weinmiller went upstairs to go to bed when appellant and Groves returned upstairs. Weinmiller testified that appellant pushed her into one of the bedrooms after Groves. Appellant then pulled out a pocket knife and threatened Weinmiller and Groves. He continued to threaten them and she was very scared. An altercation occurred between appellant and Groves, and then Groves and appellant ran out of the room. Groves was injured by the knife and required many stitches. When the police arrived, appellant was on the roof threatening to jump if the police approached him. Eventually, he returned to the inside of the house where he was arrested.

Appellant testified on his own behalf and gave a different version of the evening's events. Appellant admitted that the three did ingest cocaine and marijuana all afternoon. Appellant testified that he had quite a bit of money because he and Groves had finished some drywall work during the week. He admitted that, after he and Groves returned to 1543 Summit in the early hours of the morning, Groves received a telephone call. Appellant was feeling paranoid, "antsy" and scared after ingesting the cocaine and, based on part of the telephone call he overheard as well as stories he had heard about crime in the neighborhood, he believed that Groves and possibly others were about to rob him. He also thought the call was from a former girlfriend. He pushed Groves and Weinmiller into a bedroom, wedged the chair under the doorknob and took out the knife because he believed he was about to be robbed. He stated that he asked Groves why he was about to take his money and Groves lunged at him. Appellant tried to punch Groves and they struggled. Appellant stated he did not know how Groves was stabbed and that he did not intend to hurt Groves.

The jury found appellant guilty of felonious assault and the two counts of kidnapping. Appellant filed a timely notice of appeal.***

By the first assignment of error, appellant contends that the trial court erred in refusing to give the jury specific instructions regarding lesser included offenses. Appellant's counsel had requested instructions on both abduction and unlawful restraint.***

This issue requires a comparison of the elements of the respective offenses. R.C. 2905.01 defines kidnapping, the charged offense, as follows:

> (A) No person, by force, threat, or deception, *** by any means, shall remove another from the place where the other person is found or restrain the liberty of the other person, for any of the following purposes:
> ***
>> (2) To facilitate the commission of any felony or flight thereafter [here, felonious assault];
>> (3) To terrorize, or to inflict serious physical harm on the victim or another;
> ***
> (C) Whoever violates this section is guilty of kidnapping, a felony of the first degree. If the offender releases the victim in a safe place unharmed, kidnapping is a felony of the second degree.

R.C. 2905.02 defines abduction, as follows:

> (A) No person, without privilege to do so, shall knowingly do any of the following:
> (1) By force or threat, remove another from the place where the other person is found;
> (2) By force or threat, restrain the liberty of another person, under circumstances which create a risk of physical harm to the victim, or place the other person in fear;
> (3) Hold another in a condition of involuntary servitude.

(B) Whoever violates this section is guilty of abduction, a felony of the third degree.

R.C. 2905.03 defines unlawful restraint, as follows:

(A) No person, without privilege to do so, shall knowingly restrain another of his liberty.
(B) Whoever violates this section is guilty of unlawful restraint, a misdemeanor of the third degree.

It has previously been determined that abduction and unlawful restraint are lesser included offenses of kidnapping because abduction and unlawful restraint carry a lesser penalty than kidnapping, the essential conduct proscribed necessarily involves an abduction or unlawful restraint, and kidnapping involves additional elements which need not be established to prove abduction or unlawful restraint. *See State v. Joyner* (Mar. 23, 1999), Franklin App. No. 98AP-785.

In this case, the trial court properly denied the request for the abduction instruction. Given the injuries that Groves sustained, including three stab wounds which required many stitches, the jury could not reasonably acquit appellant of kidnapping. The trial court also properly denied the request for the unlawful restraint instruction. Given the forceful, threatening manner that both Weinmiller and Groves testified to, involving the use of the knife, the injury to Groves and appellant's threatening language, the jury could neither reasonably nor lawfully have ignored this evidence and convicted appellant only of unlawful restraint. Appellant's first assignment of error is not well-taken.***

Notes and Questions

1. As *State v. Kroesen* illustrates, the victim in a kidnapping need not be moved very far. Should there be a required distance?

2. In *Kroesen*, can you identify in each witness's testimony the point at which the kidnapping occurred? Was there more than one act of kidnapping in any version of events?

3. Why do you think the defendant's version of events did not warrant an instruction for abduction or unlawful restraint? If you were representing the defendant in *Kroesen* what arguments would you put forward for either an instruction on abduction or unlawful restraint?

B. Robbery

1. Level of Force

In order for a theft offense to rise to the level of robbery, the defendant must use force or the threat of force. The threat must be of imminent harm, not future harm. The threat need not be directed at the victim (e.g., the threat could be made to the victim's family or companion).

The first case in this chapter, *State v. Weaver*, explores how much force is necessary to elevate a theft to a robbery. In certain jurisdictions, like Ohio, robbery can occur even without the defendant using force, or the threat of force, so long as the defendant commits the theft while in possession or control of a deadly weapon. The second case in this section, *State v. Wharf,* examines how a deadly weapon, even if it is not brandished or used, can elevate a theft to a robbery.

State v. Weaver, 1993 WL 441799 (Ohio Ct. App. 1993)

GRADY, Presiding Judge.

Defendant, Duane Weaver, was indicted and tried before a jury on one count of Robbery, R.C. 2911.02(A), one count of Theft, R.C. 2913.02(A)(1) and one count of Forgery, R.C. 2913.31(A)(3). The theft and forgery counts carried a prior offense of violence specification, R.C. 2941.143. The jury found Weaver guilty as charged. At sentencing, the trial court found that the prior offense of violence specification had been proved by the State. The trial court merged the theft charge with the robbery charge, and sentenced Weaver to eight to fifteen years imprisonment on the Robbery and three to five years on the Forgery, said sentences to be served consecutively.

Weaver has timely appealed his conviction and sentence and presents four assignments of error:

> I. APPELLANT'S CONVICTION FOR ROBBERY SHOULD BE REVERSED BECAUSE THE EVIDENCE ADDUCED AT TRIAL WAS LEGALLY INSUFFICIENT TO PROVE BEYOND A REASONABLE DOUBT ALL THE ELEMENTS OF ROBBERY.

> II. THE TRIAL COURT ERRED IN NOT INCORPORATING INTO THE DEFINITION OF FORCE THE REQUIREMENT OF ACTUAL OR POTENTIAL HARM.***

As the first and second assignments of error both address the element of force in a prosecution for robbery, we shall consider them together.

Relying upon the decision of this court in *State v. Furlow* (1992), 80 Ohio App. 3d 146, Duane Weaver argues in his first assignment of error that his conviction for Robbery must be reversed because the evidence presented at trial was insufficient as a matter of law to prove "force," one of the essential elements of the offense of Robbery.

R.C. 2911.02, which defines the offense of Robbery, provides as follows:

> (A) No person, in attempting or committing a theft offense, as defined in section 2913.01 of the Revised Code, or in fleeing immediately after such attempt or offense, shall use or threaten the immediate use of force against another.

"Force" is defined in R.C. 2901.01(A) as:

> *** any violence, compulsion, or constraint physically exerted by any means upon or against a person or thing.

In Furlow, this court concluded that the defendant's act of snatching a wallet and money out of the victim's firmer than usual grip did not constitute the type of force necessary to sustain a conviction for robbery. In so concluding we noted that the Committee Comment to R.C. 2911.02 indicates that the difference between robbery and what would otherwise be a theft is the element of actual or potential harm to persons. We further stated:

> In the context of robbery, at least two appellate courts have stated that the type of force envisioned by the legislature in enacting R.C. 2911.02 is "that which poses actual or potential harm to a person." *State v. Carter* (1985), 29 Ohio App. 3d 148. In our judgment, these courts, guided by the Committee Comment to R.C. 2911.02 have properly determined that the difference between theft and robbery is an element of actual or potential harm to persons.
>
> The difference between theft and robbery can be as great as the difference between a first degree misdemeanor and an aggravated felony of the second degree. R.C. 2913.02(B), 2911.02(B). Requiring that the force necessary to elevate a theft to a robbery involve actual or potential harm provides a meaningful distinction between the two offenses.
>
> The distinction between theft and robbery we found in *Furlow* finds support in common law. Robbery is a form of theft, an unlawful taking of the property of another. In former times it frequently was accomplished by some "strongarm" method that

resulted in harm to the victim or threatened the victim with harm. Thus, to constitute robbery, the unlawful taking was (1) of the victim's property from the victim's person or the area of the victim's personal control, (2) accomplished by force or violence that harmed the victim or the threat of it that put the victim in fear of such harm. The harm or threat of harm might be inflicted to accomplish the theft or to ward off the victim's natural attempts to resist or to stop the criminal in a flight from the crime. This same component of actual or potential physical harm is reflected in the statutory definition of "force," which contemplates more than a mere touching; it requires the application of "violence" or of physical "compulsion" or "constraint" to accomplish the theft. The Committee Comment to R.C. 2911.02(A) we cited in *Furlow* articulates and perpetuates this distinction in the case of the offense of Robbery by requiring evidence of actual or potential physical harm.

The State's evidence demonstrates that as the victim, Sally Rizer, was waiting to get into a parked car, Duane Weaver ran up from behind Rizer and snatched her purse from her shoulder. The State suggests that when Weaver pulled the purse from Rizer's shoulder, the shoulder strap became detached from the purse and that Weaver left the shoulder strap behind when he fled. However, there is no evidence in the record from which that fact may be found. The evidence pertaining to the taking of Rizer's purse consisted of the following testimony by Sally Rizer:

> We came out of the Douglas Inn and we were parked across the street by the Moose Club, and we were walking over to the car; and as I was waiting for him to unlock the door for me, I had my purse on my shoulder and my hand on my shoulder strap, and someone grabbed my purse from behind, had come up running and grabbed it, took off and went down Miami Street.
> Q. And when the purse was taken from you, were you actually wearing it at that time?
> A. Yes, I had it up on my shoulder with my hand on this strap (indicating), but not on-on the purse itself.
> Q. And was it ripped away from you?
> A. Yes.
> Q. Now, Sally, I'm going to show you what's been marked as State's Exhibit 1 for identification purposes and ask you, after you have had a chance to look at it, if you can identify it for us.
> A. Yes, this is the strap.

Q. All right. Now that we have established or that you have established from your testimony that the purse was yanked off, did you see the person that stole the purse before it was taken?
A. As we were crossing the street, I noticed a man walking in front of the—Is it the Champaign Inn?
Q. Okay.
A. Walking along on that side of the street, and I—I didn't think anything of it. I just happened to notice this man walking along there. And then when I felt my purse being yanked away and he went running, I realized that was the man that I had seen.

Neither this evidence nor any other evidence in this record constitutes proof from which a jury could find, beyond a reasonable doubt, that Sally Rizer suffered actual physical harm or its potential from the Defendant's acts. Accordingly, we must conclude as we did in *Furlow* that the evidence of force was, as a matter of law, insufficient to prove robbery. Weaver's first assignment of error is sustained.

The trial court instructed the jury in this case on both robbery and the lesser included offense of theft. In instructing on robbery the court utilized the definition of force set out in R.C. 2901.01(A). Duane Weaver argues in his second assignment of error that the trial court erred in not incorporating into its jury instruction on force the requirement of actual or potential harm to persons***.

Inasmuch as our disposition of Weaver's first assignment of error renders this assignment of error moot, it is not necessary that we decide the second. See, App.R. 12(A)(1)(c). Nevertheless, we point out what we said in *Furlow*:

> The definition of "force" in R.C. 2901.01(A), without more, does not serve to sufficiently distinguish the offenses of theft and robbery, which carry very different penalties. Concomitantly, a jury instruction that incorporates into the definition of force the requirement of actual or potential harm will provide the jury with a tangible means of evaluating evidence of force in robbery prosecutions that an instruction based solely on the R.C. 2901.01(A) definition will not provide.

The judgment of the trial court finding Duane Weaver guilty of robbery and sentencing him for that offense will be reversed and vacated. The judgment to the extent that it memorializes the jury's necessary finding that Weaver was guilty of theft is left undisturbed and, therefore, is affirmed. The case will be remanded to the trial court for the purpose of sentencing Weaver for theft.***

Having sustained Duane Weaver's first assignment of error, his conviction for robbery will be vacated and the case remanded to the trial court for the purpose of sentencing Weaver on the lesser included offense of theft. Otherwise, the judgment of the trial court will be affirmed.

YOUNG J., concurring:

I find the decision and opinion here perfectly correct if we recognize it is based upon an extremely narrow and unusual set of facts. If there had been evidence that the purse strap was broken when the snatch was made, it could reasonably be inferred that the grab of the purse was done with sufficient force to have pulled Sally Rizer off balance and perhaps causing her to fall. The potential for physical harm would certainly have been present and robbery would be the appropriate charge.

My point is that the *Furlow* doctrine should be regarded as very narrow in the extreme. Almost every taking of an object from the physical control of its owner in the presence of the owner raises the possibility of physical harm or a fear of it. *Furlow* must be narrowly confined, and probably would not have been applied even in this case had the record substantiated the argument of the State.

Notes and Questions

1. Would it make a difference if the appellant in *State v. Weaver* had come face-to-face with the victim prior to snatching the purse?

2. How much force is needed for a robbery conviction? The court in *Weaver* stated that the instructions to the jury on the definition of force should include "the requirement of actual or potential harm." Does adding this phrase help? If you were on the jury hearing the *Weaver* case, how much force would you need to see in order to convict the defendant of robbery?

3. What if the purse snatching had not been executed properly e.g., a struggle ensued or the defendant had to make more than one attempt at securing the purse would that be sufficient conduct for robbery?

2. Deadly Weapon

State v. Wharf, 86 Ohio St. 3d 375 (1999)

On November 12, 1996, appellant, Stephen M. Wharf, was driving an Isuzu Trooper ("Isuzu") that he had stolen from an automobile dealership in Louisville, Kentucky. Appellant drove the Isuzu into a SuperAmerica gas station in Clermont County, Ohio, filled the vehicle's gas tank with gasoline, and drove away from the gas station without paying. Trooper Matt Evans of the Ohio State Highway Patrol proceeded, in a police vehicle, to follow the Isuzu shortly after appellant exited the gas station. After receiving a radio dispatch regarding the theft of gasoline from the SuperAmerica, Evans activated his "pursuit lights," signaling appellant to pull over. At that point, the Isuzu accelerated rapidly and appellant led Evans on a high-speed chase with speeds exceeding 100 miles per hour and spanning three counties. During the chase, Evans noticed appellant reaching in the backseat of the Isuzu for "something." That something turned out to be a .22 caliber rifle.

Evans's high-speed pursuit of appellant lasted approximately twenty minutes and also involved law enforcement personnel from several localities. The pursuit ended when law enforcement officers placed "stop sticks" across the roadway and were able to disable the Isuzu by deflating its tires. Evans testified that when he approached the Isuzu to make the arrest, appellant was pointing a rifle at him through the vehicle's passenger side window. As a result, Evans fired his weapon at appellant, striking appellant in the head. After appellant dropped his rifle, he was removed from the Isuzu and placed under arrest.

Appellant was indicted for, among other things, aggravated robbery in violation of R.C. 2911.01(A)(1). The trial court amended the indictment to robbery in violation of R.C. 2911.02(A)(1). During trial, appellant proposed a jury instruction to the trial court regarding the deadly weapon element of R.C. 2911.02(A)(1). The elements of robbery set forth in R.C. 2911.02(A)(1) are that "[n]o person, in attempting or committing a theft offense or in fleeing immediately after the attempt or offense, shall *** [h]ave a deadly weapon on or about the offender's person or under the offender's control." Appellant requested an instruction that, before the jury could find appellant guilty of robbery, they must find that appellant acted *recklessly* in having a deadly weapon on or about his person. The trial court declined to give the proposed jury instruction.

Appellant was convicted of committing robbery. On appeal, appellant claimed that the trial court erred in failing to instruct the jury that "recklessly" was the requisite mental state for the deadly weapon element of robbery in R.C. 2911.02(A)(1). The Warren County Court of Appeals disagreed. In affirming the trial court's judgment, the court of appeals held that no mental condition or actual use of a deadly weapon is required pursuant to the statute. Thereafter, the court of appeals determined its judgment to be in conflict with the judgments of the courts of appeals in *State v. Anthony* (Sept. 30, 1994), Lake App. No. 93–L–096, *unreported, 1994 WL 587882*. Accordingly, the court of appeals entered an order certifying a conflict. This cause is now before this court upon our determination that a conflict exists.

DOUGLAS, J.

The question certified by the court of appeals is "whether R.C. 2901.21(B) requires the particular robbery element, codified in R.C. 2911.02(A)(1), '[h]ave a deadly weapon on or about the offender's person or under the offender's control,' to be committed with the mens rea of recklessness." In other words, the issue presented for our determination is whether robbery, as defined by R.C. 2911.02(A)(1), requires that, in order to prove the deadly weapon element of the offense, it is necessary that the defendant had recklessness as a state of mind.

R.C. 2901.21 provides in relevant part:

> (A) Except as provided in division (B) of this section, a person is not guilty of an offense unless *** :
>   ***
>   (2) He has the requisite degree of culpability for each element as to which a culpable mental state is specified by the section defining the offense.
> (B) When the section defining an offense does not specify any degree of culpability, and plainly indicates a purpose to impose strict criminal liability for the conduct described in such section, then culpability is not required for a person to be guilty of the offense. When the section neither specifies culpability nor plainly indicates a purpose to impose strict liability, recklessness is sufficient culpability to commit the offense.

As previously mentioned, the offense of robbery is defined in R.C. 2911.02. Appellant was convicted of violating R.C. 2911.02(A)(1), which provides:

> No person, in attempting or committing a theft offense or in fleeing immediately after the attempt or offense, shall *** [h]ave a deadly weapon on or about the offender's person or under the offender's control.

The parties agree that there is no mental state for culpability specified in R.C. 2911.02(A)(1). Because R.C. 2911.02(A)(1) is silent as to the necessary mental state of the offender, the certified question before us can be resolved by determining whether this statute plainly indicates an intent on the part of the General Assembly to impose strict criminal liability.

Appellant contends that the deadly weapon element set forth in R.C. 2911.02(A)(1) does not plainly indicate that robbery was intended to be a strict liability offense. In contrast, appellee argues that while the predicate offense to robbery, i.e., theft, requires a mental state of knowingly, no separate mens rea requirement should be read into the deadly weapon element of the offense of robbery. Appellee contends that possession alone of a deadly weapon is sufficient to find an offender in violation of the robbery statute.

Our reading of the statute leads us to conclude that the General Assembly intended that a theft offense, committed while an offender was in possession or control of a deadly weapon, is robbery and no intent beyond that required for the theft offense must be proven. According to the statutory language, possession of a deadly weapon is all that is required to elevate a theft offense to robbery. See *State v. Merriweather* (1980), 64 Ohio St. 2d 57[.] In fact, R.C. 2911.02(A)(1) provides that the offender need not have actual physical possession of the weapon but only that it be "under [his or her] control." See *State v. Brown* (1992), 63 Ohio St. 3d 349. Furthermore, one need not have the weapon in one's possession or under one's control while committing or attempting to commit a theft offense. A violation of R.C. 2911.02(A)(1) will also be found if the offender has a deadly weapon on or about his person, or under his control, while fleeing after such offense or attempt. Thus, no use, display, or brandishing of a weapon, or intent to do any of the aforementioned acts, is necessary according to the plain language of the statute. Had the legislature so intended, it certainly could have required a level of conduct more severe than it did in order to show a violation of the statute. Thus, by employing language making mere possession or control of a deadly weapon, as opposed to actual use or intent to use, a violation, it is clear to us that the General Assembly intended that R.C. 2911.02(A)(1) be a strict liability offense.

Furthermore, the 1973 Legislative Service Commission Comment to Am. Sub. H.B. No. 511 clearly indicates that the legislature, in defining the offenses of robbery and aggravated robbery, intended to punish the potential for harm to persons as well as actual harm. See Committee Comment to Am. Sub. H.B. No. 511, R.C. 2911.01 and 2911.02. In this regard, we find the rationale of *State v. Edwards* (1976), 50 Ohio App. 2d 63, 4 O.O.3d 44, 361 N.E.2d 1083, compelling. At issue in *Edwards* was the deadly weapon element of former R.C. 2911.01(A)(1), which contained essentially the same statutory language at issue here. The Montgomery County Court of Appeals construed the statutory language of former R.C. 2911.01(A)(1), as well as the legislative comments, and held that "[a] person who commits a theft offense is guilty of aggravated robbery, *** if at the time he has possession or control of a deadly weapon, even though he does not display, use or intend to use such weapon." *Id.* at syllabus. The *Edwards* court noted that "[t]he thrust and philosophy of [Am. Sub.] H.B. [No.] 511 is to remove the potential for harm that exists while one is committing a theft offense. The anti-social act is the theft offense, committed while armed with a weapon. Merely *having* the weapon is the potentially dangerous factual condition warranting the more severe penalty. As to the weapon, no mental condition or actual use is necessary or required under the statute." (Emphasis in original.) *Id.* at 66–67, 4

O.O.3d at 46, 361 N.E.2d at 1086. We find the reasoning in *Edwards* to be persuasive.

We are mindful of the appellate court decisions, cited *supra*, holding that "recklessness" is the mental state necessary to prove the deadly weapon element of R.C. 2911.02(A)(1). However, for the following reasons, we find the reasoning behind those decisions not persuasive.

The Summit County Court of Appeals in Gulley, the Lake County Court of Appeals in Anthony, and the Licking County Court of Appeals in Westbrook based their decisions largely on the case of *State v. Crawford* (1983), 10 Ohio App. 3d 207, 10 OBR 280, 461 N.E.2d 312. As appellee points out, reliance on *Crawford* in resolving the issue at hand is misplaced. *Crawford* involved former R.C. 2911.01(A)(2), aggravated robbery, which provided in pertinent part that "[n]o person, in attempting or committing a theft offense, *** or in fleeing immediately after such attempt or offense, shall *** [i]nflict, or attempt to inflict serious physical harm on another.*" (Emphasis added.) Am. Sub. H.B. No. 511, 134 Ohio Laws, Part II, 1866, 1922. In *Crawford*, the Hamilton County Court of Appeals held "recklessness [to] be the standard which the prosecution must meet in proving, beyond a reasonable doubt, that the defendant inflicted, or attempted to inflict, serious physical harm on another." *Crawford*, 10 Ohio App. 3d 207, paragraph one of the syllabus. Accordingly, we conclude that the physical harm element of former R.C. 2911.01(A)(2) and the deadly weapon element of R.C. 2911.02(A)(1) are not analogous provisions and cannot be compared in deciding the question, herein, certified to us for determination.

The Defiance County Court of Appeals did not rely on *Crawford* in reaching its decision in the *Steel* case. That court instead cited *State v. Merriweather* (1980), 64 Ohio St. 2d 57, for the proposition that recklessness was the mental state necessary to prove the deadly weapon element of R.C. 2911.02(A)(1). We respectfully disagree. We find, instead, that *Merriweather* stands for the proposition that "robbery under [former] R.C. 2911.02 [was] not a lesser-included offense of the crime of aggravated robbery under [former] R.C. 2911.01(A)(1)." *Merriweather*, 64 Ohio St. 2d 57. In fact, the court in *Merriweather* stated, in dictum, that "as long as the accused merely possesses a deadly weapon or dangerous ordnance during the commission of a theft[,]" the accused could be convicted of aggravated robbery pursuant to former R.C. 2911.01(A)(1). *Id.* at 59. Conversely, *McSwain* did involve the "physical harm" element of former R.C. 2911.01(A)(2) and, thus, in resolving the issue in *McSwain*, the Cuyahoga County Court of Appeals placed proper reliance on *Crawford*. However, we have already noted that the premise that *Crawford* and the physical harm element of former R.C. 2911.01(A)(2) are analogous is not well taken.

It is apparent that this case bears out precisely the potential type of harm the General Assembly sought to prevent when it enacted R.C. 2911.02(A)(1). Appellant committed a relatively minor theft offense. However, in attempting to elude law enforcement officials, the severity of appellant's unlawful actions and the risk of harm quickly escalated due, in large measure, to a deadly weapon being readily accessible to appellant. This was not a case of neglect, innocent mistake, or pure accident on the part of appellant. This was a situation where the potential for violence was greatly enhanced because appellant, in fleeing after committing a theft offense, had in his possession a firearm.

By making offenders like appellant strictly accountable for this type of conduct, the General Assembly clearly had in mind the laudable goal of protecting not only law enforcement officers, but also members of the general public from any potential increased risks of harm. It is axiomatic that an effective means of achieving that goal would be the reduction of criminal activity involving the use of firearms. Accordingly, we answer the certified question in the negative and hold that the deadly weapon element of R.C. 2911.02(A)(1), to wit, "[h]ave a deadly weapon on or about the offender's person or under the offender's control[,]" does not require the mens rea of recklessness. In order to prove a violation of R.C. 2911.02(A)(1), no specific mental state is necessary regarding the deadly weapon element of the offense of robbery. The judgment of the court of appeals is affirmed.

Judgment affirmed.

Notes and Questions

1. How far away can the weapon be from the defendant and still fulfill the possession element of robbery in Ohio? Do you think it would have mattered to the Ohio Supreme Court in *State v. Wharf* if the weapon was in the appellant's trunk rather than in the backseat?

2. What public policy arguments exist for treating the deadly weapon element of robbery under a strict liability standard? What about treating that same element under a reckless standard?

PART IV
Crimes Against Property

Chapter 13
Larceny and False Pretenses

A. Larceny

Early common law did not punish theft of personal property unless the defendant used force or threatened the victim (i.e., committed robbery). As society advanced, especially economically, it became clear that the common law needed to expand to cover the taking of personal property without force or threat of force. Thus, sometime during the Middle Ages, the common law created the crime of larceny which was defined as the "trespassory taking and carrying away the personal property of another with the intent to permanently deprive." Larceny, which involves the defendant obtaining possession of the property but not title, is a specific intent crime.

While the definition of larceny is fairly straightforward, the case law surrounding it is not. This is primarily because larceny was a capital offense at common law, which caused many judges to strictly apply its elements in order to avoid finding certain defendants guilty of the crime. This in turn left some thefts of personal property unpunished. These gaps in the law were later filled-in legislatively through the creation of new crimes such as embezzlement and false pretenses.

Over time, jurisdictions found the various laws regulating the unlawful taking of personal property to be both redundant and unnecessarily complex. As a result, most jurisdictions, including Ohio, turned to a catchall theft statute that incorporates the various ways in which individuals unlawfully obtain the personal property of another. While it is important to know the modern theft statutes, it is equally important to be able to trace these laws back to their historical antecedents.

1. Custody vs. Possession

United States v. Mafnas, 701 F. 2d 83 (1983)

PER CURIAM:

Appellant (Mafnas) was convicted in the U.S. District Court of Guam of stealing money from two federally insured banks in violation of 18 U.S.C. § 2113(b) which makes it a crime to ". . . take . . . with intent to steal . . . any money belonging to . . . any bank . . . ."

Mafnas was employed by the Guam Armored Car Service (Service), which was hired by the Bank of Hawaii and the Bank of America to deliver bags of money.

On three occasions Mafnas opened the bags and removed money. As a result he was convicted of three counts of stealing money from the banks.

This Circuit has held that § 2113(b) applies only to common law larceny which requires a trespassory taking. Mafnas argues his taking was embezzlement rather than larceny as he had lawful possession of the bags, with the consent of the banks, when he took the money.

This problem arose centuries ago, and common law has evolved to handle it. The law distinguishes between possession and custody. R. Perkins and R. Boyce, Criminal Law 296-302 (1982), 3 Wharton's Criminal Law 346-57 (C. Torcia, 14th ed. 1980).

> Ordinarily, . . . if a person receives property for a limited or temporary purpose, he is only acquiring custody. Thus, if a person receives property from the owner with instructions to deliver it to the owner's house, he is only acquiring custody; therefore, his subsequent decision to keep the property for himself would constitute larceny.

3 Wharton's Criminal Law, at 353.

The District Court concluded that Mafnas was given temporary custody only, to deliver the money bags to their various destinations. Ex. R. at 8. The later decision to take the money was larceny, because it was beyond the consent of the owner, who retained constructive possession until the custodian's task was completed. This rationale was used in *United States v. Pruitt,* 446 F.2d 513, 515 (6th Cir. 1971). There, Pruitt was employed by a bank as a messenger. He devised a plan with another person to stage a fake robbery and split the money which Pruitt was delivering for the bank. The Sixth Circuit found that Pruitt had mere custody for the purpose of delivering the money, and that his wrongful conversion constituted larceny.

Mafnas distinguishes *Pruitt, supra,* because the common law sometimes differentiates between employees, who generally obtain custody only, and others (agents), who acquire possession. Although not spelled out, Mafnas essentially claims that he was a bailee, and that the contract between the banks and Service resulted in Service having lawful possession, and not mere custody over the bags. *See Lionberger v. United States,* 371 F.2d 831, 840, 178 Ct. Cl. 151 (Ct. Cl.) *cert. denied,* ("A bailment situation is said to arise where an owner, while retaining title, delivers personalty to another for some particular purpose upon an express or implied contract.")

The common law also found an answer to this situation. A bailee who "breaks bulk" commits larceny.

> Under this doctrine, the bailee-carrier was given possession of a bale, but not its contents. Therefore, when the bailee pilfered the entire bale, he was not guilty of larceny; but when he broke open the bale and took a portion or all of the contents, he was guilty of larceny because his taking was trespassory and it was from the constructive possession of another.

Wharton's Criminal Law 353-54.

Either way, Mafnas has committed the common law crime of larceny, replete with trespassory taking.

Mafnas also cannot profit from an argument that any theft on his part was from Service and not from the banks. Case law is clear that since what was taken was property belonging to the banks, it was property or money "in the care, custody, control, management, or possession of any bank" within the meaning of 18 U.S.C. § 2113(b), notwithstanding the fact that it may have been in the possession of an armored car service serving as a bailee for hire. *See United States v. Jakalski,* 237 F.2d 503 (7th Cir. 1956), *cert. denied.*

Therefore, his conviction is AFFIRMED.

2. Trespassory Taking

Rex v. Pear, 1 Leach 212, 168 English Report 208 (1779)

The prisoner was indicted for stealing a black horse, the property of Samuel Finch. It appeared in evidence that Samuel Finch was a Livery-Stable keeper in the Borough; and that the prisoner, on the 2nd of July 1779, hired the horse of him to go to Sutton, in the county of Surry, and back again, saying on being asked where he lived, that he lodged at No. 25 in King-street, and should return about eight o'clock the same evening. He did not return; and it was proved that he had sold the horse on the very day he had hired it, to one William Hollist, in Smithfield Market; and that he had no lodging at the place to which he had given the prosecutor directions.

The learned Judge said: There had been different opinions on the law of this class of cases; that the general doctrine then was that if a horse be let for a particular portion of time, and after that time is expired, the party hiring, instead of returning the horse to its owner, sell it and convert the money to his own use, it is felony, because there is then no privity of contract subsisting between the parties; that in the present case the horse was hired to take a journey into Surry, and the prisoner sold him the same day, without taking any such journey; that there were also other circumstances which imported that at the time of the hiring the prisoner had it in intention to sell the horse, as his saying that he lodged at a place where in fact he was not known. He therefore left it with the Jury to consider, Whether the prisoner meant at the time of the hiring to take such journey, but was afterwards tempted to sell the horse? For if so he must be acquitted; but that if they were of opinion that at the time of the hiring the journey was a mere pretence to get the horse into his possession, and he had no intention to take such journey but intended to sell the horse, they would find that fact specially for the opinion of the Judges.

The Jury found that the facts above stated were true; and also that the prisoner had hired the horse with a fraudulent view and intention of selling it immediately.

The question was referred to the Judges, Whether the delivery of the horse by the prosecutor to the prisoner, had so far changed the possession of the property, as to render the subsequent conversion of it a mere breach of trust, or whether the conversion was felonious?

The judges differed greatly in opinion on this case; and delivered their opinions *seriatim* upon it at Lord Chief Justice De Gray's house on 4th February 1780 and on the 22nd of the same month Mr. Baron Perryn delivered their opinion on it. The majority of them thought, That the question, as to the original intention of the prisoner in hiring the horse, had been properly left to the jury; and as they had found, that his view in so doing was fraudulent, the parting with the property had not changed the nature of the possession, but that it remained unaltered at the time of the conversion; and that the prisoner was therefore guilty of felony.

Notes and Questions

1. *Rex v. Pear* illustrates one of the ways to commit larceny. Here, the defendant committed larceny by trick. With larceny by trick, the trespassory taking is accomplished by a misrepresentation or a false promise of a past or present fact. Under the majority view, a false future promise which the promisor does not

intend to keep at the time made will also meet the requirements of larceny by trick. What false misrepresentations did the defendant make to Samuel Finch? Can you think of other ways the defendant may trespassorily take someone else's property?

2. In *Pear*, what was the exact issue before the court on appeal? Why was it necessary for the jury to determine the prisoner's intentions when he first obtained possession of the horse?

3. Asportation

State v. Cadle, 2008-Ohio-3639 (Ohio Ct. App. 2008)

SLABY, Presiding Judge

Defendant-Appellant, Kevin Cadle, appeals his conviction and sentence by the Summit County Court of Common Pleas. We affirm.

On July 28, 2006, employees of the Home Depot in Cuyahoga Falls saw three men who, in their judgment, were acting suspiciously. Defendant was seen pushing a flat cart loaded with a vanity toward the checkout area. Before he reached the checkout, Defendant left the cart behind. He then exited the store. Employees found numerous Dewalt power tools concealed within the vanity, and Defendant was arrested at a nearby restaurant. On September 8, 2006, he was indicted on a charge of theft in violation of R.C. 2913.02(A)(1)/(3), a fifth-degree felony. Defendant was found guilty by a jury and, on January 2, 2008, the trial court sentenced him to a six-month prison term. Defendant timely appealed.***

R.C. 2913.02(A)(3), which prohibits theft, provides that "No person, with purpose to deprive the owner of property or services, shall knowingly obtain or exert control over either the property or services *** [b]y deception[.]" To deprive one of property is to:

> (1) Withhold property of another permanently, or for a period that appropriates a substantial portion of its value or use, or with purpose to restore it only upon payment of a reward or other consideration;
>
> (2) Dispose of property so as to make it unlikely that the owner will recover it; [or]
>
> (3) Accept, use, or appropriate money, property, or services, with purpose not to give proper consideration in return for the money, property, or services, and without reasonable justification or excuse for not giving proper consideration. R.C. 2913.01(C).

Deprivation, however, need not be complete:

> "The least removing of items with an intent to deprive the owner of it is a sufficient asportation, though the property is not removed from the premises of the owner nor retained in the possession of the thief. ***" [This] comports with common sense, for to wait until the suspect leaves the store with the stolen merchandise may indeed jeopardize the successful apprehension of the suspect. *State v. Williams* (1984), 16 Ohio App. 3d 232, 234.

Consequently, courts have concluded that a theft has occurred when a defendant conceals merchandize on his person in a retail establishment even if he is detained or discards the merchandise before leaving the premises. "The state need only prove that appellant exerted control over the merchandise with the intent to deprive the store of its property, regardless of whether [the defendant] was still in the store. The slightest act of removal or hiding of property, coupled with the requisite intent, is a sufficient asportation in the eyes of the law." ***

Mr. Marc Garnek, a Home Depot employee assigned to "Asset Protection," worked the afternoon shift at Home Depot on July 28, 2006. Mr. Garnek's job was to "walk the stores and look for potential shoplifters" while dressed in plainclothes. Mr. Garnek testified that as he patrolled the aisles on July 28th, he recognized two individuals with whom Home Depot had problems with theft in the past: Brian Stanton and Chad Doyle. According to Mr. Garnek, Stanton and Doyle were accompanied by a third individual, whom he identified as Defendant. Mr. Garnek, whose testimony accompanied a surveillance video from the store, testified that Defendant entered the Home Depot through the lumber entrance with an empty flat cart. Mr. Garnek recalled that he noticed behavior from Stanton, Doyle, and Defendant that raised his suspicions. Specifically, he observed that the three were located in an aisle in which the view was partially obscured by two large doors that had been placed on a cart and that Doyle and Defendant appeared to be acting as lookouts. He testified that Stanton and Doyle selected Dewalt power tools from an end-of-aisle display at least four times and returned with the tools to a flat cart that contained a vanity.

As Mr. Garnek watched, Defendant took possession of the cart containing the vanity, left the aisle, and proceeded toward the main checkout area. Prior to leaving the store, however, Defendant abandoned the cart and left empty handed. Mr. Garnek followed Defendant from the store and saw Stanton and Doyle sitting in a van watching the doors from which Defendant exited. The two pulled out from the parking space after Defendant left with Mr. Garnek close behind, and Defendant continued across the parking lot. Mr. Garnek testified that the vanity found on the cart was "packed very neatly" and "filled with Dewalt power tools." The value of the items, including the vanity in which they were stowed, was $3,434.00. Mr. Garnek acknowledged that all of the tools were recovered and that Home Depot did not suffer a loss.***

Having reviewed the evidence in this case, along with the reasonable inferences that can be drawn therefrom, this Court concludes that Defendant's conviction for theft is not against the manifest weight of the evidence. The testimony at trial established that Defendant did not leave Home Depot with any contraband. It also established, however, that Defendant exerted control over the tools with the intent to deprive Home Depot of its merchandise.***

Defendant's characterization of attempted theft as a lesser included offense of theft is incorrect. Attempt is one of "three groups of lesser offenses on which, when supported by the evidence at trial, [a jury] must be charged and on which it may reach a verdict[.]" *State v. Deem* (1988), 40 Ohio St. 3d 205, paragraph one of the syllabus. In this respect, attempt is similar to, yet conceptually distinct from, lesser included offenses and crimes that represent inferior degrees of the indicted offense:

> Each of these groups of offenses is conceptually separate and distinct from the group of lesser "included" offenses also provided for in the statute and rule.
>
> Attempts, as criminal offenses, arise from R.C. 2923.02 and need not be included within the indictment for the completed offense. Rather, if during the course of trial the defendant presents sufficient evidence that his conduct was unsuccessful in constituting the indicted offense, an instruction to the jury on attempt would be proper. *Id.* at 208.

Defendant argues that an attempted theft charge was warranted in this case because "he abandoned any effort to commit the offense by walking out of the store without trying to take any merchandise and without being approached by anyone from Home Depot in regards to any of his actions while in the store." As set forth in this Court's disposition of Defendant's first and second assignments of error, however, Defendant's actions were sufficient to constitute a completed theft. See, e.g., *State v. Bateman* (June 26, 1997), 10th Dist. No. 96APA09-1159, at *6 (concluding that the defendant's actions were sufficient to constitute a completed theft and that an attempt instruction was not warranted). In this case, an instruction on attempted theft was not required because the evidence did not support the conclusion that Defendant was unsuccessful in committing the offense of theft. See *Deem* at 208. Because the trial court was not required to instruct the jury regarding attempted theft, it follows that an abandonment instruction was not required either. See, e.g., R.C. 2923.02(D).***

Judgment affirmed.

Notes and Questions

1. According to *State v. Cadle*, must the defendant actually leave the store with merchandise to be convicted of theft? At what point had the defendant met all the elements for theft? As to the asportation element, how much movement of the merchandise is necessary?

2. If the defendant in *Cadle* had returned all the items on the cart back to the shelf where he obtained them before he made his way to the checkout, could he be convicted of theft? What about attempted theft? If you were the prosecutor in this case, would you have pursued a charge of theft or attempted theft? Why might you choose attempted theft in this case?

3. If the defendant was unaware of the power tools in the vanity and then proceeded to exit the store could he have been convicted of larceny? What element of larceny would be difficult for the prosecution under this scenario?

4. As a practical matter, why do you think a store manager or loss prevention officer would wait until a shoplifter has gone beyond the last point of sale before attempting to apprehend or stop the suspect for theft?

4. Intent to Permanently Deprive and the Continuing Trespass Doctrine

To be convicted of larceny at common law, the defendant at the time of the trespassory taking had to have the intent to permanently deprive the victim of possession of his or her property. If the defendant developed the intent to steal after the trespassory taking then it was not larceny. To combat this concurrence requirement, courts created a legal fiction entitled "continuing trespass." Thus, if the defendant wrongfully (as opposed to innocently) takes the property of another, his initial trespass continues so long as the wrongdoer remains in possession of the property.

Most of the cases applying the continuing trespass doctrine do not involve larceny by trick. Also, it is an open question whether the continuing trespass doctrine even applies to larceny by trick.

5. Lost and Abandoned Property

Brooks v. State, 35 Ohio St. 46 (1878)

The plaintiff in error, George Brooks, at the February term, 1879, of the Court of Common Pleas of Trumbull county, was convicted of larceny in stealing $200 in bank bills, the property of Charles B. Newton. It appears from the evidence, that Newton resided at Newton Falls, in the county of Trumbull, and that, on the 24th of October, 1878, he came to the city of Warren in a buggy to attend to some business. He fastened his horse to a hitching post on Market street. On his way home, in the forenoon of the same day, he discovered that he had lost the package of bank bills in question. He made search for it in various places where he had been, but failed to find it. He looked where he hitched his horse on Market street, but he states that he did not look there very carefully, as there was a team of horses hitched there at the time. Notice of the loss was published in the two newspapers printed in Warren, and in one printed in Leavittsburgh, which also had a circulation in Warren.

On Wednesday, the 20th of November following, the defendant, who resided in Warren, while working on Market street, near the post at which Newton hitched his horse, found the roll or package of bank bills. The package was found "five or six feet from the hitching post." He was, at the time, working in company with several other laborers. At the time he found the money one of these laborers was within ten feet and another within twenty feet of him, but he did not let any of them know that he had found the money. He states, in his testimony, that he put it in his pocket as soon as he found it. Just after finding the package, he picked up a one dollar bill, which he did show to them. This bill was wet and muddy, and he sold it to one of them for twenty-five cents, saying if none of them bought it he would keep it himself. He testifies the reason he sold it was that he did not want them to know at the time that he had found the other money. This bill was shown to several persons at the time, and was put on the hitching post to dry. Within a half hour after finding the money, at the time of stopping for dinner, he quit work, and, at his request, was paid off. He spent part of the money, the same day, for a pair of boots, and for other purposes, and let a Mrs. Lease have fifty dollars of it the same day, with which to purchase furniture for his wife, and for other purposes. Mrs. Lease saw him have the money at his house the afternoon of the same day. At the time of receiving the money she told him that she did not want to take the money if it was stolen or was counterfeit. He told her he received it from an uncle, and, as another time, on being asked by her about it, said, "what if I found it?"

Evidence was also given that the defendant, with his wife, shortly afterward left Warren, and that he attempted to secrete himself before he left. The evidence did not show that the defendant saw any of the notices of the loss of the money published in the newspapers, or that he had any notice of the loss by Newton at the time it was found. Much other evidence was given, but the foregoing is sufficient to show the character of the legal questions raised.

The evidence being closed, the defendant's counsel asked the court to instruct the jury as follows: "To render the finder of lost property guilty of larceny, he must know who the owner is at the time he acquires possession, or have the means of identifying him *instanter*, or have reason to believe that he knows who the owner is." This instruction was refused.

The defendant's counsel also, among other things, asked the court to instruct the jury as follows:

> That it is not enough to render the finder of lost property guilty of larceny, that he has the general means of discovering the owner by honest diligence. In order to convict the finder of lost property of larceny, the jury must be satisfied that the taking of the property was with a felonious intent. It is not sufficient that, after finding the money, it was converted to the owner's use with a felonious intent.

This instruction was refused in the form asked; but, in the general charge, the court instructed the jury on the subject as follows:

> But though the money was actually lost, and the defendant found it, and at the time of finding supposed it to be lost, and appropriated it with intent to take entire dominion over it, yet really believing that the owner could not be found, that was not larceny and he can not be convicted. The intent to steal must have existed at the time of the taking. . . . It is not enough that he had the general means of discovering the owner by honest diligence. He was not bound to inquire on the streets or at the printing offices for the owner, though if at the time of the taking he knew he had reasonable means of ascertaining that fact, that might be taken as showing a belief that the owner of the money could be found. In order to convict, it must be shown that the taking of the property was with felonious intent, that is with intent to steal, under the definition I have given you; and it is not sufficient that afterward, after finding the money, it was converted to his own use with felonious intent. The intent must have existed at the time of the finding.

To the refusal to charge as asked exceptions were taken.

WHITE, J.

We find no ground in the record for reversing the judgment.

The first instruction asked was properly refused. It was not necessary to the conviction of the accused that he should, at the time of taking possession of the property, have known, or have had reason to believe he knew, the *particular person* who owned it, or have had the means of identifying him *instanter*. The charge asked was liable to this construction, and there was no error in its refusal.

The second instruction asked was substantially given in the general charge.

Larceny may be committed of property that is casually lost as well as of that which is not. The title to the property, and its constructive possession, still remains in the owner; and the finder, if he takes possession of it for his own use, and not for the benefit of the owner, would be guilty of trespass, unless the circumstances were such as to show that it had been abandoned by the owner.

The question is, under what circumstances does such property become the subject of larceny by the finder?

In *Baker v. The State,* 29 Ohio St. 184, the rule stated by Baron Park, in Thurborn's case, was adopted. It was there laid down, that "when a person finds goods that have actually been lost, and takes possession with intent to appropriate them to his own use, really believing, at the time, or having good ground to believe, that the owner can be found, it is larceny."

It must not be understood from the rule, as thus stated, that the finder is bound to use diligence or to take pains in making search for the owner. His belief, or grounds of belief, in regard to finding the owner, is not to be determined by the degree of diligence that he might be able to use to accomplish that purpose, but by the circumstances apparent to him at the time of finding the property. If the property has not been abandoned by the owner, it is the subject of larceny by the finder, when, at the time he finds it, he has reasonable ground to believe, from the nature of the property, or the circumstances under which it is found, that if he does not conceal but deals honestly with it, the owner will appear or be ascertained. But before the finder can be guilty of larceny, the intent to steal the property must have existed at the time he took it into his possession.

There are cases in conflict with the foregoing view; but we believe it correct in principle, and well supported by authority.***

The case was fairly submitted to the jury; and from an examination of the evidence, we find no ground for interfering with the action of the court below in refusing a new trial.

Judgment affirmed.

OKEY, J., dissenting.

I do not think the plaintiff was properly convicted. A scavenger, while in the performance of his duties in cleaning the streets, picked up from the mud and water in the gutter, a roll of money, consisting of bank bills of the denominations of five, ten, and twenty dollars, and amounting, in the aggregate, to two hundred dollars. It had laid there several weeks, and the owner had ceased to make search for it. The evidence fails to show that the plaintiff had any information of a loss previous to the finding, and in his testimony he denied such notice. There was no mark on the money to indicate the owner, nor was there any thing in the attending circumstances pointing to one owner more than another. He put the money in his pocket, without calling the attention of his fellow-workmen to the discovery, and afterward, on the same day, commenced applying it to his own use.

No doubt the plaintiff was morally bound to take steps to find the owner. An honest man would not thus appropriate money, before he had made the finding public, and endeavored to find the owner. But in violating the moral obligation, I do not think the plaintiff incurred criminal liability.

Baker's case, 29 Ohio St. 184, was correctly decided. It is stated in the opinion not only that when he took the goods he intended to appropriate them to his own use, but that he had reasonable ground for believing that Alden was the owner. A passage from *Regina v. Thurborn*, 1 Den. C.C. 387, is cited in that case as containing a correct statement of the law. But a careful examination of *Regina v. Thurborn* will show that the court which rendered the decision would not have sustained this conviction; and that case has been repeatedly followed in England and this country. *R. v. Preston*, 2 Den. C.C. 351.

The obligation, stated in the syllabus, that the finder must deal "honestly" with the money, is too indefinite; and the opinion contains no satisfactory explanation of it. This leaves both law and fact to the jury, without any rule to guide them. What one jury might think was honest dealing, another jury might think was the reverse. The adverb *properly or rightfully* would have been as certain.

Notes and Questions

1. Someone who finds abandoned property is not guilty of larceny; however, lost property is something different. To be guilty of larceny as a finder of lost property, the defendant must intend to steal it and either know who the owner is or have reason to believe that the owner's identity could be discovered? If the intent to steal occurs after the finder obtains possession of the property, this would not be larceny.

2. Do you think the defendant in *Brooks v. State* was guilty of larceny? If the defendant had come to you for legal advice on what to do with the money, what would you have told him?

6. Mistaken Transfer of Property

R v. Middleton, **Crown Cases Reserved, 7 June 1873**

The case came on to be argued in the ordinary course before five Judges, but on the argument they were not agreed, and the case was adjourned to be argued before all the Judges. Pollock, B, was absent at chambers, and Quain, J, was unwell. The above-named 15 Judges heard the case, and, after time taken to consider, 11 of them were of opinion that the conviction ought to be affirmed, but Martin, B, Bramwell, B, Brett, J, and Cleasby, B, dissented.

At the session of the Central Criminal Court held on Monday, 23 September 1872, George Middleton was tried before me for feloniously stealing certain money to the amount of £ 8 16s 10d, the moneys of the Postmaster-General.

The ownership of the money was laid in other counts in the Queen and in the mistress of the local post-office.

It was proved by the evidence that the prisoner was a depositor in a post-office savings bank, in which a sum of 11s stood to his credit.

In accordance with the practice of the bank he duly gave notice to withdraw 10s, stating in such notice the number of his depositor's book, the name of the post-office, and the amount to be withdrawn.

A warrant for 10s was duly issued to the prisoner, and a letter of advice was duly sent to the post-office at Notting Hill to pay the prisoner 10s. He presented himself at that post-office and handed in his depositor's book and the warrant to the clerk, who, instead of referring to the proper letter of advice for 10s, referred by mistake to another letter of advice for £ 8 16s 10d, and placed upon the counter a £ 5 note, three sovereigns, a half sovereign, and silver and copper, amounting altogether to £ 8 16s 10d.

The clerk entered the amount paid, viz. £ 8 16s 10d in the prisoner's depositor's book, and stamped it, and the prisoner took up the money and went away.

The mistake was afterwards discovered and the prisoner was brought

back, and upon being asked for his depositor's book said he had burnt it. Other evidence of the prisoner having had the money was given.

It was objected by counsel for the prisoner that there was no larceny because the clerk parted with the property and intended to do so, and because the prisoner did not get possession by any fraud or trick.

The jury found that the prisoner had the animus furandi at the moment of taking the money from the counter, and that he knew the money to be the money of the Postmaster-General when he took it up.

A verdict of guilty was recorded, and I reserved for the opinion of the Court for Crown Cases Reserved the question whether, under the circumstances above disclosed, the prisoner was properly found guilty of larceny.

I discharged the prisoner on recognizance with sureties to appear and receive judgment when called upon.

(Signed) THOMAS CHAMBERS

PIGOTT B., Concurring.

I agree in the judgment of the majority of the court; except that I do not adopt the reasons which are there assigned for holding that the mistaken intention of the clerk did not under the circumstances here prevent the case from being one of larceny on the part of the prisoner. I quite accede to that proposition, but my reason is that, in the view I take of the facts, the intention and acts of the clerk are not material in determining the nature of the prisoner's act and intent; because the transaction between them stopped short of placing the money completely in the prisoner's possession, and could in no way have misled the prisoner. The case states, the clerk placed the money on the counter. He then entered the amount of it in the prisoner's book and stamped it. This no doubt gave the prisoner the opportunity of taking up the money, and he did so in the presence of the clerk; but before doing so he must have seen by the amount that the clerk was in error, and that the money could not really be intended in payment of his order, and therefore was not for him, but for another person. It was with full knowledge of this mistake that he resolved to avail himself of it and, in fact, to steal the money. The interval afforded him the opportunity, and he did in fact conceive the animus furandi, while as yet he had not taken the money in his manual possession. The dividing line may appear to be a fine one; but it is, I think, very distinct and well defined in fact, for it was with this formed intention in his mind that he took possession of the money. If complete possession had been given by the clerk to the prisoner, so that no act of the latter were required to complete it after his discovery of the mistake and his own formed intention to steal it, I should not feel myself at liberty to affirm this conviction. In that case the prisoner would have done nothing to defraud the clerk, and the latter intending (to the extent to which he had such intention) as much to pass the property as the possession in the money, there would be nothing to deprive the matter of the character of a business transaction fully completed. I desire to adhere to the law stated in the 3rd Institute, p ll0: "The intent to steal must be when it cometh to his hands or possession; for if he hath the possession of it once lawfully, though he hath animus furandi afterwards, and carrieth it away, it is no larceny." But the facts satisfy me, and the jury have found upon them, that the prisoner had the animus furandi while the money was yet on the counter, and that at the moment of taking it up he knew the money to be the Postmaster-General's. The case is therefore very much like that of a finder who immediately on finding it knows or has the means of knowing the owner and yet determines to steal it. (2 Russell, 169.) The same facts satisfy the requirements in the definition of larceny, that the taking must be invito domino. The loser does not intend to be robbed of his property, nor did the clerk in this case; and the prisoner's conduct is unaffected by the clerk's apparent consent, in ignorance of its real nature. I therefore agree in affirming the conviction.

DISPOSITION:
Conviction affirmed.

Notes and Questions

1.   If you are at your local grocery store and you pay for your groceries in cash and the clerk makes a mistake and gives you back too much change and you accept the money, have you committed larceny at common law? Would it matter when you discovered the clerk's mistake? For example, does it make a difference if you discover the mistake at the moment you receive the money or after you exit the store and review the receipt?

B. False Pretenses

False pretenses was one of the first gap fillers created by statute to address thefts not covered by larceny.   False pretenses was necessary because larceny at common law did not punish individuals who through a false misrepresentation obtained title of the property. The first two cases in this chapter, *Winnett v. State* and *Chaplin v. United States*, explore the term "material misrepresentation" and whether an intention or future promise can meet the elements of false pretenses.

In many ways, false pretenses resembles larceny by trick.   The main difference between false pretenses and larceny by trick is that the defendant only obtains possession of the property with larceny by trick while false pretenses provides the defendant with title. As illustrated by *Blackledge v. United States*, the last case in this chapter, it is not always easy to determine whether the defendant obtained possession or title of the property. Generally speaking, the best way to make this determination is to look at whether the victim intends to transfer title to the defendant.

1. Past or Present Fact and Material Misrepresentation

Winnett v. State, 18 Ohio C.C. 515 (1899)

VOORHEES, J.

The case of Albert E. Winnett, plaintiff in error, against the state of Ohio, defendant in error, is in this court on error. The plaintiff contends that the court below erred in overruling a demurrer to the indictment upon which he was tried and convicted. The indictment charged plaintiff in error with obtaining the signature of one Swartz to a promissory note for two hundred dollars, by false pretenses.

> The indictment is founded upon sec. 7076, Rev. Stat., which provides: "Whoever, by any false pretense, with intent to defraud, obtains from any person anything of value, or procures the signature of any person as maker, indorser or guarantor thereof, to any bond, bill, receipt, promissory note, draft or check, or any other evidence of indebtedness, *** shall, if the value of the property or instrument so procured is thirty-five dollars or more, be imprisoned in the penitentiary," etc.

The indictment in this case is drawn upon the above section of the statute, and, omitting formal parts, is as follows:

> The defendant, Albert E. Winnett, about October 7, 1896, at the county of Stark and state of Ohio, did unlawfully and falsely pretend, with intent to defraud one Calvin Swartz, that he wanted to show to one Harmon, who was at his house and a special friend of Winnett, that he, Winnett, had a good standing in the community of Middlebranch, Ohio, where he, Winnett, lived, and that he had friends there who had confidence in him, who would sign and indorse bankable paper for him; and did further unlawfully and falsely pretend that he wanted him, Swartz, to make, sign and indorse some promissory notes with him, Winnett, for the purpose aforesaid, and for no other purpose; and that the notes would then and there be left in the possession of him, the said Winnett; that he would keep the said notes in his possession, and he would then destroy them; by which said false pretenses theretofore made by Winnett, he did unlawfully procure the signature of said Swartz as maker to a certain promissory note of the value of two hundred dollars (a copy of the note is set forth in the indictment) whereas in truth and in fact he, Winnett, did not want to show to said Harmon that he, Winnett, had a good standing in the community of Middlebranch, Ohio, where he lived, and did not want to show that he had friends there who had confidence in him, who would sign and indorse bankable paper for him; that he did not want Swartz to make, sign and indorse some or any promissory notes for him for the purpose aforesaid, but did want said signature to said note for the purpose of raising money thereon; nor did he

intend said notes would be left in the possession of him, Winnett, nor keep them in his possession, or destroy the same; and at the time he did pretend as aforesaid, he well knew said false pretenses to be false.

To constitute the offense described in the statute and set forth in the indictment, it is not sufficient simply to follow the language of the statute. The particular pretense or pretenses by which the signature of the person to the instrument was procured must be specifically stated, and the indictment must aver all the material facts which it is necessary to prove to produce a conviction, and with such reasonable certainty as to advise the accused what he may expect to meet on the trial. Four things must concur, and four distinct averments must be proved:

> First—There must be an intent to defraud.
> Second—There must be an actual fraud committed.
> Third—False pretenses must be used for the purpose of perpetrating the fraud; and
> Fourth—The fraud must be accomplished by means of the false pretenses made use of for the purpose, viz., they must be the cause which induced the party to sign the instrument or part with his property.

The pretense or pretenses relied upon must relate to a past event or an existing fact; and that any representation or assurance in relation to future transactions, however false or fraudulent it may be, is not, within the meaning of the statute, a false pretense which lays the foundation for a criminal prosecution. *Dillingham v. State*, 5 Ohio St., 280, 283; *Commonwealth v. Drew*, 19 Pick., 179, 185.

It is contended on behalf of the state that the intent, the mental operation of the mind of the accused, existing at the time he procured the signature of Swartz to the note, was an existing fact, and, although such existing intent or mental action was coupled with a promise as to what he would do in the future with the note, would constitute a crime under the statute.

The defendant went to Swartz and requested him to sign a note, pretending he wanted to show the note to his friend Harmon, whom, he represented, was then at his, Winnett's, home. It is not alleged in the indictment that Harmon was not at his home and his representation was, therefore, false. Such a statement or pretense would have related to an existing fact. Representing that Harmon was at his house, and in using that pretense for the purpose and with the intent to get the signature of Swartz to the note, and he did so get it, and it was untrue, this would be a statement or assurance of an existing fact.

What influenced Swartz to sign the note?

It was not that Winnett wanted to show the note to Harmon that induced him to sign the note; but rather his promise that he would retain that note in his possession and would destroy it, influenced his action. The indictment does not negative the statement that Winnett did not retain the note in his possession or did not destroy it. These are material matters.

But, first, was there a pretense or a representation made of a past or existing fact?

An indictment for false pretenses cannot be founded upon an assertion of an existing intention, although the intention did not in fact exist; there must be a false representation as to an existing fact.

People v. Blanchard, 90 New York, 314, is an authority in point here.

That case was an indictment for obtaining property under false pretenses. The representations alleged to be false were that the accused "was agent for Otto Gulick, of Utica, and that he wanted to buy 18 cattle for Gulick, and that Gulick wanted him to buy for and send him 18 cattle; and that he had a contract with Gulick for buying cattle for him, and Gulick had agreed to pay him $1 a head for buying cattle." "This," says the judge announcing the opinion, on page 318, "taking this accusation as a whole, and construing it in the ordinary sense and acceptation of the language used, charges a false representation or agency in the purchase of the cattle for Gulick. It is impossible to misunderstand the tenor of these representations, taken together. They import an agency existing, action desired and intended under such agency, and a compensation of $1 a head as a reward for the services rendered."

But the court says, at page 319: "Disregarding entirely the alleged claim of agency, two statements were culled from the representations recited in the indictment, and made the sole basis of the conviction. These were, that Blanchard said he wanted to buy 18 cattle for Otto Gulick, and that Otto Gulick wanted him to buy for him and send him 18 cattle; and the meaning attached by the court and jury to these words was that Blanchard represented that he had wanted to buy in his own name and on his own responsibility for Otto Gulick, a customer of his, and that Gulick stood ready as such customer to make the purchase and take the property." And continuing, at page 324: "This brings us to the final question of the nature of this representation. It declares an intention, and involves a promise. It states a present purpose and design to sell the cattle, when bought, to Gulick, and a promise to apply the proceeds resulting from such sale to the payment of the post dated check. 'I am buying for Gulick,' 'I want these cattle for Otto,' could mean only that the defendant bought with a then present intention of sending them to Gulick. It was a statement of the design and motive of the accused in making the purchase. It represented what was at the time in his mind, and constituted his intention, and so far as it tended to affect or influence the seller, it was essentially a promise, and related to the future. *** So far as this intention and promise were concerned, the seller necessarily took the risk of its fulfillment. He had to rely alone upon the supposed honesty and integrity of the defendant, and he was cheated, not by any false statement of facts, but by reliance upon a promise and intention not meant to be fulfilled."

When Winnett applied to Swartz to get his signature to the note, he represented that he wanted to show it to Harmon. Grant that this was false, and that such intention did not exist, he having no such intention in his mind—under the New York case this was not the representation or assurance of an existing or past fact. Winnett's declaration and intention to show the note to Harmon were coupled with a promise that, after he did so, he would retain the note in his possession or would destroy it. He wanted to get the note to show to Harmon to convince him that he had good standing in that community; that his friends would indorse for him. This is what he represented he wanted the note for, and what he intended to do with it; but, so far as the intention and promise were concerned, Swartz, like the seller of the cattle in *People v. Blanchard, supra,* took the risk that after Winnett had shown the note to Harmon, to convince him that he had friends who would indorse for him, he would destroy the note or keep it. Swartz took the responsibility on himself, or the risk, that Winnett would do so. He had to rely upon the supposed honesty and integrity of the defendant, and he was deceived; not by any false statement of a fact, but in relying upon a promise and intention not meant to be fulfilled.

In *Archer's* case, Dearsley's C.C., 453, Pollock, C. B., describes the present case very nearly in his statement, that if a man says: "I want goods for a certain house, and I mean to send them to that house; sell them to me," that would not be a representation of an existing fact. Other authorities lead to the same conclusion. 2 Whart., 2118; *West's* Case, I D. & B. C. C., 575; *Ranney v. People*, 22 N. Y., 417; *Reg. v. Bates*, 3 Cox's C.C., 201, 203; *Reg. v. Jennison*, 9 Id., 158; *Rex v. Goodhall, Russ & Ry.*, 461; *People v. Thompkins*, 1 Park Cr. Cas., 238.

It is claimed, and this is the contention on the part of the state, that a promise or an intention—the intention existing in the mind of the party, and at the same time not meant to be fulfilled—is an existing fact. We think the authorities will not sustain this contention.

In 12 Am. & Eng. Enc., 2d Ed., on page 811, the author says:

> False representations amounting to mere promises, or professions of intentions, though they induce the defrauded party to part with his property, are not false pretenses, for they have reference to future events. Citing in note among cases from other states, *Dillingham v. State*, 5 Ohio St., 280.

In *Commonwealth v. Warren*, 94 Ky., 615, it is held:

> To constitute the offense of obtaining the signature of
> another to a writing by false pretense, the false pretense must be
> a statement of some pretended past occurrence or existing fact,
> made for the purpose of inducing the party injured to sign the
> writing. No statement or representation of anything to take place
> in future is a pretense in the meaning of the statute, whether it
> be in the form of a promise or not. One who induces another to
> sign a note upon the representation that it is to be used as a
> renewal of an existing note upon which the person signing is
> bound, does not violate the statute, although he intends to and
> does use the note for another purpose.

To same effect is *Com. v. Moore*, 99 Pa. St., 570; s. c., 4 Am. Crim. R., 230.
In *Reg. v. Woodman*, 28 Cox C.C., 561; s. c., 14 Cox C.C., 179,

> "An indictment charged one Gregory with having obtained
> £30 from the prosecutor, Woodman, on the false pretense that
> he, the said Gregory, then wanted the loan of £30 to enable him
> to take a public house at Melksham, by means of which said false
> pretense the said Gregory did then unlawfully and fraudulently
> obtain the said sum from the said Samuel Woodman with intent
> to defraud. Whereas the said Gregory was not then going to take
> a public house at Melksham, as he, the said Gregory, well knew.
> And whereas the said Gregory did not want a loan of £30 or any
> money to enable him to take said house: Held, not a false
> pretense as to an existing fact." To a suggestion of the
> prosecutor, in the above case, "that there the existing fact was
> the intention of the prisoner," Mellor, J., replied: "How can you
> define a man's mind? It is a mere promissory false pretense."***

To constitute a false pretense within the purview of the statute, the
representation must be such as either with or without the co-operation of other
causes, had a decisive influence upon the mind of the party defrauded, so that
without its weight he would not have parted with his property. The only possible
thing that could have influenced Swartz in the representation or assurance made
to him by Winnett which could have induced him to sign the note, was the
statement that Winnett would keep the note in his possession, after showing it
to Harmon, and would destroy it. And this is nowhere negatived in the
indictment. It is entirely consistent with all its averments, that Winnett still has

the note, or has destroyed it as he promised he would. This omission alone would make the indictment defective. *Dillingham v. State*, 5 Ohio St., 280-284.***

Chaplin v. United States, 81 U.S. App. D.C. 80 (1946)

Opinion by: CLARK

This is an appeal from a conviction under the first count of an indictment charging appellant and his wife with obtaining money by false pretenses.

Of the several points raised by appellant we think one to be of controlling significance. He urges that the indictment failed to charge a crime because the one statement which he is alleged to have made relating to a subsisting fact was not traversed and no evidence was introduced to prove that the one statement was false.

To examine this contention, we turn to the indictment. It is there charged that appellant and his wife, co-defendant below, with intent to defraud, feloniously did pretend and represent to one Violette McMullen, then and there being, that they, the said Sydney A. Chaplin and the said Dorothy Chaplin, were engaged in the wine and liquor business in Alexandria, Virginia, and that if she, the said Violette McMullen, would advance certain money, they, would purchase certain liquor stamps with said money and would return any money so advanced. In the traversing clause, it is charged that the defendants would not purchase such liquor stamps and would not return the money advanced as they well knew.

It appears from the indictment that the prosecution's case was necessarily founded on the defendants' intention, at the time of acquiring the money, not to do two things promised: (1) buy stamps, and (2) repay the money. Both of these promises relate to things the defendants were to do in the future. The prosecution did not prove that the defendants misrepresented their business connection. On the contrary, it appears from the record that the appellant and his wife were in the liquor business, that they did own a large quantity of wine for which state stamps were required and that they did buy some small amount of tax stamps. The question for our decision comes down to whether the "present intention" of the defendants not to return the money and not to buy the stamps as they said they would relates to a "present or past existing fact" such as will support a conviction for the crime of false pretenses. The rule stated in Wharton's Criminal Law, 12th Ed., Sec. 1439, is that: "A false pretense, under the statute, must relate to a past even[t] or existing fact. Any representation with regard to a future transaction is excluded. Thus, for instance, a false statement, that a draft which has been received from a house of good credit abroad, and is for a valuable consideration, on the faith of which he obtains the prosecutor's goods, is within the law; a promise to deposit with him such a draft at some future time, though wilfully and intentionally false, and the means of prosecutor's parting possession with his property, is not. So a pretense that the party would do an act that he did not mean to do (as a pretense that he would pay for goods on delivery) was ruled by all the judges not to be a false pretense under the Statute of Geo. II., and the same rule is distinctly recognized in this country, it being held that the statement of an intention is not a statement of an existing fact." We think the great weight of authority sustains this statement of the rule and compels us to answer the question in the negative.

In its brief, the government was most candid on this point, stating that *Commonwealth v. Althause*, 207 Mass. 32, 93 N.E. 202, 31 L.R.A., N.S., 999, from which a quotation of dictum was taken did not represent the weight of authority. The same may be said for the other two cases cited to support the prosecutions's position on the point. It appears from a study of these cases that the courts concerned found no difficulty in applying the rule on "intention" which has long been used in action at law for fraud and deceit. We think it unnecessary to discuss the advisability of transplanting this concept to criminal actions. There is a vast difference between subjecting a defendant to criminal penalties and providing for the redress of wrong through civil actions.

A majority of the courts having this problem placed before them have not subscribed to the theory that "intention," as manifest by false and misleading promises, standing alone, is a fact in the sense required for a conviction on the charge of false pretenses.

Not only is the rule deeply rooted in our law, but moreover, we think the reasons upon which it is founded are no less cogent today that they were when the early cases were decided under the English statute cited by Wharton, supra. It is of course true that then, as now, the intention to commit certain crimes was ascertained by looking backward from the act and finding that the accused intended to do what he did do. However, where, as here, the act complained of— namely, failure to repay money or use it as specified at the time of borrowing— is as consonant with ordinary commercial default as with criminal conduct, the danger of applying this technique to prove the crime is quite apparent. Business affairs would be materially incumbered by the ever present threat that a debtor might be subjected to criminal penalties if the prosecutor and jury were of the view that at the time of borrowing he was mentally a cheat. The risk of prosecuting one who is guilty of nothing more than a failure or inability to pay his debts is a very real consideration. It is not enough to say that if innocent the accused would be found not guilty. The social stigma attaching to one accused of a crime as well as the burdens incident to the defense would, irrespective of the outcome, place a devastating weapon in the hands of a disgruntled or disappointed creditor.

The business policy, as well as the difficulties and dangers inherent in a contrary rule are illustrated by the earlier English cases. In *Rex v. Goodhall*, 1821, Russ. & R.C.C. 461, the accused was found to have obtained a quantity of meat, promising to pay for it but not so intending. In reversing the jury's verdict of guilty the court said: "It was merely a promise for future conduct, and common prudence and caution would have prevented any injury arising from the breach of it." Again, in *Reg. v. Oates*, 1855, Dears C.C. 469, 6 Cox C.C. 540, where the accused was charged with making a fraudulent overcharge for work performed the court discharged the prisoner saying: "Is a shopkeeper who knowingly charges for an article more than it is worth, liable to an indictment under this statute? To hold the statute applicable to such a case would shake many transactions which, though certainly not fair in themselves are still not indictable."

If we were to accept the government's position the way would be open for every victim of a bad bargain to resort to criminal proceedings to even the score with a judgment proof adversary. No doubt in the development of our criminal law the zeal with which the innocent are protected has provided a measure of shelter for the guilty. However, we do not think it wise to increase the possibility of conviction by broadening the accepted theory of the weight to be attached to the mental attitude of the accused.

Reversed.

EDGERTON, Associate Justice (dissenting).

The court holds that "the great weight of authority compels us." This is a new rule and an important one. I think it is erroneous.

Usually there are good reasons for a doctrine which is widely accepted, and uniformity itself has some value even in criminal law. Accordingly, we should consider the weight of authority elsewhere for what it may be worth. But we should not determine our action by a count of foreign cases regardless of logic, consistency, and social need. The social value of a rule has become a test of growing power and importance. We should decide the question before us in accordance with present-day standards of wisdom and justice rather than in accordance with some outworn and antiquated rule of the past' which was never adopted here. To let judges who lived and died in other times and places make our decisions would be to abdicate as judges and serve as tellers.

Considered without regard to the foreign cases on which the court relies, the indictment is plainly valid. No doubt a promise is commonly an undertaking, but it is always an assertion of a present intention to perform. "I will" means among other things "I intend to." It is so understood and it is meant to be so understood. Intention is a fact and present intention is a present fact. A promise made without an intention to perform is therefore a false statement about a present fact. This factual and declarative aspect of a promise is not a new discovery. It has come to be widely recognized in civil actions for deceit.

In criminal cases, most courts and text writers have clung to an old illusion that the same words cannot embody both a promise and a statement of fact. But this tradition that in a criminal case "the statement of an intention is not a statement of an existing fact" has begun to break down. It is an obvious fiction. The meaning of words is the same whether their author is prosecuted civilly or criminally or not at all. The fiction that a promise made without intent to perform does not embody a misrepresentation conflicts with the facts, with the deceit cases, and with the interest of society in protecting itself against fraud. An Act of Congress makes it a crime in the District of Columbia to obtain money "by any false pretense, with intent to defraud." Congress did not exempt, and the court should not exempt, a pretense conveyed by words which also convey a promise. As a matter of plain English there could be no clearer case of false and fraudulent pretense than a borrower's pretense that he intends to repay money which he actually does not intend to repay.

The old illusion that a promise states no facts is not the only source of the old tolerance of falsehoods regarding intention. That a fool and his money are soon parted was once accepted as a sort of natural law. In 1821 the fact that common prudence and caution would have prevented any injury seemed to an English court a good reason for refusing to penalize an injury which had been intentionally inflicted by a false promise. The fact that common agility in dodging an intentional blow would have prevented any injury would not have seemed a reason for refusing to penalize a battery. Fools were fair game though cripples were not. But in modern times, no one not talking law would be likely to deny that society should protect mental as well as physical helplessness against intentional injuries.

Though the court decides the case on the basis of authority, the opinion concludes with a defense of the prevailing rule. But to justify this rule it would be necessary to show that false pretenses regarding intention are a harmless way of obtaining money, or else that intention cannot be proved in prosecutions for false pretenses as it is constantly proved in other criminal prosecutions and in civil actions for deceit.

Difficulties of proof are seldom greater in criminal cases than in civil, except that the prosecution must prove its case beyond a reasonable doubt. No peculiar difficulty of proof distinguishes this crime from others. Intention of one sort or another must be proved in most criminal cases. They are usually proved by conduct. It is inherently no more difficult to prove an intent not to perform a promise than, for example, an intent to monopolize, to commit a felony, or to receive goods knowing them to be stolen. Appellant's conduct showed his intent. After getting $375 from a nurse by promising to buy liquor stamps and repay the money, he made the same promise a few days later and got $700 more. He said he needed the money to get the stamps. Yet he bought less than $40 worth of stamps, if any, during the next six weeks, and there is no evidence that he bought any stamps at any later time. Meanwhile he continued to borrow money from the woman. He made no repayments at any time. The jury might well conclude, as it did, that the difference between his promises and his performance was not accidental but was part of his original plan. The court does not suggest that the proof of his original intention was insufficient. If it were thought to be insufficient, the conviction should be reversed on that ground. The rule which the court adopts will make prosecutions impossible even when admissions or other evidence make guilt obvious.

Notes and Questions

1. In *Winnett v. State*, how does the prosecution address the issue of material misrepresentation of a past or present fact? Were you persuaded by the prosecution's argument?

2. Didn't the defendant in *Winnett* make several misrepresentations to the victim? Are these misrepresentations sufficient to establish the elements for false pretenses?

3. Is *Winnett* more about material misrepresentations or future promises?

4. In *Chaplin v. United States*, what is the court's main concern with convicting people based of future promises?

2. Passing Title

Blackledge v. United States, 447 A.2d 46 (D.C. Ct. App. 1982)

GALLAGHER, Associate Judge, Retired.

Appellant, Ervin Blackledge, was convicted of receiving stolen property (Shell credit card), D.C. Code 1981, § 22-2205, and attempted false pretenses, *id.* §§ 22-103, -1301. This appeal is based primarily on the ground that there is insufficient evidence to support appellant's conviction on either count. Specifically, appellant contends that the government failed to prove beyond a reasonable doubt that appellant had the required intent to commit the crimes of receipt of stolen property and attempted false pretenses. Appellant also contends that, even if all the facts in this case are viewed in the light most favorable to the government, the government could not prove that appellant obtained property in reliance on the charged misrepresentation that is, appellant's implicit representation that he was authorized to use the Shell credit card and that, therefore, the government could prove neither the completed crime of false pretenses nor the crime of attempted false pretenses. We reject appellant's arguments and affirm his conviction.

I

The government presented evidence that, in September 1979, while shopping in a supermarket in McLean, Virginia, Ann Fleury placed her purse on a shopping cart and then turned away from the cart. She returned minutes later to find her purse gone. Among the items in the stolen purse was a Shell credit card bearing the name of her husband, G. J. Fleury, M.D., on its face, and her signature on the back of the card.

On May 21, 1980, appellant drove into the Parkway Shell station in Northeast Washington, D.C. and asked James Jones, a station attendant, for ten dollars worth of gasoline. After Jones put the gasoline in the car, appellant presented him with the Fleury credit card. Jones checked the Fleury credit card against a list of "bad cards," discovered that the Fleury credit card was on the list of "bad cards," and reported his discovery to a fellow attendant. He then told appellant that the card was "bad" and that he would have to pay for the gasoline in cash. Appellant became angry and attempted to drive away. After he moved the car approximately three feet, his path was blocked by Officer Hawkins, who had been flagged over by Jones' co-worker. Officer Hawkins placed appellant under arrest and advised him of his rights. Later, at the police station and again at trial, appellant claimed that a woman whom he had known for about three years named Shirley Brown, had given him the credit card. Appellant's explanation for his possession and use of the credit card was that Ms. Brown had given him the Shell credit card, and that she assured him that the card belonged to her uncle and had not been stolen, and that he could use the card to purchase gasoline

II

Both the crime of receiving stolen property and the crime of attempted false pretenses require that appellant possessed a fraudulent intent. In prosecutions for receiving stolen property, the government must prove that a (1) stolen (2) item of value (3) was received by the defendant (4) with an intent to defraud and (5) while the defendant knew or had reason to know that the item was stolen. *Brock v. United States,* D.C. App., 404 A.2d 955, 958 n.2 (1979). To convict a defendant for the crime of false pretenses, the government must prove that the defendant made a false representation with knowledge of its falsity and an intent to defraud; that the defrauded party relied on the misrepresentation; and that the defendant obtained (title to) something of value as a result of the misrepresentation. *Hymes v. United States*, D.C. App., 260 A.2d 679, 680 (1970*). See generally* W. LaFave & A. Scott, Criminal Law § 90, at 655 (2d ed. 1972). To prove the crime of attempted false pretenses, the government must prove, as in any other attempt case, that appellant had the intent to commit the crime and that he performed some act towards its commission. *Marganella v. United States,* D.C. App., 268 A.2d 803, 804 (1970).

Appellant contends there was insufficient evidence to establish that he received the credit card with guilty knowledge that it was stolen or with a fraudulent intent. He contends that he simply presented a card which he thought he was authorized to use, and that by using the card, he had no intent to defraud the gas station attendant and the Shell station. The essence of appellant's argument is that, because appellant gave an explanation for his allegedly innocent possession and use of the stolen credit card, he could not have had the requisite intent for receiving stolen property or for attempted false pretenses. This argument is clearly without merit.***

III

Appellant makes an additional argument to attack his conviction for attempted false pretenses. The first portion of appellant's argument is based on a narrow view of what occurred at the gas station and of what can constitute the completed crime of false pretenses. It is appellant's position that because he presented the Fleury credit card just after rather than just before the gasoline was pumped into his car, the gas station attendant did not rely and could not have relied on any misrepresentation associated with the presentation of the credit card. *See Hymes v. United States, supra* at 680 (reliance is an essential element of the crime of false pretenses). Therefore, appellant argues, even if the gas station attendant had not checked the "bad card" list and appellant had left the gas station with the gasoline under the recited circumstances, appellant could not be convicted of the completed crime of false pretenses. The second portion of appellant's argument is essentially that, because the factual sequence in this case and the attendant's ultimate discovery that the credit card was "bad" make it impossible for there to have been actual reliance and for appellant to have been convicted of the completed crime of false pretenses, appellant cannot be convicted of an attempt to commit that crime that is, he cannot be said to have taken a step toward the completion of the crime of false pretenses. We reject this argument.

Appellant was charged with attempted false pretenses. The government was therefore not required to prove the crime of false pretenses, but rather "an intent to commit it, the doing of some act toward its commission and the failure to consummate its commission." *Marganella v. United States, supra* at 804. "And it is not necessary in order to establish an intent that the potential victim was deceived and had parted with [something of value]." *Id.*, (citations omitted). Therefore, the focus must be placed on appellant's intent. Whether Mr. Jones relied on his representations to his detriment is essentially immaterial in the context of an attempted false pretense charge.

In resolving this issue, the incident at the gas station must be viewed in its entirety. Appellant made an implicit representation that he would render lawful payment when he drove into the station and asked Mr. Jones for $10 worth of gasoline. In accordance with common practice among gasoline stations, of which this court may take judicial notice, the means of payment apparently was not established before the gasoline was placed in the car. However, since the gasoline was placed in the car on the basis of an implied agreement that lawful payment would be made, it is equally clear that appellant's authority to assert ownership or title over the gasoline was contingent of such lawful payment. Therefore, when appellant produced the stolen credit card and falsely represented that he was the owner of that card and was authorized to use it, he stood in the same position as an individual who has selected merchandise in a store, placed it in a cart, taken it to the checkout counter where it is rung up on the cash register and placed in a bag, and is then required to make payment before he can assert ownership. *See Henson v. United States,* D.C. App., 287 A.2d 106 (1972). At the time appellant produced the credit card and made his false representations, he was merely in possession of the gasoline. In making his false representations, appellant was attempting to obtain title to the gasoline so that he could drive his car away from the station. Had Mr. Jones not discovered the stolen nature of the card, appellant would perhaps have been given a semblance of voidable title and permitted to leave. Mr. Jones made it quite clear in his testimony that he had no intention of letting appellant leave the station without paying and planned to siphon the gasoline from the car. Ownership and the ability to use the gasoline was clearly of value, and in a very practical sense, was what appellant sought when he entered the gas station. In short, appellant obtained a limited, contingent possessory right in the gasoline prior to his misrepresentation. The misrepresentation was made to complete the transaction and effect the transfer of title.

This court has recognized that the false pretenses statute was enacted before credit cards were widely in use and that as a result "this new mode of possible criminal activity does suggest that the form of proof will differ from that usually found in past cases." *Hymes v. United States, supra* at 680. In *Hymes* the defendant was convicted of seven counts of false pretenses involving the unauthorized use of a stolen gasoline credit card. The government's case rested largely on the credit card receipts linked to appellant by handwriting analysis. The gas station attendants were not able to testify to the individual transactions. This court upheld the convictions, holding that it could be inferred from the credit receipts that the gasoline was provided on reliance on the validity of the card and appellant's authorized use. *Accord, Teves v. State,* 237 Md. 653, 207 A.2d 614 (1965). In the instant case, the only thing that averted a completed false pretense was Mr. Jones' discovery that the card was stolen. In *Hymes* this court did not concern itself with whether Mr. Hymes presented his stolen card before or after the gasoline was placed in his car. Rather, the court looked at the overall situation and held that it could be inferred that the attendants relied on the false representations.

We hold that where a false pretenses charge stems from the unauthorized use of a credit card, it is not necessarily significant that the credit card was presented immediately after rather than just prior to receipt of the goods in what is virtually a simultaneous exchange. An initial implicit false promise of lawful payment coupled with the presentation of a stolen credit card, which occur in a single and continuous transaction, can support a conviction for false pretenses or attempted false pretenses, provided that together they induce or would have induced the victim to surrender title to the property.

In this case, a reasonable jury could conclude that appellant was guilty of receiving stolen property (*i.e.*, Shell credit card) and of attempted false pretenses. Appellant took steps toward the commission of the crime of false pretenses by driving into the Shell station and presenting the Fleury credit card to complete his purchase of gasoline. The fact that there was no ultimate reliance on the Fleury credit card does not preclude the jury from reasonably concluding that appellant committed the offense charged. We affirm appellant's conviction on both counts.

Affirmed.

Notes and Questions

1. In *Blackledge v. United States*, would the defendant be guilty of false pretenses or larceny by trick if he drove up to a gas station and told the clerk to fill up his tank and then subsequently sped off without paying for the gas he received?

2. If you were a juror in *Blackledge*, would you have been able to find the defendant guilty of false pretenses on the state's evidence? What facts support finding that each element of the crime has been proven beyond a reasonable doubt?

3. For a successful prosecution for false pretenses, must the victim rely on the bogus misrepresentation or does the prosecution need only prove that the defendant intended for the victim to rely on the misrepresentation?

Chapter 14
Embezzlement, Receipt of Stolen Property, and Forgery

A. Embezzlement

Like false pretenses, embezzlement was created as a stop-gap law to cover certain thefts left unpunished by larceny. Specifically, embezzlement addresses situations where the defendant is in lawful possession of another's property but then decides to convert the property to his own use. Since embezzlement is a creature of statute, its definition varies by jurisdiction. Generally speaking, the requirements for embezzlement are as follows: (1) the fraudulent (2) conversion of (3) the property (4) of another (5) by one who is already in lawful possession of it.

Rex v. Bazeley, 2 Leach 835 (1799)

At the Old Bailey in February Session 1799, Joseph Bazeley was tried before John Silvester, Esq. Common Serjeant of the city of London, for feloniously stealing on the 18th January preceding, a Bank-note of the value of one hundred pounds, the property of Peter Esdaile, Sir Benjamin Hammett, William Esdaile, and John Hammett.

The following facts appeared in evidence. The prisoner, Joseph Bazeley, was the principal teller at the house of Messrs. Esdaile's and Hammett's, bankers, in Lombard-street, at the salary of £100 a year, and his duty was to receive and pay money, notes, and bills, at the counter. The manner of conducting the business of this banking-house is as follows: There are four tellers, each of whom has a separate money-book, a separate money-drawer, and a separate bag. The prisoner being the chief teller, the total of the receipts and payments of all the other money-books were every evening copied into his, and the total balance or rest, as it is technically called, struck in his book, and the balances of the other money-books paid, by the other tellers, over to him. When any monies, whether in cash or notes, are brought by customers to the counter to be paid in, the teller who receives it counts it over, then enters the Bank-notes or drafts, and afterwards the cash, under the customer's name, in his book; and then, after casting up the total, it is entered in the customer's book. The money is then put into the teller's bag, and the Bank-notes or other papers, if any, put into a box which stands on a desk behind the counter, directly before another clerk, who is called the cash book-keeper, who makes an entry of it in the received cash-book in the name of the person who has paid it in, and which he finds written by the receiving teller on the back of the bill or note so placed in the drawer. The prisoner was treasurer to an association called "The Ding Dong Mining Company"; and in the course of the year had many bills drawn on him by the Company, and many bills drawn on other persons remitted to him by the Company. In the month of January 1799, the prisoner had accepted bills on account of the Company, to the amount of £112, 4s. 1d. and had in his possession a bill of £166, 7s. 3d. belonging to the Company, but which was not due until the 9th February. One of the bills, amounting to £100, which the prisoner had accepted, became due on 18th January. Mr. William Gilbert, a grocer, in the Surry-road, Black-friars, kept his cash at the banking-house of the prosecutors, and on the 18th January 1799, he sent his servant, George Cock, to pay in £137. This sum consisted of £122 in Bank-notes, and the rest in cash. One of these Bank-notes was the note which the prisoner was indicted for stealing. The prisoner received this money from George Cock, and after entering the £137 in Mr. Gilbert's Bank-book, entered the £15 cash in his own money-book, and put over the £22 in Bank-notes into the drawer behind him, keeping back the £100 Bank-note, which he put into his pocket, and afterwards paid to a banker's clerk the same day at a clearing-house in Lombard-street, in discharge of the £100 bill which he had accepted on account of the Ding Dong Mining Company. To make the sum in Mr. Gilbert's Bank-book, and the sum in the book of the banking-house agree, it appeared that a unit had been added to the entry of £37 to the credit of Mr. Gilbert, in the book of the banking-house, but it did not appear by any direct proof that this alteration had been made by the prisoner; it appeared however that he had made a confession, but the confession having been obtained under a promise of favour, it was not given in evidence.

Const and Jackson, the prisoner's Counsel, submitted to the Court, that to constitute a larceny, it was necessary in point of law that the property should be taken from the possession of the prosecutor, but that it was clear from the evidence in this case, that the Bank-note charged to have been stolen, never was either in the actual or the constructive possession of Esdaile and Hammett, and that even if it had been in their possession, yet that from the manner in which it had been secreted by the prisoner, it amounted only to a breach of trust.

The Court left the facts of the case to the consideration of the Jury, and on their finding the prisoner Guilty, the case was reserved for the opinion of the Twelve Judges on a question, whether under the circumstances above stated, the taking of the Bank-note was in law a felonious taking, or only a fraudulent breach of trust.

The case was accordingly argued before nine of the Judges (Lord Kenyon, L.C.J.; C.J. Eyre, C.B. Macdonald, Mr. Baron Hotham, Mr. B. Perryn, Mr. Baron Thompson, Mr. J. Grose, Mr. J. Lawrence, Mr. J. Rooke) in the Exchequer Chamber, on Saturday, 27th April 1799, by Const for the prisoner, and by Fielding for the Crown.

Const, for the prisoner, after remarking that the prosecutor never had actual possession of the Bank-note, and defining the several offences of larceny, fraud, and breach of trust, viz. that Larceny is the taking of valuable property from the possession of another without his consent and against his will. Secondly, That Fraud consists in obtaining valuable property from the possession of another with his consent and will, by means of some artful device, against the subtilty of which common prudence and caution are not sufficient safeguards. And, Thirdly, That Breach of Trust is the abuse or misusing of that property which the owner has, without any fraudulent seducement, and with his own free will and consent, put, or permitted to be put, either for particular or general purposes, into the possession of the trustee, proceeded to argue the case upon the following points.

First, That the prosecutors cannot, in contemplation of law, be said to have had a constructive possession of this Bank-note, at the time the prisoner is charged with having tortiously converted it to his own use.

Secondly, That supposing the prosecutors to have had the possession of this note, the prisoner, under the circumstances of this case, cannot be said to have tortiously taken it from that possession with a felonious intention to steal it.

Thirdly, That the relative situation of the prosecutors and the prisoner makes this transaction merely a breach of trust; and,

Fourthly, That this is not one of those breaches of trust which the Legislature has declared to be felony.

The first point, viz. That the prosecutor cannot, in contemplation of law, be said to have had a constructive possession of this Bank-note at the time the prisoner is charged with having tortiously converted it to his own use.—To constitute the crime of larceny, the property must be taken from the possession of the owner; this possession must be either actual or constructive; it is clear that he prosecutors had not, upon the present occasion, the actual possession of the Bank-note, and therefore the inquiry must be, whether they had the constructive possession of it? or, in other words, whether the possession of the servant was, under the circumstances of this case, the possession of the master? Property in possession is said by Sir William Blackstone (2Bl. Com. 389, 396) to subsist only where a man hath both the right to, and also the occupation of, the property. The prosecutors in the present case had only a right or title to possess the note, and not the absolute or even qualified possession of it. It was never in their custody or under their controul. There is no difference whatever as to the question of possession between real and personal property; and if after the death of an ancestor, and before the entry of his heir upon the descending estate, or if after the death of a particular tenant, and before the entry of the remainder-man, or reversioner, a stranger should take possession of the vacant land, the heir in the one case, and the remainder-man, or reversioner in the other, would be, like the prosecutor in the present case, only entitled to, but not possessed of, the estate; and each of them must recover possession of it by the respective remedies which the law has in such cases made and provided. Suppose the prisoner had not parted with the note, but had merely kept it in his own custody, and refused, on any pretense whatever, to deliver it over to his employers, they could only have recovered it by means of an action of trover or detinue, the first of which presupposes the person against whom it is brought, to have obtained possession of the property by lawful means, as by delivery, or finding; and the second, that the right of property only, and not the possession of it, either really or constructively, is in the person bringing it. The prisoner received this note by the permission and consent of the prosecutors, while it was passing from the possession of Mr. Gilbert to the possession of Messrs. Esdaile's and Hammett's; and not having reached its destined goal, but having been thus intercepted in its transitory state, it is clear that it never came to the possession of the prosecutors. It was delivered into the possession of the prisoner, upon an implied confidence on the part of the prosecutors, that he would deliver it over into their possession, but which, from the pressure of temporary circumstances, he neglected to do: at the time therefore of the supposed conversion of this note, it was in the legal possession of the prisoner. To divest the prisoner of this possession, it certainly was not necessary that he should have delivered this note into the hands of the prosecutors, or of any other of their servants personally; for if he had deposited it in the drawer kept for the reception of this species of property, it would have been a delivery of it into the possession of his masters; but he made no such deposit: and instead of determining in any way his own possession of it, he conveyed it immediately from the hand of Mr. Gilbert's clerk into his own pocket. Authorities are not wanting to support this position. In the Year-book, 7 Hen. 6, fol. 43, it is said, "if a man delivers goods to another to keep, or lend goods to another, the deliverer or lender may commit felony of them himself, for he hath but *jus proprietatis*; the *jus possessionis* being with the bailee," and permitting one man to receive goods to the use of another, who never had any possession of them, is a stronger case. So long ago as the year 1687, the following case was solemnly determined in the Court of King's Bench on a special verdict. The prisoner had been a servant, or journeyman, to one John Fuller, and was employed to sell goods and receive money for his master's use; in the course of his trade he sold a large parcel of goods; received one hundred and sixty guineas for them from the purchaser; deposited ten of them in a private place in the chamber where he slept; and, on his being discharged from his service, took away with him the remaining one hundred and fifty guineas, but he had not put any of the money into his master's till, or in any way given it into his possession. Before this embezzlement was discovered, he suddenly decamped from his master's service, leaving his trunk, containing some of his clothes and the ten guineas so secreted behind him; but he afterwards, in the night-time, broke open his master's house, and took away with him the ten guineas which he had hid privately in his bed-chamber; and this was held to be no burglary, because the taking of the money was no felony: for although it was the master's money in right, it was the servant's money in possession, and the first original act no felony. This case was cited by Sir B. Shower, in his argument in the case of *Rex* v. *Meeres* (1 Shower, 53), and is said to be reported by Gouldsborough, 186: but I have been favoured with a manuscript report of it, extracted from a collection of cases in the possession of the late Mr. Reynolds, Clerk of the Arraigns, at the Old Bailey, under the title of *Rex* v. *Dingley*, by which it appears that the special verdict was found at the Easter Session 1687, and argued in the King's Bench in Hilary Term, 3 Jac. IId., and in which it is said to have been determined that this offence was not burglary, but trespass only. The law of this case has been recently confirmed by the case of *The King* v. *Bull*. The prisoner, Thomas Bull, was tried at the Old Bailey January Session 1797, before Mr. Justice Heath, on an indictment charging him with having stolen, on the 7th of the same month, a half-crown and three shillings, the property of William Tilt, who was a confectioner, in Cheapside, with whom the prisoner lived as a journeyman; and Mr. Tilt having had, for some time before, strong suspicion that the prisoner had robbed him, adopted the following method for the purpose of detecting him:--On the 7th January, the day laid in the indictment, he left only four sixpences in the till; and taking two half-crowns, thirteen shillings, and two sixpences, went to the house of Mr. Garner, a watchmaker, who marked the two half-crowns, several of the shillings, and the sixpences, with a tool used in his line of business, that impressed a figure something like a half-moon. Mr. Tilt, having got the money thus marked, went with it to the house of a Mrs. Hill; and giving a half-crown and three of the shillings to Ann Wilson, one of her servants, and five of the shillings and the other sixpence to Mary Bushman, another of her servants, desired them to proceed to his house, and purchase some of his goods of the prisoner, whom he had left in care of the shop. The two women went accordingly to Mr. Tilt's shop, where Ann Wilson purchased confectionary of the prisoner to the amount of five shillings and three-pence, gave him the half-crown and three shillings, and received three-pence in change; and Mary Bushman purchased of him articles to the amount of four shillings and sixpence, for which she paid him out of the monies she had so received, and returned the other shilling to her mistress, Mary Hill: but neither of these women observed whether the prisoner put either the whole or any part of the money into the till or into his pocket. While the women, however, were purchasing these things, Mr. Tilt and Mr. Garner were waiting, with a constable, at a convenient distance, on the outside of the shop-door; and when they observed the women come out, they went immediately into the shop, where, on examining the prisoner's pockets, they found among the silver coin, amounting to fifty-three shillings, which he had in his waistcoat pocket, the marked half-crowns, and three of the marked shillings, which had been given to Wilson and Bushman; only seven shillings and sixpence were found in the till; and it appeared that Mrs. Tilt had taken one shilling in the shop, and put it into the till, during her husband's absence; so that the two shillings which had been left therein in the morning, the one shilling which Mrs. Tilt had put into it, the four shillings and sixpence laid out by Mary Bushman, and the five shillings and sixpence marked money which was found in the prisoner's pocket, made up the sum which ought to have been put into the till. The prisoner upon this evidence was found guilty, and received sentence of transportation; but a case was reserved for the opinion of the Twelve Judges (see 2 East's P.C. 572, *notis*), Whether, as Mr. Tilt had divested himself of this money by giving it to Mary Hill, who had given it to her servants in the manner and for the purpose above described, and as it did not appear that the prisoner had, on receiving it from them, put it into the till, or done anything with it that could be construed a restoring of it to the possession of his master, the converting of it to his own use by putting it into his pocket, could amount to the crime of larceny, it being essential to the commission of that offence that the goods should be taken from the possession of the owner; and, although no opinion was ever publicly delivered upon this case, the prisoner was discharged. [15] After these determinations, it cannot be contended that the possession of the servant is the possession of the master; for, independently of these authorities, the rule, that the possession of the servant is the possession of the master, cannot be extended to a case in which the property never was in the master's possession, however it may be so construed in cases where the identical thing stolen is delivered by the master, or where the question is between the master and a third person. "If," says Sir Matthew Hale (1 Hale, P.C. 688), "I deliver my servant a bond to receive money, or deliver goods to him to sell, and he receives the money upon the bond or goods, and go away with it, this is not felony; for though the bond or goods were delivered to him by the master, yet the money was not delivered to him by the master": but he admits, that "if taken away from the servant by a trespasser, the master may have a general action of trespass"; which shews that the law, in a criminal case, will not, under such circumstances, consider the master to have a constructive possession of the property. Such a possession arises by mere implication of law; and it is an

---

[15] On the consultation among the Judges on this case, they were of opinion that Bull was not guilty of felony, but only of a breach of trust; the money never having been put into the till, and therefore not having been in the possession of the master as against the defendant; and *Rex* v. *Waite, ante*, p. 28, case 14, was very mainly relied on to shew that this was a mere breach of trust. 2 East, P.C. 572.

established rule, that no man's life shall be endangered by any intendment or implication whatsoever.

Secondly, Supposing the prosecutor to have had the possession of this note, yet the prisoner, under the circumstances of this case, cannot be said to have tortiously taken it from that possession with a felonious intent to steal it. It may be said that this was a fact for the opinion of the Jury, and that they have found by the verdict of "Guilty," that he did take it with that design; but a special case, saved for the opinion of the Judges, brings under their consideration all the evidence that was given at the trial, in the same manner as a special verdict would have brought forwards all the facts found therein; for it is said by Mr. Justice Grose, in reporting the opinion of the Judges in the case of *Rex* v. *Brown* and *Parkes*, at the Old Bailey, that in a criminal case it is never too late to review the circumstances of it;[16] and in that case the evidence of the intention with which Brown had uttered the note, and of his knowledge of its having been forged, formed part of the judgment given thereon. In the present case there was no evidence whatever to shew that any such intention existed in his mind at the time the note came to his hands; and if so, it is within the principles laid down in the case of *Rex* v. *Charlewood* (*ante*, p. 409, case 189). Besides, the prisoner had given a bond to account faithfully for the monies that should come to his hands; he was the agent of a trading company, and had the means of converting bills into cash, which would have enabled him, at the time, to repay to the prosecutor the £100, which he detained for his own use; but if, at the very time he received the note, he had no intent to steal it, it is no felony; for Sir Edward Coke (3 Inst. 107, and all the writers on Crown Law agree, that the intent to steal must be when the property comes to his hands or possession; and that if he have the possession of it once lawfully, though he hath the *animus furandi* afterwards, when he carrieth it away, it is no larceny.***

Fielding, for the Crown, argued the case entirely on the question, Whether the prosecutors, Esdaile and Hammett, had such a constructive possession of the Bank-note as to render the taking of it by the prisoner felony? He insisted, that in the case of personal chattels, the possession in law follows the right of property; and, that as Gilbert's clerk did not deposit the notes with Bazeley as a matter of trust to him; for they were paid at the counter, and in the banking-house of the prosecutors, of which Bazeley was merely one of the organs; and, therefore, the payment to him was in effect a payment to them, and his receipt of them vested the property *eo instanter* in their hands, and gave them the legal possession of it. He said that this case was distinguishable from the case of *Rex* v. *Bull*, inasmuch as Bull had authority to sell the goods of his master, and was only accountable to him for the monies he received for them; but that Bank-notes

---

[16] The same is also declared by Mr. Justice Buller, in delivering the opinion of the Judges in the case of *Rex* v. *Tilley, ante,* p. 662.

CR. CA. I.-17*

could not be considered articles of dealing, and Bazeley had no authority to dispose of any from the shop; and from the case of *Rex* v. *Waite*, inasmuch as the India bonds in that case were a personal deposit with Waite, as one of the cashiers, pursuant to the directions of the statute 12 Geo. I. c. 32, which designates the person and character with whom the bonds are to be placed, namely, with the cashier of the Bank; and he cited the cases of *Rex* v. *Abrahat* (*ante*, p. 824, case 306), and *Rex* v. *Spears* (ante, p. 825, case 307), to shew that a servant may be guilty of larceny, upon the principle that the possession of the servant is to be considered as the possession of the master.

The Judges, it is said, were of opinion, upon the authority of *Rex* v. *Waite*, that this Bank-note never was in the legal custody or possession of the prosecutors, Messrs. Esdailes and Hammett; but no opinion was ever publicly delivered;[17] and the prisoner was included in the Secretary of State's letter as a proper object for a pardon.

offender his adviser, procurer, aider or abettor, shall be liable to be transported for any term not exceeding fourteen years, in the discretion of the Court."[18]

---

[17] On consultation among the Judges, some doubt was at first entertained; but at last all assembled agreed that it was not felony, inasmuch as the note was never in the possession of the bankers, distinct from the possession of the prisoner: though it would have been otherwise if the prisoner had deposited it in the drawer, and had afterwards taken it. (*Vide Chipchase's* case, *ante*, p. 699.) And they thought that this was not to be differed from the cases of *Rex* v. *Waite*, ante, p. 28, and *Rex* v. *Bull*, ante, p. 841, which turned on this consideration, that the thing was not taken by the prisoner out of the possession of the owner: and here it was delivered into the possession of the prisoner. That although to many purposes the note was in the actual possession of the masters, yet it was also in the actual possession of the servant, and that possession not to be impeached; for it was a lawful one. Eyre, C.J. also observed that the cases ran into one another very much, and were hardly to be distinguished: That in the case of *Rex* v. *Spears*, *ante,* p. 825, the corn was in the possession of the master under the care of the servant: and Lord Kenyon said that he relied much on the Act of Parliament respecting the Bank not going further than to protect the Bank.
2 East, C.L. 574.

[18] At the Old Bailey in April Session 1800, John Patinson was convicted on this statute, for embezzling one shilling and fourpence as the servant to Barnjum and Raindon. On the 15th March 1800, he carried, on account of his master, household goods, belonging to one Roach, for the carriage of which Roach paid him three shillings and six-pence; but he only accounted for two and two-pence.

Notes and Questions

1. Shortly after this case was decided, the English Parliament created the crime of embezzlement, which punished the fraudulent conversion of money or goods received by an employee for his employer (39 Geo. III, c. 85 (1799)).

> "An Act to protect Masters and others against Embezzlement, by their Clerks or Servants"; and after reciting, that whereas Bankers, Merchants, and others, are, in the course of their dealings and transactions, frequently obliged to entrust their servants, clerks, and persons employed by them in the like capacity, with receiving, paying, negotiating, exchanging, or transferring money, goods, bonds, bills, notes, bankers' drafts, and other valuable effects and securities; that doubts had been entertained, whether the embezzling the same by such servants, clerks, and others, so employed by their masters, amounts to felony by the laws of England; and that it is expedient that such offences should be punished in the same manner in both parts of the United Kingdom"; it enacts and declares, "That if any servant or clerk, or any person employed for the purpose in the capacity of a servant or clerk[19] to any person or persons whomsoever, or to any body corporate or politic, shall, by virtue of such employment, receive or take into his possession any money, goods, bond, bill, note, banker's draft, or other valuable security or effects, for or in the name, or on the account of his master or masters, or employer or employers, and shall fraudulently embezzle, secrete, or make away with the same, or any part thereof; every such offender shall be deemed to have feloniously stolen the same from his master or masters, employer or employers, for whose use, or in whose name or names, or on whose account, the same was or were delivered to, or taken into the possession of, such servant, clerk, or other person so employed, although such money, &c. was or were no otherwise received into the possession of such master or masters, employer or employers, than by the actual possession of his or their

---

[19] See also 52 Geo. III. c.63, by which the offence of embezzlement is extended to bankers, merchants, brokers, attornies, agents, of any description whatsoever, as to certain descriptions of property entrusted to their care, and 50 Geo. III. c. 59, as to embezzlements by collectors of the public monies, and the case of *Rex* v. *Walsh*, 4 Taunton's Rep. 266.

servant, clerk, or other person so employed;[20] and every such offender his adviser, procurer, aider or abettor, shall be liable to be transported for any term not exceeding fourteen years, in the discretion of the Court."

2. Historical Note: *Rex v. Bazeley* mentioned the case *Rex v. Bull*. In *Bull*, the defendant was sentenced to "transportation." British courts during the eighteenth century would oftentimes sentence defendants to live in America or Australia as opposed to face incarceration in England.

1. Intent to Defraud

Ambrose v. United States, 45 App. D.C. 112 (1916)

The COURT in the opinion stated the facts as follows:

This appeal is from a judgment in the supreme court of the District convicting the defendant, William E. Ambrose, appellant here, of embezzlement and sentencing him to imprisonment for ten years.

Two indictments, containing a large number of counts, were consolidated for trial. At the conclusion of the evidence the government elected to stand on the 6th count of the first indictment and the 7th count of the second indictment, and there was a verdict of guilty as to each.

The first of the above counts charged that the defendant, on May 7, 1912, was guardian of Clarence Limerick and Robert Limerick, and that on said date, as such guardian, he had in his possession $2,250 of the property of said minors, which had come into his possession as such guardian, and that he "did then and there unlawfully and fraudulently convert and appropriate the same to his own use, and did thereby then and there embezzle the same." The second of the above counts charged that on May 17, 1912, the defendant was guardian of Agnes Limerick and Oliver Limerick, and that he then had in his possession as such guardian the sum of $2,400, the property of said minors, which he unlawfully and fraudulently converted, as set forth in the first count.

The evidence for the government was in brief as follows: On April 24, 1912, defendant was appointed guardian of the above-named children in place of Mr. Floyd E. Davis, who had resigned. The oldest of these children, Agnes Limerick

---

[20] One Jones was convicted at Winton Spring Assizes 1800, for larceny at Common Law in stealing wearing apparel from his master, and it was contended that under the above Act there must be judgment of transportation; but Mr. Justice Lawrence and Mr. Serjeant Palmer, who tried the prisoner, were both of opinion that in order to found a judgment on this statute the indictment must be specially drawn so as to bring the case within it. 2 East, P.C. 576. See *Rex* v. *John McGregor*, O.B. September Session, 1801, *post*.

Allen, would be of age on September 11th, following. Defendant duly qualified, giving a bond in the penalty of $7,000. There was turned over to him an overdue note of a Mr. Weeks for $2,250, secured by a deed of trust (a similar note of Mary E. Lynham for $2,000, but not here involved); two notes of a Mr. Richards for $200 each, and two notes of Mr. Richards for $1,000 each. In addition to these notes, $224.60 in cash came into his hands. The Weeks' note was the property of Robert and Clarence Limerick, and the four Richards's notes, aggregating $2,400, were the property of Agnes and Oliver Limerick. The former guardian having made overpayments to these minors aggregating $466.10, the defendant immediately, out of his own moneys, refunded that amount. The father of these children was dead, but the mother was living, and the former guardian had paid the mother $30 per month towards the maintenance of the children.

The defendant immediately petitioned the court and was granted leave to sell the Richard's notes at not less than their face value, which he did, receiving therefor cash or its equivalent. What was done with this money the government did not attempt to prove.

It next was shown that the defendant collected the overdue Weeks' note, the proceeds of which were placed in bank to his individual credit and mingled with his individual funds. The government then proved by bank officials that after the date of the deposit, on May 27, 1912, of the proceeds of the Weeks' note, the defendant issued checks against his account so that on July 31st following, the account showed an overdraft of $4.17.

Here the government rested.

Thereupon the defendant took the stand and explained that when he was appointed guardian, Agnes Allen was within a few months of reaching majority, at which time it would be necessary to settle with her; that he already had advanced some of his own money to the prior guardian, Mr. Davis, on account of the overpayments previously mentioned; that he did not remember whether he deposited the proceeds of the Richards's notes "in one account or in another account;" that when the Weeks' note was paid, "he charged himself as guardian with the receipt of the principal and the accumulated interest;" that he did not open any special account for this guardianship case. Upon being shown an account bearing the file mark of the clerk of the court June 15, 1914, entitled "Guardianship of Agnes Limerick, et al., First individual account, *final as to Agnes,*" he identified it as the account which he had filed, and also identified a number of vouchers accompanying the account and testified that those vouchers were for disbursements. Thereupon the account and voucher were offered in evidence. The government objecting, the court inquired as to "the date of the last entry made by the bank officer, who testified as to the closing of the account" (bank account), and, being informed that it was in July, 1912, sustained the objection, over defendant's exception.

The witness further testified that he paid $466 to Mr. Davis, the prior guardian, before he received either the notes or the cash from Mr. Davis. Upon stating that he had no independent recollection of the various receipts and dates of payment, he was shown a receipt, and testified that he made a payment of $30 to Mrs. Pote, mother of the minors, for their support on May 23, 1912, and offered the receipt in evidence. Thereupon counsel for the Government announced his intention to move the striking out of this receipt unless the defendant showed "some connection between these particular funds." Thereupon the court ruled that, to make this admissible, it must appear that these payments "came from the particular money deposited in the particular institution where he placed it to his individual credit, rather than to his credit as the fiduciary." Counsel for the defendant then offered to prove monthly payments of $30, commencing with the first payment on May 23, 1912, down to and including March, 1914. The district attorney then inquired whether these payments were by check out of a particular fund. Defendant's counsel answered that it was "by check out of these funds. I am not limiting it to any particular fund." Counsel for the defendant further offered to prove that out of the fund received from the proceeds of the Richards's notes and other funds in which Agnes Limerick Allen had a share, there was paid to her in full settlement, when she became of age in September, 1912, $2,276.51, and by error she was overpaid by the defendant to the extent of $265.37. Counsel further offered to prove the state of the other accounts, showing that defendant had the proper balance on deposit in the Security Savings & Commercial Bank, when he filed his account on June 15, 1914. The government objected to all the evidence thus offered and the court sustained the objection, to which ruling an exception was noted.

On cross-examination the government was permitted, over defendant's objection, to inquire concerning various cases in which he had acted in a fiduciary capacity.

The defendant was asked whether he reinvested the proceeds of the notes he collected as guardian, and replied that he used the proceeds in his business, "and accounted for it when I was called on for it." The latter part of the answer, upon motion of the district attorney and over the objection of the defendant, was stricken out by the court. The defendant's financial condition then was gone into, he testifying, in answer to the question whether in May of 1912 and for two years prior thereto he had not been in financial distress, that in 1912 he was making an average of $16,000 a year, and that he had interests in various properties "which he then believed and now believes to have been worth at that time many thousands of dollars in excess of his liabilities. That he had no conception of any difficulties." He further testified that his income at that time was steadily increasing, and that in 1913 it was over $22,000.***

MR. JUSTICE ROBB delivered the opinion of the Court:

Embezzlement is a creature of the statute, not being an offense at common law. Generally speaking, it may be defined as the fraudulent conversion of another's personal property by one to whom it has been intrusted, with the intention of depriving the owner thereof. *Masters* v. *United States,* 42 App. D. C. 350, Ann. Cas. 1916A, 1243. In 9 R. C. L. at page 1265, it is said: "It must be borne in mind, however, that the safest guide in determining what constitutes the crime of embezzlement, and what persons are amenable to the charge, is the statutes of the particular state in which the crime is prosecuted." Under the common-law definition it was found that many wrongdoers escaped; first, because it was necessary that the stolen goods should have been at some time in the complaining party's possession; and, second, because if the possession of the goods was lawfully acquired, no subsequent conversion during the bailment constituted larceny. It was to meet these defects that embezzlement statutes were enacted. It is at once apparent that the principal difference between larceny and embezzlement lies in the manner in which possession of the property is acquired. In larceny there is a trespass, accompanied by an intent to steal, while in embezzlement there is a *fraudulent* conversion of property the possession of which was lawfully acquired. *Moore v. United States*, 160 U.S. 268. In either case, however, except under special statutes, evil intent must be shown. In many jurisdictions it is provided that a public officer who knowingly and unlawfully appropriates funds in his keeping to his own use is guilty of embezzlement, the purpose of such statutes being to prevent such public officials from using money coming to them in their official capacity for any purpose other than that for which it came to them. Such a statute was the 3d section of the act of June 14, 1866, "to regulate and secure the safe-keeping of public money." 14 Stat. at L. 65, chap. 122.

The statute involved in the present case is of a different character from those to which reference has just been made. It is section 841 of the Code [31 Stat. at L. 1326, chap. 854], relating to "Executors and Other Fiduciaries," including guardians, and provides that if any such fiduciary "shall *fraudulently* convert or appropriate" property in his possession to his own use, he shall, in addition to forfeiting all claims to commissions, costs, and charges thereon, be deemed guilty of embezzlement. Section 834, relating to "Embezzlement By Agent, Attorney, Clerk, or Servant," denounces a *wrongful* conversion; and we have recently held that evil intent is an essential element of this crime. *Masters v. United States,* 42 App. D.C. 350. There is even greater reason for ruling that evil intent, that is intent to defraud, is an essential element of the crime denounced by section 841 than for so interpreting section 834, for the duties and powers of an executor or guardian are broader with respect to the management or control of funds coming into his hands than are generally exercised by an agent, attorney, or clerk. A guardian has complete charge of the property of his ward that comes into his possession, and must keep it properly and safely invested. While, of course, it is the better way for the guardian to keep money of his ward entirely separate from his own, the mere fact that he does not do so affords no sufficient basis for a presumption of evil intent. He is required to give a bond for the faithful discharge of his duties, and if he carelessly deposits funds of his ward in his own name or mingles such funds in a deposit of his own, and any loss results, he and his bondsman are responsible therefor. *Mades v. Miller,* 2 App. D.C. 455. In the case last cited, it was ruled that to entitle a guardian to protection from the loss of funds of his ward by the failure of a bank in which he deposited them, the deposit must clearly show that it was made by him as such guardian, and the letters "Guar" after his name, in the certificate of deposit, are insufficient.

We now will briefly review such cases as we think bear upon the questions here involved.***

In *State v. Reynolds,* 65 N. J. L. 424, it was ruled that in all cases "which are of an uncertain, or general, or special agency, where the time for the return of the funds collected is indefinite, or not fixed, or which is at the pleasure of the agent or servant, there a demand or other evidence of a fraudulent intent to convert may be necessary to put the defendant in a position of having fraudulently converted the money to his own use. It should be said, however, that a demand and refusal does not of itself in any case establish conversion, or conversion by a defendant to his own use, but that it is only evidence to go to the jury upon the question of the defendant's fraudulent conversion."

A pertinent suggestion was made by the court in *State v. Strasser,* 83 N. J. L. 691, a prosecution of an attorney for embezzlement, as follows: "The defendant was not being tried for unprofessional conduct, or even for a breach of a civil contract, but for the criminal conversion of another's money."

In the light of the foregoing, let us now consider the facts of the present case. The government contented itself with merely showing, in the one instance, the receipt of funds of the ward by the defendant, and, in the other, the receipt of funds, the mingling of those funds by the defendant with his own, the evidence tending to show conversion thereof. Had the defendant rested at this point and moved for an instructed verdict, it would have been the duty of the court to have granted the motion. No statute or rule of court was shown to have been violated. It was perfectly proper for the defendant to collect the overdue note, and it can hardly be contended that there was any culpability in the same of the Richards's notes, because that sale was expressly authorized by the probate court. There was no evidence whatever upon which the jury legitimately could have based a finding that there had been a fraudulent conversion of those funds. As the court remarked in the *Page Case,* 116 Cal. 386, the defendant all along may have had the funds on deposit in another bank or in his safe, ready to respond to any proper demand upon him as guardian. In the absence of proof to the contrary, the presumption would be that he did. In other words, the presumption of innocence is not overthrown by mere rumor or suspicion.

The question naturally arises, how is intent to be proved or disproved. Manifestly, it must be proved by the circumstances surrounding a given case, and disproved by evidence tending to explain those circumstances. It is competent for the government to prove the financial condition of the accused at or immediately prior to the alleged offense. *State* v. *Moyer, supra; Govatos v. State,* 116 Ga. 592. This upon the theory that a man is presumed to know the natural and probable consequences of his acts. Hence if a guardian, without adequate available means to meet all his obligations as guardian, should mingle guardianship funds with his own and thereafter deplete the common fund, a jury would not be likely to attach much credence to his denial of an intent to defraud his ward. In other words, if the guardian's financial condition is such that it fairly may be said that any misappropriation of his ward's funds will be likely to result in loss to the ward, then that fact will have an important bearing upon the question of intent, as well as upon the related question of motive. Failure to account for or turn over funds in the hands of the defendant is a circumstance, as we have seen, which may be considered along with the other evidence. *State* v. *Reynolds, supra.****

In the present case the court rejected all evidence as to payments from the defendant to his wards, and as to the account subsequently filed and approved by the probate court. This was upon the theory, first, that it had not been shown that those payments "came from the particular money deposited in the particular institution" to the credit of the wards; and, second, as to the account, that it had not been filed until after the depletion of the defendant's bank account, to which reference has been made. In our view, the evidence clearly was admissible. Evidence that the defendant met all his guardianship obligations promptly and in due course tended to throw light upon the question of intent. So all the authorities hold. Even in a case where the mere conversion of public funds by a public officer constitutes the offense, it has been held that the return of the property is a circumstance which should go to the jury for what it may be worth, as reflecting the motive of the trustee at the time of the appropriation, that is, as tending to disprove the allegation that the defendant was guilty of an appropriation. *Baxter v. State*, 91 Ohio St. 167. It would be a very unjust rule, indeed, that would permit the government to show failure on the part of the fiduciary to account for and pay over the funds in his hands, as tending to show fraudulent conversion, and preclude the defendant, where there was no evidence of such failure, affirmatively to prove both an accounting and payment, or offer of payment. The suggestion of the government, which seems to have been entertained by the learned trial justice, that when the account was filed with the probate court the crime of embezzlement already had been committed, does not take into account the very important consideration that the jury weighing all the evidence, including this account, might conclude there never had been a fraudulent conversion by the defendant of the guardianship funds coming into his hands. It is not for us to assume the defendant's guilt, for that question is for the jury to determine in the light of all the circumstances surrounding the transaction.

The defendant was interrogated concerning estates which had been closed in 1910, or long prior to his appointment in the present case. From what we have said it is apparent that the answer to this inquiry could throw no light upon the issue involved, and the defendant's objection should have been sustained.

It is unnecessary further to discuss the assignments of error, since they are covered by our general discussion of the case.

The judgment must be reversed and a new trial awarded.

Reversed.

Notes and Questions

1. According to *Ambrose v. United States,* why was it necessary to create the crime of embezzlement?

2. What specific acts by the defendant in *Ambrose* did the trial court find sufficient to demonstrate an intent to defraud? Why was the appellate court less persuaded by those same facts?

B. Larceny, False Pretenses, and Embezzlement

Eiseman & Landsman v. State, 1932 WL 1699 (Ohio Ct. App. 1932)

STATEMENT OF FACTS

Eiseman and Landsman were by indictment charged with the larceny of $22,000, the property of Sarah Silverberg. They were found guilty. Eiseman was sentenced to the penitentiary and Landsman to the State Reformatory. They both prosecute error to that judgment by separate petitions in error. In this court the cases are heard together upon the same bill of exceptions.

MAUCK, PJ.

***The principal question in the case is whether under the established facts the accused were guilty of the crime of larceny. Certainly the most hopeful view that might be taken of their case is that they were guilty of obtaining money under false pretenses or of embezzlement, and not of the technical charge of larceny.

Mrs. Silverberg and her daughters were living for a season in New York City where they made the acquaintance, under another name, of the defendant who is known in this record as George Eiseman. There is some question as to whether Mrs. Silverberg made the acquaintance of Landsman through a marriage broker or not, but there is some evidence that Mrs. Silverberg looked with favor upon Landsman as a possible son in law. She invited him to come to Cleveland when she resumed her residence in this city, and this he did. He and Eiseman made their headquarters at a hotel in the vicinity of Mrs. Silverberg's home. Mrs. Silverberg was known by the defendants to have a large amount of easily accessible cash and they knew that she had lost a sum of money in a bank failure in New York City. They conducted a sedulous campaign to prejudice her against Cleveland banks, advising her to draw out her money and give it to them to embark in some ambitious real estate projects which they attempted to convince her offered safety and profits. After a short campaign they induced Mrs. Silverberg to withdraw something like $22,000 in different Cleveland banks, and they generously furnished a brief case in which she could put the money. She took the money to her home where it was concealed over night. On the next day Landsman was in her home. All parties agree that he went to the Silverberg residence without the money and all agree that he left the home with the money. How he got possession of the money is disputed. Landsman was expected back at the Silverberg home for dinner. He did not show up. It was then learned that immediately after getting the $22,000 both defendants had checked out of the hotel and their trunk was traced to Detroit. They were soon located in a hotel at Detroit under the names under which they were indicted and tried, which were not at all the names by which they were known to Mrs. Silverberg and her family. The money taken consisted of twenty-one $1,000 bills and other currency. Some of this had been spent for a diamond ring. The larger bills had been exchanged for bills of smaller denominations. This money had been placed in a safety deposit box in Detroit, the keys therefor being found in Eiseman's possession. Landsman upon his arrest denied any knowledge of the Silverbergs and any connection with the transaction. The evidence shows that on more than one occasion when Mrs. Silverberg had been with these men she was taken sick, and there is some intimation that she had been drugged but there is nothing definite shown along this line. It is apparent, however, that if she were not drugged she was in a highly nervous condition and suffering from some physical disorders that account for her lack of definite knowledge upon some of the features of the case. Some of the testimony of her and her daughter indicates that without her consent Landsman took the money at her home, and some support to this view is given by the fact that the brief case was left, and in it some paper and glass, well calculated to deceive one lifting the brief case in the belief that it still contained the money that Landsman had walked away with. Other parts of Mrs. Silverberg's testimony indicate that more or less voluntarily she yielded the custody of this money to Landsman. The evidence is, however, clear enough that if she did voluntarily yield custody of the money to him that custody had been obtained by trickery and fraud of these reptiles, and that this trickery and fraud is sufficient to take the place of the trespass that is said to constitute one of the essential elements of the crime of larceny. We deem it unnecessary to recite the details more fully.

The Supreme Court of Massachusetts in *Commonwealth v. Barry,* 124 Mass. 325, distinguishes between the offense of embezzlement, obtaining property under false pretenses and larceny in a particularly lucid way. We quote:

> If a person honestly receives the possession of the goods, chattels or money of another upon any trust, express or implied, and after receiving them fraudulently converts them to his own use, he may be guilty of the crime of embezzlement but can not be of that of larceny except as embezzlement is by statute made larceny. If the possession of said property is obtained by fraud, and the owner of it intends to part with his title as well as his possession, the offense is that of obtaining property by false pretenses, provided the means by which they are acquired are such as are in law false pretenses. If the possession is fraudulently obtained, with intent on the part of the person obtaining it at the time he receives it to convert the same to his own use, and the person parting with it intends to part with his possession merely, and not with his title to the property, the offense is larceny.

These distinctions were approved and followed in *People v. Miller,* 169 N. Y. 339, 88 Am. St. 546. The principle referred to is discussed and the supporting cases collected in *Channock v. United States,* 11 A.L.R. 799-803.

The defendants in this case, if in fact they took this property with the owner's knowledge, did so intending at the time to convert it to their own use, and Mrs. Silverberg never had any intention of parting with her title to the money. In whatever manner the defendants acquired custody of the money larceny was accomplished.

The record is free from error.

The Judgment is affirmed.

Notes and Questions

1. The court in *Eiseman & Landsman v. State* found that the defendants committed larceny. Was this larceny by trick? If you think it was larceny by trick, what was the material misrepresentation?

2. Can you make an argument that rather than larceny the defendants in *Eiseman & Landsman* committed either embezzlement or false pretenses?

3. Towards the end of the case, the court notes some differences among larceny, false pretenses, and embezzlement. What additional differences, not noted by the court, exist among the three crimes?

4. As discussed previously, most jurisdictions consolidate the crimes of larceny, false pretenses, and embezzlement into a generic theft statute. Ohio's Theft statute (ORC 2913.02) reads as follows:

> (A) No person, with purpose to deprive the owner of property or services, shall knowingly obtain or exert control over either the property or services in any of the following ways:
>> (1) Without the consent of the owner or person authorized to give consent;
>> (2) Beyond the scope of the express or implied consent of the owner or person authorized to give consent;
>> (3) By deception;
>> (4) By threat;
>> (5) By intimidation.

C. Receipt of Stolen Property

State v. Diephaus, 55 Ohio App. 3d 90 (1989)

PER CURIAM.

In this appeal, the defendant-appellant, Donald Diephaus, seeks for a second time to challenge the legal sufficiency of the evidentiary fundament relied upon by a judge of the Hamilton County Municipal Court to convict him of receiving stolen property in violation of R.C. 2913.51. In an earlier appeal, we reversed the judgment of conviction that resulted from a plea of no contest, holding that certain procedural irregularities had worked, contrary to the intentions of all those involved in the prosecution below, to foreclose meaningful appellate review of what had become the pivotal issue in the case: whether the property that Diephaus had allegedly received could, in a legal sense, be considered stolen. *State v. Diephaus* (May 4, 1988), Hamilton App. No. C-870141, *unreported*. On remand, those irregularities identified in our decision were overcome when Diephaus elected to proceed upon a plea of not guilty and to have the charge against him resolved, by stipulation, on the basis of evidence that had already been presented to the court in connection with several pretrial motions. We now reverse the conviction that has stemmed from the proceedings held on remand

and discharge Diephaus from further prosecution on the charge of receiving stolen property.

The material facts underpinning the challenged conviction are themselves not in dispute. According to the record, there is no question that Diephaus agreed to purchase, and did in fact receive, from an individual who had been persuaded to work as an informant in concert with police officers, several cartons of cigarettes, including one that the informant had been caught shoplifting from a grocery store located in a suburban area near the city of Cincinnati. The shoplifted carton, which was the one piece of evidence essential to the success of the prosecution below, had been recovered on behalf of its rightful owner by a store security guard when the informant was apprehended at the scene of the shoplifting offense. From that location, the guard took the carton, along with the informant, to a police station house in Cincinnati, where a Cincinnati police officer devised a plan that called for the informant to sell cigarettes, as part of a "sting" operation, to various individuals who were suspected of black-market dealings in stolen goods. The shoplifted carton then remained directly under the control of the Cincinnati officer for some four hours until it was ultimately removed from the trunk of a car and delivered to Diephaus, among a quantity of cigarettes purchased for $4 per carton, at a drinking establishment known as the Good Luck Cafe.

In the only assignment of error given to us for review, Diephaus now asserts that his conviction must be held contrary to law on the basis of the following proposition:

> One cannot be convicted of Receiving Stolen Property when the owner of the property or his agent recovers and possesses said property before delivery to the intended receiver, because the property loses its identity as stolen property when recovered by the owner.

The proposition that Diephaus would have us adopt is essentially a restatement of the rule that prevailed under the common law to bar a conviction for receiving stolen property once the goods in question had been recovered by the owner or his recognized agent. See Annotation, Conviction of Receiving Stolen Property, or Related Offenses, Where Stolen Property Previously Placed Under Police Control (1989), 72 A.L.R. 4th 838, 840. That common-law bar has survived in the modern era, in one form or another, even where the statutory codification of the criminal law has not explicitly incorporated or referred to it, see, *e.g.*, *United States v. Johnson* (C.A.8, 1985); and in our judgment, following a review of the various case authorities touching upon the subject, there is no persuasive reason for concluding that the bar has not similarly survived in Ohio, where the offense of receiving stolen property has been codified in R.C.

2913.51(A), without specific reference to what effect, if any, attends the recovery of the stolen goods.

In reaching this conclusion, we are aware that some courts, including one in this state, have attempted to create a distinction that would render the rule we have followed here inapplicable in cases where "police gain possession of stolen goods within a criminal scheme of which the defendant is a part and possess those goods [only] for a short period of time" before "they are transported to the defendant pursuant to the [same] criminal scheme." *State v. Pyle* (Dec. 30, 1983), Lake App. No. 9-237. To the extent that there may be some basis in law to support such a distinction, we are convinced that it cannot be invoked to save the conviction obtained against Diephaus for at least two reasons: (1) the extent of the actual possession and control of the stolen cigarettes asserted by the police here cannot, under the circumstances demonstrated in this record, be trivialized, either in degree or in duration; and (2) there is no evidence that the recovery of the cigarettes from the informant, and the ensuing transfer of the goods to the Cincinnati police, was, in any way, part of the criminal scheme under which the cigarettes were ultimately sold to Diephaus (as far as this record is concerned, the criminal scheme was plotted only after the cigarettes were recovered and the theft offense made known to the Cincinnati police).

Because the shoplifted carton of cigarettes was not stolen property at the time it was received by Diephaus, we hold that the evidence upon which the court below relied was legally insufficient to support a conviction under R.C. 2913.51. The assignment of error presented to us is, accordingly, well-taken, and we therefore reverse the judgment of the Hamilton County Municipal Court and order that the defendant-appellant be discharged from further prosecution.

Judgment accordingly.

Notes and Questions

1. Subsequent to *State v. Diephaus*, Ohio amended its Receipt of Stolen Property statute (2913.51) to read as follows:

> (A) No person shall receive, retain, or dispose of property of another knowing or having reasonable cause to believe that the property has been obtained through commission of a theft offense.
> (B) It is not a defense to a charge of receiving stolen property in violation of this section that the property was obtained by means other than through the commission of a theft offense if the property was explicitly represented to the accused person as being obtained through the commission of a theft offense

2. Based on this statute, can price (e.g., the four dollar cigarette cartons in *State v. Diephaus*) alone ever be sufficient to show that a defendant knew or should have known that the product in question had been obtained through the commission of a theft offense? If you were on a jury, what factors would you look at to determine whether the defendant had adequate knowledge of the stolen status of the property?

D. Forgery

In re Clemons, 168 Ohio St. 83 (1958)

MATTHIAS, Judge.

The single issue before us is whether the making and issuance, with intent to defraud, of a check signed by the maker with his own name but drawn on a bank in which such maker has no 'checking account' constitute a violation of Section 2913.01, Revised Code, i. e., whether the petitioner was convicted of a crime over which the Common Pleas Court of Gallia County had jurisdiction pursuant to the indictment hereinbefore set out.

Section 2913.01, Revised Code, reads in part as follows:

> "No person, with intent to defraud, shall falsely make *** a *** check *** or, with like intent, utter or publish as true and genuine such false *** matter, knowing it to be false ***.
> "Whoever violates this section is guilty of forgery ***."

In rendering its decision in this cause, the Court of Appeals for Franklin County followed a precedent of that court which is evidenced by the case of State ex rel. Bailey v. Henderson, 76 Ohio App. 547, 63 N.E.2d 830, and it is essentially the differences between that case and the case of State v. Havens, supra, 91 Ohio App. 578, 109 N.E.2d 48, which this court must resolve.

The Court of Appeals for Franklin County, in the Bailey case, held that every offense defined by Section 2913.01 must be a forgery in the common-law sense of the word, which, it stated, includes only the signing of a name other than that of the signer.

However, in the Havens case, the Court of Appeals for Sandusky County held that the General Assembly can define the offenses described in Section 2913.01 in any manner it sees fit, and that, even though there are included among the acts described therein acts which may not be forgery in the common-law dictionary sense of that word, such acts are nevertheless punishable as 'forgery' under the terms of Section 2913.01, Revised Code.

Section 1307.03, Revised Code, defines "check" as follows:

> "A check is a bill of exchange drawn on a bank payable on demand."

Section 1305.02, Revised Code, defines a bill of exchange as follows:

> "A bill of exchange is an unconditional order in writing, addressed by one person to another, signed by the person giving it, requiring the person to whom it is addressed to pay, on demand or at a fixed or determinable future time, a sum certain in money to order or to bearer."

Although it is true that a check is merely an order to a bank to pay on demand a certain sum, in order for a check to be considered a genuine instrument the maker must have a *right to make such order, i. e.,* he must have money in the drawee bank.

It seems perfectly clear to this court that the making of an instrument purporting to be a check, with intent to defraud, drawn on a bank wherein the maker has no "checking account" constitutes the false making of a check within the purview of the statute, regardless of whether the maker signs his own name or that of another, and that such act was intended by the General Assembly to be included in its definition of "forgery" as set out in Section 2913.01, Revised Code.

In fully sustaining the position of the Court of Appeals for Sandusky County, we find that we cannot improve on the following language of explanation used by Judge Fess of that court, in the Havens case, supra [91 Ohio App. 578, 109 N.E.2d 49]:

> "Forgery at common law is defined by Blackstone as the fraudulent making or altering of a writing to the prejudice of another's right, and by East as the false making or altering, *malo animo*, of any written instrument for the purposes of fraud and deceit. In 1865, in In re Windsor, 6 Best & Smith, 522, Cockburn, C.J., declared that forgery 'by universal acceptation *** is understood to mean, the making or altering a writing so as to make the writing or alteration purport to be the act of some other person, which it is not.' But in 1869, in Rey v. Ritson, 1 Law Reports, Crown Cases, 200, it was held that forgery is the fraudulent making of an instrument in words purporting to be what they are not, to the prejudice of another's rights. In the same case, Blackburn, J., adopted Comyn's definition that forgery is where a man fraudulently writes or publishes a false deed or

writing to the prejudice of another. 2 Wharton's Criminal Law (12 Ed.), 1162, Section 859. It is apparent that the cases in the United States have departed from the broad common-law definition and have followed the more narrow rule pronounced by Cockburn in In re Windsor. In its ordinary sense, forgery is the false signing of another's name, but in the Snyder [Snyder v. State, 8 Ohio Cir. Ct. R. 463] and Henderson cases the courts overlook the fact that Section 13083 of the Ohio General Code [Section 2913.01, Revised Code] is much broader and more inclusive than the Cockburn definition. It recites that 'whoever, with intent to defraud, falsely makes, alters, forges, counterfeits, prints or photographs *** bank bill or note, check, bill of exchange, contract, promissory note *** or, with like intent, utters or publishes as true and genuine such false, altered, forged, counterfeited *** matter, knowing it to be' such, is guilty of forgery.

"No language is to be found in the section denouncing in explicit terms the false making or forging of another's signature. No such language was necessary, because the statute says 'forges,' which includes forgery in the limited sense of forging another's signature. But in addition to the word, 'forges,' the Legislature says, 'falsely makes, alters, counterfeits, prints,' etc. In construing the statute, regard must be had to the additional language employed.

"It is true that criminal statutes are to be strictly construed. But the rule of strict construction is subordinate to the rule of reasonable, sensible and fair construction according to the expressed legislative intent, having due regard to the plain, ordinary and natural meaning and scope of the language employed.

"In other words, although it is settled that a penal statute is not to be extended by construction to persons or acts not within its descriptive terms, yet it is just as well settled that the provisions of a penal statute are to be fairly construed according to the expressed legislative intent, and mere verbal nicety or forced construction is not to be resorted to in order to exonerate persons committing acts plainly within the terms of the statute. To hold that the making of a false instrument is not within a criminal statute directed against the false making of an instrument, as was held by the Supreme Court of Nebraska in Goucher v. State, 113 Neb. 352, 204 N.W. 967, 41 A.L.R. 227, requires an artificial and narrow interpretation which, it seems to us, would defeat the apparent purpose and intent of the Legislature to include as forgery the making of a false instrument regardless of whether the signature itself was genuine.

"The state of Illinois has a statute defining forgery somewhat similar to the Ohio statute. It provides that every person who shall falsely make, alter, forge or counterfeit any one of a specified number of instruments shall be guilty of forgery. In People v. Kramer, 1933, 352 Ill. 304, 185 N.E. 590, the Supreme Court held that the essence of forgery is the making of a false writing with intent that it be received as the act of another, and can not be committed by the making of a genuine instrument though the statements made therein are untrue. But in People v. Kubanek, 1939, 370 Ill. 646, 19 N.E.2d 573, the court held that the Illinois statute was not directed solely against the forgery of signatures, but includes false making, uttering and counterfeiting, when done with intent to defraud. In People v. Mau, 1941, 377 Ill. 199, 36 N.E.2d 235, the court held that a person may be guilty of a 'false making' of an instrument within the meaning of the common-law definition of 'forgery' where the instrument is false in any material part and calculated to induce another to give credit to it as genuine and authentic, notwithstanding the fact that the person signs and executes the instrument in his own name."

Following his lucid explanation, Judge Fess drew this conclusion, which is hereby adopted as the conclusion of the Supreme Court on the subject:

"We, therefore, *** hold that under Section *** [2913.01, Revised Code], a person is guilty of the false making of a check where the check is drawn upon a bank in which the maker has no funds or deposit account and is calculated to induce another to give credit to it as genuine and authentic, even though such person signs his own name thereto and likewise that one who utters such a check [with knowledge of its falsity] is guilty of forgery."

Since the acts committed by petitioner constituted a violation of Section 2913.01, Revised Code, it follows that he pleaded guilty to a crime over which the convicting court had jurisdiction under the indictment, and, such jurisdiction being the essential test of the validity of this petition in habeas corpus, such petition is without merit, and the judgment of the Court of Appeals is reversed and the petitioner remanded to custody.

Judgment reversed.

WEYGANDT, C. J., and ZIMMERMAN, STEWART, BELL and HERBERT, JJ., concur.

TAFT, Judge (dissenting).

As the statement of the instant case indicates, the indictment charged only that petitioner "did falsely make, forge and counterfeit." The majority opinion apparently recognizes that the words "forge" and "counterfeit" could not describe the acts with which petitioner was charged. We are therefore only concerned with the portion of the statute quoted at the beginning of the majority opinion (Section 2913.01, Revised Code) and providing that "no person, with intent to defraud, shall falsely make *** a *** check" and not with the latter portion relative to uttering or publishing "as true and genuine such false *** matter" except as that latter part of the statute may indicate the legislative intent with respect to the portion with which we are concerned.

Of course the General Assembly can specify that certain elements will constitute the crime of forgery, even though such elements would not have amounted to forgery at common law. The question still remains whether the General Assembly in Section 2913.01, Revised Code, did specify that what petitioner was charged with doing in the instant case could constitute the crime of forgery. Undoubtedly, what petitioner was charged with doing in the instant case would have amounted to a crime under Section 1115.23, Revised Code, and perhaps under other statutes, but petitioner was indicted only under Section 2913.01, Revised Code.

Here, the so-called "false making" of a "check" with which petitioner was charged was his signing a check with his own name on a bank in which he had no account.

A check is simply a written order addressed by its maker to a bank and directing the bank to pay on demand a sum certain *90 in money to the payee or on the order of the payee or to the bearer. Sections 1307.02 and 1305.02, Revised Code. It gives the payee or the bearer to whom it is delivered no right of action against the bank before the bank accepts it. It is "simply an order which may be countermanded and payment forbidden by the drawer any time before it is actually cashed or accepted." If the check is not paid or accepted when presented to the bank an immediate right of recourse against the drawer accrues to its holder. Section 1305.26, Revised Code.

Although the check drawn in the instant case was almost certain to be dishonored by the bank upon which it was drawn, it was exactly what it purported to be, that is, a check drawn by petitioner who signed his own name to it.

As stated in 23 American Jurisprudence, 678, Section 7:

"*** the term 'falsely,' as applied to making *** a writing in order to make it a forgery, does not refer to the contents or tenor of the writing or to the facts stated therein, but implies that the paper or writing is not genuine, that in itself it is false or counterfeit. Hence, although there is some authority to the contrary, as a general rule, forgery cannot be committed by the genuine making of an instrument for the purpose of defrauding."

Also in 37 C.J.S. Forgery § 5, p. 36, it is said:

"Subject to statutory variations, the false making or alteration of some instrument in writing is an essential element of the crime of forgery. The essence of the offense is the making of a false writing with the intent that it shall be received as the act of another than the party signing it ***. Forgery cannot be committed by the making of a genuine instrument, although the statements made therein are untrue. The term 'falsely' has reference not to the contracts or tenor of the writing, or to the fact stated in the writing, but it implies that the paper or writing is false, not genuine, fictitious, not a true writing, without regard to the truth or falsehood of the statement it contains."

In 37 C.J.S. Forgery § 15, p. 42, it is stated:

"*** while there can be no forgery without a fraudulent intent *** it does not follow that every intent to defraud, although coupled with a written instrument, is forgery. *** Making *** a writing genuine in itself, but containing false statements, is not within a statute providing a punishment for falsely making *** a writing ***."

In the annotation at 41 A.L.R. 229, it is said:

"The term 'genuine making' is employed in the annotation to denote cases in which the instrument *** charged to have been forged, was in fact the writing of the person purporting to have executed it ***.
"***
"*** the better view, and that supported by the majority opinion, is that under the common law and under statutes defining forgery in the substantial language of the common-law

definitions, the genuine making of an instrument for the purpose of defrauding does not constitute the crime of forgery.

"***.

"To forge or to counterfeit is falsely to make, and an alteration of a writing must be falsely made to make it forgery at common law, or by a statute defining the crime substantially as defined by the common-law writers. The term 'falsely,' as applied to making or altering a writing in order to make it forgery, has reference not to the contracts or tenor of the writing or to the facts stated in the writing, because a writing containing a true statement may be forged or counterfeited as well as any other, but it implies that the paper or writing is false, not genuine, fictitious, not a true writing, without regard to the truth or falsehood of the statement it contains-a writing which is the counterfeit of something which is or has been a genuine writing, or one which purports to be a genuine writing or an instrument when it is not."

As the foregoing statements clearly indicate, our statute by defining a "false making" of a writing as a forgery has not thereby made something a forgery which was not within the common-law definition of a forgery. In short, those words were always used in defining the common-law crime of forgery.

Apart from the two Courts of Appeals' opinions referred to therein, the majority opinion does not refer to any authorities dealing with the question whether one may be guilty of forgery either at common law or under a statute similar to the Ohio statute where the act with which he is charged is the signing of his name to a check on a bank in which he had no account. The dearth of such authority is further indicated by the absence from Judge Fess' opinion (which is quoted in the majority opinion) of reference to any cases considering that precise question; and that very dearth of authority on the question suggests that very few have heretofore even contended that one could be found guilty of forgery, as that crime is defined in our statute, where he signed his own name to a check on a bank in which he had no account even though he may have done so with intent to defraud and might be guilty of some other statutory crime by reason of his having done so.

Although recognizing that two other Ohio intermediate appellate courts had previously reached a different conclusion, Judge Fess, in support of his conclusion which has been adopted as the basis for the conclusion in the majority opinion, relied principally on the cases of People v. Mau, 377 Ill. 199, 36 N.E.2d 235, and People v. Kubanek, 370 Ill. 646, 19 N.E.2d 573. The Mau case did not even involve a check. It involved the making of another kind of written instrument containing false statements with regard to facts that it was the legal duty of the maker thereof to state correctly. The Kubanek case involved the filling in of blanks in a check in a way not authorized by its maker and would seem to represent a decision contrary to that rendered by this court in Schryver v. Hawkes, 22 Ohio St. 308.

Apparently the only case on the precise question, other than Ohio intermediate appellate court decisions, is Wright v. United States, 9 Cir., 172 F.2d 310, holding that one who signs his own name as drawer of a check on a bank in which he has no account is not guilty of forgery under a statute, defining that crime as it is defined in the Ohio statute, even though he may have done so with intent to defraud.

Notes and Questions

1. Who had the stronger argument in *In re Clemons,* the majority or the dissent? Which side adhered more closely to the common law?

1. Forgery Mensa Rea

Morales-Algerin v. Gonzales, 449 F. 3d 1051 (2006)

BERZON, Circuit Judge.

The Board of Immigration Appeals (BIA) held that Francisco Morales-Alegria was removable because he had been convicted of an "aggravated felony" within the meaning of Immigration and Nationality Act (INA) section 101(a)(43)(R), 8 U.S.C. § 1101(a)(43)(R). Morales-Alegria maintains that his conviction for forgery under California Penal Code section 476 does not qualify as an "aggravated felony." He contends that (1) a conviction under section 476 is not necessarily "an offense relating to . . . forgery" because it does not require knowledge of the fictitious nature of the instrument***

With respect to Morales-Alegria's first claim, we hold that a conviction under section 476 does require knowledge of the fictitious nature of the instrument and therefore is not broader than the federal definition of "offense relating to . . . forgery" on that account.

I

Pursuant to INA section 237(a)(2)(A)(iii), an alien who, at any time after admission, is convicted of an aggravated felony-defined to include "an offense relating to . . . forgery . . . for which the term of imprisonment is at least one year," 8 U.S.C. § 1101(a)(43)(R)-may be removed from the country. The government charged Morales-Alegria, a native and citizen of Guatemala, with removal for having committed an aggravated felony. The basis for removal was his prior conviction under California Penal Code section 476, entitled, "Forgery; fictitious or altered bills, notes or checks," which the government stated satisfied § 1101(a)(43)(R).

After a hearing, the Immigration Judge (IJ) issued an oral decision holding that Morales-Alegria was removable as charged, which Morales-Alegria appealed.***

III

Morales-Alegria argues that section 476 includes a broader range of conduct than generic "forgery." Specifically, Morales-Alegria maintains that an individual may be convicted of forgery under Penal Code section 476 without a showing that he had knowledge of the fictitious nature of the instrument, while the generic definition of forgery requires such knowledge. We hold that while the generic definition of forgery does require such knowledge, so does section 476.

A

Forgery offenses developed from the common-law crime of "larceny." 3 Wayne R. Lafave, Substantive Criminal Law § 19.7(a), (j)(5) (2d ed. 2003)[hereinafter Substantive Criminal Law]. We therefore use the first approach and consider the generic, core meaning of the crime.*** Morales-Alegria only disputes the mens rea for the crime of which he was convicted. Accordingly, we only consider the knowledge and intent requirements traditionally included in the offense of forgery.

B

The crime of forgery stems from the related crime of false pretenses, developed to fill a gap left in the evolution of the common-law crime of larceny. SUBSTANTIVE CRIMINAL LAW §§ 19.1(b), 19.2. Common-law larceny was originally limited to "(1) trespassory (2) taking and (3) carrying away of the (4) personal property (5) of another (6) with intent to steal it." *Id.* § 19.2. Although "[t]he definition of larceny . . . was expanded by judicial interpretation to include cases where the owner merely was deemed to be in possession," "[b]y the late 18th century, courts were less willing to expand common-law definitions." As a result, no crime punishing individuals who obtained title to, rather than only physical possession of, property through fraudulent means existed under the common-law. *Id.*; 3 Wharton's Criminal Law § 343 (15th ed. 2005).

The crime of obtaining property by false pretenses was first created by the English Parliament in 1757 to fill this gap. The English statute punished those who "knowingly and designedly, by false pretence or pretences, shall obtain from any person or persons, money, goods, wares or merchandises, with intent to cheat or defraud any person or persons of the same." Substantive Criminal Law § 19.7(a) (internal quotation marks omitted) (quoting 1757, 30 Geo. II, c. 24 (Eng.)). At least one American jurisdiction recognized the English offense of "false pretenses" as part of the common-law. *Id.* § 19.7(a). Most jurisdictions, however, adopted false pretenses as a statutory crime. Although the statutory definition varies some from jurisdiction to jurisdiction, it generally consists of five elements: "(1) a false representation of a material present or past fact (2) which causes the victim (3) to pass title to (4) his property to the wrongdoer, (5) who (a) *knows his representation to be false* and (b) *intends thereby to defraud* the victim." *Id.* § 19.7 (emphases added).

Forgery, a crime closely related to false pretenses, is "aimed primarily at safeguarding confidence in the genuineness of documents relied upon in commercial and business activity." *Id.* § 19.7(j)(5). Jurisdictions that recognize forgery as a common-law crime provide that "the essential elements of the crime are (1) a false making of some instrument in writing; (2) a fraudulent intent; [and] (3) an instrument apparently capable of effecting a fraud." Furthermore, crimes of forgery require that one have knowledge of the falsity of the document.

State statutory definitions of forgery rarely depart from common-law definitions, as they "do not repeal the common law, but merely codify existing case law." 36 Am. Jur. 2D *Forgery* § 3 (2005). Under the modern offense, then, "the intent to injure or defraud, and proof of a specific intent to defraud, such as through a showing that the person passing the instrument knew that it was forged, is essential to a conviction of the offense." *Id.* § 5 (footnote omitted). The Model Penal Code recognizes a similar definition:

> A person is guilty of forgery if, *with purpose to defraud or injure anyone,* or *with knowledge that he is facilitating a fraud or injury to be perpetrated by anyone,* the actor:
>
> (a) alters any writing of another without his authority; or
>
> (b) makes, completes, executes, authenticates, issues or transfers any writing so that it purports to be the act of another who did not authorize that act, or to have been executed at a time or place or in a numbered sequence other than was in fact the case, or to be a copy of an original when no such original existed; or
>
> (c) utters any writing which he knows to be forged in a manner specified in paragraphs (a) or (b).[21]

---

[21] The MPC definition implicitly or explicitly requires knowledge of the false nature of the document in question. Under subsections (a) and (b), a person *must* know that a document is forged if she alters, makes, completes, executes, authenticates, issues or transfers a writing without authorization and with an intent to defraud or injure or with knowledge that he or she is facilitating a

Model Penal Code § 224.1(1) (2001) (emphasis added).

In short, the common-law and generic state statutory definitions of "forgery" generally require both an intent to defraud and knowledge of the fictitious nature of the instrument.

C

The Third Circuit, in *Drakes v. Zimski,* 240 F.3d 246 (3d Cir. 2001), is the only other circuit that has analyzed the mental state requirements of forgery to determine whether an offense under a state statute constitutes an aggravated felony for the purposes of § 1101(a)(43)(R). In *Drakes,* the court considered a Delaware statute that criminalizes a variety of acts committed while "intending to defraud, deceive or injure another person," *Drakes,* 240 F.3d at 248 (internal quotation marks omitted) (quoting Del. Code Ann._tit. 11, § 861). While concluding that the Delaware statute was an offense "relating to . . . forgery," *Drakes* noted that "[c]ourts generally define traditional common-law forgery as requiring an intent to defraud[,]" "state forgery statutes frequently cite intent to defraud as the sole requisite intent," and federal statutes often require an intent to defraud.

Drakes does not address whether knowledge of the fictitious nature of the instrument is required. "Intent to defraud," however, has been interpreted by federal courts as requiring such knowledge.

Given that the common-law and modern state statutory definitions of the mental state requirements for forgery are consistent with each other, as well as with the federal statutes reviewed in *Drakes,* we adopt a generic, core definition of forgery which requires intent to defraud and includes a mental state requirement of knowledge of the fictitious nature of the instrument.

D

Because in California knowledge of the falsity of the document is "inherent in the concept of intent to defraud," *see id.,* the lack of an explicit "knowledge" requirement in section 476 does not make that section broader than the generic, core definition of forgery that we adopt. We hold, therefore, that Morales-Alegria's claim-that his conviction under section 476 is not categorically a forgery offense because the generic definition, but not section 476, requires a showing of knowledge-fails.

V

---

fraud or injury. Under subsection (c), the crime of "uttering" explicitly requires knowledge

We reject Morales-Alegria's claim that his conviction under section 476 is not categorically a forgery offense because the generic definition, but not section 476, requires a showing of knowledge. Morales-Alegria's claim that his sentence for forgery was not "at least one year" as required by § 1101(a)(43)(R) was not raised before the BIA. Morales-Alegria therefore did not exhaust that claim, and this court lacks jurisdiction to decide it.

PETITION DENIED.

Chapter 15
Burglary, Arson, and Vandalism

A. Burglary

At common law, burglary is the breaking and entering the dwelling house of another at night with the intent to commit a felony therein. The first part of this definition, "breaking and entering," is examined in greater detail in *Goins v. State*. The last part of this definition, "with the intent to commit a felony therein," is discussed in greater detail in *In re L.D.* and *State v. Gardner*. *In re L.D.* explores the point at which the defendant has to have the intent to commit the felony. *Gardner* examines the specific underlying felony to be committed by the defendant and what proof requirements must be put forth by the government to demonstrate that the defendant did indeed intend to commit the felony within the dwelling.

1. Breaking and Entering

Goins v. State, 90 Ohio St. 176 (1914)

NEWMAN, J.

The only means of ingress to and egress from the chicken house was through a doorway of ordinary size. On the evening before the chickens were stolen the door of the chicken house, which was hung upon hinges, was open about 15 or 18 inches, being held open by means of a fence post placed on one side thereof and a brick on the other side. The owner of the property, Mary Linton, testified that the door had been propped open in that way, "just so that the chickens and myself could pass in and out." She stated that the door was not open wide enough to permit her to walk in—she "had to take hold of the edge of the door and then pull around the corner." It appears from the evidence that the morning after the chickens were stolen the door was from one-half to two-thirds open, and the fence post and brick were moved out of place.

That the chicken house was entered by plaintiffs in error and chickens of the value of $15 were stolen by them is not controverted. Counsel insist, however, that the crime of burglary was not established, that there was no evidence tending to show that there was a forcible breaking and entering of the chicken house, and that the court erred in refusing to give to the jury two certain special instructions, requested by them to be given before argument. These instructions are as follows:

> If the jury find from the evidence that the building charged in the indictment to have been forcibly, feloniously, and burglariously broken and entered was a chicken house, and if the mode of ingress to and egress from was through a common sized door hung upon hinges, and that the said door was so adjusted that it was left open, or partly open, so that the owner and the chickens could pass in and out, and you further find that said door was in that condition at the time when it is claimed that it was broken and entered, as charged in the indictment, then I charge you that your verdict should be not guilty of breaking and entering said building.

> If the jury find from the evidence that the building in question was a chicken house, and that the only mode of ingress to and egress from said chicken house was through a common sized door hung upon hinges, and a brick or piece of brick was so placed between the sill of said building and said door as to leave said door open for a space of from 15 to 18 inches, and that upon the outside of said door there was placed upon the ground a piece of fence post to prevent the door from swinging wide open, and that through the space thus left the owner could pass into and from said building, and that said door was in that condition at the time it is charged it was broken and entered, then I charge you that your verdict must be not guilty of breaking and entering said building.

The objection to these instructions is that there is an assumption that the door was open sufficiently wide so that any person might pass in and out of the chicken house. This was a question for the jury, and, in view of the fact that the fence post and brick were moved, and the door was found to be from one-half to two-thirds open after the chickens were stolen, the jury was justified in finding that the opening was not large enough to admit plaintiffs in error and that it was necessary to move the obstacles which had been placed against the door to hold it in position before they could gain an entrance to the house.

The court, in its general charge, properly instructed the jury that if it found from the evidence that the door of the chicken house was partly open, so that a person or persons could enter the same, and it was not necessary to remove the brick or post that had been placed against the door to hold it in that position when making an entrance, then that would not constitute a forcible breaking in the sense the statute uses the term.

The court further instructed the jury that if it found that the door was partly open and it was necessary to remove the post or brick placed against it to hold it in the position in which it was, and that the entrance could not have been made into the building without the removal of the brick or post, and that if the brick or post was so removed by plaintiffs in error, or either of them, and an entrance made into the chicken house, then this would constitute a forcible breaking. We are of the opinion that the court charged correctly on this proposition.

Counsel rely upon the following statement in the opinion in *Timmons v. State*, 34 Ohio St. 426:

> The law on the point is, that if the owner leaves his doors open, or partly open, or his windows raised, or partly raised and unfastened, it will be such negligence or folly on his part, as is calculated to induce or tempt a stranger to enter; and if he does so through the open door or window, or by pushing open the partly opened door, or further raising the window that is a little up, it will not be burglary.

This doctrine, as was stated by the judge delivering the opinion, had no application in that case, and, as we view it, was clearly obiter. We are aware, however, that it is the holding in a number of cases that where a door or window is partly open and an entrance is gained by pushing open the partly open door or further raising the window it is not a breaking, and will not constitute burglary. This rule finds favor with the English authorities, with the courts of Massachusetts, and is approved by some text-writers. But there is a tendency on the part of a number of courts to depart from the strict construction of the common law, which required an actual breaking. They have adopted what we consider to be the more reasonable and logical rule, holding that but the slightest force is necessary to constitute a breaking. If any force at all is necessary to effect an entrance into a building through any place of ingress, usual or unusual, whether open, partly open, or closed, such entrance is a breaking sufficient in law to constitute is a breaking other elements of the offense are present.***

In the common-law definition of burglary the word "forcibly" is not used in connection with the word "break," nor does it appear in the statutes of some of the states whose courts have adopted the rule to which we subscribe. It is used in the Ohio statute, but, as was stated in *Ducher v. State*, 18 Ohio, 308, the offense is not changed by the statute which adds the word "forcibly" as a qualifying term. And in *Timmons v. State, supra*, the court say that the application of the rule does not depend upon the degree of force used, but upon the fact that force of some degree, however slight, was used. In that case the court held:

> The force necessary to push open a closed, but unfastened, transom, that swings horizontally on hinges over an outer door of a dwelling house, is sufficient to constitute a breaking in burglary under our statute, which requires a forcible breaking.

We think, as was said by the court in *Claiborne v. State, supra*, that to hold that the opening of a door or window which is closed but not fastened is sufficient evidence of breaking, but that the further opening of a door or window partly open, in order to gain an entrance is not sufficient evidence, is a useless refinement.

In the case under consideration, if the door of the chicken house was further opened, in order to make the opening sufficiently wide to admit the plaintiffs in error (and this was a question for the jury) unquestionably some force was required, and, however slight it may have been, it was all that was required to constitute a "forcible breaking" under the statute, and, taken with the other facts established, made a case of burglary. The trial court, therefore, properly refused to direct a verdict of not guilty and committed no error in refusing to give the two special instructions requested.***

There being no error in the record prejudicial to plaintiffs in error, the judgment of the court of appeals is affirmed.

Judgment affirmed.

United States v. Eichman, 756 F. Supp. 143 (1991)

OPINION

SAND, District Judge.

This criminal case involves charges arising from acts allegedly committed by the defendants at the United States Armed Forces Recruiting Station at Times Square in New York City. Count three of the indictment, brought pursuant to the Assimilative Crimes Act, 18 U.S.C. § 13 (1988), charges the defendants with burglary in the third degree in violation of N.Y. Penal Law § 140.20 (McKinney 1988). Presently before this Court are the defendants' motions to dismiss count three of the indictment, or, in the alternative, to permit an inspection of the grand jury minutes.

The issue raised by defendants' motions is what constitutes "enter[ing] . . . in a building with intent to commit a crime therein" under the burglary provisions of the New York Penal Law. The government opposes defendants' motions but asks this Court to issue a ruling on how the jury will be charged on the burglary count. For the reasons given below, this Court denies the motion to dismiss and the motion to inspect. However, we grant the government's request and set forth our determination as to how the jury will be charged with respect to the elements of the burglary count.

I. BACKGROUND

The government and the defendants are in substantial agreement as to the facts of this case. On September 11, 1990, defendants Shawn Eichman and Joseph Urgo went to the Armed Forces Recruiting Station at Times Square and climbed onto the roof of the one story structure using a ladder. Once on the roof the defendants poured motor oil over the surface of the roof and onto the exterior signs of the building. The defendants then lowered the American flag flying over the building, doused it with lighter fluid and set it on fire. Defendants claim that their activities were acts of political protest symbolizing their objection to American policy in the Persian Gulf.

Shortly after they ignited the flag, defendants were arrested on the roof by New York City police officers. The next day they were arraigned on a complaint charging attempted arson of the recruiting station. The government subsequently decided not to pursue the arson charge. Instead, the indictment returned by the grand jury charged defendants with three other crimes: (1) injuring and committing depredations against property of the United States, in violation of 18 U.S.C. §§ 1361, 1362 (1988); (2) reckless endangerment, in violation of 18 U.S.C. §§ 7, 13 (1988) and N.Y. Penal Law § 120.20 (McKinney 1988); and (3) burglary in the third degree, in violation of 18 U.S.C. §§ 7, 13 and N.Y. Penal Law § 140.20.

On November 16, 1990, defendants made a request for a Bill of Particulars. The government responded the same day with a letter which states, in part, that "the Government does not contend that the defendants entered within the four walls and beneath the roof of the Recruiting Station. Rather, the Government contends that the defendants unlawfully entered upon the roof of the Recruiting Station." *See* Government's Memorandum of Law, p. 4.

On December 17, 1990, defendants moved to dismiss the burglary count of the indictment on the ground that absent an allegation that defendants entered within the four walls of the recruiting station, the government would be unable to prove the "entry" element of the burglary count at trial. Defendants moved in the alternative to inspect the minutes of the grand jury proceedings. The government argues that the defendants' motions should be denied because the indictment pleads all the necessary elements of burglary under New York law. However, the government nonetheless asks this Court to reach the merits of defendants' argument regarding the entry element. *See* Government's Memorandum of Law, p. 6. The government suggests that it would be appropriate for this Court to address the issue in the form of a ruling on how the jury will be charged at trial with regard to the entry element of the burglary charge.

II. DISCUSSION

A. Defendants' Motion to Dismiss

***In this case, count three of the indictment pleads all of the elements of the offense of burglary. Under New York law, a person is guilty of burglary in the third degree when he "knowingly enters or remains unlawfully in a building with intent to commit a crime therein." N.Y. Penal Law § 140.20. The third count tracks the statutory language, charging that the defendants "knowingly entered and remained in . . . [the recruiting station] with intent to commit one or more crimes therein." Assuming the factual allegations contained in count three to be true, the count properly pleads the charge of burglary in the third degree. Consequently, the motion to dismiss must be denied.

Defendants argue that while the third count may plead all the elements of burglary, it should be dismissed nonetheless because the government's statements in the Bill of Particulars demonstrate that the government will not be able to prove the element of "entry" at trial. This argument is without merit. Statements made by the government in a Bill of Particulars are not deemed to modify the indictment. *See United States v. Fischbach & Moore, Inc.,* 750 F.2d 1183, 1189 (3d Cir. 1984), *cert. denied,* 470 U.S. 1029, 105 S. Ct. 1397, 84 L. Ed. 2d 785 (1985). So long as the indictment properly pleads an offense, it is not subject to challenge on the ground of lack of evidence. *See Costello v. United States,* 350 U.S. 359, 363-64, 76 S. Ct. 406, 408-09, 100 L. Ed. 397 (1956). Consequently, even if the defendants are correct that the statements in the Bill of Particulars show that the government will have insufficient evidence to prove the crime of burglary, the indictment is not subject to challenge on that ground.***

C. Government's Request for Ruling on Charge to Jury

In its Memorandum of Law in opposition to defendants' motions and again at oral argument, the government argued that while the motions should be denied, this Court nonetheless should reach the substantive issue raised therein. The government asks that we rule on how the jury would be charged with regard to the burglary count, on the ground that resolution of that question at this time is likely to advance the resolution of this case. We treat the government's request as being in the nature of a motion *in limine* and grant the request.

The underlying issue raised by defendants' motions is whether the defendants can be convicted of burglary under New York law if the government does not attempt to prove that they ever entered within the four walls or beneath the roof of the recruiting station. This court is convinced that they cannot.

Under New York law, a person must "enter or remain unlawfully in a building" in order to be guilty of burglary in the third degree. N.Y. Penal Law § 140.20. In defining unlawful entry the Penal Law focuses on the requirement of unlawfulness, defining it in terms of lack of license or privilege to be in a building. *See* N.Y. Penal Law § 140.00(5). However, the Penal Law does not define the breadth of the concept of entering *in* a building.

In the absence of statutory guidance, the parties place their reliance on a recent Court of Appeals decision, *People v. King,* 61 N.Y.2d 550, 463 N.E.2d 601, 475 N.Y.S.2d 260 (1984). In *King,* the defendant appealed his conviction for attempted burglary of a jewelry store. The store was on the ground floor and had a metal security gate covering the display windows and the vestibule area which led past the display windows and into the interior of the store. The defendant was apprehended after he cut a small hole in the part of the security gate directly in front of the vestibule area.

The defendant's first contention in *King* was that he should not have been convicted because it would have been impossible for him to enter the store in that the hole was not big enough for his body to pass through. The Court rejected this contention, holding that because the Penal Law does not define "enter" the term retains its common law meaning, which is that entry is accomplished when a person "intrudes within a building, no matter how slightly." Because the defendant could have put a part of his body through the hole, the entry requirement was satisfied.

The defendant's second contention was that the vestibule area was not part of the "building" within the meaning of the statute, such that his attempt to enter it was not attempted burglary. The Court also rejected this contention, holding that the "existence of the security gate, which can be pulled down to completely enclose the vestibule area from public access, albeit with a temporary fourth wall, makes the vestibule functionally indistinguishable from the space inside the display cases or the rest of the store." *Id.*

In this case, both parties focus on the part of the *King* opinion which discusses the vestibule area. The government reads that part as standing for the proposition that the element of entering is satisfied so long as the defendant goes into "an area of or related to a building to which the public has been or can be denied access." Government's Memorandum of Law at 7. The defendants interpret *King* to mean that in order to be guilty of burglary, the defendant must intrude into some enclosed space in or connected to a building.

In deciding which view of *King* is correct, the appropriate starting point is the common law of burglary since, according to the *King* Court, the element of entry still retains its common law meaning in New York. At common law, burglary was the breaking and entering of a dwelling house at night with the intent to commit a felony therein. The predominate impetus of common law burglary was "to protect the security of the home, and the person within his home." Note,

Statutory Burglary—The Magic of Four Walls and a Roof, 100 U. Pa. L. Rev. 401, 427 (1951). The offense was directed at preserving the internal security of the dwelling; consequently, an entry into the structure itself was an essential element of the crime. The intrusion of any part of the defendant's body, or of an object held in his hand, was sufficient to establish the element of entry. Yet there had to be some movement by the defendant across the external boundaries of the structure, some breaking of the planes created by the threshold and the four walls. *See* 3 *Wharton's Criminal Law* §§ 331-332 (C. Torcia 14th ed. 1980); 4 W. Blackstone, *Commentaries on the Laws of England* 227 (1988) (reprint of original edition). Activity conducted outside the external boundaries of a dwelling, no matter how felonious, was not burglary at common law.[22]

The scope of common law burglary was expanded somewhat through the concept of curtilage. Curtilage was defined as the area within close proximity to the dwelling house. *See* 3 *Wharton's Criminal Law, supra,* § 336. Outbuildings within the curtilage were deemed to be part of the dwelling house, such that an unlawful entry into the outbuilding was burglary. *See id.* In essence, then, the effect of the concept of curtilage was to expand the definition of dwelling house; however, it did not alter the entry requirement. Thus a defendant might be convicted of burglary for stealing from a homeowner's barn, but only if he actually entered within the four walls of the barn.

Because the common law required that a defendant penetrate the exterior walls of a structure in order to be guilty of burglary, such penetration is required for the commission of statutory burglary in New York. *See King,* 61 N.Y.2d at 555, 463 N.E.2d at 603, 475 N.Y.S.2d at 262 (entry requirement in burglary statute adopts common law definition). Thus in this case, the defendants may be convicted of burglary only if the government can prove that they actually entered within the four walls or beneath the roof of the recruiting station.

This conclusion comports with the Court of Appeal's decision in *King* and the case law of New York's lower courts. In *King,* the vestibule of the jewelry store was within the planes created by the four exterior walls of the building. *See id.* Thus the defendant was guilty of attempted burglary because he tried to gain entrance to the vestibule. In *People v. Bright,* 162 A.D.2d 212, 556 N.Y.S.2d 585, 586 (1990), the defendant's conviction for burglary was upheld where he was apprehended inside the vestibule area of a store, which was within the area encompassed by the four walls of the building. In *People v. Pringle,* 96 A.D.2d 873, 873-74, 465 N.Y.S.2d 742, 743 (App. Div. 1983), the defendant's conviction for burglary was upheld where he entered a separately secured nurse's station within a prison and committed an assault. The common thread in these cases is that in all three instances, the defendants actually entered into the interiors of enclosed and separately secured structures.

---

[22] Thus Lord Hale maintained that firing a gun into a house was not burglary unless some part of the weapon crossed the threshold.

In addition to its consonance with the case law of New York, the view of the entry requirement adopted by this Court comports with the restraints imposed by the rule of lenity. That rule, sometimes referred to as the principle of legality, is implicit in the concept of due process. As expressed by the Supreme Court, the rule of lenity requires that "before a man can be punished as a criminal under the federal law, his case must be 'plainly and unmistakably' within the provisions of some statute." *United States v. Gradwell,* 243 U.S. 476, 485, 37 S. Ct. 407, 410, 61 L. Ed. 857 (1917) (criminal statute must give person of ordinary intelligence fair notice of conduct forbidden by a statute). Courts should decline to interpret a criminal statute to encompass situations which a reasonable layperson could not foresee as being within the ambit of the statute. In this case, there is little doubt but that the defendants knew that their actions on the rooftop of the recruiting station violated the law. Trespass, destruction of government property, reckless endangerment and perhaps even attempted arson were foreseeable charges stemming from their conduct. That the defendants could reasonably have foreseen the charge of burglary is, however, a much more doubtful proposition.

In sum, this Court is of the view that the New York Penal Law requires that a defendant actually enter within the four walls or beneath the roof of a building in order to be guilty of burglary in the third degree. At trial, the jury will be instructed that they may not convict the defendants of the burglary charge unless they find that such an entry occurred. Of course, if the government presents no evidence of such entry then the count will be dismissed.

CONCLUSION

For the reasons given above, defendants' motion to dismiss the third count of the indictment and their motion to inspect the grand jury minutes are denied. The government's request for a ruling on the charge to be given to the jury is granted. At trial, the jury will be instructed in the manner discussed above.

SO ORDERED.

Notes and Questions

1. After reading *Goins v. State*, how much force do you think is necessary to fulfill the "breaking" element of burglary at common law?

2. Suppose in *Goins* that the defendant had gained access to the chicken house without using any type of force e.g., through an open window, would this still be burglary at common law? What if the defendant used fraud to gain access to the chicken house (e.g., he told the owner of the house that he was a government inspector who had come to inspect the chickens)? In the first example, the defendant would not meet the breaking requirement; however, in the second

example the defendant would meet the requirement. Why do you think the common law made this distinction?

3. *United States v. Eichman* has a very unique procedural posture. Why do you think the government requested a ruling on the jury charge? Based on the ruling would you go forward with the burglary charge if you were prosecuting this case?

4. The court in *Eichman* states that the common law expanded the reach of burglary. In what way did the common law expand burglary? Does this expansion comport with the original purpose behind creating the crime of burglary?

2. Felony Therein

In re L.D., 63 Ohio Misc. 2d 303 (Ohio Ct. Com. P. 1993)

[Previously Discussed in the chapter on Concurrence]

Notes and Questions

1. In this case, the court found that the minor formed the intent to steal after entry. As a prosecutor, how might you find otherwise?

2. The court is concerned with violent offenders and over-crowding in jails. Should this be a concern for the court or the legislature? Would the court have found differently in this case if the juvenile had assaulted someone after trespassing? Should it make a difference?

State v. Gardner, 118 Ohio St. 3d 420 (2008)

O'CONNOR, J.

Appellee, Reginald Gardner Jr., was indicted on one count of aggravated burglary in violation of R.C. 2911.11(A)(2), with a firearm specification; one count of felonious assault in violation of R.C. 2903.11(A)(2), with a firearm specification; and one count of burglary in violation of R.C. 2911.12(A)(2). At trial, the jury found him guilty of aggravated burglary with the firearm specification but acquitted him on the other offenses.

Gardner appealed, asserting that his due process rights were violated because the jury instructions did not specify that the jury needed to agree unanimously as to which criminal offense Gardner intended to commit during the course of the aggravated burglary. The court of appeals agreed and vacated his conviction. We now reverse.

RELEVANT BACKGROUND

On the evening of April 25, 2005, Ebony Lee prepared dinner in her home for her three children. Her boyfriend, James Pippins, was present at the time.

While the children were eating, Lee telephoned Gardner to purchase marijuana from him. A short time later, Gardner arrived at Lee's home accompanied by a friend, codefendant Turrell Justice.

Lee spoke with Gardner and Justice from her back porch. Gardner and Justice argued over whether Justice could have some of the marijuana that Gardner had brought for Lee.

The State's Case: Aggravated Burglary

From inside the house, Pippins heard the raised voices and, apparently believing that Gardner and Justice were arguing with Lee, confronted Gardner. But upon learning that he had misunderstood the situation, he calmed down, admitted his mistake, and went back inside. Gardner, however, was not pleased.

Despite Pippins's retreat, Gardner continued to yell at Pippins and repeatedly threatened to kill him. Lee no longer wanted to purchase the marijuana and opened the screen door to go back into her apartment. Gardner grabbed the door from Lee's hand, pushed her out of the way, and entered her home.

After entering Lee's home, Gardner assaulted Pippins. The men fought, and Pippins eventually "slammed" Gardner on the floor.

At that time, Justice, who had also entered Lee's apartment without her permission, attempted to assist Gardner. Lee grabbed Justice by the back of his shirt to prevent him from doing so, and Lee and Justice then "tussl[ed]." Justice stepped back, lifted his shirt, pulled a gun from his pants, and pointed it at Pippins's back.

Gardner repeatedly demanded that Justice give him the gun to kill Pippins. Justice refused, stating, "No, we got three kids in here. I got three kids, I know how it is. We going to catch [Pippins] in the 'hood. We going to kill him." Gardner and Justice then left Lee's apartment.

During the state's closing statements to the jury, it argued that this initial entry without permission constituted the aggravated-burglary offense. In its brief before this court, the state avers that the felonious-assault count of the indictment also arose from this initial portion of the incident. Our review of the record, however, establishes that the state's real theory at trial was that a subsequent portion of the incident, described below, served as the basis for the felonious-assault and burglary charges.

The State's Case: Felonious Assault and Burglary

Lee testified that after Gardner and Justice left her home, she called the police. She then arranged for her cousin to pick her up. The police responded and began to search the neighborhood for Gardner and Justice. As they did so, Lee gathered her children, and she and Pippins prepared to leave the premises and stay with relatives.

Before they could leave, however, Gardner and Justice allegedly returned to Lee's home with approximately eight people, whom Gardner referred to as his "killers." As Gardner approached Lee's back door, he reiterated his threats to kill Pippins. Pippins attempted to placate him, but to no avail. While the men argued, Lee gathered her children into her cousin's car.

Lee testified that as she and her family were driven to a nearby parking lot to safely await the police's arrival, she observed Gardner kick in her back door. Although she "assumed" that Gardner entered her apartment because she no longer saw him, her testimony was equivocal on that point.

Lee also testified that as Gardner kicked in the back door, the group of men that had accompanied him ran to the front of her apartment, apparently to trap Pippins. Before they got there, Pippins escaped through the front door, jumped a fence, and fled down the street.

Lee and other witnesses at trial testified that either Justice or Gardner, or both, were shooting at Pippins as he ran from the scene. That testimony was somewhat confused and, at times, contradictory.

The Defense

Justice and Gardner were tried together. Neither testified at trial. Defense counsel conceded that Justice and Gardner had gone to Lee's apartment to sell her marijuana and that there had been a disagreement there between Gardner and Pippins. They asserted their clients' innocence of the crimes charged, however, claiming that their clients had been falsely accused and that the state's case lacked factual and legal bases.

Justice's attorney argued that Justice had merely attempted to break up the fight between Gardner and Pippins and that Justice had no intent to commit a crime in Lee's home. He also stated that after the fight ended, Justice and Gardner left the scene. Defense counsel denied that Justice had had a gun and stressed repeatedly that there was no physical evidence of a firearm or of a shooting at the scene.

Gardner's counsel's theme was similar to Justice's. He suggested that as Lee spoke to Gardner about the marijuana, Pippins went into "a jealous fit of rage" and began yelling at Gardner, a reaction that angered Gardner and led to the men fighting on Lee's back porch. Counsel asserted that as Gardner and Pippins fought, they "[got] up against the [back] door," the door opened, and the men "fell" into Lee's apartment.

Gardner's counsel conceded that Pippins was victorious in the fight. He argued that Gardner had chased Pippins out of the house, but that Gardner had done so only because he wanted to even the score. Counsel claimed that Gardner abandoned the chase and went home, never returning to Lee's apartment.***

The Jury's Instructions, the Verdicts, and the Appeal

The jury instruction on aggravated burglary, which tracked the indictment and the language of R.C. 2911.11(A)(2), stated:

> In Count Three of the indictment, Mr. Reginald Gardner is charged with aggravated burglary. Before you can find Mr. Gardner guilty of this offense, you must find beyond a reasonable doubt that on or about April 25, 2005, in Montgomery County, Ohio, he did, by force, stealth or deception, trespass in an occupied structure, to-wit [Lee's apartment], or in a separately secured or separately occupied portion of the occupied structure, when another person, other than an accomplice of the offender, was present, with the purpose to commit in the structure or in the separately secured or separately occupied portion of the structure any criminal offense, and did have a deadly weapon or dangerous ordnance, to-wit, a handgun, on or about his person or under his control.***

***[T]he judge did not give a more specific unanimity instruction, and he did not instruct the jury that it needed to agree as to which offense Gardner had intended to commit in the home. Nor did the judge instruct the jury on any specific crime that Gardner allegedly committed that would satisfy the "any criminal offense" prong of the statute.

After deliberating for a day, the jury returned its verdicts. It acquitted both Justice and Gardner of felonious assault and Gardner of burglary. However, it found both men guilty of aggravated burglary and the related firearm specification.

Gardner appealed, raising several propositions. The court of appeals rejected most of his claims, including his argument that the convictions were supported by insufficient evidence and were against the manifest weight of the evidence. *State v. Gardner*, Montgomery App. No. 21357, 2007-Ohio-182, ¶ 9-20. It agreed, however, with Gardner's assertion that "by failing to specify the underlying criminal offense he had a purpose to commit, the court's instruction permitted the jurors to return a verdict of guilty on a finding that he had a purpose to commit some criminal offense, but without necessarily arriving at a unanimous agreement about what that offense was, depriving [Gardner] of his due process right to a unanimous verdict required by Crim. R. 31(A)." Id. at ¶ 54.

The court of appeals acknowledged that Gardner did not object to the instruction, but found plain error and reversed the conviction. Id. at ¶ 54-55, 67.***

Ohio's Aggravated-Burglary Statute

***The General Assembly, like most state legislatures, has broadened the scope of many crimes, including aggravated burglary, well beyond their elements at common law. See Legislative Service Commission Notes to R.C. 2911.11; *State v. Barker* (Sept. 27, 2001), Licking App. No. 01-CA-0027, 2001 WL 1169561 (describing the expansion of Ohio's aggravated-burglary statute and the legislative intent "to broaden the common law concept of the offense of burglary from one of an offense against security of habitation, to one concerned with the risk of harm created by the actual or likely presence of a person in a structure of any nature"); *Taylor v. United States* (1990), 495 U.S. 575, 593, 110 S. Ct. 2143, 109 L. Ed. 2d 607 (noting that "the contemporary understanding of 'burglary' has diverged a long way from its common-law roots" and that most states have expanded the offense). As our courts of appeals have found, it is obvious that the General Assembly's intent in doing so was to broaden the concept of burglary from an offense against the security of the home to one against the security of persons who may be inside. *State v. Bennie* (Mar. 17, 1993).

In order to convict Gardner under R.C. 2911.11(A)(2), the state was required to establish that (1) he trespassed in Lee's home by use of force, stealth, or deception, (2) while someone other than Justice was present, (3) with the purpose to commit "any criminal offense" inside, (4) while carrying a deadly weapon or dangerous ordnance. Our analysis in this case focuses on the third prong, the "any criminal offense" element.

Our cases make clear that the state was required to show that Gardner invaded the dwelling for the purpose of committing a crime or that he formed that intent during the trespass. *State v. Fontes* (2000), 87 Ohio St. 3d 527, 721 N.E.2d 1037, syllabus (to be guilty of aggravated burglary, "a defendant may form the purpose to commit a criminal offense at any point during the course of a trespass"). In broadening the scope of the crime, the legislature has expanded the mens rea element from an intent to commit a felony to an intent to commit "any criminal offense," which is the mental state required in the current version of R.C. 2911.11. Given the General Assembly's use of the term "any" in the phrase "any criminal offense," we presume that it intended to encompass "every" and "all" criminal offenses recognized by Ohio. See, e.g., *Cales v. Armstrong World Industries, Inc.*, Scioto App. No. 02CA2851, 2003-Ohio-1776, ¶17, fn. 8 (citing cases defining "any" as meaning "every" and "all"); *Motor Cargo, Inc. v. Richfield Twp. Bd. of Twp. Trustees* (C.P. 1953).***

In doing so, we hold that Ohio's burglary statutes proscribe a single crime that may be carried out in more than one manner or method. As the court explained in *State v. Hammer* (1997), 216 Wis.2d 220, 576 N.W.2d 285,

> [t]he language of the [burglary] statute indicates that the
> crime here is one single offense with multiple modes of
> commission. The pertinent language states that burglary is
> committed when an actor unlawfully enters a dwelling with an
> "intent to *** commit a felony." The statute does not set forth
> any alternatives with respect to the intent element. The language
> indicates that the emphasis is on the fact that the defendant had
> the intent to commit a felony and it does not matter which felony
> formed the basis of that intent. There are different means of
> accomplishing this crime, but the different ways do not create
> separate and distinct offenses."

In adopting that reasoning, we believe that the nature of the burglary offense is particularly suitable to the *Schad* analysis and contrary to the limited *Richardson* rule.***

Conversely, the *Schad* rule applies when the jury's focus is on a defendant's acts that *are* morally equivalent. Thus, a defendant charged with murder is not deprived of any right to jury unanimity if some jurors believe that he committed the murder with premeditation while others believe that he committed it as part of the commission of a felony, because those actions may legitimately be characterized as morally equivalent. "Whether or not everyone would agree that the mental state that precipitates death in the course of robbery is the moral equivalent of premeditation, it is clear that such equivalence could reasonably be found, which is enough to rule out the argument that this moral disparity bars treating them as alternative means to satisfy the mental element of a single offense." *Schad,* 501 U.S. at 644, 111 S. Ct. 2491, 115 L. Ed. 2d 555. Similarly, we do not require all jurors to agree whether a defendant raped a victim orally, vaginally, or anally, because all three constitute "sexual conduct" in violation of the rape statute. In such cases, there is no violation of the jury unanimity rule as long as all of the jurors agree that there was sufficient penetration to satisfy the "sexual conduct" element of the crime of rape. *Thompson*, 33 Ohio St. 3d at 11, 514 N.E.2d 407. It is no great leap to extend this rationale to the crime of burglary. To the contrary, that evolution began in other states more than 40 years ago. See, e.g., *Failla*, 64 Cal.2d at 567, 51 Cal. Rptr. 103, 414 P.2d 39 (noting that the question of whether jurors must agree to the underlying felony in a burglary case "appears to be one of first impression in a burglary context, but we are not without guidance," citing cases rejecting a unanimity requirement as to the state's theory in a murder or theft case).

In enacting and amending our burglary statutes over the past 35 years, the General Assembly has removed distinctions between daytime and nighttime break-ins, the type of property entered, and the motive for entering. See 1974

Committee Comment to R.C. 2911.11. The legislative focus in enacting the burglary statute was not on the underlying offense, but rather, on "the reduction or elimination of the high risk of harm to persons that exists when one forcibly enters an occupied structure." *State v. Ramirez*, Clermont App. No. CA2004-06-046, 2005-Ohio-2662.

In the context of burglary, the legislature has erased the moral distinctions between the underlying crimes that the defendant intended to commit after he gained access, requiring only that the crime be a felony. There is nothing unusual about that legislative prerogative, and nothing about it that is constitutionally offensive.

Ohio's definition of burglary is similar to Arizona's definition of first-degree murder in that both use alternative bases for the intent element, both are widely used, and both have a long history. See *People v. Griffin,* 90 Cal.App.4th at 752, 109 Cal. Rptr. 2d 273. "According to Justice Scalia's concurrence in *Schad*, this factor alone would be sufficient to conclude that due process is not offended ***." *Id*. at fn. 8. "It is clear from the statute that the legislature focused on the intent to commit a felony, not any particular felony. Therefore, all the felonies are conceptually similar for the purposes of unanimity because each and every felony provides the predicate intent element. There is no difference in penalty irrespective of which underlying felony or combination of felonies was intended. Rather, it is [the defendant's] single entry into the dwelling with the requisite intent that constitutes the crime." *Hammer,* 216 Wis. 2d at 222, 576 N.W.2d 285.

Thus, a defendant charged with burglary is not deprived of a unanimous verdict "simply because the jury was not required to agree unanimously as to the nature of the crime the defendant intended to commit at the time he entered unlawfully into the victim's building. 'In situations where "the alternatives of the mens rea [intent] component give rise to the same criminal culpability, it does not appear critical that the jury may have reached different conclusions regarding the nature of the defendant's intent if such differences do not reflect disagreement on the facts pertaining to the defendant's conduct." *State v. Suggs,* 209 Conn. 733, 763 (1989). Here, the precise nature of the defendant's intent does not implicate any lack of unanimity regarding the defendant's conduct.' *State v. Marsala*, 43 Conn. App. 527, 539.

We proceed with these considerations in mind.

In determining whether jury instructions that allow the jury to disagree on the underlying crime in an aggravated-burglary case violate due process, a court must be guided by the evidence in the case before it and by general principles of fundamental fairness. See generally *In re C.S.,* 115 Ohio St. 3d 267.

As previously indicated, R.C. 2911.11(A) requires proof that the defendant trespassed "with purpose to commit *** any criminal offense." Contrary to the view taken by the court of appeals in this case, we do not discern in this language a statutory requirement that the jury be instructed on the elements of whatever offense the defendant intended to commit. We agree with the Supreme Court of Washington, whose burglary statute is similar to Ohio's, that "the specific crime or crimes intended to be committed inside burglarized premises is *not* an element of burglary that must be included in the *** jury instructions ***." (Emphasis sic.) *State v. Bergeron*, 105 Wash. 2d at 16.

We do agree, however, that the state must prove the defendant's intent to commit a crime—"any criminal offense"—beyond a reasonable doubt. The breadth of the phrase "any criminal offense" is such that in some cases, it may invite a fatally "patchwork" verdict based on conceptually distinct groupings of crimes or on multiple acts. We believe that in such cases, due process requires that the jurors must be instructed as to the specific criminal act(s) that the defendant intended to commit inside the premises. See *Johnson*, 46 Ohio St. 3d at 105 ("where there appears a possibility of jury confusion in light of the allegations made and the statute charged, an augmented general instruction may be necessary to ensure that the jury understands its duty to unanimously agree *to a particular set of facts*" [emphasis added]). We believe that in such cases, the usual general instruction on unanimity "would provide too little protection in too many instances." *United States v. Beros* (C.A.3, 1987), 833 F.2d 455, 461. A specific charge instructing the jury that it must be unanimous as to each component of the criminal offense the defendant had "purpose to commit" once inside the premises will help ensure against improper juror divergence.

We think that it is preferable for the trial judge to instruct the jury in all aggravated-burglary cases as to which criminal offense the defendant is alleged to have intended to commit once inside the premises and the elements of that offense. Such instructions provide an important road map for the jury in its deliberations and help ensure that jurors focus on specific conduct that constitutes a criminal offense.

Nevertheless, we do not require this instruction in every case. Prudence may strongly suggest such a precaution, but we are not persuaded that it is appropriate in all circumstances. Trial judges are in the best position to determine the content of the instructions based on the evidence at trial and on whether the case presents an alternative-means or multiple-acts scenario.

In so holding, we reject the dissent's call to afford a defendant greater protection under the Ohio Constitution than he enjoys under the federal Constitution.***

There is no suggestion of jury confusion in this case. The jury did not question the meaning of the "any criminal offense" element, and the state did not present evidence of an array of crimes that Gardner may have intended to commit in Lee's home. Indeed, the evidence here supported only crimes within a single conceptual grouping—assault, felonious assault, or menacing.

If, as the state argues in this court, the underlying crime was felonious assault against Pippins in Lee's home, we are not persuaded that the outcome of the trial would have been different if the instructions had specified that offense and its elements. After all, the jury was well aware of those elements from other portions of the instructions, and its acquittal of Gardner and Justice indicates that it considered those elements carefully.

The acquittal, however, does not suggest that Gardner's aggravated-burglary conviction cannot stand. To the contrary, the Supreme Court has made clear that a verdict that convicts a defendant of one crime and acquits him of another, when the first crime requires proof of the second, may not be disturbed merely because the two findings are irreconcilable. "'Consistency in the verdict is not necessary. Each count in an indictment is regarded as if it was a separate indictment.'" *United States v. Powell* (1984), 469 U.S. 57. "[I]nconsistent verdicts – even verdicts that acquit on a predicate offense while convicting on the compound offense – should not necessarily be interpreted as a windfall for the Government at the defendant's expense." *Powell*, 469 U.S. at 65. As *Powell* notes, "[i]t is equally possible that the jury, convinced of guilt, properly reached its conclusion on the compound offense, and then through mistake, compromise, or lenity, arrived at an inconsistent conclusion on the lesser offense." *Id.*

Gardner's acquittal on the felonious-assault charge is not dispositive, because there is no requirement in Ohio law that the criminal offense underlying an aggravated-burglary charge be completed in order for the latter charge to stand. R.C. 2911.11(A) (an accused need only have a "purpose to commit" a criminal offense); *State v. Castell* (Aug. 20, 1992), Cuyahoga App. No. 61352, 1992 WL 205130.

Nor are we persuaded that a manifest injustice occurred when we view the case in the manner in which the case was initially presented to the jury, i.e., that the felonious-assault charge arose from the allegation that Gardner, Justice, or both shot at Pippins upon their return to Lee's home.

Although the jury was not given a specific crime to consider in determining Gardner's intent in entering Lee's home, a reasonable jury could conclude that Gardner's attack on Pippins or his threat to kill him was a "criminal offense" of some form, even without the benefit of the elements of assault, R.C. 2903.13, or menacing, R.C. 2903.22. Indeed, Ohio courts have recognized that one who forcibly enters a dwelling in the manner depicted in this case may reasonably be assumed to do so with the intent to commit a criminal act within. See, e.g., *State v. Robinson*, Cuyahoga App. No. 82261, 2003-Ohio-4666, ¶ 24. Consistent with the court of appeals in this case, we find that Gardner's conviction in this case is not against the manifest weight of the evidence and that there is sufficient evidence to sustain it. Accordingly, we find no manifest injustice.

Given the evidence and the inference arising from it that Gardner entered Lee's home to commit an assault on Pippins, the absence of any apparent jury confusion about the "any criminal offense" element, and that the state did not present a multiple-acts case or suggest that the "any criminal offense" element was satisfied by crimes of distinct conceptual groupings, we find no risk of manifest injustice here. Accordingly, we reverse the court of appeals' decision and remand the cause to the court of appeals to consider the claims of error it did not address in its opinion.

Judgment reversed and cause remanded.

LANZINGER, J., dissenting.

The lengthy opinion of the majority essentially concludes that the phrase "with the purpose to commit *** any criminal offense" in R.C. 2911.11(A) does not constitute an essential element of aggravated burglary. I dissent and would hold that this phrase defines the mens rea that the state must prove beyond a reasonable doubt, and therefore, I would require as a matter of due process that the jury be instructed on the elements of the particular crime that a defendant intended to commit "in the structure or in the separately secured or separately occupied portion of the structure" before it may convict for the offense of aggravated burglary.***

The holding in this case should be simple—that the trial judge must instruct a jury in an aggravated burglary case on the elements of the criminal offense that the defendant is alleged to have had the purpose to commit once inside the premises. But instead of mandating that judges follow the current Ohio Jury Instructions in aggravated burglary cases by identifying and informing the jury that the underlying intended offense is an element of the crime, the majority holds that a trial judge must analyze whether the case involves "alternative means" or "multiple acts," whether the indictment is divided into two or more "distinct conceptual groupings," and whether the jury's focus is on a defendant's acts that are "morally equivalent." Then the trial court may decide if a more specific instruction is "preferable." The majority's rule is confusing, at the very least.***

The Ohio Jury Instructions, while not binding legal authority, are helpful as an example of the generally accepted interpretation of the aggravated burglary statute in Ohio. The instructions inform jurors that they must agree that a defendant had the "purpose to commit the offense of" and then requires the judge to "insert [the] name of [the] criminal offense." 4 Ohio Jury Instructions (2000), Section 511.11. Comment 3 to Section 511.11 states, "The court must instruct the jury on the elements of the underlying criminal offense, together with the meaning of particular words and phrases." *Id*. By requiring the jury to specifically agree on the intended offense, the instructions treat the underlying intended crime as an element of aggravated burglary. I would hold that the standard Ohio Jury Instructions are correct in treating the underlying intended crime in such a manner.

A jury cannot be asked to decide if there is proof beyond a reasonable doubt that a defendant had the purpose to commit a criminal offense unless the jurors have been instructed on the definition of the particular offense intended. The fact that the statute does not specify a particular offense does not relieve the state of its burden to prove that an offense was intended. In closing statements to the jury, the state argued merely that Gardner's initial entry into Lee's home without permission constituted the aggravated burglary offense; however, these facts are insufficient to show Gardner's intent to commit any crime there.

The trial court's instruction tracked the language of R.C. 2911.11(A)(2), but failed to identify or legally define the crime that Gardner had the purpose to commit. The majority states, "Although the jury was not given a specific crime to consider in determining Gardner's intent in entering Lee's home, a reasonable jury could conclude that Gardner's attack on Pippins or his threat to kill him was a 'criminal offense' *of some form*, even without the benefit of the elements of assault, R.C. 2903.13, or menacing, R.C. 2903.22." (Emphasis added.) In fact, the majority also states that the term "any crime" encompasses "every" and "all" criminal offenses recognized by Ohio.

If, as the state insists in this case, Gardner intended to commit felonious assault on Pippins when he trespassed into Lee's home, the prosecution did not prove the mens rea element beyond a reasonable doubt unless the jury unanimously found that Gardner had trespassed "with purpose" to commit felonious assault. When the judge has failed to identify or instruct on the elements of the underlying crime intended, the jury's finding of proof beyond a reasonable doubt of the required mens rea element is called into question. When the jury has acquitted on the separate charge of felonious assault, the questions are even more serious.

The majority thus permits a conviction for aggravated burglary even if no two jurors agree on the underlying crime that a defendant intended to commit. I would hold that because "with purpose to commit *** any criminal offense" is an element of aggravated burglary, the majority's interpretation strips defendant of his right to have proof beyond a reasonable doubt on every element of the offense charged. As Justice White noted in his dissent in *Schad*, "it violates due process for a State to invoke more than one statutory alternative, each with different specified elements, without requiring that the jury indicate on which of the alternatives it has based the defendant's guilt." 501 U.S. at 656. The majority goes even further by allowing the jury to speculate, without any instruction, on what criminal offense the defendant may have had the purpose to commit.***

Of all the crimes with which he was charged, Gardner was convicted only of aggravated burglary. Although he was also charged with felonious assault, the jury ultimately found him not guilty of that offense. This acquittal raises additional questions over whether the jurors were unanimous in deciding exactly which crime Gardner intended to commit and whether the state carried its burden of proving the mens rea element of the crime of aggravated burglary beyond a reasonable doubt.

The majority correctly notes that inconsistencies in a verdict do not necessarily require that a conviction be vacated. Here, however, the jury was never fully instructed on all elements of the offense of aggravated burglary. There was no unanimous jury interrogatory answered that Gardner had a purpose to commit a specific crime. Because the incomplete jury instructions resulted in a jury verdict that raises the question of whether aggravated burglary was proved beyond a reasonable doubt, Gardner's substantial rights were affected, resulting in a manifest injustice. I conclude that plain error does exist.

CONCLUSION

Because I would hold that the particular offense that was intended to be committed in the occupied structure is part of the mens rea element of aggravated burglary, and because the jury was not instructed on the particular offense that was intended to be committed, plain error occurred. I would affirm the decision of the court of appeals.

Notes and Questions

1. Who has the stronger argument in *State v. Gardner*, the majority or the dissent? At what point during the altercation in *Gardner* did the defendant "form the purpose to commit a criminal offense" in the home of Ebony Lee.

2. In *Gardner*, the court discusses how Ohio has modified the common law definition of burglary. What were some of those modifications? What was the rationale proffered by the court for these changes?

3. To convict the defendant of aggravated burglary in *Gardner*, the jurors had to find that he had the purpose to commit a criminal offense inside the premises. If the defendant was acquitted on felonious assault, what crime was he going to commit in the apartment?

B. Arson

John Poulos, *The Metamorphosis of the Law of Arson*, 51 Mo. L. Rev. 295 (1986)

Arson, at common law, was the malicious burning of the dwelling house of another. Like most of the other common law felonies, it was punishable by death. Anciently, the convicted incendiary was burned to death, but before Lord Hale wrote, the method of execution had been changed to death by hanging.

The primary purpose of common law arson was to preserve the security of the habitation, to protect the dwellers within the building from injury or death by fire, although it functioned to protect the possessory interest in the house as well. Of the common law felonies, it was considered to be one of the worst. Sir William Blackstone explains why this was so:

> This is an offense of very great malignity, and much more pernicious to the public than simple theft: because, first, it is an offense against that right, of habitation, which is acquired by the law of nature as well as by the laws of society: next, because of the terror and confusion that necessarily attends it; and, lastly, because in simple theft the thing stolen only changes it's master, but still remains *in esse* for the benefit of the public, whereas by burning the very substance is absolutely destroyed. It is also frequently more destructive than murder itself, of which too it is often the cause: Since murder, atrocious as it is, seldom extends beyond the felonious act designed; whereas fire too frequently involves in the common calamity persons unknown to the incendiary, and not intended to be hurt by him, and friends as well as enemies.

*** Since the primary purpose of the law of arson was to protect the physical safety of the inhabitants of the dwelling house, the "of another" requirement meant that the dwelling house had to be in the possession of someone other than the incendiary. Accordingly, an owner could be guilty of common law arson by burning a dwelling house in the possession of someone else, as where a landlord burned a house occupied by tenant, or where an owner burned a dwelling in the possession of any other person. And, of course, the burning of a dwelling house by the person in actual possession of the premises was not common law arson. For the same reason, it was not arson for one occupant to burn a dwelling house which was shared with another when both possessed the entire building. For example, if a wife burned the dwelling house in which she, her husband and her family resided, it was not arson at common law. ***

What then was meant by "burning"? The common law required the *actual combustion* of a portion of the material of which the dwelling house was composed. Or to put it another way, there had to be an ignition of the material by the application of an external heat source. In the parlance of the street, some part of the material had to be destroyed or consumed by fire. And in the language of the law, many courts said that a "charring" of the material was necessary. "Combustion," "ignition," "destroyed or consumed by fire," and "charring" were all synonymously used to describe the common law "burning" requirement. On the other hand, damage from heat insufficient to cause combustion or ignition (or the synonymous terms) was not a "burning." Thus, if the material were only discolored by heat, singed, scorched, or damaged by smoke, there was no arson.

But once the material began to burn, once it was ignited, there was no requirement that it burn for any substantial period of time. Liability attached the instant the burning began, and it made no difference whether the fire was immediately extinguished or went out by itself. Nor was it necessary for the material ever to be ablaze; the only requirement was that it burn—smoldering would do.

Finally, the manner by which the arsonist caused the dwelling to burn was equally of no importance as long as all of the elements of the crime were met. Any method of applying heat to the dwelling which caused it to burn, regardless of how unique or exotic it was, sufficed for arson. Even an explosive would suffice, so long as the house burned rather than first being torn apart by the blast. And it made no difference whether the burning was caused by directly applying the source of heat to the dwelling, or by more indirect methods. For example, although it was not arson to burn one's own dwelling house (or any other building not within the curtilage of the dwelling house of another except, of course, one's own apartment in an apartment house), if one did so under circumstances which created an extremely high risk of burning another dwelling house (or another building within its curtilage) and the adjoining building was burned, it was arson of the adjoining building, provided the act was done with the necessary *mens rea*.***

Although the *mens rea* of arson is generally described as "maliciously," accompanied by either "willfully" or "voluntarily," the latter words add nothing to the concept of "malice." Hence it is entirely accurate to define arson at common law as the *malicious* burning of the dwelling house of another. Of course, since either intentional burnings or wanton burnings may be subject to legal justification or excuse, the *mens rea* of arson at common law would exclude all forms of justification or excuse in the definition of the malicious state of mind. To summarize, the *mens rea* of arson, "malice," is composed of two distinct mental states: (1) intentional burning without justification or excuse; and (2) wanton burning without justification or excuse. Later we will see how the common law notion of malice for the law of arson has changed in some jurisdictions to accommodate statutory changes in the law of arson.

Notes and Questions

1. Re-read *State v. Boggs* from Chapter 1. Which opinion adhered to the common law, the majority or the dissent?

2. In what way has Ohio modified the common law definition of arson?

C. Vandalism

State v. Sullivan, 2010-Ohio-5357 (Ohio Ct. App. 2010)

PATRICIA ANN BLACKMON, P.J.

Appellant Vincent Sullivan appeals his conviction for vandalism and assigns the following two errors for our review:

> "I. The defendant's conviction of vandalism was not supported by sufficient evidence, in violation of defendant's right to due process of law under Article I, Section 14 of the Ohio Constitution, and the 14th Amendment to the United States Constitution."
>
> "II. The defendant was denied effective assistance of counsel, in violation of defendant's right to counsel under Article I, Section 10 of the Ohio Constitution, and the 6th and 14th Amendments to the United States Constitution."

Having reviewed the record and relevant law, we reverse and vacate Sullivan's conviction. The apposite facts follow.

The Cuyahoga County Grand Jury indicted Sullivan for one count of felonious assault under R.C. 2923.11(A)(2), causing or attempting to cause physical harm with a deadly weapon, and one count of vandalism under R.C. 2909.05(B)(1)(b), causing harm to property that was "necessary in order for its owner or possessor to engage in the owner's or possessor's profession, business, trade, or occupation." The counts were unrelated as they occurred on different days and involved different facts; however, both offenses were tried jointly. Because Sullivan is not appealing his assault conviction, we will only relate the facts that are relevant to his vandalism charge.

FACTS

During the early morning hours of June 8, 2009, a window at the Goodrich and Gannett Neighborhood Center was broken. The center is located at 1400 East 55th Street in Cleveland and operates a licensed childcare center and also provides programs for senior citizens.

Officer Crites responded to the scene at 2:00 a.m., after receiving a report that someone was attempting to break into the center. When he arrived at the scene, he observed Sullivan standing in the parking lot about ten feet away from a broken window. No one else was present. Sullivan had a canvas bag containing a hammer, a chisel, and gloves. The officer placed Sullivan under arrest and transported him to the police station. At the station, officers found shards of glass in the cuff of Sullivan's pants.

4:00 a.m., Lee DeAngelis, the operations director of the center, received a call from the center's alarm company, informing him that there had been an attempted break-in at the center. When DeAngelis arrived at the scene around 4:45 a.m., he observed the damaged window. The size of the window was approximately 3' by 3' and faced the parking lot. DeAngelis stayed at the scene for security reasons until staff arrived. He later called a company to replace the glass. The window was not repaired until two weeks later because the glass had to be ordered. However, in the meantime, the glass replacement company installed a wood covering where the window had been. The total cost of the repairs was approximately $571.

The jury found Sullivan guilty of vandalism. The trial court sentenced him to nine months in prison.***

R.C. 2909.05(B)(1)(b) provides:

> "(1) No person shall knowingly cause physical harm to property that is owned or possessed by another, when either of the following applies:
> "(a) ***
> "(b) Regardless of the value of the property or the amount of damage done, the property or its equivalent is necessary in order for its owner or possessor to engage in the owner's or possessor's profession, business, trade, or occupation."

In the instant case, there was no evidence presented that the window was necessary for the center to conduct business. In fact, the evidence showed that the broken window had no effect on the center's ability to conduct business. A board was installed over the window to secure it until the glass was replaced two weeks later. There was no evidence that the center had to remain closed during this two week period.

The Committee Comment to R.C. 2909.05(B)(1)(b) gave examples of the type of vandalism that would impede the ability to conduct business as follows:

> "Examples of this type of violation include rifling and scattering current case files of an attorney, damaging samples of a traveling salesman, or destroying a plumber's tools. When the property is merely used in its owner's or possessor's occupation, as opposed to its being necessary to carry on his occupation, then the value of the property or the amount of damage done must be $150 or more [the current requirement is $500 or more] for there to be a violation of this part of the section."

Here, the evidence did not indicate the window was "necessary" for the center to operate. While securing the premises was a concern, once the wooden board was installed, security was no longer an issue.[23]

The state did present evidence to prove vandalism under R.C. 2909.05(B)(1)(a), which only requires showing damages in excess of $500. Evidence presented showed that the repair of the window cost over $500. However, the fact that sufficient evidence was presented under (B)(1)(a) does not support Sullivan's conviction under (B)(1)(b) because Sullivan was not indicted under (B)(1)(a) nor was the jury instructed regarding this section.

This court in *State v. Hart,* Cuyahoga App. No. 79564, 2002-Ohio-1984 and *State v. Hamley* (2001), 142 Ohio App. 3d 615, 756 N.E.2d 702, had the converse situation. That is, sufficient evidence was presented to support a conviction that the damaged property was "necessary" to conduct business, but the evidence was not sufficient to support a conviction that the damage was in excess of $500. In those cases, we concluded that because the indictment specifically recited the section of the vandalism statute that applied, and because the state did not seek to amend the indictment to refer to the other section, the defendant could not be convicted of the section not set forth in the indictment. Additionally, the trial court only instructed the jury on the section contained in the indictment.

We have the identical situation here. Sullivan's indictment recited verbatim section (B)(1)(b), and the state did not attempt to amend the indictment. The trial court also only instructed the jury regarding section (B)(1)(b). Accordingly, because the state failed to present evidence on an essential element of the vandalism offense, insufficient evidence existed to support the vandalism conviction. Sullivan's sole assigned error is well-taken. Sullivan's vandalism conviction is reversed and vacated. Although Sullivan requests to be discharged he has already served his sentence.

Due to our disposition of the first assigned error, the second assigned error is moot and need not be addressed. App. R. 12(A)(1)(c).

Judgment is reversed and vacated.

It is ordered that appellant recover of appellee his costs herein taxed.

The court finds there were reasonable grounds for this appeal.

FRANK D. CELEBREZZE, JR., J., concurs.

---

[23] The state cites to this court's decision in *State v. Stewart,* Cuyahoga App. No. 81157, 2002-Ohio-6855, in which the defendant who damaged a door to a bar was convicted pursuant to R.C. 2909.05(B)(1)(b). However, in that case, we did not discuss the element of whether the property damaged was necessary to conduct business. Instead, we focused on whether "serious physical harm" was proven, requiring an instruction thereon.

ANN DYKE, J., Dissenting.

I respectfully dissent. I would conclude that there is sufficient evidence to support the vandalism conviction. I would find that a rational jury could conclude that the window was "necessary in order for its owner or possessor to engage in the owner's or possessor's profession, business, trade or occupation," under R.C. 2909.05(B)(1)(b), as the child care center and senior center require safe and secure premises. I also would apply this court's decision in *State v. Stewart,* Cuyahoga App. No. 81157, 2002-Ohio-6855. In *Stewart,* this court considered the sufficiency of the evidence of defendant's conviction for vandalism where he shot a door to a bar and determined that the state established that defendant knowingly caused physical harm to property that is necessary in order for its owner or possessor to engage in the owner's or possessor's profession, business, trade, or occupation.

PART V
Inchoate Crimes and Accomplice Liability

Chapter 16
Attempt

A. Background

Some define an "inchoate crime" as an "incomplete crime," but the more precise definition is "anticipatory crime." Inchoate crimes consist of attempt, solicitation, and conspiracy, all of which will be examined in depth. With these three crimes, society is seeking to punish the defendant before actual harm occurs. With inchoate crimes, society is able to go after those who are intent on committing crimes, but have not yet done so.

At common law, attempt was a specific intent crime. Today, most jurisdictions view attempt crimes as a lesser offense of the completed or underlying crime, which is generally punished more severely. If the defendant actually completes the crime, the attempt charge merges with the underlying crime. The critical question with attempt is: how far must the defendant progress in order to satisfy the elements of attempt? Society does not want to punish defendants for merely having bad thoughts. Yet, neither does society want the defendant to go free when criminal intent to commit the crime is present.

In order to determine when the defendant has gone beyond mere preparation, courts and the MPC have established various tests. Some jurisdictions follow the dangerous proximity test. This forward-looking test examines what steps are necessary to actually complete the crime. In contrast, is the substantial step test that has been adopted by Ohio and the MPC. Here, the court looks backwards to determine if the defendant has taken a substantial step towards completion of the crime. Other tests employed by various jurisdictions include abnormal step, probability desistance, unequivocality, physical proximity, and indispensable element.

Defenses to attempt include abandonment, which has been adopted by both Ohio and the MPC. For withdrawal to be an effective defense, the defendant must manifest a complete and voluntary renunciation of his criminal purpose. At common law, withdrawal was not a recognized defense.

Other defenses, such as factual and legal impossibility, have proven less successful to charges of attempt. Factual impossibility (e.g., pickpocket reaches into an empty pocket) has never been a defense to attempt. Pure legal impossibility (i.e., the law does not prohibit defendant's conduct) has been a valid defense to attempt. Hybrid legal impossibility (i.e., defendant's conduct is illegal but commission of the offense was impossible because of some fact unknown to him), which can also be viewed as a factual impossibility, has been a defense at common law and in a limited number of jurisdictions.

Today, most jurisdictions, including Ohio, do not recognize the hybrid legal impossibility defense. Following in the footsteps of the MPC, most jurisdictions will find the defendant guilty of attempt if he purposely engages in conduct that would constitute a crime if the attendant circumstances were as he believed them to be. An attendant circumstance is a fact or condition that must be present at the time the defendant engages in the prohibited conduct and or causes the prohibited result that constitutes the social harm of the offense.

The first two cases in this chapter, *State v. Group* and *Unites States v. Mandujano*, examine whether actions by the defendant are sufficient to find that he has made a substantial step towards completion of the crime. *State v. Brown* looks at whether legal impossibility is still a defense in Ohio. The final case, *State v. Arnold*, explores abandonment.

B. Substantial Step

United States v. Mandujano, 499 F.2d 370 (1974)

Mandujano appeals from the judgment of conviction and fifteen-year sentence imposed by the district court, based upon the jury's verdict finding him guilty of attempted distribution of heroin in violation of 21 U.S.C. 846. We affirm.

The government's case rested almost entirely upon the testimony of Alfonso H. Cavalier, Jr., a San Antonio police officer assigned to the Office of Drug Abuse Law Enforcement. Agent Cavalier testified that, at the time the case arose, he was working in an undercover capacity and represented himself as a narcotics trafficker. At about 1:30 p.m. on the afternoon of March 29, 1973, pursuant to information Cavalier had received, he and a government informer went to the Tally-Ho Lounge, a bar located on Guadalupe Street in San Antonio. Once inside the bar, the informant introduced Cavalier to Roy Mandujano. After some general conversation, Mandujano asked the informant if he was looking for "stuff." Cavalier said, "Yes." Mandujano then questioned Cavalier about his involvement in narcotics. Cavalier answered Mandujano's questions, and told Mandujano he was looking for an ounce sample of heroin to determine the quality of the material. Mandujano replied that he had good brown Mexican heroin for $650.00 an ounce, but that if Cavalier wanted any of it he would have to wait until later in the afternoon when the regular man made his deliveries. Cavalier said that he was from out of town and did not want to wait that long. Mandujano offered to locate another source, and made four telephone calls in an apparent effort to do so. The phone calls appeared to be unsuccessful, for Mandujano told Cavalier he wasn't having any luck contacting anybody. Cavalier stated that he could not wait any longer. Then Mandujano said he had a good contact, a man who kept narcotics around his home, but that if he went to see this man, he would need the money "out front." To reassure Cavalier that he would not simply abscond with the money, Mandujano stated, "You are in my place of business. My wife is here. You can sit with my wife. I am not going to jeopardize her or my business for $650.00." Cavalier counted out $650.00 to Mandujano, and Mandujano left the premises of the Tally-Ho Lounge at about 3:30 p.m. About an hour later, he returned and explained that he had been unable to locate his contact. He gave back the $650.00 and told Cavalier he could still wait until the regular man came around. Cavalier left, but arranged to call back at 6:00 p.m. When Cavalier called at 6:00 and again at 6:30, he was told that Mandujano was not available. Cavalier testified that he did not later attempt to contact Mandujano, because, "Based on the information that I had received, it would be unsafe for either my informant or myself to return to this area."

The only other government witness was Gerald Courtney, a Special Agent for the Drug Enforcement Administration. Agent Courtney testified that, as part of a surveillance team in the vicinity of the Tally-Ho Lounge on March 29, 1973, he had observed Mandujano leave the bar around 3:15 or 3:30 p.m. and drive off in his automobile. The surveillance team followed Mandujano but lost him almost immediately in heavy traffic. Courtney testified that Mandujano returned to the bar at about 4:30 p.m.

II

Section 846 of Title 21, entitled "Attempt and conspiracy," provides that,

> Any person who attempts or conspires to commit any offense defined in this subchapter is punishable by imprisonment or fine or both which may not exceed the maximum punishment prescribed for the offense, the commission of which was the object of the attempt or conspiracy.

The theory of the government in this case is straightforward: Mandujano's acts constituted an attempt to distribute heroin; actual distribution of heroin would violate section 841(a)(1) of Title 21; therefore, Mandujano's attempt to distribute heroin comes within the terms of section 846 as an attempt to commit an offense defined in the subchapter.

Mandujano urges that his conduct as described by agent Cavalier did not rise to the level of an attempt to distribute heroin under section 846. He claims that at most he was attempting to acquire a controlled substance, not to distribute it; that it is impossible for a person to attempt to distribute heroin which he does not possess or control that his acts were only preparation, as distinguished from an attempt; and that the evidence was insufficient to support the jury's verdict.

Apparently there is no legislative history indicating exactly what Congress meant when it used the word "attempt" in section 846. There are two reported federal cases which discuss the question of what constitutes an attempt under this section. In *United States v. Noreikis*, 7 Cir. 1973, 481 F.2d 1177, where the defendants possessed the various chemicals necessary to synthesize Dimethyltryptamine (DMT), a controlled substance, the court held that the preparations had progressed to the level of an attempt to manufacture a controlled substance. In its discussion, the court commented that,

> While it seems to be well settled that mere preparation is not sufficient to constitute an attempt to commit a crime, 22 C.J.S. Criminal Law 75(2)b, at 230 et seq., it seems equally clear that the semantical distinction between preparation and attempt is one incapable of being formulated in a hard and fast rule. The procuring of the instrument of the crime might be preparation in one factual situation and not in another. The matter is sometimes equated with the commission of an overt act, the "doing something directly moving toward, and bringing him nearer, the crime he intends to commit." 22 C.J.S., supra at 231.

481 F.2d at 1181.

In *United States v. Heng Awkak Roman*, S.D.N.Y.1973, 356 F. Supp. 434, where the defendants' actions would have constituted possession of heroin with intent to distribute in violation of section 841 if federal agents had not substituted soap powder for the heroin involved in the case, the court held that the defendants' acts were an attempt to possess with intent to distribute. The district court in its opinion acknowledged that "Attempt, as used in section 846, is not defined. Indeed, there is no comprehensive statutory definition of attempt in federal law." The court concluded, however, that it was not necessary in the circumstances of the case to deal with the "complex question of when conduct crosses the line between 'mere preparation' and 'attempt.'" 356 F. Supp. at 437.

The courts in many jurisdictions have tried to elaborate on the distinction between mere preparation and attempt. See the Comment at 39-48 of Tent. Draft No. 10, 1960 of the Model Penal Code. In cases involving statutes other than section 846, the federal courts have confronted this issue on a number of occasions.***

Gregg v. United States, 8 Cir. 1940, 113 F.2d 687, involved in part a conviction for an attempt to import intoxicating liquor into Kansas. The court in this case acknowledges with apparent approval the definition of attempt urged by appellant Gregg:

> He calls attention to the fact that an attempt is an endeavor to do an act carried beyond mere preparation, but falling short of execution, and that it must be a step in the direct movement towards the commission of the crime after preparations have been made. *People v. Collins*, 234 N.Y. 355, 137 N.E. 753. The act must "carry the project forward within dangerous proximity to the criminal end to be attained." Cardozo, J., in *People v. Werblow*, 241 N.Y. 55, 148.

The court held, however, that Gregg's conduct went beyond "mere preparation":

> The transportation of goods into a state is essentially a continuing act not confined in its scope to the single instant of passage across a territorial boundary. In our view the appellant advanced beyond the stage of mere preparation when he loaded the liquor into his car and began his journey toward Kansas. From that moment he was engaged in an attempt to transport liquor into Kansas within the clear intent of the statute. 113 F.2d at 691.

In *United States v. Coplon*, 2 Cir. 1950, 185 F.2d 629, where the defendant was arrested before passing to a citizen of a foreign nation classified government documents contained in defendant's purse, Judge Learned Hand surveyed the law and addressed the issue of what would constitute an attempt:

> Because the arrest in this way interrupted the consummation of the crime one point upon the appeal is that her conduct still remained in the zone of "preparation," and that the evidence did not prove an "attempt." This argument it will be most convenient to answer at the outset. A neat doctrine by which to test when a person, intending to commit a crime which he fails to carry out, has "attempted" to commit it, would be that he has done all that it is within his power to do, but has been prevented by intervention from outside; in short, that he has passed beyond any locus poenitentiae. Apparently that was the original notion, and may still be law in England; but it is certainly not now generally the law in the United States, for there are many decisions which hold that the accused has passed beyond "preparation," although he has been interrupted before he has

taken the last of his intended steps. The decisions are too numerous to cite, and would not help much anyway, for there is, and obviously can be, no definite line; but Judge Cullen's discussion in *People v. Sullivan*, 1 and Mr. '1. 173 N.Y. 122. Justice Holmes' in two Massachusetts decisions, 2 are particularly enlightening. '2. *Commonwealth v. Kennedy*, 170 Mass. 18; *Commonwealth v. Peaslee*, 177 Mass. 267.

In the second of the Massachusetts opinions Holmes, J., said:

> Preparation is not an attempt. But some preparations may amount to an attempt. It is a question of degree. If the preparation comes very near to the accomplishment of the act, the intent to complete it renders the crime so probable that the act will be a misdemeanor, although there is still a locus poenitentiae, the need of a further exertion of the will to complete the crime.

In *Mims v. United States*, 5 Cir. 1967, 375 F.2d 135, 148, we noted that, "Much ink has been spilt in an attempt to arrive at a satisfactory standard for telling where preparations ends and attempt begins," and that the question had not been decided by this Court. The Court in *Mims*, at 148 n. 40, did note that the following test from *People v. Buffum*, 40 Cal.2d 709, has been "frequently approved":

> Preparation alone is not enough, there must be some appreciable fragment of the crime committed, it must be in such progress that it will be consummated unless interrupted by circumstances independent of the will of the attempter, and the act must not be equivocal in nature. ***

Although the foregoing cases give somewhat varying verbal formulations, careful examination reveals fundamental agreement about what conduct will constitute a criminal attempt. First, the defendant must have been acting with the kind of culpability otherwise required for the commission of the crime which he is charged with attempting.

Second, the defendant must have engaged in conduct which constitutes a substantial step toward commission of the crime. A substantial step must be conduct strongly corroborative of the firmness of the defendant's criminal intent. The use of the word "conduct" indicates that omission or possession, as well as positive acts, may in certain cases provide a basis for liability. The phrase "substantial step," rather than "overt act," is suggested by *Gregg v. United States, supra* ("a step in the direct movement toward the commission of the crime"); *United States v. Coplon, supra* ("before he has taken the last of his intended steps") and *People v. Buffum, supra* ("some appreciable fragment of the crime") and indicates that the conduct must be more than remote preparation. The requirement that the conduct be strongly corroborative of the firmness of the defendant's criminal intent also relates to the requirement that the conduct be more than "mere preparation," and is suggested by the Supreme Court's emphasis upon ascertaining the intent of the defendant, *United States v. Quincy, supra*, and by the approach taken in *United States v. Coplon, supra* 185 F.2d at 633 (". . . some preparation may amount to an attempt. It is a question of degree").

III

The district court charged the jury in relevant part as follows:

> Now, the essential elements required in order to prove or to establish the offense charged in the indictment, which is, again, that the defendant knowingly and intentionally attempted to distribute a controlled substance, must first be a specific intent to commit the crime, and next that the accused wilfully made the attempt, and that a direct but ineffectual overt act was done toward its commission, and that such overt act was knowingly and intentionally done in furtherance of the attempt.*** In determining whether or not such an act was done, it is necessary to distinguish between mere preparation on the one hand and the actual commencement of the doing of the criminal deed on the other. Mere preparation, which may consist of planning the offense or of devising, obtaining or arranging a means for its commission, is not sufficient to constitute an attempt, but the acts of a person who intends to commit a crime will constitute an attempt where they, themselves, clearly indicate a certain unambiguous intent to wilfully commit that specific crime and in themselves are an immediate step in the present execution of the criminal design, the progress of which would be completed unless interrupted by some circumstances not intended in the original design.

These instructions, to which the defendant did not object, are compatible with our view of what constitutes an attempt under section 846.

After the jury brought in a verdict of guilty, the trial court propounded a series of four questions to the jury:

> (1) Do you find beyond a reasonable doubt that on the 29th day of March, 1973, Roy Mandujano, the defendant herein, knowingly, wilfully and intentionally placed several telephone

calls in order to obtain a source of heroin in accordance with his negotiations with Officer Cavalier which were to result in the distribution of approximately one ounce of heroin from the defendant Roy Mandujano to Officer Cavalier?

(2) Do you find beyond a reasonable doubt that the telephone calls inquired about in question no. (1) constituted overt acts in furtherance of the offense alleged in the indictment?

(3) Do you find beyond a reasonable doubt that on the 29th day of March, 1973, Roy Mandujano, the defendant herein, knowingly, wilfully and intentionally requested and received prior payment in the amount of $650.00 for approximately one ounce of heroin that was to be distributed by the defendant Roy Mandujano to Officer Cavalier?

(4) Do you find beyond a reasonable doubt that the request and receipt of a prior payment inquired about in question no. (3) constituted an overt act in furtherance of the offense alleged in the indictment?

Neither the government nor the defendant objected to this novel procedure. After deliberating, the jury answered "No" to question (1) and "Yes" to questions (3) and (4). The jury's answers indicate that its thinking was consistent with the charge of the trial court.

The evidence was sufficient to support a verdict of guilty under section 846. Agent Cavalier testified that at Mandujano's request, he gave him $650.00 for one ounce of heroin, which Mandujano said he could get from a "good contact." From this, plus Mandujano's comments and conduct before and after the transfer of the $650.00, as described in Part I of this opinion, the jury could have found that Mandujano was acting knowingly and intentionally and that he engaged in conduct—the request for and the receipt of the $650.00—which in fact constituted a substantial step toward distribution of heroin. From interrogatory (4), it is clear that the jury considered Mandujano's request and receipt of the prior payment a substantial step toward the commission of the offense. Certainly, in the circumstances of this case, the jury could have found the transfer of money strongly corroborative of the firmness of Mandujano's intent to complete the crime. Of course, proof that Mandujano's "good contact" actually existed, and had heroin for sale, would have further strengthened the government's case; however, such proof was not essential.

State v. Group, 98 Ohio St. 3d 248 (2002)

***[Mrs. Lozier was going to testify against Scott Group in a capital case. Group was accused of shooting Mrs. Lozier and killing her husband during a robbery.] Adam Perry was another Mahoning County Jail inmate at the time of Group's pretrial incarceration. Awaiting trial on pending charges, Perry was incarcerated with Group from December 1997 to May 1998. Perry was released on bond in May 1998.

In a letter postmarked March 20, 1998, before Perry's release, Group begged for Perry's help with his case:

> If you do bond out, let me know. There's something you may be able to do to help me with concerning my case. And I'm telling you, I need all the help I can get. *** But seriously man, and this is no joke, I need your help with something if you get out. Please don't leave me hanging? We've known each other a long time and if anyone in your family needs help, you know I'll be there.

Before Perry was released, Group asked him to firebomb Mrs. Lozier's house. Group assured Perry that Mrs. Lozier no longer lived there. However, he told Perry that "[h]e didn't want Sandy Lozier to testify against him," and he wanted Perry to "firebomb the lady's house to either scare her from testifying or to lead the police into investigating others."

Group told Perry that he had $300,000 hidden away. He offered Perry half of it in exchange for his help. Group also offered to dissuade a witness from testifying in Perry's trial.

Group explained to Perry how to make a firebomb by mixing gasoline with dish soap in a bottle, with a rag in the neck for a fuse. He instructed Perry to light the rag and throw it through the front window and then to drop a key chain with the name "Charity" on it on the front lawn. "[W]hat he wanted to do," Perry explained, "was to mislead the police into thinking that the firebomb and the murder was [sic] all involved as far as Charity's abduction and murder."

In a letter postmarked May 6, 1998, Group wrote to Perry: "So I need to know on everything if that party is still on where your sister lived. The party has to happen and happen the way we last talked. I've got to know bro, so I can figure some other things out in the next few weeks." Perry understood "the party" to refer to the planned firebombing of Mrs. Lozier's house.

Group also corresponded with Perry after Perry's release. State's Exhibit 37, a letter from Group to Perry, contains the following passage: "[Y]ou said you would take care of that flat tire for me and now that your [sic] out, I hope you do because it's a matter of life or death (mine)[.]" In the next sentence, Mrs. Lozier's address appears next to the name "Agee."

Group then wrote: "If you take care of the flat, please take care of it with that two step plan we talked about. *** Theres [sic] $300,000.00 in a wall of a certain house ***. Half goes to you to do what you like."

The second page of State's Exhibit 37 contains Mrs. Lozier's address and describes the house as ranch-style. It also lists the following items: "Cheap key chain or ID bracelet—name (Charity)" and "3 liter wine jug—mix gas & dish soap."

In June 1998, Perry knocked on Mrs. Lozier's door. When she answered, he asked her whether a "Maria something lived there." Mrs. Lozier said no, and Perry left. Perry testified that he did not want to hurt Mrs. Lozier and so, after finding her at home, he took no further action. Perry later told the prosecutor about Group's plan.

Group was indicted for the aggravated murder of Robert Lozier under R.C. 2903.01(B). The aggravated-murder count had two death specifications: R.C. 2929.04(A)(5) (purposeful attempt to kill two persons) and R.C. 2929.04(A)(7) (murder during aggravated robbery). The indictment also contained a count charging Group with the attempted aggravated murder of Mrs. Lozier on January 18, 1997, and a count charging aggravated robbery, R.C. 2911.01(A)(1). Each count had a firearm specification, R.C. 2941.145(A).

After Perry told the prosecutor about the firebombing plan, a superseding indictment was filed, containing the above counts plus two new ones: (1) the attempted aggravated murder of Mrs. Lozier "on or about or between April 1, 1998 and June 5, 1998," and (2) one count of intimidating a witness—Mrs. Lozier—"on or about or between December 1, 1997 and June 5, 1998."

Group was convicted on all counts and specifications. After a penalty hearing, he was sentenced to death.***

In his seventh proposition, Group contends that the state introduced insufficient evidence to prove him guilty of attempted aggravated murder. When a defendant challenges the legal sufficiency of the state's evidence, "the relevant question is whether, after viewing the evidence in the light most favorable to the prosecution, *any* rational trier of fact could have found the essential elements of the crime beyond a reasonable doubt." (Emphasis sic.) *Jackson v. Virginia* (1979), 443 U.S. 307.

The state's evidence showed that Group had asked Adam Perry to firebomb Mrs. Lozier's house. In exchange, Group said he would give Perry $150,000 and would dissuade a witness from testifying in Perry's trial. Group gave Perry Mrs. Lozier's address, gave him instructions for making a firebomb, and instructed him to drop a key chain with the name "Charity" on it.

However, Perry took no further action in furtherance of the plan against Mrs. Lozier after knocking on her door and finding that she was still living in her house. Perry testified that he had no intention of killing Mrs. Lozier and that Group had assured him that the house was vacant.

Group argues that "based upon [Perry's] testimony there is absolutely no evidence of an attempted aggravated murder of Sandra Lozier at the time of this incident." The state contends that Group's actions in this case— repeatedly asking Perry to firebomb the house, giving him the address and the firebomb recipe, offering to reward him, instructing him to leave a false trail— were enough to permit the jury to find him guilty of attempted aggravated murder.

The crime of attempt is defined by R.C. 2923.02(A), which provides: "No person, purposely or knowingly, and when purpose or knowledge is sufficient culpability for the commission of an offense, shall engage in conduct that, if successful, would constitute or result in the offense."

We have elaborated on the statutory definition as follows: "A 'criminal attempt' is when one purposely does or omits to do anything which is an act or omission constituting a substantial step in a course of conduct planned to culminate in his commission of the crime." *State v. Woods* (1976), 48 Ohio St. 2d 127, paragraph one of the syllabus. A "substantial step" requires conduct that is "strongly corroborative of the actor's criminal purpose." *Id.* "[T]his standard does properly direct attention to overt acts of the defendant which convincingly demonstrate a firm purpose to commit a crime, while allowing police intervention *** in order to prevent the crime when the criminal intent becomes apparent." *Id.* at 132.

Two Ohio courts have concluded that merely soliciting another person to commit a crime does not constitute an attempt. *See State v. Dapice* (1989), 57 Ohio App. 3d 99, 104 ("mere preparation" does not itself constitute an attempt); *State v. Valenta* (June 28, 2001), Cuyahoga App. No. 78232, 2001 WL 723247. That also appears to be the majority view nationally.

However, Group did more than merely solicit the firebombing of Mrs. Lozier's house. He took all action within his power, considering his incarceration, to ensure that the crime would be committed. He offered Perry a large monetary reward and a reciprocal favor. He gave Perry Mrs. Lozier's address and told him how to make the bomb. He repeatedly wrote to Perry urging him to complete the act.

Some courts have found the elements of a criminal attempt in cases factually similar to the case at bar. In *State v. Urcinoli* (1999), 321 N.J. Super. 519, the defendant hired a fellow inmate to kill someone outside the jail. The defendant expected the other inmate to be released soon; he and the other inmate discussed how the plan would be carried out and how the other inmate would be paid for the murder; and the defendant gave the other inmate identifying details about the intended victim. These discussions were held to be a substantial step, sufficient for an attempted-murder conviction. *Id.* at 537.

The court reached a similar conclusion in *Braham v. State* (Alaska 1977), 571 P.2d 631. The defendant in Braham hired someone to kill a third person. After the defendant and his hired killer agreed on the contract price, the defendant instructed the killer to visit the victim in order to get close to him and gain his trust in preparation for his murder. The hired killer did, in fact, visit the victim. After doing so, the killer abandoned the scheme and cooperated with police. On these facts, the court held the evidence sufficient to support a conviction of attempted murder. 571 P.2d at 637-638.

"The federal courts have generally rejected a rigid or formalistic approach to the attempt offense. Instead they commonly recognize that '[t]he determination whether particular conduct constitutes *** [an attempt] is so dependent on the particular facts of each case that, of necessity, there can be no litmus test to guide the reviewing courts.' *** Following this analysis, which we consider the better reasoned approach, several federal courts have concluded that a solicitation accompanied by the requisite intent may constitute an attempt." *United States v. Am. Airlines, Inc.* (C.A.5, 1984), 743 F.2d 1114, 1121, quoting *United States v. Ivic* (C.A.2, 1983), 700 F.2d 51, 66.

We agree with the federal courts that "a rigid or formalistic approach to the attempt offense" should be avoided. Nothing in the language of R.C. 2923.02(A), or in our own precedents, compels such an approach. R.C. 2923.02(A) defines attempt broadly as "conduct that, if successful, would constitute or result in the offense." In *State v. Woods*, supra, 48 Ohio St. 2d 127, paragraph one of the syllabus, we defined a "criminal attempt" as "an act or omission constituting a substantial step in a course of conduct planned to culminate in [the actor's] commission of the crime." A "substantial step" requires conduct that is "strongly corroborative of the actor's criminal purpose." *Id.*

With reference to "overt acts," we said in *Woods* that the "substantial step" standard "properly direct[s] attention to overt acts of the defendant which convincingly demonstrate a firm purpose to commit a crime, while allowing police intervention *** in order to prevent the crime when the criminal intent becomes apparent." *Id.* at 132. Thus, we conclude that an "overt act" is simply an act that meets the "substantial step" criterion enunciated in *Woods*.

Group's acts—offering Perry $150,000 to throw a firebomb through the window of Mrs. Lozier's house, providing him with her address, repeatedly importuning him to commit the crime, and instructing him how to make the bomb and how to misdirect any subsequent police investigation—strongly corroborate Group's criminal purpose, and therefore constitute a substantial step in a course of conduct planned to culminate in the aggravated murder of Mrs. Lozier. We therefore find that the evidence presented was sufficient to prove the essential elements of attempted aggravated murder.

Notes and Questions

1. In *United States v. Mandujano,* how does the court know that a defendant has gone beyond mere preparation and has actually attempted to commit the crime?

2. Imagine, in *State v. Group*, that the activities of the defendant and Adam Perry were being monitored by law enforcement. If you were the prosecutor supervising the surveillance, at what point would you tell law enforcement to step in? Remember, you need sufficient evidence to prove a charge of attempted aggravated murder. However, you want to ensure the safety of Mrs. Lozier.

> A. Defendant asks Perry to firebomb Mrs. Lozier's house while both are incarcerated. Defendant instructs Perry how to build a firebomb and promised him $150,000 if he would indeed firebomb Mrs. Lozier's house.
> B. Defendant sends a March 20, 1998 letter to Perry reiterating his request to firebomb Mrs. Lozier's house.
> C. Perry released from jail.
> D. Defendant sends a May 6, 1998 letter to Perry again requesting the firebombing.
> E. Perry goes to visit Mrs. Lozier's house in June 1998.
> F. Perry knocks on Mrs. Lozier's door.
> G. Perry talks with Mrs. Lozier.

3. If the defendant in *Group* was not incarcerated, do you believe that the Ohio Supreme Court would have found his conduct sufficient for attempted aggravated murder?

4. As *Group* and *Mandujano* illustrate, determining whether or not the defendant has gone far enough to constitute a substantial step is a very fact-sensitive inquiry. Below is the MPC section on attempt. In Section 5.01(2), the MPC describes conduct that might support finding that the defendant has made a substantial step towards committing a crime. Do you find the examples listed here helpful? Can you think of additional examples?

Model Penal Code
Section 5.01. Criminal Attempt

(1) <u>Definition of Attempt</u>. A person is guilty of an attempt to commit a crime if, acting with the kind of culpability otherwise required for commission of the crime, he:

> (a) purposely engages in conduct which would constitute the crime if the attendant circumstances were as he believes them to be; or

(b) when causing a particular result is an element of the crime, does or omits to do anything with the purpose of causing or with the belief that it will cause such result without further conduct on his part; or

(c) purposely does or omits to do anything which, under the circumstances as he believes them to be, is an act or omission constituting a substantial step in a course of conduct planned to culminate in his commission of the crime.

(2) Conduct That May Be Held Substantial Step Under Subsection (1)(c). Conduct shall not be held to constitute a substantial step under Subsection (1)(c) of this Section unless it is strongly corroborative of the actor's criminal purpose. Without negativing the sufficiency of other conduct, the following, if strongly corroborative of the actor's criminal purpose, shall not be held insufficient as a matter of law:

(a) lying in wait, searching for or following the contemplated victim of the crime;

(b) enticing or seeking to entice the contemplated victim of the crime to go to the place contemplated for its commission;

(c) reconnoitering the place contemplated for the commission of the crime;

(d) unlawful entry of a structure, vehicle or enclosure in which it is contemplated that the crime will be committed;

(e) possession of materials to be employed in the commission of the crime, which are specially designed for such unlawful use or which can serve no lawful purpose of the actor under the circumstances;

(f) possession, collection or fabrication of materials to be employed in the commission of the crime, at or near the place contemplated for its commission, where such possession, collection or fabrication serves no lawful purpose of the actor under the circumstances;

(g) soliciting an innocent agent to engage in conduct constituting an element of the crime.

5. The MPC, as discussed in the following comment, also lists additional methods or tests for determining whether or not the defendant has attempted a crime. If you were a state legislator tasked with reforming your state criminal code on attempt, which test would you choose? If none of the examples from the MPC appeal to you, can you think of your own test?

Model Penal Code
Section 5.01. Criminal Attempt
Comment

This comment to the Model Penal Code catalogues a number of formulations which have been adopted or suggested, including the following:

(a) The physical proximity doctrine—the overt act required for an attempt must be proximate to the completed crime, or directly tending toward the completion of the crime, or must amount to the commencement of the consummation.

(b) The dangerous proximity doctrine—a test given impetus by Mr. Justice Holmes whereby the greater the gravity and probability of the offense, and the nearer the act to the crime, the stronger is the case for calling the act an attempt.

(c) The indispensable element test—a variation of the proximity tests which emphasizes any indispensable aspect of the criminal endeavor over which the actor has not yet acquired control.

(d) The probable desistance test—the conduct constitutes an attempt if, in the ordinary and natural course of events, without interruption from an outside source, it will result in the crime intended.

(e) The abnormal step approach—an attempt is a step toward crime which goes beyond the point where the normal citizen would think better of his conduct and desist.

(f) The res ipsa loquitur or unequivocality test—an attempt is committed when the actor's conduct manifests an intent to commit a crime.

C. Legal Impossibility

State v. Brown, 1996 WL 139626 (Ohio Ct. App. 1996)

DECISION AND JUDGMENT ENTRY

On November 1, 1994, the grand jury sitting in Ottawa County issued a four count indictment against appellant, Central L. Brown. The first three counts in the indictment charged appellant with attempted murder in violation of R.C. 2923.02. The fourth count charged appellant as follows:

Count # Four

On or about the 17th day of October, 1994, in Ottawa County, aforesaid did knowingly attempt to cause physical harm to another by means of a deadly weapon, as defined in Section 2923.11 of the Ohio Revised Code, the victim of said offense being a peace officer, and in violation of Section 2903.11(A)(2) of the Ohio Revised Code, and against the peace and dignity of the State of Ohio.

***On February 23, 1995, the jury verdict in this case was filed in the Ottawa County Court of Common Pleas. The jury verdict reads: "We, the jury, find the defendant, Central Brown, (*) *Guilty* of Felonious Assault as alleged in the fourth count of the indictment. (*) Guilty or Not Guilty" The verdict also contains a finding by the jury that appellant did have a firearm on his person or in his control when the offense was committed. A judgment was entered by the Ottawa County Court of Common Pleas on March 21, 1995, in which the court stated that the jury was unable to reach a verdict on any of the three counts for attempted murder.

The state initially filed a notice of intent to retry appellant on the three counts of attempted murder. However, on April 24, 1995, the state filed a motion to dismiss the three counts, informing the court that appellant had "agreed to cooperate in the investigation and prosecution of co-defendants involved in this matter ***." On April 27, 1995, the trial court granted the motion to dismiss the attempted murder charges.

The trial court sentenced appellant by judgment entry on May 26, 1995. The court ordered appellant to serve five to twenty-five years for his felonious assault conviction, and ordered appellant to serve three years of actual incarceration for the firearm specification. The three years of actual incarceration were ordered to be served "prior to and consecutive with the sentence of incarceration for felonious assault of a peace officer." Following sentencing, appellant filed this appeal.

Appellant presents five assignments of error for review which are:

> ERROR NO. 1: THE COURT ERRED IN OVERRULING DEFENDANT'S MOTION FOR ACQUITTAL PURSUANT TO RULE 29 AT THE CLOSE OF THE STATE'S CASE.
> ERROR NO. 2: THE VERDICT IS AGAINST THE MANIFEST WEIGHT OF THE EVIDENCE.
> ERROR NO. 3: THE COURT ERRED SENTENCING THE DEFENDANT ON AN AGGRAVATED FELONY OF THE FIRST DEGREE.
> ERROR NO. 4: THE DEFENDANT WAS DENIED DUE PROCESS OF LAW AND EQUAL PROTECTION OF THE LAW.
> ERROR NO. 5: THE DEFENDANT WAS DENIED EFFECTIVE ASSISTANCE OF COUNSEL AT THE TRIAL.

We begin by considering appellant's contentions in support of his first and second assignments of error that the evidence in this case did not support his conviction for felonious assault of a peace officer. In his first assignment of error appellant raises the issue that he was entitled to an acquittal because the evidence presented does not overcome his defense of legal or factual impossibility. In his second assignment of error he contends that the evidence was insufficient to prove his guilt beyond a reasonable doubt.***

Both tests require an examination of the essential elements of the crime of felonious assault of a peace officer. To discern what those essential elements are, we must refer to the version of R.C. 2903.11 that was in effect when appellant was charged. The statute then in effect read:

> (A) No person shall knowingly:
> "***
>
> > (2) Cause or attempt to cause physical harm to another by means of a deadly weapon or dangerous ordnance, as defined in section 2924.11 of the Revised Code.
> >
> > (B) Whoever violates this section is guilty of felonious assault, an aggravated felony of the second degree. If the victim of the offense is a peace officer, as defined in section 2935.01 of the Revised Code, felonious assault is an aggravated felony of the first degree. R.C. 2903.11 (effective 7-1-83).

The elements of the first degree felony of felonious assault of a peace officer that were contained in the statute are: (1) no person shall knowingly; (2) cause or attempt to cause physical harm to another; (3) by means of a deadly weapon or dangerous ordnance; (4) the victim of the offense is a peace officer. Keeping these elements in mind, we now consider the evidence that was presented at trial.

The state called two witnesses who testified they were in a car with appellant on October 17, 1994. The first witness testified that he was driving the car in which appellant was a passenger. The second witness testified that he was a passenger in the back seat of the car and that appellant was a passenger in the front seat of the car. Both witnesses testified that during the course of time they were in the car with appellant, six gun shots were fired by occupants of the car. However, their testimony differed as to whether appellant was the only person who fired the shots.

The driver of the car testified that appellant first fired two shots into an empty field. The driver stated that he became frightened following the firing of the two shots but that he did not say anything because he was afraid appellant would shoot him or someone else. He testified that he continued driving and stated:

> During this time, the windows were rolled down in my car, and he was—he had the gun in his hands, and he was like waving it around and stuff, you know, messing around with it, and I told

him that there was a cop's house up on the right and to keep the
gun down because I didn't want anybody to get suspicious.

He testified that as they drove by the police officer's house, appellant fired four gun shots at the house from the passenger side of the car.

The passenger who was seated in the back of the car testified that the driver of the car, rather than appellant, fired the first two shots into an empty field. His testimony regarding the location of that field differed somewhat from the testimony of the driver of the car. However, like the driver, he testified that appellant fired four gun shots at the police officer's house.

The girlfriend of the driver of the car testified. She stated that she met her boyfriend and the passengers in his car at a drive-thru on the evening of October 17, 1994. She testified that appellant was a passenger in the car and that she had a conversation with him. During the conversation, he told her he shot an officer's house.

The state presented testimony that established that the house identified by the driver and passenger of the car as the site where appellant fired four gun shots was the home of a peace officer and his fiancee. The state also presented testimony and evidence that three bullets were fired into the house on the evening of October 17, 1994 and that three persons were in the house; the police officer's fiancee and her parents. Because they were in different rooms in the house, lights were on in several rooms across the front of the house. The lights could easily be seen from the road. The evidence showed that bullets pierced the walls of the rooms in which the three persons were located, but none of the persons were injured. Testimony presented by witnesses called by the state also established that the peace officer was not home when the shooting occurred, because he was on duty.

Appellant first argues that an essential element was not proved in this case; namely, a peace officer was not the victim of the crime because the peace officer was not present when he fired shots into the peace officer's home. Appellant also focuses on the element of attempt. He concedes that simply attempting to cause physical harm to another with a dangerous ordnance or deadly weapon is sufficient to constitute felonious assault, since attempt is included as an element of R.C. 2903.11. However, he argues that because the legislature has not separately defined attempt in the felonious assault statute, the trial court and this court must recognize his assertion of the common law defense of impossibility as a complete defense to the attempt.

To support his argument, appellant cites to a case decided by this court in 1988, *State v. Collins (1988)*, 54 Ohio App. 3d 134. However, appellant's use of this case is misguided. First, *State v. Collins* involved the interpretation of the statutory provisions then in effect that set forth the elements of the separate crime of attempt. *Id.* at 135-136. Appellant was not charged in this case with the separate crime of attempt, he was only charged with felonious assault, which can be committed with a mere attempt to cause another physical harm if the attempt includes the use of a dangerous ordnance or deadly weapon. Second, while appellant correctly points out that in *State v. Collins* this court concluded that the common law defense of legal impossibility was still a viable defense to the separate crime of attempt, because in a subsection of the attempt statute the legislature had specifically eliminated factual impossibility as a defense but did not also bar the defense of legal impossibility, *id.* at 136, appellant fails to acknowledge the impact of the events which occurred following this court's decision in *State v. Collins.*

Following the *State v. Collins* decision, the Ohio legislature amended the attempt statute. R.C. 2923.02 now contains the following pertinent provisions:

> (A) No person, purposely or knowingly, and when purpose or knowledge is sufficient culpability for the commission of an offense, shall engage in conduct which, if successful, would constitute or result in the offense.
>
> (B) It is no defense to a charge under this section that, in retrospect, commission of the offense which was the object of the attempt was either factually or legally impossible under the attendant circumstances, if that offense could have been committed had the attendant circumstances been as the actor believed them to be. R.C. 2923.02.

While appellant is correct that the legislature specified that factual or legal impossibility are eliminated as defenses only for persons charged under the attempt statute, we do not accept his assertion that as a result we are constrained to recognize the defenses of legal or factual impossibility as viable for persons charged with a principle crime that encompasses an attempt.

The legislature's action to amend R.C. 2923.02(B) to eliminate all impossibility defenses for a charge of attempt was limited to that statute alone because this court was only interpreting that specific statute in *State v. Collins,* 54 Ohio App. 3d at 135-136. However, by responding as it did, the legislature sent a clear signal that public policy in Ohio will no longer tolerate an impossibility defense for any crime that incorporates attempt as an element. Furthermore, since the impossibility defenses arose in common law, they can be eliminated by common law. See *State v. Platt* (June 10, 1981), Brown App. No. 376, unreported (Stephenson, J. Concurring). Accordingly, this court holds that common law will no longer recognize an impossibility defense to attempt and rejects appellant's contention that he has a viable impossibility defense to the element of attempt contained in R.C. 2903.11.

Having found that impossibility is no defense to an attempt under the felonious assault statute, we now consider what evidence was presented relating to each of the elements of the crime of felonious assault of a peace officer. The first element of the crime, no person shall knowingly, requires consideration of the meaning of the term knowingly. Knowingly is defined as follows in R.C. 2901.22(B):

> (B) A person acts knowingly, regardless of his purpose, when he is aware that his conduct will probably cause a certain result or will probably be of a certain nature. A person has knowledge of circumstances when he is aware that such circumstances probably exist.

The testimony of the driver of the car, the back seat passenger and the girlfriend of the driver of the car all established that appellant was aware that he was shooting bullets into a peace officer's house. The testimony presented at trial also showed that persons could infer from what they could see from the road that occupants were inside the house at the time shots were fired. From this evidence, a rational trier of fact could conclude that the state proved beyond a reasonable doubt that appellant, a person, acted knowingly.

As we previously noted, the second element of the crime of felonious assault is: cause or attempt to cause physical harm to another. Physical harm to persons is defined in R.C. 2901.01(C) as: "any injury, illness, or other physiological impairment, regardless of its gravity or duration." Attempt is defined in R.C. 2923.02(A) as: "No person, purposely or knowingly, and when purpose or knowledge is sufficient culpability for the commission of an offense, shall engage in conduct which, if successful, would constitute or result in the offense." R.C. 2923.02(A).3 The evidence that appellant purposely fired bullets into a house that he knew to be a peace officer's home when the house was fully lighted from the inside is sufficient to allow a rational trier of fact to conclude beyond a reasonable doubt that appellant attempted to cause physical harm to another.

The third element is by means of a deadly weapon or dangerous ordnance. "Deadly weapon" is defined in R.C. 2923.11(A) as: "any instrument, device, or thing capable of inflicting death, and designed or specially adapted for use as a weapon, or possessed, carried, or used as a weapon." The evidence in this case showed that a fully operational gun was used in the commission of the crime. Accordingly, a rational trier of fact could conclude that the use of a deadly weapon was proved beyond a reasonable doubt.

The final element is that the victim is a peace officer. R.C. 2935.01 provides in pertinent part: "'Peace officer' includes a *** deputy sheriff ***." R.C. 2935.01(B). The state called the owner of the house that was the site of the shooting on October 17, 1994, to the stand. He testified that he is a deputy sheriff with the Ottawa County Sheriff's Department. However, as appellant has correctly argued, the witness also testified that he was not present when appellant fired bullets into his home. His absence from the site is only one factor for consideration. The evidence clearly shows that appellant's actions were a knowing attempt to cause physical harm by means of a deadly weapon to a peace officer; he fired the bullets into a well lighted house after he was told the house was the dwelling place of a peace officer. As previously discussed, appellant cannot escape conviction for an attempt to feloniously assault a peace officer just because the attempt was legally or factually impossible to complete. Accordingly, a rational trier of fact could conclude that all of the essential elements of felonious assault of a peace officer were proved beyond a reasonable doubt.

United States v. Farner, 251 F. 3d 510 (2001)

KAZEN, Chief Judge:

Robert E. Farner ("Farner") appeals his conviction for attempting to persuade and entice a minor to engage in criminal sexual activity in violation of 18 U.S.C. § 2422(b). He argues that the evidence against him was insufficient as a matter of law based on the defense of legal impossibility. We affirm the conviction.

I

The undisputed facts of this case derive from the stipulated evidence at trial. Farner, an adult male living in Dallas, first met "Cindy" through America Online's Internet service. He sent a real-time instant message to a person using the screen name "CIN136419," who told him that she was a 14-year-old girl named Cindy. Farner sent Cindy a message asking if she was looking for an older man. She responded affirmatively. He then told her that he would like to meet her in person. For the next three months, Farner kept in contact with Cindy through instant messaging, e-mail and telephone calls. During these conversations, Farner attempted to persuade, induce, entice, and coerce Cindy into having sexual relations with him. Farner also sent her four pornographic pictures depicting adults participating in various sexual acts.

After one particular conversation, Farner made arrangements with Cindy to meet in Houston to engage in sexual activity. They agreed to meet at a local restaurant. Farner drove from Dallas to Houston, where he was to attend a medical conference. After checking into a hotel, he drove to the parking lot of the restaurant, where he was confronted and arrested by law enforcement officials. Cindy was, in fact, an adult Federal Bureau of Investigation agent named Kathy Crawford, participating in an undercover sting operation.

At the FBI office, Farner waived his *Miranda* rights and confessed that he had traveled to Houston to meet Cindy. He claimed that he had no specific plans with Cindy, but he would have done anything she wanted to do. He further admitted that he had planned to take her into his hotel room, and that he had discussed sex with her prior to traveling to Houston. A search of his hotel room revealed a box of condoms and a tube of surgilube lubricant.

A federal grand jury indicted Farner for attempting to persuade, induce, entice, and coerce a minor to engage in criminal sexual activity in violation of 18 U.S.C. § 2422(b). Farner waived a jury and proceeded to trial on stipulated evidence. The district court found him guilty, and sentenced him to 15 months' confinement.

On appeal, Farner claims that the district court should have granted his motion for judgment of acquittal because it was legally impossible for him to have committed the crime since the "minor" involved in this case was actually an adult. We review de novo a court's denial of a motion for judgment of acquittal.

II

Relying on *United States v. Contreras,* 950 F.2d 232, 237 (5th Cir. 1991), *cert. denied*, the district court held that "factual impossibility is not a defense if the crime could have been committed had the attendant circumstances been as the actor believed them to be." The court found beyond a reasonable doubt that Farner believed Cindy to be a minor and acted on that belief. On appeal, Farner insists that his defense was not factual impossibility, but rather legal impossibility.

The distinction between factual and legal impossibility is elusive at best. *See, e.g., United States v. Everett,* 700 F.2d 900, 905 (3rd Cir. 1983) (stating that the doctrine has become a "source of utter frustration" and a "morass of confusion"). Most federal courts have repudiated the distinction or have at least openly questioned its usefulness. *See Osborn v. United States,* 385 U.S. 323, (1966) (questioning whether "the doctrine of 'impossibility' with all its subtleties" should have continued validity); *United States v. Powell,* 1 F. Supp. 2d 1419, 1421 (N.D. Ala. 1998), *aff'd*, 177 F.3d 982 ("In the Eleventh Circuit . . . traditional factual impossibility/legal impossibility analysis has been discarded"); *United States v. Darnell,* 545 F.2d 595, 597 (8th Cir. 1976) ("[B]eyond the logical problem is the pragmatic: the difficulty of categorization [of the two impossibilities]. The tidy dichotomy of the theoretician becomes obscure in the courtroom"); *United States v. Duran,* 884 F. Supp. 577, 580 n. 5 (D.D.C. 1995) ("[C]ategorizing a case as involving legal versus factual impossibility is difficult, if not pointless"); *United States v. Quijada,* 588 F.2d 1253, 1255 (9th Cir. 1978) (rejecting impossibility defense).

The illusory distinction between the two defenses is evident in the instant case. Thus, Farner says this is a case of legal impossibility because Kathy Crawford was an adult, and the statute does not address attempted sexual activity between adults. On the other hand, the district court viewed the impossibility as factual, because the defendant unquestionably intended to engage in the conduct proscribed by law but failed only because of circumstances unknown to him. We think the latter view is correct.

In any event, this circuit has properly eschewed the semantical thicket of the impossibility defense in criminal attempt cases and has instead required proof of two elements: first, that the defendant acted with the kind of culpability otherwise required for the commission of the underlying substantive offense, and, second, that the defendant had engaged in conduct which constitutes a substantial step toward commission of the crime. The substantial step must be conduct which strongly corroborates the firmness of defendant's criminal attempt. In this case, the district court correctly concluded from the stipulated evidence, beyond a reasonable doubt, that Farner intended to engage in sexual acts with a 14-year-old girl and that he took substantial steps toward committing the crime.

We need not hold that there can never be a case of true legal impossibility, although such a case would be rare. The typical definition of that defense is a situation "when the actions which the defendant performs or sets in motion, even if fully carried out *as he desires,* would not constitute a crime." *United States v. Oviedo,* 525 F.2d at 883 (emphasis added). The one case cited by Farner which arguably invokes that doctrine is *United States v. McInnis,* 601 F.2d 1319 (5th Cir. 1979). The defendants there were charged with, among other things, conspiracy to violate the federal kidnapping statute, 18 U.S.C. § 1201. The intended scheme of the alleged co-conspirators was to entice the victim to travel into Mexico on his own volition so that he could be kidnaped in Mexico. The co-conspirators "planned neither to cross state or international borders themselves nor to follow the abduction of (the victim) with international travel." *Id.* at 1326. This court concluded that even if the scheme had been implemented exactly as planned, it did not violate the federal kidnapping statute. The situation in the instant case is quite different. Defendant Farner's scheme, if fully carried out as he "desired" or "planned," was not to engage in sexual relations with an adult FBI officer. By his own stipulation, the person whom he desired to entice was a 14-year-old girl. The only reason he failed was because the true facts were not as he believed them to be.

The judgment is affirmed.

Notes and Questions

1. Why do you think Ohio modified its laws to remove legal impossibility as a defense? What argument supports allowing legal impossibility?

2. *State v. Brown* illustrates one of the challenges of studying the common law. Here, the court stated, "since the impossibility defenses arose in common law, they can be eliminated by common law . . . [a]ccordingly, this court holds that the common law will no longer recognize an impossibility defense to attempt." If individual courts are permitted to determine the law, how can attorneys, law students, or even laypersons be expected to know the current state of the law?

3. Does ORC 2903.11(A)(2) require the offender to know that the victim is a peace officer or is it a strict liability offense as it pertains to this particular element of the crime?

4. Did the defendant's conduct in *United Sates v. Farner* constitute a factual or legal impossibility?

5. Can a defendant be convicted of an attempt crime that involves pure legal impossibility?

D. Abandonment

State v. Arnold, 9 Ohio Misc. 2d 14 (Hamilton County Mun. Ct. 1983)

PAINTER, J.

Defendant, Michael W. Arnold, was charged with the violation of R.C. 2923.02, the "attempt" section. The affidavit stated that Mr. Arnold "with purpose to deprive the 7-11 store did remove 4 packs of bacon value $2.85 each from the meat cooler and did put the bacon inside his coat. The defendant then turned to leave the store, saw he was being watched by the store manager and put the bacon back into the cooler and fled the store."

The testimony elicited at trial was that the defendant, after having placed the bacon in his coat, was observed by the store manager, whereupon he replaced the bacon. These facts were uncontradicted at trial, defendant raising the sole argument that he was not guilty of attempted theft, because he had abandoned or renounced his criminal intent prior to his apprehension.

R.C. 2923.02(D) states as follows: "It is an affirmative defense to a charge under this section that the actor abandoned his effort to commit the offense or otherwise prevented its commission, under circumstances manifesting a complete and voluntary renunciation of his criminal purpose."

Of course, the defendant bears the burden of proof on an affirmative defense. R.C. 2901.05. We have been cited no Ohio cases which would be of any guidance given this state of facts; however, the case of *State* v. *Cooper* (1977), 52 Ohio St. 2d 163, vacated in part on other grounds (1978), 438 U.S. 911, stands for the proposition that, once a criminal intent has been formed, coupled with an overt act toward the commission of an offense, abandonment is no defense. We are not quite certain of this reasoning, in light of the clear meaning of R.C. 2923.02(D). We do not need to reach that issue, because we believe that the issue in the case before us is whether the abandonment was voluntary, as required by R.C. 2923.02(D).

The court has no doubt, and finds as a fact that the defendant abandoned his criminal enterprise only upon discovery by the store manager. That being the case, we believe the Committee Comment to Section 501(4) of the Model Penal Code, quoted in 4 O.J.I. 523.02, at page 339, is helpful. The comment states as follows:

> Within the meaning of this Article, renunciation of criminal purpose is not voluntary if it is motivated, in whole or in part, by circumstances, not present or apparent at the inception of the actor's course of conduct, which increase the probability of detection or apprehension or which make more difficult the accomplishment of the criminal purpose. ***

This court believes the above reasoning is persuasive. Because we are convinced beyond a reasonable doubt that defendant intended to commit a theft offense, and because defendant has failed in his affirmative defense, the defendant is found guilty.

Defendant guilty.

Notes and Questions

1. In *State v. Arnold*, at what point had the defendant completed the substantial step for theft? Based on your answer, do you think the defendant could have been convicted of theft rather than attempted theft? Why or why not?

2. What are the policy reasons behind allowing the defense of abandonment?

Chapter 17
Solicitation

A. Introduction

At common law, solicitation involved requesting, encouraging, inciting, inducing, urging, or soliciting another to commit a crime with the specific intent that the person commit the crime. Solicitation is complete at the moment the defendant communicates the request to another. Jurisdictions differ as to whether the failure of the communication to reach the intended party serves as a defense to solicitation. For example, an email sent but undelivered may or may not constitute solicitation depending on the jurisdiction. In contrast, the Model Penal Code states that failure to communicate the solicitation to the intended party is not a defense. Another difference between the MPC and the common law with respect to solicitation is renunciation. The MPC allows renunciation as a defense while the common law is less definitive on whether such a defense exists.

Ohio does not have a general solicitation statute. However, a defendant may be charged with complicity (accomplice liability) if the underlying crime is committed with encouragement from the defendant. In addition, as noted in the previous chapter, solicitation can fulfill the substantial step requirement necessary for attempt.

While Ohio does not have a general solicitation statute, it, like many states, has a law forbidding individuals from soliciting others to engage in sexual activity for hire. The first case in this chapter, *State v. Short*, illustrates how broadly some courts have interpreted the term 'solicit.'

Finally, since solicitation generally involves communication either written or oral, some defendants may raise the First Amendment as a potential defense. *United States v. White* examines how the court addresses the crime of solicitation in the context of the First Amendment.

1. Solicit Another

State v. Short, 2017 WL 3446990

OPINION

FROELICH, J.

Kenneth Short appeals from his conviction after a bench trial in the Dayton Municipal Court for soliciting, in violation of R.C. 2907.24(A)(1), a misdemeanor of the third degree. Short was sentenced to ten days in jail, all of which were suspended. He was also sentenced to one year of community control with the requirements that he complete HIV testing and "Johns' School" and that he forfeit his seized cash totaling $130.

Short appeals from his conviction, claiming that his conviction for soliciting was based on insufficient evidence. For the following reasons, the trial court's judgment will be affirmed.

I. RECORD ON APPEAL

On October 7, 2015, Short was tried to the court on orally-stipulated facts. Upon review of the record, we find it necessary to detail what the parties represented to the trial court and what is now properly before us for consideration.

At the beginning of trial, the prosecutor indicated, and defense counsel agreed, that the evidence would be a joint stipulation as to what Detective Melanie Phelps-Powers's testimony would have been, as well as two joint exhibits: the police report and a printout of the text messages between Short and the detective. After that representation to the trial court, the prosecutor outlined the following facts.

On March 18, 2015, the RANGE Task Force was conducting an undercover prostitution sting operation at the Marriott Hotel in Dayton. The day before, Detective Phelps-Powers had placed an advertisement on the Backpage website in the "sex for money" section of the website. During the morning of March 18, Phelps-Powers began to receive text messages from multiple individuals. One of those individuals was Short, who texted the undercover detective at 10:09 a.m. The pertinent conversation between Short and Phelps-Powers read:

> Short: Hi sexy
> Detective: Mornin
> Short: Free today?
> Detective: How long
> Short: I tell me[.] U tell me
> Detective: What r u wantin

> Short: Bj [blow job]? Hot hand job? Hot sex?
> Detective: Hr 125, half 80
> Short: Ok . . . where

Detective Phelps-Powers told Short to come to the Marriott, and the two texted each other photographs to identify themselves. Short repeatedly asked the detective to send a picture of her breasts so that he would know that she was "not a cop;" the detective texted a photo of bare breasts, but the photo did not include a face.

Short went to the Marriott and met Phelps-Powers in the lobby. The two recognized each other from previous contacts, but were initially unable to recall from where. They figured out that Short used to be a regular customer at a restaurant at which Phelps-Powers had worked. As they walked down the hallway, Short told Phelps-Powers that "he doesn't do this" and that her "secret was safe with him."

The two went to the hotel room where, unbeknownst to Short, the sting was going to occur. When Phelps-Powers opened the door, other undercover detectives were (mistakenly) in the room. Short saw the detectives, became scared, and fled, but he was apprehended after getting in his vehicle and trying to leave. Short was brought back to the hotel room and identified. When Short was apprehended, he had $130 and a condom in his possession. Short was charged with soliciting.

The police report included narrative discussions and property inventories regarding Phelps-Powers's interactions with Short, as well as two other individuals who were arrested as a result of the sting operation. (At trial, the parties did not discuss the factual circumstances regarding the other individuals.) Defense counsel questioned the prosecutor's mentioning of the condom, indicated that she (defense counsel) was stipulating to "whatever is stated in the police report and whatever is stated in the text messages." After reviewing the police report, the parties and the trial court agreed that a condom belonging to Short was listed in the property inventory portion of the police report.

The trial court then asked defense counsel, "[Defense counsel,] everything that [the prosecutor] has just read into the record stipulation you agree to that, correct?" Defense counsel responded, "Yes[,] Your Honor." The court also asked defense counsel if there was anything that she would like to add. Defense counsel responded, "No[,] I believe that is the total content of what we had decided to stipulate to." The parties and the court then established a timetable for post-trial briefing. No Crim. R. 29 motion was made.

In Short's post-trial memorandum, filed on November 6, 2015, Short argued that the State failed to prove that he had made an offer to have sex for hire. He argued that his actions were, at most, an acceptance of an offer made by the undercover officer. He emphasized that he never mentioned money to the undercover officer and never inquired as to whether the sexual activity would be for money or how much.

Short's post-trial memorandum stated, in a footnote, that the "sex for money" description of the Backpage website was not included in the police report and that the defense had stipulated only to the contents of the police report and text messages between Short and the detective. Short further indicated that, "[o]ff the record the State agreed that description would not be included for purposes of arguing the issues." (Short included the same footnote in his appellate brief.) The parties did not file a joint motion or other document with the trial court, seeking to modify the stipulations that had been made at trial.

The statement of facts in the State's post-trial memorandum (and its appellate brief) indicated that Phelps-Powers had placed an ad on Backpage; it did not mention the section of the website in which the ad was placed. Although this perhaps demonstrated implicit agreement with footnote 1 of Short's post-trial memorandum, the State did not mention any agreement with Short to modify the stipulated facts.

As to the sufficiency of the evidence against Short, the State argued to the trial court: "In response to the detective's open ended inquiry, the Defendant stated the specific sexual services that he was interested in receiving. The Defendant consummated his offer when he readily agreed to the price(s) quoted, and subsequently made contact with the detective at the predetermined time and location."

Both Short and the State relied on *State v. West*, 2d Dist. Montgomery No. 22966, 2009-Ohio-6270, to support their arguments regarding the sufficiency of the evidence.

The trial court found Short guilty of soliciting, in violation of R.C. 2907.24(A). It concluded that Short had committed the "actus reas of the offense," i.e., that he made an offer to have sex for hire and that the State had proven every element of soliciting beyond a reasonable doubt. The trial court's written verdict did not include a statement of facts, and it is unclear whether the court considered the fact that the ad was placed in a "sex for money" section of the Backpage website.

Upon our review of the record, Short stipulated at trial that Detective Phelps-Powers placed an advertisement in the "sex for money" section of Backpage. The prosecutor indicated, and defense counsel agreed, that the stipulation would include "what [the prosecutor] had expected the evidence to present here today from the State's witness[,] which would have been Detective Phelps-Powers," and the two exhibits. Defense counsel never objected at trial to the reference to the "sex for money" portion of Backpage, and she agreed with the prosecutor's statement of the facts.***

III. DEFENDANT'S CONVICTION FOR SOLICITING

R.C. 2907.24(A)(1) provides that "[n]o person shall solicit another who is eighteen years of age or older to engage with such other person in sexual activity for hire."[2] "Sexual activity for hire" means "an implicit or explicit agreement to provide sexual activity in exchange for anything of value paid to the person engaging in such sexual activity, to any person trafficking that person, or to any person associated with either such person." R.C. 2907.24(E)(2).

To establish a violation of R.C. 2907.24(A)(1), the State must prove (1) the accused's solicitation of another, (2) to engage in sexual activity, (3) for hire. *West*, 2d Dist. Montgomery No. 22966, 2009-Ohio-6270, at ¶ 18. "Solicitation requires the accused to have solicited, rather than agreed, to engage in sexual activity for hire." *State v. Bennett*, 1st Dist. Hamilton Nos. C-140507, C-140508, 2015-Ohio-3246, ¶ 9, citing *State v. Swann*, 142 Ohio App. 3d 88, 90, 753 N.E.2d 984 (1st Dist. 2001). "Solicit" is generally defined as "to entice, urge, lure or ask." *E.g., State v. Eslich*, 5th Dist. Stark No. 2014CA67, 2014-Ohio-4640, ¶ 15; *State v. Renner*, 12th Dist. Clermont No. CA2010-06-042, 2011-Ohio-539, ¶ 10; *Swann* at 89.

Short claims that he did not "solicit" Detective Phelps-Powers to engage in sexual activity for hire. He relies upon *Swann*, *West*, and *State v. Howard*, 7 Ohio Misc. 2d 45, 455 N.E.2d 29 (M.C. 1983), to support his argument that he did not make an offer to the undercover detective. We have previously summarized *Swann* and *Howard*, as follows:

> *** In *Swann*, a Cincinnati police officer was patrolling for evidence of prostitution. A second officer was hidden in the trunk of the unmarked car. Upon seeing Swann walking down the street, the officer pulled to the curb and engaged Swann in conversation. The officer then invited Swann into his car, where their discussion initially was not of a sexual nature. The officer then offered Swann crack or money for oral sex, and they finally agreed on a price of $15.00. At that point, the second officer in the trunk emerged and arrested Swann.
>
> The First District determined that "Swann did not 'entice, urge, lure or ask' the officer for anything. She simply agreed to his suggestion." In reversing the trial court's judgment and discharging Swann from further prosecution, the First District relied upon *State v. Howard* (1983), 7 Ohio Misc. 2d 45, 455 N.E.2d 29. In *Howard*, an undercover policeman approached Howard near the curb and asked him if he was "dating." Howard asked if the officer had any money, and the officer indicated he did, and he asked Howard what he would "do." Howard responded that he would "do" anything. The officer asked him if

he would perform oral sex, and after Howard agreed and got into the car, he was arrested.

The court determined, "the defendant in this case did not entice, urge, lure or ask for money in return for sexual performance. What defendant did was agree to what the officer had suggested and as such he cannot be found guilty of soliciting, an offense unlike some other offenses where entrapment is raised, where the crime is in the asking."

State v. Key, 2d Dist. Montgomery No. 22609, 2009–Ohio–422, ¶ 12–14. The Tenth District discussed *Swann* and *Howard*, stating:

> In determining that the defendants in *Swann* and *Howard* were not guilty of soliciting, the courts stated that, in a soliciting case, the crime is in the asking. However, these courts did not limit soliciting cases to situations where a defendant explicitly asks for sexual activity for hire, as appellant suggests. Instead, the courts in *Swann* and *Howard* recognized that soliciting may also involve a defendant enticing, urging or luring another to engage in sex for hire. Likewise, the courts in *Swann* and *Howard* did not exonerate the defendants on the basis that the undercover law enforcement officers, and not the defendants, suggested the particular sexual activity and price. Rather, these courts concluded that the defendants were not guilty of soliciting because they merely agreed to the law enforcement officers' advances and did nothing more that rose to the level of enticing, urging, luring or asking the officers to engage in sex for hire.

Columbus v. Myles, 10th Dist. Franklin No. 04AP-1255, 2005-Ohio-3933, ¶ 22-24. In *West*, 2d Dist. Montgomery No. 22966, 2009-Ohio-6270, a case from this appellate district, a Vice Crime Unit detective drove to a busy intersection where West was speaking with the drivers of vehicles that had stopped. When the undercover detective approached the intersection, West made a hitchhiking signal, the detective stopped, and West got into his car. After they exchanged first names, the detective told West that he was "just killing time," and West asked the detective if he would like "a great blow job." The detective responded, "sure," and asked what she needed for that. West did not reply, but rubbed the detective's penis on the outside of his pants. As they drove away, the detective again asked "what she needed." West replied that she wanted a new pair of shoes that cost $24, but she would settle for $20. The detective drove to a bank where an ATM was located. Once there, West was arrested by another officer who had observed and followed them.

In affirming West's conviction for soliciting, we rejected the contention that a person accused of soliciting must not only offer to engage in sexual activity for hire, but must also have "initiated an offer that was complete in those terms." *West* at ¶ 21. We stated: "The conduct that R.C. 2907.24 prohibits is the offer. Whether it is done in the form of an initial offer, a counter offer, or in response to an open inquiry, is immaterial. *** West's request to be paid $20 demonstrates that her offer to engage in sexual activity was to do so 'for hire.' " *Id.* at ¶ 22.

We find the situation before us to be more similar to *Bennett*, 1st Dist. Hamilton Nos. C-140507, C-140508, 2015-Ohio-3246. There, the defendant drove up to an undercover officer, who was standing on the sidewalk, and asked if she was "working." The defendant stated that he was looking for a "regular," and indicated that he was interested in engaging in sexual activities with the officer. The defendant asked the officer what she charged and stated that he was not expecting any "freebies." The officer provided a price to which defendant agreed. In affirming the conviction for soliciting, the First District stated, "The fact that the officer was the first one to state a dollar amount does not negate Bennett's role in the exchange." *Id.* at ¶ 11.

Here, it was Phelps-Powers, not Short, who indicated the dollar amount for their encounter, but we cannot reasonably characterize Short's conduct as merely acquiescing in the detective's advances. Detective Phelps-Powers placed an advertisement in the "sex for money" section of the Backpage website as part of an undercover sting operation. Although the specific content of that ad is not in the record, there is nothing in the record to indicate that the advertisement itself was an offer of sexual activity for hire, and the police report reflects that, in response to the Backpage ad, the detective received multiple texts from men.

At 10:09 a.m., Short initiated contact with the undercover detective concerning sexual activity. In Short's text messages to the undercover detective, he asked if she were available that day. When the detective asked "how long," Short had responded, "U tell me." Short suggested specific sexual activity in which they could engage. After the officer texted back her hourly and half-hour rate, Short agreed to the price and asked where they would meet; he met with the undercover detective at the agreed-upon hotel. Short had sought assurances from Phelps-Powers that she was not a police officer.

Construing the evidence in the light most favorable to the State, we conclude that there was sufficient evidence that Short solicited the undercover detective to engage for hire. In response to an advertisement in a "sex for money" section of a website, Short contacted Phelps-Powers and identified specific sexual acts that he wanted from the undercover detective. Although the detective named the specific cost for those (sex) acts, there was sufficient evidence that Short was aware when he contacted Phelps-Powers that monetary payment was expected (for hire). The State presented sufficient evidence that Short committed soliciting.

Even if we were to accept the parties' proposed modification to the trial stipulations and to disregard that fact that the advertisement was placed in the "sex for money" section of Backpage, we would still conclude that the State presented sufficient evidence of soliciting. Although Short did not explicitly ask the detective to engage in sex in exchange for money and the detective suggested the price, the evidence supports a conclusion that Short engaged in "enticing, urging, and luring" conduct regarding sexual activity for hire.

Short's assignment of error is overruled.

IV. CONCLUSION

The trial court's judgment will be affirmed.

HALL, P.J. and WELBAUM, J., concur.

Notes and Questions

1. Can you pinpoint exactly where the solicitation occurred in *State v. Short*? Did the defendant solicit merely by going on Backpage.com or was it when he started to discuss specific sexual activity?

2. What did the *Short* court mean when it cited the following language: "The conduct that R.C. 2907.24 prohibits is the offer. Whether it is done in the form of an initial offer, a counter offer, or in response to an open inquiry, is immaterial." Does this statement mean that solicitation can occur by agreeing with another party? Is that what occurred in this case?

2. First Amendment

United States v. White, 610 F. 3d 956 (7th Cir. 2010)

Before POSNER, FLAUM, and WILLIAMS, Circuit Judges.
PER CURIAM.

A superseding indictment alleged that William White was the founder and content provider of a website that posted personal information about a juror who served on the Matthew Hale jury, along with postings calling for the use of violence on enemies of white supremacy. In connection with these postings, White was charged with soliciting a crime of violence in violation of 18 U.S.C. § 373. The district court dismissed the indictment, holding that White's internet posting could not give rise to a violation under § 373 because it was protected by the First Amendment. Because we find that the indictment is legally sufficient to state an offense, we reverse the district court's dismissal.

I. BACKGROUND

According to the government's indictment, William White created and maintained the website Overthrow.com. Overthrow.com was affiliated with the "American National Socialist Workers Party," an organization comprised of white supremacists who "fight for white working people" and were "disgusted with the general garbage" that the white supremacist movement had attracted. White used the website to popularize his views concerning "non-whites, Jews, homosexuals, and persons perceived by white supremacists as acting contrary to the interests of the white race." On multiple occasions, White advocated that violence be perpetrated on the "enemies" of white supremacy and praised attacks on such enemies.

A repeated topic on his website was Matthew Hale, the leader of a white supremacist organization known as the World Church of the Creator. In January 2003, Hale was charged with soliciting the murder of a federal district court judge and obstruction of justice. Hale was convicted of two counts of obstruction of justice and one count of solicitation and sentenced to 480 months' imprisonment. Specifically related to the Matthew Hale trial, White wrote on his website in March 2005 that "everyone associated with the Matt Hale trial has deserved assassination for a long time." He also wrote a posting naming individuals involved or related in some way to Hale's conviction, such as federal agents and prosecutors and other citizens advocating for Hale's arrest, stating that any of them may be the next targets of an "unknown nationalist assassin." White did not publish their personal information in that post because he felt "there is so great a potential for action."

On September 11, 2008, White posted personal information about the foreperson of the jury in the Hale trial ("Juror A"). At the time of the posting, Overthrow.com was an active website, and as such, each link and posting was contemporaneously accessible. So, a reader of this September 11 posting would have had access to the past posts about Hale, Hale's trial, and other calls for violence against "anti-racists." The September 11 entry by White was entitled "The Juror Who Convicted Matt Hale." It identified Juror A by name, featured a color photograph of Juror A and stated the following:

> Gay anti-racist [Juror A] was a juror who played a key role in convicting Matt Hale. Born [date], [he/she] lives at [address] with [his/her] gay black lover and [his/her] cat [name]. [His/Her] phone number is [phone number], cell phone [phone number], and [his/her] office is [phone number].

On the following day, White posted a follow-up entry entitled "[Juror A] Update—Since They Blocked the first photo." This posting contained all the same information as above, with the added sentence, "Note that [University A] blocked much of [Juror A's] information after we linked to [his/her] photograph."

On October 21, 2008, a federal grand jury returned a one-count indictment charging White with soliciting a crime of violence against Juror A, in violation of 18 U.S.C. § 373. On February 10, 2009, the grand jury returned a superseding indictment, maintaining the single charge of solicitation and adding additional examples of the circumstances corroborating the defendant's intent to solicit a crime of violence against Juror A. The superseding indictment charged that:

> 2. From on or about September 11, 2008, through at least on or about October 11, 2008, in the Northern District of Illinois, Eastern Division, and elsewhere, WILLIAM WHITE, defendant herein, with intent that another person engage in conduct constituting a felony that has as an element the use, attempted use, or threatened use of force against the person of Juror A, in violation of the laws of the United States, and under circumstances strongly corroborative of that intent, solicited and otherwise endeavored to persuade such other person to engage in such conduct; in that defendant solicited and otherwise endeavored to persuade another person to injure Juror A on account of a verdict assented to by Juror A, in violation of Title 18, United States Code Section 1503.

> 3. It was part of the solicitation, inducement, and endeavor to persuade that on or about September 11, 2008, defendant WILLIAM WHITE caused to be displayed on the front page of "Overthrow.com" a posting entitled, "The Juror Who Convicted Matt Hale."

. . .

> 5. The above-described solicitation, inducement, and endeavor to persuade occurred under the following circumstances, among others, strongly corroborative of defendant WILLIAM WHITE's intent that another person engage in conduct constituting a felony that has as an element the use, attempted use, or threatened use of force against the person of Juror A. . . .

White moved to dismiss the superseding indictment on the grounds that it violated the First Amendment, and on July 22, 2009, the district court granted White's motion to dismiss. The government timely appealed.

II. ANALYSIS

A. Indictment Valid on Its Face

The government argues on appeal that the superseding indictment is legally sufficient to charge the offense of solicitation. We review questions of law in a district court's ruling on a motion to dismiss an indictment de novo. *United States v. Greve,* 490 F.3d 566, 570 (7th Cir. 2007). An indictment is legally sufficient if it (1) states all the elements of the crime charged; (2) adequately informs the defendant of the nature of the charges so that he may prepare a defense; and (3) allows the defendant to plead the judgment as a bar to any future prosecutions. *See* Fed. R. Crim. P. 7(c)(1); *United States v. Smith,* 230 F.3d 300, 305 (7th Cir.2000). An indictment is reviewed on its face, regardless of the strength or weakness of the government's case. *Risk,* 843 F.2d at 1061. One that "tracks" the words of a statute to state the elements of the crime is generally acceptable, and while there must be enough factual particulars so the defendant is aware of the specific conduct at issue, the presence or absence of any particular fact is not dispositive. *Smith,* 230 F.3d at 305.

Applying these standards, the indictment here is legally sufficient. Title 18 of the United States Code, section 373(a) provides, in pertinent part:

> Whoever, with intent that another person engage in conduct constituting a felony that has as an element the use, attempted use, or threatened use of physical force against property or against the person of another in violation of the laws of the United States, and under circumstances strongly corroborative of that intent, solicits, commands, induces, or otherwise endeavors to persuade such other person to engage in such conduct.

In a solicitation prosecution, the government must establish (1) with strongly corroborative circumstances that a defendant intended for another person to commit a violent federal crime, and (2) that a defendant solicited or otherwise endeavored to persuade the other person to carry out the crime. 18 U.S.C. § 373(a); *see United States v. Hale,* 448 F.3d 971 (7th Cir.2006). A list of non-exhaustive corroborating circumstances of the defendant's intent include whether the defendant repeatedly solicited the commission of the offense, the defendant's belief as to whether the person solicited had previously committed similar offenses, and whether the defendant acquired the tools or information suited for use by the person solicited. *United States v. Gabriel,* 810 F.2d 627, 635 (7th Cir. 1987) (citing S. REP. NO. 97-307, at 183 (1982)).

The indictment here tracks the language of the statute, and lists each element of the crime. It charges White with having the intent for another person to injure Juror A, and soliciting another person to do so. It provides corroborating circumstances of White's intent. As one example of his intent, the government points to the re-posting of the information once action was taken by Juror A's employer to remove his picture from public access. As another, the government argues that White knew the persons solicited were prone to violence. The indictment properly charges a federal solicitation because injuring a juror for rendering a verdict is a federal offense under 18 U.S.C. § 1503. Finally, by adding factual allegations and dates, it makes White aware of the specific conduct against which he will have to defend himself at trial. In judging the sufficiency of this indictment, we do not consider whether any of the charges have been established by evidence or whether the government can ultimately prove its case. *United States v. Sampson,* 371 U.S. 75, 78-79, (1962). We only look to see if an offense is sufficiently charged, and on its face, this indictment adequately performs that function.

B. No First Amendment Violation

Having found that the face of the indictment is legally sufficient to charge White with solicitation, our inquiry would ordinarily end. But the district court held that the indictment's allegations could not support a prosecution under 18 U.S.C. § 373 because White's internet posting was speech protected by the First Amendment. As detailed below, this potential First Amendment concern is addressed by the requirement of proof beyond a reasonable doubt at trial, not by a dismissal at the indictment stage.

The First Amendment removes from the government any power "to restrict expression because of its message, its ideas, its subject matter, or its content." *Ashcroft v. ACLU,* 535 U.S. 564, 573, (2002) (quotation marks omitted). Even speech that a "vast majority of its citizens believe to be false and fraught with evil consequence[s]" cannot be punished. *Whitney v. California,* 274 U.S. 357, 374, (1927). This broad protection ensures that the right of the Nazi party to march in front of a town hall is protected, *Collin v. Smith,* 578 F.2d 1197, 1202 (7th Cir. 1978), as is the right of an individual to express an unpopular view against the government, *Texas v. Johnson,* 491 U.S. 397, 419-20, (1989) (holding that the First Amendment protects the expressive act of flag burning). In *Brandenburg v. Ohio,* the Supreme Court invalidated a state statute targeting people who "advocate or teach the duty, necessity, or propriety" of violence as a means of accomplishing reform, and held that even certain statements advocating violence had social value and received First Amendment protection. 395 U.S. 444, (1969). At issue were Ku Klux Klan members' statements such as, "we're not a revengent organization, but if our President . . . continues to suppress the white, Caucasian race, it's possible that there might have to be some revengeance taken." *Id.* at 446, 89 S. Ct. 1827. The Supreme Court held that "the constitutional guarantees of free speech and free press do not permit a State to forbid or proscribe advocacy of the use of force . . . except where such advocacy is directed to inciting or producing imminent lawless action and is likely to incite or produce such action." *Id.* at 447, 89 S. Ct. 1827. Speech related to the expression and advocacy of unpopular, and even violent ideas, receives *Brandenburg* protection.

Although First Amendment speech protections are far-reaching, there are limits. Speech integral to criminal conduct, such as fighting words, threats, and solicitations, remain categorically outside its protection. *United States v. Williams,* 553 U.S. 285, (2008) ("Offers to engage in illegal transactions are categorically excluded from First Amendment protection."). This type of speech "brigaded with action" becomes an overt act or conduct that can be regulated. *Brandenburg,* 395 U.S. at 456, (Black, J., concurring). For this reason, a state cannot forbid individuals from burning crosses to express an opinion, but it can forbid individuals from burning crosses with the intent to intimidate others. *See Virginia v. Black,* 538 U.S. 343, (2003). In the case of a criminal solicitation, the speech—asking another to commit a crime—is the punishable act. Solicitation is an inchoate crime; the crime is complete once the words are spoken with the requisite intent, and no further actions from either the solicitor or the solicitee are necessary. *See* Wayne R. LaFave, *2 Substantive Criminal Law* § 11.1 (2d ed. 2009). Also, a specific person-to-person request is not required. *United States v. Rahman,* 189 F.3d 88, 117-18 (2d Cir.1999).

For example, in *United States v. Sattar,* a district court, without requiring any evidence or allegations of further acts, found sufficient an indictment where the alleged solicitation consisted of a generally issued fatwa urging Muslims to "fight the Jews and to kill them wherever they are." 272 F. Supp. 2d 348, 373-74 (S.D.N.Y.2003). In *United States v. Rahman,* Rahman was convicted of soliciting violence based on his public speeches calling for an attack on military installations and the murder of an Egyptian president. 189 F.3d at 117. Furthermore, that a request for criminal action is coded or implicit does not change its characterization as a solicitation. In *United States v. Hale,* this court held sufficient evidence existed to uphold a solicitation conviction where Hale never explicitly asked his chief enforcer to do anything. He simply asked his chief enforcer to locate a judge's home address and made statements such as "that information's been pro-, provided. If you wish to, ah, do anything yourself, you can, you know?" 448 F.3d 971, 979 (7th Cir. 2006). Hale's multiple attempts to distance himself from any illegal actions with statements such as "I'm gonna fight within the law" and "I can't take any steps to further anything illegal," were not enough to overturn the solicitation conviction. *Id.* We held that a rational jury could have inferred his true intention from the evidence, regardless of any coded or disguised language. *Id.* at 984-85.

So, whether or not the First Amendment protects White's right to post personal information about Juror A first turns on his intent in posting that information. If White's intent in posting Juror A's personal information was to request that one of his readers harm Juror A, then the crime of solicitation would be complete. No act needed to follow, and no harm needed to befall Juror A. If, on the other hand, White's intent was to make a political point about sexual orientation or to facilitate opportunities for other people to make such views known to Juror A, then he would not be guilty of solicitation because he did not have the requisite intent required for the crime.

White argues that *NAACP v. Claiborne Hardware Co.,* 458 U.S. 886, (1982), stands for the proposition that the only permissible view of his posting is to see it as a constitutionally protected expression and subject to the *Brandenburg* test. In *Claiborne,* black citizens of Claiborne County, Mississippi, sent a letter to white merchants with a list of particularized demands for racial equality and integration. After receiving an unsatisfactory response, they began a boycott that lasted years. Several of the white merchants sued members of the boycott to recover losses and enjoin further boycott activity, and won. The Mississippi Supreme Court upheld liability as to 92 participants by finding that members had agreed to use force, violence and threats to ensure compliance with the boycott, but the Supreme Court reversed, holding that an individual could not be held liable for his mere association with an organization whose members engage in illegal acts. *Id.* at 920, 102 S. Ct. 3409. *Claiborne* primarily focused on the constitutionality of group-based liability, but it also concluded that Charles Evers, the field secretary of the NAACP and chief proponent of the boycott at the time, could not be held liable based on his "emotionally charged rhetoric." *Id.* at 928, 102 S. Ct. 3409. In speeches given before and during the boycott, Evers stated that there would be "discipline" coming to those who did not participate in the boycott, and that any "uncle toms" would "have their necks broken." *Id.* at 900 n.28, 102 S. Ct. 3409.

White reads too much into *Claiborne.* A careful reading of the Court's analysis of Evers's liability does not provide the support White believes it does. Given that the speeches were mainly an "impassioned plea" for unity, support, and nonviolent participation in the boycott, and the few choice phrases were the only example of threatening language, the Court found there was no evidence that Evers authorized violence or threatened anyone. In this context, the speeches did not exceed the bounds of *Brandenburg*-protected advocacy and could not be the basis of liability. But, the Supreme Court acknowledged that there would be no constitutional problem with imposing liability for losses caused by violence and threats of violence, *id.* at 916, 102 S. Ct. 3409, and that if there was evidence of such "wrongful conduct" the speeches could be used to corroborate that evidence, *id.* at 929, 102 S. Ct. 3409.

White's argument boils down to this: his posting was not a solicitation and because it is not a solicitation, it is speech deserving of First Amendment protection. The government sees the posting in the opposite light: the posting and website constitute a solicitation and as such, fall outside the parameters of First Amendment protection. This dispute turns out not to be an argument about the validity of the indictment in light of the First Amendment, but is instead a dispute over the meaning and inferences that can be drawn from the facts. The government informed us at oral argument that it has further evidence of the website's readership, audience, and the relationship between White and his followers which will show the posting was a specific request to White's followers, who understood that request and were capable and willing to act on it. This evidence is not laid out in the indictment and does not need to be. *Sampson,* 371 U.S. at 78-79. The existence of strongly corroborating circumstances evincing White's intent is a jury question. *Hale,* 448 F.3d at 983. Of course, the First Amendment may still have a role to play at trial. Based on the full factual record, the court may decide to instruct the jury on the distinction between solicitation and advocacy, and the legal requirements imposed by the First Amendment. *See, e.g., United States v. Freeman,* 761 F.2d 549, 552 (9th Cir.1985). The government has the burden to prove, beyond a reasonable doubt, that White intended, through his posting of Juror A's personal information, to request someone else to harm Juror A. After the prosecution presents its case, the court may decide that a reasonable juror could not conclude that White's intent was for harm to befall Juror A, and not merely electronic or verbal harassment. But, this is not a question to be decided now. We have no idea what evidence or testimony will be produced at trial. The government has laid out the elements of the crime and the statute that White is accused of violating, along with some specific factual allegations for support, and that is all it is required to do. The question of White's intent and the inferences that can be drawn from the facts are for a jury to decide, as the indictment is adequate to charge the crime of solicitation. The indictment is legally sufficient and should not have been dismissed.

III. CONCLUSION

We REVERSE and REMAND for further proceedings consistent with this opinion.

Notes and Questions

1. What exactly did the defendant in *United States v. White* do that was illegal at least according to the government?

2. Suppose you have a client, a noted firebrand for a local organization, that comes to you for advice. The client plans on giving a speech to members of her organization and hopes to motivate them to action. However, she does not want to violate the law. What advice would you give her? Can you provide her a clear distinction between solicitation and advocacy?

3. Model Penal Code

Section 5.02. Criminal Solicitation

(1) <u>Definition of Solicitation</u>. A person is guilty of solicitation to commit a crime if with the purpose of promoting or facilitating its commission he commands, encourages or requests another person to engage in specific conduct which would constitute such crime or an attempt to commit such crime or which would establish his complicity in its commission or attempted commission.

(2) <u>Uncommunicated Solicitation</u>. It is immaterial under Subsection (1) of this Section that the actor fails to communicate with the person he solicits to commit a crime if his conduct was designed to effect such communication.

(3) <u>Renunciation of Criminal Purpose</u>. It is an affirmative defense that the actor, after soliciting another person to commit a crime, persuaded him not to do so or otherwise prevented the commission of the crime, under circumstances manifesting a complete and voluntary renunciation of his criminal purpose.

4. As stated previously, the MPC, unlike the common law, allows for renunciation. What policy arguments exist for and against allowing this defense to solicitation?

5. If the person solicited agrees to carry out the crime in question does that create an additional crime? Potentially, both the solicitor and the person solicited may be liable for conspiracy, which will be discussed in greater detail in the next chapter. It should be noted that solicitation merges into the crime of conspiracy.

Chapter 18
Conspiracy

A. Background

At common law, conspiracy, a specific intent crime, consisted of an agreement between two or more persons to accomplish some criminal or unlawful act. At least two co-conspirators had to have so-called "guilty minds" (i.e., an intent to commit the object of the conspiracy). The conspiracy was completed once the two guilty minds reached an agreement. Also, at common law, defendants could be charged with the subsequent crimes of their co-conspirators, pursuant to *Pinkerton* liability, even if they did not participate in those crimes so long as the acts were in furtherance of the conspiracy.

The Model Penal Code has dramatically modified common law conspiracy. The MPC relies on unilateral, rather than bilateral, conspiracy. Thus, to be prosecuted for conspiracy under the MPC, the defendant's co-conspirator need not have a guilty mind or an intent to carry out the conspiracy, e.g., the defendant can conspire with an undercover police officer. The MPC, unlike the common law, also requires an overt act by the defendant in order to prove conspiracy for certain crimes.

As for potential defenses, there were few available at common law for conspiracy. When a defendant withdrew from a conspiracy at common law, he was withdrawing from subsequent crimes by co-conspirators. There was no withdrawal from the crime of conspiracy itself once the conspiracy elements were met. In contrast, the MPC allows the defendant to both withdraw and abandon the conspiracy under certain conditions.

Finally, some jurisdictions like Ohio merge conspiracy into the underlying crime (e.g., conspiracy to commit robbery and robbery result in a sentence for only robbery if the defendant is convicted of both crimes). The MPC also merges conspiracy with the underlying offense unless the prosecution proves that the conspiracy involved additional offenses not yet committed or attempted.

In contrast, at common law, both the conspiracy and the underlying object of the conspiracy were separate crimes (e.g., the defendant could be convicted for both conspiring to commit robbery and the actual robbery itself).

The first case in this chapter, *State v. Marian*, looks at whether Ohio should adopt the unilateral or bilateral approach to conspiracy. The second case, *State v. Baugh*, examines two specific features of conspiracy-overt act and withdrawal. The third case, *Pinkerton v. United States*, addresses co-conspirator liability. The fourth case, *Iannelli v. United States*, explores Wharton's Rule.

B. Unilateral vs. Bilateral

State v. Marian, 62 Ohio St. 2d 250 (1980)

***On December 3, 1977, Joseph Marian was arrested and charged with the crime of conspiracy to commit aggravated murder in violation of R.C. 2923.01(A)(1). An indictment was returned on the charges on January 26, 1978, and Marian was arraigned on February 3.

Marian filed a number of motions on April 14, 1978, including a motion to dismiss the indictment. On August 8, 1978, Marian filed a waiver of his right to speedy trial.

The indictment charges Marian with planning the murder of his wife, Patricia, with another, John Protain. It charges that in supplying Protain with a gun and with $500, Marian had committed a substantial overt act in furtherance of the conspiracy.

The parties stipulated, for purposes of the motion to dismiss the indictment, that immediately upon being informed of the plan, Protain determined that he would not commit the offense and feigned participation, and that Protain notified law enforcement authorities of his entire relationship with Marian at the first opportunity, which was prior to the alleged performance of any overt act set forth in the indictment. It was further stipulated that Protain proceeded to act in accordance with instructions from law enforcement authorities.

Following a hearing, the Court of Common Pleas of Mahoning County sustained Marian's motion and dismissed the indictment. That court held that R.C. 2923.01(A)(1) and (B), in defining the conspiracy offense, required that there be a "planning" between at least two people regarding the achievement of an unlawful objective and the commission of a substantial overt act toward its completion. Under the facts that are stipulated, Protain never intended to participate prior to the commitment of a substantial overt act.

The Court of Appeals reversed the trial court, holding that the provisions of R.C. 2923.01 prohibited situations where one person believes he is agreeing with another to achieve an unlawful purpose even though that other person does not intend to achieve that objective. The court also held that the facts alleged in the indictment constituted substantial overt acts, in furtherance of the conspiracy.

The cause is now before this court pursuant to the allowance of a motion for leave to appeal.***

CELEBREZZE, Chief Justice.

R.C. 2923.01 defines the crime of conspiracy. R.C. 2923.01(A), states, in part:

> No person, with purpose to commit or to promote or facilitate the commission of aggravated murder or murder, kidnapping, compelling prostitution or promoting prostitution, aggravated arson or arson, aggravated robbery or robbery, aggravated burglary or burglary, or a felony offense of unauthorized use of a vehicle, corrupting another with drugs, trafficking in drugs, theft of drugs, or illegal processing of drug documents shall do either of the following:
>
> (1) With another person or persons, plan or aid in planning the commission of any such offense.

R.C. 2923.01(B) states that:

> No person shall be convicted of conspiracy unless a substantial overt act in furtherance of the conspiracy is alleged and proved to have been done by him or a person with whom he conspired, subsequent to the accused's entrance into the conspiracy. For purposes of this section, an overt act is substantial when it is of such character as to manifest a purpose on the part of the actor that the object of the conspiracy should be completed.

Under this statute one who is guilty of conspiring to commit one of the enumerated crimes is generally guilty of a crime to the next lesser degree than the most serious offense which is the object of the conspiracy. A conspiracy to commit murder or aggravated murder is a felony of the first degree.

Traditionally a criminal conspiracy has existed only if there has been a meeting of the minds of two or more people to act together to achieve an unlawful purpose. However, in 1962, the Model Penal Code defined conspiracy to include situations where only one of the participants actually intended to achieve the unlawful purpose. This has been called the "unilateral approach" of conspiracy and it has been adopted in many jurisdictions.

The Model Penal Code very clearly enacted the unilateral approach. In Section 5.03, the code states:

(1) Definition of Conspiracy. A person is guilty of conspiracy with another person or persons to commit a crime if with the purpose of promoting or facilitating its commission he:

(a) agrees with such other person or persons that they or one or more of them will engage in conduct which constitutes such crime or an attempt or solicitation to commit such crime; or

(b) agrees to aid such other person or persons in the planning or commission of such crime or of an attempt or solicitation to commit such crime.

Section 5.04 states, in part:

(1) *** it is immaterial to the liability of a person who solicits or conspires with another to commit a crime that:

(a) he or the person whom he solicits or with whom he conspires does not occupy a particular position or have a particular characteristic which is an element of such crime, if he believes that one of them does; ***.

The language in R.C. 2923.01(A) is similar to that used in Section 5.03, but the statute has no provision equivalent to Section 5.04. It is unclear whether the General Assembly intended to adopt the unilateral approach and as a consequence this issue is before this court.

In *State v. St. Christopher* (1975), 305 Minn. 226, 232 N.W.2d 798, the Minnesota Supreme Court held that an analogous statute, Minn. St. 609.175(2), prohibits unilateral as well as traditional conspiracies. The Minnesota statute states that "(w)hoever conspires with another to commit a crime and in furtherance of the conspiracy *** does some overt act *** " is to be sentenced as a criminal conspirator. Because the legislature had significantly altered the old statute, Minn. St. (1961) 613.70, which had made it a crime for "two or more persons" to conspire, and because the court agreed with the policy behind the unilateral approach, the Minnesota court held that the statute prohibited unilateral conspiracies, even though it had no provision similar to Model Penal Code Section 5.04.

The Ohio General Assembly has also significantly altered its definition of conspiracy. The earlier conspiracy statute, former R.C. 2901.34, which was limited to abduction cases, stated:

"If two or more persons conspire together to commit any offense under sections 2901.26 to 2901.33, inclusive, of the Revised Code, and one or more of such persons do any act to effect the object of such conspiracy, each of the persons who is

a party to such conspiracy shall be imprisoned not less than five
nor more than thirty years.

By changing the statutory language from requiring that two or more persons conspire to requiring that one person plan with another, the General Assembly indicated, in much the same manner as the Minnesota legislature, an intent to include unilateral conspiracies in the conspiracy offense. In addition, the General Assembly did not enact a solicitation provision, apparently recognizing that solicitation offenses encompass dangers similar to those protected against by a unilateral conspiracy provision.

The unilateral approach has been the subject of much criticism. Some have argued that conspiracy, which is basically an inchoate crime, is designed to protect society against the dangers inherent in group criminal conduct. They contend that the unilateral approach makes an attempted inchoate crime criminal, that it punishes what is only an evil state of mind, and as such that it is not properly a part of our criminal justice system. See Marcus, Prosecution and Defense of Criminal Conspiracy Cases, Section 2.04. Despite this criticism, we are persuaded that the prohibition of such unilateral conduct is justified.

It is true that a unilateral conspiracy makes participation in a group, rather than actual group conduct, criminal, and that it is thereby more inchoate than a traditional conspiracy. Further, participation in a group where there is not a meeting of the minds may be less dangerous to society than the actual presence of a group. However, the acts and intent of the unilateral conspirator are dangerous and his conduct is the proper subject of a criminal offense. It must now be determined whether that offense is the same conspiracy offense as the one engaged in by the participant in a more traditional conspiracy.

The acts and intent of the unilateral conspirator are identical to those of the conspirator who is part of a group where an actual meeting of the minds exists. The unilateral conspirator's culpability is the same as the participant in a more traditional conspiracy. This is in contrast to the person guilty of an attempt; he has not acted in the same manner as the man actually guilty of the crime. Consequently, once it is decided that participation in unlawful group conduct is the proper subject of a criminal offense even in the absence of a meeting of the minds, it becomes proper to make such participation a conspiracy even though it may be inchoate in nature. The unilateral approach is properly a part of our criminal justice system.

This is particularly true when the legislature has recognized and dealt with the inchoate nature of unilateral conspiracies. R.C. 2923.01(B) requires that there be a substantial overt act, insuring that purely a state of mind is not punishable. R.C. 2923.01(F) merges the conspiracy offense, due to its inchoate nature, into the substantive offenses which are the object of the conspiracy. In addition, the legislature has not provided a separate provision for the highly inchoate solicitation offense.

We hold that a person is guilty of conspiracy under R.C. 2923.01, when with purpose to commit, promote, or facilitate the commission of one of the offenses listed in R.C. 2923.01(A), he plans the commission of the crime with another and does a substantial overt act in furtherance of the conspiracy, even though the other person feigns agreement and at no time intends to go through with the plan.

The judgment of the Court of Appeals is affirmed.

Notes and Questions

1. In *State v. Marian*, what grounds does the court give for following the unilateral approach? Do you agree with the court's rationale? Should we as a society be more concerned with criminals who act in a group rather than alone?

2. How does the *Marian* court address the two major criticisms of the unilateral approach? In what ways is a unilateral conspiracy different from a solicitation? How does a substantial overt act compare to a substantial step as required in attempt. In *Marian*, would you prosecute the defendant for attempt? Can he be convicted of both attempt and conspiracy?

C. Overt Act and Withdrawal

State v. Baugh, 1978 WL 216550 (Ohio Ct. App. 1978)

It is agreed by appellant as well as by the state that on a certain date in February, 1977, Baugh and the three others mentioned in the indictment planned the aggravated robbery of Wade's Corner Cafe, hereinafter Wade's. Baugh was an adult (age 18); the other three were juveniles. The conspiracy statute requires, *inter alia*, proof of planning the commission of an offense to establish a violation thereof. There can be no doubt that this condition of the statute was satisfied. The four definitely planned the robbery. Further developments in the *scenario* are as explained below.

On arrival at Wade's Corner, the young men parked close to the cafe. They decided to go in, and the appellant and two of the juveniles did enter Wade's. There is evidence that Baugh at that time had a loaded .32 caliber pistol in his possession, and one of the juveniles also entering Wade's carried on his person a loaded .22 caliber pistol. It is uncontroverted that the juvenile had a loaded weapon with him in Wade's. It is equally uncontroverted that Baugh had a loaded weapon in his possession in the automobile before entering Wade's, but the evidence conflicts as to whether he took it into the establishment. The other member of the trio carried a pillow case into Wade's. The evidence tended to show that the purpose for going into Wade's was to rob it. For instance, Gary Worley testified as follows:

> Q. And the three of you were going to go into Wade's Corner?
> A. (Worley). Yeah.
> Q. What was your purpose at this point in going in?
> A. *We were going to rob it.*
> (T.p. 40. Emphasis supplied.)

As completely conceded by appellant in his brief, the testimony of one of the other boys, Jeff Niehaus, also demonstrates that the robbery plan was still viable *at the time the boys entered the cafe*. (Brief, p. 6.) We look to appellant's brief for a narration of what then transpired:

On entering the cafe the boys asked the location of the men's restroom and proceeded to such location, in the basement of the establishment. After a brief period Worley and Cain returned from the restroom and seated themselves in a section of the cafe operated as a tavern. Appellant, Ricky Baugh, left the men's restroom after the other two boys, and entered a portion of Wade's Corner that is operated as a delicatessen. Worley and Cain remained for a few minutes in the tavern and then left the premises. While in the tavern they did not display any weapons or talk to anyone. Ricky Baugh remained in the delicatessen portion of the cafe for approximately 10 minutes before leaving. He did not display a weapon, and with the exception of buying a Coca Cola, he did not converse with anyone in the delicatessen.

The three boys were in the cafe for a period covering approximately 15 minutes. During the time they were in the cafe they either wore, or had in their possession, knit toboggan caps; however, at no time did any of the boys make any attempt to cover or obscure their faces.

While the appellant and the other two boys were in Wade's Corner the police were called. Apparently, the officers responded after Greg Cain and Gary Worley had left the premises but while Ricky Baugh was still inside. It does not appear that Ricky Baugh, or the others, were aware of their presence. Baugh first encountered a police officer when he left the cafe. At such time he was approached by Officer Glen Taylor. Officer Taylor conducted a "pat-down" search of appellant. Said search did not disclose a weapon. Officer Taylor talked with the appellant for approximately 10 minutes before leaving to respond to an "officer needs assistance" call. When Officer Taylor did not find a policeman requiring assistance at the designated location, a radio broadcast was issued to stop the automobile in which the appellant was believed to be riding. The automobile, which contained the appellant and the other three juveniles, was stopped in the

4100 block of Florida Avenue as it was proceeding away from the Wade's Corner Cafe. After the automobile was stopped a search was conducted; said search disclosed the two pistols and a pillow case.

Additionally, the record reveals that some of the quartet were looking through the window of Wade's before they eventually entered.***

Since it is uncontroverted that Messrs. Baugh, Worley, Cain and Niehaus planned the commission of aggravated robbery, we next consider whether the state proved beyond a reasonable doubt the element of a substantial overt act or acts in furtherance of the conspiracy as thus required by R. C. 2923.01(P):

> No person shall be convicted of conspiracy unless a substantial overt act in furtherance of the conspiracy is alleged and proved to have been done by him or a person with whom he conspired, subsequent to the accused's entrance into the conspiracy. For purposes of this section, an overt act is substantial when it is of such character as to manifest a purpose on the part of the actor that the object of the conspiracy should be completed.

Black's Law Dictionary, Revised Fourth Edition, defines "overt" and "overt act" as follows:

> OVERT. Open; manifest; public; issuing in action, as distinguished from that which rests merely in intention or design.
> OVERT ACT. In criminal law. An open manifest act from which criminality may be implied. An outward act done in pursuance and manifestation of an intent or design. An open act, which must be manifestly proved.

The text writer in 15A C.J.S. Conspiracy §43(2) states:

> The overt act must at least start to carry the conspiracy into effect or must reach far enough toward the accomplishment of the desired result to amount to the commencement of the consummation; but if it is done with the purpose of putting the unlawful agreement in effect, and it shows that action on the conspiracy has begun, it is sufficient, although it has no tendency to accomplish its object, or it has additional objectives which happen to be lawful. The conspiracy is complete on the forming of the criminal agreement and the performance of at least one overt act in furtherance thereof. . . .

The overt act, if in furtherance of the unlawful design, need not be in itself a criminal or unlawful act. A *fortiori* it is not necessary that the overt act should constitute the very crime which is the object of the conspiracy, although it may constitute such crime. . . .

Case references follow which provide interpretations by various courts of the purport of the concept of "overt act."

In *Ashcraft v. United States Fidelity and G. Co.* (1953), 255 S.W.2d 485, 37 ALR 2d 1078, the Kentucky Court of Appeals in construing a policy of insurance against loss by robbery held the word "overt" to mean "open to view."

In *Commonwealth v. Cohen* (1964), 203 Pa. Super. 34, 199 A.2d 139, the Supreme Court of Pennsylvania held that signing a check and delivering it to a payee were two overt acts, and proceeded to define an overt act as one "which is done openly by one of the co-conspirators to accomplish the purpose of the conspiracy. . . ."

In *United States v. Armone* (1966), 363 F.2d 385, the defendants were convicted in the U.S. District Court of New York for conspiracy to violate federal narcotics laws and they appealed to the U.S. Court of Appeals, Second Circuit. *Armone* is a lengthy and involved opinion. One of the headnotes, which is faithful to the holding in the decision itself, states:

> Conspiracy. The principal reason for the overt act requirement in a conspiracy prosecution is to manifest that the conspiracy is at work and is neither a project still resting solely in minds of conspirators nor a fully completed operation no longer in existence.

Furthermore, the Second Circuit Court held that conversations qualify as an "act." The decision states:

> Appellants seem to argue that conversation cannot be an "act," and that, in any event, this conversation was not in furtherance of the conspiracy. However, such talk is "action" with direct legal consequences; e.g., people "decide," "promise," and "reject." Cf. decisions holding telephone conversations to be overt acts. *Singer v. United States,* 208 F.2d 477, 480 (6th Cir. 1953); *Bartoli v. United States,* 192 F.2d 130, 132 (4th Cir. 1951); *Smith v. United States,* 92 F.2d 460, 461 (9th Cir. 1937). Here we have a warning to coconspirator Hedges by defendant Armone, after the conspirators had gone to the trouble of tracing the source of the counterfeit bill. *We hold that this conversation qualified as an "act."* (P. 401; emphasis supplied.)

The court in *People v. George* (1925), 74 Cal. App. 440, was confronted with an appeal from a conviction of conspiracy to obtain money from an insurance company by false pretenses that insured had accidentally drowned. The court held the following facts to satisfy the statutory requirement of some overt act:

a) Taking out of the insurance policy;
b) Procuring the boat, the Catalina Flyer;
c) Procuring of garb for purposes of disguise, and
d) Embarkation upon the boat.

A California appellate court had before it a criminal conviction of conspiracy to kidnap a famous and popular movie star, Mary Pickford Fairbanks, in *People v. Stevens* (1926), 78 Cal. App. 395, 248 P. 696. The court held:

> (4) It is contended by appellants that their act in stationing themselves before the Mary Pickford Studio was not an overt act within the meaning of the statutes of this state upon the subject of criminal conspiracy. In disposing of this point, we deem it sufficient to refer to *People v. George, supra. We think the act here shown was an overt act* within the rules laid down in that case. This conclusion presupposes, of course, that the conspiracy here charged was formulated before appellants made their trip to the studio gates. Whether it had been formulated before that event is a point later to be considered. (Emphasis supplied.)

The Third District Court of Appeals of California decided *People v. Beck,* 60 Cal. App. 417, in 1923, and consequently the examples of overt acts delineated by the court understandably are representative of the times. Nevertheless, the illustrations in *Beck* are in point in the instant matter to exemplify the type of activity the California court readily accepted as overt acts. In the decision it is stated:

> The following have been held sufficient overt acts under charges of conspiracy: Provisioning and sailing of a vessel in a conspiracy to smuggle Chinese into the United States, *Daly v. United States,* 170 Fed. 321. Telegraphic orders by one conspirator to another to make shipments of intoxicating liquors in a conspiracy to unlawfully ship such liquors. *Witte v. Shelton,* 240 Fed. 265. Cutting telegraph wires and *going to or near the place at which the offense was to be committed in a conspiracy to rob* the United States mail. *Collier v. United States,* 255 Fed. 328. Calling upon a coconspirator in pursuance of and to effect

the object of the conspiracy. *Gruher v. United States,* 255 Fed. 474. Registration of an illegal voter in a conspiracy to procure such person to vote. *State v. Nugent,* 77 N. J. Law 84. (Emphasis added.)

In *People v. Delk* (5th Dist., Appellate Ct. of Ill. 1976), 34 N.E.2d 197, the court declared that:

> The crux of defendants' argument is that entering a tavern while armed with a deadly weapon, albeit with intent to commit a robbery therein, is nothing more than mere preparation which does not amount to a substantial step toward the commission of the offense. *This contention lacks merit.* (345 N.E.2d at 202; emphasis added.)

In the instant matter, we find *substantial overt acts* in furtherance of the conspiracy to commit aggravated robbery in Wade's, to be, in part, at least:

> 1) Driving to Wade's with two loaded pistols in the possession of two of the conspirators pursuant to an agreement to commit robbery;
> 2) Casing the cafe before entering—activity witnessed by those in the establishment and prompting two calls to the police department because of apprehension about the presence in the vicinity of the conspirators;
> 3) One boy remaining outside of the cafe in a car as a lookout and inferentially the escape driver;
> 4) Entrance of three conspirators into Wade's with at least one loaded pistol in their possession and arguably, a second;
> 5) Carrying a pillow case;
> 6) Three conspirators entering a one-person rest room in Wade's and remaining there for a period of time before exiting the tavern.

Although possession of toboggan type hats or ski masks, and gloves, traditional paraphernalia in robberies, might arguably be included in the list, we elect not to rely upon them. However, it must be observed that all of these substantial overt acts followed an agreement to rob Wade's and as indicated above, two of the conspirators themselves testified that entry thereof was for the purpose to commit robbery.

The Ohio conspiracy statute does not render thoughts or intentions alone as criminal. Before there can be a conviction thereunder there must be planning with another person or persons to commit the offenses proscribed in R.C.

2923.01; there must be proof of at least one substantial overt act in furtherance of the conspiracy, and the state must prove beyond a reasonable doubt that there was no abandonment of the conspiracy. Thus the statute does not punish a criminal intention *unless* the intention is followed by a substantial overt act or acts. The legislature's interest in discouraging alliances for illicit purposes impresses us as a constitutional, legitimate and entirely reasonable area of legislative action. Moreover, although this appeal fails to raise the constitutionality of R. C. 2923.01, we note only parenthetically that the statute suffers from no facial constitutional infirmities.

III

This, then, at last brings us to an examination of the abandonment provisions in R. C. 2923.01. Although reproduced *supra* in the initial footnote, for simplicity's sake we repeat the applicable sections below:

> (E) A conspiracy terminates when the offense or offenses which are its objects are committed, *or when it is abandoned by all conspirators*.
>
> ***
>
> (I) The following are affirmative defenses to a charge of conspiracy:...
>
> (1) . . .
>
> (2) After conspiring to commit an offense, the actor abandoned the conspiracy prior to the commission of or attempt to commit any offense which was the object of the conspiracy, either by advising all other conspirators of his abandonment, or by informing any law enforcement authority of the existence of the conspiracy and of his participation therein. (Underscoring ours.)

We elect to evaluate (I)(2) before considering section (E). Our understanding of the state's burden vis-a-vis (I)(2) is that it must prove beyond a reasonable doubt that one charged with a violation of R.C. 2923.01 did not abandon the conspiracy either by advising all other conspirators of his abandonment, or by informing any law enforcement authority of the existence of the conspiracy and of his participation therein. We conclude that the state proved that Baugh did not satisfy *either* of the two conditions in (I)(2) necessary for an abandonment. He did not advise the two juveniles in Wade's with him of any abandonment; they walked out on him, and he followed five or ten minutes later arguably because the contemplated joint activity aborted and he was left very much alone. Nor did he advise Jeff Niehaus, driver and lookout. Moreover, the record contains nothing that indicates that Baugh informed "any law enforcement authority of the existence of the conspiracy and of his participation therein"—the alternative in (I)(2) for an [Illegible text] abandonment.

At this point in our discussion, the decision of the United States Supreme Court in *United States v. U.S. Gypsum Co.*, 46 U.S.L.W. 4937 (U.S. June 29, 1978) becomes relevant. In this antitrust case one of the issues was the abandonment of a conspiracy. The charge to the jury had included the following language:

> To withdraw, a defendant either must have affirmatively notified each other member of the conspiracy he will no longer participate in the undertaking so they understand they can no longer expect his participation or acquiescence or he must make disclosures of the illegal scheme to law enforcement officials.

The Supreme Court, in holding that the charge unduly limited the jury's consideration, concluded that the jury should have been allowed to consider other evidence of affirmative action indicating withdrawal from the enterprise. The court wrote:

> Affirmative acts inconsistent with the object of the conspiracy and communicated in a manner reasonably calculated to reach co-conspirators have generally been regarded as sufficient to establish withdrawal or abandonment.

With this guideline in mind, we proceed to paragraph (E) of the statute. We experience grave difficulty in validating the judgment below in the light of Section E, and the rationale of *Gypsum, supra*, and thus ultimately decide we are unable to do so. After reading and rereading the transcript of proceedings we believe the state failed to negative an abandonment "by all conspirators," including, of course, appellant. It is uncontroverted that the four actors left the cafe and drove away in their car. We have struggled with the issue of whether *all four* abandoned their criminal plans voluntarily or whether the presence of police officers on the scene prompted the renunciation. It is especially puzzling to determine the driver-lookout's motivation, but we come to the conclusion that it is just as reasonable to find that he abandoned—with the others—for reasons independent of the police officers' presence. Section (I)(1) of the conspiracy statute—a section inapposite to the factual pattern before us—refers to *"voluntary* renunciation," and R.C. 2923.02, Attempt, includes the phrase "[i]t is an affirmative defense to a charge under this section that the actor abandoned. . . . under circumstances manifesting a complete and *voluntary* renunciation of his criminal purpose." Nevertheless section (E) seems not to require a *voluntary* abandonment if in fact all conspirators abandon their criminal purpose. (Our underscoring.) Let us assume, *arguendo*, that in the factual pattern before us the change of heart and abandonment (by all) had to be voluntary. Even so, and ascribing significance to the police on the scene, the state failed to prove beyond a reasonable doubt that the renunciation was anything but voluntary. In other words, that Niehaus—the driver—abandoned because of the presence of the police was not proven. The transcript certainly contains no admission on his part that such caused him to forsake the criminal plan. A reasonable explanation is that he perceived the getaway activities of his three companions and joined the exodus.

Resultantly, section (E) of R.C. 2923.01 requires us to sustain the assignments of error. Thus we reverse the judgment below and discharge the appellant.

PALMER, P. J., CONCURRING.

I concur in the judgment of reversal since I entertain no doubt that the record here manifests an abandonment of the criminal enterprise by all of the conspirators. R.C. 2923.01(E). I would prefer, however, that it be clearly understood that this is the only rule of the case.

Thus, the issue of the constitutionality of the statute not having been raised in this appeal, it is supererogatory to comment on the issue, and I would prefer not to indicate any predisposition on my part therein. As to the statute being a "legitimate and entirely reasonable area of legislative action," as the opinion of my brother, Judge Keefe, states, I have reservations both technical and substantive. As a technical matter, the reasonableness or legitimacy of a criminal statute is solely a matter of legislative concern unless the constitutional fundament for the exercise of legislative authority, *e.g.*, the police power, is properly called into question. Such was not the case here; the comment is, therefore, both *obiter* and gratuitous.

Were the issue before us, and if my opinion of the statute somehow became judicially relevant, I would certainly wish to preserve my freedom to subject this legislation to a close and searching scrutiny of the very issues assumed in the above extract quoted from the majority opinion. Moreover, I would do so, as is I believe wholly proper, out of an awareness that statutes proscribing conspiracy, and similar inchoate crimes, clearly and designedly impinge upon regulation of the cognitive process, that they therefore derive not from the common law but from Star Chamber tradition, and that they are not, in sum, truly indigenous to native soil.*** It may well be that modern corporate crime has made this kind of legislation, if not desirable, at least necessary; and it may well be—and certainly there is abundant authority to support it—that such statutes can be made to comport with a constitutional exercise of the police power. But I do not think it desirable to preclude a full debate of these important issues in a case which does not require or merit such decision.

Notes and Questions

1. The appellate judges in *State v. Baugh* decided not to rely on "possession of toboggan type hats or ski masks, and gloves, traditional paraphernalia in robberies," as proof of overt acts by the defendants. Why do you think the judges decided against using this evidence?

2. Do you think the age of the conspirators influenced the opinion of the judges in *Baugh*? Do you think a judge is more likely to find that the defendants abandoned a conspiracy if they are younger?

3. If you were deciding this case, would you have found that the defendants had abandoned the robbery? If so, what actions of the defendants would have been most compelling to you? Also, do you think that it was too late for the defendants to abandon the conspiracy?

D. Pinkerton Liability

Pinkerton v. United States, 328 U.S. 640 (1946)

Mr. Justice DOUGLAS delivered the opinion of the Court.

Walter and Daniel Pinkerton are brothers who live a short distance from each other on Daniel's farm. They were indicted for violations of the Internal Revenue Code. The indictment contained ten substantive counts and one conspiracy count. The jury found Walter guilty on nine of the substantive counts and on the conspiracy count. It found Daniel guilty on six of the substantive counts and on the conspiracy count. Walter was fined $500 and sentenced generally on the substantive counts to imprisonment for thirty months. On the conspiracy count he was given a two year sentence to run concurrently with the other sentence. Daniel was fined $1,000 and sentenced generally on the substantive counts to imprisonment for thirty months. On the conspiracy count he was fined $500 and given a two year sentence to run concurrently with the other sentence.***

A single conspiracy was charged and proved. Some of the overt acts charged in the conspiracy count were the same acts charged in the substantive counts. Each of the substantive offenses found was committed pursuant to the conspiracy. Petitioners therefore contend that the substantive counts became merged in the conspiracy count, and that only a single sentence not exceeding the maximum two-year penalty provided by the conspiracy statute (Criminal Code s 37, 18 U.S.C. s 88, 18 U.S.C.A. s 88) could be imposed. Or to state the matter differently, they contend that each of the substantive counts became a separate conspiracy count but since only a single conspiracy was charged and proved, only single sentence for conspiracy could be imposed. They rely on *Braverman v. United States*, 317 U.S. 49.

In the *Braverman* case the indictment charged no substantive offense. Each of the several counts charged a conspiracy to violate a different statute. But only one conspiracy was proved. We held that a single conspiracy, charged under the general conspiracy statute, however diverse its objects may be, violates but a single statute and no penalty greater than the maximum provided for one conspiracy may be imposed. That case is not apposite here. For the offenses charged and proved were not only a conspiracy but substantive offenses as well.

Nor can we accept the proposition that the substantive offenses were merged in the conspiracy. There are, of course, instances where a conspiracy charge may not be added to the substantive charge. One is where the agreement of two persons is necessary for the completion of the substantive crime and there is no ingredient in the conspiracy which is not present in the completed crime. *See United States v. Katz*, 271 U.S. 354. Another is where the definition of the substantive offense excludes from punishment for conspiracy one who voluntarily participates in another's crime. *Gebardi v. United States, supra.* But those exceptions are of a limited character. The common law rule that the substantive offense, if a felony, was merged in the conspiracy, has little vitality in this country. It has been long and consistently recognized by the Court that the commission of the substantive offense and a conspiracy to commit it are separate and distinct offenses. The power of Congress to separate the two and to affix to each a different penalty is well established. *Clune v. United States*, 159 U.S. 590.***

It is contended that there was insufficient evidence to implicate Daniel in the conspiracy. But we think there was enough evidence for submission of the issue to the jury.

There is, however, no evidence to show that Daniel participated directly in the commission of the substantive offenses on which his conviction has been sustained, although there was evidence to show that these substantive offenses were in fact committed by Walter in furtherance of the unlawful agreement or conspiracy existing between the brothers. The question was submitted to the jury on the theory that each petitioner could be found guilty of the substantive offenses, if it was found at the time those offenses were committed petitioners were parties to an unlawful conspiracy and the substantive offenses charged were in fact committed in furtherance of it.

Daniel relies on *United States v. Sall, supra.* That case held that participation in the conspiracy was not itself enough to sustain a conviction for the substantive offense even though it was committed in furtherance of the conspiracy. The court held that, in addition to evidence that the offense was in fact committed in furtherance of the conspiracy, evidence of direct participation in the commission of the substantive offense or other evidence from which participation might fairly be inferred was necessary.

We take a different view. We have here a continuous conspiracy. There is here no evidence of the affirmative action on the part of Daniel which is necessary to establish his withdrawal from it. *Hyde v. United States*, 225 U.S. 347. As stated in that case, "having joined in an unlawful scheme, having constituted agents for its performance, scheme and agency to be continuous until full fruition be secured, until he does some act to disavow or defeat the purpose he is in no situation to claim the delay of the law. As the offense has not been terminated or accomplished, he is still offending. And we think, consciously offending,— offending as certainly, as we have said, as at the first moment of his confederation, and consciously through every moment of its existence." *Id.*, 225 U.S. at page 369. And so long as the partnership in crime continues, the partners act for each other in carrying it forward. It is settled that "an overt act of one partner may be the act of all without any new agreement specifically directed to that act." *United States v. Kissel*, 218 U.S. 601. Motive or intent may be proved by the acts or declarations of some of the conspirators in furtherance of the common objective.***The criminal intent to do the act is established by the formation of the conspiracy. Each conspirator instigated the commission of the crime. The unlawful agreement contemplated precisely what was done. It was formed for the purpose. The act done was in execution of the enterprise. The rule which holds responsible one who counsels, procures, or commands another to commit a crime is founded on the same principle. That principle is recognized in the law of conspiracy when the overt act of one partner in crime is attributable to all. An overt act is an essential ingredient of the crime of conspiracy under s 37 of the Criminal Code, 18 U.S.C. s 88, 18 U.S.C.A. s 88. If that can be supplied by the act of one conspirator, we fail to see why the same or other acts in furtherance of the conspiracy are likewise not attributable to the others for the purpose of holding them responsible for the substantive offense.

A different case would arise if the substantive offense committed by one of the conspirators was not in fact done in furtherance of the conspiracy, did not fall within the scope of the unlawful project, or was merely a part of the ramifications of the plan which could not be reasonably foreseen as a necessary or natural consequence of the unlawful agreement. But as we read this record, that is not this case.

Affirmed.

MR. JUSTICE RUTLEDGE, dissenting in part.

The judgment concerning Daniel Pinkerton should be reversed. In my opinion it is without precedent here and is a dangerous precedent to establish.

Daniel and Walter, who were brothers living near each other, were charged in several counts with substantive offenses, and then a conspiracy count was added naming those offenses as overt acts. The proof showed that Walter alone committed the substantive crimes. There was none to establish that Daniel participated in them, aided and abetted Walter in committing them, or knew that he had done so. Daniel in fact was in the penitentiary, under sentence for other crimes, when some of Walter's crimes were done.

There was evidence, however, to show that over several years Daniel and Walter had confederated to commit similar crimes concerned with unlawful possession, transportation, and dealing in whiskey, in fraud of the federal revenues. On this evidence both were convicted of conspiracy. Walter also was convicted on the substantive counts on the proof of his committing the crimes charged. Then, on that evidence without more than the proof of Daniel's criminal agreement with Walter and the latter's overt acts, which were also the substantive offenses charged, the court told the jury they could find Daniel guilty of those substantive offenses. They did so.***

The old doctrine of merger of conspiracy in the substantive crime has not obtained here. But the dangers for abuse, which in part it sought to avoid, in applying the law of conspiracy have not altogether disappeared. *Cf. Kotteakos v. United States*, 66 S. Ct. 1239. There is some evidence that they may be increasing. The looseness with which the charge may be proved, the almost unlimited scope of vicarious responsibility for others' acts which follows once agreement is shown, the psychological advantages of such trials for securing convictions by attributing to one proof against another, these and other inducements require that the broad limits of discretion allowed to prosecuting officers in relation to such charges and trials be not expanded into new, wider and more dubious areas of choice. If the matter is not generally of constitutional proportions, it is one for the exercise of this Court's supervisory power over the modes of conducting federal criminal prosecutions within the rule of *McNabb v. United States*, 318 U.S. 332.

I think that power should be exercised in this case with respect to Daniel's conviction. If it does not violate the letter of constitutional right, it fractures the spirit. *United States v. Sall, supra.* I think the ruling in that case was right, and for the reasons stated. It should be followed here. Daniel has been held guilty of the substantive crimes committed only by Walter on proof that he did no more than conspire with him to commit offenses of the same general character. There was no evidence that he counseled, advised or had knowledge of those particular acts or offenses. There was, therefore, none that he aided, abetted or took part in them. There was only evidence sufficient to show that he had agreed with Walter at some past time to engage in such transactions generally. As to Daniel this was only evidence of conspiracy, not of substantive crime.

The court's theory seems to be that Daniel and Walter became general partners in crime by virtue of their agreement and because of that agreement without more on his part Daniel became criminally responsible as a principal for everything Walter did thereafter in the nature of a criminal offense of the general sort the agreement contemplated, so long as there was not clear evidence that Daniel had withdrawn from or revoked the agreement. Whether or not his commitment to the penitentiary had that effect, the result is a vicarious criminal responsibility as broad as, or broader than, the vicarious civil liability of a partner for acts done by a co-partner in the course of the firm's business.

Such analogies from private commercial law and the law of torts are dangerous, in my judgment, for transfer to the criminal field. See Sen. Rep. No. 163, 72d Cong., 1st Sess., 20. Guilt there with us remains personal, not vicarious, for the more serious offenses. It should be kept so. The effect of Daniel's conviction in this case, to repeat, is either to attribute to him Walter's guilt or to punish him twice for the same offense, namely, agreeing with Walter to engage in crime. Without the agreement Daniel was guilty of no crime on this record. With it and no more, so far as his own conduct is concerned, he was guilty of two.***

Notes and Questions

1. If Daniel was in prison when Walter committed the substantive crimes, how did the Supreme Court justify holding Daniel accountable for the conduct of Walter? Why does the dissent say that Daniel is being punished twice for the same act?

2. After reading the following two sections of the MPC that cover accomplice liability and conspiracy, can you determine whether or not the MPC accepts Pinkerton Liability? If you believe that the MPC does not adhere to Pinkerton Liability, what sections in the MPC would support your argument?

3. The *Pinkerton* court found that conspiracy did not merge into the underlying crime. The MPC, as indicated in Section 5.03, has taken an opposite approach. What arguments support the MPC approach of merging conspiracy with the underlying offense?

Model Penal Code
Section 2.06. Liability for Conduct of Another; Complicity.
(1) A person is guilty of an offense if it is committed by his own conduct or by the conduct of another person for which he is legally accountable, or both.
(2) A person is legally accountable for the conduct of another person when:
    (a) acting with the kind of culpability that is sufficient for the commission of the offense, he causes an innocent or irresponsible person to engage in such conduct; or

(b) he is made accountable for the conduct of such other person by the Code or by the law defining the offense; or

(c) he is an accomplice of such other person in the commission of the offense.

(3) A person is an accomplice of another person in the commission of an offense if:

(a) with the purpose of promoting or facilitating the commission of the offense, he

(i) solicits such other person to commit it, or

(ii) aids or agrees or attempts to aid such other person in planning or committing it, or

(iii) having a legal duty to prevent the commission of the offense, fails to make proper effort so to do; or...

Model Penal Code
Section 5.03. Criminal Conspiracy.

(1) Definition of Conspiracy. A person is guilty of conspiracy with another person or persons to commit a crime if with the purpose of promoting or facilitating its commission he:

(a) agrees with such other person or persons that they or one or more of them will engage in conduct that constitutes such crime or an attempt or solicitation to commit such crime; or

(b) agrees to aid such other person or persons in the planning or commission of such crime or of an attempt or solicitation to commit such crime.

(2) Scope of Conspiratorial Relationship. If a person guilty of conspiracy, as defined by Subsection (1) of this Section, knows that a person with whom he conspires to commit a crime has conspired with another person or persons to commit the same crime, he is guilty of conspiring with such other person or persons, whether or not he knows their identity, to commit such crime.

(3) Conspiracy with Multiple Criminal Objectives. If a person conspires to commit a number of crimes, he is guilty of only one conspiracy so long as such multiple crimes are the object of the same agreement or continuous conspiratorial relationship.

(4) Joinder and Venue in Conspiracy Prosecutions.

(a) Subject to the provisions of paragraph (b) of this Subsection, two or more persons charged with criminal conspiracy may be prosecuted jointly if:

(i) they are charged with conspiring with one another; or

(ii) the conspiracies alleged, whether they have the same or different parties, are so related that they constitute different aspects of a scheme of organized criminal conduct.

(b) In any joint prosecution under paragraph (a) of this Subsection:

(i) no defendant shall be charged with a conspiracy in any county [parish or district] other than one in which he entered into such conspiracy or in which an overt act pursuant to such conspiracy was done by him or by a person with whom he conspired; and

(ii) neither the liability of any defendant nor the admissibility against him of evidence of acts or declarations of another shall be enlarged by such joinder; and

(iii) the Court shall order a severance or take a special verdict as to any defendant who so requests, if it deems it necessary or appropriate to promote the fair determination of his guilt or innocence, and shall take any other proper measures to protect the fairness of the trial.

(5) Overt Act. No person may be convicted of conspiracy to commit a crime, other than a felony of the first or second degree, unless an overt act in pursuance of such conspiracy is alleged and proved to have been done by him or by a person with whom he conspired.

(6) Renunciation of Criminal Purpose. It is an affirmative defense that the actor, after conspiring to commit a crime, thwarted the success of the conspiracy, under circumstances manifesting a complete and voluntary renunciation of his criminal purpose.

(7) Duration of Conspiracy. For purposes of Section 1.06(4):

(a) conspiracy is a continuing course of conduct that terminates when the crime or crimes that are its object are committed or the agreement that they be committed is abandoned by the defendant and by those with whom he conspired; and

(b) such abandonment is presumed if neither the defendant nor anyone with whom he conspired does any overt act in pursuance of the conspiracy during the applicable period of limitation; and

(c) if an individual abandons the agreement, the conspiracy is terminated as to him only if and when he advises those with whom he conspired of his abandonment or he informs the law enforcement authorities of the existence of the conspiracy and of his participation therein.

E. Wharton's Rule

Iannelli v. United States, **420 U.S. 770 (1975)**

Each of the eight petitioners, along with seven unindicted coconspirators and six codefendants, was charged with conspiring to violate (18 U.S.C. 371), and with violating, 18 U.S.C. 1955, a provision of the Organized Crime Control Act of 1970 (Act) aimed at large-scale gambling activities; and each petitioner was convicted and sentenced under both counts. The Court of Appeals affirmed, finding that prosecution and punishment for both offenses were permitted by a recognized exception to Wharton's Rule. Under that Rule an agreement by two persons to commit a particular crime cannot be prosecuted as a conspiracy when the crime is of such a nature as necessarily to require the participation of two persons for its commission, in such a case the conspiracy being deemed to have merged into the completed offense. Held: Petitioners were properly convicted and punished for violating 18 U.S.C. 1955 and for conspiring to violate that statute, it being clear that Congress in enacting the Act intended to retain each offense as an independent curb in combating organized crime.***

MR. JUSTICE POWELL delivered the opinion of the Court.

This case requires the Court to consider Wharton's Rule, a doctrine of criminal law enunciating an exception to the general principle that a conspiracy and the substantive offense that is its immediate end are discrete crimes for which separate sanctions may be imposed.

I

Petitioners were tried under a six-count indictment alleging a variety of federal gambling offenses. Each of the eight petitioners, along with seven unindicted coconspirators and six codefendants, was charged, inter alia, with conspiring to violate and violating 18 U.S.C. 1955, a federal gambling statute making it a crime for five or more persons to conduct, finance, manage, supervise, direct, or own a gambling business prohibited by state law. Each petitioner was convicted of both offenses, and each was sentenced under both the substantive and conspiracy counts. The Court of Appeals for the Third Circuit affirmed, finding that a recognized exception to Wharton's Rule permitted prosecution and punishment for both offenses, 477 F.2d 999 (1973). We granted certiorari to resolve the conflicts caused by the federal courts' disparate approaches to the application of Wharton's Rule to conspiracies to violate 1955. 417 U.S. 907 (1974). For the reasons now to be stated, we affirm.

II

Wharton's Rule owes its name to Francis Wharton, whose treatise on criminal law identified the doctrine and its fundamental rationale:

> When to the idea of an offense plurality of agents is logically necessary, conspiracy, which assumes the voluntary accession of a person to a crime of such a character that it is aggravated by a plurality of agents, cannot be maintained. . . . In other words, when the law says, "a combination between two persons to effect a particular end shall be called, if the end be effected, by a certain name," it is not lawful for the prosecution to call it by some other name; and when the law says, such an offense—e.g., adultery—shall have a certain punishment, it is not lawful for the

prosecution to evade this limitation by indicting the offense as conspiracy. 2 F. Wharton, Criminal Law 1604, p. 1862 (12th ed. 1932).

The Rule has been applied by numerous courts, state and federal alike. It also has been recognized by this Court, although we have had no previous occasion carefully to analyze its justification and proper role in federal law.

The classic formulation of Wharton's Rule requires that the conspiracy indictment be dismissed before trial. Wharton's description of the Rule indicates that, where it is applicable, an indictment for conspiracy "cannot be maintained," *** however, the courts held that the Rule's purposes can be served equally effectively by permitting the prosecution to charge both offenses and instructing the jury that a conviction for the substantive offense necessarily precludes conviction for the conspiracy.

Federal courts likewise have disagreed as to the proper application of the recognized "third-party exception," which renders Wharton's Rule inapplicable when the conspiracy involves the cooperation of a greater number of persons than is required for commission of the substantive offense. *See Gebardi v. United States, supra*, at 122 n. 6. In the present case, the Third Circuit concluded that the third-party exception permitted prosecution because the conspiracy involved more than the five persons required to commit the substantive offense, 477 F.2d 999 a view shared by the Second Circuit, *United States v. Becker*, 461 F.2d 230, 234 (1972), *vacated and remanded on other grounds*, 417 U.S. 903 (1974). The Seventh Circuit reached the opposite result, however, reasoning that since 1955 also covers gambling activities involving more than five persons, the third-party exception is inapplicable. *United States v. Hunter*, 478 F.2d 1019.

The Courts of Appeals are at odds even over the fundamental question whether Wharton's Rule ever applies to a charge for conspiracy to violate 1955. The Seventh Circuit holds that it does. *Hunter, supra*. The Fourth and Fifth Circuits, on the other hand, have declared that it does not. *United States v. Bobo*, 477 F.2d 974 (1973).

As this brief description indicates, the history of the application of Wharton's Rule to charges for conspiracy to violate 1955 fully supports the Fourth Circuit's observation that "rather than being a rule, [it] is a concept, the confines of which have been delineated in widely diverse fashion by the courts." *United States v. Bobo, supra*, at 986. With this diversity of views in mind, we turn to an examination of the history and purposes of the Rule.

III

A

Traditionally the law has considered conspiracy and the completed substantive offense to be separate crimes. Conspiracy is an inchoate offense, the essence of which is an agreement to commit an unlawful act. *See, e.g., United States v. Feola*, ante, p. 671, the conspiracy to commit an offense and the subsequent commission of that crime normally do not merge into a single punishable act. *Pinkerton v. United States, supra*, at 643. Thus, it is well recognized that in most cases separate sentences can be imposed for the conspiracy to do an act and for the subsequent accomplishment of that end. *Feola, supra; Callanan v. United States*, 364 U.S. 587 (1961). Indeed, the Court has even held that the conspiracy can be punished more harshly than the accomplishment of its purpose. *Clune v. United States*, 159 U.S. 590 (1895).

The consistent rationale of this long line of decisions rests on the very nature of the crime of conspiracy. This Court repeatedly has recognized that a conspiracy poses distinct dangers quite apart from those of the substantive offense.

> This settled principle derives from the reason of things in dealing with socially reprehensible conduct: collective criminal agreement—partnership in crime—presents a greater potential threat to the public than individual delicts. Concerted action both increases the likelihood that the criminal object will be successfully attained and decreases the probability that the individuals involved will depart from their path of criminality. Group association for criminal purposes often, if not normally, makes possible the attainment of ends more complex than those which one criminal could accomplish. Nor is the danger of a conspiratorial group limited to the particular end toward which it has embarked. Combination in crime makes more likely the commission of crimes unrelated to the original purpose for which the group was formed. In sum, the danger which a conspiracy generates is not confined to the substantive offense which is the immediate aim of the enterprise. *Callanan v. United States, supra*, at 593-594.

As Mr. Justice Jackson, no friend of the law of conspiracy observed: "The basic rationale of the law of conspiracy is that a conspiracy may be an evil in itself, independently of any other evil it seeks to accomplish." *Dennis v. United States*, 341 U.S. 494, 573 (1951) (concurring opinion).

B

The historical difference between the conspiracy and its end has led this Court consistently to attribute to Congress "a tacit purpose—in the absence of any inconsistent expression—to maintain a long-established distinction between offenses essentially different; a distinction whose practical importance in the criminal law is not easily overestimated." *Ibid.*; *Callanan, supra*, at 594. Wharton's Rule announces an exception to this general principle.

The Rule traces its origin to the decision of the Pennsylvania Supreme Court in *Shannon v. Commonwealth*, 14 Pa. 226 (1850), a case in which the court ordered dismissal of an indictment alleging conspiracy to commit adultery that was brought after the State had failed to obtain conviction for the substantive offense. Prominent among the concerns voiced in the *Shannon* opinion is the possibility that the State could force the defendant to undergo subsequent prosecution for a lesser offense after failing to prove the greater. The *Shannon* court's holding reflects this concern, stating that "where concert is a constituent part of the act to be done, as it is in fornication and adultery, a party acquitted of the major cannot be indicted of the minor." *Id.*, at 227-228.

Wharton's treatise first reported the case as one based on principles of double jeopardy, see F. Wharton, Criminal Law 198 (2d ed. 1852), and indicated that it was limited to that context. Subsequently, however, Wharton came to view the principle as one of broader application. The seventh edition of Wharton's treatise reported the more general rule which is repeated in similar form today. *Shannon v. Commonwealth* was said to be an application of the principle rather than its source. 2 F. Wharton, Criminal Law 634 (7th ed. 1874).

This Court's previous discussions of Wharton's Rule have not elaborated upon its precise role in federal law. In most instances, the Court simply has identified the Rule and described it in terms similar to those used in Wharton's treatise. But in *United States v. Holte*, 236 U.S. 140 (1915), the sole case in which the Court felt compelled specifically to consider the applicability of Wharton's Rule, it declined to adopt an expansive definition of its scope. In that case, Wharton's Rule was advanced as a bar to prosecution of a female for conspiracy to violate the Mann Act. Rejecting that contention, the Court adopted a narrow construction of the Rule that focuses on the statutory requirements of the substantive offense rather than the evidence offered to prove those elements at trial:

> The substantive offence might be committed without the woman's consent, for instance, if she were drugged or taken by force. Therefore the decisions that it is impossible to turn the concurrence necessary to effect certain crimes such as bigamy or duelling into a conspiracy to commit them do not apply. *Id.*, at 145.

Wharton's Rule first emerged at a time when the contours of the law of conspiracy were in the process of active formulation. The general question whether the conspiracy merged into the completed felony offense remained for some time a matter of uncertain resolution. That issue is now settled, however, and the Rule currently stands as an exception to the general principle that a conspiracy and the substantive offense that is its immediate end do not merge upon proof of the latter. *See Pinkerton v. United States*, 328 U.S. 640 (1946). If the Rule is to serve a rational purpose in the context of the modern law of conspiracy, its role must be more precisely identified.

C

This Court's prior decisions indicate that the broadly formulated Wharton's Rule does not rest on principles of double jeopardy, *see Pereira v. United States*, 347 U.S. 1, 11 (1954). Instead, it has current vitality only as a judicial presumption, to be applied in the absence of legislative intent to the contrary. The classic Wharton's Rule offenses—adultery, incest, bigamy, dueling—are crimes that are characterized by the general congruence of the agreement and the completed substantive offense. The parties to the agreement are the only persons who participate in commission of the substantive offense, and the immediate consequences of the crime rest on the parties themselves rather than on society at large. *See United States v. Bobo*, 477 F.2d, at 987. Finally, the agreement that attends the substantive offense does not appear likely to pose the distinct kinds of threats to society that the law of conspiracy seeks to avert. It cannot, for example, readily be assumed that an agreement to commit an offense of this nature will produce agreements to engage in a more general pattern of criminal conduct.

The conduct proscribed by 1955 is significantly different from the offenses to which the Rule traditionally has been applied. Unlike the consequences of the classic Wharton's Rule offenses, the harm attendant upon the commission of the substantive offense is not restricted to the parties to the agreement. Large-scale gambling activities seek to elicit the participation of additional persons—the bettors—who are parties neither to the conspiracy nor to the substantive offense that results from it. Moreover, the parties prosecuted for the conspiracy need not be the same persons who are prosecuted for commission of the substantive offense. An endeavor as complex as a large-scale gambling enterprise might involve persons who have played appreciably different roles, and whose level of culpability varies significantly. It might, therefore, be appropriate to prosecute the owners and organizers of large-scale gambling operations both for the conspiracy and for the substantive offense but to prosecute the lesser participants only for the substantive offense. Nor can it fairly be maintained that agreements to enter into large-scale gambling activities are not likely to generate additional agreements to engage in other criminal endeavors. As shown in Part IV hereof, the legislative history of 1955 provides documented testimony to the contrary.

Wharton's Rule applies only to offenses that require concerted criminal activity, a plurality of criminal agents. In such cases, a closer relationship exists between the conspiracy and the substantive offense because both require collective criminal activity. The substantive offense therefore presents some of the same threats that the law of conspiracy normally is thought to guard against, and it cannot automatically be assumed that the Legislature intended the conspiracy and the substantive offense to remain as discrete crimes upon consummation of the latter. Thus, absent legislative intent to the contrary, the Rule supports a presumption that the two merge when the substantive offense is proved.

But a legal principle commands less respect when extended beyond the logic that supports it. In this case, the significant differences in characteristics and consequences of the kinds of offenses that gave rise to Wharton's Rule and the activities proscribed by 1955 counsel against attributing significant weight to the presumption the Rule erects. More important, as the Rule is essentially an aid to the determination of legislative intent, it must defer to a discernible legislative judgment. We turn now to that inquiry.

IV

The basic purpose of the Organized Crime Control Act of 1970, Pub. L. No. 91-452, 84 Stat. 922, 923, was "to seek the eradication of organized crime in the United States by strengthening the legal tools in the evidence-gathering process, by establishing new penal prohibitions, and by providing enhanced sanctions and new remedies to deal with the unlawful activities of those engaged in organized crime." The content of the Act reflects the dedication with which the Legislature pursued this purpose. In addition to enacting provisions to facilitate the discovery and proof of organized criminal activities, Congress passed a number of relatively severe penalty provisions. For example, Title X, codified in 18 U.S.C. 3575-3578, identifies for harsher sentencing treatment certain "dangerous special offenders," among them persons who initiate, direct, or supervise patterns of criminal conduct or conspiracies to engage in such conduct, and persons who derive substantial portions of their income from those activities. 3575 (e).

Major gambling activities were a principal focus of congressional concern. Large-scale gambling enterprises were seen to be both a substantive evil and a source of funds for other criminal conduct. See S. Rep. No. 91-617, pp. 71-73 (1969). Title VIII thus was enacted "to give the Federal Government a new substantive weapon, a weapon which will strike at organized crime's principal source of revenue: illegal gambling." *Id.*, at 71. In addition to declaring that certain gambling activities violate federal as well as state law, 18 U.S.C. 1955, Title

VIII provides new penalties for conspiracies to obstruct state law enforcement efforts for the purpose of facilitating the conduct of these activities. 18 U.S.C. 1511.

In drafting the Organized Crime Control Act of 1970, Congress manifested its clear awareness of the distinct nature of a conspiracy and the substantive offenses that might constitute its immediate end. The identification of "special offenders" in Title X speaks both to persons who commit specific felonies during the course of a pattern of criminal activity and to those who enter into conspiracies to engage in patterns of criminal conduct. 18 U.S.C. 3575 (e). And Congress specifically utilized the law of conspiracy to discourage organized crime's corruption of state and local officials for the purpose of facilitating gambling enterprises. 18 U.S.C. 1511.

But the 1955 definition of "gambling activities" pointedly avoids reference to conspiracy or to agreement, the essential element of conspiracy. Moreover, the limited 1955 definition is repeated in identifying the reach of 1511, a provision that specifically prohibits conspiracies. Viewed in this context, and in light of the numerous references to conspiracies throughout the extensive consideration of the Organized Crime Control Act, we think that the limited congressional definition of "gambling activities" in 1955 is significant. The Act is a carefully crafted piece of legislation. Had Congress intended to foreclose the possibility of prosecuting conspiracy offenses under 371 by merging them into prosecutions under 1955, we think it would have so indicated explicitly. It chose instead to define the substantive offense punished by 1955 in a manner that fails specifically to invoke the concerns which underlie the law of conspiracy.

Nor do we find merit to the argument that the congressional requirement of participation of "five or more persons" as an element of the substantive offense under 1955 represents a legislative attempt to merge the conspiracy and the substantive offense into a single crime. The history of the Act instead reveals that this requirement was designed to restrict federal intervention to cases in which federal interests are substantially implicated. The findings accompanying Title VIII, see note following 18 U.S.C. 1511, would appear to support the assertion of federal jurisdiction over all illegal gambling activities. Congress did not, however, choose to exercise its power to the fullest. Recognizing that gambling activities normally are matters of state concern, Congress indicated a desire to extend federal criminal jurisdiction to reach only "those who are engaged in an illicit gambling business of major proportions." S. Rep. No. 91-617, p. 73 (1969). It accordingly conditioned the application of 1955 on a finding that the gambling activities involve five or more persons and that they remain substantially in operation in excess of 30 days or attain gross revenues of $2,000 in a single day. 18 U.S.C. 1955 (b) (1) (iii) (1970 ed. and Supp. III). Thus the requirement of "concerted activity" in 1955 reflects no more than a concern to avoid federal prosecution of small-scale gambling activities which pose a limited threat to federal interests and normally can be combated effectively by local law enforcement efforts.

Viewed in the context of this legislation, there simply is no basis for relying on a presumption to reach a result so plainly at odds with congressional intent. We think it evident that Congress intended to retain each offense as an "independent curb" available for use in the strategy against organized crime. *Gore v. United States*, 357 U.S. 386, 389 (1958). We conclude, therefore, that the history and structure of the Organized Crime Control Act of 1970 manifest a clear and unmistakable legislative judgment that more than outweighs any presumption of merger between the conspiracy to violate 1955 and the consummation of that substantive offense.

V

In expressing these conclusions we do not imply that the distinct nature of the crimes of conspiracy to violate and violation of 1955 should prompt prosecutors to seek separate convictions in every case, or judges necessarily to sentence in a manner that imposes an additional sanction for conspiracy to violate 1955 and the consummation of that end. Those decisions fall within the sound discretion of each, and should be rendered in accordance with the facts and circumstances of a particular case. We conclude only that Congress intended to retain these traditional options. Neither Wharton's Rule nor the history and structure of the Organized Crime Control Act of 1970 persuade us to the contrary.

Affirmed.

Notes and Questions

1. What is the policy argument for and against Wharton's Rule? One reason for the limitation is that the rule has been traditionally limited to offenses like adultery, incest, bigamy, and duelling. In *Iannelli v. United States*, the U.S. Supreme Court stated that the consequences for these types of crimes "rest on the parties themselves rather than on society at large." Do you agree with this statement?

2. An exception to Wharton's Rule is when the number of conspirators exceeds the number of essential participants in the completed crime. Thus, if X and Y participate in a duel they cannot be convicted of both duelling and conspiracy to duel pursuant to Wharton's Rule. However, if X, Y, and Z all engage in a duel then all three can be convicted of duelling and conspiracy to duel. Why do you think jurisdictions have carved out this exception?

3. The court in *Iannelli* says, "the broadly formulated Wharton's Rule does not rest on principles of double jeopardy." If this is correct, then what legal principles support the rule?

F. LEGISLATIVELY PROTECTED CLASS

Gebardi v. United States, 287 U.S. 112 (1932)

Mr. Justice STONE delivered the opinion of the Court.

This case is here on certiorari to review a judgment of conviction for conspiracy to violate the Mann Act (36 Stat. 825, 18 U.S.C. s 397 et seq. (18 USCA s 397 et seq.)). Petitioners, a man and a woman, not then husband and wife, were indicted in the District Court for Northern Illinois, for conspiring together, and with others not named, to transport the woman from one state to another for the purpose of engaging in sexual intercourse with the man. At the trial without a jury there was evidence from which the court could have found that the petitioners had engaged in illicit sexual relations in the course of each of the journeys alleged; that the man purchased the railway tickets for both petitioners for at least one journey; and that in each instance the woman, in advance of the purchase of the tickets, consented to go on the journey and did go on it voluntarily for the specified immoral purpose. There was no evidence supporting the allegation that any other person had conspired. The trial court overruled motions for a finding for the defendants, and in arrest of judgment, and gave judgment of conviction, which the Court of Appeals for the Seventh Circuit affirmed

The only question which we need consider here is whether, within the principles announced in that case, the evidence was sufficient to support the conviction. There the defendants, a man and a woman, were indicted for conspiring together that the man should transport the woman from one state to another for purposes of prostitution. In holding the indictment sufficient, the court said "As the defendant is the woman, the district court sustained a demurrer on the ground that although the offense could not be committed without her, she was no party to it, but only the victim. The single question is whether that ruling is right. We do not have to consider what would be necessary to constitute the substantive crime under the act of 1910 (the Mann Act), or what evidence would be required to convict a woman under an indictment like this; but only to decide whether it is impossible for the transported woman to be guilty of a crime in conspiring as alleged." The court assumed that there might be a degree of co-operation which would fall short of the commission of any crime, as in the case of the purchaser of liquor illegally sold. But it declined to hold that a woman could not under some circumstances not precisely defined, be guilty of a violation of the Mann Act and of a conspiracy to violate it as well. Light is thrown upon the intended scope of this conclusion by the supposititious case which the court put: "Suppose, for instance, that a professional prostitute, as well able to look out for herself as was the man, should suggest and carry out a journey within the act of 1910 in the hope of black-mailing the man, and should buy the railroad tickets, or should pay the fare from Jersey City to New York,-she would be within the letter of the act of 1910 and we see no reason why the act should not be held to apply. We see equally little reason for not treating the preliminary agreement as a conspiracy that the law can reach, if we abandon the illusion that the woman always is the victim."

In the present case we must apply the law to the evidence; the very inquiry which was said to be unnecessary to decision in United States v. Holte, supra.

First. Those exceptional circumstances envisaged in United States v. Holte, supra, as possible instances in which the woman might violate the act itself, are clearly not present here. There is no evidence that she purchased the railroad tickets or that hers was the active or moving spirit in conceiving or carrying out the transportation. The proof shows no more than that she went willingly upon the journeys for the purposes alleged.

Section 2 of the Mann Act (18 U.S.C. s 398 (18 USCA s 398)), violation of which is charged by the indictment here as the object of the conspiracy, imposes the penalty upon "any person who shall knowingly transport or cause to be transported, or aid or assist in obtaining transportation for, or in transporting, in interstate or foreign commerce *** any woman or girl for the purpose of prostitution or debauchery, or for any other immoral purpose. ***" Transportation of a woman or girl whether with or without her consent, or causing or aiding it, or furthering it in any of the specified ways, are the acts punished, when done with a purpose which is immoral within the meaning of the law.

The act does not punish the woman for transporting herself; it contemplates two persons-one to transport and the woman or girl to be transported. For the woman to fall within the ban of the statute she must, at the least, "aid or assist" some one else in transporting or in procuring transportation for herself. But such aid and assistance must, as in the case supposed in United States v. Holte be more active than mere agreement on her part to the transportation and its immoral purpose. For the statute is drawn to include those cases in which the woman consents to her own transportation. Yet it does not specifically impose any penalty upon her, although it deals in detail with the person by whom she is transported. In applying this criminal statute we cannot infer that the mere acquiescence of the woman transported was intended to be condemned by the general language punishing those who aid and assist the transporter, any more than it has been inferred that the purchaser of liquor was to be regarded as an abettor of the illegal sale. The penalties of the statute are too clearly directed against the acts of the transporter as distinguished from the consent of the subject of the transportation. So it was intimated in United States v. Holte, supra, and this conclusion is not disputed by the government here, which contends only that the conspiracy charge will lie though the woman could not commit the substantive offense.

Second. We come thus to the main question in the case, whether, admitting that the woman by consenting, has not violated the Mann Act, she may be convicted of a conspiracy with the man to violate it. Section 37 of the Criminal Code (18 U.S.C. s 88 (18 USCA s 88)), punishes a conspiracy by two or more persons "to commit any offense against the United States." The offense which she is charged with conspiring to commit is that perpetrated by the man, for it is not questioned that in transporting her he contravened section 2 of the Mann Act. Cf. Hence we must decide whether her concurrence, which was not criminal before the Mann Act, nor punished by it, may, without more, support a conviction under the conspiracy section, enacted many years before.

As was said in the Holte Case an agreement to commit an offense may be criminal, though its purpose is to do what some of the conspirators may be free to do alone. Incapacity of one to commit the substantive offense does not necessarily imply that he may with impunity conspire with others who are able to commit it. For it is the collective planning of criminal conduct at which the statute aims. The plan is itself a wrong which, if any act be done to effect its object, the state has elected to treat as criminal. And one may plan that others shall do what he cannot do himself.

But in this case we are concerned with something more than an agreement between two persons for one of them to commit an offense which the other cannot commit. There is the added element that the offense planned, the criminal object of the conspiracy, involves the agreement of the woman to her transportation by the man, which is the very conspiracy charged.

Congress set out in the Mann Act to deal with cases which frequently, if not normally, involve consent and agreement on the part of the woman to the forbidden transportation. In every case in which she is not intimidated or forced into the transportation, the statute necessarily contemplates her acquiescence. Yet this acquiescence, though an incident of a type of transportation specifically dealt with by the statute, was not made a crime under the Mann Act itself. Of this class of cases we say that the substantive offense contemplated by the statute itself involves the same combination or community of purpose of two persons only which is prosecuted here as conspiracy. If this were the only case covered by the act, it would be within those decisions which hold, consistently with the theory upon which conspiracies are punished, that where it is impossible under any circumstances to commit the substantive offense without co-operative action, the preliminary agreement between the same parties to commit the offense is not an indictable conspiracy either at common law. But criminal transportation under the Mann Act may be effected without the woman's consent as in cases of intimidation or force (with which we are not now concerned). We assume, therefore, for present purposes, as was suggested in the Holte Case that the decisions last mentioned do not in all strictness apply. We do not rest our decision upon the theory of those cases, nor upon the related one that the attempt is to prosecute as conspiracy acts identical with the substantive offense. We place it rather upon the ground that we perceive in the failure of the Mann Act to condemn the woman's participation in those transportations which are effected with her mere consent, evidence of an affirmative legislative policy to leave her acquiescence unpunished. We think it a necessary implication of that policy that when the Mann Act and the conspiracy statute came to be construed together, as they necessarily would be, the same participation which the former contemplates an an inseparable incident of all cases in which the woman is a voluntary agent at all, but does not punish, was not automatically to be made punishable under the latter. It would contravene that policy to hold that the very passage of the Mann Act effected a withdrawal by the conspiracy statute of that immunity which the Mann Act itself confers.

It is not to be supposed that the consent of an unmarried person to adultery with a married person, where the latter alone is guilty of the substantive offense, would render the former an abettor or a conspirator, compare In re Cooper, 162 Cal. 81, 85, 121 P. 318, or that the acquiescence of a woman under the age of consent would make her a co-conspirator with the man to commit statutory rape upon herself. Compare Queen v. Tyrrell, (1894) 1 Q.B. 710. The principle, determinative of this case, is the same.

On the evidence before us the woman petitioner has not violated the Mann Act and, we hold, is not guilty of a conspiracy to do so. As there is no proof that the man conspired with anyone else to bring about the transportation, the convictions of both petitioners must be

Reversed.

Mr. Justice CARDOZO concurs in the result.

Chapter 19
Accomplice Liability

A. Background

State v. Mitzel, 1989 WL 110827 (Ohio Ct. App. 1989)

The original concepts of "aiding and abetting" have their roots in common law. The participants in a crime were separated into four categories:

> (1) principals in the first degree who actually perpetrated the offense; (2) principals in the second degree who were actually or constructively present at the scene of the crime and aided or abetted its commission; (3) accessories before the fact who aided or abetted the crime, but were not present at its commission; and (4) accessories after the fact who rendered assistance after the crime was complete. *Standefer v. U.S.* (1980), 447 U.S. 10, 15. (Citations omitted.)

The principal in the first degree was the actual perpetrator of the crime, the person whose hand was actively involved in the commission of the crime. The principal in the second degree was the individual who was actually or constructively present at the scene and aided and abetted by doing some affirmative act or providing advice or encouragement. See, *e.g., State v. Mitchell* (1975), 24 N.C. App. 484.

Ohio has codified the crime of "aiding and abetting" in the complicity statute in R.C. 2923.03(A)(2). It provides:

> (A) No person, acting with the kind of culpability required for the commission of an offense, shall do any of the following:
> ***

2) Aid or abet another in committing the offense; R.C. 2923.03(A)(2).

This was interpreted in *State v. Sims* (1983), 10 Ohio App. 3d 56, where the court held in paragraph two of the syllabus:

The definition of an "aider and abettor" within the meaning of R.C. 2923.03(A)(2), is one who assists or encourages another to commit a crime, and participates in the commission thereof by some act, deed, word, or gesture. ***

It is defined in 25 Ohio Jurisprudence 3d (1981), 177, Criminal Law, Section 75:

To "aid" means to help to assist, or to strengthen; to "abet" means to encourage, to counsel, to incite, or to assist in a criminal act;

and, in 4 Ohio Jury Instructions (1988), Section 523.03, at 341:

AIDED. "Aid" means to help, assist, or strengthen.
ABETTED. "Abet" means to encourage, counsel, incite, or assist.****

Notes and Questions

1. As illustrated by *State v. Mitzel*, most jurisdictions no longer use the common law terms of principals in the first or second degree or accessories before or after the fact.

2. At common law, principals in the first or second degree and accessories before the fact were liable for the crime in which they aid, abet, encourage or assist another to commit. In contrast, the accessory after the fact was not liable for the underlying felony that had been committed. Instead, that defendant was charged with obstruction of justice or misprision.

B. Mere Presence

State v. Johnson, 93 Ohio St. 3d 240 (2001)

LUNDBERG STRATTON, J.

On June 10, 1996, members of the street gang known as the Bloods opened fire on members of another gang, the Crips. Edward McGaha, a member of the Crips, was wounded. Defendant-appellee, Leslie Johnson, also a Crips member, was present during the attack. One of the primary shooters in the attack was Richard Miles ("Boom"), a Bloods gang member and crack dealer.

Later that day, McGaha returned home from the hospital and was sitting on the front porch of his mother's home with some other Crips gang members and associates, including defendant, when a carload of Bloods pulled up and opened fire a second time. The Crips returned fire, but no one was injured in the exchange.

After the second exchange of gunfire, defendant, McGaha, Antwan Jones, Neil Bunkley, and Denicholas Stoutmire drove over to the house of a fellow Crips member known only as Heavy. At Heavy's, the group drank beer, smoked marijuana, and talked about how McGaha almost lost his life. According to McGaha, the group talked about going to "get them," and "everybody was just down with me." Neil Bunkley was so angry about the shooting that he punched out a window afterwards. The group decided to go after Boom for his involvement in the McGaha shooting.

Some of the Crips gang members stole two cars and they borrowed a third car from a "feener," a person who uses drugs. Around 12:30 a.m., a group of gang members, including defendant, got into the three cars and left Heavy's house. McGaha and Bunkley were in the stolen black Buick, and McGaha had a sawed-off shotgun. Gary Drayton and Antwan Jones were in a Chevette, and Drayton had a .380 gun. Denicholas Stoutmire was driving the stolen Bonneville, with Damian Williams, who had a .45 automatic, in the passenger seat, and defendant and Sidney Cornwell in the backseat. According to Bunkley, defendant was in possession of a .380 gun earlier that day. The passengers of the three cars were looking for Boom. They planned to shoot him if they found him.

First, the caravan drove to the south side of town, known to be Bloods territory. After splitting up briefly, the cars later met on Edwards Street on the south side of town. The cars then drove around and stopped on South Avenue, where Cornwell and defendant got out of the Bonneville to get a lighter from Jones. Defendant and Cornwell then got back in the Bonneville and decided to go back to Heavy's.

However, rather than going back to Heavy's, the lead car, the Bonneville, pulled up at Oak Park, an apartment complex that Boom was known to frequent.

The caravan pulled up side by side in front of the apartments and the occupants discussed kicking down the apartment door to go in and look for Boom. McGaha testified that they planned to kill Boom if they found him. Williams testified that he told the group that kicking in the door was a bad idea because one of them might get shot. Williams also testified that the group got together to go find and kill Boom and that Cornwell was "getting angrier and angrier." Williams testified that "common sense" told them what they needed to do.

The caravan of cars pulled around to the back of the apartments. Both the Buick and the Chevette drove past the back of the apartment, but the Bonneville stopped behind the apartment. Although the lighting was dim, McGaha testified that he was able to see a female and a male on the porch.

Susan Hamlett, a resident of the apartment complex, and Donald Meadows, her date, were on the back porch at 2:20 a.m. when Hamlett's three-year-old niece, Jessica Ballew, came out on the porch, wanting a drink of water. Hamlett was on her way back into the apartment with Jessica when the three cars came up the alley behind the apartment building.

Hamlett could see four people in the Bonneville. Cornwell asked if Boom was at the apartment. When Hamlett and Meadows replied that Boom was not at the apartment, Cornwell asked again, "Where is Boom?" Hamlett replied, "He don't live here." Cornwell said, "Well, tell Boom this," and he opened fire. Samuel Lagese and Marilyn Conrad, who were inside the apartment, and Meadows were struck and wounded. Three-year-old Jessica Ballew was killed.

A jury convicted defendant of one count of complicity to commit aggravated murder, in violation of R.C. 2923.03(A)(2) and 2903.01(A), and three counts of complicity to commit attempted aggravated murder, in violation of R.C. 2923.03(A)(2), 2923.02(A), and 2903.01(A). In addition, each count carried a firearm specification pursuant to R.C. 2941.141 and former 2929.71(A), now R.C. 2929.14. The Court of Appeals for Mahoning County relied on *State v. Sims* (1983), 10 Ohio App. 3d 56 and reversed the convictions and discharged the defendant.

The cause is now before this court upon the allowance of a discretionary appeal.

The issue before the court today is whether the actions of the defendant constituted complicity by aiding and abetting pursuant to R.C. 2923.03(A)(2). We find that they do, and for the reasons that follow, we reverse the judgment of the court of appeals and reinstate the defendant's convictions and sentence.

Defendant was convicted of complicity to commit aggravated murder, a violation of R.C. 2923.03(A)(2) and 2903.01(A), for the killing of Jessica Ballew. R.C. 2923.03 provides:

> (A) No person, acting with the kind of culpability required for the commission of an offense, shall do any of the following:

***

(2) Aid or abet another in committing the offense.

R.C. 2903.01(A) provides a definition of aggravated murder:

> No person shall purposely, and with prior calculation and design, cause the death of another ***.

With regard to the three other victims of these crimes, defendant was charged with and convicted of complicity to commit attempted aggravated murder, in violation of R.C. 2923.03(A)(2), 2903.01(A), and 2923.02(A).

R.C. 2923.02(A) provides a definition of attempt:

> No person, purposefully or knowingly, and when purpose or knowledge is sufficient culpability for the commission of an offense, shall engage in conduct that, if successful, would constitute or result in the offense.

Ohio's complicity statute, R.C. 2923.03, does not provide a definition of the terms "aid or abet." As a result, this court is now called upon to provide a definition. Black's Law Dictionary defines "aid and abet" as "[t]o assist or facilitate the commission of a crime, or to promote its accomplishment." Black's Law Dictionary (7 Ed. Rev. 1999) 69.

This court has held that "the mere presence of an accused at the scene of a crime is not sufficient to prove, in and of itself, that the accused was an aider and abettor." *State v. Widner* (1982), 69 Ohio St. 2d 267. This rule is to protect innocent bystanders who have no connection to the crime other than simply being present at the time of its commission.

We find, however, on these facts, much more than "mere presence" and we find that the court of appeals misapplied this legal concept. The court of appeals relied heavily on a case that is often cited by other appellate courts and defines "aider and abettor" as "one who assists or encourages another to commit a crime, and participates in the commission thereof by some act, deed, word, or gesture." *State v. Sims* (1983), 10 Ohio App. 3d 56, paragraph two of the syllabus. *Sims* held that "[a] person cannot be convicted of aiding and abetting a principal offender in the commission of an offense in the absence of evidence that the person assisted, incited or encouraged the principal to commit the offense." *Id.*, paragraph three of the syllabus.

Of course, *Sims* is not controlling legal authority. It is also distinguishable. In *Sims,* the defendant, who was convicted of aiding and abetting receiving stolen property and aiding and abetting possession of criminal tools, was a passenger in the back seat of a stolen car being driven by another male who was the apparent thief. The only evidence adduced indicated that Sims was "'associated' with Sanders [the principal], in that he was a passenger in the car with Sanders for about thirty seconds when he and his women companions were ordered out of the car by police." *Id.* at 59.

This case is clearly distinguishable from *Sims*. The prosecution in *Sims* obviously failed to prove that the defendant was anything more than merely present at the scene of the crime. Defendant in this case was a member of the Crips gang. Based on the record, which chronicles three separate gang-related shootings in a twenty-four-hour period, violence and revenge were a way of life for these rival gang members. Defendant went along on that fateful night as protection and support for his fellow gang members who had recently been "disrespected." He also had his own reason for revenge, as he himself had been shot at earlier that day.

Defendant was present when the Bloods shot at defendant, McGaha, and other Crips earlier in the day, wounding McGaha. Williams testified that he was driving around when he saw McGaha lying in the driveway, looking "almost dead." Williams testified that he talked with defendant at the scene and defendant told him that Boom had shot McGaha.

Defendant was present at the home of McGaha's mother later that afternoon when the Bloods shot at the Crips a second time. Defendant was present at Heavy's house when the Crips got together to discuss the prior shootings. Defendant was present when the group decided to "go get" Boom.

After other Crips members and associates went out and stole two cars to use in their plan to get Boom, defendant got into one of the stolen cars and rode around town in areas known to be frequented by rival Bloods gang members for over an hour looking for Boom. At one point during the evening, the cars converged, and defendant got out of the stolen Bonneville to get a light for his cigarette. Defendant could have abandoned the plan to kill Boom at that point or several other points throughout the day and night, but he did not. Instead, he chose to continue on with the three-car caravan in search of Boom so that the gang could seek revenge on Boom, their rival. As McGaha testified, "Everybody was just down with me."

Defendant was in the lead stolen car when the caravan pulled up in front of the Oak Park apartment, known to be frequented by Boom. Although no one told Stoutmire where to go on Oak Park, Williams agreed that Stoutmire knew where he was going, since they were looking for Boom and intended to shoot him if they found him. The gang members discussed the best way to enter the apartment in order to kill Boom. Williams testified about talk of kicking the door down to go in after Boom, but Williams testified that he told the gang that he thought that that was a bad idea. Again, defendant was reassured that a murder was about to take place, and he yet he failed to renounce or abandon the plan.

Defendant was still present in the stolen Bonneville when it pulled around behind the Oak Park apartment and up to the back porch, where his cohort, Sidney Cornwell, shot and killed three-year-old Jessica Ballew and wounded Meadows, Lagese, and Conrad. After these shootings, defendant and some of his fellow Crips gang members continued to stay together and went into hiding until defendant and others were ultimately arrested and charged with these crimes.

Defendant would have this court conclude that because no witness pinpointed a specific statement by defendant of his intent to join the plan to kill Boom, there is insufficient evidence to support a conviction for complicity based on aiding and abetting. This position defies not only the law but common sense.

Accordingly, we find that the court of appeals' decision went astray when it held that although the evidence at trial could reasonably support a finding that defendant was involved in a conspiracy to kill Boom, such a finding was insufficient to support convictions of complicity to commit aggravated murder and attempted aggravated murder based on appellant's alleged aiding and abetting of the principal offender. The court of appeals concluded that had the state elected to charge defendant with complicity based on his involvement in a conspiracy pursuant to R.C. 2923.03(A)(3), it was free to do so. But, by charging defendant solely under R.C. 2923.03(A)(2) as an aider and abettor, the court of appeals found that the state failed to provide defendant with sufficient legal notice that he could be convicted for the offense based on his role as a conspirator. We disagree and hold that defendant's actions did constitute aiding and abetting as set forth in R.C. 2923.03(A)(2).

Defendant was not an innocent bystander who was merely along for the ride. In fact, he intended to assist with the murder of Boom. We agree with the proposition that "[p]articipation in criminal intent may be inferred from presence, companionship and conduct before and after the offense is committed." *State v. Pruett* (1971), 28 Ohio App. 2d 29.

Defendant's cohort, Williams, defined what the gang intended to do not as a plan but as a "common sense" understanding of what needed to be done. When asked why they did what they did, Bunkley responded, "To seek revenge for something that he did to my friend. *** I mean, he [Boom] tried to kill my friend, so-you know, you bold enough to take a life, you'll get yours, too." When asked whether killing Boom was the plan of all eight people who were at Oak Park that night, Bunkley responded, "There was no plan. We all knew what we had to do. *** Get rid of Boom. *** Cause physical harm, kill him, shoot him, whatever you want to call it."

The fact that defendant did not articulate his intent will not allow him to escape responsibility for his clear actions of complicity by aiding and abetting in the commission of these crimes. Accordingly, we hold that to support a conviction for complicity by aiding and abetting pursuant to R.C. 2923.03(A)(2), the evidence must show that the defendant supported, assisted, encouraged, cooperated with, advised, or incited the principal in the commission of the crime, and that the defendant shared the criminal intent of the principal. Such intent may be inferred from the circumstances surrounding the crime.

Defendant and his fellow gang members hatched a calculated plan to kill Boom in order to avenge the shooting of their fellow gang member, McGaha. Defendant rode in the lead car with the shooter looking for their intended target. Sidney Cornwell and his associates, including defendant, intended to shoot Boom, but they killed Jessica Ballew and injured three others instead, and for those acts defendant is responsible as a complicitor.

Accordingly, we reverse the judgment of the court of appeals and reinstate defendant's convictions and sentence.

Judgment reversed.

PFEIFER, J., dissenting.

This court should have adopted *State v. Sims* (1983), 10 Ohio App. 3d 56, as the controlling Ohio authority on what constitutes an aider or abettor. *Sims,* as the majority points out, has been relied upon by other Ohio appellate jurisdictions, and appears to provide a useable definition for a somewhat slippery term. In my mind, the *Sims* definition creates a necessary distinction between an aider or abettor and a conspirator. The *Sims* definition requires participation in the commission of the act rather than in the planning of the act. I agree with the court of appeals that Johnson may well have been guilty of conspiracy, but he was not so charged. Instead, the prosecution overreached and failed to present any evidence of *Sims*-required actual participation. I would affirm the judgment of the appellate court.

Notes and Questions

1. According to the Ohio Supreme Court, how did the defendant in *State v. Johnson* aid and abet another in the killing of the three-year-old child? What specifically did he do? Is riding around in a car with a bunch of criminals sufficient to support a complicity conviction?

2. Was the defendant in *Johnson* properly charged? If you were the prosecutor in this case, would you have charged the defendant with complicity or conspiracy? How about both crimes? Why do you think the appellate court found that the evidence at trial could reasonably support a finding that the defendant was involved in a conspiracy to kill Boom, but was insufficient to support convictions of complicity to commit aggravated murder and attempted aggravated murder?

3. Looking back at *State v. Tomaino* in Chapter 3, the court suggested that the defendant might have been charged under an accomplice liability theory. Based on what you know about accomplice liability, would you have charged the defendant under that theory?

C. Actions of the Principal

In re T.K., 109 Ohio St. 3d 512 (2006)

ALICE ROBIE RESNICK, J.

In the early evening of July 30, 2003, Carolyn Pinson and members of her family gathered at her home for a birthday celebration. Several members of a local gang, Seven All, walked down Pinson's street, stopping in front of her home. The members of Seven All had come to the house in search of one of Carolyn Pinson's nephews, who had been previously involved in an altercation with a member of the gang. Witnesses testified to seeing a handgun passed between members of the gang and to hearing the appellee, T.K., a minor, shout out "Shoot" and "Shoot the [expletive]." Shots were fired, and Carolyn Pinson, her minor nephew, D.W., and a neighbor, Julio Hines, were wounded.

Appellee, T.K., was charged with three counts of delinquency by having committed a violation of law that, if committed by an adult, would be felonious assault in violation of R.C. 2903.11(A)(2) and one count of a violation that, if committed by an adult, would be aggravated riot in violation of R.C. 2917.02(A)(2). All charges against the appellee contained a one-year and a three-year firearm specification and a gang specification.

After a trial, the juvenile court found the appellee to be delinquent on two counts of felonious assault for the shootings of Pinson and her nephew, D.W., and delinquent on one count of aggravated riot with a one-year firearm specification and a gang specification. In reaching its decision, the court reasoned that the appellee knew that a gun was present at the scene and that he specifically intended his words to be put into action. Further, although the court expressed some uncertainty as to which victim the appellee's words were intended to target, the court found that the state sufficiently showed transferred intent to support the court's finding of complicity to commit felonious assault. The juvenile court committed the appellee to the institutional care of the Ohio Department of Youth Services for a minimum of 30 months, not to exceed his attainment of 21 years of age.

The appellee appealed his convictions to the Eighth District Court of Appeals. The appellate court unanimously upheld the appellee's conviction for aggravated riot, but a majority reversed his convictions on the two counts of felonious assault. *In re T.K.,* 8th Dist. No. 84934, 2005-Ohio-2321, ¶ 16. The majority determined that the evidence presented was "so riddled with conflicting testimony" that the juvenile court could not identify the principal or determine the intended target. *Id.* at ¶ 10. Consequently, a majority of the appellate court held that the evidence presented was insufficient to support the appellee's convictions of felonious assault. *Id.* at ¶ 11.

The dissenting judge asserted that the juvenile court's findings of delinquency on the charges of felonious assault were proper under the principle of complicity by aiding and abetting, given evidence that the appellee had actively encouraged a member of his gang to shoot at someone associated with Carolyn Pinson at her home. *Id.* at ¶ 20, 22. The dissenter argued that the juvenile court's uncertainty over the identity of the specific target of the shooter was not fatal to the court's finding of delinquency, because the juvenile court had determined that the appellee knew that members of his gang had a gun at the scene and that he acted with the specific intent to harm someone. *Id.* at ¶ 19.

The cause is now before our court pursuant to our acceptance of a discretionary appeal.

Ohio's complicity statute, R.C. 2923.03, reads:

> (A) No person, acting with the kind of culpability required for the commission of an offense, shall do any of the following:
>   ***
>   (2) Aid or abet another in committing the offense.
> ***
> (F) Whoever violates this section is guilty of complicity in the commission of an offense, and shall be prosecuted and punished as if he were a principal offender. A charge of complicity may be stated in terms of this section, or in terms of the principal offense.

This court has held that the state need not establish the identity of the principal in order to convict an offender of complicity. *State v. Perryman* (1976), 49 Ohio St. 2d 14, paragraph four of the syllabus. Rather, "[to] support a conviction for complicity by aiding and abetting pursuant to R.C. 2923.03(A)(2), the evidence must show that the defendant supported, assisted, encouraged, cooperated with, advised, or incited the principal in the commission of the crime, and that the defendant shared the criminal intent of the principal." *State v. Johnson* (2001), 93 Ohio St. 3d 240, syllabus. Such criminal intent can be inferred from the presence, companionship, and conduct of the defendant before and after the offense is committed. *Id.* at 245.

As these precedents indicate, the identity of the principal is not an element that the state must prove to establish the offense of complicity by aiding and abetting pursuant to R.C. 2923.03(A)(2). Therefore, the juvenile court's inability to identify the principal did not prevent it from finding the appellant delinquent on the two counts of felonious assault. The juvenile court evaluated the evidence and determined that the appellee was more than a mere bystander at the scene of the shootings. Specifically, the court found that the appellee was guilty of the two counts of felonious assault because he knew that a member of his gang possessed a gun at the scene, and with that knowledge and the specific intent to cause harm, he actively encouraged the shooter to shoot at someone at Pinson's home.

Further, under the doctrine of transferred intent, an offender who intentionally acts to harm someone but ends up accidentally harming another is criminally liable as if the offender had intended to harm the actual victim. *See State v. Solomon* (1981), 66 Ohio St. 2d 214, 217. We hold that the doctrine of transferred intent applies in complicity cases.

The juvenile court's uncertainty over the identity of the intended targets in this case is essentially immaterial. If the victims were the intended targets, the appellee, as an aider and abettor, can be prosecuted and punished as if he were the shooter. R.C. 2923.03(F). Moreover, even if the victims were not the intended targets, under the doctrine of transferred intent, the appellee is as criminally culpable for the harm caused to the actual victims as he would be if they had been the intended targets.

Overall, we must emphasize that the weight of the evidence and the credibility of the witnesses are matters primarily for the trier of fact. *State v. DeHass* (1967), 10 Ohio St. 2d 230, paragraph one of the syllabus. In this case, the juvenile court evaluated the evidence, determined that the appellee had actively encouraged a member of his gang to shoot at someone at the Pinson home with the specific intent to cause harm, and found that the state had sufficiently showed transferred intent to support the court's finding of complicity in two counts of felonious assault. The juvenile court's inability to identify the principal or determine the intended targets did not weaken the court's findings so as to prevent the court's adjudication of the appellee as delinquent on the charges of felonious assault.

Accordingly, we reverse the judgment of the court of appeals.

Judgment reversed.

Notes and Questions

1. Why do you think the appellate court in *In re T.K.* was so concerned with identifying the principal? If you were drafting new legislation on accomplice liability would you require that the principal be identified before convicting the accomplice?

2. The court in *In re T.K.* found the defendant guilty even though the principal was never charged with a crime. Would the outcome change for an accessory if the principal was acquitted? At common law, an accessory could not be tried before the principal. Furthermore, the accessory could not be convicted unless the principal was also convicted. This is no longer true today in most jurisdictions. However, the prosecution still has to prove at trial that a crime has been committed.

3. How might a prosecutor use accomplice liability when the state is unable to determine which defendant actually caused the harm? For example, if two offenders shoot into a crowd killing one person, can the state charge both under the complicity statute?

D. Mens Rea

John F. Decker, *The Mental State Requirement for Accomplice Liability in American Criminal Law*
60 S.C. L. Rev. 237 (2008)

Due to the inconsistency between the plain language of states' accomplice liability legislation and its respective interpretation in the state courts, many states' accomplice laws present a confused picture in terms of the law's stance on accomplice liability. No aspect of this law is more complex than that relating to the mental state requirement for accomplice liability. Nevertheless, if one engages in a cursory examination of the legal literature, case law, and state legislation concerning the mental state requirement for accomplice liability, essentially three approaches surface. These approaches differ in the degree to which they hold an individual culpable for the conduct of another. First, there is the perspective (which is particularly popular in the academic community) that favors a very limited, narrow approach whereby accomplice liability is dependent upon a finding that an accused's "purpose [was] to encourage or assist another in the commission of a crime." Meanwhile, a second perspective (which the Model Penal Code follows to some extent) tolerates a more expansive approach whereby an accomplice's liability turns on whether the accomplice harbored the mental state required of the substantive crime allegedly aided or abetted. Finally, the third and broadest approach holds an accomplice liable for the "natural and probable" consequences of a principal's conduct that the accomplice somehow assisted or encouraged, regardless of the accomplice's mental state.

Ⓥ The first approach, which this Article will refer to as the Category I approach, asserts that an individual should only be liable for the acts of a principal if that individual acted with the specific intent to promote or assist the principal's commission of the crime. This theory holds that a mental state of knowledge or recklessness on the part of an alleged accomplice is insufficient to hold the alleged accomplice culpable. Jurisdictions following this approach will only hold an alleged accomplice liable for the crimes that the alleged accomplice intended a perpetrator commit. Also, if the perpetrator commits a secondary crime in pursuance of the intended crime, the accomplice is not liable for the secondary crime unless the accomplice intended to promote or facilitate this offense as well. So long as the alleged accomplice intended to somehow assist or encourage the principal's criminality, the accomplice is liable even if the substantive crime only requires recklessness or negligence on the part of the principal. Thus, if A loans his gun to B knowing B intends to use it to shoot his neighbor's barking dog, A would not be an accomplice to B's act unless he himself intends that B's neighbor's dog be shot. Likewise, if X gives the keys of her car to Y, who is intoxicated, knowing Y intends to drive the car, X would not be criminally liable if Y's reckless driving kills or injures an innocent person. Thus, this might simply be described as the "specific intent" approach.

The second approach, which this study refers to as the Category II model, is what might be called the "statutorily prescribed mental state" approach. According to this somewhat more expansive view, an individual may be liable for a crime the individual did not specifically intend for the perpetrator to commit. Rather, liability attaches if the alleged accomplice acted "with the mental culpability required for the commission" of the offense. Thus, states following this approach will hold an individual liable for the conduct of another if that individual possessed the mental state prescribed by the state's substantive criminal statute, whether the requisite mental state for conviction is intent, knowledge, recklessness, or criminal negligence. Returning to the hypotheticals discussed above, where A loans his gun knowing of B's intent to shoot the neighbor's barking dog, A would now be criminally liable for the knowing, unauthorized infliction of injury or death on an animal, even though A has no intent for the crime occur. Likewise, where X gives her car keys to the intoxicated Y knowing Y will drive her car and Y recklessly kills Z, X would be liable for reckless homicide along with Y if we agree X harbors a reckless state of mind. Both A and X would be liable because each acts with the mental culpability required for the commission of their respective offenses.

Category II states can be divided into two subcategories: (1) states that articulate the Category II approach statutorily, and (2) states whose courts have judicially interpreted the Category II approach from statutes void of Category II language. The states that statutorily follow the Category II approach can be further divided into states that require the statutorily prescribed mental state with regard to result-oriented crimes alone, and those that do not differentiate between conduct- and result-oriented crimes. The Model Penal Code, codified by a number of states, allows for liability if an accomplice possessed the requisite mental state for conviction of a perpetrator when "causing a particular result is an element" of the crime (e.g., the "death" in homicide; the "injury" in battery). However, if the crime focuses on the conduct of the actor rather than the result (e.g., the "unauthorized entry" in burglary; the "substantial step" in criminal attempt), it is necessary that the accomplice have the specific intent that the principal commit the crime. States that do not distinguish between conduct- and result-oriented crimes will hold an individual liable for the conduct of another as long as the individual possessed the statutorily prescribed mental state for the substantive crime.

 The third approach, which this Article refers to as Category III, is the most expansive of the approaches. States following this approach will hold an actor liable for all the natural and probable consequences of the intended crime. Although some jurisdictions may not use this exact language, these states reject the necessity of proving the accomplice had either the specific intent required by the Category I approach or the statutorily prescribed mental state mandated by the Category II approach. Therefore, if the principal committed a secondary crime in the course of carrying out the target crime even if the accomplice had no way of knowing or anticipating that an incidental or secondary crime would occur, a court will nonetheless convict the accomplice of the incidental crime if the court determines it to be a natural and probable consequence of the intended crime. Now the hypotheticals above become really interesting. Assume after B shoots his neighbor's barking dog with A's gun, the neighbor, C, becomes angry and engages B in a physical altercation during which B shoots and injures C. If we agree the altercation and resultant injury suffered by C are natural and probable consequences of A's arming B while knowing of B's intentions, A would be liable as an accomplice for B's battery of C. In the example where X gives her keys to the intoxicated Y (which itself is a violation of the state's motor vehicle code), now assume Y not only recklessly becomes involved in a fatal vehicle crash but also that Y collides with a gasoline truck, which explodes and causes a nearby building to catch fire. If we agree that when X gives the intoxicated Y the keys to her car she should be held accountable for all natural and probable consequences, it is arguable that X is liable not only for reckless homicide if Y is involved in a fatal collision while driving X's car but also for criminal damage to property or perhaps arson. Or, worse yet, if a firefighter or building occupant dies in the fire, it might even be asserted that X is liable for manslaughter.

Members of the academic community, including Professors Wayne LaFave, Joshua Dressler, and Audrey Rogers, have strongly criticized the Category III approach because it holds an individual to the same culpability as a principal for a crime the commission of which the accomplice had no knowledge of or intent to assist in. Scholars have also asserted that "this foreseeable-offense extension of the complicity doctrine is clearly a minority view." In any event, under this view one is held accountable for the incidental crime as a result of choosing to enter into the criminal arena, an environment where history has shown criminality has a tendency to spread like fast growing cancer cells.

Notes and Questions

1. Of the three approaches discussed which one do you prefer? What are the strengths and weaknesses of each one?

2. Can you identify the approach used by the courts in *State v. Johnson* and *In re T.K.*?

PART VI
Defenses

PART VI
Defense

Chapter 20
Self-Defense and Defense of Others

A. Background

At early common law, self-defense was viewed as an excuse defense, where now it is viewed as a justification defense. Today, a non-aggressor may use a reasonable amount of force against another when he reasonably believes that he is in immediate danger of unlawful bodily harm and that the use of force is necessary to avoid this danger. If the individual is facing serious physical harm or death, he may use lethal force.

B. Burden of Proof

Similar to voluntary manslaughter, the question of who has the burden of proof routinely arises with respect to self-defense. The first case in this chapter, *Martin v. Ohio*, addresses the issue of whether placing the burden of proving self-defense onto the defendant violates the constitution.

Martin v. Ohio, 480 U.S. 228 (1987)

Justice WHITE delivered the opinion of the Court.

The Ohio Code provides that "[e]very person accused of an offense is presumed innocent until proven guilty beyond a reasonable doubt, and the burden of proof for all elements of the offense is upon the prosecution. The burden of going forward with the evidence of an affirmative defense, and the burden of proof by a preponderance of the evidence, for an affirmative defense, is upon the accused." Ohio Rev. Code Ann. 2901.05(A) (1982). An affirmative defense is one involving "an excuse or justification peculiarly within the knowledge of the accused, on which he can fairly be required to adduce supporting evidence." Ohio Rev. Code Ann. 2901.05(C)(2) (1982). The Ohio courts have "long determined that self-defense is an affirmative defense," 21 Ohio St. 3d 91 (1986), and that the defendant has the burden of proving it as required by 2901.05(A).

As defined by the trial court in its instructions in this case, the elements of self-defense that the defendant must prove are that (1) the defendant was not at fault in creating the situation giving rise to the argument; (2) the defendant had an honest belief that she was in imminent danger of death or great bodily harm, and that her only means of escape from such danger was in the use of such force; and (3) the defendant did not violate any duty to retreat or avoid danger. App. 19. The question before us is whether the Due Process Clause of the Fourteenth Amendment forbids placing the burden of proving self-defense on the defendant when she is charged by the State of Ohio with committing the crime of aggravated murder, which, as relevant to this case, is defined by the Revised Code of Ohio as "purposely, and with prior calculation and design, caus[ing] the death of another." Ohio Rev. Code Ann. 2903.01 (1982).

The facts of the case, taken from the opinions of the courts below, may be succinctly stated. On July 21, 1983, petitioner Earline Martin and her husband, Walter Martin, [480 U.S. 228, 231] argued over grocery money. Petitioner claimed that her husband struck her in the head during the argument. Petitioner's version of what then transpired was that she went upstairs, put on a robe, and later came back down with her husband's gun which she intended to dispose of. Her husband saw something in her hand and questioned her about it. He came at her, and she lost her head and fired the gun at him. Five or six shots were fired, three of them striking and killing Mr. Martin. She was charged with and tried for aggravated murder. She pleaded self-defense and testified in her own defense. The judge charged the jury with respect to the elements of the crime and of self-defense and rejected petitioner's Due Process Clause challenge to the charge placing on her the burden of proving self-defense. The jury found her guilty.

Both the Ohio Court of Appeals and the Supreme Court of Ohio affirmed the conviction. Both rejected the constitutional challenge to the instruction requiring petitioner to prove self-defense. The latter court, relying upon our opinion in *Patterson v. New York*, 432 U.S. 197 (1977), concluded that the State was required to prove the three elements of aggravated murder but that *Patterson* did not require it to disprove self-defense, which is a separate issue that did not require Mrs. Martin to disprove any element of the offense with which she was charged. The court said, "the state proved beyond a reasonable doubt that appellant purposely, and with prior calculation and design, caused the death of her husband. Appellant did not dispute the existence of these elements, but rather sought to justify her actions on grounds she acted in self defense." 21 Ohio St. 3d, at 94. There was thus no infirmity in her conviction. We granted certiorari, 475 U.S. 1119 (1986), and affirm the decision of the Supreme Court of Ohio.

In re Winship, 397 U.S. 358, 364 (1970), declared that the Due Process Clause "protects the accused against conviction except upon proof beyond a reasonable doubt of every fact [480 U.S. 228, 232] necessary to constitute the crime with which he is charged." A few years later, we held that *Winship's* mandate was fully satisfied where the State of New York had proved beyond reasonable doubt each of the elements of murder, but placed on the defendant the burden of proving the affirmative defense of extreme emotional disturbance, which, if proved, would have reduced the crime from murder to manslaughter. *Patterson v. New York, supra*. We there emphasized the preeminent role of the States in preventing and dealing with crime and the reluctance of the Court to disturb a State's decision with respect to the definition of criminal conduct and the procedures by which the criminal laws are to be enforced in the courts, including the burden of producing evidence and allocating the burden of persuasion. 432 U.S., at 201-202. New York had the authority to define murder as the intentional killing of another person. It had chosen, however, to reduce the crime to manslaughter if the defendant proved by a preponderance of the evidence that he had acted under the influence of extreme emotional distress. To convict of murder, the jury was required to find beyond a reasonable doubt, based on all the evidence, including that related to the defendant's mental state at the time of the crime, each of the elements of murder and also to conclude that the defendant had not proved his affirmative defense. The jury convicted Patterson, and we held there was no violation of the Fourteenth Amendment as construed in *Winship*. Referring to *Leland v. Oregon*, 343 U.S. 790 (1952), and *Rivera v. Delaware*, 429 U.S. 877 (1976), we added that New York "did no more than *Leland* and *Rivera* permitted it to do without violating the Due Process Clause" and declined to reconsider those cases. 432 U.S., at 206, 207. It was also observed that "the fact that a majority of the States have now assumed the burden of disproving affirmative defenses—for whatever reasons—[does not] mean that those States that strike a different balance are in violation of the Constitution." *Id.*, at 211. [480 U.S. 228, 233]

As in *Patterson*, the jury was here instructed that to convict it must find, in light of all the evidence, that each of the elements of the crime of aggravated murder has been proved by the State beyond reasonable doubt, and that the burden of proof with respect to these elements did not shift. To find guilt, the jury had to be convinced that none of the evidence, whether offered by the State or by Martin in connection with her plea of self-defense, raised a reasonable doubt that Martin had killed her husband, that she had the specific purpose and intent to cause his death, or that she had done so with prior calculation and design. It was also told, however, that it could acquit if it found by a preponderance of the evidence that Martin had not precipitated the confrontation, that she had an honest belief that she was in imminent danger of death or great bodily harm, and that she had satisfied any duty to retreat or avoid danger. The jury convicted Martin.

We agree with the State and its Supreme Court that this conviction did not violate the Due Process Clause. The State did not exceed its authority in defining the crime of murder as purposely causing the death of another with prior calculation or design. It did not seek to shift to Martin the burden of proving any of those elements, and the jury's verdict reflects that none of her self-defense evidence raised a reasonable doubt about the State's proof that she purposefully killed with prior calculation and design. She nevertheless had the opportunity under state law and the instructions given to justify the killing and show herself to be blameless by proving that she acted in self-defense. The jury thought she had failed to do so, and Ohio is as entitled to punish Martin as one guilty of murder as New York was to punish Patterson.

It would be quite different if the jury had been instructed that self-defense evidence could not be considered in determining whether there was a reasonable doubt about the State's case, i. e., that self-defense evidence must be put aside for all purposes unless it satisfied the preponderance [480 U.S. 228, 234] standard. Such an instruction would relieve the State of its burden and plainly run afoul of *Winship's* mandate. 397 U.S., at 364. The instructions in this case could be clearer in this respect, but when read as a whole, we think they are adequate to convey to the jury that all of the evidence, including the evidence going to self-defense, must be considered in deciding whether there was a reasonable doubt about the sufficiency of the State's proof of the elements of the crime.

We are thus not moved by assertions that the elements of aggravated murder and self-defense overlap in the sense that evidence to prove the latter will often tend to negate the former. It may be that most encounters in which self-defense is claimed arise suddenly and involve no prior plan or specific purpose to take life. In those cases, evidence offered to support the defense may negate a purposeful killing by prior calculation and design, but Ohio does not shift to the defendant the burden of disproving any element of the state's case. When the prosecution has made out a prima facie case and survives a motion to acquit, the jury may nevertheless not convict if the evidence offered by the defendant raises any reasonable doubt about the existence of any fact necessary for the finding of guilt. Evidence creating a reasonable doubt could easily fall far short of proving self-defense by a preponderance of the evidence. Of course, if such doubt is not raised in the jury's mind and each juror is convinced that the defendant purposely and with prior calculation and design took life, the killing will still be excused if the elements of the defense are satisfactorily established. We note here, but need not rely on, the observation of the Supreme Court of Ohio that "[a]ppellant did not dispute the existence of [the elements of aggravated murder], but rather sought to justify her actions on grounds she acted in self-defense." 21 Ohio St. 3d, at 94. [480 U.S. 228, 235]

Petitioner submits that there can be no conviction under Ohio law unless the defendant's conduct is unlawful, and that because self-defense renders lawful what would otherwise be a crime, unlawfulness is an element of the offense that the state must prove by disproving self-defense. This argument founders on state law, for it has been rejected by the Ohio Supreme Court and by the Court of Appeals for the Sixth Circuit. *White v. Arn*, 788 F.2d 338, 346-347 (1986). It is true that unlawfulness is essential for conviction, but the Ohio courts hold that the unlawfulness in cases like this is the conduct satisfying the elements of aggravated murder—an interpretation of state law that we are not in a position to dispute. The same is true of the claim that it is necessary to prove a "criminal" intent to convict for serious crimes, which cannot occur if self-defense is shown: the necessary mental state for aggravated murder under Ohio law is the specific purpose to take life pursuant to prior calculation and design. *See White v. Arn, supra*, at 346.

As we noted in Patterson, the common-law rule was that affirmative defenses, including self-defense, were matters for the defendant to prove. "This was the rule when the Fifth Amendment was adopted, and it was the American rule when the Fourteenth Amendment was ratified." 432 U.S., at 202. Indeed, well into this century, a number of States followed the common-law rule and required a defendant to shoulder the burden of proving that he acted in self-defense. Fletcher, Two Kinds of Legal Rules: A Comparative Study of Burden-of-Persuasion Practices in Criminal Cases, 77 Yale [480 U.S. 228, 236] L. J. 880, 882, and n. 10 (1968). We are aware that all but two of the States, Ohio and South Carolina, have abandoned the common-law rule and require the prosecution to prove the absence of self-defense when it is properly raised by the defendant. But the question remains whether those States are in violation of the Constitution; and, as we observed in *Patterson*, that question is not answered by cataloging the practices of other States. We are no more convinced that the Ohio practice of requiring self-defense to be proved by the defendant is unconstitutional than we are that the Constitution requires the prosecution to prove the sanity of a defendant who pleads not guilty by reason of insanity. We have had the opportunity to depart from *Leland v. Oregon*, 343 U.S. 790 (1952), but have refused to do so. *Rivera v. Delaware*, 429 U.S. 877 (1976). These cases were important to the *Patterson* decision and they, along with *Patterson*, are authority for our decision today.

The judgment of the Ohio Supreme Court is accordingly

Affirmed.

Justice POWELL, with whom Justice BRENNAN and Justice MARSHALL join, and with whom Justice BLACKMUN joins with respect to Parts I and III, dissenting.

Today the Court holds that a defendant can be convicted of aggravated murder even though the jury may have a reasonable doubt whether the accused acted in self-defense, and thus whether he is guilty of a crime. Because I think this decision is inconsistent with both precedent and fundamental fairness, I dissent.

I

Petitioner Earline Martin was tried in state court for the aggravated murder of her husband. Under Ohio law, the elements of the crime are that the defendant has purposely killed another with "prior calculation and design." Ohio Rev. Code Ann. 2903.01 (1982). Martin admitted that she [480 U.S. 228, 237] shot her husband, but claimed that she acted in self-defense. Because self-defense is classified as an "affirmative" defense in Ohio, the jury was instructed that Martin had the burden of proving her claim by a preponderance of the evidence. Martin apparently failed to carry this burden, and the jury found her guilty.

The Ohio Supreme Court upheld the conviction, relying in part on this Court's opinion in *Patterson v. New York*, 432 U.S. 197 (1977). The Court today also relies on the *Patterson* reasoning in affirming the Ohio decision. If one accepts *Patterson* as the proper method of analysis for this case, I believe that the Court's opinion ignores its central meaning.

In *Patterson*, the Court upheld a state statute that shifted the burden of proof for an affirmative defense to the accused. New York law required the prosecutor to prove all of the statutorily defined elements of murder beyond a reasonable doubt, but permitted a defendant to reduce the charge to manslaughter by showing that he acted while suffering an "extreme emotional disturbance." See N.Y. Penal Law 125.25, 125.20 (McKinney 1975 and Supp. 1987). The Court found that this burden shifting did not violate due process, largely because the affirmative defense did "not serve to negative any facts of the crime which the State is to prove in order to convict of murder." 432 U.S., at 207. The clear implication of this ruling is that when an affirmative defense does negate an element of the crime, the state may not shift the burden. *See White v. Arn*, 788 F.2d 338, 344-345 (1986). In such a case, *In re Winship*, 397 U.S. 358 (1970), requires the state to prove the nonexistence of the defense beyond a reasonable doubt.

The reason for treating a defense that negates an element of the crime differently from other affirmative defenses is plain. If the jury is told that the prosecution has the burden of proving all the elements of a crime, but then also is instructed [480 U.S. 228, 238] that the defendant has the burden of disproving one of those same elements, there is a danger that the jurors will resolve the inconsistency in a way that lessens the presumption of innocence. For example, the jury might reasonably believe that by raising the defense, the accused has assumed the ultimate burden of proving that particular element. Or, it might reconcile the instructions simply by balancing the evidence that supports the prosecutor's case against the evidence supporting the affirmative defense, and conclude that the state has satisfied its burden if the prosecution's version is more persuasive. In either case, the jury is given the unmistakable but erroneous impression that the defendant shares the risk of nonpersuasion as to a fact necessary for conviction.

Given these principles, the Court's reliance on *Patterson* is puzzling. Under Ohio law, the element of "prior calculation and design" is satisfied only when the accused has engaged in a "definite process of reasoning *in advance* of the killing," i.e., when he has given the plan at least some "studied consideration." App. 14 (jury instructions) (emphasis added). In contrast, when a defendant such as Martin raises a claim of [480 U.S. 228, 239] self-defense, the jury also is instructed that the accused must prove that she "had an honest belief that she was in *imminent* danger of death or great bodily harm." 2 *Id.*, at 19 (emphasis added). In many cases, a defendant who finds himself in immediate danger and reacts with deadly force will not have formed a prior intent to kill. The Court recognizes this when it states:

> It may be that most encounters in which self-defense is claimed arise suddenly and involve no prior plan or specific purpose to take life. In those cases, evidence offered to support the defense may negate a purposeful killing by prior calculation and design . . . . Ante, at 234.

Under *Patterson*, this conclusion should suggest that Ohio is precluded from shifting the burden as to self-defense. The Court nevertheless concludes that Martin was properly required to prove self-defense, simply because "Ohio does not shift to the defendant the burden of disproving any element of the state's case." *Ibid*.

The Court gives no explanation for this apparent rejection of *Patterson*. The only justification advanced for the Court's decision is that the jury could have used the evidence of self-defense to find that the State failed to carry its burden of proof. Because the jurors were free to consider both Martin's and the State's evidence, the argument goes, the verdict of guilt necessarily means that they were convinced that the defendant acted with prior calculation and design, and were unpersuaded that she acted in self-defense. Ante, at 233. The Court thus seems to conclude that as long as the jury is told that the state has the burden of proving all elements of the crime, the overlap between the offense and defense is immaterial. [480 U.S. 228, 240]

This reasoning is flawed in two respects. First, it simply ignores the problem that arises from inconsistent jury instructions in a criminal case. The Court's holding implicitly assumes that the jury in fact understands that the ultimate burden remains with the prosecutor at all times, despite a conflicting instruction that places the burden on the accused to disprove the same element. But as pointed out above, the *Patterson* distinction between defenses that negate an element of the crime and those that do not is based on the legitimate concern that the jury will mistakenly lower the state's burden. In short, the Court's rationale fails to explain why the overlap in this case does not create the risk that *Patterson* suggested was unacceptable.

Second, the Court significantly, and without explanation, extends the deference granted to state legislatures in this area. Today's decision could be read to say that virtually all state attempts to shift the burden of proof for affirmative defenses will be upheld, regardless of the relationship between the elements of the defense and the elements of the crime. As I understand it, *Patterson* allowed burden shifting because evidence of an extreme emotional disturbance did not negate the mens rea of the underlying offense. After today's decision, however, even if proof of the defense does negate an element of the offense, burden shifting still may be [480 U.S. 228, 241] permitted because the jury can consider the defendant's evidence when reaching its verdict.

I agree, of course, that States must have substantial lee-way in defining their criminal laws and administering their criminal justice systems. But none of our precedents suggests that courts must give complete deference to a State's judgment about whether a shift in the burden of proof is consistent with the presumption of innocence. In the past we have emphasized that in some circumstances it may be necessary to look beyond the text of the State's burden-shifting laws to satisfy ourselves that the requirements of *Winship* have been satisfied. In *Mullaney v. Wilbur*, 421 U.S. 684, 698-699 (1975) we explicitly noted the danger of granting the State unchecked discretion to shift the burden as to any element of proof in a criminal case. The Court today fails to discuss or even cite *Mullaney*, despite our unanimous agreement in that case that this danger would justify judicial intervention in some cases. Even *Patterson*, from which I dissented, recognized that "there are obviously constitutional limits beyond which the States may not go [in labeling elements of a crime as an affirmative defense]." 5 432 U.S., at 210. Today, however, the Court simply asserts that Ohio law properly allocates the burdens, without giving any indication of where those limits lie.

Because our precedent establishes that the burden of proof may not be shifted when the elements of the defense and the elements of the offense conflict, and because it seems clear [480 U.S. 228, 242] that they do so in this case, I would reverse the decision of the Ohio Supreme Court.***

III

In its willingness to defer to the State's legislative definitions of crimes and defenses, the Court apparently has failed to recognize the practical effect of its decision. Martin alleged that she was innocent because she acted in self-defense, a complete justification under Ohio law. *See State v. Nolton*, 19 Ohio St. 2d 133 (1969). Because she had the burden of proof on this issue, the jury could have believed that it was just as likely as not that Martin's conduct was justified, and yet still have voted to convict. In other words, even though the jury may have had a substantial doubt whether Martin committed a crime, she was found guilty under Ohio law. I do not agree that the Court's authority [480 U.S. 228, 244] to review state legislative choices is so limited that it justifies increasing the risk of convicting a person who may not be blameworthy. *See Patterson v. New York, supra*, at 201-202 (state definition of criminal law must yield when it "'offends some principle of justice so rooted in the traditions and conscience of our people as to be ranked as fundamental'" (*quoting Speiser v. Randall*, 357 U.S. 513, 523 (1958)). The complexity of the inquiry as to when a State may shift the burden of proof should not lead the Court to fashion simple rules of deference that could lead to such unjust results.

Notes and Questions

1. In *Martin v. Ohio*, the majority wrote the following language, "[i]t would be quite different if the jury had been instructed that self-defense evidence could not be considered in determining whether there was a reasonable doubt about the State's case, i.e., that self-defense evidence must be put aside for all purposes unless it satisfied the preponderance." Is the majority saying that jurors are able to apply the same set of facts to the evidence presented by both the prosecution and defense under the appropriate legal standards? As a practical matter, do you agree or disagree with this assertion?

2. After *Martin*, how far could a state go in redefining its crimes? Could a state redefine murder in such a way as to remove a critical element and in turn require the defendant to prove that element if he wants to assert it as a defense?

C. Castle Doctrine

A majority of jurisdictions around the country do not require an individual to retreat before using deadly force. A minority of jurisdictions, including Ohio, do require the individual to retreat if he can safely do so before resorting to deadly force. The next case examines an exception to this duty to retreat before using deadly force.

State v. Kozlosky, 195 Ohio App. 3d 343 (2011)

JURY TRIAL.

McNaughton testified again and described her eight-year on-and-off tumultuous relationship with Coleman, which was fraught with physical abuse. About two months prior to the shooting, she began renting the upstairs of

Kozlosky's home, and about a week later, she asked Kozlosky to allow Coleman to move into the house, and Kozlosky consented. However, because of the constant fights between her and Coleman, Kozlosky ultimately evicted Coleman.

McNaughton testified that around 4 a.m., on September 20, 2009, Nicki, a woman she casually knew, Doug Kapel, and Coleman arrived in a red truck. Nicki invited McNaughton to party with them, and she accepted. They stopped to buy crack cocaine and proceeded to a motel, where they remained for several hours abusing drugs.

McNaughton testified that after consuming all the crack cocaine they had purchased, they bought more, returned to the motel, and consumed more crack cocaine. McNaughton stated that once they had consumed all of the crack cocaine, Coleman encouraged her to make sexual advances towards Kapel in an effort to influence Kapel to buy more drugs. McNaughton refused, and Coleman became angry. As a ruse to leave the motel, McNaughton told Coleman that she needed to meet someone who had agreed to advance her drugs.

McNaughton testified that the foursome drove to the parking lot of a Save-A-Lot supermarket located near Kozlosky's home. McNaughton exited the truck while the others remained inside; she then surreptitiously slipped away and made her way back home. Once home, McNaughton told Kozlosky that she had left Coleman a few streets away, that he was very upset, and that he would be there shortly looking for her.

A short time later, McNaughton observed Coleman exiting the red truck driven by Kapel, via a computer-operated security camera that monitors Kozlosky's driveway. McNaughton hysterically began yelling that Coleman had arrived and that they should lock the doors. Coleman immediately began banging on the locked back door; he kicked out the bottom panel and entered the house.

McNaughton stated that Kozlosky told Coleman he was not allowed on the property, but Coleman pushed past him and came towards her in the living room. McNaughton yelled that the police had been called and that Kapel was pulling out of the driveway, which prompted Coleman to retreat and exit Kozlosky's house.

McNaughton hid in the garage until Coleman left; she stayed for about 10 minutes, and reentered the house when she thought it was safe. When she entered the house, McNaughton found Coleman standing in the kitchen. Coleman immediately started yelling at McNaughton to give him money, followed her into the living room, grabbed her by the hair, threw her to the ground, and began hitting her. McNaughton testified that as Coleman was beating her, Kozlosky fired two shots, hitting Coleman, who spun around and fell to the ground. McNaughton testified that Kozlosky proceeded to shoot Coleman several times as he lay on the floor.

At trial, 54-year-old Kozlosky, a laid-off engineer and part-time community college professor, as well as a United States Air Force veteran, took the stand in his own defense. Kozlosky testified that in June 2009, after being laid off from his job with Sprint in 2008, he rented the upstairs unit of his house to Carolyn Walker. McNaughton occasionally visited Walker and later sought Kozlosky's permission to share the unit with Walker. Kozlosky consented, and McNaughton moved in July 2009.

Walker moved out of the house at the end of July 2009, and McNaughton sought permission from Kozlosky for Coleman to move in, which he granted. From the very beginning, Coleman and McNaughton argued and fought constantly, with Coleman violently beating McNaughton, especially when he was coming down from a crack-cocaine high. Kozlosky testified that by the end of August 2009, the fighting between Coleman and McNaughton had become so frequent and disruptive to himself and his neighbors that he had ordered him to leave his house. Kozlosky escorted Coleman off his property and told him not to return. But Coleman was uncooperative. A loud argument ensued, and neighbors summoned the police. Coleman eventually left, and Kozlosky was cited for disorderly conduct. Kozlosky wore a leather pocket holster with a gun. He had a concealed carry permit; however, the police took the weapon and told him he could pick it up the next week.

After Coleman's departure, McNaughton warned him about Coleman's violent past. McNaughton showed Kozlosky information on Cuyahoga County's website regarding Coleman's 1990 conviction for shooting a man to death, a conviction for carrying a concealed weapon, and numerous drug-related offenses.

Kozlosky testified that on September 20, 2009, Coleman, despite protests, entered his house three separate times. First, Coleman began banging on the locked door shortly after McNaughton had arrived home. Kozlosky and McNaughton shouted that Coleman was not allowed inside, but he ignored them, kicked out the bottom panel of the door, and crawled through into the kitchen. Coleman finally left when McNaughton told him that the police had been called.

While Kozlosky was repairing the door that Coleman had kicked in, Coleman returned. Kozlosky demanded that he leave, but Coleman brushed passed him, asked if Kozlosky wanted to "shoot it out," and proceeded to search for McNaughton. While Kozlosky was in the house, Coleman held one hand behind his back signaling that he had a gun. Coleman left after his attempts to locate McNaughton proved unsuccessful.

Coleman returned a third time while Kozlosky was still repairing the broken door. Again, Kozlosky demanded that Coleman leave, at which time McNaughton entered the house. Coleman immediately grabbed McNaughton by her hair and began beating her. Kozlosky protested, as McNaughton yelled for help. Kozlosky demanded that Coleman stop the assault, but when Coleman reached behind his back for his gun, Kozlosky pulled his revolver and shot Coleman. Kozlosky testified that when he shot Coleman, Coleman spun around, fell to the ground, and began to twitch, a scenario that prompted Kozlosky to fire several more times.

Kozlosky described his thoughts at the moment of the shooting: "I thought I was dead. I thought, I was panicking, I thought it just about, I thought he was going to shoot me. My gun was brand new, I never tried it. I didn't even know if it would work. I was afraid it would fail me and he was going to shoot me. I was pretty much panicking at the time." Kozlosky maintained, "I thought he was going to shoot me."

The jury found Kozlosky guilty of murder and the attached one-and three-year firearm specifications. The trial court sentenced Kozlosky to a prison term of 15 years to life for the murder conviction and three years for the firearm specifications. Kozlosky now appeals.

Self-defense is an affirmative defense that, if proved, relieves a defendant of criminal liability for the force that the defendant used. "'The burden of going forward with the evidence of an affirmative defense, and the burden of proof, by a preponderance of the evidence, for an affirmative defense, is upon the accused.'" *State v. Suarez*, 2d Dist. No. 10CA0008, 2011-Ohio-1438, ¶ 10, quoting R.C. 2901.05(A).

ELEMENTS (3)

The accused must show each of three elements in order to establish self-defense: (1) the accused was not at fault in creating the situation; (2) the accused had a bona fide belief that he or she was in imminent danger of death or great bodily harm and that the only means of escape was the use of force; (3) the accused did not violate any duty to retreat or avoid the danger. *State v. Clellan*, 10th Dist. No. 09AP-1043. *See also State v. Melchior* (1978), 56 Ohio St. 2d 15

R.C. 2901.09(B) codifies a form of self-defense known as the "Castle Doctrine" and provides:

> For purposes of any section of the Revised Code that sets forth a criminal offense, a person who lawfully is in that person's residence has no duty to retreat before using force in self-defense, defense of another, or defense of that person's residence, and a person who lawfully is an occupant of that person's vehicle or who lawfully is an occupant in a vehicle owned by an immediate family member of the person has no duty to retreat before using force in self-defense or defense of another.

This statute creates a rebuttable presumption, and the burden to prove that the charged individual was not acting in self-defense falls on the state. See Senate Bill 184 ("S.B. 184"). "Under the Castle Doctrine [S.B. 184], a person is presumed to have acted in self-defense when attempting to expel or expelling another from [his] home who is unlawfully present. Further, under the Castle Doctrine, a person attempting to expel or expelling another is allowed to use deadly force or force great enough to cause serious bodily harm. There is also no duty to retreat inside one's home anymore." *State v. Johnson*, Cuyahoga App. No. 92310, 2010-Ohio-145, ¶ 18.

In the instant case, nothing in the record indicates that Kozlosky was at fault in creating the incident that led to Coleman's death. To the contrary, at trial, the evidence unequivocally established that Coleman, who had previously been evicted from the residence, was unlawfully in the house on the day he was shot and killed by Kozlosky.

It is undisputed that Coleman entered Kozlosky's home three times without permission and against protestations and that he ignored all demands to leave. In his first unlawful entry, Coleman kicked out the bottom panel of the back door, crawled through, and, with impunity, remained in the house until McNaughton yelled that the police had been summoned. Coleman returned a second time within minutes after going next door to search for McNaughton. He then menacingly searched throughout the house for McNaughton, despite Kozlosky's repeated demands that he leave.

In his third unlawful entry, Coleman immediately attacked McNaughton and began beating her. Kozlosky testified:

> Q. What happens next?
> A. She yelled out to me, yelled out my name. So I say "Stop that, you can't be doing that." He turns to her, looks over at me and he goes to pull his gun out from behind his back. When he does that, as soon as his arms starts to move, I draw my gun and hold it. I watched his hand come out from behind his back. As soon as I see he had something in it, I begin to fire and pulled the trigger as fast as I can.
> Q. How many times did you shoot, do you remember?
> A. I can't remember, but I—I looked down at my gun to make sure it was pointing in this direction. *** He turned like this until his back was facing me. When I saw that, that's when I stopped. Then he fell forward like that, with his feet out here and his head between the two couches.
> Q. After you fired the shots, at some point, what did you do?
> A. After I fired and he fell, I walked over to see if he was moving or if I hit him. I tried to see if he was moving or if I hit him. I tried to see if I had actually hit him or if I missed or what ***.
> Q. At some point, what did you do after you were looking over him?
> A. Well I am looking over close. I did have my gun there pointing, holding it right next to him just to make sure, in case I just grazed him or he's about to jump back up at me. I saw movement and I panicked and pulled the trigger again, and I don't know if the gun

actually went off or if I had shot all the rounds already or if I did fire again.

***

Q. Now, Mr. Kozlosky, what is going through your mind at the time in which this is occurring?

A. I thought I was dead, I thought, I was panicking, I thought it just about, I thought he was going to shoot me. My gun was brand new, I never tried it. I didn't even know if it would work. I was afraid it would fail me and he was going to shoot me. I was pretty much panicking at the time.

Here, Kozlosky's testimony establishes that he had a bona fide belief that he was in imminent danger of death or great bodily harm at the hands of Coleman and that the only means of escape was the use of force. Kozlosky had recently learned from McNaughton that Coleman had killed a man in 1990 and had been convicted of carrying a concealed weapon, and he had personally observed Coleman's violent behavior towards McNaughton. Given this knowledge and Coleman's actions of unlawfully entering the house three separate times that day, as well as Coleman's statement about "shooting it out," Kozlosky's belief that he was in imminent danger was well founded.

Finally, under the Castle Doctrine, Kozlosky had no duty to retreat inside his own home. *Johnson*, 2010-Ohio-145. Therefore, we find that Kozlosky has established all three elements of the affirmative defense of self-defense, and the Castle Doctrine fully applies to the facts of the instant case. We also find that the jury appeared confused about the jury instruction, as evidenced by questions regarding the definition of "unlawful entry" and "Castle Doctrine." Further, the jurors queried whether the Castle Doctrine applied to both self-defense of the owner of the home and anyone in the home.

Finally, the record indicates that two of the jurors did independent research on the Castle Doctrine and discussed it with the other jurors. We conclude that the jury lost its way in the instant case, and Kozlosky's convictions are against the manifest weight of the evidence. Accordingly, we sustain the tenth assigned error and reverse his convictions. We reluctantly remand the matter for a new trial because we are restrained by the standard of review under the manifest weight of the evidence and cannot discharge Kozlosky. *Thompkins*, 78 Ohio St. 3d 380.

Our disposition of the tenth assigned error renders the remaining errors moot. See App. R. 12(A)(1)(c).

Notes and Questions

1. The *Kozlosky* court discusses Ohio's unique rebuttable presumption rule with respect to the Castle Doctrine. What policy arguments can be made in support and against this presumption?

2. The *Kozlosky* court also determined that the defendant was not at fault. Do you agree? If you were prosecuting this case, what argument would you put forth to show that the defendant was at fault?

3. It should also be noted that at common law deadly force may be used to prevent dangerous or violent felonies. However, lethal force may not be used solely to protect property.

D. Initial Aggressor and Proportionality

The two cases in this section, *Stewart v. State* and *United States v. Peterson*, explore the viability of self-defense when the defendant is the initial aggressor.

Stewart v. State, 1 Ohio St. 66 (1852)

THURMAN, J.

***The homicide was committed Monday, September 9, 1850. On the Saturday night previous, a difficulty took place between Stewart, Dotey, McCartney and Jennings, in relation to a small debt, twenty-five cents, due by Dotey, or McCartney, to Stewart. In the forenoon of the next day, as George Huff testified, Stewart showed witness the knife, with which Dotey was afterwards killed. He opened it and greased it, and said if he had had it the night before when he was attacked, he did not think Dotey would have got out of the bar-room safe; that if he ever attacked him again—he or any of the crowd that was with him-he would cut his d___d guts out.

Spinning testified, that Stewart called on him as a justice of the peace, on Monday, September 9, 1850, wanted a capias against McCartney, and told witness the difficulty existing between them. He said, that on Saturday evening, Dotey, McCartney, and another met him at the tavern and had a dispute about the debt; that they came upon him apparently with the intention to whip him; that they did not succeed in molesting him; that if he had had a knife he would have put it into MaCartney, or into them, witness did not recollect which; that he would have put the knife into the one that was pushing on to him the strongest. Witness observed to him, that certainly for so small an offence he would not lay himself liable to go to the penitentiary. He replied he would be justified in doing it. Witness asked if they had any Bowie knives, pistols, or other arms, that would justify him in doing it. He said, No, he did not know that they had. Witness asked if they had him so cornered up, or any dangerous weapons over him, that he could not retreat. He said he did not know that they had any weapons, but that there were two or three of them, and on that ground he would be justified. I, the witness, replied, that I was sorry he would endanger himself for so small an affair; that I did not consider he would be justified.

Beall testified as follows: On Sunday morning, I had a conversation with Stewart. He stated that Dotey owed him some money, and when he asked him for it, he attempted to whip him. He wanted to know what I would do in such a case. I told him I would not be bullied out of my rights. He then drew a knife out of his pocket, a large knife, which opened with a spring, and said that if he had had it the night before, he would have cut his d___d guts out; that he intended to carry it and ask him for the money whenever he saw him again, and that if he attemped to whip him, he would cut his d___d guts out; that he would dun him every time that he met him.

This is the testimony of the three witnesses named***

The fifth error assigned is, that the court erred and misdirected the jury in the charge delivered to them as to the law of homicide in self-defence, and in refusing certain charges asked by the accused.

The charge complained of was in these words; "The homicide in self-defence, which is considered as excusable, rather than justifiable, is that, whereby a man may protect himself from an assault in the course of a sudden, casual, affray, by killing him who assaults him. In such a case, however, the law requires of the party to have quitted the combat before a mortal wound shall have been given, if in his power to retreat, as far as he can with safety, and at last to kill from mere urgent necessity, for the preservation of his life, or to avoid enormous bodily harm. He is supposed to kill his adversary under the impression of an absolute necessity to do so, in order to save his own life, or to save himself from enormous bodily harm. If the person killing was not in any supposed or real imminent danger of his own life, or of enormous bodily harm, and if the jury find that the prisoner could not reasonably have apprehended from the deceased, and did not so apprehend any danger of his own life or of enormous bodily harm, then the killing is not excusable homicide."

It is not denied that this charge has a great weight of authority in its support. Indeed it was more lenient to the accused than the doctrine of many adjudicated cases, in this, that it makes the homicide excusable, if the slayer had reasonable cause to apprehend, and did apprehend, danger to his life, or great bodily harm, although such danger may not, in fact, have existed. And the court, at the prisoner's request, also charged, that "the law does not measure nicely, the degree of force which may be employed by a person attacked, and that if he employ more force than necessary he is not responsible for it unless it is so disproportioned to his apparent danger as to show wantonness, revenge, or a malicious purpose to injure the assailant."

But the part of the charge which seems to be objected to is that which relates to the necessity of quitting the combat, if it could be done with safety, before taking the life of the assailant; and it is urged that the law in Ohio is, that

OH LAW

a person assailed may, in all cases, without retreating, take his assailant's life, if he reasonably believe it necessary to do so, in order to save his own life, or to avoid great bodily harm; and this, although he could, without increasing his danger retire, and thereby escape all necessity of slaying his adversary.

As to what is the precise state of the law on this subject, there is some diversity of opinion among the members of this court, and, therefore, without attempting, at this time, to lay it down, we prefer to dispose of the case upon a view which is satisfactory to us all. And we do this the more willingly because there is not a full bench sitting upon the case. Whether a person assaulted is, or is not, bound to quit the combat, if he can safely do so, before taking life, it will not be denied that in order to justify the homicide he must, at least, have reasonably apprehended the loss of his own life or great bodily harm, to prevent which, and under a real, or at least, supposed necessity, the fatal blow must be given. And again, the combat must not have been of his own seeking, and he must not have put himself in the way of being assaulted, in order that when assaulted and hard pressed, he might take the life of his assailant. It will also be admitted, that in a criminal, as well as a civil cause, before the judgment can be reversed for error in the charge to the jury, it must appear that some evidence was given tending to prove a state of case in which the charge would be material. If the charge was upon a mere abstract question of law, that could not arise upon the testimony, and could not influence the decision of the jury, its character, however erroneous, furnishes no ground to reverse the sentence. And such, we are clearly of opinion, was the case under consideration. We find no evidence tending to prove that Stewart, when he slew Dotey, was in danger of loss of life, or limb, or of great bodily harm, or that he apprehended such danger. Were there any evidence, however slight, tending to show that he reasonably believed such danger to exist, we would feel bound to decide upon the correctness of the charge complained of; but we see no such testimony. And we are equally satisfied that the combat did not occur without blame on his part. On Sunday, the day previous to the murder, he showed George Huff the knife with which he afterwards killed Dotey. It was a very deadly weapon, the blade of which opened with a spring. He opened it and prepared it for use by greasing it, and said that if he had had it the night before, when he was attacked, he did not think that Dotey would have got out of the bar-room safe; and that if Dotey ever attacked him again—he or any of the crowd that was with him-he would cut his d___d guts out. On the same day he made similar declarations to the witness Beall, and showed him the knife, and told him he intended to carry it, and ask Dotey for the money whenever he saw him again, and if he attempted to whip him he would cut his d___d guts out; that he would dun him every time he met him. He made similar statements to Pierson Spinning, Monday morning. The affray took place just after supper, Monday evening. John Huff testifies that before supper, that evening, "I was sitting on the bench by the bar-room door, and Stewart said to me, John, there will be war here to-night. I thought he referred to the military that were encamping in town, and replied, that I reckoned not. Stewart replied, Yes, he guessed there would be war; that McCartney and Dotey were coming down there to whip him if he asked them for the money they owed him, and he said he intended to ask them for it." Shortly after supper, Stewart came out of the hotel, his boarding house, and saw Dotey and McCartney standing on the pavement. Dotey was leaning against a post. Stewart came forward to near where he was standing, and said, John and Jim, I want to know if you are going to pay me the money you owe me. Dotey told him to go away about his business, he did not want any thing to do with him, or to say to him. Stewart replied, that he had paid for Dotey's dinner, and he ought to be man enough to pay for that. Dotey said he had meant to pay, but Stewart had acted so meanly in dunning him in the street, at every opportunity, that he did not intend to pay. Stewart said he had asked him for it in private. Dotey denied it. Stewart reaffirmed his statement, and Dotey replied, It's a lie. Steward rejoined: "It's a damned lie," or "You are a damned liar." Dotey said: "I won't take that," and advanced towards Stewart, with his hand raised to strike him, and struck at him. Stewart did not move, and as soon as Dotey came within reach, he stabbed him, and, repeating his blows, gave him five stabs—one in the abdomen which severed the intestines, one in the back, two through the left arm, and one between the shoulder-blade and ribs. Dotey cried out, "Take him away, he has a knife." They were then separated by some of the bystanders, and Dotey afterwards died of the wounds. Stewart received no injury except a cut in his hand, made by his own knife, no doubt. When Dotey started towards Stewart, they were but a few feet apart, and the conflict lasted but a few seconds. It does not appear that Dotey had any weapon. He certainly attempted to use none. Stewart neither showed his knife, nor said that he had one, before using it. He appears to have concealed it from Dotey until he gave the fatal stabs.

Now it does seem clear to us that Stewart sought to bring on the affray, that he desired to be assaulted, and intended, if assaulted, to make good his previous threats of using his knife. True, he had a right to dun Dotey for his money, but he had no right to do so for the purpose of bringing on an affray in order to afford him a pretext to stab his enemy. There is some testimony tending to prove that Dotey went to the hotel that night to whip Stewart. It is not impossible that such was the fact; but if so, and the combat was mutual, the case is no better for the accused. Again, it does not appear that Stewart was, at any time, in danger of a serious injury, or that he apprehended it. There is no testimony tending to prove either the danger or the belief of it.

We have next to consider the refusal to charge as requested by the accused. He asked the court to direct the jury: "that if a man is attacked by a person of strength superior to his own, he is not bound to flee, but may use such force, and such weapons as may be sufficient to resist the force employed against him, and if the assailant is killed, it is neither murder in the first or the second degree, or manslaughter." Which instruction the court refused to give. As to so much of this instruction as relates to the necessity of retreating, it was immaterial, for the reasons we have given. As to the residue of the instruction, if it had any application to the case, it amounted in substance to this, that Stewart, when assailed by an unarmed man, might repel the assault by the use of a deadly and concealed weapon, even though it might have been as well resisted by other means. The court were not asked to tell the jury that a man, in his defence, may employ sufficient force to repel the assailant. That they had already charged. But they were asked in effect to say, that he may employ any weapon sufficient for that purpose. If this is so, a man upon whom an ordinary assault and battery is committed may pierce his assailant with a sword, or knock him down with an axe, for each of these is a weapon "sufficient to resist the force employed." We do not think such is the law.***

The judgment of the Common Pleas is affirmed with costs.

United States v. Peterson, 483 F. 2d 1222 (1973)

SPOTTSWOOD W. ROBINSON, III, Circuit Judge:

Indicted for second-degree murder, and convicted by a jury of manslaughter as a lesser included offense, Bennie L. Peterson urges three grounds for reversal.*** He complains, lastly, that the judge twice erred in the instructions given the jury in relation to his claim that the homicide was committed in self-defense. One error alleged was an instruction that the jury might consider whether Peterson was the aggressor in the altercation that immediately foreran the homicide. The other was an instruction that a failure by Peterson to retreat, if he could have done so without jeopardizing his safety, might be considered as a circumstance bearing on the question whether he was justified in using the amount of force which he did. After careful study of these arguments in light of the trial record, we affirm Peterson's conviction.

The events immediately preceding the homicide are not seriously in dispute. The version presented by the Government's evidence follows. Charles Keitt, the deceased, and two friends drove in Keitt's car to the alley in the rear of Peterson's house to remove the windshield wipers from the latter's wrecked car. While Keitt was doing so, Peterson came out of the house into the back yard to protest. After a verbal exchange, Peterson went back into the house, obtained a pistol, and returned to the yard. In the meantime, Keitt had reseated himself in his car, and he and his companions were about to leave.

Upon his reappearance in the yard, Peterson paused briefly to load the pistol. "If you move," he shouted to Keitt, "I will shoot." He walked to a point in the yard slightly inside a gate in the rear fence and, pistol in hand, said, "If you come in here I will kill you." Keitt alighted from his car, took a few steps toward

Peterson and exclaimed, "What the hell do you think you are going to do with that?" Keitt then made an about-face, walked back to his car and got a lug wrench. With the wrench in a raised position, Keitt advanced toward Peterson, who stood with the pistol pointed toward him. Peterson warned Keitt not to "take another step" and, when Keitt continued onward shot him in the face from a distance of about ten feet. Death was apparently instantaneous. Shortly thereafter, Peterson left home and was apprehended 20-odd blocks away.***

III

More than two centuries ago, Blackstone, best known of the expositors of the English common law, taught that "all homicide is malicious, and of course, amounts to murder, unless . . . justified by the command or permission of the law; excused on the account of accident or self-preservation; or alleviated into manslaughter, by being either the involuntary consequence of some act not strictly lawful, or (if voluntary) occasioned by some sudden and sufficiently violent provocation."

Tucked within this greatly capsulized schema of the common law of homicide is the branch of law we are called upon to administer today. No issue of justifiable homicide, within Blackstone's definition is involved.[24] But Peterson's consistent position is that as a matter of law his conviction of manslaughter—alleviated homicide—was wrong, and that his act was one of self-preservation-excused homicide. The Government, on the other hand, has contended from the beginning that Keitt's slaying fell outside the bounds of lawful self-defense. The questions remaining for our decision inevitably track back to this basic dispute.

Self-defense, as a doctrine legally exonerating the taking of human life, is as viable now as it was in Blackstone's time, and in the case before us the doctrine is invoked in its purest form. But "[t]he law of self defense is a law of necessity;" the right of self-defense arises only when the necessity begins, and equally ends with the necessity; and never must the necessity be greater than when the force employed defensively is deadly. The "necessity must bear all semblance of reality, and appear to admit of no other alternative, before taking life will be justifiable as excusable." Hinged on the exigencies of self-preservation, the doctrine of homicidal self-defense emerges from the body of the criminal law as

---

[24] By the early common law, justification for homicide extended only to acts done in execution of the law, such as homicides in effecting arrests and preventing forcible felonies, and homicides committed in self-defense were only excusable. The distinction between justifiable and excusable homicide was important because in the latter case the slayer, considered to be not wholly free from blame, suffered a forfeiture of his goods. F. Wharton, Homicide Sec. 3 at 211 (1855). However, with the passage of 24 Henry VIII, ch. 5 (1532), the basis of justification was enlarged, and the distinction has largely disappeared. More usually the terms are used interchangeably, each denoting a legally non-punishable act, entitling the accused to an acquittal.

a limited though important exception to legal outlawry of the arena of self-help in the settlement of potentially fatal personal conflicts.

So it is that necessity is the pervasive theme of the well defined conditions which the law imposes on the right to kill or maim in self-defense. There must have been a threat, actual or apparent, of the use of deadly force against the defender. The threat must have been unlawful and immediate. The defender must have believed that he was in imminent peril of death or serious bodily harm, and that his response was necessary to save himself therefrom. These beliefs must not only have been honestly entertained, but also objectively reasonable in light of the surrounding circumstances. It is clear that no less than a concurrence of these elements will suffice.

Here the parties' opposing contentions focus on the roles of two further considerations. One is the provoking of the confrontation by the defender. The other is the defendant's failure to utilize a safe route for retreat from the confrontation. The essential inquiry, in final analysis, is whether and to what extent the rule of necessity may translate these considerations into additional factors in the equation. To these questions, in the context of the specific issues raised, we now proceed.

IV

The trial judge's charge authorized the jury, as it might be persuaded, to convict Peterson of second-degree murder or manslaughter, or to acquit by reason of self-defense. On the latter phase of the case, the judge instructed that with evidence of self-defense present, the Government bore the burden of proving beyond a reasonable doubt that Peterson did not act in self-defense; and that if the jury had a reasonable doubt as to whether Peterson acted in self-defense, the verdict must be not guilty. The judge further instructed that the circumstances under which Peterson acted, however, must have been such as to produce a reasonable belief that Keitt was then about to kill him or do him serious bodily harm, and that deadly force was necessary to repel him. In determining whether Peterson used excessive force in defending himself, the judge said, the jury could consider all of the circumstances under which he acted.

These features of the charge met Peterson's approval, and we are not summoned to pass on them. There were, however, two other aspects of the charge to which Peterson objected, and which are now the subject of vigorous controversy. The first of Peterson's complaints centers upon an instruction that the right to use deadly force in self-defense is not ordinarily available to one who provokes a conflict or is the aggressor in it. Mere words, the judge explained, do not constitute provocation or aggression; and if Peterson precipitated the altercation but thereafter withdrew from it in good faith and so informed Keitt by words or acts, he was justified in using deadly force to save himself from imminent danger or death or grave bodily harm. And, the judge added, even if

Keitt was the aggressor and Peterson was justified in defending himself, he was not entitled to use any greater force than he had reasonable ground to believe and actually believed to be necessary for that purpose. Peterson contends that there was no evidence that he either caused or contributed to the conflict, and that the instructions on that topic could only misled the jury.

It has long been accepted that one cannot support a claim of self-defense by a self-generated necessity to kill. The right of homicidal self-defense is granted only to those free from fault in the difficulty; it is denied to slayers who incite the fatal attack, encourage the fatal quarrel or otherwise promote the necessitous occasion for taking life. The fact that the deceased struck the first blow, fired the first shot or made the first menacing gesture does not legalize the self-defense claim if in fact the claimant was the actual provoker. In sum, one who is the aggressor in a conflict culminating in death cannot invoke the necessities of self-preservation. Only in the event that he communicates to his adversary his intent to withdraw and in good faith attempts to do so is he restored to his right of self-defense.

This body of doctrine traces its origin to the fundamental principle that a killing in self-defense is excusable only as a matter of genuine necessity. Quite obviously, a defensive killing is unnecessary if the occasion for it could have been averted, and the roots of that consideration run deep with us. A half-century ago, in *Laney v. United States*, this court declared that, before a person can avail himself of the plea of self-defense against the charge of homicide, he must do everything in his power, consistent with his safety, to avoid the danger and avoid the necessity of taking life. If one has reason to believe that he will be attacked, in a manner which threatens him with bodily injury, he must avoid the attack if it is possible to do so, and the right of self-defense does not arise until he has done everything in his power to prevent its necessity.

And over the many years since *Laney*, the court has kept faith with its precept.

In the case at bar, the trial judge's charge fully comported with these governing principles. The remaining question, then, is whether there was evidence to make them applicable to the case. A recapitulation of the proofs shows beyond peradventure that there was.

It was not until Peterson fetched his pistol and returned to his back yard that his confrontation with Keitt took on a deadly cast. Prior to his trip into the house for the gun, there was, by the Government's evidence, no threat, no display of weapons, no combat. There was an exchange of verbal aspersions and a misdemeanor[25] against Peterson's property was in progress but, at this juncture, nothing more. Even if Peterson's post-arrest version of the initial encounter were accepted—his claim that Keitt went for the lug wrench before he armed himself—

---

[25] It is well settled that deadly force cannot be employed to arrest or prevent the escape of a misdemeanant.

the events which followed bore heavily on the question as to who the real aggressor was.

The evidence is uncontradicted that when Peterson reappeared in the yard with his pistol, Keitt was about to depart the scene. Richard Hilliard testified that after the first argument, Keitt reentered his car and said, "Let's go." This statement was verified by Ricky Gray, who testified that Keitt "got in the car and . . . they were getting ready to go;" he, too, heard Keitt give the direction to start the car. The uncontroverted fact that Keitt was leaving shows plainly that so far as he was concerned the confrontation was ended. It demonstrates just as plainly that even if he had previously been the aggressor, he no longer was.

Not so with Peterson, however, as the undisputed evidence made clear. Emerging from the house with the pistol, he paused in the yard to load it, and to command Keitt not to move. He then walked through the yard to the rear gate and, displaying his pistol, dared Keitt to come in, and threatened to kill him if he did. While there appears to be no fixed rule on the subject, the cases hold, and we agree, that an affirmative unlawful act reasonably calculated to produce an affray foreboding injurious or fatal consequences is an aggression which, unless renounced, nullifies the right of homicidal self-defense. We cannot escape the abiding conviction that the jury could readily find Peterson's challenge to be a transgression of that character.

The situation at bar is not unlike that presented in *Laney*. There the accused, chased along the street by a mob threatening his life, managed to escape through an areaway between two houses. In the back yard of one of the houses, he checked a gun he was carrying and then returned to the areaway. The mob beset him again, and during an exchange of shots one of its members was killed by a bullet from the accused's gun. In affirming a conviction of manslaughter, the court reasoned:

> It is clearly apparent . . . that, when defendant escaped from the mob into the back yard . . . he was in a place of comparative safety, from which, if he desired to go home, he could have gone by the back way, as he subsequently did. The mob had turned its attention to a house on the opposite side of the street. According to Laney's testimony, there was shooting going on in the street. His appearance on the street at that juncture could mean nothing but trouble for him. Hence, when he adjusted his gun and stepped out into the areaway, he had every reason to believe that his presence there would provoke trouble. We think his conduct in adjusting his revolver and going into the areaway was such as to deprive him of any right to invoke the plea of self-defense.

Similarly, in *Rowe v. United States*, the accused was in the home of friends when an argument, to which the friends became participants, developed in the street in front. He left, went to his nearby apartment for a loaded pistol and returned. There was testimony that he then made an insulting comment, drew the pistol and fired a shot into the ground. In any event, when a group of five men began to move toward him, he began to shoot at them, killing two, and wounding a third. We observed that the accused "left an apparently safe haven to arm himself and return to the scene," and that "he inflamed the situation with his words to the men gathered there, even though he could have returned silently to the safety of the [friends'] porch." We held that

> [t]hese facts could have led the jury to conclude that [the accused] returned to the scene to stir up further trouble, if not actually to kill anyone, and that his actions instigated the men into rushing him. Self-defense may not be claimed by one who deliberately places himself in a position where he has reason to believe "his presence . . . would provoke trouble."

We noted the argument "that a defendant may claim self-defense if he arms himself in order to proceed upon his normal activities, even if he realizes that danger may await him;" we responded by pointing out "that the jury could have found that the course of action defendant here followed was for an unlawful purpose." We accordingly affirmed his conviction of manslaughter over his objection that an acquittal should have been directed.

We are brought much the readier to the same conclusion here. We think the evidence plainly presented an issue of fact as to whether Peterson's conduct was an invitation to and provocation of the encounter which ended in the fatal shot. We sustain the trial judge's action in remitting that issue for the jury's determination.

V

The second aspect of the trial judge's charge as to which Peterson asserts error concerned the undisputed fact that at no time did Peterson endeavor to retreat from Keitt's approach with the lug wrench. The judge instructed the jury that if Peterson had reasonable grounds to believe and did believe that he was in imminent danger of death or serious injury, and that deadly force was necessary to repel the danger, he was required neither to retreat nor to consider whether he could safely retreat. Rather, said the judge, Peterson was entitled to stand his ground and use such force as was reasonably necessary under the circumstances to save his life and his person from pernicious bodily harm. But, the judge continued, if Peterson could have safely retreated but did not do so, that failure was a circumstance which the jury might consider, together with all others, in determining whether he went further in repelling the danger, real or apparent, than he was justified in going.

Peterson contends that this imputation of an obligation to retreat was error, even if he could safely have done so. He points out that at the time of the shooting he was standing in his own yard, and argues he was under no duty to move. We are persuaded to the conclusion that in the circumstances presented here, the trial judge did not err in giving the instruction challenged.

Within the common law of self-defense there developed the rule of "retreat to the wall," which ordinarily forbade the use of deadly force by one to whom an avenue for safe retreat was open. This doctrine was but an application of the requirement of strict necessity to excuse the taking of human life, and was designed to insure the existence of that necessity. Even the innocent victim of a vicious assault had to elect a safe retreat if available, rather than resort to defensive force which might kill or seriously injure.

In a majority of American jurisdictions, contrarily to the common law rule, one may stand his ground and use deadly force whenever it seems reasonably necessary to save himself. While the law of the District of Columbia on this point is not entirely clear, it seems allied with the strong minority adhering to the common law. In 1856, the District of Columbia Criminal Court ruled that a participant in an affray "must endeavor to retreat, . . . that is, he is obliged to retreat, if he can safely." The court added that "[a] man may, to be sure, decline a combat when there is no existing or apparent danger, but the retreat to which the law binds him is that which is the consequence." In a much later era this court, adverting to necessity as the soul of homicidal self-defense, declared that "no necessity for killing an assailant can exist, so long as there is a safe way open to escape the conflict." Moreover, the common law rule of strict necessity pervades the District concept of pernicious self-defense, and we cannot ignore the inherent inconsistency of an absolute no-retreat rule. Until such time as the District law on the subject may become more definitive, we accept these precedents as ample indication that the doctrine of retreat persists.

That is not to say that the retreat rule is without exceptions. Even at common law it was recognized that it was not completely suited to all situations. Today it is the more so that its precept must be adjusted to modern conditions nonexistent during the early development of the common law of self-defense. One restriction on its operation comes to the fore when the circumstances apparently foreclose a withdrawal with safety. The doctrine of retreat was never intended to enhance the risk to the innocent; its proper application has never required a faultless victim to increase his assailant's safety at the expense of his own. On the contrary, he could stand his ground and use deadly force otherwise appropriate if the alternative were perilous, or if to him it reasonably appeared to be. A slight variant of the same consideration is the principle that there is no duty to retreat from an assault producing an imminent danger of death or grievous bodily harm. "Detached reflection cannot be demanded in the presence of an uplifted knife," nor is it "a condition of immunity that one in that situation should pause to consider whether a reasonable man might not think it possible to fly with safety or to disable his assailant rather than to kill him."

The trial judge's charge to the jury incorporated each of these limitations on the retreat rule. Peterson, however, invokes another—the so-called "castle" doctrine. It is well settled that one who through no fault of his own is attacked in his home is under no duty to retreat therefrom. The oft-repeated expression that "a man's home is his castle" reflected the belief in olden days that there were few if any safer sanctuaries than the home. The "castle" exception, moreover, has been extended by some courts to encompass the occupant's presence within the curtilage outside his dwelling. Peterson reminds us that when he shot to halt Keitt's advance, he was standing in his yard and so, he argues, he had no duty to endeavor to retreat.

Despite the practically universal acceptance of the "castle" doctrine in American jurisdictions wherein the point has been raised, its status in the District of Columbia has never been squarely decided. But whatever the fate of the doctrine in the District law of the future, it is clear that in absolute form it was inapplicable here. The right of self-defense, we have said, cannot be claimed by the aggressor in an affray so long as he retains that unmitigated role. It logically follows that any rule of no-retreat which may protect an innocent victim of the affray would, like other incidents of a forfeited right of self-defense, be unavailable to the party who provokes or stimulates the conflict. Accordingly, the law is well settled that the "castle" doctrine can be invoked only by one who is without fault in bringing the conflict on. That, we think, is the critical consideration here.

We need not repeat our previous discussion of Peterson's contribution to the altercation which culminated in Keitt's death. It suffices to point out that by no interpretation of the evidence could it be said that Peterson was blameless in the affair. And while, of course, it was for the jury to assess the degree of fault, the evidence well nigh dictated the conclusion that it was substantial.

The only reference in the trial judge's charge intimating an affirmative duty to retreat was the instruction that a failure to do so, when it could have been done safely, was a factor in the totality of the circumstances which the jury might consider in determining whether the force which he employed was excessive. We cannot believe that any jury was at all likely to view Peterson's conduct as irreproachable. We conclude that for one who, like Peterson, was hardly entitled to fall back on the "castle" doctrine of no retreat, that instruction cannot be just cause for complaint.***

Notes and Questions

1. If the court in *Stewart v. State* had found that the defendant was not the initial aggressor, do you think the defendant's self-defense claim would have been successful? Is a defendant justified in using lethal force if he himself is not facing serious bodily harm or death?

2. Can an initial aggressor, like the defendants in *Stewart* and *United States v. Peterson,* ever regain his right to self-defense? The answer to this question is "yes." Restoration of self-defense generally occurs under two circumstances. The first instance arises when the aggressor uses nondeadly force but is met by the victim's use of deadly force. The second instance arises when the aggressor effectively withdraws from the fray with the victim. Did the defendant in *Peterson* effectively withdraw?

3. Besides the exceptions listed in #2, can you think of other instances where the initial aggressor might justifiably use self-defense?

4. Why was the court in *Peterson* so reluctant to allow the defendant to raise the Castle Doctrine?

5. How was the defendant in *Peterson* found to be the initial aggressor? Wasn't he merely confronting several thieves who had come to his house to steal items from his car?

6. The court in *Peterson* wrote "a defendant may claim self-defense if he arms himself in order to proceed upon his normal activities, even if he realizes that danger may await him; we responded by pointing out that the jury could have found that the course of action defendant here followed was for an unlawful purpose." What did the court mean by this statement?

E. Defense of Others

One question that arises with the defense of others is whether an individual must have a relationship with the person she aids. Some early English cases intimidated that a relationship was necessary before an individual could use force to defend another; however, few, if any, jurisdictions follow that rule today. Instead, the prevailing modern rule is that an individual may use reasonable force in defense of another, even a stranger, in order to prevent serious bodily harm.

If the good samaritan is mistaken in her assessment of the situation and the presumed victim is not really a victim, the good samaritan will not be liable in most jurisdictions so long as she had a reasonable belief in the necessity of force. In contrast, the good samaritan might be criminally liable in a jurisdiction that adheres to the "alter-ego" rule. Pursuant to the alter ego rule, the good samaritan's right to defend another is coextensive with the so-called victim. Thus, if the presumptive victim could not use self-defense, then defense of others is unavailable to the good samaritan. The next case explores the alter-ego rule.

City of Columbus v. Wenger, 1978 Ohio App. LEXIS 7886

REILLY, J.

The transcript shows that appellant, a resident of Cleveland, came to Columbus, September 5, 1977, to demonstrate against a Ku Klux Klan rally held at the Ohio Statehouse grounds that day. The complainant, Officer Joseph Whalen, was part of a special group of officers of the Columbus Police Department, called the SWAT Unit, who were present at the rally. The SWAT Unit members were instructed to dress in ordinary street clothes and mingle with the crowd, conduct a general surveillance, and arrest persons whom they observed breaking the law.

Officer Whalen testified that he saw one of the demonstrators, Ms. Cathy Pekel, throwing eggs in the direction of the Ku Klux Klan members. After the rally Officer Whalen approached Ms. Pekel, identified himself as a police officer, and informed her she was under arrest. At this point the testimony is conflicting. At any rate, Officer Whalen testified that he physically grabbed Ms. Pekel by the arm to effectuate the arrest, while appellant testified that Officer Whalen grabbed her by the neck. He stated that Ms. Pekel resisted the arrest and attempted to break away.

Appellant, who was a short distance away, observed these activities and came to Ms. Pekel's assistance, and hit Officer Whalen in the lower back area with the dowel portion of a placard he had been carrying during the demonstration. Appellant testified that he perceived Ms. Pekel to be in a dangerous circumstance and intervened in the struggle as a protective measure. Moreover, he testified that he was not aware that Officer Whalen was a police officer performing an arrest. He stated that he would not have intervened had he been aware of such fact.

The jury rendered verdicts in appellant's favor upon obstructing official business and resisting arrest; but in favor of the State for assault. This appeal has now been perfected.

Appellant's first assignment of error reads as follows:

> 1. The trial court erred by failing to give the jury the requested instruction concerning "defense of another » where

factual support existed for said instruction, thus denying appellant's right to a fair trial and due process of law, as protected by the Fourteenth Amendment of the United States Constitution and Article I, Section 16 of the Ohio Constitution.

This assignment of error is without merit. The transcript shows the following statement made by the trial court prior to closing arguments concerning the requested instruction:

> The defense has given the Court a requested special instruction to be incorporated as a part of the charge, which reads verbatim as follows: "The Court instructs you that the use of force upon or toward the person of another is justifiable to protect a third person when: Under the circumstances as the actor believes them to be, the person whom he seeks to protect would be justified in using such protective force; and the actor believes that his intervention is necessary for the protection of such other person."

The citation given to the Court by defense counsel for this particular charge is Section 3.05 Article 3 Model Penal Code.

MR. MEEKS: That's correct.
THE COURT: The Court has attempted to review the case law in regard to this matter and has elected not to grant the defense request for that particular charge.

The basis for the Court's ruling is the Assault and Battery Section of 5 O. Jur. 2d, specifically, Section 13, dealing with the defense of third parties.

In addition to that, the unreported case from the Franklin County Court of Appeals, Case Number 76 A, as in Albert, P, as in Paul, dash 962, entitled State of Ohio versus Hendlay, H-e-n-d-l-a-y, Eugene Miller and the case of People versus Young, citation, 183 NE 2d 319, which is the Court of Appeals of New York, 1962 decision, and additional reference to Commonwealth versus Martin, cited 341 NE 2d 885, 1976 decision out of Massachusetts.

In going over the testimony in this matter along with the cases that the Court has cited, the Court believes that the only testimony in this case is that on September the 5th, 1977, undercover officers of the Columbus Police Department, in particular one Officer Whalen, who testified in this matter, lawfully arrested one Cathy Pekel.

MR. MEEKS: P-e-k-e-l.
THE COURT: The testimony is unrefuted that the officers observed Miss Pekel during the demonstration of the KKK, throwing eggs at said KKK members.

After waiting until the KKK demonstration was ended, Officer Whalen attempted to effectuate a legal arrest of Miss Pekel. At said time, Miss Pekel attempted to resist said arrest.

After said attempt a slight—strike the word "slight" and substitute "altercation," between Officer Whalen and Miss Pekel ensued. At this point in time, the incident was noted for the first time by the defendant in this matter, Mr. ——

MR. MEEKS: Wenger.

THE COURT: --Wenger.

Under Ohio law, the Court believes that Mr. Wenger could only intervene in behalf of Miss Pekel and take such action as Miss Pekel could have taken herself.

Inasmuch as—The Court feels that the evidence is uncontroverted that the arrest of Miss Pekel was legal, and, consequently, she could not use any type of self-defense in order to resist said arrest.

The Court further believes that there was no testimony indicating that the arresting officer used any type of undue force or extreme measures in attempting to effectuate the arrest of Miss Pekel.

Consequently, as the Court understands the law, Mr. Wenger could only lawfully use force against the officer that could have been used by Miss Pekel. Inasmuch as the Court believes she was entitled to use no force whatsoever, the Court does not believe that Mr. Wenger would be entitled to the proposed instructions requested by his counsel, Mr. Meeks.

In any event, it is reiterated that appellant was found guilty of assault, which is defined in R. C. 2903.13 as follows:

> (A) No person shall knowingly cause or attempt to cause physical harm to another.
>
> (B) No person shall recklessly cause serious physical harm to another.
>
> (C) Whoever violates this section is guilty of assault, a misdemeanor of the first degree.

Moreover, R. C. 2901.21(A)(2) reads as follows:

> (A) Except as provided in division (B) of this section, a person is not guilty of an offense unless both of the following apply:
>
>   ***
>
> (2) He has the requisite degree of culpability for each element as to which a culpable mental state is specified by the section defining the offense.

Consequently, it is only necessary, for a conviction of assault, for the State to show that appellant knowingly caused or attempted physical harm to another. As to the meaning of "knowingly," R. C. 2901.22(B) reads as follows:

> (B) A person acts knowingly, regardless of his purpose, when he is aware that his conduct will probably cause a certain result or will probably be of a certain nature. A person has knowledge of circumstances when he is aware that such circumstances probably exist.

Therefore, appellant's purpose, motive, or mistake of fact were not significant on a charge of assault because the requisite mental element of knowledge involved the nature of the conduct and not the nature of the circumstances. There is sufficient testimony in the transcript to support the jury's verdict that appellant knowingly caused harm to Officer Whalen, and therefore was guilty of assault.

Appellant's right to come to the defense of Ms. Pekel was no greater than his right to come to his own defense. Since Ms. Pekel was under arrest, she did not have a right to resist the officer. We note *Columbus v. Fraley* (1975), 41 Ohio St. 2d 173, the third paragraph of the syllabus:

> 3. In the absence of excessive or unnecessary force by an arresting officer, a private citizen may not use force to resist arrest by one he knows, or has good reason to believe, is an authorized police officer engaged in the performance of his duties, whether or not the arrest is illegal under the circumstances.

Therefore, considering that appellant was found guilty of assault, and not guilty of the other charges; as well as noting our rationale in reaching the same conclusion is somewhat different; it was not prejudicial error when the trial court did not give the requested instruction as indicated above. Accordingly, appellant's first assignment of error is not well taken and is overruled.***

McCORMAC, J., dissenting

Appellant's first assignment of error should be sustained and the case should be remanded for a new trial.

The defendant presented evidence which, if believed by the jury, proved that he believed a third person to be in a dangerous circumstance where his intervention was necessary as a protective measure. However, the jury was not permitted to consider this defense since the trial court ruled that an intervening third party, irrespective of the reasonableness of his beliefs, could not intervene unless the person whom he sought to aid had the right to use the actions which were used. Since it was conceded that the person whom defendant aided had no such right, in essence the jury was instructed to find defendant guilty of assault.

The question is solely a choice of law. One body of cases takes the position taken by the majority that a third party intervenor stands in the shoes of the person whom he is aiding and it is immaterial whether a reasonable person would have acted as did the intervening defendant. The policy of this rule of law is to require the intervenor to make certain of his rights before acting.

The contrary rule of law is that an intervenor may aid another if it appears to be reasonably necessary even though based on a mistaken belief, even in the situation where the person who is aided would not have had the same right. The policy behind this rule of law is to encourage a person to assist another without being deterred by the knowledge that irrespective of good faith, notice, or apparent necessity, he may be criminally liable if mistaken.

There appears to be no Ohio Supreme Court decision directly deciding this issue. However, it is believed that the modern position is that reflected in the American Law Institute Model Penal Code from which defendant's requested charge was taken verbatim, as cited in the majority opinion. Explicit in the Model Penal Code provision is the rejection of the older common law doctrine placing the defendant in the same legal position as the person he assists, thereby requiring that the intervenor act at his own peril if he uses force in the defense of another. The reason for the rejection of this principle code is explained in the Model Penal Code as follows:

> *** This emasculates the privilege of protection of much of its content, introducing a liability without fault which is indefensible in principle. The cautious potential actor who knows the law will, in the vast majority of cases, refrain from acting at all. The result may well be that an innocent person is injured without receiving assistance from bystanders. It seems far preferable, therefore, to predicate the justification upon the actor's belief, safeguarding if thought necessary against abuse of the privilege by the imposition of a requirement of proper care in evolving the belief. *** Model Penal Code, Reprint-Tentative Drafts Nos. 8, 9, and 10.

The Washington Supreme Court specifically adopted the aforesaid provision of the Model Penal Code, recently stating that the "*** test of whether person may use force in defense of another person is not what facts actually were, but whether circumstances as they appeared to defendant made it reasonably necessary for him to protect himself or another." *State v. Penn* (Washington Supreme Court, 1977), 568 P. 2d 797.

Many other jurisdictions have adopted the "modern rule," which I believe to be the better rule after consideration of the competing policy considerations, particularly in view of the fact that many citizens are already reluctant to get involved or to come to the aid of another. A jury is capable of rejecting the defense when there is not an honest or reasonable belief in the necessity of intervention.

The judgment of the trial court should be reversed and the case should be remanded for a new trial.

Notes and Questions

1. The dissent in *City of Columbus v. Wenger* puts forward a very persuasive argument as to why the court should follow the MPC with respect to the defense of others. Why do you think the majority went with the so-called "alter-ego" rule? Can you think of any policy reasons why you would want to limit the protections afforded to so-called good samaritans?

F. Defensive Force and Law Enforcement

City of Columbus v. Fraley, 41 Ohio St. 2d 173 (1975)

***The facts in case No. 74-125 are:

On November 1, 1971, Columbus police investigated two complaints by a white family in an interracial neighborhood. On the first occasion, two officers entered the area to investigate; on the second, they were joined by a police sergeant and two additional officers.

While the second complaint was being investigated, an argument broke out between the police and black residents of the neighborhood, one of whom was appellant, Imogene Fraley. According to the testimony of police officials, appellant became "boisterous and loud," called the officers "motherfucker" and "pigs," and made the statement that "*** if (blacks) had called the police, they wouldn't have got this much motherfucking police protection." When two of the officers attempted to place the appellant under arrest, she allegedly started swinging her arms, yelled, kicked them, broke away, and ran across the street into her house.

Appellant was subsequently arrested and charged with disorderly conduct, in violation of Section 2327.01 of the Columbus Code of Ordinances, and for using violence against a police officer, in violation of Section 2355.01 of the Columbus Code. The trial judge instructed the jury that to find appellant guilty of violating Section 2327.01, it would have to determine that her language was obscene or profane. The jury found her guilty on both charges, and judgment was entered upon the verdict. Upon appeal, the judgment was affirmed. Appellant's conviction for violating Section 2327.01 was affirmed on the theory that her language constituted "fighting words."***

PAUL W. BROWN, Justice.

***III

In case No. 74-125, appellant Fraley was also convicted for violating Section 2355.01 of the Columbus Code of Ordinances. That section provides that:

> "No person shall strike or assault a police officer or draw or lift any weapon or offer any violence against a police officer, when said police officer is in the execution of his office."

Appellant contends that if her arrest for the alleged use of obscene language was illegal, she was privileged to use force in resisting it. We disagree.

At common law, the right to resist an unlawful arrest was unquestioned. The United States Supreme Court applied the doctrine in John Bad Elk v. United States (1900), 177 U.S. 529, and Ohio courts have done likewise. Columbus v. Holmes (1958), 107 Ohio App. 391; Columbus v. Guidotti (1958), Ohio App., 160 N.E.2d 355.

More recently, however, the rule has been severely criticized. Section 5 of the Uniform Arrest Act abrogates the right whenever "a person has reasonable ground to believe that he is being arrested by a peace officer *** regardless of whether or not there is a legal basis for the arrest." Section 3.04(2)(a) (i) of the American Law Institute's Model Penal Code prohibits the use of force "to resist an arrest which the actor knows is being made by a peace officer, although the arrest is unlawful." At least six states have abolished the common-law doctrine by statute, and at least three others have done so by judicial decision.

The reason for such change is clear. Since 1709, when the doctrine was pronounced in The Queen v. Tooley (1709), 2 Ld. Raym. 1296, 92 Eng. Rep. 349, society has changed drastically. Nations once rural and agrarian have become urban and industrialized. Policemen who once employed staves and swords to effect arrests now use guns and sophisticated weapons. The era "when most arrests were made by private citizens, when bail for felonies was usually unattainable, and when years might pass before the royal judges arrived for a jail delivery," is past. Warner, The Uniform Arrest Act, 28 Va. L. Rev. 315, Modern-day defendants reap the benefits of "liberal bonding policies, appointed counsel in the case of indigency, and the opportunity to be taken before a magistrate for immediate arraignment and preliminary hearing." State v. Richardson (1973), 95 Idaho 446.

Considerations of this type have prompted both courts and legislatures to look anew at, and often abandon, the common law rule. Thus, in State v. Koonce (1965), 89 N.J. Super. 169, the Appellate Division of the New Jersey Superior Court declared:

> "*** an appropriate accommodation of society's interests in securing the right of individual liberty, maintenance of law enforcement, and prevention of death or serious injury not only of the participants in an arrest fracas but of innocent third persons, precludes tolerance of any formulation which validates an arrestee's resistance of a police officer with force merely because the arrest is ultimately adjudged to have been illegal. Force begets force, and escalation into bloodshed is a frequent probability. The right or wrong of an arrest is often a matter of close debate as to which even lawyers and judges may differ. In this era of constantly expanding legal protections of the rights of the accused in criminal proceedings, one deeming himself illegally arrested can reasonably be asked to submit peaceably to arrest by a police officer, and to take recourse in his legal remedies for regaining his liberty and defending the ensuing prosecution against him. At the same time, police officers attempting in good faith, although mistakenly, to perform their duties in effecting an arrest should be relieved of the threat of physical harm at the hands of the arrestee."

Similarly, in Miller v. State (Alaska 1969), 462 P.2d 421, the Supreme Court of Alaska stated:

> "The control of man's destructive and aggressive impulses is one of the great unsolved problems of our society. Our rules of law should discourage the unnecessary use of physical force between man and man. Any rule which promotes rather than inhibits violence should be re-examined. Along with increased sensitivity to the rights of the criminally accused there should be a corresponding awareness of our need to develop rules which facilitate decent and peaceful behavior by all."

We agree with those courts and legislatures which have chosen to abandon the rule allowing forcible resistance to arrest. We believe it essential that potentially violent conflicts be resolved, not in the streets, but in the courts. Thus, we hold that in the absence of excessive or unnecessary force by an arresting officer, a private citizen may not use force to resist arrest by one he knows, or has good reason to believe, is an authorized police officer engaged in the performance of his duties, whether or not the arrest is illegal under the circumstances.

In the present case, appellant Fraley was arrested by uniformed police officers for an alleged violation of Section 2327.01 of the Columbus Code. No evidence whatever indicates that police officials used excessive or unnecessary force. Rather, the record shows that when police officials attempted to place appellant under arrest, she swung her arms, yelled, kicked them, broke away, and ran across the street into her house. Such conduct was clearly sufficient to warrant her conviction for using violence against a police officer under Section 2355.01.

The judgment of the Court of Appeals in case No. 74-125, affirming appellant's conviction for violating Section 2355.01 of the Columbus Code of Ordinances, is affirmed.

In case No. 74-177, judgment reversed.

In case No. 74-125, judgment affirmed in part and reversed in part.

C. WILLIAM O'NEILL, C. J., and HERBERT, CORRIGAN, STERN, CELEBREZZE and WILLIAM B. BROWN, JJ., concur.

Tennessee v. Garner, 471 U.S. 1 (1985)

Justice WHITE delivered the opinion of the Court.

This case requires us to determine the constitutionality of the use of deadly force to prevent the escape of an apparently unarmed suspected felon. We conclude that such force may not be used unless it is necessary to prevent the escape and the officer has probable cause to believe that the suspect poses a significant threat of death or serious physical injury to the officer or others.

I

At about 10:45 p.m. on October 3, 1974, Memphis Police Officers Elton Hymon and Leslie Wright were dispatched to answer a "prowler inside call." Upon arriving at the scene they saw a woman standing on her porch and gesturing toward the adjacent house. She told them she had heard glass breaking and that "they" or "someone" was breaking in next door. While Wright radioed the dispatcher to say that they were on the scene, Hymon went behind the house. He heard a door slam and saw someone run across the backyard. The fleeing suspect, who was appellee-respondent's decedent, Edward Garner, stopped at a 6-feet-high chain link fence at the edge of the yard. With the aid of a flashlight, Hymon was able to see Garner's face and hands. He saw no sign of a weapon, and, though not certain, was "reasonably sure" and "figured" that Garner was unarmed. App. 41, 56; Record 219. He thought Garner was 17 or 18 years old and about 5'5" or 5'7" tall. While Garner was crouched at the base of the fence, Hymon called out "police, halt" and took a few steps toward him. Garner then began to climb over the fence. Convinced that if Garner made it over the fence he would elude capture, Hymon shot him. The bullet hit Garner in the back of the head. Garner was taken by ambulance to a hospital, where he died on the operating table. Ten dollars and a purse taken from the house were found on his body.

In using deadly force to prevent the escape, Hymon was acting under the authority of a Tennessee statute and pursuant to Police Department policy. The statute provides that "[i]f, after notice of the intention to arrest the defendant, he either flee or forcibly resist, the officer may use all the necessary means to effect the arrest." Tenn. Code Ann. § 40-7-108 (1982). The Department policy was slightly more restrictive than the statute, but still allowed the use of deadly force in cases of burglary. App. 140-144. The incident was reviewed by the Memphis Police Firearm's Review Board and presented to a grand jury. Neither took any action. *Id.,* at 57.

Garner's father then brought this action in the Federal District Court for the Western District of Tennessee, seeking damages under 42 U.S.C. § 1983 for asserted violations of Garner's constitutional rights. The complaint alleged that the shooting violated the Fourth, Fifth, Sixth, Eighth, and Fourteenth Amendments of the United States Constitution. It named as defendants Officer Hymon, the Police Department, its Director, and the Mayor and city of Memphis. After a 3-day bench trial, the District Court entered judgment for all defendants. It dismissed the claims against the Mayor and the Director for lack of evidence. It then concluded that Hymon's actions were authorized by the Tennessee statute, which in turn was constitutional. Hymon had employed the only reasonable and practicable means of preventing Garner's escape. Garner had "recklessly and heedlessly attempted to vault over the fence to escape, thereby assuming the risk of being fired upon." App. to Pet. for Cert. A10.

The Court of Appeals for the Sixth Circuit affirmed with regard to Hymon, finding that he had acted in good-faith reliance on the Tennessee statute and was therefore within the scope of his qualified immunity.***

The Court of Appeals reversed and remanded. It reasoned that the killing of a fleeing suspect is a "seizure" under the Fourth Amendment, and is therefore constitutional only if "reasonable." The Tennessee statute failed as applied to this case because it did not adequately limit the use of deadly force by distinguishing between felonies of different magnitudes—"the facts, as found, did not justify the use of deadly force under the Fourth Amendment." *Id.,* at 246. Officers cannot resort to deadly force unless they "have probable cause . . . to believe that the suspect [has committed a felony and] poses a threat to the safety of the officers or a danger to the community if left at large." *Ibid.*

The State of Tennessee, which had intervened to defend the statute appealed to this Court. The city filed a petition for certiorari. We noted probable jurisdiction in the appeal and granted the petition.

II

Whenever an officer restrains the freedom of a person to walk away, he has seized that person. *United States v. Brignoni-Ponce,* 422 U.S. 873, (1975).***

A

A police officer may arrest a person if he has probable cause to believe that person committed a crime. Petitioners and appellant argue that if this requirement is satisfied the Fourth Amendment has nothing to say about *how* that seizure is made. This submission ignores the many cases in which this Court, by balancing the extent of the intrusion against the need for it, has examined the reasonableness of the manner in which a search or seizure is conducted. To determine the constitutionality of a seizure "[w]e must balance the nature and quality of the intrusion on the individual's Fourth Amendment interests against the importance of the governmental interests alleged to justify the intrusion." *United States v. Place,* 462 U.S. 696, (1983).***

B

*** The intrusiveness of a seizure by means of deadly force is unmatched. The suspect's fundamental interest in his own life need not be elaborated upon. The use of deadly force also frustrates the interest of the individual, and of society, in judicial determination of guilt and punishment. Against these interests are ranged governmental interests in effective law enforcement. It is argued that overall violence will be reduced by encouraging the peaceful submission of suspects who know that they may be shot if they flee. Effectiveness in making arrests requires the resort to deadly force, or at least the meaningful threat thereof. "Being able to arrest such individuals is a condition precedent to the state's entire system of law enforcement." Brief for Petitioners 14.

Without in any way disparaging the importance of these goals, we are not convinced that the use of deadly force is a sufficiently productive means of accomplishing them to justify the killing of nonviolent suspects. The use of deadly force is a self-defeating way of apprehending a suspect and so setting the criminal justice mechanism in motion. If successful, it guarantees that that mechanism will not be set in motion. And while the meaningful threat of deadly force might be thought to lead to the arrest of more live suspects by discouraging escape attempts, the presently available evidence does not support this thesis. The fact is that a majority of police departments in this country have forbidden the use of deadly force against nonviolent suspects.

The use of deadly force to prevent the escape of all felony suspects, whatever the circumstances, is constitutionally unreasonable. It is not better that all felony suspects die than that they escape. Where the suspect poses no immediate threat to the officer and no threat to others, the harm resulting from failing to apprehend him does not justify the use of deadly force to do so. It is no doubt unfortunate when a suspect who is in sight escapes, but the fact that the police arrive a little late or are a little slower afoot does not always justify killing the suspect. A police officer may not seize an unarmed, nondangerous suspect by shooting him dead. The Tennessee statute is unconstitutional insofar as it authorizes the use of deadly force against such fleeing suspects.

It is not, however, unconstitutional on its face. Where the officer has probable cause to believe that the suspect poses a threat of serious physical harm, either to the officer or to others, it is not constitutionally unreasonable to prevent escape by using deadly force. Thus, if the suspect threatens the officer with a weapon or there is probable cause to believe that he has committed a crime involving the infliction or threatened infliction of serious physical harm, deadly force may be used if necessary to prevent escape, and if, where feasible, some warning has been given. As applied in such circumstances, the Tennessee statute would pass constitutional muster.

III

A

It is insisted that the Fourth Amendment must be construed in light of the common-law rule, which allowed the use of whatever force was necessary to effect the arrest of a fleeing felon, though not a misdemeanant. As stated in Hale's posthumously published Pleas of the Crown:

> "[I]f persons that are pursued by these officers for felony or the just suspicion thereof . . . shall not yield themselves to these officers, but shall either resist or fly before they are apprehended or being apprehended shall rescue themselves and resist or fly, so that they cannot be otherwise apprehended, and are upon necessity slain therein, because they cannot be otherwise taken, it is no felony." 2 M. Hale, Historia Placitorum Coronae 85 (1736).

See also 4 W. Blackstone, Commentaries. Most American jurisdictions also imposed a flat prohibition against the use of deadly force to stop a fleeing misdemeanant, coupled with a general privilege to use such force to stop a fleeing felon.

The State and city argue that because this was the prevailing rule at the time of the adoption of the Fourth Amendment and for some time thereafter, and is still in force in some States, use of deadly force against a fleeing felon must be "reasonable." It is true that this Court has often looked to the common law in evaluating the reasonableness, for Fourth Amendment purposes, of police activity.*** Because of sweeping change in the legal and technological context, reliance on the common-law rule in this case would be a mistaken literalism that ignores the purposes of a historical inquiry.

B

It has been pointed out many times that the common-law rule is best understood in light of the fact that it arose at a time when virtually all felonies were punishable by death. "Though effected without the protections and formalities of an orderly trial and conviction, the killing of a resisting or fleeing felon resulted in no greater consequences than those authorized for punishment of the felony of which the individual was charged or suspected."

Neither of these justifications makes sense today. Almost all crimes formerly punishable by death no longer are or can be. And while in earlier times "the gulf between the felonies and the minor offences was broad and deep," 2 Pollock & Maitland 467, n.3; *Carroll v. United States, supra,* 267 U.S., at 158, 45 S. Ct., at 287, today the distinction is minor and often arbitrary. Many crimes classified as misdemeanors, or nonexistent, at common law are now felonies. Wilgus, 22 Mich. L. Rev., at 572–573. These changes have undermined the concept, which was questionable to begin with, that use of deadly force against a fleeing felon is merely a speedier execution of someone who has already forfeited his life. They have also made the assumption that a "felon" is more dangerous than a misdemeanant untenable. Indeed, numerous misdemeanors involve conduct more dangerous than many felonies.

There is an additional reason why the common-law rule cannot be directly translated to the present day. The common-law rule developed at a time when weapons were rudimentary. Deadly force could be inflicted almost solely in a hand-to-hand struggle during which, necessarily, the safety of the arresting officer was at risk. Handguns were not carried by police officers until the latter half of the last century. L. Kennett & J. Anderson, The Gun in America 150–151 (1975). Only then did it become possible to use deadly force from a distance as a means of apprehension. As a practical matter, the use of deadly force under the standard articulation of the common-law rule has an altogether different meaning—and harsher consequences—now than in past centuries. See Wechsler & Michael, A Rationale for the Law of Homicide: I, 37 Colum. L. Rev. 701, 741 (1937).

One other aspect of the common-law rule bears emphasis. It forbids the use of deadly force to apprehend a misdemeanant, condemning such action as disproportionately severe.

In short, though the common-law pedigree of Tennessee's rule is pure on its face, changes in the legal and technological context mean the rule is distorted almost beyond recognition when literally applied.

C

***It cannot be said that there is a constant or overwhelming trend away from the common-law rule. In recent years, some States have reviewed their laws and expressly rejected abandonment of the common-law rule. Nonetheless, the long-term movement has been away from the rule that deadly force may be used against any fleeing felon, and that remains the rule in less than half the States.

D

Actual departmental policies are important for an additional reason. We would hesitate to declare a police practice of long standing "unreasonable" if doing so would severely hamper effective law enforcement. But the indications are to the contrary. There has been no suggestion that crime has worsened in any way in jurisdictions that have adopted, by legislation or departmental policy, rules similar to that announced today. *Amici* noted that "[a]fter extensive research and consideration, [they] have concluded that laws permitting police officers to use deadly force to apprehend unarmed, non-violent fleeing felony suspects actually do not protect citizens or law enforcement officers, do not deter crime or alleviate problems caused by crime, and do not improve the crime-fighting ability of law enforcement agencies." *Id.,* at 11. The submission is that the obvious state interests in apprehension are not sufficiently served to warrant the use of lethal weapons against all fleeing felons. See *supra,* at 1700–1701, and n.10.

Nor do we agree with petitioners and appellant that the rule we have adopted requires the police to make impossible, split-second evaluations of unknowable facts. See Brief for Petitioners 25; Brief for Appellant 11. We do not deny the practical difficulties of attempting to assess the suspect's dangerousness. However, similarly difficult judgments must be made by the police in equally uncertain circumstances. See, *e.g., Terry v. Ohio,* 392 U.S., at 20, 27, 88 S. Ct., at 1879, 1883. Nor is there any indication that in States that allow the use of deadly force only against dangerous suspects, see nn.15, 17–19, *supra,* the standard has been difficult to apply or has led to a rash of litigation involving inappropriate second-guessing of police officers' split-second decisions. Moreover, the highly technical felony/misdemeanor distinction is equally, if not more, difficult to apply in the field. An officer is in no position to know, for example, the precise value of property stolen, or whether the crime was a first or second offense. Finally, as noted above, this claim must be viewed with suspicion in light of the similar self-imposed limitations of so many police departments.

IV

The District Court concluded that Hymon was justified in shooting Garner because state law allows, and the Federal Constitution does not forbid, the use of deadly force to prevent the escape of a fleeing felony suspect if no alternative means of apprehension is available. See App. to Pet. for Cert. A9-A11, A38. This conclusion made a determination of Garner's apparent dangerousness unnecessary. The court did find, however, that Garner appeared to be unarmed, though Hymon could not be certain that was the case. *Id.,* at A4, A23. See also App. 41, 56; Record 219. Restated in Fourth Amendment terms, this means Hymon had no articulable basis to think Garner was armed.

In reversing, the Court of Appeals accepted the District Court's factual conclusions and held that "the facts, as found, did not justify the use of deadly force." We agree. Officer Hymon could not reasonably have believed that Garner—young, slight, and unarmed—posed any threat. Indeed, Hymon never attempted to justify his actions on any basis other than the need to prevent an escape. The District Court stated in passing that "[t]he facts of this case did not indicate to Officer Hymon that Garner was 'non-dangerous.'" App. to Pet. for Cert. A34. This conclusion is not explained, and seems to be based solely on the fact that Garner had broken into a house at night. However, the fact that Garner was a suspected burglar could not, without regard to the other circumstances, automatically justify the use of deadly force. Hymon did not have probable cause to believe that Garner, whom he correctly believed to be unarmed, posed any physical danger to himself or others.

The dissent argues that the shooting was justified by the fact that Officer Hymon had probable cause to believe that Garner had committed a nighttime burglary. *Post,* at 1711, 1712. While we agree that burglary is a serious crime, we cannot agree that it is so dangerous as automatically to justify the use of deadly force. The FBI classifies burglary as a "property" rather than a "violent" crime. See Federal Bureau of Investigation, Uniform Crime Reports, Crime in the United States 1 (1984). Although the armed burglar would present a different situation, the fact that an unarmed suspect has broken into a dwelling at night does not automatically mean he is physically dangerous. This case demonstrates as much.

Justice O'CONNOR, with whom THE CHIEF JUSTICE and Justice REHNQUIST join, dissenting.

The Court today holds that the Fourth Amendment prohibits a police officer from using deadly force as a last resort to apprehend a criminal suspect who refuses to halt when fleeing the scene of a nighttime burglary. This conclusion rests on the majority's balancing of the interests of the suspect and the public interest in effective law enforcement. *Ante,* at 1699. Notwithstanding the venerable common-law rule authorizing the use of deadly force if necessary to apprehend a fleeing felon, and continued acceptance of this rule by nearly half the States, *ante,* at 1703–1704, the majority concludes that Tennessee's statute is unconstitutional inasmuch as it allows the use of such force to apprehend a burglary suspect who is not obviously armed or otherwise dangerous. Although the circumstances of this case are unquestionably tragic and unfortunate, our constitutional holdings must be sensitive both to the history of the Fourth

Amendment and to the general implications of the Court's reasoning. By disregarding the serious and dangerous nature of residential burglaries and the longstanding practice of many States, the Court effectively creates a Fourth Amendment right allowing a burglary suspect to flee unimpeded from a police officer who has probable cause to arrest, who has ordered the suspect to halt, and who has no means short of firing his weapon to prevent escape. I do not believe that the Fourth Amendment supports such a right, and I accordingly dissent.

Notes and Questions

1. Why did the court in *City of Columbus v. Fraley* abandon the common law?

2. *Tennessee v. Garner* was a civil suit brought by the father of the decedent. If you were the chief prosecutor for Shelby County, Tennessee would you have brought criminal charges against the police officer? Why or why not?

3. In *Garner*, the Supreme Court determined that the police officer's "seizure" of Garner was not justified. However, the court declined to find the Tennessee statute in question unconstitutional. Why?

Chapter 21
Insanity

A. Background

Legal issues concerning the defendant's sanity arise at three different junctures of the criminal justice process. First, the court must ensure that the defendant is competent at the time of trial. To be deemed competent, the defendant must be able to consult with her attorney and understand the nature and consequences of the proceedings. If found incompetent, the court can commit the defendant until competency is restored and also forcibly medicate the defendant.

If found competent to stand trial, the defendant may present an insanity defense to all charges. Here, the court looks at whether the defendant was insane at the time of the crime. At the outset, it should be noted that the medical definition of insanity is not the same as the legal definition. In fact, there are at least four different methods of determining whether someone is legally insane in the United States. Also, some states have slight variations of these four traditional methods, while other states have completely abolished the defense. The different approaches to address the defendant's sanity can be traced to the historical evolution of the defense in this country. This evolution has been primarily guided by both advancements in diagnosing mental health illnesses and high-profile trials involving the insanity defense, for example, John Hinckley and Daniel M'Naghten.

The final issue with respect to the defendant's sanity involves capital punishment. The Supreme Court has ruled that the execution of an insane person constitutes cruel and unusual punishment in violation of the Eighth Amendment.

This chapter will explore the various ways courts have defined insanity to include what proof requirements may be imposed on the defendant. In addition, this chapter will examine diminished capacity through the lens of *State v. Wilcox* and *Clark v. Arizona*.

Queen v. M'Naghten, 10 Cl. & F. 200, 8 Eng. Rep. 718 (House of Lords 1843)

[Daniel M'Naghten believed that the Tory party was persecuting him. Thus, he wanted to assassinate the English Prime Minister Robert Peel. Believe that the Prime Minister was in his personal carriage, M'Naghten shot into the carriage. However, the only person present was Peel's secretary, Edward Drummond who succumbed to his wounds. At trial M'Naghten was found not guilty by reason of insanity. The public was not pleased with the verdict. As a result, the House of Lords debated the decision to include posing questions to the judiciary. The questions and answers are what follows next.]

Lord Chief Justice TINDAL:

The first question proposed by your Lordship is this: What is the law respecting alleged crimes committed by persons afflicted with insane delusion, in respect of one or more particular subjects or persons; as, for instance, where at the time of the commission of the alleged crime, the accused knew he was acting contrary to law, but did the act complained of with a view, under the influence of insane delusion, of redressing or revenging some supposed grievance or injury, or of producing some supposed public benefit?

Assuming that your Lordships' inquiries are confined to those persons who labour under such partial delusions only, and are not in other respects insane, we are of opinion that, notwithstanding the party accused did the act complained of with a view, under the influence of insane delusion, of redressing or revenging some supposed grievance or injury, or of producing some public benefit, he is nonetheless punishable according to the nature of the crime committed, if he knew at the time of committing such crime that he was acting contrary to law; by which expression we understand your Lordships to mean the law of the land.

Your Lordships are pleased to inquire of us, secondly, "What are the proper questions to be submitted to the jury, when a person alleged to be afflicted with insane delusion respecting one or more particular subjects or persons, is charged with the commission of a crime (murder, for example), and insanity is set up as a defence?" And, thirdly, "In what terms ought the question to be left to the jury, as to the prisoner's state of mind at the time when the act was committed? As these two questions appear to us to be more conveniently answered together, we have to submit our opinion to be that the jury ought to be told in all cases that every man is presumed to be sane, and to possess a sufficient degree of reason to be responsible for his crimes, until the contrary be proved to their satisfaction; and that, to establish a defence on the ground of insanity, it must be clearly proved that at the time of committing the act, the party accused was labouring under such a defect of reason, from disease of the mind, as not to know the nature and quality of the act he was doing, or if he did know it that he did not know he was doing what was wrong. The mode of putting the latter part of the question to jury on these occasions has generally been, whether the accused at the time of doing the act knew the difference between right and wrong; which mode, though rarely, if ever, leading to any mistake with the jury, is not, as we conceive, so accurate when put generally and in the abstract, as when put with reference to the party's knowledge of right and wrong in respect to the very act with which he is charged. If the question were to be put as to the knowledge of the accused solely and exclusively with reference to the law of the land, it might tend to confound the jury by inducing them to believe that an actual knowledge of the law of the land was essential in order to lead to a conviction; whereas the law is administered on the principle that everyone must be taken conclusively to know it, without proof that he does know it. If the accused was conscious that the act was one which he ought not to do, and if that act was at the same time contrary to the law of the land, he is punishable, and the usual course therefore has been to leave the question to the jury whether the accused had a sufficient degree of reason to know he was doing an act that was wrong; and this course we think is correct, accompanied with such observations and explanations as the circumstances of each case may require.

The fourth question which your Lordships have proposed to us is this: "If a person under an insane delusion, as to existing facts, commits an offence in consequence thereof, is he thereby excused? The answer must of course depend on the nature of the delusion: but, making the same assumptions as we did before, namely, that he labours under such partial delusion only, and is not in other respects insane, we think he must be considered in the same situation as to responsibility as if the facts with respect to which the delusion exists were real. For example, if under the influence of his delusion he supposes another man to be in the act of attempting to take away his life, and he kills that man, as he supposes in self-defense, he would be exempt from punishment. If his delusion was that the deceased had inflicted a serious injury on his character and fortune, and he killed him in revenge for such supposed injury, he would be liable to punishment.

The question lastly proposed by your Lordship is: "Can a medical man conversant with the disease of insanity, who never saw the prisoner previously to the trial, but who was present during the whole trial and at the examination of all the witnesses, be asked his opinion as to the state of the prisoner's mind at the time of the commission of the alleged crime, or his opinion whether the prisoner was conscious at the time of doing the act, that he was acting contrary to law, or whether he was labouring under any and what delusion at the time?" "In answer thereto, we state to your lordships that we think the medical man, under the circumstances supposed, cannot in strictness be asked his opinion in the terms above stated, because each of those questions involves the determination of the truth of the facts deposed to, which it is for the jury to decide, and the questions are not mere questions upon a matter of science, in which case such evidence is admissible. But where the facts are admitted or not dispute, and the question become substantially one of science only, it may be convenient to allow the question to be put in that general form, though the same cannot be insisted on as a matter of right.

State v. Staten, 247 N.E. 2d 293 (Ohio 1969)

TAFT, Chief Justice.

This appeal is based upon the contention that the proper test was not used by the three-judge Common Pleas Court in determining whether defendant should be found not guilty by reason of insanity.

The argument of defendant's counsel to the trial court represented in large part an attack upon the *M'Naghten* test for determining the defense of insanity.

After hearing that argument and the argument of the prosecutor, the presiding judge at the court stated:

> At this time, I will state that the court feels that the *McNaughten* (sic) rule is the law of Ohio.

There is nothing further in the record to indicate what test the trial court used in determining that defendant should not be acquitted by reason of insanity.

In *M'Naghten's* case (1843), 4 St.Tr. N.S. 847, it was stated that:

> *** jurors ought to be told in all cases that every man is to be presumed to be be sane, and to possess a sufficient degree of reason to be responsible for his crimes, until the contrary be proved to their satisfaction; and that to establish a defense on the ground of insanity, it must by clearly proved that, at the time of the committing of the act, the party accused was labouring under such a defect of reason, from disease of the mind, as not to know the nature and quality of the act he was doing; or, if he did know it, that he did not know he was doing what was wrong. The mode of putting the latter part of the question to the jury *** has generally been, whether the accused at the time of doing the act knew the difference between right and wrong *** in respect to the very act with which he is charged, ***

It has been stated that Ohio, along with most jurisdictions, follows the so-called *M'Naghten* rule as the "sole test" of criminal responsibility.

In determining what unsoundness of mind may excuse an accused from criminal responsibility for his acts, this court has almost always, both before and after the *Ross* case, been more liberal to those accused of crime than were the judges who promulgated the so-called *M'Naghten* rule. Furthermore in giving the reasons for its determinations, generally this court has not even mentioned the *M'Naghten* rule, although it has always stated the substance of that rule as a part of its own test for determining whether an accused should be relieved of criminal responsibility for an act.

In *Clark v. State* (1843), 12 Ohio 483 (decided in the same year as *M'Naghten*'s case), at page 494, there appears "portions of the charge to the jury, by Judge Birchard," which were "reduced to writing, and approved by the other (3) judges." Those portions read in part:

> *** Purposely implies an act of the will; an intention; a design to do the act. It presupposes the free agency of the actor. Deliberation and premeditation require action of the mind. They are operations of the intellectual faculties, and require an exercise of reason, reflection, judgment and decision, and can not happen in any case where the faculties of the mind are deranged, destroyed, or do not exist. The crime of murder in the first degree can, therefore, only be perpetrated by a free agent, capable of acting or of abstaining from action-free to embrace the right and to reject the wrong. He must have a sound intellect, capable of reason, reflection, premeditation, and under the control of the will.

In *Farrer v. State* (1853), 2 Ohio St. 54, it is said in the opinion by Corwin, J., at page 70:

> *** The power or self-control—"free agency"—is said to be quite as essential to criminal accountability as the power to distinguish between right and wrong. And I have no doubt that every correct definition of sanity, either expressly or by necessary construction, must suppose freedom of will, to avoid a wrong, no less than the power to distinguish between the wrong and the right. ***

In those early cases, it is quite apparent that this court held that an accused was not responsible for a criminal act by reason of insanity, if either (1) at the time of the act he did not know what he was doing, or (2) at that time he did not know that that act was wrong, or (3) at that time he could not refrain from doing that act.

Unfortunately, paragraph eight of the syllabus of *Loeffner v. State* (1857), 10 Ohio St. 598, does not mention the inability of a defendant to refrain from doing a criminal act as excusing him from criminal responsibility therefor. However, subsequently, in *Blackburn v. State* (1872), 23 Ohio St. 146, it was contended (page 155) that, "no one is criminally responsible for an act which he had no power whatever to refrain from doing." In answer to that contention it is stated in the opinion by Welch, J., at page 164:

> *** The form of question submitted to the jury is substantially the same as laid down in *Clark's* case, 12 Ohio 494 (note), and seems to us to embody the true rule, namely: Was the accused a free agent in forming the purpose to kill? Was he at the time capable of judging whether that act was right or wrong? And did he know at the time that it was an offense against the laws of God and man?'

Although we have some doubt whether this statement, or its counterpart in paragraph four of the syllabus of the case, could justify the conclusion that the inability of an accused to refrain from doing a criminal act would excuse him from criminal responsibility for doing it, the charge of Birchard, J., in *State v. Clark, supra* (12 Ohio 494), which was expressly approved by Judge Welch in his opinion in the *Blackburn* case, certainly would so excuse him. As hereinbefore pointed out, that charge stated that defendant could not be held criminally responsible for his act if he established that he was not a "free agent, capable of acting or abstaining from action—free to embrace the right and to reject the wrong."

Subsequent decisions of this court have made it clear that an accused will have no criminal responsibility for an act if he had no ability to refrain from doing that act. Thus, paragraph 15 of the syllabus of *State v. Frohner* (1948), 150 Ohio St. 53, and paragraph four of the syllabus of *State v. Stewart* (1964), 176 Ohio St. 156, read:

> A person accused of a crime who knows and recognizes the difference between right and wrong in respect to the crime with which he is charged and has the ability to choose the right and abjure the wrong is legally sane.

Defendant contends that one accused of criminal conduct should not be responsible for such criminal conduct if, at the time of such conduct, as a result of mental disease or defect, he lacks substantial capacity either to appreciate the wrongfulness of his conduct or to conform his conduct to the requirements of law.

This would represent a correct statement of the law of Ohio, as previously declared in our decisions, if the words "does not have the" were used instead of the words "lacks substantial," and if the word "know" was used instead of the word "appreciate."

In other words, defendant asks this court to adopt a rule that would eliminate criminal responsibility for an act of an accused, even though the accused knew that the act was wrong and had the ability to refrain from doing it, if either the capacity of the accused to know the wrongfulness of the act of his capacity to refrain from doing the act had been substantially impaired.

It may be observed that the rule contended for by defendant represents a substantial retreat from the so-called *Durham* rule, under which an accused could be relieved of criminal responsibility where his criminal act was merely a product of his mental abnormality. Under that rule, it was apparently not even necessary to establish that such abnormality was a proximate or substantial cause of the criminal act. *See Durham v. United States* (1954), 94 U.S. App. D.C. 228.

The so-called *Durham* rule and much of the confusion with regard to whether an accused should be excused from responsibility for criminal conduct on account of mental abnormalities have resulted from a failure to consider why an accused should be so excused. The defense accorded an accused by reason of his mental abnormalities has been labeled as the defense of insanity. Insanity encompasses a great many mental abnormalities. Those who criticize the so-called defense of insanity in criminal cases in Ohio usually do so merely because that defense does not encompass all the mental abnormalities which medical science recognizes as encompassed within the term "insanity." Such criticism fails to consider the reasons why there should be any defense of insanity in criminal cases.

One of the justifications for criminal sanctions is that they provide the public with protection against those addicted to criminal acts. Those who question whether there should be any defense of insanity in criminal cases do so because they believe that that defense deprives the public of that protection. In our opinion, this apprehension is not justified in Ohio.

Section 2943.03, Revised Code, provides in part:

> A defendant who does not plead not guilty by reason of insanity is conclusively presumed to have been sane at the time of the commission of the offense charged. The court may, for good cause shown, allow a change of plea at any time before the commencement of the trial.

Section 2945.39, Revised Code, provides in part:

> When a defendant pleads "not guilty by reason of insanity," and is acquitted on the sole ground of his insanity, such fact shall be found by the jury in its verdict, and it is presumed that such insanity continues. In such case the court shall forthwith direct that the accused be confined in the Lima state hospital, and shall

forthwith commit him to such hospital, and such person shall not be released from confinement in said hospital until the judge of the court of common pleas of Allen county, the superintendent of the Lima state hospital, an alienist to be designated by said judge and superintendent, or a majority of them, after notice and hearing, find and determine that said defendant's sanity has been restored, and that his release will not be dangerous. If said release is granted, it may be final or on condition, or such person may be released on parole, and thereafter, in the discretion of said judge or superintendent, said defendant may be returned to said hospital. *** This section does not deprive said defendant of his constitutional privilege to the writ of habeas corpus. (Emphasis added.)

It is apparent therefore that Ohio provides its public with adequate protection against those who are found not guilty by reason of insanity.

Other reasons for criminal sanctions against a convicted defendant are that he should be punished because his punishment will (1) tend to deter him from further criminal activities and (2) will deter others from such criminal activities.

This court, by its pronouncements, has apparently concluded that a person should not be punished for what he does, if, by reason of mental disease, he either does not know that what he did was wrong or could not prevent himself from doing it; and that punishing such an irresponsible individual will deter neither him nor others from doing what he did.

Although we have some doubt as to whether such an insane defendant's punishment would not have a deterrent effect on others, we cannot escape the conclusion that one, who does not know that his action is wrong or does not have the capacity to avoid such actions, is not a proper subject for punishment. See United States v. Currens (C.A.3, 1961), 290 F.2d 751. To punish such an individual would be like inflicting punishment upon an inanimate object, such as a machine, because it had, without any intelligent human intervention, caused some damage.

However, if an accused knows that his criminal act is wrong and has the ability to refrain from that act, we see no reason for not punishing him for doing that act, even where his capacity for knowing the wrongfulness of that act or his capacity to refrain therefrom has been diminished. Such diminished capacity may represent a reason for a diminished punishment but not for an absence of any punishment. In such an event, we believe that punishment would have a deterrent effect on others, especially those who might be inclined to feign such a diminished capacity.

In our opinion, therefore, the so-called defense of insanity, as recognized in Ohio in criminal cases, should not be criticized because that defense cannot be established by proving any one or more of the many mental abnormalities that may be included within "insanity," as that term is recognized by the medical profession.

Our conclusion is that, where the defense of insanity has been raised by a plea in a criminal prosecution, that defense and the burden of proof with respect thereto should be defined, in language that a jury may understand, as follows:

> In order to establish the defense of insanity, the accused must establish by a preponderance of the evidence that disease or other defect of his mind had so impaired his reason that, at the time of the criminal act with which he is charged, either he did not know that such act was wrong or he did not have the ability to refrain from doing that act.

Judgment reversed.

Notes and Questions

1. What do you think is the biggest weakness of M'Naghten? Many believe that M'Naghten focuses exclusively on the cognitive capacity of the defendant and ignores those who are incapable of controlling their own behavior.

2. Is the insanity test requested by the defendant in *State v. Staten* different from the one adopted by the Ohio Supreme Court? Of the two tests, which one is most similar to *M'Naghten*?

3. How does the court in *Staten* respond to the argument that the insanity defense puts the public at risk? Are you satisfied by this explanation?

4. According to the *Staten* court, society does not punish those who are legally insane because it would not serve as a specific deterrence. The court went on to say, "we have some doubt as to whether such an insane defendant's punishment would not have a deterrent effect on others." Do you agree with this statement? How could punishing an insane person ever have a deterrent effect?

B. Mens Rea and Level of Proof

State v. Curry, 45 Ohio St. 3d 109 (1989)

On the morning of June 3, 1986, defendant, Barbara M. Curry, was driving a beige three-quarter-ton Chevrolet truck eastbound on U.S. Route 20A in Williams County, Ohio. At a point approximately one-half mile from the village of West Unity, Curry's truck approached a flat-bed truck traveling in the opposite direction and being driven by Donald Leonard. Curry's truck crossed the center line into the path of Leonard's truck, but Leonard avoided a collision by swerving to the far right edge of the road. Leonard noticed that the woman driving the oncoming truck (Curry) "was sitting up right[,] had both hands on the wheel and her eyes were closed."

Curry's truck continued eastbound on U.S. Route 20A. The truck again crossed the center line, this time into the path of an oncoming red half-ton Ford truck being driven by Dennis B. Fletcher. Fletcher's effort to avoid an accident was unsuccessful, and the trucks collided head on. Fletcher was killed, and Curry suffered personal injuries. The parties stipulated that "[t]he crash of the two vehicles caused the death of [Fletcher] ***."

On December 30, 1986, Curry was charged with negligent vehicular homicide in violation of R.C. 2903.07(A). Curry entered a plea of not guilty, subsequently amended to not guilty by reason of insanity. Curry demanded a jury trial but later withdrew that demand. Following several continuances the case was tried to the court. Rejecting Curry's insanity defense, the court found her guilty as charged. The court sentenced Curry to six months and stayed execution of said sentence pending appeal.

On appeal, Curry argued that the evidence concerning her mental state at the time of the accident was sufficient to establish a defense of insanity, and thus that she was entitled to a judgment of not guilty by reason of insanity. The state disputed the sufficiency of the evidence and also argued that insanity is not an available defense to a charge of negligent vehicular homicide. The court of appeals reversed, holding: (1) insanity is a defense to negligent vehicular homicide; and (2) Curry had established her insanity defense by a preponderance of the evidence. Accordingly, the court of appeals reversed the judgment of the trial court and entered a judgment finding Curry not guilty by reason of insanity.***

OPINION

WRIGHT, Justice.

The state raises two questions for review: first, whether insanity is a defense to negligent vehicular homicide, and second, if insanity is a defense, whether Curry has established the defense by a preponderance of the evidence. We answer the first question in the affirmative and the second question in the negative. Accordingly, the judgment of the court of appeals is reversed, and the decision of the trial court is reinstated.

I

Appellee was charged with a violation of R.C. 2903.07(A), which provides in pertinent part: "No person, while operating *** a motor vehicle, *** shall negligently cause the death of another."

"Negligence" for purposes of the criminal code is defined in R.C. 2901.22(D):

> A person acts negligently when, because of a substantial lapse from due care, he fails to perceive or avoid a risk that his conduct may cause a certain result or may be of a certain nature. A person is negligent with respect to circumstances when, because of a substantial lapse from due care, he fails to perceive or avoid a risk that such circumstances may exist.

In its first proposition of law, the state argues that "[i]nsanity is not a defense to the crime of negligent vehicular homicide." In the state's view, insanity is only a defense to a criminal charge where it negates the intent element of the offense. Accordingly, the state argues, since negligent vehicular homicide is not a crime requiring an intent to kill, insanity is not available as a defense. We believe this argument misperceives the fundamental bases of the insanity defense.

In *State v. Staten* (1969), 18 Ohio St. 2d 13, this court reviewed at length the history of the insanity defense in Ohio. We noted that "[i]n determining what unsoundness of mind may excuse an accused from criminal responsibility for his acts, this court has almost always *** been more liberal to those accused of crime than were the judges who promulgated the so-called *M'Naghten* rule." *Id.* at 15. While the *M'Naghten* rule focuses strictly on the cognitive ability of the defendant to distinguish right from wrong, see *M'Naghten's Case* (1843), 8 Eng.Rep. 718, the insanity defense adopted in Ohio also considers the defendant's volition or "free agency" such that he will have no criminal responsibility for an act if he was unable to refrain from doing that act. *Staten, supra,* at 17. Accordingly, we held at paragraph one of the syllabus: "One accused of criminal conduct is not responsible for such criminal conduct if, at the time of such conduct, as a result of mental disease or defect, he does not have the capacity either to know the wrongfulness of his conduct or to conform his conduct to the requirements of law. *** " (Citations omitted.)

In arguing that the insanity defense is limited to offenses of which intent is an element, the state appears to confuse the insanity defense with the defense of "diminished capacity," under which an accused is permitted to introduce evidence of a mental disease or defect to prove that he did not have the particular state of mind that is an element of the offense charged. This court, however, expressly rejected the diminished capacity defense in *State v. Wilcox* (1982), 70 Ohio St. 2d 182. Thus, it is clear from our decision in *Wilcox* that in Ohio the insanity defense operates independently of the mental element of an offense. *See Mullaney v. Wilbur* (1975), 421 U.S. 684 (Rehnquist, J., concurring) (noting that "the existence or nonexistence of legal insanity bears no necessary relationship to the existence or nonexistence of the required mental elements of the crime").

This conclusion also follows from the fact that under Ohio law, a plea of not guilty by reason of insanity is an affirmative defense. *State v. Humphries* (1977), 51 Ohio St. 2d 95, paragraph one of the syllabus. In *State v. Poole* (1973), 33 Ohio St. 2d 18, this court described the nature of affirmative defenses as follows: "[T]hey represent not a mere denial or contradiction of evidence which the prosecution has offered as proof of an essential element of the crime charged, but, rather, they represent a substantive or independent matter 'which the defendant claims exempts him from liability even if it is conceded that the facts claimed by the prosecution are true.' " In other words, "the applicability of a defense becomes an issue only after all the elements of a crime have been satisfied. If an element is missing, the defendant is simply not guilty, and there is no need to resort to a defense. *** " Mickenberg, A Pleasant Surprise: The Guilty but Mentally Ill Verdict Has Both Succeeded in Its Own Right and Successfully Preserved the Traditional Role of the Insanity Defense (1987), 55 U. Cin. L. Rev. 943, 952. Since, for example, the diminished capacity defense goes directly to the mental element of an offense, successful use of that defense would negate that element and the accused would be entitled to acquittal of the crime charged (though he may be guilty of a lesser degree offense). Conversely, where the state has proved every element of the crime beyond a reasonable doubt, including the mental element, the accused may present evidence that he was insane at the time of the offense and thus should not be held criminally responsible. Rather than leading to a simple judgment of acquittal, however, successful use of the insanity defense results in a judgment of not guilty by reason of insanity, followed by committal proceedings pursuant to R.C. 2945.40.

Thus, the insanity defense is and always has been broader in scope than the posture argued by the state. While it is true that a legally insane defendant may lack the capacity to form the specific intent to commit a particular crime, criminal intent or lack thereof is not the focus of the insanity question. Rather, the insanity defense goes to the very root of our criminal justice system and is founded on the broader principle that an insane person may not be held criminally responsible for his conduct. *See Kuhn v. Zabotsky* (1967), 9 Ohio St. 2d 129. As explained in *Staten, supra,* "one, who does not know that his action is wrong or does not have the capacity to avoid such action, is not a proper subject for punishment. *** To punish such an individual would be like inflicting punishment upon an inanimate object, such as a machine, because it had, without any intelligent human intervention, caused some damage." *Id.* at 20. Thus, insanity may be a defense to any crime regardless of whether the particular offense requires that the defendant's conduct be purposeful, knowing, reckless, or negligent. Accordingly, we hold specifically that insanity is a defense to negligent vehicular homicide. *Accord Minneapolis v. Altimus* (1976), 306 Minn. 462, 238 N.W.2d 851, paragraph two of the syllabus (temporary insanity due to involuntary intoxication is a defense to traffic offenses requiring proof of a general criminal intent or negligence).

II

In its second proposition the state argues that the evidence is insufficient to establish Curry's insanity defense. The test of insanity is set forth in *Staten, supra,* at paragraph two of the syllabus:

> In order to establish the defense of insanity where raised by plea in a criminal proceeding, the accused must establish by a preponderance of the evidence that disease or other defect of his mind had so impaired his reason that, at the time of the criminal act with which he is charged, either he did not know that such act was wrong or he did not have the ability to refrain from doing that act.

Over the state's continuing objection, several witnesses testified concerning the defendant's emotional condition during the days preceding the accident. This testimony, along with the defendant's testimony, reveals that the defendant and her husband experienced marital problems arising from his involvement with another woman. The couple was separated for two and one-half months, during which time the defendant became increasingly involved in her religion. She spent a considerable amount of time reading the Bible and interpreting the Scriptures.

Much of the testimony focused on the sequence of events occurring between Friday, May 30, 1986 and the morning of Tuesday, June 3, 1986, the morning of the accident. All the witnesses testified that the defendant was emotionally distraught during this period. They also agreed that the defendant had gotten little, if any, sleep during this period.

As to the defendant's mental condition during the days before the accident, the defendant's sister testified that the defendant at times was in "a real deep stare." The defendant's mother testified that when she visited the defendant on the day before the accident the defendant " *** was staring at the Bible, just staring she wasn't reading, she was just staring." A deacon who had met with the defendant that evening testified that she was "just too much in a daze." Finally, the babysitter with whom the defendant had stayed the night before the accident stated that they had prayed and discussed the Scriptures but that "in the state she [the defendant] was at, you know, I don't think she was comprehending what I was telling her."

The state argues that Curry's mental condition as described above is attributable primarily to the fact that she had gotten little sleep during this period. Three of the witnesses quoted above testified that Curry appeared to be very tired and in need of sleep. The defendant's sister admitted that she did not know the symptoms of a person who is deprived of sleep.

The defendant testified that she was extremely upset during this period as a result of the separation from her husband and the fact that, while a reconciliation was attempted, her husband was forcing her to choose between him and her religion. She further testified that she had gone without sleep from Friday, May 30 until Tuesday, June 3. As to the particular circumstances of the accident, Curry recalled that she left the babysitter's residence and was intending to drive home but did not. Apparently, Curry drove past the turn-off to her home and continued driving on through West Unity. When asked where she was going, Curry testified:

> In my mind, at that time, I thought I was going to heaven. And, that's all I could think about, I thought well, if I go this way— this way is home and that way would be heaven and so I followed the sun and to me at that time it was the Son of God and if I followed, I'd go. So, I kept going.

The defense also offered the deposition of Dr. Thomas G. Sherman, a forensic psychiatrist who had examined the defendant on two occasions beginning approximately three months after the accident. Dr. Sherman stated "to a reasonable degree of psychiatric certainty" that the defendant at the time of the accident suffered from "schizophreniform disorder," or a "profound disorganization of thought." Dr. Sherman stated that, in his opinion, the defendant's mental disease on the date of the accident rendered her incapable of appreciating the criminality of the act with which she was charged, and that "had the mental illness not been present, an act such as the auto accident in its current form would have never occurred." The state objected to these statements of opinion. On cross-examination, Dr. Sherman further explained that when he examined the defendant in August 1986 her mental illness was "in remission," and that he had never seen her in a state of psychosis.

Having fully set forth the evidence relevant to Curry's insanity defense, we must consider whether that defense was proven by a preponderance of the evidence. Although the statement of the trial court is somewhat unclear, the judge did state that "I do give considerable weight to the testimony of Doctor Sherman." Since Dr. Sherman's testimony was relevant solely to Curry's insanity defense, it can scarcely be doubted that the trial court considered the defense and found that it had not been established.

The trial judge also stated that "I find that the defendant's mental state at that time was such that she was not able to mentally concern herself with traffic laws ***." The court of appeals held that this statement "establishes that *** [Curry] was legally insane at the time of the accident since it establishes that she did not know her act of driving left of center was wrong." We disagree.

This court held in *State v. Thomas* (1982), 70 Ohio St. 2d 79: "The weight to be given the evidence and the credibility of the witnesses concerning the establishment of the defense of insanity in a criminal proceeding are primarily for the trier of the facts. *** " (Citations omitted.) *Id.* at syllabus. Here the trial court considered the deposition of Dr. Sherman, the numerous state objections recorded therein, and the substance and credibility of the testimony presented by the defense. The trial court was obviously in the best position to determine whether Curry was insane at the time of the offense.

Contrary to the conclusion reached by the court of appeals below, the finding by the trial court that Curry "was not able to mentally concern herself with traffic laws" is *not* equivalent to a finding that Curry was insane at the time of the accident. The trial court stated that Curry's condition was "caused by a combination of her personal problems and self imposed lack of sleep[,]" and that "it was negligent for the defendant to be operating a motor vehicle at all in the mental state that she was in. Just as though she had been intoxicated." As suggested by the trial court, a voluntarily intoxicated person may be unable to "concern himself with traffic laws," yet such intoxication would not be a defense to negligent vehicular homicide, specific intent not being an element of that offense. *See, generally, State v. Fox* (1981), 68 Ohio St. 2d 53. Similarly, a person who operates a motor vehicle in a negligent manner following a self-imposed lack of sleep, and thereby causes the death of another, may be convicted of negligent vehicular homicide.

This is not a case of overwhelming evidence of the defendant's insanity. *Cf. State v. Brown* (1983), 5 Ohio St. 3d 133. The witnesses on Curry's behalf testified that she was emotionally distraught and had gone without sleep prior to the accident. Dr. Sherman stated that she was suffering from a disorganization of thought which rendered her incapable of appreciating the criminality of her conduct. The trial court duly considered this evidence and the state's objections to Dr. Sherman's legal conclusions. Thus, we will not disturb the trial court's finding that Curry failed to overcome the presumption of her sanity by a preponderance of the evidence.

For the foregoing reasons, the judgment of the court of appeals, finding appellee not guilty by reason of insanity, is reversed, and the judgment of the trial court is reinstated.

Judgment accordingly.

Notes and Questions

1. Historically, the prosecution had to prove the defendant's insanity. Today, however, most jurisdictions place the burden, at least initially on the defendant. If you were in a jurisdiction looking to reform its laws on insanity, would you place the burden of proof on the defendant? If so, why? Also, what level of proof must the defendant meet? In Ohio, like in many jurisdictions, the level of proof is the preponderance of the evidence.

2. The prosecution in *State v. Curry* argued that insanity could not apply to negligent vehicular manslaughter. In making this argument, the state said that insanity "is limited to offenses of which intent is an element." How did the court address this claim?

3. In *Curry*, the defense's expert witness said that the defendant was "incapable of appreciating the criminality of her conduct." If the trial judge found this to be true, would the defense have met the test for insanity in Ohio?

4. What was the defendant's criminal conduct in *Curry*? Was it driving while sleep deprived or disobeying traffic laws? Would defining the negligent conduct as either of these benefit her insanity defense?

5. In 1990, Ohio codified its new insanity test at ORC 2901.01(A)(14). In this new test, the state legislature removed the volitional portion of the insanity test as created by the *Staten* court. Why do you think the state legislature decided to modify the holding in *Staten*? Do you think legislators were bothered by cases like *Curry* or can you think of other reasons for changing the test for insanity?

O.R.C. 2945.391
Not guilty by reason of insanity finding.

For purposes of sections 2945.371, 2945.40, 2945.401, and 2945.402 and Chapters 5122. and 5123. of the Revised Code, a person is "not guilty by reason of insanity" relative to a charge of an offense only as described in division (A)(14) of section 2901.01 of the Revised Code. Proof that a person's reason, at the time of the commission of an offense, was so impaired that the person did not have the ability to refrain from doing the person's act or acts, does not constitute a defense.

O.R.C. 2901.01
General provisions definitions.

(A)(14) A person is "not guilty by reason of insanity" relative to a charge of an offense only if the person proves, in the manner specified in section 2901.05 of the Revised Code, that at the time of the commission of the offense, the person did not know, as a result of a severe mental disease or defect, the wrongfulness of the person's acts.

C. Diminished Capacity

State v. Wilcox, 70 Ohio St. 2d 182 (1982)

SWEENEY, Justice.

The question before the court in the instant appeal is whether appellee is entitled to a new trial at which he may present expert psychiatric testimony relating to his alleged incapacity to form the requisite specific intent to commit aggravated murder and aggravated burglary. The state, finding support in the dissent below, contends that "all relevant admissible evidence related to the mental status of Moses Wilcox was before the jury." As a consequence thereof, the state further contends that "any additional psychiatric testimony if offered would not have altered anything in the trial" and therefore the trial court's refusal to admit the additional evidence even if erroneous constituted non-prejudicial, harmless error. Appellee argues that the Court of Appeals did not err in ordering a new trial because the "defense of diminished capacity is properly proveable in the state of Ohio and that where the trial court frustrates or otherwise fails to admit relevant testimony in furtherance of its proof, as in the instant case, it has committed reversible error."

The parties herein and the court below, relied on *State v. Nichols* (1965), 3 Ohio App. 2d 182, as authority for the proposition that the partial defense of diminished capacity is recognized in Ohio. The case of *State v. Jackson* (1972), 32 Ohio St. 2d 203, has gone unnoticed, or at the very least uncited, at any stage of these proceedings. In *Jackson* the question of whether Ohio would recognize the diminished capacity defense was briefed, argued, and explicitly, albeit cursorily, rejected by this court. *Id.* at page 206, 291 N.E.2d 432. We adhere to the rule adopted in *Jackson* but shall endeavor in this opinion to spell out our objections to the diminished capacity defense and thereby overcome whatever confusion our nearly invisible treatment of diminished capacity in *Jackson* has engendered among bench and bar.

I

At the outset we note that there are a number of variations on the diminished capacity theme and a variety of labels have been applied to the doctrine. Inasmuch as the Court of Appeals below referred to *United States v. Brawner* (1972), 471 F.2d 969, for the doctrinal underpinning of its diminished capacity formulation, it is appropriate for us to use the *Brawner* model of diminished capacity to provide a working definition of the doctrine for purposes of our discussion herein. According to *Brawner*, at page 998, "expert testimony as to a defendant's abnormal mental condition may be received and considered, as tending to show, in a responsible way, that defendant did not have the specific mental state required for a particular crime or degree of crime—even though he was aware that his act was wrongful and was able to control it, and hence was not entitled to complete exoneration." If the *Brawner* rule were applied to the case at bar, then appellee, even though legally sane, could present psychiatric testimony as to his abnormal mental condition (diminished capacity) to show that he did not have the specific mental state—in this instance, the purpose—required to commit the crimes with which he stands charged. However, our review of the history and policies underlying the diminished capacity concept and the experience of jurisdictions that have attempted to apply the doctrine militate against the adoption of a *Brawner*-type rule in Ohio.

The diminished capacity defense originated in Scotland more than a century ago "to reduce the punishment of the 'partially insane' from murder to culpable homicide, a non-capital offense. *See HM Advocate v. Dingwall*, (1867) J.C. 466." Arenella, supra, at page 830, fn. 16. The doctrine has been widely accepted overseas, see Arenella, supra, and Comment, Criminal Law-Partial Insanity-Evidentiary Relevance Defined, 16 Rutgers L. Rev. 174, 176-77, fn. 8, but most American jurisdictions, with the notable exception of California, have been slow to embrace the concept. See Lewin, supra, at pages 1055, 1059, and Appendix; Goldstein, The Insanity Defense, at 195 (hereinafter Goldstein). While a number of states followed California's lead in adopting one form or another of the diminished capacity defense, see Annotation, 22 A.L.R.3d 1228, the *Brawner* court may have overstated the case when it found that the doctrine was being "adopted by the overwhelming majority of courts that have recently faced the question." 471 F.2d at page 1000. A post-*Brawner* student note determined that the supposed trend detected in *Brawner* was continuing, stating that "in recent years a growing number of jurisdictions have recognized the concept of diminished capacity." Note, Diminished Capacity—Recent Decisions and an Analytical Approach, 30 Vand. L. Rev. 213, 214. At this juncture, however, it appears that enthusiasm for the diminished capacity defense is on the wane and that there is, if anything, a developing movement away from diminished capacity although the authorities at this point are still quite mixed in their views.

The diminished capacity defense developed as a covert judicial response to perceived inequities in the criminal law. The purported justifications for the doctrine include the following:

> (1) it ameliorates defects in a jurisdiction's insanity test criteria; (2) it permits the jury to avoid imposing the death penalty on mentally disabled killers who are criminally responsible for their acts; and (3) it permits the jury to make more accurate individualized culpability judgments. *Arenella, supra*, at page 853.

In addition the diminished capacity defense has a certain logical appeal when juxtaposed against the settled rule that evidence of voluntary intoxication may be considered in determining whether an accused acted with the requisite specific intent. *See State v. Fox* (1981), 68 Ohio St. 2d 53. The analogy to the partial defense of voluntary intoxication figured prominently in the *Brawner* court's analysis. The court stated:

> Neither logic nor justice can tolerate a jurisprudence that defines the elements of an offense as requiring a mental state such that one defendant can properly argue that his voluntary drunkenness removed his capacity to form the specific intent but another defendant is inhibited from a submission of his contention that an abnormal mental condition, for which he was in no way responsible, negated his capacity to form a particular specific intent, even though the condition did not exonerate him from all criminal responsibility. 471 F.2d at page 999. See, also, Lewin, supra, at page 1092, and Weihofen and Overholser, Mental Disorder Affecting the Degree of a Crime, 56 Yale L.J. 959, 962-963 (hereinafter "Weihofen").

Upon examination, however, we find none of the foregoing justifications for the defense of diminished capacity sufficiently compelling as to warrant its adoption, particularly in light of the problems posed by the doctrine, problems even its proponents acknowledge.

I A

The diminished capacity defense does serve to ameliorate the limitations of the traditional, *M'Naghten*, right from wrong test for insanity. It is no coincidence that California, which pioneered the diminished capacity defense, for many years adhered to a strict *M'Naghten* standard. Justice Mosk of the California Supreme Court explicitly acknowledged the ameliorative effect of California's diminished capacity defense in *People v. Kelly* (1973), 10 Cal.3d 565, 579-80 (Concurring opinion):

> Efforts to "get around" the *M'Naghten* rule were undertaken in New Hampshire as long ago as 1870 (*State v. Pike*, 49 N.H. 399, 429), by Judge Bazelon in 1954 in *Durham v. United States*, 214 F.2d 862 (C.A.D.C.), by Chief Judge Biggs of the Third Circuit in *United States v. Currens* (1961) 290 F.2d 751, 774, and by this court when in 1949 we adopted a significant variation of *M'Naghten* in *People v. Wells* (1949) 33 Cal. 2d 330, 202, a thoughtful concept developed by Justice Schauer, and further explicated in *People v. Gorshen* (1959) 51 Cal. 2d 716.
>
> *** (I)n *People v. Henderson* (1963) 60 Cal.2d 482, 490, Justice Traynor frankly conceded the Wells-Gorshen "purpose and effect are to ameliorate the law governing criminal responsibility prescribed by the M'Naghten rule," ***.

The ameliorative argument loses much of its force, however, in jurisdictions that have abandoned or expanded upon the narrow *M'Naghten* standard. The test for insanity in Ohio is set forth in *State v. Staten* (1969), 18 Ohio St. 2d 13, paragraph one of the syllabus, as follows:

> One accused of criminal conduct is not responsible for such criminal conduct if, at the time of such conduct, as a result of mental disease or defect, he does not have the capacity either to know the wrongfulness of his conduct or to conform his conduct to the requirements of law. *** (Citations omitted.)

While this standard is arguably less expansive than that espoused by the drafters of the Model Penal Code it is considerably more flexible than the *M'Naghten* rule. The record in the case at bar, which is replete with expert testimony going to the question of appellee's sanity, illustrates the relative liberality of Ohio's insanity rule. Thus we see no reason to fashion a halfway measure, e.g., diminished capacity, when an accused may present a meaningful insanity defense in a proper case.

The interplay between the diminished capacity doctrine and the insanity defense, moreover, is not limited to the supposed ameliorative effect of the former on the latter. Rather, as Dr. Diamond, among others, has observed, "(e)xperience with the diminished responsibility (or capacity) defense has been extensive in England and in California, and indicates that this defense does not just supplement the insanity defense, but tends to supersede it *** " Futile Journey, supra, at page 124. Dr. Diamond, a leading proponent of the diminished capacity concept whose testimony is quoted at some length in Gorshen, supra, attributes the supersession of the insanity defense to the fact that a diminished capacity formulation "may well be a much more rational solution to the problem of the mentally ill offender." Futile Journey, supra, at page 124. Other commentators are far less sanguine about the tendency of diminished capacity to supplant the insanity defense:

> *** "partial responsibility" becomes an important alternative to the plea of insanity, particularly when the question of capital punishment is removed. The defendant facing a murder charge must then choose between, on the one hand, insanity and indeterminate commitment and, on the other, conviction and a long sentence, which may be reduced by parole. Some indication of how they choose is afforded by the recent English experience with "diminished responsibility." That plea has become so popular that it threatens to displace the insanity defense entirely. Goldstein, supra, at pages 195-196.

Professor Arenella notes that "(s)eriously disturbed defendants can avoid an indefinite commitment to a mental hospital for the criminally insane by relying on the diminished responsibility defense which frequently leads to a reduced term in prison." According to this view, the principal practical effect of the diminished capacity defense is to enable mentally ill offenders to receive shorter and more certain sentences than they would receive if they were adjudged insane. Having satisfied ourselves that Ohio's test for criminal responsibility adequately safeguards the rights of the insane, we are disinclined to adopt an alternative defense that could swallow up the insanity defense and its attendant commitment provisions. See R.C. 2945.40.

I B

We can quickly dispose of the argument that the diminished capacity defense alleviates the harshness of the death penalty when mentally ill but nonetheless sane defendants are convicted of capital crimes. While this rationale formerly had considerable force, and indeed may have been the underlying basis of People v. Wells, supra, recent United States Supreme Court decisions have limited capital crimes to a narrow range of cases. Appellee faced no death penalty threat because Ohio's former capital punishment statute was struck down as unconstitutional in Lockett v. Ohio, supra. Moreover, under Ohio's recently enacted death penalty statute, which was not in effect when the instant case arose and on which we express no opinion herein, " *** (w)hen death may be imposed as a penalty, the court, upon request of the defendant *** shall require a mental examination to be made ***." R.C. 2929.03(D)(1). Mental capacity is a formal mitigating factor in capital cases under current Ohio law at the punishment stage of the now bifurcated proceedings. Thus the ameliorative purpose served by the diminished capacity defense in capital cases has largely been accomplished by other means.

<h2 style="text-align:center">I C</h2>

The justifications for diminished capacity relating to the defense's potential for more accurate, individualized culpability judgments and its logical relevance are based largely on analogies to the insanity defense and the defense of intoxication, respectively. These arguments were discussed at some length in *Bethea v. United States* (D.C. App. 1976), 365 A.2d 64, wherein the court voiced persuasive objections to the diminished capacity doctrine. *Bethea*, moreover, is of particular significance because the court expressly rejected the *Brawner* model of diminished capacity for the District of Columbia notwithstanding the fact that *Brawner* was a District of Columbia case. The following language from *Bethea*, at pages 86-88, is relevant to the case at bar:

> Our principal objection to the *Brawner* dicta is its apparent abandonment of traditional legal theory. The essence of the diminished capacity concept embraced in that decision is that the circumstance of mental deficiency should not be confined to use as an all-or-nothing defense. *** It is true, of course, that the existence of the required state of mind is to be determined subjectively in the sense that the issue must be resolved according to the particular circumstances of a given case. However, this fact may not be allowed to obscure the critical difference between the legal concepts of mens rea and insanity. *** The former refers to the existence in fact of a "guilty mind;" insanity, on the other hand, connotes a presumption that a particular individual lacks the capacity to possess such a state of mind. It is upon this distinction that the "logic" of the diminished capacity doctrine founders. *** The concept of insanity is simply a device the law employs to define the outer limits of that segment of the general population to whom these presumptions concerning the capacity for criminal intent shall not be applied. The line between the sane and the insane for the purposes of criminal adjudication is not drawn because for one group the actual existence of the necessary mental state (or lack thereof) can be determined with any greater certainty, but rather because those whom the law declares insane are demonstrably so

aberrational in their psychiatric characteristics that we choose to make the assumption that they are incapable of possessing the specified state of mind. Within the range of individuals who are not "insane," the law does not recognize the readily demonstrable fact that as between individual criminal defendants the nature and development of their mental capabilities may vary greatly.

In the same vein as *Bethea*, the Wisconsin Supreme Court in *Steele v. State* (1979), 97 Wis. 2d 72, recently made the following pertinent observations:

"*** The determination of capacity to form an intent—to find whether or not the alleged offender intended to do, in the sense of the criminal law, what he in fact did—requires a fine tuning of an entirely different nature than that required for the admission of evidence on the general question of insanity for the determination of whether or not there should be criminal responsibility ***. To make *** (the insanity) determination requires no fine tuning. It is, rather, a gross evaluation that a person's conduct and mental state is so beyond the limits of accepted norms that to hold him criminally responsible would be unjust. This is a far cry from accepting testimony which purports to prove or disprove a specific intent, as distinguished from criminal responsibility. While some courts may have blind faith in all phases of psychiatry, this court does not. There is substantial doubt whether evidence such as was sought to be introduced here is scientifically sound, and there is substantial legal doubt that it is probative on the point for which it was asserted in this case. *Id.* at pages 96-97.

Theoretically the insanity concept operates as a bright line test separating the criminally responsible from the criminally irresponsible. The diminished capacity concept on the other hand posits a series of rather blurry lines representing gradations of culpability. As Professor Arenella notes, at page 860,

(t)he analogy to the insanity defense is misleading because the diminished responsibility doctrine asks the expert witness and the jury to make a far more subtle distinction. The insanity defense asks both to distinguish between a large group of offenders who are punishable for their acts despite their mental deficiencies, and a small class of offenders who are so mentally disabled that they cannot be held accountable because they lack the minimal capacity to act voluntarily. The diminished responsibility doctrine attempts to divide the first large group of responsible sane offenders into two subgroups: a group of "normal" fully culpable criminal offenders, and a group of mentally abnormal but sane offenders with reduced culpability.

In light of the linedrawing difficulties courts and juries face when assessing expert evidence to make the "bright line" insanity determination, we are not at all confident that similar evidence will enable juries, or the judges who must instruct them, to bring the blurred lines of diminished capacity into proper focus so as to facilitate principled and consistent decision-making in criminal cases. In short, the fact that psychiatric evidence is admissible to prove or disprove insanity does not necessarily dictate the conclusion that it is admissible for purposes unrelated to the insanity defense.

The *Brawner* court emphasized the apparent illogic of permitting evidence of voluntary intoxication to be introduced to negate specific intent while precluding the introduction of evidence of an abnormal mental condition not amounting to insanity for the same purpose. While we concede that there is a superficial attractiveness to the intoxication-diminished capacity analogy, upon closer examination we, like the court in *Bethea*, find the concepts to be quite disparate. The *Bethea* court addressed this precise point and stated as follows:

> The rule that evidence of intoxication may be employed to demonstrate the absence of specific intent figured prominently in the *Brawner* court's advocacy of consistency in the treatment of expert evidence of mental impairment. The asserted analogy is flawed, however, by the fact that there are significant evidentiary distinctions between psychiatric abnormality and the recognized incapacitating circumstances. Unlike the notion of partial or relative insanity, conditions such as intoxication, medication, epilepsy, infancy, or senility are, in varying degrees, susceptible to quantification or objective demonstration, and to lay understanding. As the Ninth Circuit observed in *Wahrlich v. Arizona*, 479 F.2d 1137, 1138 (9th Cir.):
>
> "Exposure to the effects of age and of intoxicants upon state of mind is a part of common human experience which fact finders can understand and apply; indeed, they would apply them even if the state did not tell them they could. The esoterics of psychiatry are not within the ordinary ken."

It takes no great expertise for jurors to determine whether an accused was "so intoxicated as to be mentally unable to intend anything (unconscious),"

Jackson, supra, 32 Ohio St. 2d at page 206, whereas the ability to assimilate and apply the finely differentiated psychiatric concepts associated with diminished capacity demands a sophistication (or as critics would maintain a sophistic bent) that jurors (and officers of the court) ordinarily have not developed. We are convinced as was the *Bethea* court, that these "significant evidentiary distinctions" preclude treating diminished capacity and voluntary intoxication as functional equivalents for purposes of partial exculpation from criminal responsibility.

II

We have examined the commonly asserted justifications for diminished capacity and have found them wanting. We have also looked at the leading California cases, which attempted to apply the diminished capacity concept in a principled manner, and have concluded that the California experience with diminished capacity does not inspire imitation. The California courts struggled to evolve a coherent diminished capacity framework but the difficulties inherent in the doctrine, e.g., its subjectivity, its non-uniform and exotic terminology, its open-endedness, and its quixotic results in particular cases, were not overcome, and therefore consistent and predictable application of the diminished capacity concept in California became an elusive and unachieved goal.

Commentators, including proponents as well as opponents of diminished capacity, attempted to untangle the several strands of the California diminished capacity defense. Their conclusions are not overly heartening.***

The upshot of the doctrinal confusion and the public outcry over cases like *People v. White, supra*, finally prompted the California legislature to abolish the diminished capacity defense by statute. Thus the diminished capacity concept has been repudiated in the very jurisdiction that formerly gave the greatest credence to the doctrine.

The open-endedness of the diminished capacity doctrine troubles us as well. Under the California rule evidence of diminished capacity could only be introduced to negate the mental element in crimes requiring specific intent. The specific intent limitation imposed by the California courts did not, however, flow from the theory underlying the diminished capacity doctrine and, indeed, may have been in direct conflict therewith. The *Bethea* court, at page 90 acknowledged this theoretical incongruity in its discussion of *Brawner*:

> "The *Brawner* court did indicate that for the time being the admission of psychiatric evidence of diminished capacity would be limited to the trial of offenses involving specific intent. *** We are not satisfied that the rule could be confined to easily. Assuming the competency of experts to testify as to an accused's capacity for specific intent we see no logical bar to their

observations as to the possible existence or lack of malice or general intent. Moreover, it does not appear to us that the balance between the evidentiary value of medical testimony and its potential for improper impact upon the trier would vary sufficiently as between the various degrees of mens rea to warrant such an artificial distinction." (Citation omitted.)

If however, in the interests of doctrinal purity evidence of diminished capacity were admitted to disprove the mental element in general intent crimes, then "successful application of the diminished capacity doctrine *** would create the anomalous result of a 'partial defense' leading to outright acquittal of the defendant because of the absence of a lesser included offense." Arenella, supra, at page 832, fn. 25. This "anomalous result," although a theoretical possibility is unlikely to be countenanced by courts because "(t)he complete acquittal of such offenders would release from state control the very persons society should probably fear most-because their endowments are fewer, because they are more suggestible, more manipulable, more fearful." Goldstein, supra, at page 202.Nevertheless, the potential applicability of diminished capacity as a complete defense to crimes of general intent dramatically highlights the paradox inhering in the doctrine:

> "The subjective (diminished capacity) theory classes as less serious the offender who is less culpable; assuming him to be less 'guilty,' it proceeds to class him as less dangerous and either reduces the length of time he may be detained or releases him entirely. Yet his objective behavior may mark him as extremely dangerous and seriously in need not only of correction and treatment but of detention as well." *Id.*

This paradox did not escape notice in *Bethea*, wherein the court quoted the pre-*Brawner* case of *Fisher v. United States* (1945), 149 F.2d 28, *affirmed* 328 U.S. 463, (1946), for the proposition that "'it is obvious that brutal murders are not committed by normal people. To give (such) an instruction *** is to tell the jury that they are at liberty to acquit one who commits a brutal crime because he has the abnormal tendencies of persons capable of such crimes.'" *Bethea, supra*, at page 85, *quoting Fisher, supra*, at page 29. Under a diminished capacity regime, however, the more brutal, bizarre, or sensational the crime, the greater is the likelihood of a successful diminished capacity defense. "Psychiatry's elastic definitions of mental abnormality easily encompass anyone who kills another human being without justification or excuse because such an act demonstrates a serious deviation from cultural and social norms. From such abnormality, the expert can readily infer that the accused had extreme difficulty in obeying the law and is therefore entitled to formal mitigation." Arenella, supra, at page 858. In other words, the commission of the offense in most instances becomes ipso facto evidence of diminished capacity.

"While there may be superficial appeal to the idea that the standards of criminal responsibility should be applied as subjectively as possible, the overriding danger of the disputed doctrine is that it would discard the traditional presumptions concerning mens rea without providing for a corresponding adjustment in the means whereby society is enabled to protect itself from those who cannot or will not conform their conduct to the requirements of the law." *Bethea, supra*, at page 90. Thus, the effect of adopting a diminished capacity model transcends the doctrine's potential to transform criminal trials into psychiatric shouting matches. Rather, the diminished capacity theory forcefully challenges conventional concepts of culpability and "involve(s) a fundamental change in the common law theory of responsibility." *Fisher, supra*, 328 U.S. at 476. Echoing *Bethea*, "(w)e conclude that the potential impact of concepts such as diminished capacity or partial insanity—however labeled—is of a scope and magnitude which precludes their proper adoption by an expedient modification of the rules of evidence. If such principles are to be incorporated into our law of criminal responsibility, the change should lie within the province of the legislature." *Bethea, supra*, at page 92.

We hold, therefore, that the partial defense of diminished capacity is not recognized in Ohio (*State v. Jackson, supra* (32 Ohio St. 2d 203) followed) and consequently, a defendant may not offer expert psychiatric testimony, unrelated to the insanity defense, to show that the defendant lacked the mental capacity to form the specific mental state required for a particular crime or degree of crime.

For the reasons hereinbefore stated, the judgment of the Court of Appeals is reversed.

Judgment reversed.

Clark v. Arizona, 548 U.S. 735 (2006)

Justice SOUTER delivered the opinion of the Court.

The case presents two questions: whether due process prohibits Arizona's use of an insanity test stated solely in terms of the capacity to tell whether an act charged as a crime was right or wrong; and whether Arizona violates due process in restricting consideration of defense evidence of mental illness and incapacity to its bearing on a claim of insanity, thus eliminating its significance directly on the issue of the mental element of the crime charged (known in legal shorthand as the *mens rea,* or guilty mind). We hold that there is no violation of due process in either instance.

In the early hours of June 21, 2000, Officer Jeffrey Moritz of the Flagstaff Police responded in uniform to complaints that a pickup truck with loud music blaring was circling a residential block. When he located the truck, the officer turned on the emergency lights and siren of his marked patrol car, which prompted petitioner Eric Clark, the truck's driver (then 17), to pull over. Officer Moritz got out of the patrol car and told Clark to stay where he was. Less than a minute later, Clark shot the officer, who died soon after but not before calling the police dispatcher for help. Clark ran away on foot but was arrested later that day with gunpowder residue on his hands; the gun that killed the officer was found nearby, stuffed into a knit cap.

Clark was charged with first-degree murder under Ariz. Rev. Stat. Ann. § 13-1105(A)(3) (West Supp. 2005) for intentionally or knowingly killing a law enforcement officer in the line of duty.[26] In March 2001, Clark was found incompetent to stand trial and was committed to a state hospital for treatment, but two years later the same trial court found his competence restored and ordered him to be tried. Clark waived his right to a jury, and the case was heard by the court.

At trial, Clark did not contest the shooting and death, but relied on his undisputed paranoid schizophrenia at the time of the incident in denying that he had the specific intent to shoot a law enforcement officer or knowledge that he was doing so, as required by the statute. Accordingly, the prosecutor offered circumstantial evidence that Clark knew Officer Moritz was a law enforcement officer. The evidence showed that the officer was in uniform at the time, that he caught up with Clark in a marked police car with emergency lights and siren going, and that Clark acknowledged the symbols of police authority and stopped. The testimony for the prosecution indicated that Clark had intentionally lured an officer to the scene to kill him, having told some people a few weeks before the incident that he wanted to shoot police officers. At the close of the State's evidence, the trial court denied Clark's motion for judgment of acquittal for failure to prove intent to kill a law enforcement officer or knowledge that Officer Moritz was a law enforcement officer.

In presenting the defense case, Clark claimed mental illness, which he sought to introduce for two purposes. First, he raised the affirmative defense of insanity, putting the burden on himself to prove by clear and convincing evidence, § 13-502(C) (West 2001), that "at the time of the commission of the criminal act [he] was afflicted with a mental disease or defect of such severity that [he] did not

---

[26] Section 13–1105(A)(3) provides that "[a] person commits first degree murder if . . . [i]ntending or knowing that the person's conduct will cause death to a law enforcement officer, the person causes the death of a law enforcement officer who is in the line of duty."

know the criminal act was wrong," § 13-502(A).[27] Second, he aimed to rebut the prosecution's evidence of the requisite *mens rea,* that he had acted intentionally or knowingly to kill a law enforcement officer. See, *e.g.,* Record in No. CR 2000–538 (Ariz. Super. Ct.), Doc. 374 (hereinafter Record).

The trial court ruled that Clark could not rely on evidence bearing on insanity to dispute the *mens rea.* The court cited *State v. Mott,* 187 Ariz. 536, 931 P.2d 1046 , which "refused to allow psychiatric testimony to negate specific intent," 187 Ariz., at 541, 931 P.2d, at 1051, and held that "Arizona does not allow evidence of a defendant's mental disorder short of insanity . . . to negate the *mens rea* element of a crime."

As to his insanity, then, Clark presented testimony from classmates, school officials, and his family describing his increasingly bizarre behavior over the year before the shooting. Witnesses testified, for example, that paranoid delusions led Clark to rig a fishing line with beads and wind chimes at home to alert him to intrusion by invaders, and to keep a bird in his automobile to warn of airborne poison. There was lay and expert testimony that Clark thought Flagstaff was populated with "aliens" (some impersonating government agents), the "aliens" were trying to kill him, and bullets were the only way to stop them. A psychiatrist testified that Clark was suffering from paranoid schizophrenia with delusions about "aliens" when he killed Officer Moritz, and he concluded that Clark was incapable of luring the officer or understanding right from wrong and that he was thus insane at the time of the killing. In rebuttal, a psychiatrist for the State gave his opinion that Clark's paranoid schizophrenia did not keep him from appreciating the wrongfulness of his conduct, as shown by his actions before and after the shooting (such as circling the residential block with music blaring as if to lure the police to intervene, evading the police after the shooting, and hiding the gun).

At the close of the defense case consisting of this evidence bearing on mental illness, the trial court denied Clark's renewed motion for a directed verdict grounded on failure of the prosecution to show that Clark knew the victim was a police officer. The judge then issued a special verdict of first-degree murder, expressly finding that Clark shot and caused the death of Officer Moritz beyond a reasonable doubt and that Clark had not shown that he was insane at the time. The judge noted that though Clark was indisputably afflicted with paranoid schizophrenia at the time of the shooting, the mental illness "did not . . . distort his perception of reality so severely that he did not know his actions were wrong." App. 334. For this conclusion, the judge expressly relied on "the facts of the crime, the evaluations of the experts, [Clark's] actions and behavior both before and

---

[27] Section 13-1105(A)(3) provides that "[a] person commits first degree murder if . . . [i]ntending or knowing that the person's conduct will cause death to a law enforcement officer, the person causes the death of a law enforcement officer who is in the line of duty."

after the shooting, and the observations of those that knew [Clark]." *Id.,* at 333. The sentence was life imprisonment without the possibility of release for 25 years.

Clark moved to vacate the judgment and sentence, arguing, among other things, that Arizona's insanity test and its *Mott* rule each violate due process. As to the insanity standard, Clark claimed (as he had argued earlier) that the Arizona Legislature had impermissibly narrowed its standard in 1993 when it eliminated the first part of the two-part insanity test announced in *M'Naghten's Case,* 10 Cl. & Fin. 200, 8 Eng. Rep. 718 (1843). The court denied the motion.

The Court of Appeals of Arizona affirmed Clark's conviction, treating the conclusion on sanity as supported by enough evidence to withstand review for abuse of discretion, and holding the State's insanity scheme consistent with due process. App. 336. As to the latter, the Court of Appeals reasoned that there is no constitutional requirement to recognize an insanity defense at all, the bounds of which are left to the State's discretion. Beyond that, the appellate court followed *Mott,* reading it as barring the trial court's consideration of evidence of Clark's mental illness and capacity directly on the element of *mens rea.* The Supreme Court of Arizona denied further review.

We granted certiorari to decide whether due process prohibits Arizona from thus narrowing its insanity test or from excluding evidence of mental illness and incapacity due to mental illness to rebut evidence of the requisite criminal intent. 546 U.S. 1060 (2005). We now affirm.

II

Clark first says that Arizona's definition of insanity, being only a fragment of the Victorian standard from which it derives, violates due process. The landmark English rule in *M'Naghten's Case, supra,* states that

"the jurors ought to be told . . . that to establish a defence on the ground of insanity, it must be clearly proved that, at the time of the committing of the act, the party accused was laboring under such a defect of reason, from disease of the mind, as not to know the nature and quality of the act he was doing; or, if he did know it, that he did not know he was doing what was wrong." *Id.,* at 210, 8 Eng. Rep., at 722.

The first part asks about cognitive capacity: whether a mental defect leaves a defendant unable to understand what he is doing. The second part presents an ostensibly alternative basis for recognizing a defense of insanity understood as a lack of moral capacity: whether a mental disease or defect leaves a defendant unable to understand that his action is wrong.

When the Arizona Legislature first codified an insanity rule, it adopted the full *M'Naghten* statement (subject to modifications in details that do not matter here):

"A person is not responsible for criminal conduct if at the time of such conduct the person was suffering from such a mental disease or defect as not to know the nature and quality of the act or, if such person did know, that such person did not know that what he was doing was wrong." Ariz. Rev. Stat. Ann. § 13-502 (West 1978).

In 1993, the legislature dropped the cognitive incapacity part, leaving only moral incapacity as the nub of the stated definition. Under current Arizona law, a defendant will not be adjudged insane unless he demonstrates that "at the time of the commission of the criminal act [he] was afflicted with a mental disease or defect of such severity that [he] did not know the criminal act was wrong," Ariz. Rev. Stat. Ann. § 13-502(A) (West 2001).

A

Clark challenges the 1993 amendment excising the express reference to the cognitive incapacity element. He insists that the side-by-side *M'Naghten* test represents the minimum that a government must provide in recognizing an alternative to criminal responsibility on grounds of mental illness or defect, and he argues that elimination of the *M'Naghten* reference to nature and quality " 'offends [a] principle of justice so rooted in the traditions and conscience of our people as to be ranked as fundamental.' "

***Even a cursory examination of the traditional Anglo–American approaches to insanity reveals significant differences among them, with four traditional strains variously combined to yield a diversity of American standards. The main variants are the cognitive incapacity, the moral incapacity, the volitional incapacity, and the product-of-mental-illness tests. The first two emanate from the alternatives stated in the *M'Naghten* rule. The volitional incapacity or irresistible-impulse test, which surfaced over two centuries ago (first in England, then in this country), asks whether a person was so lacking in volition due to a mental defect or illness that he could not have controlled his actions. And the product-of-mental-illness test was used as early as 1870, and simply asks whether a person's action was a product of a mental disease or defect. Seventeen States and the Federal Government have adopted a recognizable version of the *M'Naghten* test with both its cognitive incapacity and moral incapacity components. One State has adopted only *M'Naghten's* cognitive incapacity test, and 10 (including Arizona) have adopted the moral incapacity test alone. Fourteen jurisdictions, inspired by the Model Penal Code, have in place an amalgam of the volitional incapacity test and some variant of the moral incapacity test, satisfaction of either (generally by showing a defendant's substantial lack of capacity) being enough to excuse. Three States combine a full *M'Naghten* test with a volitional incapacity formula. And New Hampshire alone stands by the product-of-mental-illness test. The alternatives are multiplied further by variations in the prescribed insanity verdict: a significant number of these jurisdictions supplement the traditional "not guilty by reason of insanity" verdict with an alternative of "guilty but mentally ill." Finally, four States have no affirmative insanity defense, though one provides for a "guilty and mentally ill" verdict. These four, like a number of others that recognize an affirmative insanity defense, allow consideration of evidence of mental illness directly on the element of *mens rea* defining the offense.

With this varied background, it is clear that no particular formulation has evolved into a baseline for due process, and that the insanity rule, like the conceptualization of criminal offenses, is substantially open to state choice. Indeed, the legitimacy of such choice is the more obvious when one considers the interplay of legal concepts of mental illness or deficiency required for an insanity defense, with the medical concepts of mental abnormality that influence the expert opinion testimony by psychologists and psychiatrists commonly introduced to support or contest insanity claims.***

B

Nor does Arizona's abbreviation of the *M'Naghten* statement raise a proper claim that some constitutional minimum has been shortchanged. Clark's argument of course assumes that Arizona's former statement of the *M'Naghten* rule, with its express alternative of cognitive incapacity, was constitutionally adequate (as we agree). That being so, the abbreviated rule is no less so, for cognitive incapacity is relevant under that statement, just as it was under the more extended formulation, and evidence going to cognitive incapacity has the same significance under the short form as it had under the long.

Though Clark is correct that the application of the moral incapacity test (telling right from wrong) does not necessarily require evaluation of a defendant's cognitive capacity to appreciate the nature and quality of the acts charged against him, see Brief for Petitioner 46-47, his argument fails to recognize that cognitive incapacity is itself enough to demonstrate moral incapacity. Cognitive incapacity, in other words, is a sufficient condition for establishing a defense of insanity, albeit not a necessary one. As a defendant can therefore make out moral incapacity by demonstrating cognitive incapacity, evidence bearing on whether the defendant knew the nature and quality of his actions is both relevant and admissible. In practical terms, if a defendant did not know what he was doing when he acted, he could not have known that he was performing the wrongful act charged as a crime. Indeed, when the two-part rule was still in effect, the Supreme Court of Arizona held that a jury instruction on insanity containing the moral incapacity part but not a full recitation of the cognitive incapacity part was fine, as the cognitive incapacity part might be "'treated as adding nothing to the requirement that the accused know his act was wrong.' " *State v. Chavez,* 143 Ariz. 238, (1984) (quoting A. Goldstein, The Insanity Defense 50 (1967)).

The Court of Appeals of Arizona acknowledged as much in this case, too, see App. 350 ("It is difficult to imagine that a defendant who did not appreciate the 'nature and quality' of the act he committed would reasonably be able to perceive that the act was 'wrong' "), and thus aligned itself with the long-accepted understanding that the cognitively incapacitated are a subset of the morally incapacitated within the meaning of the standard *M'Naghten* rule, see, *e.g.,* Goldstein, *supra,* at 51 ("In those situations where the accused does not know the nature and quality of his act, in the broad sense, he will not know that it was wrong, no matter what construction 'wrong' is given"); 1 W. LaFave, Substantive Criminal Law § 7.2(b)(3), p. 536 (2d ed. 2003) ("Many courts feel that knowledge of 'the nature and quality of the act' is the mere equivalent of the ability to know that the act was wrong" (citing cases)); *id.,* § 7.2(b)(4), at 537 ("If the defendant does not know the nature and quality of his act, then quite obviously he does not know that his act is 'wrong,' and this is true without regard to the interpretation given to the word 'wrong' "); cf. 1 R. Gerber, Criminal Law of Arizona 502-7, n. 1 (2d ed. 1993).

Clark, indeed, adopted this very analysis himself in the trial court: "[I]f [Clark] did not know he was shooting at a police officer, or believed he had to shoot or be shot, even though his belief was not based in reality, this would establish that he did not know what he was doing was wrong." Record, Doc. 374, at 1. The trial court apparently agreed, for the judge admitted Clark's evidence of cognitive incapacity for consideration under the State's moral incapacity formulation. And Clark can point to no evidence bearing on insanity that was excluded. His psychiatric expert and a number of lay witnesses testified to his delusions, and this evidence tended to support a description of Clark as lacking the capacity to understand that the police officer was a human being. There is no doubt that the trial judge considered the evidence as going to an issue of cognitive capacity, for in finding insanity not proven he said that Clark's mental illness "did not . . . distort his perception of reality so severely that he did not know his actions were wrong," App. 334.

We are satisfied that neither in theory nor in practice did Arizona's 1993 abridgment of the insanity formulation deprive Clark of due process.

III

Clark's second claim of a due process violation challenges the rule adopted by the Supreme Court of Arizona in *State v. Mott,* 187 Ariz. 536.

A

Understanding Clark's claim requires attention to the categories of evidence with a potential bearing on *mens rea*. First, there is "observation evidence" in the everyday sense, testimony from those who observed what Clark did and heard what he said; this category would also include testimony that an expert witness might give about Clark's tendency to think in a certain way and his behavioral characteristics. This evidence may support a professional diagnosis of mental disease and in any event is the kind of evidence that can be relevant to show what in fact was on Clark's mind when he fired the gun. Observation evidence in the record covers Clark's behavior at home and with friends, his expressions of belief around the time of the killing that "aliens" were inhabiting the bodies of local people (including government agents),[28] his driving around the neighborhood before the police arrived, and so on. Contrary to the dissent's characterization, see *post,* at 2738-2739 (opinion of Kennedy, J.), observation evidence can be presented by either lay or expert witnesses.

Second, there is "mental-disease evidence" in the form of opinion testimony that Clark suffered from a mental disease with features described by the witness. As was true here, this evidence characteristically but not always comes from professional psychologists or psychiatrists who testify as expert witnesses and base their opinions in part on examination of a defendant, usually conducted after the events in question. The thrust of this evidence was that, based on factual reports, professional observations, and tests, Clark was psychotic at the time in question, with a condition that fell within the category of schizophrenia.

Third, there is evidence we will refer to as "capacity evidence" about a defendant's capacity for cognition and moral judgment (and ultimately also his capacity to form *mens rea*). This, too, is opinion evidence. Here, as it usually does, this testimony came from the same experts and concentrated on those specific details of the mental condition that make the difference between sanity and insanity under the Arizona definition. In their respective testimony on these details the experts disagreed: the defense expert gave his opinion that the symptoms or effects of the disease in Clark's case included inability to appreciate the nature of his action and to tell that it was wrong, whereas the State's psychiatrist was of the view that Clark was a schizophrenic who was still sufficiently able to appreciate the reality of shooting the officer and to know that it was wrong to do that.***

B

It is clear that *Mott* itself imposed no restriction on considering evidence of the first sort, the observation evidence. We read the *Mott* restriction to apply, rather, to evidence addressing the two issues in testimony that characteristically comes only from psychologists or psychiatrists qualified to give opinions as expert witnesses: mental-disease evidence (whether at the time of the crime a defendant suffered from a mental disease or defect, such as schizophrenia) and

---

[28] Section 13-1105(A)(3) provides that "[a] person commits first degree murder if . . . [i]ntending or knowing that the person's conduct will cause death to a law enforcement officer, the person causes the death of a law enforcement officer who is in the line of duty."

capacity evidence (whether the disease or defect left him incapable of performing or experiencing a mental process defined as necessary for sanity such as appreciating the nature and quality of his act and knowing that it was wrong).

Mott was careful to distinguish this kind of opinion evidence from observation evidence generally and even from observation evidence that an expert witness might offer, such as descriptions of a defendant's tendency to think in a certain way or his behavioral characteristics; the Arizona court made it clear that this sort of testimony was perfectly admissible to rebut the prosecution's evidence of *mens*. Thus, only opinion testimony going to mental defect or disease, and its effect on the cognitive or moral capacities on which sanity depends under the Arizona rule, is restricted.

In this case, the trial court seems to have applied the *Mott* restriction to all evidence offered by Clark for the purpose of showing what he called his inability to form the required *mens rea.* Thus, the trial court's restriction may have covered not only mental-disease and capacity evidence as just defined, but also observation evidence offered by lay (and expert) witnesses who described Clark's unusual behavior. Clark's objection to the application of the *Mott* rule does not, however, turn on the distinction between lay and expert witnesses or the kinds of testimony they were competent to present.

C

There is some, albeit limited, disagreement between the dissent and ourselves about the scope of the claim of error properly before us.

*** The point on which we disagree with the dissent, however, is this: did Clark apprise the Arizona courts that he believed the trial judge had erroneously limited the consideration of observation evidence, whether from lay witnesses like Clark's mother or (possibly) the expert witnesses who observed him? This sort of evidence was not covered by the *Mott* restriction, and confining it to the insanity issue would have been an erroneous application of *Mott* as a matter of Arizona law. For the following reasons we think no such objection was made in a way the Arizona courts could have understood it, and that no such issue is before us now. We think the only issue properly before us is the challenge to *Mott* on due process grounds, comprising objections to limits on the use of mental-disease and capacity evidence.***

At no point did the trial judge specify any particular evidence that he refused to consider on the *mens rea* issue. Nor did defense counsel specify any observation or other particular evidence that he claimed was admissible but wrongly excluded on the issue of *mens rea,* so as to produce a clearer ruling on what evidence was being restricted on the authority of *Mott* and what was not. He made no "offer of proof" in the trial court; and although his brief in the Arizona Court of Appeals stated at one point that it was not inconsistent with *Mott* to consider nonexpert evidence indicating mental illness on the issue of *mens rea,* and argued that the trial judge had failed to do so, Appellant's Opening Brief in No. 1CA-CR-03-0851 etc., pp. 48-49 (hereinafter Appellant's Opening Brief), he was no more specific than that, see, *e.g., id.,* at 52 ("The Court's ruling in *Mott* and the trial court's refusal to consider whether as a result of suffering from paranoid schizophrenia [Clark] could not formulate the *mens rea* necessary for first degree murder violated his right to due process"). Similarly, we read the Arizona Court of Appeals to have done nothing more than rely on *Mott* to reject the claim that due process forbids restricting evidence bearing on *"[a]bility to [f]orm [m]ens [r]ea,"* App. 351 (emphasis in original), (*i.e.,* mental-disease and capacity evidence) to the insanity determination.***

E

1

The first reason supporting the *Mott* rule is Arizona's authority to define its presumption of sanity (or capacity or responsibility) by choosing an insanity definition, as discussed in Part II, *supra,* and by placing the burden of persuasion on defendants who claim incapacity as an excuse from customary criminal responsibility. No one, certainly not Clark here, denies that a State may place a burden of persuasion on a defendant claiming insanity. And Clark presses no objection to Arizona's decision to require persuasion to a clear and convincing degree before the presumption of sanity and normal responsibility is overcome.

But if a State is to have this authority in practice as well as in theory, it must be able to deny a defendant the opportunity to displace the presumption of sanity more easily when addressing a different issue in the course of the criminal trial. Yet, as we have explained, just such an opportunity would be available if expert testimony of mental disease and incapacity could be considered for whatever a factfinder might think it was worth on the issue of *mens rea.* As we mentioned, the presumption of sanity would then be only as strong as the evidence a factfinder would accept as enough to raise a reasonable doubt about *mens rea* for the crime charged; once reasonable doubt was found, acquittal would be required, and the standards established for the defense of insanity would go by the boards.***

2

A State's insistence on preserving its chosen standard of legal insanity cannot be the sole reason for a rule like *Mott,* however, for it fails to answer an objection the dissent makes in this case. See *post,* at 2742-2747 (opinion of KENNEDY, J.). An insanity rule gives a defendant already found guilty the opportunity to excuse his conduct by showing he was insane when he acted, that is, that he did not have the mental capacity for conventional guilt and criminal responsibility. But, as the dissent argues, if the same evidence that affirmatively shows he was not guilty by reason of insanity (or "guilty except insane" under

Arizona law, Ariz. Rev. Stat. Ann. § 13-502(A) (West 2001)) also shows it was at least doubtful that he could form *mens rea,* then he should not be found guilty in the first place; it thus violates due process when the State impedes him from using mental-disease and capacity evidence directly to rebut the prosecution's evidence that he did form *mens rea.*

Are there, then, characteristics of mental-disease and capacity evidence giving rise to risks that may reasonably be hedged by channeling the consideration of such evidence to the insanity issue on which, in States like Arizona, a defendant has the burden of persuasion? We think there are: in the controversial character of some categories of mental disease, in the potential of mental-disease evidence to mislead, and in the danger of according greater certainty to capacity evidence than experts claim for it.

To begin with, the diagnosis may mask vigorous debate within the profession about the very contours of the mental disease itself. See, *e.g.,* American Psychiatric Association, Diagnostic and Statistical Manual of Mental Disorders xxxiii (4th ed. text rev. 2000) (hereinafter DSM-IV-TR) ("DSM-IV reflects a consensus about the classification and diagnosis of mental disorders derived at the time of its initial publication. New knowledge generated by research or clinical experience will undoubtedly lead to an increased understanding of the disorders included in DSM-IV, to the identification of new disorders, and to the removal of some disorders in future classifications. The text and criteria sets included in DSM-IV will require reconsideration in light of evolving new information"); P. Caplan, They Say You're Crazy: How the World's Most Powerful Psychiatrists Decide Who's Normal (1995) (criticism by former consultant to the DSM against some of the DSM's categories). And Members of this Court have previously recognized that the end of such debate is not imminent. See *Jones,* 463 U.S., at 365, n.13, 103 S. Ct. 3043 (" 'The only certain thing that can be said about the present state of knowledge and therapy regarding mental disease is that science has not reached finality of judgment' " (quoting *Greenwood v. United States,* 350 U.S. 366, 375, 76 S. Ct. 410, 100 L. Ed. 412 (1956))); *Powell v. Texas,* 392 U.S. 514, 537, 88 S. Ct. 2145, 20 L. Ed. 2d 1254 (1968) (plurality opinion) ("It *775 is simply not yet the time to write into the Constitution formulas cast in terms whose meaning, let alone relevance, is not yet clear . . . to doctors"). Though we certainly do not "condem[n mental-disease evidence] wholesale," Brief for American Psychiatric Association et al. as *Amici Curiae* 15, the consequence of this professional ferment is a general caution in treating psychological classifications as predicates for excusing otherwise criminal conduct.

Next, there is the potential of mental-disease evidence to mislead jurors (when they are the factfinders) through the power of this kind of evidence to suggest that a defendant suffering from a recognized mental disease lacks cognitive, moral, volitional, or other capacity, when that may not be a sound conclusion at all. Even when a category of mental disease is broadly accepted and the assignment of a defendant's behavior to that category is uncontroversial, the classification may suggest something very significant about a defendant's capacity, when in fact the classification tells us little or nothing about the ability of the defendant to form *mens rea* or to exercise the cognitive, moral, or volitional capacities that define legal sanity. See DSM-IV-TR xxxii-xxxiii ("When the DSM-IV categories, criteria, and textual descriptions are employed for forensic purposes, there are significant risks that diagnostic information will be misused or misunderstood. These dangers arise because of the imperfect fit between the questions of ultimate concern to the law and the information contained in a clinical diagnosis. In most situations, the clinical diagnosis of a DSM-IV mental disorder is not sufficient to establish the existence for legal purposes of . . . 'mental diseas[e]' or 'mental defect.' In determining whether an individual meets a specified legal standard (e.g., for . . . criminal responsibility . . .), additional information is usually required beyond that contained in the DSM-IV diagnosis"). The limits of the utility of a professional disease diagnosis are evident in the dispute between the two testifying experts in this case; they agree that Clark was schizophrenic, but they come to opposite conclusions on whether the mental disease in his particular case left him bereft of cognitive or moral capacity. Evidence of mental disease, then, can easily mislead; it is very easy to slide from evidence that an individual with a professionally recognized mental disease is very different, into doubting that he has the capacity to form *mens rea,* whereas that doubt may not be justified. And of course, in the cases mentioned before, in which the categorization is doubtful or the category of mental disease is itself subject to controversy, the risks are even greater that opinions about mental disease may confuse a jury into thinking the opinions show more than they do. Because allowing mental-disease evidence on *mens rea* can thus easily mislead, it is not unreasonable to address that tendency by confining consideration of this kind of evidence to insanity, on which a defendant may be assigned the burden of persuasion.

There are, finally, particular risks inherent in the opinions of the experts who supplement the mental-disease classifications with opinions on incapacity: on whether the mental disease rendered a particular defendant incapable of the cognition necessary for moral judgment or *mens rea* or otherwise incapable of understanding the wrongfulness of the conduct charged. Unlike observational evidence bearing on *mens rea,* capacity evidence consists of judgment, and judgment fraught with multiple perils: a defendant's state of mind at the crucial moment can be elusive no matter how conscientious the enquiry, and the law's categories that set the terms of the capacity judgment are not the categories of psychology that govern the expert's professional thinking. Although such capacity judgments may be given in the utmost good faith, their potentially tenuous character is indicated by the candor of the defense expert in this very case. Contrary to the State's expert, he testified that Clark lacked the capacity to appreciate the circumstances realistically and to understand the wrongfulness of what he was doing, App. 48-49, but he said that "no one knows exactly what was on [his] mind" at the time of the shooting, *id.,* at 48. And even when an expert is confident that his understanding of the mind is reliable, judgment addressing the basic categories of capacity requires a leap from the concepts of psychology, which are devised for thinking about treatment, to the concepts of legal sanity, which are devised for thinking about criminal responsibility.***

It bears repeating that not every State will find it worthwhile to make the judgment Arizona has made, and the choices the States do make about dealing with the risks posed by mental-disease and capacity evidence will reflect their varying assessments about the presumption of sanity as expressed in choices of insanity rules. The point here simply is that Arizona has sensible reasons to assign the risks as it has done by channeling the evidence.

F

Arizona's rule serves to preserve the State's chosen standard for recognizing insanity as a defense and to avoid confusion and misunderstanding on the part of jurors. For these reasons, there is no violation of due process under *Chambers* and its progeny, and no cause to claim that channeling evidence on mental disease and capacity offends any " 'principle of justice so rooted in the traditions and conscience of our people as to be ranked as fundamental,' " *Patterson,* 432 U.S., at 202, 97 S. Ct. 2319.

***

The judgment of the Court of Appeals of Arizona is, accordingly, affirmed.

It is so ordered.

Justice KENNEDY, with whom Justice STEVENS and Justice GINSBURG join, dissenting.

In my submission the Court is incorrect in holding that Arizona may convict petitioner Eric Clark of first-degree murder for the intentional or knowing killing of a police officer when Clark was not permitted to introduce critical and reliable evidence showing he did not have that intent or knowledge. The Court is wrong, too, when it concludes the issue cannot be reached because of an error by Clark's counsel. Its reasons and conclusions lead me to file this respectful dissent.

Since I would reverse the judgment of the Arizona Court of Appeals on this ground, and the Arizona courts might well alter their interpretation of the State's criminal responsibility statute were my rationale to prevail, it is unnecessary for me to address the argument that Arizona's definition of insanity violates due process.

I

Clark claims that the trial court erred in refusing to consider evidence of his chronic paranoid schizophrenia in deciding whether he possessed the knowledge or intent required for first-degree murder. Seizing upon a theory invented here by the Court itself, the Court narrows Clark's claim so he cannot raise the point everyone else thought was involved in the case. The Court says the only issue before us is whether there is a right to introduce mental-disease evidence or capacity evidence, not a right to introduce observation evidence. See *ante,* at 2724-2729. This restructured evidentiary universe, with no convincing authority to support it, is unworkable on its own terms. Even were that not so, however, the Court's tripartite structure is something not addressed by the state trial court, the state appellate court, counsel on either side in those proceedings, or the briefs the parties filed with us. The Court refuses to consider the key part of Clark's claim because his counsel did not predict the Court's own invention. It is unrealistic, and most unfair, to hold that Clark's counsel erred in failing to anticipate so novel an approach. If the Court is to insist on its approach, at a minimum the case should be remanded to determine whether Clark is bound by his counsel's purported waiver.

The Court's error, of course, has significance beyond this case. It adopts an evidentiary framework that, in my view, will be unworkable in many cases. The Court classifies Clark's behavior and expressed beliefs as observation evidence but insists that its description by experts must be mental-disease evidence or capacity evidence. See *ante,* at 2724-2726. These categories break down quickly when it is understood how the testimony would apply to the question of intent and knowledge at issue here. The most common type of schizophrenia, and the one Clark suffered from, is paranoid schizophrenia. See P. Berner et al., Diagnostic Criteria for Functional Psychoses 37 (2d ed. 1992). The existence of this functional psychosis is beyond dispute, but that does not mean the lay witness understands it or that a disputed issue of fact concerning its effect in a particular instance is not something for the expert to address. Common symptoms of the condition are delusions accompanied by hallucinations, often of the auditory type, which can cause disturbances of perception. *Ibid.* Clark's expert testified that people with schizophrenia often play radios loudly to drown out the voices in their heads. See App. 32. Clark's attorney argued to the trial court that this, rather than a desire to lure a policeman to the scene, explained Clark's behavior just before the killing. *Id.,* at 294-295. The observation that schizophrenics play radios loudly is a fact regarding behavior, but it is only a relevant fact if Clark has schizophrenia.

Even if this evidence were, to use the Court's term, mental-disease evidence, because it relies on an expert opinion, what would happen if the expert simply were to testify, without mentioning schizophrenia, that people with Clark's symptoms often play the radio loudly? This seems to be factual evidence, as the term is defined by the Court, yet it differs from mental-disease evidence only in forcing the witness to pretend that no one has yet come up with a way to classify the set of symptoms being described. More generally, the opinion that Clark had paranoid schizophrenia—an opinion shared by experts for both the prosecution and defense—bears on efforts to determine, as a factual matter, whether he knew he was killing a police officer. The psychiatrist's explanation of Clark's condition was essential to understanding how he processes sensory data and therefore to deciding what information was in his mind at the time of the shooting. Simply put, knowledge relies on cognition, and cognition can be affected by schizophrenia. See American Psychiatric Association, Diagnostic and Statistical Manual of Mental Disorders 299 (4th ed. text rev. 2000) ("The characteristic symptoms of Schizophrenia involve a range of cognitive and emotional dysfunctions that include perception"); *ibid.* (Symptoms include delusions, which are "erroneous beliefs that usually involve a misinterpretation of perceptions or experiences"). The mental-disease evidence at trial was also intertwined with the observation evidence because it lent needed credibility. Clark's parents and friends testified Clark thought the people in his town were aliens trying to kill him. These claims might not be believable without a psychiatrist confirming the story based on his experience with people who have exhibited similar behaviors. It makes little sense to divorce the observation evidence from the explanation that makes it comprehensible.

Assuming the Court's tripartite structure were feasible, the Court is incorrect when it narrows Clark's claim to exclude any concern about observation evidence. In deciding Clark's counsel failed to raise this issue, the Court relies on a series of perceived ambiguities regarding how the claim fits within the Court's own categories. See *ante,* at 2726-2729. The Court cites no precedent for construing these ambiguities against the claimant and no prudential reason for ignoring the breadth of Clark's claim. It is particularly surprising that the Court does so to the detriment of a criminal defendant asserting the fundamental challenge that the trier of fact refused to consider critical evidence showing he is innocent of the crime charged.

The alleged ambiguities are, in any event, illusory. The evidence at trial addressed more than the question of general incapacity or opinions regarding mental illness; it went further, as it included so-called observation evidence relevant to Clark's mental state at the moment he shot the officer. There was testimony, for example, that Clark thought the people in his town, particularly government officials, were not human beings but aliens who were trying to kill him.***

The Court holds, nonetheless, that "we cannot be sure" whether the trial court failed to consider this evidence. *Ante,* at 2728-2729. It is true the trial court ruling was not perfectly clear. Its language does strongly suggest, though, that it did not consider any of this testimony in deciding whether Clark had the knowledge or intent required for first-degree murder. After recognizing that "much of the evidence that [the defense is] going to be submitting, in fact all of it, as far as I know . . . that has to do with the insanity could also arguably be made . . . as to form and intent and his capacity for the intent," the court concluded "we will be focusing, as far as I'm concerned, strictly on the insanity defense." App. 9. In announcing its verdict, the trial court did not mention any of the mental-illness evidence, observation or otherwise, in deciding Clark's guilt. *Id.,* at 331-335. The most reasonable assumption, then, would seem to be that the trial court did not consider it, and the Court does not hold otherwise. See *ante,* at 2726.

Clark's objection to this refusal by the trier of fact to consider the evidence as it bore on his key defense was made at all stages of the proceeding. In his post-trial motion to vacate the judgment, Clark argued that "prohibiting consideration of *any* evidence reflecting upon a mentally ill criminal defendant's ability to form the necessary *mens rea* violates due process." Record, Doc. 406, p. 8. Clark pressed the same argument in the Arizona Court of Appeals. See Appellant's Opening Brief in No. 1CA-CR-03-0851 etc., pp. 46-52 (hereinafter Appellant's Opening Brief). He also noted that the trial judge had erred in refusing to consider nonexpert testimony—presumably what the Court would call observation evidence—on Clark's mental illness. *Id.,* at 47-48 ("The trial court therefore violated [Clark's] right to present a defense because [the] court refused to consider *any evidence,* including the multiple testimonials of *lay* witnesses . . . in deciding whether he could form the requisite *mens rea*"). The appeals court decided the issue on the merits, holding that the trial court was correct not to consider the evidence of mental illness in determining whether Clark had the *mens rea* for first-degree murder. See App. 351-353. It offered no distinction at all between observation or mental-disease evidence.

Notwithstanding the appeals court's decision, the Court states that the issue was not clearly presented to the state courts.***

First, Clark's claim goes well beyond an objection to *Mott.* In fact, he specifically attempted to distinguish *Mott* by noting that the trial court in this case refused to consider all evidence of mental illness. See Record, Doc. 406, at 8; see also *** Appellant's Opening Brief 48. The Court notices these arguments but criticizes Clark's counsel for not being specific about the observation evidence he wanted the trial court to consider. See *ante,* at 2727-2728. There was no reason, though, for Clark's counsel to believe additional specificity was required, since there was no evident distinction in Arizona law between observation evidence and mental-disease testimony.

Second, *Mott's* holding was not restricted to mental-disease evidence. The Arizona Supreme Court did not refer to any distinction between observation and mental-disease evidence, or lay and expert testimony. Its holding was stated in broad terms: "Arizona does not allow evidence of a defendant's mental disorder short of insanity either as an affirmative defense or to negate the *mens rea* element of a crime." ("The legislature's decision . . . evidences its rejection of the use of psychological testimony to challenge the *mens rea* element of a crime"). The Court attempts to divine a fact/opinion distinction in *Mott* based on *Mott's* distinguishing a case, *State v. Christensen,* 129 Ariz. 32, 628 P.2d 580 (1981), where evidence about behavioral tendencies was deemed admissible. *Christensen,* though, also addressed an expert opinion; the difference was that the evidence there concerned a "character trait of acting reflexively in response to stress," not a mental illness. Since the Court recognizes the Arizona Court of Appeals relied on *Mott,* the expansive rule of exclusion in *Mott*—without any suggestion of a limitation depending on the kind of evidence—should suffice for us to reach the so-called observation-evidence issue. Even if, as the Court contends, see *ante,* at 2724, *Mott* is limited to expert testimony, the Court's categories still do not properly interpret *Mott,* because the Court's own definition of observation evidence includes some expert testimony, see *ante,* at 2724-2725.

It makes no difference that in the appeals court Clark referred to the issue as inability to form knowledge or intent. He did not insist on some vague, general incapacity. He stated, instead, that he "suffered from a major mental illness and was psychotic at the time of the offense." *Id.,* at 48. Even if Clark's arguments were insufficient to apprise the state court of the argument, "[o]ur traditional rule is that '[o]nce a federal claim is properly presented, a party can make any argument in support of that claim; parties are not limited to the precise arguments they made below.' " *Lebron v. National Railroad Passenger Corporation,* 513 U.S. 374, (1995). The claim is clear. Though it seems to be obscure to this Court, it was understood by the Arizona Court of Appeals, which stated: "Clark argues that the trial court erred in refusing to consider evidence of his mental disease or defect in determining whether he had the requisite *mens rea* to commit first-degree murder." App. 351. When the question is what the state court held, it is not instructive for this Court to recast the words the state court used.

The razor-thin distinction the Court draws between evidence being used to show incapacity and evidence being used to show lack of *mens rea* directly does not identify two different claims. Clark's single claim, however characterized, involves the use of the same mental-illness evidence to decide whether he had the requisite knowledge or intent. The various ways in which the evidence is relevant in disproving *mens rea* hardly qualify as separate claims.***

II

The central theory of Clark's defense was that his schizophrenia made him delusional. He lived in a universe where the delusions were so dominant, the theory was, that he had no intent to shoot a police officer or knowledge he was doing so. It is one thing to say he acted with intent or knowledge to pull the trigger. It is quite another to say he pulled the trigger to kill someone he knew to be a human being and a police officer. If the trier of fact were to find Clark's evidence sufficient to discount the case made by the State, which has the burden to prove knowledge or intent as an element of the offense, Clark would not be guilty of first-degree murder under Arizona law.

The Court attempts to diminish Clark's interest by treating mental-illness evidence as concerning only "judgment," rather than fact. *Ante,* at 2735-2736. This view appears to derive from the Court's characterization of Clark's claim as raising only general incapacity. See *ibid.* This is wrong for the reasons already discussed. It fails to recognize, moreover, the meaning of the offense element in question here. The *mens rea* element of intent or knowledge may, at some level, comprise certain moral choices, but it rests in the first instance on a factual determination. That is the fact Clark sought to put in issue. Either Clark knew he was killing a police officer or he did not.

The issue is not, as the Court insists, whether Clark's mental illness acts as an "excuse from customary criminal responsibility," *ante,* at 2732, but whether his mental illness, as a factual matter, made him unaware that he was shooting a police officer. If it did, Clark needs no excuse, as then he did not commit the crime as Arizona defines it. For the elements of first-degree murder, where the question is knowledge of particular facts—that one is killing a police officer—the determination depends not on moral responsibility but on empirical fact. Clark's evidence of mental illness had a direct and substantial bearing upon what he knew, or thought he knew, to be the facts when he pulled the trigger; this lay at the heart of the matter.

The trial court's exclusion was all the more severe because it barred from consideration on the issue of *mens rea* all this evidence, from any source, thus preventing Clark from showing he did not commit the crime as defined by Arizona law.***

Arizona's rule is problematic because it excludes evidence no matter how credible and material it may be in disproving an element of the offense.***

This is not to suggest all general rules on the exclusion of certain types of evidence are invalid. If the rule does not substantially burden the defense, then it is likely permissible.***

In the instant case Arizona's proposed reasons are insufficient to support its categorical exclusion. While the State contends that testimony regarding mental illness may be too incredible or speculative for the jury to consider, this does not explain why the exclusion applies in all cases to all evidence of mental illness.***

The risk of jury confusion also fails to justify the rule. The State defends its rule as a means to avoid the complexities of determining how and to what degree a mental illness affects a person's mental state. The difficulty of resolving a factual issue, though, does not present a sufficient reason to take evidence away from the jury even when it is crucial for the defense.***

Even assuming the reliability and jury-confusion justifications were persuasive in some cases, they would not suffice here. It does not overcome the constitutional objection to say that an evidentiary rule that is reasonable on its face can be applied as well to bar significant defense evidence without any rational basis for doing so.***

The Court undertakes little analysis of the interests particular to this case. By proceeding in this way it devalues Clark's constitutional rights. The reliability rationale has minimal applicability here. The Court is correct that many mental diseases are difficult to define and the subject of great debate. Schizophrenia , however, is a well-documented mental illness, and no one seriously disputes either its definition or its most prominent clinical manifestations. The State's own expert conceded that Clark had paranoid schizophrenia and was actively psychotic at the time of the killing. See App. 254-257. The jury-confusion rationale, if it is at all applicable here, is the result of the Court's own insistence on conflating the insanity defense and the question of intent. Considered on its own terms, the issue of intent and knowledge is a straightforward factual question. A trier of fact is quite capable of weighing defense testimony and then determining whether the accused did or did not intend to kill or knowingly kill a human being who was a police officer. True, the issue can be difficult to decide in particular instances, but no more so than many matters juries must confront.

The Court says mental-illness evidence "can easily mislead," *ante,* at 2735, and may "tel[l] us little or nothing about the ability of the defendant to form *mens rea,*" *ibid.* These generalities do not, however, show how relevant or misleading the evidence in this case would be (or explain why Arizona Rule of Evidence 403 is insufficient for weighing these factors). As explained above, the evidence of Clark's mental illness bears directly on *mens rea,* for it suggests Clark may not have known he was killing a human being. It is striking that while the Court discusses at length the likelihood of misjudgment from placing too much emphasis on evidence of mental illness, see *ante,* at 2733–2736, it ignores the risk of misjudging an innocent man guilty from refusing to consider this highly relevant evidence at all. Clark's expert, it is true, said no one could know exactly what was on Clark's mind at the time of the shooting. See *ante,* at 2736. The expert testified extensively, however, about the effect of Clark's delusions on his perceptions of the world around him, and about whether Clark's behavior around the time of the shooting was consistent with delusional thinking. This testimony was relevant to determining whether Clark knew he was killing a human being. It also bolstered the testimony of lay witnesses, none of which was deemed unreliable or misleading by the state courts.

For the same reasons, the Court errs in seeking support from the American Psychiatric Association's statement that a psychiatrist may be justifiably reluctant to reach legal conclusions regarding the defendant's mental state. See *ibid.* In this very case, the American Psychiatric Association made clear that psychiatric evidence plays a crucial role regardless of whether the psychiatrist testifies on the ultimate issue: "Expert evidence of mental disorders, presented by qualified professionals and subject to adversarial testing, is both relevant to the mental-state issues raised by *mens rea* requirements and reliable . . . . Such evidence could not be condemned wholesale without unsettling the legal system's central reliance on such evidence." Brief for American Psychiatric Association et al. as *Amici Curiae* 15.

Contrary to the Court's suggestion, see *ante,* at 2735, the fact that the state and defense experts drew different conclusions about the effect of Clark's mental illness on his mental state only made Clark's evidence contested; it did not make the evidence irrelevant or misleading. The trial court was capable of evaluating the competing conclusions, as factfinders do in countless cases where there is a dispute among witnesses. In fact, the potential to mislead will be far greater under the Court's new evidentiary system, where jurors will receive observation evidence without the necessary explanation from experts.

The fact that mental-illness evidence may be considered in deciding criminal responsibility does not compensate for its exclusion from consideration on the *mens rea* elements of the crime. Cf. *ante,* at 2733–2734. The evidence addresses different issues in the two instances. Criminal responsibility involves an inquiry into whether the defendant knew right from wrong, not whether he had the *mens rea* elements of the offense. While there may be overlap between the two issues, "the existence or nonexistence of legal insanity bears no necessary relationship to the existence or nonexistence of the required mental elements of the crime." *Mullaney v. Wilbur,* 421 U.S. 684, (1975).

***While defining mental illness is a difficult matter, the State seems to exclude the evidence one would think most reliable by allowing unexplained and uncategorized tendencies to be introduced while excluding relatively well-understood psychiatric testimony regarding well-documented mental illnesses. It is unclear, moreover, what would have happened in this case had the defendant wanted to testify that he thought Officer Moritz was an alien. If disallowed, it would be tantamount to barring Clark from testifying on his behalf to explain his own actions. If allowed, then Arizona's rule would simply prohibit the corroboration necessary to make sense of Clark's explanation. In sum, the rule forces the jury to decide guilt in a fictional world with undefined and unexplained behaviors but without mental illness. This rule has no rational justification and imposes a significant burden upon a straightforward defense: He did not commit the crime with which he was charged.

These are the reasons for my respectful dissent.

Notes and Questions

1. After reading *State v. Wilcox*, do you believe that the move by states away from recognizing voluntary intoxication as a defense signaled the death knell for diminished capacity?

2. How is diminished capacity both similar and dissimilar to insanity? What are the benefits to the defendant in choosing one defense over the other?

3. In *Wilcox*, the court holds that diminished capacity is not an available defense in Ohio. As such, psychiatric testimony may not be used to show a defendant's lack of diminished capacity. As a defense attorney, what evidence might you use to show that your client lacked the requisite mental state if your client does not meet the test for insanity?

4. In *Clark v. Arizona*, who had the better argument the majority or the dissent? If you agree with the majority, how is it possible to have both a mental abnormality like Clark's but still have the specific intent to commit a crime?

Chapter 22
Infancy and Intoxication

A. Infancy

Deluca v. Bowden, 42 Ohio St. 2d 392 (1975)

*** The basic dilemma of all these cases is that a child of tender years has only some dim and imponderable responsibility for his acts—and yet those acts, as those of an adult, may cause injury to others. It is probable inevitable as a part of growing up that in rare cases a child will cause severe injuries to others. Yet it is most difficult to attach blame to a child of tender years for those injuries in any sense comparable to the blame attachable to an adult, whom we hold responsible for his acts. Our laws and our moral concepts assume actors capable of legal and moral choices, of which a young child is incapable. See Bohlen, Liability in Tort of Infants and Insane Persons, 23 Mich. L. Rev. 9. For that reason, a child under seven years of age was at common law considered incapable of criminal responsibility. For the same reason, we cannot accept those rules which hold a child strictly liable, or which permit a jury to find liability, in cases of intentional tort. Our choice is between rules which permit the imposition of a legal judgment upon a young child for his intentional acts, and a rule which holds that members of society must accept the damage done by very young children to be no more subject to legal action than some force of nature or act of God. Our choice is the latter rule. The same public policy considerations which led this court in *Holbrock* to hold that children under the age of seven are not liable for contributory negligence, convince us that children under the age of seven also should not be held liable for intentional torts.***

In re Washington, 75 Ohio St. 3d 390 (1996)

*** The issues before this court are whether a rebuttable presumption exists that a child under the age of fourteen is incapable of committing the crime of rape and whether sufficient evidence existed to support the trial court's finding that appellee was delinquent. For the following reasons, we find that (1) no such presumption exists in Ohio, and (2) in the present case the evidence was sufficient to support the trial court's finding that appellee was delinquent. Accordingly, we reverse the court of appeals' judgment.***

In finding that insufficient evidence existed to support the trial court's finding of rape, the court of appeals relied on cases from the 1800s such as *Williams v. State* (1846), 14 Ohio 222, and *Hiltabiddle v. State* (1878), 35 Ohio St. 52, the latter of which held that "[a]n infant under the age of fourteen years is presumed to be incapable of committing the crime of rape, or an attempt to commit it; but that the presumption may be rebutted by proof that he has arrived at the age of puberty and is capable of emission and consummating the crime." *Williams, supra,* at 227. This case law came about because until 1877, the emission of semen was an essential element of rape. Thus, the rule that a child under age fourteen was presumed incapable of committing the crime involved this element and could be rebutted only upon evidence that the rapist could emit semen. However, such a rule is now unnecessary, as the present statute does not require this element. As succinctly stated by the Second District Court of Appeals in *In re Wilson* (Dec. 1, 1988), Montgomery App. No. 10909, *unreported,* 1988 WL 129176: "A rule which requires proof of the capacity to emit a seed when there is proof of penetration by force against the victim's will is archaic and has no place in today's society." *See, also, In re Smith* (1992), 80 Ohio App. 3d 502. As noted by the court in *In re Wilson,* the General Assembly in 1974 further expanded the class of persons who may be convicted of rape when it established that mere penetration, however slight, constituted rape. Thus, to adhere to this old English common-law rule would be to override the clear intent of the General Assembly to broaden the class of persons who can be convicted of rape. Accordingly, we abolish the common law that held a child under the age of fourteen is rebuttably presumed incapable of committing rape.

Notes and Questions

1. At common law, children under the age of seven did not have the ability to form the mens rea to commit a crime. Children between the ages of 7 and 14 were presumed incapable of committing a crime. However, this presumption could be rebutted by the prosecution. Children over 14 had no type of infancy defense. Many jurisdictions like Ohio have eliminated the common law's protections of children 14 and under. Thus, even very young children may be prosecuted for crimes. These minors, especially if they are below the age of 14, are tried in juvenile court.

B. Intoxication

State v. Johnston, 2015-Ohio-450 (Ohio Ct. App. 2015)

Defendant-appellant, Jason E. Johnston, Jr., appeals from his conviction in the Montgomery County Court of Common Pleas after pleading no contest to rape, gross sexual imposition, sexual battery, felonious assault, and multiple counts of kidnapping and aggravated menacing. Johnston claims the trial court erred and abused its discretion in precluding his expert witness from testifying at trial. Additionally, Johnston contends his no contest plea was not knowingly and voluntarily made. For the reasons outlined below, the judgment of the trial court will be affirmed.

FACTS AND COURSE OF PROCEEDINGS

On September 21, 2012, the Montgomery County Grand Jury returned a twelve-count indictment against Johnston charging him with two counts of kidnapping in violation of R.C. 2905.01(A)(2); three counts of kidnapping in violation of R.C. 2905.01(A)(3); one count of kidnapping in violation of R.C. 2905.01(A)(4), which included a sexual motivation specification; one count of rape in violation of R.C. 2907.02(A)(2); one count of gross sexual imposition in violation of R.C. 2907.05(A)(1); two counts of aggravated menacing in violation of R.C. 2903.21(A); one count of sexual battery in violation of R.C. 2907.03(A)(5); and one count of felonious assault in violation of R.C. 2903.11(A)(2). All counts, except for the two counts of aggravated menacing, included a three-year firearm specification.

Following his indictment, on October 18, 2012, Johnston filed a written plea of not guilty by reason of insanity, moving for an examination to determine his competency to stand trial and his mental state at the time of the alleged offenses. The trial court ordered the requested examinations to be completed and reported on by the Forensic Psychiatry Center for Western Ohio. After examining Johnston, the Center's psychologist submitted a written report opining that within a reasonable degree of psychological certainty, Johnston was competent to stand trial and was not legally insane at the time of the alleged offenses.

In light of the foregoing report, Johnston requested, and the trial court permitted, a second evaluation by psychologist Dr. Richard Bromberg. Dr. Bromberg examined Johnston and his report contradicted the first evaluation. Dr. Bromberg's report stated that within a reasonable degree of psychological certainty, Johnston was legally insane at the time of the alleged offenses due to an acute psychological condition of Amphetamine–Induced Psychotic Disorder and a chronic psychological condition of Mood Disorder Not Otherwise Specified.

The parties partially stipulated to the contents of the first report only with respect to the issue of Johnston's competency. The trial court subsequently found Johnston competent to stand trial. The State then filed a combined motion for a hearing pursuant to *Daubert v. Merrell Dow Pharmaceuticals, Inc.*, 509 U.S. 579 and an order in limine to: (1) determine whether Dr. Bromberg's expert opinion on Johnston's sanity was admissible under *Daubert*; and (2) preclude any testimony or evidence concerning Johnston's alleged psychiatric or psychological conditions that are related to his voluntary ingestion of drugs.

On September 30, 2013, the trial court held a hearing on the combined motion. Dr. Bromberg appeared at the hearing and testified regarding his expert opinion. Specifically, Dr. Bromberg testified that he had diagnosed Johnston with Amphetamine–Induced Psychotic Disorder with onset during intoxication. Dr. Bromberg also testified that Johnston reported taking an overdose of Ritalin on the night of the offenses, ingesting 10 to 12 times the prescribed amount as a suicide attempt. In addition, Dr. Bromberg testified that Johnston's wife had reported that Johnston ingested some of her prescription medication, which included Vistaril, Seroquel, and Propranolol. Dr. Bromberg also testified that it was reported Johnston consumed alcohol. Continuing, Dr. Bromberg testified that Johnston's initial overdose of Ritalin was voluntary, but that his state of mind thereafter changed in a manner making his continued intoxication involuntary. Dr. Bromberg also testified that if Johnston had not ingested the aforementioned substances, he would not have diagnosed him with Amphetamine–Induced Psychotic Disorder, and without that diagnosis, he would not have found Johnston not guilty by reason of insanity. Dr. Bromberg unequivocally testified that Johnston would not have been legally insane had he not taken the substances.

After the hearing, the trial court granted the State's motion in limine and issued an order excluding Dr. Bromberg's testimony on grounds that it was improper under R.C. 2901.21(C), a statute which precludes using voluntary intoxication as a defense. No ruling was made under *Daubert* as to the scientific reliability of Dr. Bromberg's expert opinion.

Following the exclusion of his expert witness, Johnston pled no contest to the charges in the indictment. At the plea hearing, defense counsel indicated on the record that Johnston entered his no contest plea because the trial court's evidentiary ruling destroyed his sole defense and he wanted the opportunity to appeal the ruling. The trial court accepted counsel's statement without any comment. Thereafter, the trial court sentenced Johnston to an aggregate 10–year prison term.

Johnston now appeals from his conviction, raising three assignments of error for review.***

That being said, we now turn to whether the trial court erred in excluding Dr. Bromberg's expert testimony regarding Johnston's sanity. While appellate courts generally review rulings on motions in limine for an abuse of discretion, this is improper if the ruling is the functional equivalent of a suppression ruling. *Greaves,* 2012-Ohio-1989, 971 N.E.2d 987 at ¶ 10. In that instance, appellate courts should use the standard of review for motions to suppress. *Id.* at ¶ 10-11.

"Under the standard of review for a motion to suppress, an appellate court must accept as true the trial court's supported findings of fact and then independently determine, without deference to the conclusion of the trial court, whether the facts satisfy the applicable legal standard." *State v. Leveck,* 2d Dist. Montgomery No. 23970, 2011-Ohio-1135.

Here, the trial court found that Dr. Bromberg's opinion that Johnston was legally insane is based upon Johnston's claimed voluntary overdose of prescription medication and alcohol immediately before the offenses were committed. The record supports this finding; therefore, we shall apply it in conducting our inquiry into whether the trial court's resolution of this matter meets the applicable legal standard.

As noted earlier, the trial court excluded Dr. Bromberg's testimony on grounds that it was improper under R.C. 2901.21(C), which provides that: "Voluntary intoxication may not be taken into consideration in determining the existence of a mental state that is an element of a criminal offense." In other words, voluntary intoxication is not a defense to any crime. (Citations omitted.) *State v. Arnold,* 2013-Ohio-5336.

While Johnston recognizes this principle, he argues that he still should have been able to present Dr. Bromberg's testimony with regards to his insanity defense, which he correctly argues is a separate legal concept from voluntary intoxication. *See State v. Smith,* 11th Dist. Trumbull No.2005-T-0080, citing R.C. 2901.01(A)(14). Nevertheless, a person is not guilty by reason of insanity only if the person proves by a preponderance of the evidence that at the time of the commission of the offense, the person did not know the wrongfulness of his acts *as the result of severe mental disease or defect. See* R.C. 2901.01(A)(14) and R.C. 2901.05(A). Here, Dr. Bromberg essentially testified that it was the voluntary overdose of medication that caused Johnston not to know the wrongfulness of his acts, not a mental disease or defect. This is reflected in the following testimony:

> State: First, would it be fair to say you diagnosed the Defendant with amphetamine-induced psychotic disorder with onset during intoxication in partial remission?
> Bromberg: Yes, sir.
> State: Okay. And would you agree with me, if the Defendant had not taken [the] medication, he would not have had the diagnosis; correct?
> Bromberg: That's correct, sir.

State: In fact, without this diagnosis you wouldn't have found him NGRI, or not guilty by reason of insanity?

Bromberg: I don't believe so. Although, there was traces of some psychosis in his psychological testing.

State: Right. But without this particular diagnosis, that—traces wouldn't have been enough for it to be an NGRI; correct?

Bromberg: Unlikely not.

State: You would agree with me that the Defendant reported taking too much medication—

Bromberg: Yes.

State:—or overdosing.

Bromberg: Yes, sir.

State: Just to be clear, the facts in this case aren't a situation where somebody was taking the normal amount of medication and then had this diagnosis. The Defendant actually took an overdose or too much and that's what caused this diagnosis, according to you?

Bromberg: That's what it appears, yes, sir.

***

State: Okay. And earlier you had talked about the Defendant taking too much medication. You agree that he took that medication voluntarily; correct?

Bromberg: He took the medication voluntarily, yes, he did.

State: Okay.

Bromberg: Although, what we have to specify here, is that he took varying amounts of different medication at different times. So his degree of voluntary taking was measured by his—the state of mind after he took the first pill, then his state of mind begins to change.

State: So if I understand what you are saying, then, his voluntariness was changed after he had started taking medication, he—maybe later on when he took medication that wouldn't be voluntary?

Bromberg: Well, if he takes—let's say he takes three pills, and he's already starting to have some toxicity. At that point I—I don't think that he is in command of his senses enough that he is voluntarily taking it, so there are different levels. When he took the first pill, I would say that that [sic] was likely done voluntarily.

State: And in his reporting to you, when he took the overdose, was that the voluntary act or was he already involuntary by that point?

Bromberg: I think it was a voluntary act when he just began.

State: Okay. And that's when he took the large quantity of Ritalin; correct? According to him?

Bromberg: Yes.

***

Court: Doctor, I want you to assume that in the minutes and the hours before the events of September 11, 2012, which lie at the heart of this case, I want you to assume that Mr. Johnston had not consumed alcohol, had not consumed his wife's prescription medication, and had not taken an overdose of his prescribed Ritalin. Would your opinion, within a reasonable medical—strike that—reasonable psychological certainty, be that Mr. Johnston would not have been insane under Ohio law at the time of the alleged offenses?

Bromberg: Had he not taken any of the substances, no.

Court: No what?

Bromberg: He would not have been insane.

Trans. (Sept. 30, 2013), p. 7-8; 11-13; 25-26.

Since Dr. Bromberg's testimony indicates that it was Johnston's voluntary overdose of medication, not a mental disease or defect, which affected his mental state on the night of the offenses, his testimony necessarily implicates voluntary intoxication as opposed to insanity. *See State v. Swanson,* 6th Dist. Wood No. WD-12-003, 2014-Ohio-549, ¶ 14 ("[w]here the insanity is simply a temporary condition brought on by the voluntary ingestion of drugs or alcohol, it does not suffice to establish [a not guilty by reason of insanity] defense"). As a result, we conclude the trial court correctly excluded Dr. Bromberg's testimony pursuant to R.C. 2901.21(C) and Johnston's argument to the contrary is overruled.

Johnston also argues that Dr. Bromberg's testimony should have been allowed because it could have established a defense of involuntary intoxication. We disagree. Unlike voluntary intoxication, involuntary intoxication is an affirmative defense. (Citation omitted.) *State v. Kortz,* 2d Dist. Montgomery No. 25041, 2013-Ohio-121, ¶ 20. Dr. Bromberg's testimony, however, does not support such a defense. As noted above, Dr. Bromberg testified that Johnston's initial overdose was ingested voluntarily. His additional testimony that Johnston's initial overdose may have rendered his subsequent bouts of intoxication involuntary creates a trivial distinction. Dr. Bromberg did not testify that someone forced Johnston to intoxicate himself. Nor did he testify that Johnston took the prescribed amount of medication and then had an adverse reaction so as to arguably make his intoxication involuntary. Rather, as the trial court found, and in which we agree, Dr. Bromberg's testimony indicates that a voluntary overdose led to Johnston's condition.

For the foregoing reasons, we find no merit in any of the arguments advanced herein; therefore, Johnston's First and Second Assignments of Error are overruled.***

Notes and Questions

1. In *State v. Johnston*, the court found that since the defendant voluntarily ingested the medication that brought on the defendant's insanity, the defendant's expert would not be allowed to testify. What if the court had found that the defendant had involuntarily ingested the medication? Would the expert then be allowed to testify?

2. Jurisdictions around the country take various approaches to addressing the affirmative defense of involuntary intoxication. About a third treat the defense like insanity. Thus, to avoid criminal liability, the defendant who claims involuntary intoxication must meet the same test for insanity for that particular jurisdiction.

Other jurisdictions, like Ohio, are more limiting and only allow the defense of involuntary intoxication to refute a culpable mental state. Thus, involuntary intoxication would not be a viable defense for a strict liability crime. Shouldn't an involuntary intoxication defense work like an insanity defense? What purpose does it serve to prosecute someone for conduct that occurs while involuntarily intoxicated?

Montana v. Egelhoff, 518 U.S. 37 (1996)

Justice SCALIA announced the judgment of the Court and delivered an opinion, in which THE CHIEF JUSTICE, Justice KENNEDY, and Justice THOMAS join.

We consider in this case whether the Due Process Clause is violated by Montana Code Annotated § 45-2-203, which provides, in relevant part, that voluntary intoxication "may not be taken into consideration in determining the existence of a mental state which is an element of [a criminal] offense."

I

In July 1992, while camping out in the Yaak region of northwestern Montana to pick mushrooms, respondent made friends with Roberta Pavola and John Christenson, who were doing the same. On Sunday, July 12, the three sold the mushrooms they had collected and spent the rest of the day and evening drinking, in bars and at a private party in Troy, Montana. Some time after 9 p.m., they left the party in Christenson's 1974 Ford Galaxy station wagon. The drinking binge apparently continued, as respondent was seen buying beer at 9:20 p.m. and recalled "sitting on a hill or a bank passing a bottle of Black Velvet back and forth" with Christenson.

At about midnight that night, officers of the Lincoln County, Montana, sheriff's department, responding to reports of a possible drunk driver, discovered Christenson's station wagon stuck in a ditch along U.S. Highway 2. In the front seat were Pavola and Christenson, each dead from a single gunshot to the head. In the rear of the car lay respondent, alive and yelling obscenities. His blood-alcohol content measured .36 percent over one hour later. On the floor of the car, near the brake pedal, lay respondent's .38-caliber handgun, with four loaded rounds and two empty casings; respondent had gunshot residue on his hands.

Respondent was charged with two counts of deliberate homicide, a crime defined by Montana law as "purposely" or "knowingly" causing the death of another human being. Mont. Code Ann. § 45-5-102 (1995). A portion of the jury charge, uncontested here, instructed that "[a] person acts purposely when it is his conscious object to engage in conduct of that nature or to cause such a result," and that "[a] person acts knowingly when he is aware of his conduct or when he is aware under the circumstances his conduct constitutes a crime; or, when he is aware there exists the high probability that his conduct will cause a specific result." Respondent's defense at trial was that an unidentified fourth person must have committed the murders; his own extreme intoxication, he claimed, had rendered him physically incapable of committing the murders, and accounted for his inability to recall the events of the night of July 12. Although respondent was allowed to make this use of the evidence that he was intoxicated, the jury was instructed, pursuant to Mont. Code Ann. § 45-2-203 (1995), that it could not consider respondent's "intoxicated condition . . . in determining the existence of a mental state which is an element of the offense." The jury found respondent guilty on both counts, and the court sentenced him to 84 years' imprisonment.

The Supreme Court of Montana reversed. It reasoned (1) that respondent "had a due process right to present and have considered by the jury all relevant evidence to rebut the State's evidence on all elements of the offense charged," 272 Mont., at 125, and (2) that evidence of respondent's voluntary intoxication was "clear[ly] . . . relevant to the issue of whether [respondent] acted knowingly and purposely," *id.,* at 122. Because § 45-2-203 prevented the jury from considering that evidence with regard to that issue, the court concluded that the State had been "relieved of part of its burden to prove beyond a reasonable doubt every fact necessary to constitute the crime charged," *id.,* at 124, and that respondent had therefore been denied due process. We granted certiorari.

II

The cornerstone of the Montana Supreme Court's judgment was the proposition that the Due Process Clause guarantees a defendant the right to present and have considered by the jury "*all relevant evidence* to rebut the State's evidence on all elements of the offense charged." 272 Mont., at 125 (emphasis added). Respondent does not defend this categorical rule; he acknowledges that the right to present relevant evidence "has not been viewed as absolute." That is a wise concession, since the proposition that the Due Process Clause guarantees the right to introduce all relevant evidence is simply indefensible.*** Of course, to say that the right to introduce relevant evidence is not absolute is not to say that the Due Process Clause places *no* limits upon restriction of that right. But it is to say that the defendant asserting such a limit must sustain the usual heavy burden that a due process claim entails***

Respondent's task, then, is to establish that a defendant's right to have a jury consider evidence of his voluntary intoxication in determining whether he possesses the requisite mental state is a "fundamental principle of justice."

Our primary guide in determining whether the principle in question is fundamental is, of course, historical practice. *See Medina v. California,* 505 U.S. 437 (1992). Here that gives respondent little support. By the laws of England, wrote Hale, the intoxicated defendant "shall have no privilege by this voluntary contracted madness, but shall have the same judgment as if he were in his right senses." 1 M. Hale, Pleas of the Crown *32-*33. According to Blackstone and Coke, the law's condemnation of those suffering from *dementia affectata* was harsher still: Blackstone, citing Coke, explained that the law viewed intoxication "as an aggravation of the offence, rather than as an excuse for any criminal misbehaviour." 4 W. Blackstone, Commentaries *25-*26. This stern rejection of inebriation as a defense became a fixture of early American law as well. The American editors of the 1847 edition of Hale wrote:

> Drunkenness, it was said in an early case, can never be received as a ground to excuse or palliate an offence: this is not merely the opinion of a speculative philosopher, the argument of counsel, or the *obiter dictum* of a single judge, but it is a sound and long established maxim of judicial policy, from which perhaps a single dissenting voice cannot be found. But if no other authority could be adduced, the uniform decisions of our own Courts from the first establishment of the government, would constitute it now a part of the common law of the land. 1 Hale, *supra,* at *32, n. 3.

In an opinion citing the foregoing passages from Blackstone and Hale, Justice Story rejected an objection to the exclusion of evidence of intoxication as follows:

This is the first time, that I ever remember it to have been contended, that the commission of one crime was an excuse for another. Drunkenness is a gross vice, and in the contemplation of some of our laws is a crime; and I learned in my earlier studies, that so far from its being in law an excuse for murder, it is rather an aggravation of its malignity." *United States v. Cornell,* 25 F. Cas. 650, 657-658 (No. 14,868) (CC R.I. 1820).

The historical record does not leave room for the view that the common law's rejection of intoxication as an "excuse" or "justification" for crime would nonetheless permit the defendant to show that intoxication prevented the requisite *mens rea.* Hale, Coke, and Blackstone were familiar, to say the least, with the concept of *mens rea,* and acknowledged that drunkenness "deprive[s] men of the use of reason," 1 Hale, *supra,* at *32; see also Blackstone, *supra,* at *25. It is inconceivable that they did not realize that an offender's drunkenness might impair his ability to form the requisite intent; and inconceivable that their failure to note this massive exception from the general rule of disregard of intoxication was an oversight. Hale's statement that a drunken offender shall have the same judgment "as if he were in his right senses" must be understood as precluding a defendant from arguing that, because of his intoxication, he could not have possessed the *mens rea* required to commit the crime. And the same must be said of the exemplar of the common-law rule cited by both Hale and Blackstone, see 1 Hale, *supra,* at *32; Blackstone, *supra,* at *26, n. w, which is Serjeant Pollard's argument to the King's Bench in *Reniger v. Fogossa,* 1 Plowd. 1, 19, 75 Eng. Rep. 1, 31 (1550): "[I]f a person that is drunk kills another, this shall be Felony, and he shall be hanged for it, and yet he did it through Ignorance, for when he was drunk he had *no Understanding* nor Memory; but inasmuch as that Ignorance was occasioned by his own Act and Folly, and he might have avoided it, he shall not be privileged thereby." (Emphasis added.)

Against this extensive evidence of a lengthy common-law tradition decidedly against him, the best argument available to respondent is the one made by his *amicus* and conceded by the State: Over the course of the 19th century, courts carved out an exception to the common law's traditional across-the-board condemnation of the drunken offender, allowing a jury to consider a defendant's intoxication when assessing whether he possessed the mental state needed to commit the crime charged, where the crime was one requiring a "specific intent." The emergence of this new rule is often traced to an 1819 English case, in which Justice Holroyd is reported to have held that "though voluntary drunkenness cannot excuse from the commission of crime, yet where, as on a charge of murder, the material question is, whether an act was premeditated or done only with sudden heat and impulse, the fact of the party being intoxicated [is] a circumstance proper to be taken into consideration." 1 W. Russell, Crimes and Misdemeanors *8 (citing *King v. Grindley,* Worcester Sum. Assizes 1819, MS). This exception was "slow to take root," however, Hall, Intoxication and Criminal Responsibility, 57 Harv. L. Rev. 1045, 1049 (1944), even in England. Indeed, in the 1835 case of *King v. Carroll,* 7 Car. & P. 145, 147, 173 Eng. Rep. 64, 65 (N.P.), Justice Park claimed that Holroyd had "retracted his opinion" in *Grindley,* and said "there is no doubt that that case is not law." In this country, as late as 1858 the Missouri Supreme Court could speak as categorically as this:

> To look for deliberation and forethought in a man maddened by intoxication is vain, for drunkenness has deprived him of the deliberating faculties to a greater or less extent; and if this deprivation is to relieve him of all responsibility or to diminish it, the great majority of crimes committed will go unpunished. This however is not the doctrine of the common law; and to its maxims, based as they obviously are upon true wisdom and sound policy, we must adhere. *State v. Cross,* 27 Mo. 332, 338 (1858).

And as late as 1878, the Vermont Supreme Court upheld the giving of the following instruction at a murder trial:

> "The voluntary intoxication of one who without provocation commits a homicide, although amounting to a frenzy, that is, although the intoxication amounts to a frenzy, does not excuse him from the same construction of his conduct, and the same legal inferences upon the question of premeditation and intent, as affecting the grade of his crime, which are applicable to a person entirely sober." *State v. Tatro,* 50 Vt. 483, 487 (1878).

Eventually, however, the new view won out, and by the end of the 19th century, in most American jurisdictions, intoxication could be considered in determining whether a defendant was capable of forming the specific intent necessary to commit the crime charged. See Hall, *supra,* at 1049; *Hopt v. People,* 104 U.S. 631 (1882) (citing cases).

On the basis of this historical record, respondent's *amicus* argues that "[t]he old common-law rule . . . was no longer deeply rooted at the time the Fourteenth Amendment was ratified." Brief for National Association of Criminal Defense Lawyers as *Amicus Curiae* 23. That conclusion is questionable, but we need not pursue the point, since the argument of *amicus* mistakes the nature of our inquiry. It is not the State which bears the burden of demonstrating that its rule is "deeply rooted," but rather respondent who must show that the principle of procedure *violated* by the rule (and allegedly required by due process) is "'so rooted in the traditions and conscience of our people as to be ranked as fundamental.'" *Patterson v. New York*, 432 U.S., at 202. Thus, even assuming that when the Fourteenth Amendment was adopted the rule Montana now defends was no longer generally applied, this only cuts off what might be called an *a fortiori* argument in favor of the State. The burden remains upon respondent to show that the "new common-law" rule—that intoxication may be considered on the question of intent—was so deeply rooted at the time of the Fourteenth Amendment (or perhaps has become so deeply rooted since) as to be a fundamental principle which that Amendment enshrined.

That showing has not been made. Instead of the uniform and continuing acceptance we would expect for a rule that enjoys "fundamental principle" status, we find that fully one-fifth of the States either never adopted the "new common-law" rule at issue here or have recently abandoned it.***

It is not surprising that many States have held fast to or resurrected the common-law rule prohibiting consideration of voluntary intoxication in the determination of *mens rea,* because that rule has considerable justification—which alone casts doubt upon the proposition that the opposite rule is a "fundamental principle." A large number of crimes, especially violent crimes, are committed by intoxicated offenders; modern studies put the numbers as high as half of all homicides, for example.***

There is, in modern times, even more justification for laws such as § 45-2-203 than there used to be. Some recent studies suggest that the connection between drunkenness and crime is as much cultural as pharmacological—that is, that drunks are violent not simply because alcohol makes them that way, but because they are behaving in accord with their learned belief that drunks are violent. This not only adds additional support to the traditional view that an intoxicated criminal is not deserving of exoneration, but it suggests that juries—who possess the same learned belief as the intoxicated offender—will be too quick to accept the claim that the defendant was biologically incapable of forming the requisite *mens rea.* Treating the matter as one of excluding misleading evidence therefore makes some sense.

In sum, not every widespread experiment with a procedural rule favorable to criminal defendants establishes a fundamental principle of justice. Although the rule allowing a jury to consider evidence of a defendant's voluntary intoxication where relevant to *mens rea* has gained considerable acceptance, it is of too recent vintage, and has not received sufficiently uniform and permanent allegiance, to qualify as fundamental, especially since it displaces a lengthy common-law tradition which remains supported by valid justifications today.

III

***

"The doctrines of *actus reus, mens rea,* insanity, mistake, justification, and duress have historically provided the tools for a constantly shifting adjustment of the tension between the evolving aims of the criminal law and changing religious, moral, philosophical, and medical views of the nature of man. This process of adjustment has always been thought to be the province of the States." *Powell v. Texas,* 392 U.S. 514 (1968) (plurality opinion). The people of Montana have decided to resurrect the rule of an earlier era, disallowing consideration of voluntary intoxication when a defendant's state of mind is at issue. Nothing in the Due Process Clause prevents them from doing so, and the judgment of the Supreme Court of Montana to the contrary must be reversed.

It is so ordered.

Justice GINSBURG, concurring in the judgment.

The Court divides in this case on a question of characterization. The State's law, Mont. Code Ann. § 45-2-203 (1995), prescribes that voluntary intoxication "may not be taken into consideration in determining the existence of a mental state which is an element of [a criminal] offense." For measurement against federal restraints on state action, how should we type that prescription? If § 45-2-203 is simply a rule designed to keep out "relevant, exculpatory evidence," Justice O'CONNOR maintains Montana's law offends due process. If it is, instead, a redefinition of the mental-state element of the offense, on the other hand, Justice O'CONNOR's due process concern "would not be at issue," for "[a] state legislature certainly has the authority to identify the elements of the offenses it wishes to punish," and to exclude evidence irrelevant to the crime it has defined.

Beneath the labels (rule excluding evidence or redefinition of the offense) lies the essential question: Can a State, without offense to the Federal Constitution, make the judgment that two people are equally culpable where one commits an act stone sober, and the other engages in the same conduct after his voluntary intoxication has reduced his capacity for self-control? For the reasons that follow, I resist categorizing § 45-2-203 as merely an evidentiary prescription, but join the Court's judgment refusing to condemn the Montana statute as an unconstitutional enactment.

Section 45-2-203 does not appear in the portion of Montana's Code containing evidentiary rules (Title 26), the expected placement of a provision regulating solely the admissibility of evidence at trial. Instead, Montana's intoxication statute appears in Title 45 ("Crimes"), as part of a chapter entitled "General Principles of Liability." Mont. Code Ann., Tit. 45, ch. 2 (1995). No less than adjacent provisions governing duress and entrapment, § 45-2-203 embodies a legislative judgment regarding the circumstances under which individuals may be held criminally responsible for their actions.

As urged by Montana and its *amici,* § 45-2-203 "extract[s] the entire subject of voluntary intoxication from the mens rea inquiry," thereby rendering evidence of voluntary intoxication logically irrelevant to proof of the requisite mental state. Thus, in a prosecution for deliberate homicide, the State need not prove that the defendant "purposely or knowingly cause[d] the death of another," Mont. Code Ann. § 45-5-102(a) (1995), in a purely subjective sense. To obtain a conviction, the prosecution must prove only that (1) the defendant caused the death of another with actual knowledge or purpose, *or* (2) that the defendant killed "under circumstances that would otherwise establish knowledge or purpose 'but for' [the defendant's] voluntary intoxication." Brief for American Alliance for Rights and Responsibilities et al. as *Amici Curiae* 6. Accordingly, § 45-2-203 does not "lighte[n] the prosecution's burden to prove [the] mental-state element beyond a reasonable doubt," as Justice O'CONNOR suggests for "[t]he applicability of the reasonable-doubt standard . . . has always been dependent on how a State defines the offense that is charged," *Patterson v. New York,* 432 U.S. 197 (1977).

Comprehended as a measure redefining *mens rea,* § 45-2-203 encounters no constitutional shoal. States enjoy wide latitude in defining the elements of criminal offenses, particularly when determining "the extent to which moral culpability should be a prerequisite to conviction of a crime," *Powell v. Texas,* 392 U.S. 514 (1968) (Black, J., concurring). When a State's power to define criminal conduct is challenged under the Due Process Clause, we inquire only whether the law "offends some principle of justice so rooted in the traditions and conscience of our people as to be ranked as fundamental." *Patterson,* 432 U.S., at 202 (internal quotation marks omitted). Defining *mens rea* to eliminate the exculpatory value of voluntary intoxication does not offend a "fundamental principle of justice," given the lengthy common-law tradition, and the adherence of a significant minority of the States to that position today.

Other state courts have upheld statutes similar to § 45-2-203, not simply as evidentiary rules, but as legislative redefinitions of the mental-state element. Legislation of this order, if constitutional in Arizona, Hawaii, and Pennsylvania, ought not be declared unconstitutional by this Court when enacted in Montana.

If, as the plurality, Justice O'Connor, and Justice Souter agree, it is within the legislature's province to instruct courts to treat a sober person and a voluntarily intoxicated person as equally responsible for conduct—to place a voluntarily intoxicated person on a level with a sober person—then the Montana law is no less tenable under the Federal Constitution than are the laws, with no significant difference in wording, upheld in sister States. The Montana Supreme Court did not disagree with the courts of other States; it simply did not undertake an analysis in line with the principle that legislative enactments plainly capable of a constitutional construction ordinarily should be given that construction.

The Montana Supreme Court's judgment, in sum, strikes down a statute whose text displays no constitutional infirmity. If the Montana court considered its analysis forced by this Court's precedent, it is proper for this Court to say what prescriptions federal law leaves to the States, and thereby dispel confusion to which we may have contributed, and attendant state-court misperception.

Justice O'CONNOR, with whom Justice STEVENS, Justice SOUTER, and Justice BREYER join, dissenting.

The Montana Supreme Court unanimously held that Mont. Code Ann. § 45-2-203 (1995) violates due process. I agree. Our cases establish that due process sets an outer limit on the restrictions that may be placed on a defendant's ability to raise an effective defense to the State's accusations. Here, to impede the defendant's ability to throw doubt on the State's case, Montana has removed from the jury's consideration a category of evidence relevant to determination of mental state where that mental state is an essential element of the offense that must be proved beyond a reasonable doubt. Because this disallowance eliminates evidence with which the defense might negate an essential element, the State's burden to prove its case is made correspondingly easier. The justification for this disallowance is the State's desire to increase the likelihood of conviction of a certain class of defendants who might otherwise be able to prove that they did not satisfy a requisite element of the offense. In my view, the statute's effect on the criminal proceeding violates due process.

I

This Court's cases establish that limitations placed on the accused's ability to present a fair and complete defense can, in some circumstances, be severe enough to violate due process. Applying our precedent, the Montana Supreme Court held that keeping intoxication evidence away from the jury, where such evidence was relevant to establishment of the requisite mental state, violated the due process right to present a defense and that the instruction pursuant to § 45-2-203 was not harmless error. In rejecting the Montana Supreme Court's conclusion, the plurality emphasizes that "any number of familiar and unquestionably constitutional evidentiary rules" permit exclusion of relevant evidence. It is true that a defendant does not enjoy an absolute right to present evidence relevant to his defense. But none of the "familiar" evidentiary rules operates as Montana's does. The Montana statute places a blanket exclusion on a category of evidence that would allow the accused to negate the offense's mental-state element. In so doing, it frees the prosecution, in the face of such evidence, from having to prove beyond a reasonable doubt that the defendant nevertheless possessed the required mental state. In my view, this combination of effects violates due process.

The proposition that due process requires a fair opportunity to present a defense in a criminal prosecution is not new. ***Due process demands that a criminal defendant be afforded a fair opportunity to defend against the State's accusations. Meaningful adversarial testing of the State's case requires that the defendant not be prevented from raising an effective defense, which must include the right to present relevant, probative evidence.***

A state legislature certainly has the authority to identify the elements of the offenses it wishes to punish, but once its laws are written, a defendant has the right to insist that the State prove beyond a reasonable doubt every element of an offense charged. Because the Montana Legislature has specified that a person commits "deliberate homicide" only if he "purposely or knowingly causes the death of another human being," Mont. Code Ann. § 45-5-102(1)(a)(1995), the prosecution must prove the existence of such mental state in order to convict. That is, unless the defendant is shown to have acted purposely or knowingly, *he is not guilty of the offense of deliberate homicide.* The Montana Supreme Court found that it was inconsistent with the legislature's requirement of the mental state of "purposely" or "knowingly" to prevent the jury from considering evidence of voluntary intoxication, where that category of evidence was relevant to establishment of that mental-state element. 272 Mont., at 122-123.

Where the defendant may introduce evidence to negate a subjective mental-state element, the prosecution must work to overcome whatever doubts the defense has raised about the existence of the required mental state. On the other hand, if the defendant may *not* introduce evidence that might create doubt in the factfinder's mind as to whether that element was met, the prosecution will find its job so much the easier. A subjective mental state is generally proved only circumstantially. If a jury may not consider the defendant's evidence of his mental state, the jury may impute to the defendant the culpability of a mental state he did not possess.***

A State's placement of a significant limitation on the right to defend against the State's accusations "requires that the competing interest be closely examined." *Chambers,* 410 U.S., at 295. Montana has specified that to prove guilt, the State must establish that the defendant acted purposely or knowingly, but has prohibited a category of defendants from effectively disputing guilt through presentation of evidence relevant to that essential element. And the evidence is indisputably relevant: The Montana Supreme Court held that evidence of intoxication is relevant to proof of mental and furthermore, § 45-2-203's exception for involuntary intoxication shows that the legislature does consider intoxication relevant to mental state. Montana has barred the defendant's use of a category of relevant, exculpatory evidence for the express purpose of improving the State's likelihood of winning a conviction against a certain type of defendant. The plurality's observation that all evidentiary rules that exclude exculpatory evidence reduce the State's burden to prove its case is beside the point. The *purpose* of the familiar evidentiary rules is not to alleviate the State's burden, but rather to vindicate some other goal or value—*e.g.,* to ensure the reliability and competency of evidence or to encourage effective communications within certain relationships. ***

II

The plurality does, however, raise an important argument for the statute's validity: the disallowance, at common law, of consideration of voluntary intoxication where a defendant's state of mind is at issue. Because this disallowance was permitted at common law, the plurality argues, its disallowance by Montana cannot amount to a violation of a "fundamental principle of justice."

From 1551 until its shift in the 19th century, the common-law rule prevailed that a defendant could not use intoxication as an excuse or justification for an offense, or, it must be assumed, to rebut establishment of a requisite mental state. "Early law was indifferent to the defence of drunkenness because the theory of criminal liability was then too crude and too undeveloped to admit of exceptions. . . . But with the refinement in the theory of criminal liability . . . a modification of the rigid old rule on the defence of drunkenness was to be expected." Singh, History of the Defense of Drunkenness in English Criminal Law, 49 L.Q. Rev. 528, 537 (1933) (footnote omitted). As the plurality concedes, that significant modification took place in the 19th century. Courts acknowledged the fundamental incompatibility of a particular mental-state requirement on the one hand, and the disallowance of consideration of evidence that might defeat establishment of that mental state on the other. In the slow progress typical of the common law, courts began to recognize that evidence of intoxication was properly admissible for the purpose of ascertaining whether a defendant had met the required mental-state element of the offense charged.

This recognition, courts believed, was consistent with the common-law rule that voluntary intoxication did not excuse commission of a crime; rather, an element of the crime, the requisite mental state, was not satisfied and therefore the crime had not been committed. As one influential mid–19th century case explained: "Drunkenness is no excuse for crime; yet, in that class of crimes and offences which depend upon guilty knowledge, or the coolness and deliberation with which they shall have been perpetrated, to constitute their commission . . . [drunkenness] should be submitted to the consideration of the Jury"; for, where the crime required a particular mental state, "it is proper to show any state or condition of the person that is adverse to the proper exercise of the mind" in order "[t]o rebut" the mental state or "to enable the Jury to judge rightly of the matter." *Pigman v. State,* 14 Ohio 555, 556-557 (1846); *accord, Cline v. State,* 43 Ohio St. 332 (1885) ("The rule is well settled that intoxication is not a justification or an excuse for crime. . . . But in many cases evidence of intoxication is admissible with a view to the question whether a crime has been committed . . . . As [mental state], in such case, is of the essence of the offense, it is possible that in proving intoxication you go far to prove that no offense was committed").

Courts across the country agreed that where a subjective mental state was an element of the crime to be proved, the defense must be permitted to show, by reference to intoxication, the absence of that element. One court commented that it seemed "incontrovertible and to be universally applicable" that "where the nature and essence of the crime are made by law to depend upon the peculiar state and condition of the criminal's mind at the time with reference to the act done, drunkenness may be a proper subject for the consideration of the jury, not to excuse or mitigate the offence but to show that it was not committed." *People v. Robinson,* 2 Park. Crim. 235, 306 (N.Y. Sup. Ct. 1855).

With similar reasoning, the Montana Supreme Court recognized the incompatibility of a jury instruction pursuant to § 45-2-203 in conjunction with the legislature's decision to require a mental state of "purposely" or "knowingly" for deliberate homicide. It held that intoxication is relevant to formation of the requisite mental state. Unless a defendant is proved beyond a reasonable doubt to have possessed the requisite mental state, he did not commit the offense. Elimination of a critical category of defense evidence precludes a defendant from effectively rebutting the mental-state element, while simultaneously shielding the State from the effort of proving the requisite mental state in the face of negating evidence. It was this effect on the adversarial process that persuaded the Montana Supreme Court that the disallowance was unconstitutional.

The Due Process Clause protects those "'principle[s] of justice so rooted in the traditions and conscience of our people as to be ranked as fundamental.'" *Patterson v. New York,* 432 U.S., at 202. At the time the Fourteenth Amendment was ratified, the common-law rule on consideration of intoxication evidence was in flux. The plurality argues that rejection of the historical rule in the 19th century simply does not establish that the "'new common-law'" rule is a principle of procedure so "deeply rooted" as to be ranked "fundamental." But to determine whether a fundamental principle of justice has been violated here, we cannot consider only the historical disallowance of intoxication evidence, but must also consider the "fundamental principle" that a defendant has a right to a fair opportunity to put forward his defense, in adversarial testing where the State must prove the elements of the offense beyond a reasonable doubt. As concepts of *mens rea* and burden of proof developed, these principles came into conflict, as the shift in the common law in the 19th century reflects.***

Justice SOUTER, dissenting.

I have no doubt that a State may so define the mental element of an offense that evidence of a defendant's voluntary intoxication at the time of commission does not have exculpatory relevance and, to that extent, may be excluded without raising any issue of due process. I would have thought the statute at issue here (Mont. Code Ann. § 45-2-203 (1995)) had implicitly accomplished such a redefinition, but I read the opinion of the Supreme Court of Montana as indicating that it had no such effect, and I am bound by the state court's statement of its domestic law.

Even on the assumption that Montana's definitions of the purposeful and knowing culpable mental states were untouched by § 45-2-203, so that voluntary intoxication remains relevant to each, it is not a foregone conclusion that our cases preclude the State from declaring such intoxication evidence inadmissible. A State may typically exclude even relevant and exculpatory evidence if it presents a valid justification for doing so. There may (or may not) be a valid justification to support a State's decision to exclude, rather than render irrelevant, evidence of a defendant's voluntary intoxication. Montana has not endeavored, however, to advance an argument to that effect. Rather, the State has effectively restricted itself to advancing undoubtedly sound reasons for defining the mental state element so as to make voluntary intoxication generally irrelevant (though its own Supreme Court has apparently said the legislature failed to do that) and to demonstrating that evidence of voluntary intoxication was irrelevant at common law (a fact that goes part way, but not all the way, to answering the due process objection). In short, I read the State Supreme Court opinion as barring one interpretation that would leave the statutory scheme constitutional, while the State's failure to offer a justification for excluding relevant evidence leaves us unable to discern whether there may be a valid reason to support the statute as the State Supreme Court appears to view it. I therefore respectfully dissent from the Court's judgment.

I

The plurality opinion convincingly demonstrates that when the Fourteenth Amendment's Due Process Clause was added to the Constitution in 1868, the common law as it then stood either rejected the notion that voluntary intoxication might be exculpatory or was at best in a state of flux on that issue. See also *ante,* at 2029-2031 (O'Connor, J., dissenting). That is enough to show that Montana's rule that evidence of voluntary intoxication is inadmissible on the issue of culpable mental state contravenes no principle "'so rooted in the traditions and conscience of our people,'" as they stood in 1868, "'as to be ranked as fundamental,'" (*quoting Patterson v. New York,* 432 U.S. 197 (1977)). But this is not the end of the due process enquiry. Justice Harlan's dissenting opinion in *Poe v. Ullman,* 367 U.S. 497 (1961), teaches that the "tradition" to which we are tethered "is a living thing." What the historical practice does not rule out as inconsistent with "the concept of ordered liberty," *Palko v. Connecticut,* 302 U.S. 319, 1937), must still pass muster as rational in today's world.

In this case, the second step of the due process enquiry leads to a line of precedent discussed in Justice O'Connor's dissent involving the right to present a defense.*** Collectively, these cases stand for the proposition, as the Court put it in *Chambers, supra, at 295,* that while the right to present relevant evidence may be limited, the Constitution "requires that the competing interest [said to justify the limitation] be closely examined."

II

*** While I therefore find no apparent constitutional reason why Montana could not render evidence of voluntary intoxication excludable as irrelevant by redefining "knowledge" and "purpose," as they apply to the mental state element of its substantive offenses, or by making some other provision for mental state, I do not believe that I am free to conclude that Montana has done so here.***

A second possible (although by no means certain) option may also be open. Even under a definition of the mental state element that would treat evidence of voluntary intoxication as relevant and exculpatory, the exclusion of such evidence is typically permissible so long as a State presents a "'valid' reason," to justify keeping it out. *Chambers* and its line of precedent certainly recognize that such evidence may often properly be excluded.

Hence, I do not rule out the possibility of justifying exclusion of relevant intoxication evidence in a case like this. At the least, there may be reasons beyond those actually advanced by Montana that might have induced a State to reject its prior law freely admitting intoxication evidence going to mental state.

A State (though not necessarily Montana) might, for example, argue that admitting intoxication evidence on the issue of culpable mental state but not on a defense of incapacity (as to which it is widely assumed to be excludable as generally irrelevant) would be irrational since both capacity to obey the law and purpose to accomplish a criminal result presuppose volitional ability. See Model Penal Code § 4.01 ("A person is not responsible for criminal conduct if at the time of such conduct as a result of mental disease or defect he lacks substantial capacity . . . to conform his conduct to the requirements of law") and § 2.02(2)(a)(i) ("A person acts purposely with respect to a material element of an offense when . . . it is his conscious object to engage in conduct of that nature or to cause such a result"). And quite apart from any technical irrationality, a State might think that admitting the evidence in question on culpable mental state but not capacity (when each was a jury issue in a given case) would raise too high a risk of juror confusion. See Brief for State of Hawaii et al. as *Amici Curiae* 16 ("[U]se of [intoxication] evidence runs an unacceptable risk of potential manipulation by defendants and [will lead to] confusion of juries, who may not adequately appreciate that intoxication evidence is to be used for the question of mental state, not for purposes of showing an excuse"). While Thomas Reed Powell reportedly suggested that "learning to think like a lawyer is when you learn to think about one thing that is connected to another without thinking about the other thing it is connected to," Teachout, Sentimental Metaphors, 34 UCLA L. Rev. 537, 545 (1986), a State might argue that its law should be structured on the assumption that its jurors typically will not suffer from this facility.

Quite apart from the fact that Montana has made no such arguments for justification here, however, I am not at all sure why such arguments would go any further than justifying redefinition of mental states (the first option above). I do not understand why they would justify the State in cutting the conceptual corner by leaving the definitions of culpable mental states untouched but excluding evidence relevant to this proof. Absent a convincing argument for cutting that corner, *Chambers* and the like constrain us to hold the current Montana statute unconstitutional. I therefore respectfully dissent.

Justice BREYER, with whom Justice STEVENS joins, dissenting.

I join Justice O'Connor's dissent. As the dissent says, and as Justice Souter agrees, the Montana Supreme Court did not understand Montana's statute to have redefined the mental element of deliberate homicide. In my view, however, this circumstance is not simply happenstance or a technical matter that deprives us of the power to uphold that statute. To have read the statute differently—to treat it as if it had redefined the mental element—would produce anomalous results. A statute that makes voluntary intoxication the legal equivalent of purpose or knowledge *but only where external circumstances would establish purpose or knowledge in the absence of intoxication,* see *ante,* at 2024 (Ginsburg, J., concurring), is a statute that turns guilt or innocence not upon state of mind, but upon irrelevant external circumstances. An intoxicated driver stopped at an intersection who unknowingly accelerated into a pedestrian would likely be found guilty, for a jury unaware of intoxication would likely infer knowledge or purpose. An identically intoxicated driver racing along a highway who unknowingly sideswiped another car would likely be found innocent, for a jury unaware of intoxication would likely infer negligence. Why would a legislature want to write a statute that draws such a distinction, upon which a sentence of life imprisonment, or death, may turn? If the legislature wanted to equate voluntary intoxication, knowledge, and purpose, why would it not write a statute that plainly says so, instead of doing so in a roundabout manner that would affect, in dramatically different ways, those whose minds, deeds, and consequences seem identical? I would reserve the question of whether or not such a hypothetical statute might exceed constitutional limits.

Notes and Questions

1. The state of Montana allows the defendant to admit evidence of involuntary intoxication but not voluntary intoxication. What arguments can you put forward for allowing one but not the other?

2. In *Montana v. Egelhoff*, why did the court find that voluntary intoxication is not a defense deeply rooted in the law so as to be a fundamental principle of justice?

3. Do the arguments for prohibiting psychiatric evidence as discussed in *Clark v. Arizona* also support barring alcohol-related evidence?

Chapter 23
Entrapment

A. Subjective vs. Objective

Entrapment is a defense that arises when police go too far in encouraging or enticing individuals to commit a crime. At the heart of entrapment is police conduct and whether law enforcement acted appropriately.

Jurisdictions generally take one of two approaches to an entrapment defense. Under the subjective approach, which is followed by the majority of jurisdictions to include the federal government, the court looks at the defendant's predisposition to commit the crime. Under the objective approach, which is followed by the Model Penal Code (2.13), the court examines the extent of law enforcement conduct in encouraging individuals to violate the law. Unlike the subjective approach that focuses on the defendant's subjective disposition to commit crime, the objective approach examines the police conduct irrespective of the defendant's predisposition. Under either approach, entrapment does not occur if the police merely provide the individual the opportunity to commit a crime.

The first case in this chapter, *State v. Doran*, explores both the subjective and objective approaches and examines why Ohio chose the former over the latter. The second case, *Jacobson v. United States*, discusses what it means for a defendant to be predisposed to commit the crime.

State v. Doran, 5 Ohio St. 3d 187 (1983)

*** In October 1980, appellant picked up a hitchhiker named Nona F. Wilson. Appellant did not know Wilson prior to this occasion. Unknown to appellant, Wilson was an agent of Medway Enforcement Group, a multi-county undercover drug enforcement group. Wilson was not a law enforcement officer, but was paid by Medway to introduce undercover police agents to prospective drug dealers. Medway paid Wilson $50 for arranging a drug buy with a first offender and $100 for arranging a buy with a repeat offender.

While appellant drove Wilson home, the two struck up a conversation and became friendly. During their conversation, Wilson asked appellant if he dealt in drugs. Appellant responded that he did not. Over the next several weeks appellant frequently spoke with Wilson over the telephone and occasionally saw her in person. Invariably Wilson relayed to appellant her desperate need for money. Wilson explained to appellant that her ex-husband had custody of her children and that she needed money to hire a lawyer to regain her children's custody. Wilson repeatedly suggested to appellant that if he could obtain drugs for her to sell, she could make the money she needed. Appellant declined and counselled Wilson to find a job.

Approximately two weeks after appellant and Wilson met, she requested that appellant meet her at a Wadsworth bar. There, Wilson introduced appellant to David High. High was introduced simply as a friend of Wilson, but was in reality an undercover narcotics agent with Medway.

In the days that followed, Wilson continued to press appellant into obtaining drugs for her to sell. Wilson's pleas became increasingly emotional and she would often break down and cry. Wilson even confessed to appellant that she was contemplating kidnapping her children in order to regain their custody. Appellant continuously resisted Wilson's pleas until finally he gave in and agreed to attempt to locate a supplier of drugs.

On November 18, 1980, appellant informed Wilson that he may have found a supplier. On that date appellant met with Wilson and High. Wilson explained to appellant that High was assisting her with the purchase of the drugs. Appellant received $200 from High, and Wilson and High then left. Shortly thereafter, Wilson and High saw appellant, at which time appellant delivered two tinfoil packets to them which contained phencyclidine (PCP).

Some time later, Wilson told appellant that she had found an apartment but needed money for a deposit in order to move in. On November 21, 1980, under circumstances similar to the earlier sale, another drug transaction was completed between appellant and High, in Wilson's presence.

A third sale took place on November 25, 1980 after Wilson told appellant that she was despondent over her inability to adequately clothe her children. This sale took place in the same manner as the earlier two sales with appellant delivering the drugs to High in Wilson's presence.

Over the next three to four months, three additional sales were completed. These last three sales were arranged and carried out between appellant and High alone. None of the latter sales involved the physical presence of Wilson, even though she continued to contact appellant and maintain that these drug transactions were necessary to satisfy a considerable gambling debt, the payment of which would prevent her from turning to prostitution. Prior to the final sale, High told appellant that only one more sale would be necessary in order for

Wilson and High to get married and finance a new beginning for themselves. After the sixth sale, appellant was arrested and indicted.

Appellant was tried before a jury and raised the defense of entrapment. Wilson testified as a *defense* witness. The trial court instructed the jury on the elements of the offenses and the requirement that the state had the burden to prove those elements beyond a reasonable doubt. With regard to entrapment, the trial court instructed the jury that entrapment is not an affirmative defense. Appellant requested an instruction to the effect that a criminal defendant would have no burden of proof on entrapment. Appellant also proposed an instruction defining inducement. The trial court refused to give either of appellant's proposed instructions. The trial court's definition of the defense of entrapment was, as set forth in his instruction:

> The defendant denies that he formed a purpose to commit a crime. He claims that he is excused because he was unlawfully entrapped by the undercover agent.
>
> Unlawful entrapment occurs when a police officer, informant or agent plants in the mind of the defendant the original idea and purpose inducing the defendant to commit a crime that he had not considered and which otherwise he had no intention of committing or would not have committed but for the inducement of the police officer, undercover agent or informant.
>
> If the defendant did not, himself, conceive the idea of committing a crime and it was suggested to him by the officer for the purpose of causing his arrest, the defendant must be found not guilty. However, if the defendant commits a crime while acting even in part in carrying out his own purpose or plan to violate the law, an entrapment is not unlawful and is not a defense even if the officer suggested the crime and provided the opportunity or facility or aided or encouraged its commission. A person is not entrapped when officers for the purpose of detecting crime merely present a defendant with an opportunity to commit an offense. Under such circumstances, craft and pretense may be used by law officers or agents to accomplish such purpose.
>
> If you find by credible evidence that the defendant had the predisposition and criminal design to commit the act into which he claims he was entrapped and that he was merely provided with opportunity to commit those acts for which he was both apt and willing, then he has not been unlawfully entrapped.

Twice the jury interrupted their deliberations to ask the trial judge to clarify his instruction on entrapment. The first time the trial judge repeated the original instruction. The second time the jury was ordered to return to their deliberations without any further instructions.

Appellant was acquitted of the aggravated trafficking charges which related to the first three buys and of the charge of permitting drug abuse. Appellant was found guilty of the remaining three counts of aggravated trafficking which arose from the buys conducted solely between appellant and High, without the physical presence of Wilson.

The court of appeals affirmed appellant's convictions and held that, even though the trial court erred in failing to refer to entrapment as an affirmative defense, the resulting error was not prejudicial.

The cause is now before this court pursuant to the allowance of a motion for leave to appeal.***

CELEBREZZE, C.J.

This appeal poses several previously unanswered questions significant to the administration of criminal justice in this state. First, we are asked to define the defense of entrapment. Second, we must decide whether entrapment is an affirmative defense. The final issue presented is whether a trial court commits prejudicial error by failing to allocate any burden of proof on the entrapment defense.

I

We must initially choose between defining entrapment under the "subjective" or "objective" test. Succinctly stated, the subjective test of entrapment focuses upon the predisposition of the accused to commit an offense whereas the objective or "hypothetical-person" test focuses upon the degree of inducement utilized by law enforcement officials and whether an ordinary law-abiding citizen would have been induced to commit an offense.

The United States Supreme Court adopted the subjective test of entrapment for federal prosecutions in *Sorrells v. United States* (1932), 287 U.S. 435. That test has withstood several challenges to its continued viability. *See Sherman v. United States* (1958), 356 U.S. 369 and *United States v. Russell* (1973), 411 U.S. 423. However, the objective test has won favor with a minority of United States Supreme Court justices and has been adopted by several states.

This court has not yet defined which test is applicable in this state. Since defining the entrapment defense under either of the above standards does not implicate federal constitutional principles, we are not bound by *Sorrells* and its progeny and are free to adopt either standard.

Appellant advocates adoption of the objective test. The approach advanced by appellant would examine the conduct of the police officer or agent and require a determination of whether the police conduct would induce an ordinary law-abiding citizen to commit a crime. Appellant's position is that the conduct of the police or their agent in this case was compelling and outrageous in continuing to induce appellant into committing a crime after appellant had repeatedly refused to succumb to these inducements.

The state urges adoption of the subjective test. The subjective test has already been utilized by several lower Ohio courts. The state suggests that the emphasis should be on the predisposition of the accused to commit a crime and that law enforcement should be free to use "artifice and stratagem" to apprehend those engaged in criminal activity.

For the reasons to follow, we hold that the defense of entrapment in Ohio will be defined under the subjective test.

We are constrained to reject the objective or hypothetical-person test because of the dangers inherent in the application of that standard. First, there is the danger that the objective approach will operate to convict those persons who should be acquitted. This is true because the objective test focuses upon the nature and degree of the inducement by the government agent and not upon the predisposition of the accused. Thus, even though the accused may not be individually predisposed to commit the crime, the inducement may not be of the type to induce a reasonably law-abiding citizen, and thus lead to the conviction of an otherwise innocent citizen.

Equally oppressive is the danger that the objective test may lead to acquittals of those who should be convicted. Again, the objective test emphasizes the effect of the inducement upon an ordinary law-abiding citizen and renders the predisposition of the accused irrelevant. If that is the case, a "career" criminal, or one who leaves little or no doubt as to his predisposition to commit a crime, will avoid conviction if the police conduct satisfies the objective test for entrapment.

A final danger is that adoption of the objective test may adversely impact on the accuracy of the fact-finding process. The determinative question of fact under the objective standard is what inducements were actually offered. Since most of these inducements will be offered in secrecy, the trial will more than likely be reduced to a swearing contest between an accused claiming that improper inducements were used and a police officer denying the accused's exhortations. Regardless of whether this situation favors the prosecution or defense, the fact-finder is still in the position of having to decide the truth solely upon the testimony of two diametrically opposed witnesses.

Conversely, the subjective test presents relatively few problems. By focusing on the predisposition of the accused to commit an offense, the subjective test properly emphasizes the accused's criminal culpability and not the culpability of the police officer. Indeed, the subjective test reduces the dangers of convicting an otherwise innocent person and acquitting one deserving of conviction. In addition, the fact-finding process is enhanced because evidence of predisposition may come from objective sources.

Our sole reservation concerning the subjective test involves the scope of admissible evidence on the issue of an accused's predisposition. While evidence relevant to predisposition should be freely admitted, judges should be hesitant to allow evidence of the accused's bad reputation, without more, on the issue of predisposition. Rather, while by no means an exhaustive list, the following matters would certainly be relevant on the issue of predisposition: (1) the accused's previous involvement in criminal activity of the nature charged, (2) the accused's ready acquiescence to the inducements offered by the police, (3) the accused's expert knowledge in the area of the criminal activity charged, (4) the accused's ready access to contraband, and (5) the accused's willingness to involve himself in criminal activity. Under this approach, the evidence on the issue of an accused's predisposition is more reliable than the evidence of the nature of inducement by police agents under the objective test.

Consequently, where the criminal design originates with the officials of the government, and they implant in the mind of an innocent person the disposition to commit the alleged offense and induce its commission in order to prosecute, the defense of entrapment is established and the accused is entitled to acquittal. *Sherman, supra,* at 372; *Sorrells, supra,* at 442. However, entrapment is not established when government officials "merely afford opportunities or facilities for the commission of the offense" and it is shown that the accused was predisposed to commit the offense. *Sherman, supra,* at 372.

II

In the case at bar, the trial court's instruction on entrapment, as previously set forth, is consonant with the definition of entrapment announced in this case. Nevertheless, our inquiry does not end at this juncture. We must now analyze whether the trial judge correctly characterized entrapment as not being an affirmative defense.

R.C. 2901.05(C)(2) states that an affirmative defense is:

> A defense involving an excuse or justification peculiarly within the knowledge of the accused, on which he can fairly be required to adduce supporting evidence.

If a defense is characterized as an affirmative defense, R.C. 2901.05(A) provides that the accused has the burden of going forward as well as the burden of proving the defense by a preponderance of the evidence.

There is no question that the defense of entrapment involves an "excuse or justification" as that phrase is used in R.C. 2901.05(C)(2). When an accused raises the defense of entrapment, the commission of the offense is admitted and the accused seeks to avoid criminal liability therefor by maintaining that the government induced him to commit an offense that he was not predisposed to commit. In this sense, entrapment is the classic confession and avoidance and clearly meets the first requirement of R.C. 2901.05(C)(2).

We must next determine whether entrapment is *either* "peculiarly within the knowledge of the accused" *or* of such nature that the accused "can fairly be required to adduce supporting evidence." We are satisfied that entrapment fits into both categories. The key consideration with the subjective test is whether the accused was predisposed to commit the offense. While proof of predisposition may come from objective sources, only the accused possesses the actual knowledge concerning his predisposition to commit the offense.

Further, we do not believe it is unfair to require the accused to adduce supporting evidence of his lack of predisposition. The accused, as a participant in the commission of the crime, will be aware of the circumstances surrounding the crime, and is at no disadvantage in relaying to the fact-finder his version of the crime as well as the reasons he was not predisposed to commit the crime. Moreover, the accused will certainly be aware of his previous involvement in crimes of a similar nature which may tend to refute the accused's claim that he was not predisposed to commit the offense. In summary, none of the evidence which is likely to be produced on the issue of predisposition would be beyond the knowledge of the accused or his ability to produce such evidence.

Accordingly, we hold that entrapment is an affirmative defense under R.C. 2901.05(C)(2).

III

Under the foregoing analysis, it becomes patent that the trial court erred in not characterizing entrapment as an affirmative defense. Finally, the question becomes whether that error was prejudicial to the rights of appellant.

The court of appeals below determined that appellant had actually benefited by the error committed at trial. The court below reasoned that, had the trial court properly instructed the jury that entrapment was an affirmative defense, appellant would have had the burden of proving that he was entrapped by a preponderance of the evidence. Since the trial court did not instruct that appellant had the burden of proving the defense, appellant was actually relieved of this burden. We disagree.

Even though we have no quarrel with the trial court's instruction defining entrapment, the trial court completely failed to allocate a burden of proof with respect to the defense other than stating that entrapment was not an affirmative defense which we have previously found to be patently erroneous. Under the trial court's treatment of entrapment, the state should have had the burden of disproving entrapment. Had the jury been so instructed, the court of appeals would have been correct in deciding that appellant had been benefited by the trial court's error. However, as instructed, the jury had no idea who had the burden to raise the defense of entrapment and either prove its existence or non-existence.

It was well-stated in *State v. Gideons* (1977), 52 Ohio App. 2d 70:

> To properly decide a criminal case, it is essential that the jury has a clear understanding of which party has the burden of proof. Without such an understanding, the jury cannot possibly perform its function. ***

We cannot say with any degree of certainty that the jury did not interpret the instruction to impose the burden of proof on entrapment on the appellant beyond a reasonable doubt. Consequently, a jury instruction which fails to allocate any burden of proof on the affirmative defense of entrapment is inherently misleading and confusing and is prejudicial error.

Accordingly, the judgment of the court of appeals below is reversed and the cause remanded to the trial court for a new trial.

Judgment reversed and cause remanded.

HOLMES, J., dissenting in part and concurring in part.

I agree that entrapment is an affirmative defense, but completely fail to understand how a jury instruction which does not state that the defense has the burden of proving such affirmative defense is prejudicial to the one asserting same. Here, the trial court incorrectly stated to the jury that entrapment was not an affirmative defense, but the error was harmless beyond a reasonable doubt. The trial court's erroneous instruction, in effect, placed a greater burden on the state by requiring the state to disprove the claim of entrapment. The incorrect instruction worked in the appellant's favor by unnecessarily enlarging the burden of proof to be discharged by the state. Such is not reversible error pursuant to *Chapman v. California* (1967), 386 U.S. 18.

Notes and Questions

1. For practical purposes, why do you think the prosecution would prefer the subjective over the objective test? If you were a defense attorney, would you prefer the subjective or objective test?

2. Are you as persuaded as the majority in *State v. Doran,* which wrote, "the subjective test presents relatively few problems"? Can you think of potential problems with the subjective test?

B. Predisposition

Jacobson v. United States, 503 U.S. 540 (1992)

Justice WHITE delivered the opinion of the Court.

On September 24, 1987, petitioner Keith Jacobson was indicted for violating a provision of the Child Protection Act of 1984 (Act), Pub. L. 98-292, 98 Stat. 204, which criminalizes the knowing receipt through the mails of a "visual depiction [that] involves the use of a minor engaging in sexually explicit conduct. . . ." 18 U.S.C. § 2252(a)(2)(A). Petitioner defended on the ground that the Government entrapped him into committing the crime through a series of communications from undercover agents that spanned the 26 months preceding his arrest. Petitioner was found guilty after a jury trial. The Court of Appeals affirmed his conviction, holding that the Government had carried its burden of proving beyond reasonable doubt that petitioner was predisposed to break the law and hence was not entrapped.

Because the Government overstepped the line between setting a trap for the "unwary innocent" and the "unwary criminal," _Sherman v. United States,_ 356 U.S. 369, 372, 78 S. Ct. 819, 821, 2 L.Ed.2d 848 (1958), and as a matter of law failed to establish that petitioner was independently predisposed to commit the crime for which he was arrested, we reverse the Court of Appeals' judgment affirming his conviction.

I

In February 1984, petitioner, a 56-year-old veteran-turned-farmer who supported his elderly father in Nebraska, ordered two magazines and a brochure from a California adult bookstore. The magazines, entitled Bare Boys I and Bare Boys II, contained photographs of nude preteen and teenage boys. The contents of the magazines startled petitioner, who testified that he had expected to receive photographs of "young men 18 years or older." Tr. 425. On cross-examination, he explained his response to the magazines:

> [PROSECUTOR]: [Y]ou were shocked and surprised that there were pictures of very young boys without clothes on, is that correct?
> [JACOBSON]: Yes, I was.
> [PROSECUTOR]: Were you offended?
> . . . .
> [JACOBSON]: I was not offended because I thought these were a nudist type publication. Many of the pictures were out in a rural

or outdoor setting. There was—I didn't draw any sexual connotation or connection with that.

The young men depicted in the magazines were not engaged in sexual activity, and petitioner's receipt of the magazines was legal under both federal and Nebraska law. Within three months, the law with respect to child pornography changed; Congress passed the Act illegalizing the receipt through the mails of sexually explicit depictions of children. In the very month that the new provision became law, postal inspectors found petitioner's name on the mailing list of the California bookstore that had mailed him Bare Boys I and II. There followed over the next 2 ½ years repeated efforts by two Government agencies, through five fictitious organizations and a bogus pen pal, to explore petitioner's willingness to break the new law by ordering sexually explicit photographs of children through the mail.

The Government began its efforts in January 1985 when a postal inspector sent petitioner a letter supposedly from the American Hedonist Society, which in fact was a fictitious organization. The letter included a membership application and stated the Society's doctrine: that members had the "right to read what we desire, the right to discuss similar interests with those who share our philosophy, and finally that we have the right to seek pleasure without restrictions being placed on us by outdated puritan morality." Record, Government Exhibit 7. Petitioner enrolled in the organization and returned a sexual attitude questionnaire that asked him to rank on a scale of one to four his enjoyment of various sexual materials, with one being "really enjoy," two being "enjoy," three being "somewhat enjoy," and four being "do not enjoy." Petitioner ranked the entry "[p]re-teen sex" as a two, but indicated that he was opposed to pedophilia.

For a time, the Government left petitioner alone. But then a new "prohibited mailing specialist" in the Postal Service found petitioner's name in a file, and in May 1986, petitioner received a solicitation from a second fictitious consumer research company, "Midlands Data Research," seeking a response from those who "believe in the joys of sex and the complete awareness of those lusty and youthful lads and lasses of the neophite [sic] age." The letter never explained whether "neophite" referred to minors or young adults. Petitioner responded: "Please feel free to send me more information, I am interested in teenage sexuality. Please keep my name confidential."

Petitioner then heard from yet another Government creation, "Heartland Institute for a New Tomorrow" (HINT), which proclaimed that it was "an organization founded to protect and promote sexual freedom and freedom of choice. We believe that arbitrarily imposed legislative sanctions restricting *your* sexual freedom should be rescinded through the legislative process." The letter also enclosed a second survey. Petitioner indicated that his interest in "[p]reteen sex-homosexual" material was above average, but not high. In response to another question, petitioner wrote: "Not only sexual expression but freedom of the press is under attack. We must be ever vigilant to counter attack right wing fundamentalists who are determined to curtail our freedoms."

HINT replied, portraying itself as a lobbying organization seeking to repeal "all statutes which regulate sexual activities, except those laws which deal with violent behavior, such as rape. HINT is also lobbying to eliminate any legal definition of 'the age of consent.'" These lobbying efforts were to be funded by sales from a catalog to be published in the future "offering the sale of various items which we believe you will find to be both interesting and stimulating." HINT also provided computer matching of group members with similar survey responses; and, although petitioner was supplied with a list of potential "pen pals," he did not initiate any correspondence.

Nevertheless, the Government's "prohibited mailing specialist" began writing to petitioner, using the pseudonym "Carl Long." The letters employed a tactic known as "mirroring," which the inspector described as "reflect[ing] whatever the interests are of the person we are writing to." Tr. 342. Petitioner responded at first, indicating that his interest was primarily in "male-male items." Record, Government Exhibit 9A. Inspector "Long" wrote back:

> My interests too are primarily male-male items. Are you satisfied with the type of VCR tapes available? Personally, I like the amateur stuff better if its [*sic*] well produced as it can get more kinky and also seems more real. I think the actors enjoy it more. *Id.,* Government Exhibit 13.

> Petitioner responded:

> As far as my likes are concerned, I like good looking young guys (in their late teens and early 20's) doing their thing together.

Petitioner's letters to "Long" made no reference to child pornography. After writing two letters, petitioner discontinued the correspondence. By March 1987, 34 months had passed since the Government obtained petitioner's name from the mailing list of the California bookstore, and 26 months had passed since the Postal Service had commenced its mailings to petitioner. Although petitioner had responded to surveys and letters, the Government had no evidence that petitioner had ever intentionally possessed or been exposed to child pornography. The Postal Service had not checked petitioner's mail to determine whether he was receiving questionable mailings from persons—other than the Government—involved in the child pornography industry.

At this point, a second Government agency, the Customs Service, included petitioner in its own child pornography sting, "Operation Borderline," after receiving his name on lists submitted by the Postal Service. Using the name of a fictitious Canadian company called "Produit Outaouais," the Customs Service mailed petitioner a brochure advertising photographs of young boys engaging in sex. Petitioner placed an order that was never filled.

The Postal Service also continued its efforts in the Jacobson case, writing to petitioner as the "Far Eastern Trading Company Ltd." The letter began:

> As many of you know, much hysterical nonsense has appeared in the American media concerning "pornography" and what must be done to stop it from coming across your borders. This brief letter does not allow us to give much comments; however, why is your government spending millions of dollars to exercise international censorship while tons of drugs, which makes yours the world's most crime ridden country are passed through easily.

The letter went on to say:

> [W]e have devised a method of getting these to you without prying eyes of U.S. Customs seizing your mail. . . . After consultations with American solicitors, we have been advised that once we have posted our material through your system, it cannot be opened for any inspection without authorization of a judge.

The letter invited petitioner to send for more information. It also asked petitioner to sign an affirmation that he was "not a law enforcement officer or agent of the U.S. Government acting in an undercover capacity for the purpose of entrapping Far Eastern Trading Company, its agents or customers." Petitioner responded. A catalog was sent, and petitioner ordered Boys Who Love Boys, a pornographic magazine depicting young boys engaged in various sexual activities. Petitioner was arrested after a controlled delivery of a photocopy of the magazine.

When petitioner was asked at trial why he placed such an order, he explained that the Government had succeeded in piquing his curiosity:

> Well, the statement was made of all the trouble and the hysteria over pornography and I wanted to see what the material was. It didn't describe the—mI didn't know for sure what kind of sexual action they were referring to in the Canadian letter.

In petitioner's home, the Government found the Bare Boys magazines and materials that the Government had sent to him in the course of its protracted investigation, but no other materials that would indicate that petitioner collected, or was actively interested in, child pornography.

Petitioner was indicted for violating 18 U.S.C. § 2252(a)(2)(A). The trial court instructed the jury on the petitioner's entrapment defense, petitioner was convicted, and a divided Court of Appeals for the Eighth Circuit, sitting en banc, affirmed, concluding that "Jacobson was not entrapped as a matter of law." 916 F.2d 467, 470 (1990). We granted certiorari.

II

There can be no dispute about the evils of child pornography or the difficulties that laws and law enforcement have encountered in eliminating it. Likewise, there can be no dispute that the Government may use undercover agents to enforce the law. "It is well settled that the fact that officers or employees of the Government merely afford opportunities or facilities for the commission of the offense does not defeat the prosecution. Artifice and stratagem may be employed to catch those engaged in criminal enterprises." *Sorrells v. United States,* 287 U.S. 435 (1932).

In their zeal to enforce the law, however, Government agents may not originate a criminal design, implant in an innocent person's mind the disposition to commit a criminal act, and then induce commission of the crime so that the Government may prosecute. *Sorrells, supra,* 287 U.S., at 442, 53 S. Ct., at 212. Where the Government has induced an individual to break the law and the defense of entrapment is at issue, as it was in this case, the prosecution must prove beyond reasonable doubt that the defendant was disposed to commit the criminal act prior to first being approached by Government agents. *United States v. Whoie,* 288 U.S. App. D.C. 261 (1991).

Thus, an agent deployed to stop the traffic in illegal drugs may offer the opportunity to buy or sell drugs and, if the offer is accepted, make an arrest on the spot or later. In such a typical case, or in a more elaborate "sting" operation involving government-sponsored fencing where the defendant is simply provided with the opportunity to commit a crime, the entrapment defense is of little use because the ready commission of the criminal act amply demonstrates the defendant's predisposition. *See United States v. Sherman,* 200 F.2d 880, 882 (1952). Had the agents in this case simply offered petitioner the opportunity to order child pornography through the mails, and petitioner—who must be presumed to know the law—had promptly availed himself of this criminal opportunity, it is unlikely that his entrapment defense would have warranted a jury instruction. *Mathews v. United States,* 485 U.S. 58, 66 (1988).

But that is not what happened here. By the time petitioner finally placed his order, he had already been the target of 26 months of repeated mailings and communications from Government agents and fictitious organizations. Therefore, although he had become predisposed to break the law by May 1987, it is our view that the Government did not prove that this predisposition was independent and not the product of the attention that the Government had directed at petitioner since January 1985. *Sorrells, supra,* 287 U.S., at 442.

The prosecution's evidence of predisposition falls into two categories: evidence developed prior to the Postal Service's mail campaign, and that developed during the course of the investigation. The sole piece of preinvestigation evidence is petitioner's 1984 order and receipt of the Bare Boys magazines. But this is scant if any proof of petitioner's predisposition to commit an illegal act, the criminal character of which a defendant is presumed to know. It may indicate a predisposition to view sexually oriented photographs that are responsive to his sexual tastes; but evidence that merely indicates a generic inclination to act within a broad range, not all of which is criminal, is of little probative value in establishing predisposition.

Furthermore, petitioner was acting within the law at the time he received these magazines. Receipt through the mails of sexually explicit depictions of children for noncommercial use did not become illegal under federal law until May 1984, and Nebraska had no law that forbade petitioner's possession of such material until 1988. Neb. Rev. Stat. § 28-813.01 (1989). Evidence of predisposition to do what once was lawful is not, by itself, sufficient to show predisposition to do what is now illegal, for there is a common understanding that most people obey the law even when they disapprove of it. This obedience may reflect a generalized respect for legality or the fear of prosecution, but for whatever reason, the law's prohibitions are matters of consequence. Hence, the fact that petitioner legally ordered and received the Bare Boys magazines does little to further the Government's burden of proving that petitioner was predisposed to commit a criminal act. This is particularly true given petitioner's unchallenged testimony that he did not know until they arrived that the magazines would depict minors.

The prosecution's evidence gathered during the investigation also fails to carry the Government's burden. Petitioner's responses to the many communications prior to the ultimate criminal act were at most indicative of certain personal inclinations, including a predisposition to view photographs of preteen sex and a willingness to promote a given agenda by supporting lobbying organizations. Even so, petitioner's responses hardly support an inference that he would commit the crime of receiving child pornography through the mails. Furthermore, a person's inclinations and "fantasies . . . are his own and beyond the reach of government. . . ." *Paris Adult Theatre I v. Slaton,* 413 U.S. 49, 67 (1973).

On the other hand, the strong arguable inference is that, by waving the banner of individual rights and disparaging the legitimacy and constitutionality of efforts to restrict the availability of sexually explicit materials, the Government not only excited petitioner's interest in sexually explicit materials banned by law but also exerted substantial pressure on petitioner to obtain and read such material as part of a fight against censorship and the infringement of individual rights. For instance, HINT described itself as "an organization founded to protect and promote sexual freedom and freedom of choice" and stated that "the most appropriate means to accomplish [its] objectives is to promote honest dialogue among concerned individuals and to continue its lobbying efforts with State Legislators." These lobbying efforts were to be financed through catalog sales. Mailings from the equally fictitious American Hedonist Society and the correspondence from the nonexistent Carl Long endorsed these themes.

Similarly, the two solicitations in the spring of 1987 raised the spectre of censorship while suggesting that petitioner ought to be allowed to do what he had been solicited to do. The mailing from the Customs Service referred to "the worldwide ban and intense enforcement on this type of material," observed that "what was legal and commonplace is now an 'underground' and secretive service," and emphasized that "[t]his environment forces us to take extreme measures" to ensure delivery. The Postal Service solicitation described the concern about child pornography as "hysterical nonsense," decried "international censorship," and assured petitioner, based on consultation with "American solicitors," that an order that had been posted could not be opened for inspection without authorization of a judge. It further asked petitioner to affirm that he was not a Government agent attempting to entrap the mail order company or its customers. *Ibid.* In these particulars, both Government solicitations suggested that receiving this material was something that petitioner ought to be allowed to do.

Petitioner's ready response to these solicitations cannot be enough to establish beyond reasonable doubt that he was predisposed, prior to the Government acts intended to create predisposition, to commit the crime of receiving child pornography through the mails. *See Sherman,* 356 U.S., at 374. The evidence that petitioner was ready and willing to commit the offense came only after the Government had devoted 2 ½ years to convincing him that he had or should have the right to engage in the very behavior proscribed by law. Rational jurors could not say beyond a reasonable doubt that petitioner possessed the requisite predisposition prior to the Government's investigation and that it existed independent of the Government's many and varied approaches to petitioner. As was explained in *Sherman,* where entrapment was found as a matter of law, "the Government [may not] pla[y] on the weaknesses of an innocent party and beguil[e] him into committing crimes which he otherwise would not have attempted." *Id.,* at 376.

Law enforcement officials go too far when they "implant in the mind of an innocent person the *disposition* to commit the alleged offense and induce its commission in order that they may prosecute." *Sorrells v. U.S.,* 287 U.S. 435 (emphasis added). Like the *Sorrells* Court, we are "unable to conclude that it was the intention of the Congress in enacting this statute that its processes of detection and enforcement should be abused by the instigation by government officials of an act on the part of persons otherwise innocent in order to lure them to its commission and to punish them." *Id.,* at 448. When the Government's quest for convictions leads to the apprehension of an otherwise law-abiding citizen who, if left to his own devices, likely would have never run afoul of the law, the courts should intervene.

Because we conclude that this is such a case and that the prosecution failed, as a matter of law, to adduce evidence to support the jury verdict that petitioner was predisposed, independent of the Government's acts and beyond a reasonable doubt, to violate the law by receiving child pornography through the mails, we reverse the Court of Appeals' judgment affirming the conviction of Keith Jacobson.

It is so ordered.

Justice O'CONNOR, with whom THE CHIEF JUSTICE and Justice KENNEDY join, and with whom Justice SCALIA joins except as to Part II, dissenting.

Keith Jacobson was offered only two opportunities to buy child pornography through the mail. Both times, he ordered. Both times, he asked for opportunities to buy more. He needed no Government agent to coax, threaten, or persuade him; no one played on his sympathies, friendship, or suggested that his committing the crime would further a greater good. In fact, no Government agent even contacted him face to face. The Government contends that from the enthusiasm with which Mr. Jacobson responded to the chance to commit a crime, a reasonable jury could permissibly infer beyond a reasonable doubt that he was predisposed to commit the crime. I agree.

The first time the Government sent Mr. Jacobson a catalog of illegal materials, he ordered a set of photographs advertised as picturing "young boys in sex action fun." He enclosed the following note with his order: "I received your brochure and decided to place an order. If I like your product, I will order more later." For reasons undisclosed in the record, Mr. Jacobson's order was never delivered.

The second time the Government sent a catalog of illegal materials, Mr. Jacobson ordered a magazine called "Boys Who Love Boys," described as: "11 year old and 14 year old boys get it on in every way possible. Oral, anal sex and heavy masturbation. If you love boys, you will be delighted with this." Along with his order, Mr. Jacobson sent the following note: "Will order other items later. I want to be discreet in order to protect you and me."

Government agents admittedly did not offer Mr. Jacobson the chance to buy child pornography right away. Instead, they first sent questionnaires in order to make sure that he was generally interested in the subject matter. Indeed, a "cold call" in such a business would not only risk rebuff and suspicion, but might also shock and offend the uninitiated, or expose minors to suggestive materials. Mr. Jacobson's responses to the questionnaires gave the investigators reason to think he would be interested in photographs depicting preteen sex.

The Court, however, concludes that a reasonable jury could not have found Mr. Jacobson to be predisposed beyond a reasonable doubt on the basis of his responses to the Government's catalogs, even though it admits that, by that time, he was predisposed to commit the crime. The Government, the Court holds, failed to provide evidence that Mr. Jacobson's obvious predisposition at the time of the crime "was independent and not the product of the attention that the Government had directed at petitioner." *Ante,* at 1541. In so holding, I believe the Court fails to acknowledge the reasonableness of the jury's inference from the evidence, redefines "predisposition," and introduces a new requirement that Government sting operations have a reasonable suspicion of illegal activity before contacting a suspect.

I

This Court has held previously that a defendant's predisposition is to be assessed as of the time the Government agent first suggested the crime, not when the Government agent first became involved. *Sherman v. United States,* 356 U.S. 369 (1958). Until the Government actually makes a suggestion of criminal conduct, it could not be said to have "implant[ed] in the mind of an innocent person the disposition to commit the alleged offense and induce its commission. . . ." *Sorrells v. United States,* 287 U.S. 435, 442 (1932). Even in *Sherman v. United States, supra,* in which the Court held that the defendant had been entrapped as a matter of law, the Government agent had repeatedly and unsuccessfully coaxed the defendant to buy drugs, ultimately succeeding only by playing on the defendant's sympathy. The Court found lack of predisposition based on the Government's numerous unsuccessful attempts to induce the crime, not on the basis of preliminary contacts with the defendant.

Today, the Court holds that Government conduct may be considered to create a predisposition to commit a crime, even before any Government action to induce the commission of the crime. In my view, this holding changes entrapment doctrine. Generally, the inquiry is whether a suspect is predisposed before the Government induces the commission of the crime, not before the Government makes initial contact with him. There is no dispute here that the Government's questionnaires and letters were not sufficient to establish inducement; they did not even suggest that Mr. Jacobson should engage in any illegal activity. If all the Government had done was to send these materials, Mr. Jacobson's entrapment defense would fail. Yet the Court holds that the Government must prove not only that a suspect was predisposed to commit the crime before the opportunity to commit it arose, but also before the Government came on the scene.

The rule that preliminary Government contact can create a predisposition has the potential to be misread by lower courts as well as criminal investigators as requiring that the Government must have sufficient evidence of a defendant's predisposition *before it ever seeks to contact him*. Surely the Court cannot intend to impose such a requirement, for it would mean that the Government must have a reasonable suspicion of criminal activity before it begins an investigation, a condition that we have never before imposed. The Court denies that its new rule will affect run-of-the-mill sting operations, and one hopes that it means what it says. Nonetheless, after this case, every defendant will claim that something the Government agent did before soliciting the crime "created" a predisposition that was not there before. For example, a bribetaker will claim that the description of the amount of money available was so enticing that it implanted a disposition to accept the bribe later offered. A drug buyer will claim that the description of the drug's purity and effects was so tempting that it created the urge to try it for the first time. In short, the Court's opinion could be read to prohibit the Government from advertising the seductions of criminal activity as part of its sting operation, for fear of creating a predisposition in its suspects. That limitation would be especially likely to hamper sting operations such as this one, which mimic the advertising done by genuine purveyors of pornography. No doubt the Court would protest that its opinion does not stand for so broad a proposition, but the apparent lack of a principled basis for distinguishing these scenarios exposes a flaw in the more limited rule the Court today adopts.

The Court's rule is all the more troubling because it does not distinguish between Government conduct that merely highlights the temptation of the crime itself, and Government conduct that threatens, coerces, or leads a suspect to commit a crime in order to fulfill some other obligation. For example, in *Sorrells,* the Government agent repeatedly asked for illegal liquor, coaxing the defendant to accede on the ground that "'one former war buddy would get liquor for another.'" 287 U.S., at 440. In *Sherman,* the Government agent played on the defendant's sympathies, pretending to be going through drug withdrawal and begging the defendant to relieve his distress by helping him buy drugs. 356 U.S., at 371.

The Government conduct in this case is not comparable. While the Court states that the Government "exerted substantial pressure on petitioner to obtain and read such material as part of a fight against censorship and the infringement of individual rights," one looks at the record in vain for evidence of such "substantial pressure." The most one finds is letters advocating legislative action to liberalize obscenity laws, letters which could easily be ignored or thrown away. Much later, the Government sent separate mailings of catalogs of illegal materials. Nowhere did the Government suggest that the proceeds of the sale of the illegal materials would be used to support legislative reforms. While one of the HINT letters suggested that lobbying efforts would be funded by sales from a catalog, the catalogs actually sent, nearly a year later, were from different fictitious entities (Produit Outaouais and Far Eastern Trading Company), and gave no suggestion that money would be used for any political purposes. Nor did the Government claim to be organizing a civil disobedience movement, which would protest the pornography laws by breaking them. Contrary to the gloss given the evidence by the Court, the Government's suggestions of illegality may also have made buyers beware, and increased the mystique of the materials offered: "For those of you who have enjoyed youthful material . . . we have devised a method of getting these to you without prying eyes of U.S. Customs seizing your mail." Mr. Jacobson's curiosity to see what "'all the trouble and the hysteria'" was about, is certainly susceptible of more than one interpretation. And it is the jury that is charged with the obligation of interpreting it. In sum, the Court fails to construe the evidence in the light most favorable to the Government, and fails to draw all reasonable inferences in the Government's favor. It was surely reasonable for the jury to infer that Mr. Jacobson was predisposed beyond a reasonable doubt, even if other inferences from the evidence were also possible.

II

The second puzzling thing about the Court's opinion is its redefinition of predisposition. The Court acknowledges that "[p]etitioner's responses to the many communications prior to the ultimate criminal act were . . . indicative of certain personal inclinations, including a predisposition to view photographs of preteen sex. . . ." If true, this should have settled the matter; Mr. Jacobson was predisposed to engage in the illegal conduct. Yet, the Court concludes, "petitioner's responses hardly support an inference that he would commit the crime of receiving child pornography through the mails."

The Court seems to add something new to the burden of proving predisposition. Not only must the Government show that a defendant was predisposed to engage in the illegal conduct, here, receiving photographs of minors engaged in sex, but also that the defendant was predisposed to break the law knowingly in order to do so. The statute violated here, however, does not require proof of specific intent to break the law; it requires only knowing receipt of visual depictions produced by using minors engaged in sexually explicit conduct. *See* 18 U.S.C. § 2252(a)(2). Under the Court's analysis, however, the Government must prove *more* to show predisposition than it need prove in order to convict.

The Court ignores the judgment of Congress that specific intent is not an element of the crime of receiving sexually explicit photographs of minors. The elements of predisposition should track the elements of the crime. The predisposition requirement is meant to eliminate the entrapment defense for those defendants who would have committed the crime anyway, even absent Government inducement. Because a defendant might very well be convicted of the crime here absent Government inducement even though he did not know his conduct was illegal, a specific intent requirement does little to distinguish between those who would commit the crime without the inducement and those who would not. In sum, although the fact that Mr. Jacobson's purchases of Bare Boys I and Bare Boys II were legal at the time may have some relevance to the question of predisposition, it is not, as the Court suggests, dispositive.

The crux of the Court's concern in this case is that the Government went too far and "abused" the "'processes of detection and enforcement' " by luring an innocent person to violate the law. *Ante,* at 1543, *quoting Sorrells,* 287 U.S., at 448. Consequently, the Court holds that the Government failed to prove beyond a reasonable doubt that Mr. Jacobson was predisposed to commit the crime. It was, however, the jury's task, as the conscience of the community, to decide whether Mr. Jacobson was a willing participant in the criminal activity here or an innocent dupe. The jury is the traditional "defense against arbitrary law enforcement." *Duncan v. Louisiana,* 391 U.S. 145 (1968). Indeed, in *Sorrells,* in which the Court was also concerned about overzealous law enforcement, the Court did not decide itself that the Government conduct constituted entrapment, but left the issue to the jury. 287 U.S., at 452. There is no dispute that the jury in this case was fully and accurately instructed on the law of entrapment, and nonetheless found Mr. Jacobson guilty. Because I believe there was sufficient evidence to uphold the jury's verdict, I respectfully dissent.

Notes and Questions

1. After reading *Jacobson v. United States,* do you think the majority was bothered more by the number of solicitations that the government made to the defendant or the lengthy period of time covered by the solicitations?

2. Is the Court in *Jacobson* saying that the defendant might have been predisposed to looking at nude and sexual photos of the underage boys but not predisposed to breaking the law? What is the difference?

Chapter 24
Necessity and Duress

A. Background

United States v. Contento-Pachon, 723 F. 2d 691 (1984)

This case presents an appeal from a conviction for unlawful possession with intent to distribute a narcotic controlled substance in violation of 21 U.S.C. Sec. 841(a)(1) (1976). At trial, the defendant attempted to offer evidence of duress and necessity defenses. The district court excluded this evidence on the ground that it was insufficient to support the defenses. We reverse because there was sufficient evidence of duress to present a triable issue of fact.

I. FACTS

The defendant-appellant, Juan Manuel Contento-Pachon, is a native of Bogota, Colombia and was employed there as a taxicab driver. He asserts that one of his passengers, Jorge, offered him a job as the driver of a privately-owned car. Contento-Pachon expressed an interest in the job and agreed to meet Jorge and the owner of the car the next day.

Instead of a driving job, Jorge proposed that Contento-Pachon swallow cocaine-filled balloons and transport them to the United States. Contento-Pachon agreed to consider the proposition. He was told not to mention the proposition to anyone, otherwise he would "get into serious trouble." Contento-Pachon testified that he did not contact the police because he believes that the Bogota police are corrupt and that they are paid off by drug traffickers.

Approximately one week later, Contento-Pachon told Jorge that he would not carry the cocaine. In response, Jorge mentioned facts about Contento-Pachon's personal life, including private details which Contento-Pachon had never mentioned to Jorge. Jorge told Contento-Pachon that his failure to cooperate would result in the death of his wife and three year-old child.

The following day the pair met again. Contento-Pachon's life and the lives of his family were again threatened. At this point, Contento-Pachon agreed to take the cocaine into the United States.

The pair met two more times. At the last meeting, Contento-Pachon swallowed 129 balloons of cocaine. He was informed that he would be watched at all times during the trip, and that if he failed to follow Jorge's instruction he and his family would be killed.

After leaving Bogota, Contento-Pachon's plane landed in Panama. Contento-Pachon asserts that he did not notify the authorities there because he felt that the Panamanian police were as corrupt as those in Bogota. Also, he felt that any such action on his part would place his family in jeopardy.

When he arrived at the customs inspection point in Los Angeles, Contento-Pachon consented to have his stomach x-rayed. The x-rays revealed a foreign substance which was later determined to be cocaine

At Contento-Pachon's trial, the government moved to exclude the defenses of duress and necessity. The motion was granted. We reverse.

A. Duress

There are three elements of the duress defense: (1) an immediate threat of death or serious bodily injury, (2) a well-grounded fear that the threat will be carried out, and (3) no reasonable opportunity to escape the threatened harm.***

The trial court found Contento-Pachon's offer of proof insufficient to support a duress defense because he failed to offer proof of two elements: immediacy and inescapability. We examine the elements of duress.

Immediacy: The element of immediacy requires that there be some evidence that the threat of injury was present, immediate, or impending. "[A] veiled threat of future unspecified harm" will not satisfy this requirement. *Rhode Island Recreation Center v. Aetna Casualty and Surety Co.*, 177 F.2d 603, 605 (1st Cir. 1949). The district court found that the initial threats were not immediate because "they were conditioned on defendant's failure to cooperate in the future and did not place defendant and his family in immediate danger."

Evidence presented on this issue indicated that the defendant was dealing with a man who was deeply involved in the exportation of illegal substances. Large sums of money were at stake and, consequently, Contento-Pachon had reason to believe that Jorge would carry out his threats. Jorge had gone to the trouble to discover that Contento-Pachon was married, that he had a child, the names of his wife and child, and the location of his residence. These were not vague threats of possible future harm. According to the defendant, if he had refused to cooperate, the consequences would have been immediate and harsh.

Contento-Pachon contends that he was being watched by one of Jorge's accomplices at all times during the airplane trip. As a consequence, the force of the threats continued to restrain him. Contento-Pachon's contention that he was operating under the threat of immediate harm was supported by sufficient evidence to present a triable issue of fact.

Escapability: The defendant must show that he had no reasonable opportunity to escape. *See United States v. Gordon*, 526 F.2d 406, 407 (9th Cir. 1975). The district court found that because Contento-Pachon was not physically restrained prior to the time he swallowed the balloons, he could have sought help from the police or fled. Contento-Pachon explained that he did not report the threats because he feared that the police were corrupt. The trier of fact should decide whether one in Contento-Pachon's position might believe that some of the Bogota police were paid informants for drug traffickers and that reporting the matter to the police did not represent a reasonable opportunity of escape.

If he chose not to go to the police, Contento-Pachon's alternative was to flee. We reiterate that the opportunity to escape must be reasonable. To flee, Contento-Pachon, along with his wife and three year-old child, would have been forced to pack his possessions, leave his job, and travel to a place beyond the reaches of the drug traffickers. A juror might find that this was not a reasonable avenue of escape. Thus, Contento-Pachon presented a triable issue on the element of escapability.

Surrender to Authorities: As noted above, the duress defense is composed of at least three elements. The government argues that the defense also requires that a defendant offer evidence that he intended to turn himself in to the authorities upon reaching a position of safety. Although it has not been expressly limited, this fourth element seems to be required only in prison escape cases.***

In cases not involving escape from prison there seems little difference between the third basic requirement that there be no reasonable opportunity to escape the threatened harm and the obligation to turn oneself in to authorities on reaching a point of safety. Once a defendant has reached a position where he can safely turn himself in to the authorities he will likewise have a reasonable opportunity to escape the threatened harm.

That is true in this case. Contento-Pachon claims that he was being watched at all times. According to him, at the first opportunity to cooperate with authorities without alerting the observer, he consented to the x-ray. We hold that a defendant who has acted under a well-grounded fear of immediate harm with no opportunity to escape may assert the duress defense, if there is a triable issue of fact whether he took the opportunity to escape the threatened harm by submitting to authorities at the first reasonable opportunity.

B. Necessity

The defense of necessity is available when a person is faced with a choice of two evils and must then decide whether to commit a crime or an alternative act that constitutes a greater evil. *United States v. Richardson*, 588 F.2d 1235, 1239

(9th Cir. 1978). Contento-Pachon has attempted to justify his violation of 21 U.S.C. Sec. 841(a)(1) by showing that the alternative, the death of his family, was a greater evil.

Traditionally, in order for the necessity defense to apply, the coercion must have had its source in the physical forces of nature. The duress defense was applicable when the defendant's acts were coerced by a human force. W. LaFave & A. Scott, Handbook on Criminal Law Sec. 50 at 383 (1972). This distinction served to separate the two similar defenses. But modern courts have tended to blur the distinction between duress and necessity.

It has been suggested that, "the major difference between duress and necessity is that the former negates the existence of the requisite mens rea for the crime in question, whereas under the latter theory there is no actus reus." *United States v. Micklus*, 581 F.2d 612, 615 (7th Cir. 1978). The theory of necessity is that the defendant's free will was properly exercised to achieve the greater good and not that his free will was overcome by an outside force as with duress.

The defense of necessity is usually invoked when the defendant acted in the interest of the general welfare. For example, defendants have asserted the defense as a justification for (1) bringing laetrile into the United States for the treatment of cancer patients, *Richardson*, 588 F.2d at 1239; (2) unlawfully entering a naval base to protest the Trident missile system, *United States v. May*, 622 F.2d 1000, 1008-09 (9th Cir.); (3) burning Selective Service System records to protest United States military action, *United States v. Simpson*, 460 F.2d 515, 517 (9th Cir. 1972).

Contento-Pachon's acts were allegedly coerced by human, not physical forces. In addition, he did not act to promote the general welfare. Therefore, the necessity defense was not available to him. Contento-Pachon mischaracterized evidence of duress as evidence of necessity. The district court correctly disallowed his use of the necessity defense.

II. CONCLUSION

Contento-Pachon presented credible evidence that he acted under an immediate and well-grounded threat of serious bodily injury, with no opportunity to escape. Because the trier of fact should have been allowed to consider the credibility of the proffered evidence, we reverse. The district court correctly excluded Contento-Pachon's necessity defense.

COYLE, District Judge (dissenting in part and concurring in part):

In order to establish a defense of duress, the trial court in this case required Contento-Pachon to show (1) that he or his family was under an immediate threat of death or serious bodily injury; (2) that he had a well grounded fear that the threat would be carried out; and (3) that he had no reasonable opportunity to escape the threat. Applying this three-part test, the trial court found that the defendant's offer of proof was insufficient to support a defense of duress. The government argues that this holding should be affirmed and I agree.

The government also contends that the defense of duress includes a fourth element: That a defendant demonstrate that he submitted to proper authorities after attaining a position of safety. This is not an unreasonable requirement and I believe it should be applied. I do not agree with the majority's conclusion that the fourth element of the duress defense is only required in prison escape cases. Cases applying the fourth element have not so expressly limited its application. *See, e.g., United States v. Peltier*, 693 F.2d 96, 98 (9th Cir. 1982); *United States v. Campbell*, 609 F.2d 922, 924 (8th Cir. 1979), *cert. denied*, 445 U.S. 918, 100 S. Ct. 1282, 63 L. Ed. 2d 604 (1980); *United States v. Michelson*, 559 F.2d 567, 569-70 (9th Cir. 1977). The distinction which the majority attempts to draw between prison escape cases and non-prison escape cases is not persuasive. The force of threats which allegedly excused the defendant's failure to submit to proper authorities upon his arrival in Los Angeles are no more present, immediate, or impending than the force of threats or fear of retaliation faced by a "snitch" upon his return to prison after an escape.

In granting the government's motion in limine excluding the defense of duress, the trial court specifically found Contento-Pachon had failed to present sufficient evidence to establish the necessary elements of immediacy and inescapability. In its Order the district court stated:

> The first threat made to defendant and his family about three weeks before the flight was not immediate; the threat was conditioned upon defendant's failure to cooperate in the future and did not place the defendant and his family in immediate danger or harm. Moreover, after the initial threat and until he went to the house where he ingested the balloons containing cocaine, defendant and his family were not physically restrained and could have sought help from the police or fled. *See United States v. Gordon*, 526 F.2d 406 (9th Cir. 1975). No such efforts were attempted by defendant. Thus, defendant's own offer of proof negates two necessary elements of the defense of duress.

In cases where the defendant's duress has been raised, the courts have indicated that the element of immediacy is of crucial importance. *See, e.g., United States v. Atencio*, 586 F.2d 744, 746 (9th Cir. 1978); *United States v. Patrick*, 542 F.2d 381, 388 (7th Cir. 1976); *see also United States v. Polytarides*, 584 F.2d 1350 (4th Cir. 1978). The trial court found that the threats made against the defendant and his family lacked the requisite element of immediacy. This finding is adequately supported by the record. The defendant was outside the presence of the drug dealers on numerous occasions for varying lengths of time. There is no evidence that his family was ever directly threatened or even had knowledge of the threats allegedly directed against the defendant.

Moreover, the trial court found that the defendant and his family enjoyed an adequate and reasonable opportunity to avoid or escape the threats of the drug dealers in the weeks before his flight. Until he went to the house where he ingested the balloons containing cocaine, defendant and his family were not physically restrained or prevented from seeking help. The record supports the trial court's findings that the defendant and his family could have sought assistance from the authorities or have fled. Cases considering the defense of duress have established that where there was a reasonable legal alternative to violating the law, a chance to refuse to do the criminal act and also to avoid the threatened danger, the defense will fail. Duress is permitted as a defense only when a criminal act was committed because there was no other opportunity to avoid the threatened danger. *United States v. Hernandez*, 608 F.2d 741, 750 (9th Cir. 1979); *United States v. Wood*, 566 F.2d 1108, 1109 (9th Cir. 1977); *United States v. Michelson*, 559 F.2d 567, 569 (9th Cir. 1977).***

Because the district court's decision granting the government's motion in limine is fully and adequately supported by the record, I cannot agree that the district court abused its discretion and I therefore respectfully dissent.***

Notes and Questions

1. In *United States v. Contento-Pachon*, who has the better argument, the majority or the dissent with respect to adding a fourth element to duress? If you were deciding *Contento-Pachon* would you require this fourth element?

2. What distinctions can be drawn between prisoner and non-prisoner cases that involve duress and necessity? Arguably, the prisoner has no right to be free from incarceration just a right to be free from cruel and unusual punishment.

City of Columbus v. Spingola, 144 Ohio App. 3d 76 (2001)

KENNEDY, Judge.

On June 27, 1999, defendant-appellant Charles S. Spingola, climbed a flagpole on the Ohio Statehouse grounds and cut down a rainbow flag, which was flying as a part of a gay pride celebration. For this behavior, Spingola was indicted on one count of ethnic intimidation, a violation of Columbus City Code 2331.08(A). In its indictment, plaintiff-appellant, city of Columbus, alleged that Spingola committed the predicate offense of criminal damaging and that the motive or reason for the offense was the victim's sexual orientation.

The following evidence was presented at a jury trial. Jeff Redfield, the victim of the alleged ethnic intimidation, testified that he is the executive director for

Stonewall Columbus, an organization that serves central Ohio's gay, lesbian, bisexual, and transgender community. Redfield applied for and received permission from the Capitol Square Review and Advisory Board to fly the rainbow flag, a symbol of gay pride, on the statehouse lawn as part of a gay pride celebration. Redfield supplied a rainbow flag to Ron Keller, the executive director of the Capitol Square Review and Advisory Board. Keller confirmed that his board granted Redfield's request to fly the rainbow flag. Keller testified that his staff raised the flag on the statehouse lawn on the morning of June 27, 1999.

Several witnesses testified that they saw Spingola climb the flagpole and remove the flag. Richard and Josette Bodonyi, members of Parents and Friends of Lesbians and Gays, testified that they observed Spingola among a group of protestors gathered on the statehouse lawn. According to Mr. Bodonyi, the protestors were talking about the evils of homosexuality and encouraging Spingola to climb the flagpole and remove the flag. Mrs. Bodonyi testified that Spingola had to cut or tear the flag to remove it from the pole. According to Mrs. Bodonyi, Spingola proclaimed that, while he was removing the flag, "no damn faggot flag is going to fly over" the statehouse grounds. Mark Narens, a gay rights supporter, testified that Spingola appeared to be a leader among the protestors, whom Narens characterized as loud and angry. According to Narens, Spingola tore the flag from the pole and threw it to the ground.

Spingola testified on his own behalf and described his troubled life as a child and young man. He stated that he was able to turn his life around as a result of a religious transformation at the age of twenty-three. He testified that he has been preaching his religious beliefs for the past twenty years. He stated that he believes that homosexuality is a sin and that homosexual sinners must be confronted. He testified that he learned from the media that the rainbow flag would be flying at the statehouse, and he admitted that he attended the gay pride celebration on June 27, 1999, with the intention of removing the flag from the statehouse flagpole.

Spingola testified that, on the day at issue, he watched the gay rights parade with other members of his church. When the parade concluded, Spingola walked to the statehouse lawn in order to remove the flag. He testified that he placed a pocketknife in his mouth and climbed the flagpole. When Spingola was not able to pull the flag off the pole, he "cut the flag from the pole and threw it on the ground." He testified that he was proud of his accomplishment. Spingola stated that his main motivation for removing the flag was his belief that a gay pride flag should not be flying from a government flagpole. He admitted, however, that he assumed that the owner of the flag had obtained permission to fly it on the statehouse lawn. Spingola also admitted that he did not pursue any other avenues in an effort to remove the flag. He did not speak with anyone at the statehouse to find out what he could do to have the flag removed.

The jury found Spingola guilty of the lesser-included offense of criminal damaging, and the trial court entered judgment on the jury verdict. On appeal, Spingola assigns the following errors:

ASSIGNMENT OF ERROR NUMBER ONE:
The trial court erred when it entered judgment against the defendant when it lacked subject matter jurisdiction over the matter because municipalities, with their limited power to exercise only the powers of local self-government, cannot regulate the business or property of the state government and cannot enforce local ordinances upon state property.
ASSIGNMENT OF ERROR NUMBER TWO:
The trial court erred when it overruled the defendant's request to instruct the jury on the defense of necessity as a justification for the defendant's actions.

For the reasons that follow, we overrule Spingola's assignments of error and affirm the judgment of the Franklin County Municipal Court.***

By his second assignment of error, Spingola contends that the trial court erred because it failed to instruct the jury on the necessity defense as a legal justification for Spingola's actions.***

Spingola proposed the following instructions regarding the necessity defense:

SPECIAL INSTRUCTION NO. 5: Necessity Defense
The Defendant asserts the defense of Necessity in this case. The defense of Necessity excuses criminal acts when the harm which results from compliance with the law is greater than that which results from a violation of the law.
SOURCE: *Cleveland v. Sundermeier,* 48 Ohio App. 3d 204, 207 (Cuyahoga Co. 1989).
SPECIAL INSTRUCTION NO. 6: Elements of Necessity Defense
The Necessity defense has three essential elements:
(1) the act charged must have been done to prevent a significant harm;
(2) there must have been no adequate alternative;
(3) the harm caused must not have been disproportionate to the harm avoided.
The first two elements are factual determinations which may be satisfied by the Defendant's reasonable belief. The third factor is a value determination. The accepted norms of society determine the relative harmfulness of the two alternatives.

SOURCE: *City of St. Louis v. Klocker*, 637 S.W.2d 174, 177 (Mo. App. 1982); LaFave 50 at 382-86.

Spingola's proposed instruction does not accurately recite the elements of the necessity defense under Ohio law. The common-law elements of necessity in Ohio are as follows:

> *** (1) [T]he harm must be committed under the pressure of physical or natural force, rather than human force; (2) the harm sought to be avoided is greater than, or at least equal to that sought to be prevented by the law defining the offense charged; (3) the actor reasonably believes at the moment that his act is necessary and is designed to avoid the greater harm; (4) the actor must be without fault in bringing about the situation; and (5) the harm threatened must be imminent, leaving no alternative by which to avoid the greater harm. *** *State v. Prince* (1991), 71 Ohio App. 3d 694.

Spingola's proposed instruction regarding the elements of the defense is derived from an appellate case interpreting the necessity defense under *Missouri* law, and it does not include essential elements of the defense in Ohio. Because Spingola's proposed instruction was not an accurate reflection of Ohio law, the trial court was not obligated to give the instruction.

The trial court was not required to instruct the jury regarding the necessity defense for the additional reason that the defense would not apply in light of the evidence presented at trial. "The burden of going forward with the evidence of an affirmative defense, and the burden of proof, by a preponderance of the evidence, for an affirmative defense, is upon the accused." R.C. 2901.05(A). Because Spingola failed to produce evidence sufficient to establish at least two elements of the necessity defense, the trial court was not required to instruct on the defense. *See State v. Mogul* (May 15, 1998), Trumbull App. No. 97-T-0018, 1998 WL 258164 (noting that the jury shall not be instructed regarding an affirmative defense if the defendant fails to offer sufficient evidence to establish the defense).

Spingola provided no evidence whatsoever that his damage to the flag was committed under the pressure of physical or natural force. Instead, Spingola argues that Ohio should abandon the requirement for physical or natural force in favor of a more liberal rule that would allow the necessity defense when the conduct is committed under the pressure of a human source, such as the human act of raising a flag. Even jurisdictions that allow the necessity defense for harm committed by a human source, however, require that the human source of harm must be unlawful. *See St. Louis v. Klocker* (Mo. App. 1982), 637 S.W.2d 174, 176.

Spingola failed to provide evidence from which a reasonable jury could conclude that the rainbow flag was unlawfully raised. Even under his own proposed version of the necessity defense, therefore, Spingola was not entitled to the instruction. Spingola also failed to provide evidence that he had no alternative but to cut the flag from the pole. In fact, Spingola admitted that he knew at least a day in advance that the flag would be raised but he did not speak with anyone at the statehouse about getting the flag removed. Spingola testified, "I didn't go through any avenues other than the one I took." Because Spingola's proposed instructions on the necessity defense did not correctly state the law and because the facts of the case did not establish the elements of the necessity defense, we overrule Spingola's second assignment of error.

For the foregoing reasons, we overrule Spingola's assignments of error and affirm the judgment of the Franklin County Municipal Court.

Judgment affirmed.

Notes and Questions

1. Examine the five elements of necessity in Ohio. If Ohio was a state that recognized the necessity defense for harm committed by a human source, do you think the defendant in *State v. Doran* (entrapment) could have met the five elements of necessity and thus have raised it as a defense? What challenges would he face?

B. Incarceration

State v. Cross, 58 Ohio St. 2d 482 (1979)

*** On November 1, 1977, appellant, Richard E. Cross, was arrested on a charge of aggravated arson and detained in the Belmont County jail where he remained in lieu of bond while awaiting trial. On December 23, 1977, he left the jail without authorization. Appellant made his escape through a hole in a fire door that had been made by two other prisoners. Appellant's reasons for leaving the jail were that "(i)t was so cold in there, you couldn't stand it," "(i)t was colder in there than it was outside," "(t)hey did not have no heat," the jail "hardly had any water," and because "I didn't have no lawyer; didn't know anything about my case." Generally it can be said that the appellant felt that his health, safety and legal interests were being neglected by prison officials.

The appellant fled to Mexico but returned to California and turned himself in to authorities on January 13, 1978. Appellant waived extradition and was returned to the Belmont County Jail. He was charged with violating R.C. 2921.34.

On June 6 and 7, 1978, a jury trial was held on the escape charge, and appellant's counsel attempted to introduce and proffer certain grand jury reports and other evidence of alleged inhumane conditions at the Belmont County jail as a basis for asserting the affirmative defense of "necessity" or "duress."

The trial court, however, excluded such evidence as immaterial and refused to charge the jury upon the affirmative defense of necessity as a defense to escape. A unanimous jury verdict of guilty was returned, and the defendant was sentenced to not less than eighteen months and not more than five years imprisonment.

Upon appeal to the Court of Appeals, the judgment of the trial court was affirmed on the grounds that Ohio "does not recognize any affirmative defense to a charge of breaking jail if the detention is pursuant to judicial order or in a detention facility." The Court of Appeals felt the language of R.C. 2921.34 ruled out a defense of necessity. Finding its judgment to be in conflict with a judgment of the Court of Appeals for Scioto County in *State v. Procter* (1977), 51 Ohio App. 2d 151, the Court of Appeals certified the record of the case to this court for review and final determination.

WILLIAM B. BROWN, Justice.

Appellant raises two issues in this appeal. He argues that the jury should have been instructed concerning the common-law defense of necessity as set forth in *People v. Lovercamp* (1974), 43 Cal. App. 3d 823, and that the phrase "(i)n the case of any other detention," found in R.C. 2921.34(B), is so vague, arbitrary and unreasonable as to be an unconstitutional denial of due process under the 14th Amendment to the United States Constitution.

I

We must first decide whether the affirmative defense of necessity or duress is precluded because of the language of the escape statute, R.C. 2921.34, and then decide whether the evidence presented is sufficient as a matter of law to establish such a defense.

In attempting to determine whether R.C. 2921.34(B) prohibits raising the affirmative defense of necessity or duress, we find *State v. Procter, supra*, to be helpful. In *Procter*, Judge Stephenson stated, 51 Ohio App. 2d at page 158:

> *** The evident purpose of this section is to negate such decisions as *State v. Ferguson* (1955), 100 Ohio App. 191, which holds, in substance, that a prisoner has a right to escape if his confinement is unlawful. In precluding irregularities in bringing about or maintaining detention or lack of jurisdiction as a defense, the General Assembly intended that such matters were to be remedied by means other than self help through escape.

We do not perceive, either expressly or by implication, a legislative intent therein to statutorily negate a duress defense.

We agree with these perceptions and add that the language of R.C. 2921.34(B) specifically refers to two particular defenses, i.e., irregularity in bringing about or maintaining detention or lack of jurisdiction of the detaining authority, but it does not disallow the common-law affirmative defense of necessity or duress.

In making this determination, we are involved in a balancing process. Appellant contends that intolerable, deplorable, unsanitary prison conditions provide justification for a prison escape. Yet in order to prevent mass self-help releases, we must strike a balance between the interests of society and the interests of the defendant. We agree with the reasoning set forth in *Lovercamp, supra*, 43 Cal. App. 3d at page 827, where the court stated:

> In a humane society some attention must be given to the individual dilemma. In doing so the court must use extreme caution lest the overriding interest of the public be overlooked. The question that must be resolved involves looking to all the choices available to the defendant and then determining whether the act of escape was the only viable and reasonable choice available. By doing so, both the public's interest and the individual's interest may adequately be protected. In our ultimate conclusion it will be seen that we have adopted a position which gives reasonable consideration to both interests. While we conclude that under certain circumstances a defense of necessity may be proven by the defendant, at the same time we place rigid limitations on the viability of the defense in order to insure that the rights and interests of society will not be impinged upon. ***

The restrictions and conditions we would place upon a defense of necessity or duress are adequately set forth in defendant's proposed jury instruction. Applying the rules set forth therein to the proffered evidence and viewing the evidence most favorably to the appellant, we find no specific threat of death, forcible sexual attack or substantial bodily impairment in the defendant's immediate future. At most, the evidence reveals that appellant complained of a common cold, and that in the past when he needed medical attention, he was taken to the Martins Ferry hospital for treatment.

We are not faced with a situation where an inmate may be forced to flee a burning prison to save his life (1 *Hale's Pleas of the Crown* 611 (1778)); or a situation where an inmate must choose between death, beating or homosexual advances (*Lovercamp, supra*). The evidence reveals that the conditions were not desirable, and that there was no substantial health impairment. We concur with other courts which have held that undesirable prison conditions are not sufficient to justify an escape or make one necessary. *State v. Worley* (1975), 265 S.C. 551, and cases cited in Annotation 69 A.L.R.3d 678, 689 Et seq.

One of the essential features of a necessity or duress defense is the sense of present, imminent, immediate and impending death, or serious bodily injury. *See State v. Sappienza* (1911), 84 Ohio St. 63. There is no such evidence in the present cause, for the defendant simply had a cold, saw an opening and escaped. A common cold is hardly a substantial health impairment that affected his health in an imminent way.

Neither do we find that he made any complaints to the authorities about the alleged heat and water conditions. Appellant argues that complaining would have been futile because no action had been taken even after the grand jury reports concerning prison conditions had been issued. In any event, the reports referred to lack of thermostatic temperature control and did not mention any significant lack of water.

Moreover, there was ample time and the means available to resort to the legal system. Escape was not the only viable and reasonable choice available. Appellant had access to the courts through R.C. 2921.44 and 2921.45. In addition, appellant complained that he was without counsel, and he knew nothing about the aggravated arson charge. The evidence shows that he made several phone calls during his incarceration. He was not denied access to the phone. If he wanted a lawyer, he could have called one or had a friend or relative do it.

The Coup de grace is the fact that appellant failed to turn himself in immediately after fleeing the supposed intolerable conditions. This makes it very clear what the defendant's intentions were and that he purposely escaped to flee the system and for no other reason. He fled to Mexico and only after three weeks did he turn himself into California authorities. If an affirmative defense can be raised to an escape charge, this is certainly not the case to raise it. Here, appellant saw a chance to escape and did so, and he only turned himself in because he realized he had "done wrong" and wanted to "get this mess straightened up." As a matter of law, we find that the defendant failed to produce evidence of a nature and quality sufficient to raise his defense.

We reemphasize the position taken in *Lovercamp, supra*, concerning reporting to the proper authorities. It must be understood that the defense of necessity or duress is strictly and extremely limited in application and will probably be effective in very rare occasions. It is a defense and not a conjured afterthought. All the conditions must be met, and the court must find as a matter of law that the evidence is sufficient to warrant an instruction on the affirmative defense of necessity or duress. The court may refuse to give an instruction which is not applicable to the evidence governing the case, or which is incorrect.

Callahan v. State (1871), 21 Ohio St. 306; 15A Ohio Jurisprudence 2d 550, Criminal Practice and Procedure, Section 460.***

Notes and Questions

1. If the defendant in *State v. Cross* had complained to prison authorities about his conditions and they took no action to remedy the situation, could the defendant then assert a necessity defense to the crime of escape? What if he also immediately turned himself in after escaping?

C. Homicide

State v. Grinnell, 678 N.E. 2d 231 (1996)

On April 11, 1993, a riot occurred at the Southern Ohio Correctional Facility ("Lucasville") located in Lucasville, Ohio. The riot began in mid-afternoon when a group of prisoners, who were returning to their cells from a recreation area, attacked several guards.

The prison complex at Lucasville has three main residential areas designated J-Block, K-Block and L-Block. The residential area designated L-Block is entered by passing through two large gates to a main corridor with a large gym at the end. Between the second gate and the gym, cell block ranges run off the main corridor. There are eight such ranges in L-Block, numbered L-1 through L-8. Each cell block range contains eighty cells, with twenty cells located on a lower left-hand level, twenty cells located on a lower right-hand level, twenty cells located in an upper left-hand level, and twenty cells located in an upper right-hand level. At the front of each cell block range is a console which consists of two panels with electric switches to open and close all of the doors to the cells and showers. The console area can accommodate two to three people and is designed to give a view of the entire cell block area. From the console, the operator can see the area in front of each cell door, but not necessarily into each cell.

The riot was apparently planned and instigated by a group of Muslim prisoners. The rioting prisoners seized control of various cell ranges. The events which gave rise to the charges against appellant, Timothy Grinnell, occurred in the L-6 cell block.

The Muslims were in control of the L-6 cell block, while other groups were in control of the other cell blocks. At the time the riot began, a number of things occurred simultaneously. When the inmates first took control, all of the prisoners held in L-6 were ordered out of their cells and into the corridor. Then various other prisoners were locked into the cells, allegedly for their own safety and protection, by the Muslims. Thereafter, permission had to be obtained from the inmates in charge of L-6 to enter or leave the area.

At some time on April 11, another group of seven to ten prisoners, who were not Muslims and who were also known as "the death squad," entered L-6, apparently led by Keith Lamar ("Lamar group"), with the intent of killing some of the prisoners housed in the cells in L-6 who were thought to be snitches (informers). The Lamar group was allowed to enter the L-6 area by the Muslim leaders. As the Lamar group went from cell to cell, appellant operated the console and opened the cell doors as requested by the Lamar group. The opening of the cell doors allowed the Lamar group access to various inmates, who were then beaten. Two inmates, Darrell Depina and Albert Staiano, were beaten to death. At one point, the Lamar group approached a cell holding five inmates, and demanded that appellant open the cell door; however, appellant refused and the Lamar group moved on.

Eventually the inmates surrendered and the state regained control of L-Block on April 22, 1993. As a result of his participation in the riot, appellant was indicted and charged with two counts of aggravated murder in connection with the deaths of Depina and Staiano. After a trial in which the jury found appellant guilty of both counts, he was sentenced to twenty years to life on each charge. Appellant filed a timely notice of appeal and sets forth the following assignments of error***

In his fourth assignment of error, appellant contends that the trial court erred by failing to instruct the jury that duress is a defense to murder. Appellant relies on *State v. Woods* (1976), 48 Ohio St. 2d 127 to support his contention that the jury should have been instructed that duress is a defense to murder; however, this court finds that this reliance is misplaced. In *Woods,* the Ohio Supreme Court recognized that duress or coercion as used in R.C. 2929.04(B), stating criteria for imposing death or imprisonment for a capital offense, could be used in mitigation to reduce a sentence of death to life imprisonment. *Woods* also recognized that, if the defense of duress is proved with regard to the felony underlying the aggravated murder charge, a defendant is only guilty of murder and not aggravated murder. *Woods,* however, did not recognize duress as an affirmative defense to murder. While *Woods* acknowledged that the issue has not been specifically decided in Ohio, the court noted, at 135, 2 O.O.3d at 293:

> There is strong precedent for holding that duress is not a defense to murder, but that question has not been decided in Ohio. At common law, no person can excuse himself for taking the life of an innocent person on the grounds of duress.

Here, appellant was charged with aggravated murder pursuant to R.C. 2903.01(A), not 2903.01(B). Thus, there was no underlying felony to which the defense of duress could be raised, and the state did not seek the death penalty for appellant.

Even if this court would assume that duress was available as a defense, the trial court correctly refused to give the instruction. Jury instructions which are correct, pertinent and presented in a timely manner must be included in substance in the general charge to the jury. State v. Barron (1960), 170 Ohio St. 267. However, abstract rules of law or general propositions, even though correct, should not be given unless they are specifically applicable to the facts in a given case. State v. Guster (1981), 66 Ohio St. 2d 266.

Duress consists of any conduct which overpowers a person's will and coerces or constrains his performance of an act which he otherwise would not have performed. Consequently, one who, under the pressure of a threat from another person, commits what would otherwise be a crime may, under certain circumstances, be justified in committing the act and not be guilty of the crime.

One of the essential features of the defense of duress is the sense of immediate, imminent death or serious bodily injury if the actor does not commit the act as instructed. See State v. Cross (1979), 58 Ohio St. 2d 482. The force used to compel the actor's conduct must remain constant, controlling the will of the unwilling actor during the entire time he commits the act, and must be of such a nature that the actor cannot safely withdraw. See State v. Good (1960), 110 Ohio App. 41.

Jackson and Elmore, two inmates who testified on behalf of appellant, both stated that he was threatened by Gordon. Jackson testified:

> Initially started like this. Grinnell was telling Inmate Stacey Gordon, I found out his name later on, I found out his name was Nabil, but Muslim name was Abraham. And he was arguing with Grinnell. Grinnell was telling him he couldn't come in here with his group and Stacey told Grinnell that you will do what we say do or we will deal with you, too, just go over there by that console. That's what I heard.

Elmore testified:

> So as I was looking around, and Stacey Gordon was ordering everybody out the block, but before he did that, he went over to Grinnell and told him to work the control panel or you know what will happen to you or else.

In *Woods,* the court stated:

> "In determining whether a course of conduct results in duress, the question is not what effect such conduct would have upon an ordinary man but rather the effect upon the particular person toward whom such conduct is directed, and in determining such effect the age, sex, health and mental condition of the person affected, the relationship of the parties and all the surrounding circumstances may be considered." 48 Ohio St. 2d at 135-136.

Based on the foregoing, this court finds that appellant has not shown that his criminal conduct occurred as a result of a continuous threat from another person which, because of his fear of bodily harm or death, controlled his will and compelled him to open the various cell doors. There is no evidence in the record as to whether appellant took the alleged threat by Gordon seriously, and appellant's other actions belie his claim that he acted under duress or coercion. Various inmates testified that appellant gave orders to other inmates not to leave L-6 and, instead, ordered them to act as guards or lookouts in the cell block area, ordered inmates to clean up the area where other inmates had been beaten and killed, ordered where various inmates and corrections officers should be held, and most significantly, refused access to a cell holding Trocadoro and his group, which refusal was accepted by the Lamar group.

Thus, in this case, the evidence would show that, rather than acting under duress and coercion, appellant was a willing participant in the riot and had a role of some authority. Even assuming, *arguendo,* duress to be a valid defense, this court finds that appellant has not proved by a preponderance of the evidence that his conduct is excused or justified because he was acting under the pressure of a threat from another person who would harm him if he did not do as he was told. Appellant's fourth assignment of error is overruled.***

Notes and Questions

1. At common law, duress was not a defense to murder. *State v. Grinnell* follows that common law precedent. However, the court in *Grinnell* goes on to say that the "appellant was charged with aggravated murder pursuant to R.C. 2903.01(A), not 2903.01(B). Thus, there was no underlying felony to which the defense of duress could be raised." What does the court mean by this statement? Can duress actually serve as a defense for felony murder charges? If so, how?

2. Should either duress or necessity ever be a defense to murder? Reconsider *Regina v. Dudley and Stephens* discussed at the beginning of this book. Do you

think that either Dudley or Stephens should have been allowed to raise the defense of necessity to their murder charges?

MODEL PENAL CODE

PART I. GENERAL PROVISIONS

Article 1. Preliminary

SECTION 1.01.   [Omitted]

SECTION 1.02.   PURPOSES; PRINCIPLES OF CONSTRUCTION

(1) The general purposes of the provisions governing the definition of offenses are:

> (a) to forbid and prevent conduct that unjustifiably and inexcusably inflicts or threatens substantial harm to individual
> or public interests;

> (b) to subject to public control persons whose conduct indicates that they are disposed to commit crimes;

> (c) to safeguard conduct that is without fault from condemnation as criminal;

> (d) to give fair warning of the nature of the conduct declared to constitute an offense;

> (e) to differentiate on reasonable grounds between serious and minor offenses.

(2) The general purposes of the provisions governing the sentencing and treatment of offenders are:

> (a) to prevent the commission of offenses;

> (b) to promote the correction and rehabilitation of offenders;

> (c) to safeguard offenders against excessive, disproportionate or arbitrary punishment;

(d) to give fair warning of the nature of the sentences that may be imposed on conviction of an offense;

(e) to differentiate among offenders with a view to a just individualization in their treatment;

(f) to define, coordinate and harmonize the powers, duties and functions of the courts and of administrative officers and agencies responsible for dealing with offenders;

(g) to advance the use of generally accepted scientific methods and knowledge in the sentencing and treatment of offenders;

(h) to integrate responsibility for the administration of the correctional system in a State Department of Correction [or other single department or agency].

(3) The provisions of the Code shall be construed according to the fair import of their terms but when the language is susceptible of differing constructions it shall be interpreted to further the general purposes stated in this Section and the special purposes of the particular provision involved. The discretionary powers conferred by the Code shall be exercised in accordance with the criteria stated in the Code and, insofar as such criteria are not decisive, to further the general purposes stated in this Section.

SECTION 1.03. [Omitted]

SECTION 1.04. CLASSES OF CRIMES; VIOLATIONS

(1) An offense defined by this Code or by any other statute of this State, for which a sentence of [death or of] imprisonment is authorized, constitutes a crime. Crimes are classified as felonies, misdemeanors or petty misdemeanors.

(2) A crime is a felony if it is so designated in this Code or if persons convicted thereof may be sentenced [to death or] to imprisonment for a term that, apart from an extended term, is in excess of one year.

(3) A crime is a misdemeanor if it is so designated in this Code or in a statute other than this Code enacted subsequent thereto.

(4) A crime is a petty misdemeanor if it is so designated in this Code or in a statute other than this Code enacted subsequent thereto or if it is defined by a

statute other than this Code that now provides that persons convicted thereof may be sentenced to imprisonment for a term of which the maximum is less than one year.

(5) An offense defined by this Code or by any other statute of this State constitutes a violation if it is so designated in this Code or in the law defining the offense or if no other sentence than a fine, or fine and forfeiture or other civil penalty is authorized upon conviction or if it is defined by a statute other than this Code that now provides that the offense shall not constitute a crime. A violation does not constitute a crime and conviction of a violation shall not give rise to any disability or legal disadvantage based on conviction of a criminal offense.

(6) Any offense declared by law to constitute a crime, without specification of the grade thereof or of the sentence authorized upon conviction, is a misdemeanor.

(7) An offense defined by any statute of this State other than this Code shall be classified as provided in this Section and the sentence that may be imposed upon conviction thereof shall hereafter be governed by this Code.

SECTION 1.05. ALL OFFENSES DEFINED BY STATUTE; APPLICATION OF GENERAL PROVISIONS OF THE CODE

(1) No conduct constitutes an offense unless it is a crime or violation under this Code or another statute of this State.

(2) The provisions of Part I of the Code are applicable to offenses defined by other statutes, unless the Code otherwise provides.

(3) This Section does not affect the power of a court to punish for contempt or to employ any sanction authorized by law for the enforcement of an order or a civil judgment or decree.

SECTION 1.06. [Omitted]

SECTION 1.07. METHOD OF PROSECUTION WHEN CONDUCT CONSTITUTES MORE THAN ONE OFFENSE

(1) **Prosecution for Multiple Offenses; Limitation on Convictions**. When the same conduct of a defendant may establish the commission of more than one

offense, the defendant may be prosecuted for each such offense. He may not, however, be convicted of more than one offense if:

(a) one offense is included in the other, as defined in Subsection (4) of this Section; or

(b) one offense consists only of a conspiracy or other form of preparation to commit the other; or

(c) inconsistent findings of fact are required to establish the commission of the offenses; or

(d) the offenses differ only in that one is defined to prohibit a designated kind of conduct generally and the other to prohibit a specific instance of such conduct; or

(e) the offense is defined as a continuing course of conduct and the defendant's course of conduct was uninterrupted, unless the law provides that specific periods of such conduct constitute separate offenses.

(2) **Limitation on Separate Trials for Multiple Offenses**. Except as provided in Subsection (3) of this Section, a defendant shall not be subject to separate trials for multiple offenses based on the same conduct or arising from the same criminal episode, if such offenses are known to the appropriate prosecuting officer at the time of the commencement of the first trial and are within the jurisdiction of a single court.

(3) **Authority of Court to Order Separate Trials**. When a defendant is charged with two or more offenses based on the same conduct or arising from the same criminal episode, the Court, on application of the prosecuting attorney or of the defendant, may order any such charge to be tried separately, if it is satisfied that justice so requires.

(4) **Conviction of Included Offense Permitted**. A defendant may be convicted of an offense included in an offense charged in the indictment [or the information]. An offense is so included when:

(a) it is established by proof of the same or less than all the facts required to establish the commission of the offense charged; or

(b) it consists of an attempt or solicitation to commit the offense charged or to commit an offense otherwise included therein; or

(c) it differs from the offense charged only in the respect that a less serious injury or risk of injury to the same person, property or public interest or a lesser kind of culpability suffices to establish its commission.

(5) **Submission of Included Offense to Jury.** The Court shall not be obligated to charge the jury with respect to an included offense unless there is a rational basis for a verdict acquitting the defendant of the offense charged and convicting him of the included offense.

SECTIONS 1.08-1.11.   [Omitted]

SECTION 1.12 PROOF BEYOND A REASONABLE DOUBT; AFFIRMATIVE DEFENSES; BURDEN OF PROVING FACT WHEN NOT AN ELEMENT OF AN OFFENSE; PRESUMPTIONS

(1) No person may be convicted of an offense unless each element of such offense is proved beyond a reasonable doubt. In the absence of such proof, the innocence of the defendant is assumed.

(2) Subsection (1) of this Section does not: (a) require the disproof of an affirmative defense unless and until there is evidence supporting such defense; or (b) apply to any defense that the Code or another statute plainly requires the defendant to prove by a preponderance of evidence.

(3) A ground of defense is affirmative, within the meaning of Subsection (2)(a) of this Section, when:

(a) it arises under a section of the Code that so provides; or

(b) it relates to an offense defined by a statute other than the Code and such statute so provides; or

(c) it involves a matter of excuse or justification peculiarly within the knowledge of the defendant on which he can fairly be required to adduce supporting evidence.

(4) When the application of the Code depends upon the finding of a fact that is not an element of an offense, unless the Code otherwise provides:

(a) the burden of proving the fact is on the prosecution or defendant, depending on whose interest or contention will be furthered if the finding should be made; and

(b) the fact must be proved to the satisfaction of the Court or jury, as the case may be.

(5) When the Code establishes a presumption with respect to any fact that is an element of an offense, it has the following consequences:

(a) when there is evidence of the facts that give rise to the presumption, the issue of the existence of the presumed fact must be submitted to the jury, unless the Court is satisfied that the evidence as a whole clearly negatives the presumedfact; and

(b) when the issue of the existence of the presumed fact is submitted to the jury, the Court shall charge that while the presumed fact must, on all the evidence, be proved beyond a reasonable doubt, the law declares that the jury may regard the facts giving rise to the presumption as sufficient evidence of the presumed fact.

(6) A presumption not established by the Code or inconsistent with it has the consequences otherwise accorded it by law.

SECTION 1.13.   GENERAL DEFINITIONS

In this Code, unless a different meaning plainly is required:

(1) "statute" includes the Constitution and a local law or ordinance of a political subdivision of the State;

(2) "act" or "action" means a bodily movement whether voluntary or involuntary;

(3) "voluntary" has the meaning specified in Section 2.01;

(4) "omission" means a failure to act;

(5) "conduct" means an action or omission and its accompanying state of mind, or, where relevant, a series of acts and omissions;

(6) "actor" includes, where relevant, a person guilty of an omission;

(7) "acted" includes, where relevant, "omitted to act";

(8) "person," "he" and "actor" include any natural person and, where relevant, a corporation or an unincorporated

(9) "element of an offense" means (i) such conduct or (ii) such attendant circumstances or (iii) such a result of conduct as

(a) is included in the description of the forbidden conduct in the definition of the offense; or

(b) establishes the required kind of culpability; or

(c) negatives an excuse or justification for such conduct; or

(d) negatives a defense under the statute of limitations; or

(e) establishes jurisdiction or venue;

(10) "material element of an offense" means an element that does not relate exclusively to the statute of limitations, jurisdiction, venue, or to any other matter similarly unconnected with (i) the harm or evil, incident to conduct, sought to be prevented by the law defining the offense, or (ii) the existence of a justification or excuse for such conduct;

(11) "purposely" has the meaning specified in Section 2.02 and equivalent terms such as "with purpose," "designed" or "with design" have the same meaning;

(12) "intentionally" or "with intent" means purposely;

(13) "knowingly" has the meaning specified in Section 2.02 and equivalent terms such as "knowing" or "with knowledge" have the same meaning;

(14) "recklessly" has the meaning specified in Section 2.02 and equivalent terms such as "recklessness" or "with recklessness" have the same meaning;

(15) "negligently" has the meaning specified in Section 2.02 and equivalent terms such as "negligence" or "with negligence" have the same meaning;

(16) "reasonably believes" or "reasonable belief" designates a belief that the actor is not reckless or negligent in holding.

Article 2. General Principles of Liability

SECTION 2.01. REQUIREMENTS OF VOLUNTARY ACT: OMISSION AS BASIS OF LIABILITY; POSSESSION AS AN ACT

(1) A person is not guilty of an offense unless his liability is based on conduct that includes a voluntary act or the omission to perform an act of which he is physically capable.

(2) The following are not voluntary acts within the meaning of this Section:

(a) a reflex or convulsion;

(b) a bodily movement during unconsciousness or sleep;

(c) conduct during hypnosis or resulting from hypnotic suggestion;

(d) a bodily movement that otherwise is not a product of the effort or determination of the actor, either conscious or habitual.

(3) Liability for the commission of an offense may not be based on an omission unaccompanied by action unless:

(a) the omission is expressly made sufficient by the law defining the offense; or

(b) a duty to perform the omitted act is otherwise imposed by law.

(4) Possession is an act, within the meaning of this Section, if the possessor knowingly procured or received the thing possessed or was aware of

his control thereof for a sufficient period to have been able to terminate his possession.

SECTION 2.02 GENERAL REQUIREMENTS OF CULPABILITY

(1) **Minimum Requirements of Culpability.** Except as provided in Section 2.05, a person is not guilty of an offense unless he acted purposely, knowingly, recklessly or negligently, as the law may require, with respect to each material element of the offense.

(2) **Kinds of Culpability Defined.**

(a) **Purposely**. A person acts purposely with respect to a material element of an offense when:

(i) if the element involves the nature of his conduct or a result thereof, it is his conscious object to engage in conduct of that nature or to cause such a result; and

(ii) if the element involves the attendant circumstances, he is aware of the existence of such circumstances or he believes or hopes that they exist.

(b) **Knowingly**. A person acts knowingly with respect to a material element of an offense when:

(i) if the element involves the nature of his conduct or the attendant circumstances, he is aware that his conduct is of that nature or that such circumstances exist; and

(ii) if the element involves a result of his conduct, he is aware that it is practically certain that his conduct will cause such a result.

(c) **Recklessly**. A person acts recklessly with respect to a material element of an offense when he consciously disregards a substantial and unjustifiable risk that the material element exists or will result from his conduct. The risk must be of such a nature and degree that, considering the nature and purpose of the actor's conduct and the circumstances known to him, its disregard involves a gross deviation from the standard of conduct that a law-abiding person would observe in the actor's situation.

(d) **Negligently.** A person acts negligently with respect to a material element of an offense when he should be aware of a substantial and unjustifiable risk that the material element exists or will result from his conduct. The risk must be of such a nature and degree that the actor's failure to perceive it, considering the nature and purpose of his conduct and the circumstances known to him, involves a gross deviation from the standard of care that a reasonable person would observe in the actor's situation.

(3) **Culpability Required Unless Otherwise Provided.** When the culpability sufficient to establish a material element of an offense is not prescribed by law, such element is established if a person acts purposely, knowingly or recklessly with respect thereto.

(4) **Prescribed Culpability Requirement Applies to All Material Elements.** When the law defining an offense prescribes the kind of culpability that is sufficient for the commission of an offense, without distinguishing among the material elements thereof, such provision shall apply to all the material elements of the offense, unless a contrary purpose plainly appears.

(5) **Substitutes for Negligence, Recklessness and Knowledge.** When the law provides that negligence suffices to establish an element of an offense, such element also is established if a person acts purposely, knowingly or recklessly. When recklessness suffices to establish an element, such element also is established if a person acts purposely or knowingly. When acting knowingly suffices to establish an element, such element also is established if a person acts purposely.

(6) **Requirement of Purpose Satisfied if Purpose Is Conditional.** When a particular purpose is an element of an offense, the element is established although such purpose is conditional, unless the condition negatives the harm or evil sought to be prevented by the law defining the offense.

(7) **Requirement of Knowledge Satisfied by Knowledge of High Probability.** When knowledge of the existence of a particular fact is an element of an offense, such knowledge is established if a person is aware of a high probability of its existence, unless he actually believes that it does not exist.

(8) **Requirement of Wilfulness Satisfied by Acting Knowingly.** A requirement that an offense be committed wilfully is satisfied if a person acts

knowingly with respect to the material elements of the offense, unless a purpose to impose further requirements appears.

(9) **Culpability as to Illegality of Conduct**. Neither knowledge nor recklessness or negligence as to whether conduct constitutes an offense or as to the existence, meaning or application of the law determining the elements of an offense is an element of such offense, unless the definition of the offense or the Code so provides.

(10) **Culpability as Determinant of Grade of Offense**. When the grade or degree of an offense depends on whether the offense is committed purposely, knowingly, recklessly or negligently, its grade or degree shall be the lowest for which the determinative kind of culpability is established with respect to any material element of the offense.

SECTION 2.03   CAUSAL RELATIONSHIP BETWEEN CONDUCT AND RESULT; DIVERGENCE BETWEEN RESULT DESIGNED OR CONTEMPLATED AND ACTUAL RESULT OR BETWEEN PROBABLE AND ACTUAL RESULT

(1) Conduct is the cause of a result when:

(a) it is an antecedent but for which the result in question would not have occurred; and

(b) the relationship between the conduct and result satisfies any additional causal requirements imposed by the Code or by the law defining the offense.

(2) When purposely or knowingly causing a particular result is an element of an offense, the element is not established if the actual result is not within the purpose or the contemplation of the actor unless:

(a) the actual result differs from that designed or contemplated, as the case may be, only in the respect that a different person or different property is injured or affected or that the injury or harm designed or contemplated would have been more serious or more extensive than that caused; or

(b) the actual result involves the same kind of injury or harm as that designed or contemplated and is not too remote or accidental in its occurrence to have a [just] bearing on the actor's liability or on the gravity of his offense.

(3) When recklessly or negligently causing a particular result is an element of an offense, the element is not established if the actual result is not within the risk of which the actor is aware or, in the case of negligence, of which he should be aware unless:

(a) the actual result differs from the probable result only in the respect that a different person or different property is injured or affected or that the probable injury or harm would have been more serious or more extensive than that caused; or

(b) the actual result involves the same kind of injury or harm as the probable result and is not too remote or accidental in its occurrence to have a [just] bearing on the actor's liability or on the gravity of his offense.

(4) When causing a particular result is a material element of an offense for which absolute liability is imposed by law, the element is not established unless the actual result is a probable consequence of the actor's conduct.

SECTION 2.04   IGNORANCE OR MISTAKE

(1) Ignorance or mistake as to a matter of fact or law is a defense if:

(a) the ignorance or mistake negatives the purpose, knowledge, belief, recklessness or negligence required to establish a material element of the offense; or

(b) the law provides that the state of mind established by such ignorance or mistake constitutes a defense.

(2) Although ignorance or mistake would otherwise afford a defense to the offense charged, the defense is not available if the defendant would be guilty of another offense had the situation been as he supposed. In such case, however, the ignorance or mistake of the defendant shall reduce the grade and degree of the offense of which he may be convicted to those of the offense of which he would be guilty had the situation been as he supposed.

(3) A belief that conduct does not legally constitute an offense is a defense to a prosecution for that offense based upon such conduct when:

(a) the statute or other enactment defining the offense is not known to the actor and has not been published or otherwise reasonably made available prior to the conduct alleged; or

(b) he acts in reasonable reliance upon an official statement of the law, afterward determined to be invalid or erroneous, contained in (i) a statute or other enactment; (ii) a judicial decision, opinion or judgment; (iii) an administrative order or grant of permission; or (iv) an official interpretation of the public officer or body charged by law with responsibility for the interpretation, administration or enforcement of the law defining the offense.

(4) The defendant must prove a defense arising under Subsection (3) of this Section by a preponderance of evidence.

SECTION 2.05. WHEN CULPABILITY REQUIREMENTS ARE INAPPLICABLE TO VIOLATIONS AND TO OFFENSES DEFINED BY OTHER STATUTES; EFFECT OF ABSOLUTE LIABILITY IN REDUCING GRADE OF OFFENSE TO VIOLATION

(1) The requirements of culpability prescribed by Sections 2.01 and 2.02 do not apply to:

(a) offenses that constitute violations, unless the requirement involved is included in the definition of the offense or the Court determines that its application is consistent with effective enforcement of the law defining the offense; or

(b) offenses defined by statutes other than the Code, insofar as a legislative purpose to impose absolute liability for such offenses or with respect to any material element thereof plainly appears.

(2) Notwithstanding any other provision of existing law and unless a subsequent statute otherwise provides:

(a) when absolute liability is imposed with respect to any material element of an offense defined by a statute other than the Code and a conviction is based upon such liability, the offense constitutes a violation; and

(b) although absolute liability is imposed by law with respect to one or more of the material elements of an offense defined by a statute other than the Code, the culpable commission of the offense may be charged and proved, in which event negligence with respect to such elements constitutes sufficient culpability and the classification of the offense and the sentence that may be imposed therefor upon conviction are determined by Section 1.04 and Article 6 of the Code.

(1) A person is guilty of an offense if it is committed by his own conduct or by the conduct of another person for which he is legally accountable, or both.

(2) A person is legally accountable for the conduct of another person when:

(a) acting with the kind of culpability that is sufficient for the commission of the offense, he causes an innocent or irresponsible person to engage in such conduct; or

(b) he is made accountable for the conduct of such other person by the Code or by the law defining the offense; or

(c) he is an accomplice of such other person in the commission of the offense.

(3) A person is an accomplice of another person in the commission of an offense if:

(a) with the purpose of promoting or facilitating the commission of the offense, he (i) solicits such other person to commit it, or (ii) aids or agrees or attempts to aid such other person in planning or committing it, or (iii) having a legal duty to prevent the commission of the offense, fails to make proper effort so to do; or

(b) his conduct is expressly declared by law to establish his complicity.

(4) When causing a particular result is an element of an offense, an accomplice in the conduct causing such result is an accomplice in the commission of that offense if he acts with the kind of culpability, if any, with respect to that result that is sufficient for the commission of the offense.

(5) A person who is legally incapable of committing a particular offense himself may be guilty thereof if it is committed by the conduct of another person for which he is legally accountable, unless such liability is inconsistent with the purpose of the provision establishing his incapacity.

(6) Unless otherwise provided by the Code or by the law defining the offense, a person is not an accomplice in an offense committed by another person if:

    (a) he is a victim of that offense; or

    (b) the offense is so defined that his conduct is inevitably incident to its commission; or

    (c) he terminates his complicity prior to the commission of the offense and

        (i) wholly deprives it of effectiveness in the commission of the offense; or

        (ii) gives timely warning to the law enforcement authorities or otherwise makes proper effort to prevent the commission of the offense.

(7) An accomplice may be convicted on proof of the commission of the offense and of his complicity therein, though the person claimed to have committed the offense has not been prosecuted or convicted or has been convicted of a different offense or degree of offense or has an immunity to prosecution or conviction or has been acquitted.

SECTION 2.07: LIABILITY OF CORPORATIONS, UNINCORPORATED ASSOCATIONS AND PERSONS ACTING, OR UNDER A DUTY TO ACT, IN THEIR BEHALF

    (1) A corporation may be convicted of the commission of an offense if:

        (a) the offense is a violation or the offense is defined by a statute other than the Code in which a legislative purpose to impose liability on corporations plainly appears and the conduct is performed by an agent of the corporation acting in behalf of the corporation within the scope of his office or employment, except that if the law defining the offense designates the agents for whose conduct the corporation is accountable or the circumstances under which it is accountable, such provisions shall apply; or

        (b) the offense consists of an omission to discharge a specific duty of affirmative performance imposed on corporations by law; or

        (c) the commission of the offense was authorized, requested, commanded, performed or recklessly tolerated by the board of directors or by a high managerial agent acting in behalf of the corporation within the scope of his office or employment.

(2) When absolute liability is imposed for the commission of an offense, a legislative purpose to impose liability on a corporation shall be assumed, unless the contrary plainly appears.

(3) An unincorporated association may be convicted of the commission of an offense if:

> (a) the offense is defined by a statute other than the Code that expressly provides for the liability of such an association and the conduct is performed by an agent of the association acting in behalf of the association within the scope of his office or employment, except that if the law defining the offense designates the agents for whose conduct the association is accountable or the circumstances under which it is accountable, such provisions shall apply; or

> (b) the offense consists of an omission to discharge a specific duty of affirmative performance imposed on associations by law.

> (c) the commission of the offense was authorized, requested, commanded, performed or recklessly tolerated by the board of directors or by a high managerial agent acting in behalf of the corporation within the scope of his office or employment.

(2) When absolute liability is imposed for the commission of an offense, a legislative purpose to impose liability on a corporation shall be assumed, unless the contrary plainly appears.

(3) An unincorporated association may be convicted of the commission of an offense if:

> (a) the offense is defined by a statute other than the Code that expressly provides for the liability of such an association and the conduct is performed by an agent of the association acting in behalf of the association within the scope of his office or employment, except that if the law defining the offense designates the agents for whose conduct the association is accountable or the circumstances under which it is accountable, such provisions shall apply; or

(b) the offense consists of an omission to discharge a specific duty of affirmative performance imposed on associations by law.

(4) As used in this Section:

(a) "corporation" does not include an entity organized as or by a governmental agency for the execution of a governmental program;

(b) "agent" means any director, officer, servant, employee or other person authorized to act in behalf of the corporation or association and, in the case of an unincorporated association, a member of such association;

(c) "high managerial agent" means an officer of a corporation or an unincorporated association, or, in the case of a partnership, a partner, or any other agent of a corporation or association having duties of such responsibility that his conduct may fairly be assumed to represent the policy of the corporation or association.

(5) In any prosecution of a corporation or an unincorporated association for the commission of an offense included within the terms of Subsection (1)(a) or Subsection (3)(a) of this Section, other than an offense for which absolute liability has been imposed, it shall be a defense if the defendant proves by a preponderance of evidence that the high managerial agent having supervisory responsibility over the subject matter of the offense employed due diligence to prevent its commission. This paragraph shall not apply if it is plainly inconsistent with the legislative purpose in defining the particular offense.

(6)(a) A person is legally accountable for any conduct he performs or causes to be performed in the name of the corporation or an unincorporated association or in its behalf to the same extent as if it were performed in his own name or behalf.

(b) Whenever a duty to act is imposed by law upon a corporation or an unincorporated association, any agent of the corporation or association having primary responsibility for the discharge of the duty is legally accountable for a reckless omission to perform the required act to the same extent as if the duty were imposed by law directly upon himself.

(c) When a person is convicted of an offense by reason of his legal accountability for the conduct of a corporation or an unincorporated association, he is subject to the sentence authorized by law when a natural person is convicted of an offense of the grade and the degree involved.

SECTION 2.08 INTOXICATION

(1) Except as provided in Subsection (4) of this Section, intoxication of the actor is not a defense unless it negatives an element of the offense.

(2) When recklessness establishes an element of the offense, if the actor, due to self-induced intoxication, is unaware of a risk of which he would have been aware had he been sober, such unawareness is immaterial.

(3) Intoxication does not, in itself, constitute mental disease within the meaning of Section 4.01.

(4) Intoxication that (a) is not self-induced or (b) is pathological is an affirmative defense if by reason of such intoxication the actor at the time of his conduct lacks substantial capacity either to appreciate its criminality [wrongfulness] or to conform his conduct to the requirements of law.

(5) **Definitions**. In this Section unless a different meaning plainly is required:

(a) "intoxication" means a disturbance of mental or physical capacities resulting from the introduction of substances into the body;

(b) "self-induced intoxication" means intoxication caused by substances that the actor knowingly introduces into his body, the tendency of which to cause intoxication he knows or ought to know, unless he introduces them pursuant to medical advice or under such circumstances as would afford a defense to a charge of crime;

(c) "pathological intoxication" means intoxication grossly excessive in degree, given the amount of the intoxicant, to which the actor does not know he is susceptible.

SECTION 2.09. DURESS

(1) It is an affirmative defense that the actor engaged in the conduct charged to constitute an offense because he was coerced to do so by the use of, or a threat to use, unlawful force against his person or the person of another, that a person of reasonable firmness in his situation would have been unable to resist.

(2) The defense provided by this Section is unavailable if the actor recklessly placed himself in a situation in which it was probable that he would be subjected to duress. The defense is also unavailable if he was negligent in placing himself in such a situation, whenever negligence suffices to establish culpability for the offense charged.

(3) It is not a defense that a woman acted on the command of her husband, unless she acted under such coercion as would establish a defense under this Section. [The presumption that a woman acting in the presence of her husband is coerced is abolished.]

(4) When the conduct of the actor would otherwise be justifiable under Section 3.02, this Section does not preclude such defense.

SECTION 2.10   MILITARY ORDERS

It is an affirmative defense that the actor, in engaging in the conduct charged to constitute an offense, does no more than execute an order of his superior in the armed services that he does not know to be unlawful.

SECTION 2.11   CONSENT

(1) **In General**. The consent of the victim to conduct charged to constitute an offense or to the result thereof is a defense if such consent negatives an element of the offense or precludes the infliction of the harm or evil sought to be prevented by the law defining the offense.

(2) **Consent to Bodily Injury**. When conduct is charged to constitute an offense because it causes or threatens bodily injury, consent to such conduct or to the infliction of such injury is a defense if:

> (a) the bodily injury consented to or threatened by the conduct consented to is not serious; or

> (b) the conduct and the injury are reasonably foreseeable hazards of joint participation in a lawful athletic contest or competitive sport or other concerted activity not forbidden by law; or

> (c) the consent establishes a justification for the conduct under Article 3 of the Code.

(3) **Ineffective Consent**. Unless otherwise provided by the Code or by the law defining the offense, assent does not constitute consent if:

(a) it is given by a person who is legally incompetent to authorize the conduct charged to constitute the offense; or

(b) it is given by a person who by reason of youth, mental disease or defect or intoxication is manifestly unable or known by the actor to be unable to make a reasonable judgment as to the nature or harmfulness of the conduct charged to constitute the offense; or

(c) it is given by a person whose improvident consent is sought to be prevented by the law defining the offense; or

(d) it is induced by force, duress or deception of a kind sought to be prevented by the law defining the offense.

SECTION 2.12. DE MINIMIS INFRACTIONS

The Court shall dismiss a prosecution if, having regard to the nature of the conduct charged to constitute an offense and the nature of the attendant circumstances, it finds that the defendant's conduct:

(1) was within a customary license or tolerance, neither expressly negatived by the person whose interest was infringed nor inconsistent with the purpose of the law defining the offense; or

(2) did not actually cause or threaten the harm or evil sought to be prevented by the law defining the offense or did so only to an extent too trivial to warrant the condemnation of conviction; or

(3) presents such other extenuations that it cannot reasonably be regarded as envisaged by the legislature in forbidding the offense.

The Court shall not dismiss a prosecution under Subsection (3) of this Section without filing a written statement of its
reasons.

SECTION 2.13 ENTRAPMENT

(1) A public law enforcement official or a person acting in cooperation with such an official perpetrates an entrapment if for the purpose of obtaining

evidence of the commission of an offense, he induces or encourages another person to engage in conduct constituting such offense by either:

> (a) making knowingly false representations designed to induce the belief that such conduct is not prohibited; or

> (b) employing methods of persuasion or inducement that create a substantial risk that such an offense will be committed by persons other than those who are ready to commit it.

(2) Except as provided in Subsection (3) of this Section, a person prosecuted for an offense shall be acquitted if he proves by a preponderance of evidence that his conduct occurred in response to an entrapment. The issue of entrapment shall be tried by the Court in the absence of the jury.

(3) The defense afforded by this Section is unavailable when causing or threatening bodily injury is an element of the offense charged and the prosecution is based on conduct causing or threatening such injury to a person other than the person perpetrating the entrapment.

Article 3. General Principles of Justification

SECTION 3.01 JUSTIFICATION AN AFFIRMATIVE DEFENSE; CIVIL REMEDIES UNAFFECTED

(1) In any prosecution based on conduct that is justifiable under this Article, justification is an affirmative defense.

(2) The fact that conduct is justifiable under this Article does not abolish or impair any remedy for such conduct that is available in any civil action.

SECTION 3.02 JUSTIFICATION GENERALLY: CHOICE OF EVILS

(1) Conduct that the actor believes to be necessary to avoid a harm or evil to himself or to another is justifiable, provided that:

> (a) the harm or evil sought to be avoided by such conduct is greater than that sought to be prevented by the law defining the offense charged; and

> (b) neither the Code nor other law defining the offense provides exceptions or defenses dealing with the specific situation involved; and

(c) a legislative purpose to exclude the justification claimed does not otherwise plainly appear.

(2) When the actor was reckless or negligent in bringing about the situation requiring a choice of harms or evils or in appraising the necessity for his conduct, the justification afforded by this Section is unavailable in a prosecution for any offense for which recklessness or negligence, as the case may be, suffices to establish culpability.

SECTION 3.03. EXECUTION OF PUBLIC DUTY

(1) Except as provided in Subsection (2) of this Section, conduct is justifiable when it is required or authorized by:

(a) the law defining the duties or functions of a public officer or the assistance to be rendered to such officer in the performance of his duties; or

(b) the law governing the execution of legal process; or

(c) the judgment or order of a competent court or tribunal; or

(d) the law governing the armed services or the lawful conduct of war; or

(e) any other provision of law imposing a public duty.

(2) The other sections of this Article apply to:

(a) the use of force upon or toward the person of another for any of the purposes dealt with in such sections; and

(b) the use of deadly force for any purpose, unless the use of such force is otherwise expressly authorized by law or occurs in the lawful conduct of war.

(3) The justification afforded by Subsection (1) of this Section applies:

(a) when the actor believes his conduct to be required or authorized by the judgment or direction of a competent court or tribunal or in the lawful execution of legal process, notwithstanding lack of jurisdiction of the court or defect in the legal process; and

(b) when the actor believes his conduct to be required or authorized to assist a public officer in the performance of his duties, notwithstanding that the officer exceeded his legal authority.

SECTION 3.04. USE OF FORCE IN SELF-PROTECTION

(1) Use of Force Justifiable for Protection of the Person. Subject to the provisions of this Section and of Section 3.09, the use of force upon or toward another person is justifiable when the actor believes that such force is immediately necessary for the purpose of protecting himself against the use of unlawful force by such other person on the present occasion.

(2) Limitations on Justifying Necessity for Use of Force.

(a) The use of force is not justifiable under this Section:

(i) to resist an arrest that the actor knows is being made by a peace officer, although the arrest is unlawful; or

(ii) to resist force used by the occupier or possessor of property or by another person on his behalf, where the actor knows that the person using the force is doing so under a claim of right to protect the property, except that this limitation shall not apply if:

(A) the actor is a public officer acting in the performance of his duties or a person lawfully assisting him therein or a person making or assisting in a lawful arrest; or

(B) the actor has been unlawfully dispossessed of the property and is making a re-entry or recaption justified by Section 3.06; or

(C) the actor believes that such force is necessary to protect himself against death or serious bodily injury.

(b) The use of deadly force is not justifiable under this Section unless the actor believes that such force is necessary to protect himself against death, serious bodily injury, kidnapping or sexual intercourse compelled by force or threat; nor is it justifiable if:

(i) the actor, with the purpose of causing death or serious bodily injury, provoked the use of force against himself in the same encounter; or

(ii) the actor knows that he can avoid the necessity of using such force with complete safety by retreating or by surrendering possession of a thing to a person asserting a claim of right thereto or by complying with a demand that he abstain from any action that he has no duty to take, except that:

(A) the actor is not obliged to retreat from his dwelling or place of work, unless he was the initial aggressor or is assailed in his place of work by another person whose place of work the actor knows it to be; and

(B) a public officer justified in using force in the performance of his duties or a person justified in using force in his assistance or a person justified in using force in making an arrest or preventing an escape is not obliged to desist from efforts to perform such duty, effect such arrest or prevent such escape because of resistance or threatened resistance by or on behalf of the person against whom such action is directed.

(c) Except as required by paragraphs (a) and (b) of this Subsection, a person employing protective force may estimate the necessity thereof under the circumstances as he believes them to be when the force is used, without retreating, surrendering possession, doing any other act that he has no legal duty to do or abstaining from any lawful action.

(3) Use of Confinement as Protective Force. The justification afforded by this Section extends to the use of confinement as protective force only if the actor takes all reasonable measures to terminate the confinement as soon as he knows that he safely can, unless the person confined has been arrested on a charge of crime.

SECTION 3.05. USE OF FORCE FOR THE PROTECTION OF OTHER PERSONS

(1) Subject to the provisions of this Section and of Section 3.09, the use of force upon or toward the person of another is justifiable to protect a third person when:

(a) the actor would be justified under Section 3.04 in using such force to protect himself against the injury he believes to be threatened to the person whom he seeks to protect; and

(b) under the circumstances as the actor believes them to be, the person whom he seeks to protect would be justified in using such protective force; and

(c) the actor believes that his intervention is necessary for the protection of such other person.

(2) Notwithstanding Subsection (1) of this Section:

(a) when the actor would be obliged under Section 3.04 to retreat, to surrender the possession of a thing or to comply with a demand before using force in self-protection, he is not obliged to do so before using force for the protection of another person, unless he knows that he can thereby secure the complete safety of such other person; and

(b) when the person whom the actor seeks to protect would be obliged under Section 3.04 to retreat, to surrender the possession of a thing or to comply with a demand if he knew that he could obtain complete safety by so doing, the actor is obliged to try to cause him to do so before using force in his protection if the actor knows that he can obtain complete safety in that way; and

(c) neither the actor nor the person whom he seeks to protect is obliged to retreat when in the other's dwelling or place of work to any greater extent than in his own.

(b) when the person whom the actor seeks to protect would be obliged under Section 3.04 to retreat, to surrender the possession of a thing or to comply with a demand if he knew that he could obtain complete safety by so doing, the actor is obliged to try to cause him to do so before using force in his protection if the actor knows that he can obtain complete safety in that way; and

(c) neither the actor nor the person whom he seeks to protect is obliged to retreat when in the other's dwelling or place of work to any greater extent than in his own.

SECTION 3.06. USE OF FORCE FOR THE PROTECTION OF PROPERTY

(1) **Use of Force Justifiable for Protection of Property**. Subject to the provisions of this Section and of Section 3.09, the use of force upon or toward the person of another is justifiable when the actor believes that such force is immediately necessary:

(a) to prevent or terminate an unlawful entry or other trespass upon land or a trespass against or the unlawful carrying away of tangible, movable property, provided that such land or movable property is, or is believed by the actor to be, in his possession or in the possession of another person for whose protection he acts; or

(b) to effect an entry or re-entry upon land or to retake tangible movable property, provided that the actor believes that he or the person by whose authority he acts or a person from whom he or such other person derives title was unlawfully dispossessed of such land or movable property and is entitled to possession, and provided, further, that:

(i) the force is used immediately or on fresh pursuit after such dispossession; or

(ii) the actor believes that the person against whom he uses force has no claim of right to the possession of the property and, in the case of land, the circumstances, as the actor believes them to be, are of such urgency that it would be an exceptional hardship to postpone the entry or re-entry until a court order is obtained.

(2) **Meaning of Possession**. For the purposes of Subsection (1) of this Section:

(a) a person who has parted with the custody of property to another who refuses to restore it to him is no longer in possession, unless the property is movable and was and still is located on land in his possession;

(b) a person who has been dispossessed of land does not regain possession thereof merely by setting foot thereon;

(c) a person who has a license to use or occupy real property is deemed to be in possession thereof except against the licensor acting under claim of right.

(3) **Limitations on Justifiable Use of Force**.

(a) **Request to Desist**. The use of force is justifiable under this Section only if the actor first requests the person against whom such force is used to desist from his interference with the property, unless the actor believes that:

(i) such request would be useless; or

(ii) it would be dangerous to himself or another person to make the request; or

(iii) substantial harm will be done to the physical condition of the property that is sought to be protected before the request can effectively be made.

(b) **Exclusion of Trespasser**. The use of force to prevent or terminate a trespass is not justifiable under this Section if the actor knows that the exclusion of the trespasser will expose him to substantial danger of serious bodily injury.

(c) **Resistance of Lawful Re-entry or Recaption**. The use of force to prevent an entry or re-entry upon land or the recaption of movable property is not justifiable under this Section, although the actor believes that such re-entry or recaption is unlawful, if:

(i) the re-entry or recaption is made by or on behalf of a person who was actually dispossessed of the property; and

(ii) it is otherwise justifiable under Subsection (1)(b) of this Section.

(d) **Use of Deadly Force**. The use of deadly force is not justifiable under this Section unless the actor believes that:

> (i) the person against whom the force is used is attempting to dispossess him of his dwelling otherwise than under a claim of right to its possession; or

> (ii) the person against whom the force is used is attempting to commit or consummate arson, burglary, robbery or
> other felonious theft or property destruction and either:

>> (A) has employed or threatened deadly force against or in the presence of the actor; or

>> (B) the use of force other than deadly force to prevent the commission or the consummation of the crime would expose the actor or another in his presence to substantial danger of serious bodily injury.

(4) **Use of Confinement as Protective Force**. The justification afforded by this Section extends to the use of confinement as protective force only if the actor takes all reasonable measures to terminate the confinement as soon as he knows that he can do so with safety to the property, unless the person confined has been arrested on a charge of crime.

(5) **Use of Device to Protect Property**. The justification afforded by this Section extends to the use of a device for the purpose of protecting property only if:

> (a) the device is not designed to cause or known to create a substantial risk of causing death or serious bodily injury; and

> (b) the use of the particular device to protect the property from entry or trespass is reasonable under the circumstances, as the actor believes them to be; and

> (c) the device is one customarily used for such a purpose or reasonable care is taken to make known to probable intruders the fact that it is used.

(6) **Use of Force to Pass Wrongful Obstructor.** The use of force to pass a person whom the actor believes to be purposely or knowingly and unjustifiably obstructing the actor from going to a place to which he may lawfully go is justifiable, provided that:

(a) the actor believes that the person against whom he uses force has no claim of right to obstruct the actor; and

(b) the actor is not being obstructed from entry or movement on land that he knows to be in the possession or custody of the person obstructing him, or in the possession or custody of another person by whose authority the obstructor
acts, unless the circumstances, as the actor believes them to be, are of such urgency that it would not be reasonable to
postpone the entry or movement on such land until a court order is obtained; and

(c) the force used is not greater than would be justifiable if the person obstructing the actor were using force against him to prevent his passage.

SECTION 3.07.   USE OF FORCE IN LAW ENFORCEMENT

(1) Use of Force Justifiable to Effect an Arrest. Subject to the provisions of this Section and of Section 3.09, the use of force upon or toward the person of another is justifiable when the actor is making or assisting in making an arrest and the actor believes that such force is immediately necessary to effect a lawful arrest.

(2) **Limitations on the Use of Force.**

(a) The use of force is not justifiable under this Section unless:

(i) the actor makes known the purpose of the arrest or believes that it is otherwise known by or cannot reasonably be made known to the person to be arrested; and

(ii) when the arrest is made under a warrant, the warrant is valid or believed by the actor to be valid.

(b) The use of deadly force is not justifiable under this Section unless:

(i) the arrest is for a felony; and

(ii) the person effecting the arrest is authorized to act as a peace officer or is assisting a person whom he believes to be authorized to act as a peace officer; and

(iii) the actor believes that the force employed creates no substantial risk of injury to innocent persons; and

(iv) the actor believes that:

(A) the crime for which the arrest is made involved conduct including the use or threatened use of deadly force; or

(B) there is a substantial risk that the person to be arrested will cause death or serious bodily injury if his apprehension is delayed.

(3) **Use of Force to Prevent Escape from Custody.** The use of force to prevent the escape of an arrested person from custody is justifiable when the force could justifiably have been employed to effect the arrest under which the person is in custody, except that a guard or other person authorized to act as a peace officer is justified in using any force, including deadly force, that he believes to be immediately necessary to prevent the escape of a person from a jail, prison, or other institution for the detention of persons charged with or convicted of a crime.

(4) **Use of Force by Private Person Assisting an Unlawful Arrest.**

(a) A private person who is summoned by a peace officer to assist in effecting an unlawful arrest, is justified in using any force that he would be justified in using if the arrest were lawful, provided that he does not believe the arrest is unlawful.

(b) A private person who assists another private person in effecting an unlawful arrest, or who, not being summoned, assists a peace officer in effecting an unlawful arrest, is justified in using any force that he would be justified in using if the arrest were lawful, provided that (i) he believes the arrest is lawful, and (ii) the arrest would be lawful if the facts were as he believes them to be.

(5) **Use of Force to Prevent Suicide or the Commission of a Crime.**

(a) The use of force upon or toward the person of another is justifiable when the actor believes that such force is immediately necessary to prevent such other person from committing suicide, inflicting serious bodily injury upon himself, committing or consummating the commission of a crime involving or threatening bodily injury, damage to or loss of property or a breach of the peace, except that:

(i) any limitations imposed by the other provisions of this Article on the justifiable use of force in self-protection, for the protection of others, the protection of property, the effectuation of an arrest or the prevention of an escape from custody shall apply notwithstanding the criminality of the conduct against which such force is used; and

(ii) the use of deadly force is not in any event justifiable under this Subsection unless:

(A) the actor believes that there is a substantial risk that the person whom he seeks to prevent from committing a crime will cause death or serious bodily injury to another unless the commission or the consummation of the crime is prevented and that the use of such force presents no substantial risk of injury to innocent persons; or

(B) the actor believes that the use of such force is necessary to suppress a riot or mutiny after the rioters or mutineers have been ordered to disperse and warned, in any particular manner that the law may require, that such force will be used if they do not obey.

(b) The justification afforded by this Subsection extends to the use of confinement as preventive force only if the actor takes all reasonable measures to terminate the confinement as soon as he knows that he safely can, unless the person confined has been arrested on a charge of crime.

SECTION 3.08.   USE OF FORCE BY PERSONS WITH SPECIAL RESPONSIBILITY FOR CARE, DISCIPLINE OR SAFETY OF ANOTHER

The use of force upon or toward the person of another is justifiable if:

(1) the actor is the parent or guardian or other person similarly responsible for the general care and supervision of a minor or a person acting at the request of such parent, guardian or other responsible person and:

(a) the force is used for the purpose of safeguarding or promoting the welfare of the minor, including the prevention or punishment of his misconduct; and

(b) the force used is not designed to cause or known to create a substantial risk of causing death, serious bodily injury, disfigurement, extreme pain or mental distress or gross degradation; or

(2) the actor is a teacher or a person otherwise entrusted with the care or supervision for a special purpose of a minor and:

(a) the actor believes that the force used is necessary to further such special purpose, including the maintenance of reasonable discipline in a school, class or other group, and that the use of such force is consistent with the welfare of the minor; and

(b) the degree of force, if it had been used by the parent or guardian of the minor, would not be unjustifiable under Subsection (1)(b) of this Section; or

(3) the actor is the guardian or other person similarly responsible for the general care and supervision of an incompetent person and:

(a) the force is used for the purpose of safeguarding or promoting the welfare of the incompetent person, including the prevention of his misconduct, or, when such incompetent person is in a hospital or other institution for his care and custody, for the maintenance of reasonable discipline in such institution; and

(b) the force used is not designed to cause or known to create a substantial risk of causing death, serious bodily injury, disfigurement, extreme or unnecessary pain, mental distress, or humiliation; or

(4) the actor is a doctor or other therapist or a person assisting him at his direction and:

(a) the force is used for the purpose of administering a recognized form of treatment that the actor believes to be adapted to promoting the physical or mental health of the patient; and

(b) the treatment is administered with the consent of the patient or, if the patient is a minor or an incompetent person, with the consent of his parent or guardian or other person legally competent to consent in his behalf, or the treatment is administered in an emergency when the actor believes that no one competent to consent can be consulted and that a reasonable person, wishing to safeguard the welfare of the patient, would consent; or

(5) the actor is a warden or other authorized official of a correctional institution and:

(a) he believes that the force used is necessary for the purpose of enforcing the lawful rules or procedures of the institution, unless his belief in the lawfulness of the rule or procedure sought to be enforced is erroneous and his error is due to ignorance or mistake as to the provisions of the Code, any other provision of the criminal law or the law governing the administration of the institution; and

(b) the nature or degree of force used is not forbidden by Article 303 or 304 of the Code; and

(c) if deadly force is used, its use is otherwise justifiable under this Article; or

(6) the actor is a person responsible for the safety of a vessel or an aircraft or a person acting at his direction and:

(a) he believes that the force used is necessary to prevent interference with the operation of the vessel or aircraft or obstruction of the execution of a lawful order, unless his belief in the lawfulness of the order is erroneous and his error is due to ignorance or mistake as to the law defining his authority; and

(b) if deadly force is used, its use is otherwise justifiable under this Article; or

(7) the actor is a person who is authorized or required by law to maintain order or decorum in a vehicle, train or other carrier or in a place where others are assembled, and:

(a) he believes that the force used is necessary for such purpose; and

(b) the force used is not designed to cause or known to create a substantial risk of causing death, bodily injury, or extreme mental distress.

SECTION 3.10. JUSTIFICATION IN PROPERTY CRIMES

(1) The justification afforded by Sections 3.04 to 3.07, inclusive, is unavailable when:

(a) the actor's belief in the unlawfulness of the force or conduct against which he employs protective force or his belief in the lawfulness of an arrest that he endeavors to effect by force is erroneous; and

(b) his error is due to ignorance or mistake as to the provisions of the Code, any other provision of the criminal law or the law governing the legality of an arrest or search.

(2) When the actor believes that the use of force upon or toward the person of another is necessary for any of the purposes for which such belief would establish a justification under Sections 3.03 to 3.08 but the actor is reckless or negligent in having such belief or in acquiring or failing to acquire any knowledge or belief that is material to the justifiability of his use of force, the justification afforded by those Sections is unavailable in a prosecution for an offense for which recklessness or negligence, as the case may be, suffices to establish culpability.

(3) When the actor is justified under Sections 3.03 to 3.08 in using force upon or toward the person of another but he recklessly or negligently injures or creates a risk of injury to innocent persons, the justification afforded by those Sections is unavailable in a prosecution for such recklessness or negligence towards innocent persons.

SECTION 3.11. DEFINITIONS

Conduct involving the appropriation, seizure or destruction of, damage to, intrusion on or interference with property is justifiable under circumstances that would establish a defense of privilege in a civil action based thereon, unless:

(1) the Code or the law defining the offense deals with the specific situation involved; or

(2) a legislative purpose to exclude the justification claimed otherwise plainly appears.

SECTION 3.11. DEFINITIONS

In this Article, unless a different meaning plainly is required:

(1) "unlawful force" means force, including confinement, that is employed without the consent of the person against whom it is directed and the employment of which constitutes an offense or actionable tort or would constitute such offense or tort except for a defense (such as the absence of intent, negligence, or mental capacity; duress; youth; or diplomatic status) not amounting to a privilege to use the force. Assent constitutes consent, within the meaning of this Section, whether or not it otherwise is legally effective, except assent to the infliction of death or serious bodily injury.

(2) "deadly force" means force that the actor uses with the purpose of causing or that he knows to create a substantial risk of causing death or serious bodily injury. Purposely firing a firearm in the direction of another person or at a vehicle in which another person is believed to be constitutes deadly force. A threat to cause death or serious bodily injury, by the production of a weapon or otherwise, so long as the actor's purpose is limited to creating an apprehension that he will use deadly force if necessary, does not constitute deadly force.

(3) "dwelling" means any building or structure, though movable or temporary, or a portion thereof, that is for the time being the actor's home or place of lodging.

Article 4. Responsibility

SECTION 4.01.   MENTAL DISEASE OR DEFECT EXCLUDING RESPONSIBILITY

(1) A person is not responsible for criminal conduct if at the time of such conduct as a result of mental disease or defect he lacks substantial capacity either to appreciate the criminality [wrongfulness] of his conduct or to conform his conduct to the requirements of law.

(2) As used in this Article, the terms "mental disease or defect" do not include an abnormality manifested only by repeated criminal or otherwise antisocial conduct.

SECTION 4.02.   EVIDENCE OF MENTAL DISEASE OR DEFECT WHEN RELEVANT TO ELEMENT OF THE OFFENSE; [MENTAL DISEASE OR DEFECT IMPAIRING CAPACITY AS GROUND FOR MITIGATION OF PUNISHMENT IN CAPITAL CASES]

(1) Evidence that the defendant suffered from a mental disease or defect is admissible whenever it is relevant to prove that the defendant did or did not have a state of mind that is an element of the offense.

[(2) Whenever the jury or the Court is authorized to determine or to recommend whether or not the defendant shall be sentenced to death or imprisonment upon conviction, evidence that the capacity of the defendant to appreciate the criminality [wrongfulness] of his conduct or to conform his conduct to the requirements of law was impaired as a result of mental disease or defect is admissible in favor of sentence of imprisonment.]

SECTION 4.03.   MENTAL DISEASE OR DEFECT IS AFFIRMATIVE DEFENSE; REQUIREMENT OF NOTICE; FORM OF VERDICT AND JUDGMENT WHEN FINDING OF IRRESPONSIBILTY IS MADE

(1) Mental disease or defect excluding responsibility is an affirmative defense.

(2) Evidence of mental disease or defect excluding responsibility is not admissible unless the defendant, at the time of entering his plea of not guilty or within ten days thereafter or at such later time as the Court may for good cause permit, files a written notice of his purpose to rely on such defense.

(3) When the defendant is acquitted on the ground of mental disease or defect excluding responsibility, the verdict and the judgment shall so state.

SECTION 4.04. MENTAL DISEASE OR DEFECT EXCLUDING FITNESS TO PROCEED

No person who as a result of mental disease or defect lacks capacity to understand the proceedings against him or to assist in his own defense shall be tried, convicted or sentenced for the commission of an offense so long as such incapacity endures.

SECTION 4.05. PSYCHIATRIC EXAMINATION OF DEFENDANT WITH RESPECT TO MENTAL DISEASE OR DEFECT

(1) Whenever the defendant has filed a notice of intention to rely on the defense of mental disease or defect excluding responsibility, or there is reason to doubt his fitness to proceed, or reason to believe that mental disease or defect of the defendant will otherwise become an issue in the cause, the Court shall appoint at least one qualified psychiatrist or shall request the Superintendent of the Hospital to designate at least one qualified psychiatrist, which designation may be or include himself, to examine and report upon the mental condition of the defendant. The Court may order the defendant to be committed to a hospital or other suitable facility for the purpose of the examination for a period of not exceeding sixty days or such longer period as the Court determines to be necessary for the purpose and may direct that a qualified psychiatrist retained by the defendant be permitted to witness and participate in the examination.

(2) In such examination any method may be employed that is accepted by the medical profession for the examination of those alleged to be suffering from mental disease or defect.

(3) The report of the examination shall include the following: (a) a description of the nature of the examination; (b) a diagnosis of the mental condition of the defendant; (c) if the defendant suffers from a mental disease or defect, an opinion as to his capacity to understand the proceedings against him and to assist in his own defense; (d) when a notice of intention to rely on the defense of irresponsibility has been filed, an opinion as to the extent, if any, to which the capacity of the defendant to appreciate the criminality [wrongfulness] of his conduct or to conform his conduct to the requirements of law was impaired at the time of the criminal conduct charged; and (e) when directed by the Court, an opinion as to the capacity of the defendant to have a particular state of mind that is an element of the offense charged.

If the examination cannot be conducted by reason of the unwillingness of the defendant to participate therein, the report shall so state and shall include, if possible, an opinion as to whether such unwillingness of the defendant was the result of mental disease or defect.

The report of the examination shall be filed [in triplicate] with the clerk of the Court, who shall cause copies to be delivered to the district attorney and to counsel for the defendant.

SECTION 4.06. DETERMINING OF FITNESS TO PROCEED; EFFECT OF FINDING OF UNFITNESS; PROCEEDINGS IF FITNESS IS REGAINED [; POST-COMMITMENT HEARING]

(1) When the defendant's fitness to proceed is drawn in question, the issue shall be determined by the Court. If neither the prosecuting attorney nor counsel for the defendant contests the finding of the report filed pursuant to Section 4.05, the Court may make the determination on the basis of such report. If the finding is contested, the Court shall hold a hearing on the issue. If the report is received in evidence upon such hearing, the party who contests the finding thereof shall have the right to summon and to cross-examine the psychiatrists who joined in the report and to offer evidence upon the issue.

(2) If the Court determines that the defendant lacks fitness to proceed, the proceeding against him shall be suspended, except as provided in Subsection (3) [Subsections (3) and (4)] of this Section, and the Court shall commit him to the custody of the Commissioner of Mental Hygiene [Public Health or Correction] to be placed in an appropriate institution of the Department of Mental Hygiene [Public Health or Correction] for so long as such unfitness shall endure. When the Court, on its own motion or upon the application of the Commissioner of Mental Hygiene [Public Health or Correction] or the prosecuting attorney, determines, after a hearing if a hearing is requested, that the defendant has regained fitness to proceed, the proceeding shall be resumed. If, however, the Court is of the view that so much time has elapsed since the commitment of the defendant that it would be unjust to resume the criminal proceeding, the Court may dismiss the charge and may order the defendant to be discharged or, subject to the law governing the civil commitment of persons suffering from mental disease or defect, order the defendant to be committed to an appropriate institution of the Department ofMental Hygiene [Public Health].

(3) The fact that the defendant is unfit to proceed does not preclude any legal objection to the prosecution which is susceptible of fair determination prior to trial and without the personal participation of the defendant.

[Alternative: (3) At any time within ninety days after commitment as provided in Subsection (2) of this Section, or at any later time with permission of the Court granted for good cause, the defendant or his counsel or the Commissioner of Mental Hygiene [Public Health or Correction] may apply for a special post-commitment hearing. If the application is made by or on behalf of a defendant not represented by counsel, he shall be afforded a reasonable opportunity to obtain counsel, and if he lacks funds to do so, counsel shall be assigned by the Court. The application shall be granted only if counsel for the defendant satisfies the Court by affidavit or otherwise that as an attorney he has reasonable grounds for a good faith belief that his client has, on the facts and the law, a defense to the charge other than mental disease or defect excluding responsibility.

[(4) If the motion for a special post-commitment hearing is granted, the hearing shall be by the Court without a jury. No evidence shall be offered at the hearing by either party on the issue of mental disease or defect as a defense to, or in mitigation of, the crime charged. After hearing, the Court may in an appropriate case quash the indictment or othercharge, or find it to be defective or insufficient, or determine that it is not proved beyond a reasonable doubt by the evidence, or otherwise terminate the proceedings on the evidence or the law. In any such case, unless all defects in the proceedings are promptly cured, the Court shall terminate the commitment ordered under Subsection (2) of this Section and order the defendant to be discharged or, subject to the law governing the civil commitment of persons suffering from mental disease or defect, order the defendant to be committed to an appropriate institution of the Department of Mental Hygiene [Public Health].]

SECTION 4.07. DETERMINATION OF IRRESPONSIBILITY ON THE BASIS OF REPORT; ACCESS TO DEFENDANT BY PSYCHIATRIST OF HIS OWN CHOICE; FORM OF EXPERT TESTIMONY WHEN ISSUE OF RESPONSIBILITY IS TRIED

(1) If the report filed pursuant to Section 4.05 finds that the defendant at the time of the criminal conduct charged suffered from a mental disease or defect that substantially impaired his capacity to appreciate the criminality [wrongfulness] of his conduct or to conform his conduct to the requirements of law, and the Court, after a hearing if a hearing is requested by the prosecuting attorney or the defendant, is satisfied that such impairment was sufficient to

exclude responsibility, the Court on motion of the defendant shall enter judgment of acquittal on the ground of mental disease or defect excluding responsibility.

(2) When, notwithstanding the report filed pursuant to Section 4.05, the defendant wishes to be examined by a qualified psychiatrist or other expert of his own choice, such examiner shall be permitted to have reasonable access to the defendant for the purposes of such examination.

(3) Upon the trial, the psychiatrists who reported pursuant to Section 4.05 may be called as witnesses by the prosecution, the defendant or the Court. If the issue is being tried before a jury, the jury may be informed that the psychiatrists were designated by the Court or by the Superintendent of the Hospital at the request of the Court, as the case may be. If called by the Court, the witness shall be subject to cross-examination by the prosecution and by the defendant. Both the prosecution and the defendant may summon any other qualified psychiatrist or other expert to testify, but no one who has not examined the defendant shall be competent to testify to an expert opinion with respect to the mental condition or responsibility of the defendant, as distinguished from the validity of the procedure followed by, or the general scientific propositions stated by, another witness.

(4) When a psychiatrist or other expert who has examined the defendant testifies concerning his mental condition, he shall be permitted to make a statement as to the nature of his examination, his diagnosis of the mental condition of the defendant at the time of the commission of the offense charged and his opinion as to the extent, if any, to which the capacity of the defendant to appreciate the criminality [wrongfulness] of his conduct or to conform his conduct to the requirements of law or to have a particular state of mind that is an element of the offense charged was impaired as a result of mental disease or defect at that time. He shall be permitted to make any explanation reasonably serving to clarify his diagnosis and opinion and may be cross-examined as to any matter bearing on his competency or credibility or the validity of his diagnosis or opinion.

SECTION 4.08. LEGAL EFFECT OF ACQUITTAL ON THE GROUND OF MENTAL DISEASE OR DEFECT EXCLUDING RESPONSIBILITY; COMMITMENT; RELEASE OR DISCHARGE

(1) When a defendant is acquitted on the ground of mental disease or defect excluding responsibility, the Court shall order him to be committed to the

custody of the Commissioner of Mental Hygiene [Public Health] to be placed in an appropriate institution for custody, care and treatment.

(2) If the Commissioner of Mental Hygiene [Public Health] is of the view that a person committed to his custody, pursuant to Subsection (1) of this Section, may be discharged or released on condition without danger to himself or to others, he shall make application for the discharge or release of such person in a report to the Court by which such person was committed and shall transmit a copy of such application and report to the prosecuting attorney of the county [parish] from which the defendant was committed. The Court shall thereupon appoint at least two qualified psychiatrists to examine such person and to report within sixty days, or such longer period as the Court determines to be necessary for the purpose, their opinion as to his mental condition. To facilitate such examination and the proceedings thereon, the Court may cause such person to be confined in any institution located near the place where the Court sits, which may hereafter be designated by the Commissioner of Mental Hygiene [Public Health] as suitable for the temporary detention of irresponsible persons.

(3) If the Court is satisfied by the report filed pursuant to Subsection (2) of this Section and such testimony of the reporting psychiatrists as the Court deems necessary that the committed person may be discharged or released on condition withoutdanger to himself or others, the Court shall order his discharge or his release on such conditions as the Court determines to be necessary. If the Court is not so satisfied, it shall promptly order a hearing to determine whether such person may safely be discharged or released. Any such hearing shall be deemed a civil proceeding and the burden shall be upon the committed person to prove that he may safely be discharged or released. According to the determination of the Court upon the hearing, the committed person shall thereupon be discharged or released on such conditions as the Court determines to be necessary, or shall be recommitted to the custody of the Commissioner of Mental Hygiene [Public Health], subject to discharge or release only in accordance with the procedure prescribed above for a first hearing.

(4) If, within [five] years after the conditional release of a committed person, the Court shall determine, after hearing evidence, that the conditions of release have not been fulfilled and that for the safety of such person or for the safety of others his conditional release should be revoked, the Court shall forthwith order him to be recommitted to the Commissioner of Mental Hygiene [Public Health], subject to discharge or release only in accordance with the procedure prescribed above for a first hearing.

(5) A committed person may make application for his discharge or release to the Court by which he was committed, and the procedure to be followed upon such application shall be the same as that prescribed above in the case of an application by the Commissioner of Mental Hygiene [Public Health]. However, no such application by a committed person need be considered until he has been confined for a period of not less than [six months] from the date of the order of commitment, and if the determination of the Court be adverse to the application, such person shall not be permitted to file a further application until [one year] has elapsed from the date of any preceding hearing on an application for his release or discharge.

SECTION 4.09.   [Omitted]

SECTION 4.10.   [Omitted]

Article 5. Inchoate Crimes

SECTION 5.01.   CRIMINAL ATTEMPT

(1) **Definition of Attempt**. A person is guilty of an attempt to commit a crime if, acting with the kind of culpability otherwise required for commission of the crime, he:

(a) purposely engages in conduct that would constitute the crime if the attendant circumstances were as he believes them to be; or

(b) when causing a particular result is an element of the crime, does or omits to do anything with the purpose of causing or with the belief that it will cause such result without further conduct on his part; or

(c) purposely does or omits to do anything that, under the circumstances as he believes them to be, is an act or omission constituting a substantial step in a course of conduct planned to culminate in his commission of the crime.

(2) **Conduct That May Be Held Substantial Step Under Subsection (1)(c).** Conduct shall not be held to constitute a substantial step under Subsection (1)(c) of this Section unless it is strongly corroborative of the actor's criminal purpose. Without negativing the sufficiency of other conduct, the following, if strongly corroborative of the actor's criminal purpose, shall not be held insufficient as a matter of law:

(a) lying in wait, searching for or following the contemplated victim of the crime;

(b) enticing or seeking to entice the contemplated victim of the crime to go to the place contemplated for its commission;

(c) reconnoitering the place contemplated for the commission of the crime;

(d) unlawful entry of a structure, vehicle or enclosure in which it is contemplated that the crime will be committed;

(e) possession of materials to be employed in the commission of the crime, that are specially designed for such unlawful use or that can serve no lawful purpose of the actor under the circumstances;

(f) possession, collection or fabrication of materials to be employed in the commission of the crime, at or near the place contemplated for its commission, if such possession, collection or fabrication serves no lawful purpose of the actor under the circumstances;

(g) soliciting an innocent agent to engage in conduct constituting an element of the crime.

(3) **Conduct Designed to Aid Another in Commission of a Crime**. A person who engages in conduct designed to aid another to commit a crime that would establish his complicity under Section 2.06 if the crime were committed by such other person, is guilty of an attempt to commit the crime, although the crime is not committed or attempted by such other person.

(4) **Renunciation of Criminal Purpose**. When the actor's conduct would otherwise constitute an attempt under Subsection (1)(b) or (1)(c) of this Section, it is an affirmative defense that he abandoned his effort to commit the crime or otherwise prevented its commission, under circumstances manifesting a complete and voluntary renunciation of his criminal purpose. The establishment of such defense does not, however, affect the liability of an accomplice who did not join in such abandonment or prevention. Within the meaning of this Article, renunciation of criminal purpose is not voluntary if it is motivated, in whole or in part, by circumstances, not present or apparent at the inception of the actor's course of conduct, that increase the probability of detection or apprehension or that make more difficult the accomplishment of the criminal purpose.

Renunciation is not complete if it is motivated by a decision to postpone the criminal conduct until a more advantageous time or to transfer the criminal effort to another but similar objective or victim.

SECTION 5.02.   CRIMINAL SOLICITATION

(1) **Definition of Solicitation**. A person is guilty of solicitation to commit a crime if with the purpose of promoting or facilitating its commission he commands, encourages or requests another person to engage in specific conduct that would constitute such crime or an attempt to commit such crime or would establish his complicity in its commission or attempted commission.

(2) **Uncommunicated Solicitation**. It is immaterial under Subsection (1) of this Section that the actor fails to communicate with the person he solicits to commit a crime if his conduct was designed to effect such communication.

(3) **Renunciation of Criminal Purpose**. It is an affirmative defense that the actor, after soliciting another person to commit a crime, persuaded him not to do so or otherwise prevented the commission of the crime, under circumstances manifesting a complete and voluntary renunciation of his criminal purpose.

SECTION 5.03.   CRIMINAL CONSPIRACY

(1) **Definition of Conspiracy.** A person is guilty of conspiracy with another person or persons to commit a crime if with the purpose of promoting or facilitating its commission he:

(a) agrees with such other person or persons that they or one or more of them will engage in conduct that constitutes such crime or an attempt or solicitation to commit such crime; or

(b) agrees to aid such other person or persons in the planning or commission of such crime or of an attempt or solicitation to commit such crime.

(2) **Scope of Conspiratorial Relationship.** If a person guilty of conspiracy, as defined by Subsection (1) of this Section, knows that a person with whom he conspires to commit a crime has conspired with another person or persons to commit the same crime, he is guilty of conspiring with such other person or persons, whether or not he knows their identity, to commit such crime.

(3) **Conspiracy with Multiple Criminal Objectives.** If a person conspires to commit a number of crimes, he is guilty of only one conspiracy so long as such multiple crimes are the object of the same agreement or continuous conspiratorial relationship.

(4) **Joinder and Venue in Conspiracy Prosecutions.**

(a) Subject to the provisions of paragraph (b) of this Subsection, two or more persons charged with criminal conspiracy may be prosecuted jointly if:

(i) they are charged with conspiring with one another; or

(ii) the conspiracies alleged, whether they have the same or different parties, are so related that they constitute different aspects of a scheme of organized criminal conduct.

(b) In any joint prosecution under paragraph (a) of this Subsection:

(i) no defendant shall be charged with a conspiracy in any county [parish or district] other than one in which he entered into such conspiracy or in which an overt act pursuant to such conspiracy was done by him or by a person with whom he conspired; and

(ii) neither the liability of any defendant nor the admissibility against him of evidence of acts or declarations of another shall be enlarged by such joinder; and

(iii) the Court shall order a severance or take a special verdict as to any defendant who so requests, if it deems it necessary or appropriate to promote the fair determination of his guilt or innocence, and shall take any other proper measures to protect the fairness of the trial.

(5) **Overt Act.** No person may be convicted of conspiracy to commit a crime, other than a felony of the first or second degree, unless an overt act in pursuance of such conspiracy is alleged and proved to have been done by him or by a person with whom he conspired.

(6) **Renunciation of Criminal Purpose.** It is an affirmative defense that the actor, after conspiring to commit a crime, thwarted the success of the conspiracy, under circumstances manifesting a complete and voluntary renunciation of his criminal purpose.

(7) **Duration of Conspiracy.** For purposes of Section 1.06(4):

(a) conspiracy is a continuing course of conduct that terminates when the crime or crimes that are its object are committed or the agreement that they be committed is abandoned by the defendant and by those with whom he conspired; and

(b) such abandonment is presumed if neither the defendant nor anyone with whom he conspired does any overt act in pursuance of the conspiracy during the applicable period of limitation; and

(c) if an individual abandons the agreement, the conspiracy is terminated as to him only if and when he advises those with whom he conspired of his abandonment or he informs the law enforcement authorities of the existence of the conspiracy and of his participation therein.

SECTION 5.04. INCAPACITY, IRRESPONSIBILITY OR IMMUNITY OF PARTY TO SOLICITATION OR CONSPIRACY

(1) Except as provided in Subsection (2) of this Section, it is immaterial to the liability of a person who solicits or conspires with another to commit a crime that:

(a) he or the person whom he solicits or with whom he conspires does not occupy a particular position or have a particular characteristic that is an element of such crime, if he believes that one of them does; or

(b) the person whom he solicits or with whom he conspires is irresponsible or has an immunity to prosecution or conviction for the commission of the crime.

(2) It is a defense to a charge of solicitation or conspiracy to commit a crime that if the criminal object were achieved, the actor would not be guilty of a crime under the law defining the offense or as an accomplice under Section 2.06(5) or 2.06(6)(a) or (6)(b).

SECTION 5.05. GRADING OF CRIMINAL ATTEMPT, SOLICITATION AND CONSPIRACY; MITIGATION IN CASE OF LESSER DANGER; MULTIPLE CONVICTIONS BARRED

(1) **Grading**. Except as otherwise provided in this Section, attempt, solicitation and conspiracy are crimes of the same grade and degree as the most serious offense that is attempted or solicited or is an object of the conspiracy. An attempt, solicitation or conspiracy to commit a [capital crime or a] felony of the first degree is a felony of the second degree.

(2) **Mitigation**. If the particular conduct charged to constitute a criminal attempt, solicitation or conspiracy is so inherently unlikely to result or culminate in the commission of a crime that neither such conduct nor the actor presents a public danger warranting the grading of such offense under this Section, the Court shall exercise its power under Section 6.12 to enter judgment and impose sentence for a crime of lower grade or degree or, in extreme cases, may dismiss the prosecution.

(3) **Multiple Convictions**. A person may not be convicted of more than one offense defined by this Article for conduct designed to commit or to culminate in the commission of the same crime.

SECTION 5.06.   [Omitted]

SECTION 5.07.   [Omitted]

Article 6. Authorized Disposition of Offenders

SECTION 6.01   DEGREES OF FELONIES

(1) Felonies defined by this Code are classified, for the purpose of sentence, into three degrees, as follows:

(a) felonies of the first degree;

(b) felonies of the second degree;

(c) felonies of the third degree.

A felony is of the first or second degree when it is so designated by the Code. A crime declared to be a felony, without specification of degree, is of the third degree.

(2) Notwithstanding any other provision of law, a felony defined by any statute of this State other than this Code shall constitute, for the purpose of sentence, a felony of the third degree.

SECTION 6.02. [Omitted]

SECTION 6.03. FINES

A person who has been convicted of an offense may be sentenced to pay a fine not exceeding:

(1) $10,000, when the conviction is of a felony of the first or second degree;

(2) $5,000, when the conviction is of a felony of the third degree;

(3) $1,000, when the conviction is of a misdemeanor;

(4) $500, when the conviction is of a petty misdemeanor or a violation;

(5) any higher amount equal to double the pecuniary gain derived from the offense by the offender;

(6) any higher amount specifically authorized by statute.

SECTION 6.04. PENALTIES AGAINST CORPORATIONS AND UNINCORPORATED ASSOCIATIONS; FORFEITURE OF CORPORATE CHARTER OR REVOCATION OF CERTIFICATE AUTHORIZING FOREIGN CORPORATION TO DO BUSINESS IN THE STATE

(1) The Court may suspend the sentence of a corporation or an unincorporated association that has been convicted of an offense or may sentence it to pay a fine authorized by Section 6.03.

(2)(a) The [prosecuting attorney] is authorized to institute civil proceedings in the appropriate court of general jurisdiction to forfeit the charter of a corporation organized under the laws of this State or to revoke the certificate authorizing a foreign corporation to conduct business in this State. The Court may order the charter forfeited or the certificate revoked upon finding (i) that the board of directors or a high managerial agent acting in behalf of the corporation has, in conducting the corporation's affairs, purposely engaged in a persistent course of criminal conduct and (ii) that for the prevention of future criminal conduct of the same character, the public interest requires the charter of the corporation to be forfeited and the corporation to be dissolved or the certificate to be revoked.

(b) When a corporation is convicted of a crime or a high managerial agent of a corporation, as defined in Section 2.07, is convicted of a crime committed in the conduct of the affairs of the corporation, the Court, in sentencing the corporation or the agent, may direct the [prosecuting attorney] to institute proceedings authorized by paragraph (a) of this Subsection.

(c) The proceedings authorized by paragraph (a) of this Subsection shall be conducted in accordance with the procedures authorized by law for the involuntary dissolution of a corporation or the revocation of the certificate authorizing a foreign corporation to conduct business in this State. Such proceedings shall be deemed additional to any other proceedings authorized by law for the purpose of forfeiting the charter of a corporation or revoking the certificate of a foreign corporation.

SECTION 6.05-6.13.   [Omitted]

Article 7. Authority of Court in Sentencing [Omitted]

PART II. DEFINITION OF SPECIFIC CRIMES OFFENSES INVOLVING DANGER TO THE PERSON

Article 210. Criminal Homicide

SECTION 210.0. DEFINITIONS

In Articles 210-213, unless a different meaning plainly is required:

(1) "human being" means a person who has been born and is alive;

(2) "bodily injury" means physical pain, illness or any impairment of physical condition;

(3) "serious bodily injury" means bodily injury which creates a substantial risk of death or which causes serious, permanent disfigurement, or protracted loss or impairment of the function of any bodily member or organ;

(4) "deadly weapon" means any firearm or other weapon, device, instrument, material or substance, whether animate or inanimate, which in the

manner it is used or is intended to be used is known to be capable of producing death or serious bodily injury.

SECTION 210.1. CRIMINAL HOMICIDE

(1) A person is guilty of criminal homicide if he purposely, knowingly, recklessly or negligently causes the death of another human being.

(2) Criminal homicide is murder, manslaughter or negligent homicide.

SECTION 210.2 MURDER

(1) Except as provided in Section 210.3(1)(b), criminal homicide constitutes murder when:

(a) it is committed purposely or knowingly; or

(b) it is committed recklessly under circumstances manifesting extreme indifference to the value of human life. Such recklessness and indifference are presumed if the actor is engaged or is an accomplice in the commission of, or an attempt to commit, or flight after committing or attempting to commit robbery, rape or deviate sexual intercourse by force or threat of force, arson, burglary, kidnapping or felonious escape.

(2) Murder is a felony of the first degree [but a person convicted of murder may be sentenced to death, as provided in Section 210.6].

SECTION 210.3. MANSLAUGHTER

(1) Criminal homicide constitutes manslaughter when:

(a) it is committed recklessly; or

(b) a homicide which would otherwise be murder is committed under the influence of extreme mental or emotional disturbance for which there is reasonable explanation or excuse. The reasonableness of such explanation or excuse shall be determined from the viewpoint of a person in the actor's situation under the circumstances as he believes them to be.

(2) Manslaughter is a felony of the second degree.

SECTION 210.4. NEGLIGENT HOMICIDE

(1) Criminal homicide constitutes negligent homicide when it is committed negligently.

(2) Negligent homicide is a felony of the third degree.

SECTION 210.5. CAUSING OR AIDING SUICIDE

(1) **Causing Suicide as Criminal Homicide**. A person may be convicted of criminal homicide for causing another to commit
suicide only if he purposely causes such suicide by force, duress or deception.

(2) **Aiding or Soliciting Suicide as an Independent Offense.** A person who purposely aids or solicits another to commit suicide is guilty of a felony of the second degree if his conduct causes such suicide or an attempted suicide, and otherwise of a misdemeanor.

SECTION 210.6 SENTENCE OF DEATH FOR MURDER; FURTHER PROCEEDINGS TO DETERMINE SENTENCE

§ 210.6. Withdrawn effective October 23, 2009.

<Effective October 23, 2009, The American Law Institute withdrew Section 210.6 of the Model Penal Code in light of the current intractable institutional and structural obstacles to ensuring a minimally adequate system for administering capital punishment, for the reasons stated in Part V of the Council's report to the membership at the 2009 Annual Meeting.>

Article 211. Assault; Reckless Endangering; Threats

SECTION 211.0. DEFINITIONS

In this Article, the definitions given in Section 210.0 apply unless a different meaning plainly is required.

SECTION 211.1. ASSAULT

(1) **Simple Assault**. A person is guilty of assault if he:

(a) attempts to cause or purposely, knowingly or recklessly causes bodily injury to another; or

(b) negligently causes bodily injury to another with a deadly weapon; or

(c) attempts by physical menace to put another in fear of imminent serious bodily injury.

Simple assault is a misdemeanor unless committed in a fight or scuffle entered into by mutual consent, in which case it is a petty misdemeanor.

(2) **Aggravated Assault**. A person is guilty of aggravated assault if he:

(a) attempts to cause serious bodily injury to another, or causes such injury purposely, knowingly or recklessly under circumstances manifesting extreme indifference to the value of human life; or

(b) attempts to cause or purposely or knowingly causes bodily injury to another with a deadly weapon.

Aggravated assault under paragraph (a) is a felony of the second degree; aggravated assault under paragraph (b) is a felony of the third degree.

SECTION 211.2. RECKLESSLY ENDANGERING ANOTHER PERSON

A person commits a misdemeanor if he recklessly engages in conduct which places or may place another person in danger of death or serious bodily injury. Recklessness and danger shall be presumed where a person knowingly points a firearm at or in the direction of another, whether or not the actor believed the firearm to be loaded.

SECTION 211.3 TERRORISTIC THREATS

A person is guilty of a felony of the third degree if he threatens to commit any crime of violence with purpose to terrorize another or to cause evacuation of a building, place of assembly, or facility of public transportation, or otherwise to cause serious public inconvenience, or in reckless disregard of the risk of causing such terror or inconvenience.

Article 212. Kidnapping and Related Offenses; Coercion

SECTION 212.1. KIDNAPPING

A person is guilty of kidnapping if he unlawfully removes another from his place of residence or business, or a substantial distance from the vicinity where he is found, or if he unlawfully confines another for a substantial period in a place of isolation, with any of the following purposes:

(a) to hold for ransom or reward, or as a shield or hostage; or

(b) to facilitate commission of any felony or flight thereafter; or

(c) to inflict bodily injury on or to terrorize the victim or another; or

(d) to interfere with the performance of any governmental or political function.

Kidnapping is a felony of the first degree unless the actor voluntarily releases the victim alive and in a safe place prior to trial, in which case it is a felony of the second degree. A removal or confinement is unlawful within the meaning of this Section if it is accomplished by force, threat or deception, or, in the case of a person who is under the age of 14 or incompetent, if it is accomplished without the consent of a parent, guardian or other person responsible for general supervision of his welfare.

SECTION 212.2. FELONIOUS RESTRAINT

A person commits a felony of the third degree if he knowingly:

(a) restrains another unlawfully in circumstances exposing him to risk of serious bodily injury; or

(b) holds another in a condition of involuntary servitude.

SECTION 212.3. FALSE IMPRISONMENT

A person commits a misdemeanor if he knowingly restrains another unlawfully so as to interfere substantially with his liberty.

SECTION 212.4. INTERFERENCE WITH CUSTODY

(1) **Custody of Children**. A person commits an offense if he knowingly or recklessly takes or entices any child under the age of 18 from the custody of its parent, guardian or other lawful custodian, when he has no privilege to do so. It is an affirmative defense that:

(a) the actor believed that his action was necessary to preserve the child from danger to its welfare; or

(b) the child, being at the time not less than 14 years old, was taken away at its own instigation without enticement and without purpose to commit a criminal offense with or against the child.

Proof that the child was below the critical age gives rise to a presumption that the actor knew the child's age or acted in reckless disregard thereof. The offense is a misdemeanor unless the actor, not being a parent or person in equivalent relation to the child, acted with knowledge that his conduct would cause serious alarm for the child's safety, or in reckless disregard of a likelihood of causing such alarm, in which case the offense is a felony of the third degree.

(2) **Custody of Committed Persons**. A person is guilty of a misdemeanor if he knowingly or recklessly takes or entices any committed person away from lawful custody when he is not privileged to do so. "Committed person" means, in addition to anyone committed under judicial warrant, any orphan, neglected or delinquent child, mentally defective or insane person, or other dependent or incompetent person entrusted to another's custody by or through a recognized social agency or otherwise by authority of law.

SECTION 212.5. CRIMINAL COERCION

(1) **Offense Defined**. A person is guilty of criminal coercion if, with purpose unlawfully to restrict another's freedom of action to his detriment, he threatens to:

(a) commit any criminal offense; or

(b) accuse anyone of a criminal offense; or

(c) expose any secret tending to subject any person to hatred, contempt or ridicule, or to impair his credit or business repute; or

(d) take or withhold action as an official, or cause an official to take or withhold action.

It is an affirmative defense to prosecution based on paragraphs (b), (c) or (d) that the actor believed the accusation or secret to be true or the proposed official action justified and that his purpose was limited to compelling the other to behave in a way reasonably related to the circumstances which were the subject of the accusation, exposure or proposed official action, as by desisting from further misbehavior, making good a wrong done, refraining from taking any action or responsibility for which the actor believes the other disqualified.

(2) **Grading**. Criminal coercion is a misdemeanor unless the threat is to commit a felony or the actor's purpose is felonious, in which cases the offense is a felony of the third degree.

Article 213. Sexual Offenses

SECTION 213.0. DEFINITIONS

In this Article, unless a different meaning plainly is required:

(1) the definitions given in Section 210.0 apply;

(2) "Sexual intercourse" includes intercourse per os or per anum, with some penetration however slight; emission is not required;

(3) "Deviate sexual intercourse" means sexual intercourse per os or per anum between human beings who are not husband and wife, and any form of sexual intercourse with an animal.

SECTION 213.1 RAPE AND RELATED OFFENSES

(1) **Rape**. A male who has sexual intercourse with a female not his wife is guilty of rape if:

(a) he compels her to submit by force or by threat of imminent death, serious bodily injury, extreme pain or kidnapping, to be inflicted on anyone; or

(b) he has substantially impaired her power to appraise or control her conduct by administering or employing without her knowledge drugs, intoxicants or other means for the purpose of preventing resistance; or

(c) the female is unconscious; or

(d) the female is less than 10 years old.

Rape is a felony of the second degree unless (i) in the course thereof the actor inflicts serious bodily injury upon anyone, or (ii) the victim was not a voluntary social companion of the actor upon the occasion of the crime and had not previously permitted him sexual liberties, in which cases the offense is a felony of the first degree.

(2) **Gross Sexual Imposition**. A male who has sexual intercourse with a female not his wife commits a felony of the third degree if:

(a) he compels her to submit by any threat that would prevent resistance by a woman of ordinary resolution; or

(b) he knows that she suffers from a mental disease or defect which renders her incapable of appraising the nature of her conduct; or

(c) he knows that she is unaware that a sexual act is being committed upon her or that she submits because she mistakenly supposes that he is her husband.

SECTION 213.2. DEVIATE SEXUAL INTERCOURSE BY FORCE OR IMPOSITION

(1) **By Force or Its Equivalent**. A person who engages in deviate sexual intercourse with another person, or who causes another to engage in deviate sexual intercourse, commits a felony of the second degree if:

(a) he compels the other person to participate by force or by threat of imminent death, serious bodily injury, extreme pain or kidnapping, to be inflicted on anyone; or

(b) he has substantially impaired the other person's power to appraise or control his conduct, by administering or employing without the knowledge of the other person drugs, intoxicants or other means for the purpose of preventing resistance; or

(c) the other person is unconscious; or

(d) the other person is less than 10 years old.

(2) **By Other Imposition**. A person who engages in deviate sexual intercourse with another person, or who causes another to engage in deviate sexual intercourse, commits a felony of the third degree if:

> (a) he compels the other person to participate by any threat that would prevent resistance by a person of ordinary resolution; or

> (b) he knows that the other person suffers from a mental disease or defect which renders him incapable of appraising the nature of his conduct; or

> (c) he knows that the other person submits because he is unaware that a sexual act is being committed upon him.

SECTION 213.3. CORRUPTION OF MINORS AND SEDUCTION

(1) **Offense Defined**. A male who has sexual intercourse with a female not his wife, or any person who engages in deviate sexual intercourse or causes another to engage in deviate sexual intercourse, is guilty of an offense if:

> (a) the other person is less than [16] years old and the actor is at least [four] years older than the other person; or

> (b) the other person is less than 21 years old and the actor is his guardian or otherwise responsible for general supervision of his welfare; or

> (c) the other person is in custody of law or detained in a hospital or other institution and the actor has supervisory or disciplinary authority over him; or

> (d) the other person is a female who is induced to participate by a promise of marriage which the actor does not mean to perform.

(2) **Grading**. An offense under paragraph (a) of Subsection (1) is a felony of the third degree. Otherwise an offense under this section is a misdemeanor.

SECTION 213.4. SEXUAL ASSAULT

A person who has sexual contact with another not his spouse, or causes such other to have sexual contact with him, is guilty of sexual assault, a misdemeanor, if:

(1) he knows that the contact is offensive to the other person; or

(2) he knows that the other person suffers from a mental disease or defect which renders him or her incapable of appraising the nature of his or her conduct; or

(3) he knows that the other person is unaware that a sexual act is being committed; or

(4) the other person is less than 10 years old; or

(5) he has substantially impaired the other person's power to appraise or control his or her conduct, by administering or employing without the other's knowledge drugs, intoxicants or other means for the purpose of preventing resistance; or

(6) the other person is less than [16] years old and the actor is at least [four] years older than the other person; or

(7) the other person is less than 21 years old and the actor is his guardian or otherwise responsible for general supervision of his welfare; or

(8) the other person is in custody of law or detained in a hospital or other institution and the actor has supervisory or disciplinary authority over him.

Sexual contact is any touching of the sexual or other intimate parts of the person for the purpose of arousing or gratifying sexual desire.

SECTION 213.5. INDECENT EXPOSURE

A person commits a misdemeanor if, for the purpose of arousing or gratifying sexual desire of himself or of any person other than his spouse, he exposes his genitals under circumstances in which he knows his conduct is likely to cause affront or alarm.

SECTION 213.6. PROVISIONS GENERALLY APPLICABLE TO ARTICLE 213

(1) **Mistake as to Age**. Whenever in this Article the criminality of conduct depends on a child's being below the age of 10, it is no defense that the actor did not know the child's age, or reasonably believed the child to be older than 10.

When criminality depends on the child's being below a critical age other than 10, it is a defense for the actor to prove by a preponderance of the evidence that he reasonably believed the child to be above the critical age.

(2) **Spouse Relationships**. Whenever in this Article the definition of an offense excludes conduct with a spouse, the exclusion shall be deemed to extend to persons living as man and wife, regardless of the legal status of their relationship. The exclusion shall be inoperative as respects spouses living apart under a decree of judicial separation. Where the definition of an offense excludes conduct with a spouse or conduct by a woman, this shall not preclude conviction of a spouse or woman as accomplice in a sexual act which he or she causes another person, not within the exclusion, to perform.

(3) **Sexually Promiscuous Complainants**. It is a defense to prosecution under Section 213.3 and paragraphs (6), (7) and (8) of Section 213.4 for the actor to prove by a preponderance of the evidence that the alleged victim had, prior to the time of the offense charged, engaged promiscuously in sexual relations with others.

(4) **Prompt Complaint**. No prosecution may be instituted or maintained under this Article unless the alleged offense was brought to the notice of public authority within [3] months of its occurrence or, where the alleged victim was less than [16] years old or otherwise incompetent to make complaint, within [3] months after a parent, guardian or other competent person specially interested in the victim learns of the offense.

(5) **Testimony of Complainants**. No person shall be convicted of any felony under this Article upon the uncorroborated testimony of the alleged victim. Corroboration may be circumstantial. In any prosecution before a jury for an offense under this Article, the jury shall be instructed to evaluate the testimony of a victim or complaining witness with special care in view of the emotional involvement of the witness and the difficulty of determining the truth with respect to alleged sexual activities carried out in private.

OFFENSES AGAINST PROPERTY

Article 220. Arson, Criminal Mischief, and Other Property Destruction

SECTION 220.1. ARSON RELATED OFFENSES

(1) **Arson**. A person is guilty of arson, a felony of the second degree, if he starts a fire or causes an explosion with the purpose of:

(a) destroying a building or occupied structure of another; or

(b) destroying or damaging any property, whether his own or another's, to collect insurance for such loss. It shall be an affirmative defense to prosecution under this paragraph that the actor's conduct did not recklessly endanger any building or occupied structure of another or place any other person in danger of death or bodily injury.

(2) **Reckless Burning or Exploding**. A person commits a felony of the third degree if he purposely starts a fire or causes an explosion, whether on his own property or another's, and thereby recklessly:

(a) places another person in danger of death or bodily injury; or

(b) places a building or occupied structure of another in danger of damage or destruction.

(3) **Failure to Control or Report Dangerous Fire**. A person who knows that a fire is endangering life or a substantial amount of property of another and fails to take reasonable measures to put out or control the fire, when he can do so without substantial risk to himself, or to give a prompt fire alarm, commits a misdemeanor if:

(a) he knows that he is under an official, contractual, or other legal duty to prevent or combat the fire; or

(b) the fire was started, albeit lawfully, by him or with his assent, or on property in his custody or control.

(4) **Definitions**. "Occupied structure" means any structure, vehicle or place adapted for overnight accommodation of persons, or for carrying on business therein, whether or not a person is actually present. Property is that of another, for the purposes of this section, if anyone other than the actor has a possessory or proprietary interest therein. If a building or structure is divided into separately occupied units, any unit not occupied by the actor is an occupied structure of another.

SECTION 220.2. CAUSING OR RISKING CATASTROPHE

(1) **Causing Catastrophe**. A person who causes a catastrophe by explosion, fire, flood, avalanche, collapse of building, release of poison gas,

radioactive material or other harmful or destructive force or substance, or by any other means of causing potentially widespread injury or damage, commits a felony of the second degree if he does so purposely or knowingly, or a felony of the third degree if he does so recklessly.

(2) **Risking Catastrophe**. A person is guilty of a misdemeanor if he recklessly creates a risk of catastrophe in the employment of fire, explosives or other dangerous means listed in Subsection (1).

(3) **Failure to Prevent Catastrophe**. A person who knowingly or recklessly fails to take reasonable measures to prevent or mitigate a catastrophe commits a misdemeanor if:

(a) he knows that he is under an official, contractual or other legal duty to take such measures; or

(b) he did or assented to the act causing or threatening the catastrophe.

SECTION 220.3. CRIMINAL MISCHIEF

(1) Offense Defined. A person is guilty of criminal mischief if he:

(a) damages tangible property of another purposely, recklessly, or by negligence in the employment of fire, explosives, or other dangerous means listed in Section 220.2(1); or

(b) purposely or recklessly tampers with tangible property of another so as to endanger person or property; or

(c) purposely or recklessly causes another to suffer pecuniary loss by deception or threat.

(2) Grading. Criminal mischief is a felony of the third degree if the actor purposely causes pecuniary loss in excess of $5,000, or a substantial interruption or impairment of public communication, transportation, supply of water, gas or power, or other public service. It is a misdemeanor if the actor purposely causes pecuniary loss in excess of $100, or a petty misdemeanor if he purposely or recklessly causes pecuniary loss in excess of $25. Otherwise criminal mischief is a violation.

Article 221. Burglary and Other Criminal Intrusion

SECTION 221.0. DEFINITIONS

In this Article, unless a different meaning plainly is required:

(1) "occupied structure" means any structure, vehicle or place adapted for overnight accommodation of persons, or for carrying on business therein, whether or not a person is actually present.

(2) "night" means the period between thirty minutes past sunset and thirty minutes before sunrise.

SECTION 221.1. BURGLARY

(1) **Burglary Defined**. A person is guilty of burglary if he enters a building or occupied structure, or separately secured or occupied portion thereof, with purpose to commit a crime therein, unless the premises are at the time open to the public or the actor is licensed or privileged to enter. It is an affirmative defense to prosecution for burglary that the building or structure was abandoned.

(2) **Grading**. Burglary is a felony of the second degree if it is perpetrated in the dwelling of another at night, or if, in the course of committing the offense, the actor:

(a) purposely, knowingly or recklessly inflicts or attempts to inflict bodily injury on anyone; or

(b) is armed with explosives or a deadly weapon.

Otherwise, burglary is a felony of the third degree. An act shall be deemed "in the course of committing" an offense if it occurs in an attempt to commit the offense or in flight after the attempt or commission.

(3) **Multiple Convictions**. A person may not be convicted both for burglary and for the offense which it was his purpose to commit after the burglarious entry or for an attempt to commit that offense, unless the additional offense constitutes a felony of the first or second degree.

SECTION 221.2. CRIMINAL TRESPASS

(1) **Buildings and Occupied Structures.** A person commits an offense if, knowing that he is not licensed or privileged to do so, he enters or surreptitiously remains in any building or occupied structure, or separately secured or occupied portion thereof. An offense under this Subsection is a misdemeanor if it is committed in a dwelling at night. Otherwise it is a petty misdemeanor.

(2) **Defiant Trespasser**. A person commits an offense if, knowing that he is not licensed or privileged to do so, he enters or remains in any place as to which notice against trespass is given by:

(a) actual communication to the actor; or

(b) posting in a manner prescribed by law or reasonably likely to come to the attention of intruders; or

(c) fencing or other enclosure manifestly designed to exclude intruders. An offense under this Subsection constitutes a petty misdemeanor if the offender defies an order to leave personally communicated to him by the owner of the premises or other authorized person. Otherwise it is a violation.

(3) **Defenses**. It is an affirmative defense to prosecution under this Section that:

(a) a building or occupied structure involved in an offense under Subsection (1) was abandoned; or

(b) the premises were at the time open to members of the public and the actor complied with all lawful conditions imposed on access to or remaining in the premises; or

(c) the actor reasonably believed that the owner of the premises, or other person empowered to license access thereto, would have licensed him to enter or remain.

ARTICLE 222. Robbery

SECTION 222.1. ROBBERY

(1) **Robbery Defined**. A person is guilty of robbery if, in the course of committing a theft, he:

(a) inflicts serious bodily injury upon another; or

(b) threatens another with or purposely puts him in fear of immediate serious bodily injury; or

(c) commits or threatens immediately to commit any felony of the first or second degree.

An act shall be deemed "in the course of committing a theft" if it occurs in an attempt to commit theft or in flight after the attempt or commission.

(2) **Grading**. Robbery is a felony of the second degree, except that it is a felony of the first degree if in the course of committing the theft the actor attempts to kill anyone, or purposely inflicts or attempts to inflict serious bodily injury.

Article 223. Theft and Related Offenses

SECTION 223.   DEFINITIONS

In this Article, unless a different meaning plainly is required:

(1) "deprive" means: (a) to withhold property of another permanently or for so extended a period as to appropriate a major portion of its economic value, or with intent to restore only upon payment of reward or other compensation; or (b) to dispose of the property so as to make it unlikely that the owner will recover it.

(2) "financial institution" means a bank, insurance company, credit union, building and loan association, investment trust or other organization held out to the public as a place of deposit of funds or medium of savings or collective investment.

(3) "government" means the United States, any State, county, municipality, or other political unit, or any department, agency or subdivision of any of the foregoing, or any corporation or other association carrying out the functions of government.

(4) "movable property" means property the location of which can be changed, including things growing on, affixed to, or found in land, and documents although the rights represented thereby have no physical location; "immovable

property" is all other property.

(5) "obtain" means: (a) in relation to property, to bring about a transfer or purported transfer of a legal interest in the property, whether to the obtainer or another; or (b) in relation to labor or service, to secure performance thereof.

(6) "property" means anything of value, including real estate, tangible and intangible personal property, contract rights, choses-in-action and other interests in or claims to wealth, admission or transportation tickets, captured or domestic animals, food and drink, electric or other power.

(7) "property of another" includes property in which any person other than the actor has an interest which the actor is not privileged to infringe, regardless of the fact that the actor also has an interest in the property and regardless of the fact that the other person might be precluded from civil recovery because the property was used in an unlawful transaction or was subject to forfeiture as contraband. Property in possession of the actor shall not be deemed property of another who has only a security interest therein, even if legal title is in the creditor pursuant to a conditional sales contract or other security agreement.

SECTION 223.1. CONSOLIDATION OF THEFT OFFENSES; GRADING; PROVISIONS APPLICABLE TO THEFT GENERALLY

(1) **Consolidation of Theft Offenses**. Conduct denominated theft in this Article constitutes a single offense. An accusation of theft may be supported by evidence that it was committed in any manner that would be theft under this Article, notwithstanding the specification of a different manner in the indictment or information, subject only to the power of the Court to ensure fair trial by granting a continuance or other appropriate relief where the conduct of the defense would
be prejudiced by lack of fair notice or by surprise.

(2) **Grading of Theft Offenses**.

(a) Theft constitutes a felony of the third degree if the amount involved exceeds $500, or if the property stolen is a firearm, automobile, airplane, motorcycle, motor boat, or other motor-propelled vehicle, or in the case of theft by receiving stolen property, if the receiver is in the business of buying or selling stolen property.

(b) Theft not within the preceding paragraph constitutes a misdemeanor, except that if the property was not taken from the person or by threat, or in breach of a fiduciary obligation, and the actor proves by a preponderance of the evidence that the amount involved was less than $50, the offense constitutes a petty misdemeanor.

(c) The amount involved in a theft shall be deemed to be the highest value, by any reasonable standard, of the property or services which the actor stole or attempted to steal. Amounts involved in thefts committed pursuant to one scheme or course of conduct, whether from the same person or several persons, may be aggregated in determining the grade of the offense.

(3) **Claim of Right**. It is an affirmative defense to prosecution for theft that the actor:

(a) was unaware that the property or service was that of another; or

(b) acted under an honest claim of right to the property or service involved or that he had a right to acquire or dispose of it as he did; or

(c) took property exposed for sale, intending to purchase and pay for it promptly, or reasonably believing that the owner, if present, would have consented.

(4) **Theft from Spouse**. It is no defense that theft was from the actor's spouse, except that misappropriation of household and personal effects, or other property normally accessible to both spouses, is theft only if it occurs after the parties have ceased living together.

SECTION 223.2. THEFT BY UNLAWFUL TAKING OR DISPOSITION

(1) **Movable Property**. A person is guilty of theft if he unlawfully takes, or exercises unlawful control over, movable property of another with purpose to deprive him thereof.

(2) **Immovable Property**. A person is guilty of theft if he unlawfully transfers immovable property of another or any interest therein with purpose to benefit himself or another not entitled thereto.

SECTION 223.3 THEFT BY DECEPTION

A person is guilty of theft if he purposely obtains property of another by deception. A person deceives if he purposely:

(1) creates or reinforces a false impression, including false impressions as to law, value, intention or other state of mind; but deception as to a person's intention to perform a promise shall not be inferred from the fact alone that he did not subsequently perform the promise; or

(2) prevents another from acquiring information which would affect his judgment of a transaction; or

(3) fails to correct a false impression which the deceiver previously created or reinforced, or which the deceiver knows to be influencing another to whom he stands in a fiduciary or confidential relationship; or

(4) fails to disclose a known lien, adverse claim or other legal impediment to the enjoyment of property which he transfers or encumbers in consideration for the property obtained, whether such impediment is or is not valid, or is or is not a matter of official record.

The term "deceive" does not, however, include falsity as to matters having no pecuniary significance, or puffing by
statements unlikely to deceive ordinary persons in the group addressed.

SECTION 223.4. THEFT BY EXTORTION

A person is guilty of theft if he purposely obtains property of another by threatening to:

(1) inflict bodily injury on anyone or commit any other criminal offense; or

(2) accuse anyone of a criminal offense; or

(3) expose any secret tending to subject any person to hatred, contempt or ridicule, or to impair his credit or business repute; or

(4) take or withhold action as an official, or cause an official to take or withhold action; or

(5) bring about or continue a strike, boycott or other collective unofficial action, if the property is not demanded or received for the benefit of the group in whose interest the actor purports to act; or

(6) testify or provide information or withhold testimony or information with respect to another's legal claim or defense; or

(7) inflict any other harm which would not benefit the actor. It is an affirmative defense to prosecution based on paragraphs (2), (3) or (4) that the property obtained by threat of accusation, exposure, lawsuit or other invocation of official action was honestly claimed as restitution or indemnification for harm done in the circumstances to which such accusation, exposure, lawsuit or other official action relates, or as compensation for property or lawful services.

SECTION 223.5. THEFT OF PROPERTY LOST, MISLAID, OR DELIVERED BY MISTAKE

A person who comes into control of property of another that he knows to have been lost, mislaid, or delivered under a mistake as to the nature or amount of the property or the identity of the recipient is guilty of theft if, with purpose to
deprive the owner thereof, he fails to take reasonable measures to restore the property to a person entitled to have it.

SECTION 223.6. RECEIVING STOLEN PROPERTY

(1) **Receiving**. A person is guilty of theft if he purposely receives, retains, or disposes of movable property of another knowing that it has been stolen, or believing that it has probably been stolen, unless the property is received, retained, or disposed with purpose to restore it to the owner. "Receiving" means acquiring possession, control or title, or lending
on the security of the property.

(2) **Presumption of Knowledge**. The requisite knowledge or belief is presumed in the case of a dealer who:

(a) is found in possession or control of property stolen from two or more persons on separate occasions; or

(b) has received stolen property in another transaction within the year preceding the transaction charged; or
(c) being a dealer in property of the sort received, acquires it for a consideration which he knows is far below its reasonable value.

"Dealer" means a person in the business of buying or selling goods including a pawnbroker.

SECTION 223.7. THEFT OF SERVICES

(1) A person is guilty of theft is he purposely obtains services which he knows are available only for compensation, by deception or threat, or by false token or other means to avoid payment for the service. "Services" includes labor, professional service, transportation, telephone or other public service, accommodation in hotels, restaurants or elsewhere, admission to exhibitions, use of vehicles or other movable property. Where compensation for service is ordinarily paid immediately upon the rendering of such service, as in the case of hotels and restaurants, refusal to pay or absconding without payment or offer to pay gives rise to a presumption that the service was obtained by deception as to intention to pay.

(2) A person commits theft if, having control over the disposition of services of others, to which he is not entitled, he knowingly diverts such services to his own benefit or to the benefit of another not entitled thereto.

SECTION 223.8. [Omitted]

SECTION 223.9. UNAUTHORIZED USE OF AUTOMOBILES AND OTHER VEHICLES

A person commits a misdemeanor if he operates another's automobile, airplane, motorcycle, motorboat, or other motorpropelled vehicle without consent of the owner. It is an affirmative defense to prosecution under this Section that the actor reasonably believed that the owner would have consented to the operation had he known of it.

Article 224. Forgery and Fraudulent Practices

SECTION 224.0. DEFINITIONS

In this Article, the definitions given in Section 223.0 apply unless a different meaning plainly is required.

SECTION 224.1. FORGERY

(1) **Definition**. A person is guilty of forgery if, with purpose to defraud or injure anyone, or with knowledge that he is facilitating a fraud or injury to be perpetrated by anyone, the actor:

> (a) alters any writing of another without his authority; or

> (b) makes, completes, executes, authenticates, issues or transfers any writing so that it purports to be the act of another who did not authorize that act, or to have been executed at a time or place or in a numbered sequence other than was in fact the case, or to be a copy of an original when no such original existed; or

> (c) utters any writing which he knows to be forged in a manner specified in paragraphs (a) or (b).

"Writing" includes printing or any other method of recording information, money, coins, tokens, stamps, seals, credit cards, badges, trademarks, and other symbols of value, right, privilege, or identification.

(2) **Grading**. Forgery is a felony of the second degree if the writing is or purports to be part of an issue of money, securities, postage or revenue stamps, or other instruments issued by the government, or part of an issue of stock, bonds or other instruments representing interests in or claims against any property or enterprise. Forgery is a felony of the third degree if the writing is or purports to be a will, deed, contract, release, commercial instrument, or other document evidencing, creating, transferring, altering, terminating, or otherwise affecting legal relations. Otherwise forgery is a misdemeanor.

SECTIONS 224.2.-224.4. [Omitted]

SECTION 224.5. BAD CHECKS

A person who issues or passes a check or similar sight order for the payment of money, knowing that it will not be honored by the drawee, commits a misdemeanor. For the purpose of this Section as well as in any prosecution for theft committed by means of a bad check, an issuer is presumed to know that the check or order (other than a post-dated check or order) would not be paid, if:

> (1) the issuer had no account with the drawee at the time the check or order was issued; or

(2) payment was refused by the drawee for lack of funds, upon presentation within 30 days after issue, and the issuer failed to make good within 10 days after receiving notice of that refusal.

Table of Cases